UNLOCKING
TORTS

3rd edition

Chris Turner

HODDER
EDUCATION
AN HACHETTE UK COMPANY

Orders: please contact Bookpoint Ltd, 130 Milton Park, Abingdon, Oxon OX14 4SB.
Telephone: (44) 01235 827720. Fax: (44) 01235 400454. Lines are open from 9.00 – 5.00,
Monday to Saturday, with a 24 hour message answering service. You can also order through
our website www.hoddereducation.co.uk

If you have any comments to make about this, or any of our other titles, please send them to
educationenquiries@hodder.co.uk

British Library Cataloguing in Publication Data
A catalogue record for this title is available from the British Library

ISBN: 978 1 444 10918 4

First Edition Published 2004
Second Edition Published 2007
This Edition Published 2010
Impression number 10 9 8 7 6 5 4 3
Year 2014 2013 2012 2011

Hachette UK's policy is to use papers that are natural, renewable and
recyclable products and made from wood grown in sustainable forests.
The logging and manufacturing processes are expected to conform to the
environmental regulations of the country of origin.

Illustrations by Peter Bull
Cover photo © Gytis Mikulicus/iStockphoto.com
Typeset by Dorchester Typesetting Group Ltd
Printed in Italy for Hodder Education, an Hachette UK Company, 338 Euston Road,
London NW1 3BH

Contents

Acknowledgements

The books in this series are a departure from traditional law texts and represent one view of a type of learning resource that we feel is particularly useful to students. The series editors would therefore like to thank the publishers for their support in making the project a reality. In particular we would also like to thank Alexia Chan for her continued faith in the project from its first conception.

The authors would like to thank Sukhwinder Chhokar for his work in ensuring that the book is as accurate and readable as possible.

© Crown copyright material is reproduced with permission of the Controller of HMSO.

The publishers apologise if inadvertently any sources remain unacknowledged and will be glad to make the necessary arrangements at the earliest opportunity.

Guide to the book

In the Unlocking the Law books all the essential elements that make up the law are clearly defined to bring the law alive and make it memorable. In addition, the books are enhanced with learning features to reinforce learning and test your knowledge as you study. Follow this guide to make sure you get the most from reading this book.

AIMS AND OBJECTIVES

Defines what you will learn in each chapter.

definition
Find key legal terminology at-a-glance

SECTION

Highlights sections from Acts.

ARTICLE

Defines Articles of the EC Treaty or of the European Convention on Human Rights or other Treaty.

tutor tip

Provides key ideas from lecturers on how to get ahead

CLAUSE

Shows a Bill going through Parliament or a draft Bill proposed by the Law Commission.

CASE EXAMPLE

Illustrates the law in action.

JUDGMENT

Provides extracts from judgments on cases.

Indicates that you will be able to test yourself further on this topic using the Key Questions and Answers section of this book on www.unlockingthelaw.co.uk.

QUOTATION

Encourages you to engage with primary sources.

ACTIVITY

Enables you to test yourself as you progress through the chapter.

student mentor tip

Offers advice from law graduates on the best way to achieve the results you want.

SAMPLE ESSAY QUESTIONS

Provide you with real-life sample essays and show you the best way to plan your answer.

SUMMARY

Concludes each chapter to reinforce learning.

Preface

The *Unlocking the Law* series is an entirely new style of undergraduate law textbooks. Many student texts are very prose dense and have little in the way of interactive materials to help a student feel his or her way through the course of study on a given module.

The purpose of this series, then, is to try to make learning each subject area more accessible by focusing on actual learning needs, and by providing a range of different supporting materials and features.

All topic areas are broken up into 'bite size' sections with a logical progression and extensive use of headings and numerous sub-headings. Each book in the series will also contain a variety of charts, diagrams and key fact summaries to reinforce the information in the body of the text. Diagrams and flow charts are particularly useful because they can provide a quick and easy understanding of the key points, especially when revising for examinations. Key facts charts not only provide a quick visual guide through the subject but are useful for revision purposes also.

The books have a number of common features in the layout. Important cases are separated out for easy access and have full citation in the text as well as the table of cases for ease of reference. The emphasis of the series is on depth of understanding much more than breadth. For this reason each text also includes key extracts from judgments where appropriate. Extracts from academic comment from journal articles and leading texts are also included to give some insight into the academic debate on complex or controversial areas. In both cases these are indented to make them clear from the body of the text.

Finally, the books also include much formative 'self-testing', with a variety of activities ranging through subject specific comprehension, application of the law, and a range of other activities to help the student gain a good idea of his or her progress in the course.

Note also that all incidental references to 'he', 'him', his, etc are intended to be gender neutral.

A study of the law of torts can prove fascinating because it is really all about people, the problems that they have and the ways that these might be overcome in law. Tort law covers civil wrongs and in this way the topic areas vary widely in their content and context from basic negligence actions for motoring accidents, through assaults encountered in sporting activities, to the interference of problem neighbours. Since tort is also essentially a common law area much of this book is devoted to cases and case notes and these are separated out in the text for easy reference.

The book is designed to cover all of the main topic areas on undergraduate and professional tort syllabuses and help provide a full understanding of each.

We hope that you will gain as much enjoyment in reading about the law of torts and testing your understanding with the various activities in the book as we have had in writing it, and that you gain much enjoyment and interest from your study of the law.

The law is stated as we believe it to be on 1st January 2010.

Chris Turner
Sue Hodge

Table of Cases

Table of statutes and other instruments

1

The origins and character of tortious liability

AIMS AND OBJECTIVES

After reading this chapter you should be able to:

- Understand the basic character of torts
- Understand the basic principles of tortious liability
- Understand the basic aims of tortious liability
- Understand the basic interests protected by the Law of Torts
- Understand the relevance of specific mental states in pursuing tort actions
- Be able to discriminate between fault liability and no fault liability
- Be able to discriminate between joint liability and several liability and understand how and why contributions can be made between different tortfeasors
- Understand how human rights legislation impacts on the Law of Torts

1.1 The origins of tort

tort

Tort is a French word meaning 'wrong' – so is a general word used to describe civil wrongs

trespass

Torts based on trespass tend to involve interference, eg with rights over land, or property or indeed with their 'bodily integrity'

actionable *per se*

An action for a tort where the claimant does not have to prove that damage occurred only that the tort occurred

The law of **tort**, or torts, is part of the English common law which has developed incrementally since Norman times. Academic writers are not agreed whether there is a law of tort or a law of torts. A law of tort implies some general common rules relevant to all parts of the law. A law of torts recognises that there are various separate and distinct aspects but also implies that the separate parts have something in common. The writers of this book incline to the idea that there is a law of torts, each tort being governed by similar underlying principles. It is a nice subject for a debate but of little practical importance.

Although some modern torts have been created by statute, the law is still generally to be found in common law principles. The origins of torts can be traced back to the fourteenth century when the word '**trespass**' was given a much wider legal meaning than it has today. It originally referred to 'any direct and forcible injury to the person, land or property (chattels)'.

Trespass was one of two medieval forms of action, the second being 'trespass on the case' or simply 'case'. Case covered 'injury which was consequential to a wrong but the wrong was neither forcible nor direct'.

The distinction can still be seen in the law of torts today – torts which are **actionable *per se***, ie without proof of damage, such as trespass to land and trespass to the person, generally originate from the old form of trespass, while those torts which require proof of damage, for example negligence and nuisance, generally come from case.

In the past, the distinction was of crucial importance as using the wrong form of action

claimant
The person who brings an action in tort

could result in the **claimant** being left without any remedy. Today, although there may be cost penalties, the Rules of Court allow for the amendment of pleadings (subject to the provisions of the Limitation Act 1980 which are discussed in Chapter 20). The legal historian will be able to find traces of the old rules in modern law but for practical purposes the distinction is of little relevance. Both Lord Atkin and Lord Denning MR have made this clear. In his judgment in *United Australia Ltd v Barclays Bank* [1941] AC 1, Lord Atkin said

JUDGMENT

'When these ghosts of the past stand in the path of justice clanking their medieval chains the proper course for the judge is to pass through them undeterred.'

CASE EXAMPLE

Letang v Cooper [1965] 1 QB 232

The claimant decided to sunbathe on a grass area which was also used as a car park. The defendant drove in. He did not see the claimant lying on the grass and ran over her legs. The problem for the claimant was caused by the date on which she tried to commence her action. She was out of time to bring an action for negligence (a descendant of case) where the usual time limit is three years. If she was able to use trespass, then the action could stand as the time limit was six years. It was argued that the old rules should apply, her injury was direct and forcible.

The Court of Appeal held that the old rules no longer apply. Intentional injury will give a claim based in trespass, but unintentional injury gives a claim based in negligence. The claimant was unsuccessful. In the course of his judgment Lord Denning said:

JUDGMENT

'These forms of action have served their day. They did at one time form a guide to substantive rights; but they do so no longer. Lord Atkin told us what to do about them.'

Before leaving this introduction, mention should be made of the tort of defamation. Slander has its roots in the old ecclesiastical law. Libel stems from the old prerogative law which regarded certain written statements as prejudicial to the state. Both libel and slander eventually found a home in the common law courts. As will be seen in Chapter 14, the tort of defamation continues to have its own unique characteristics.

1.2 General principles of liability

1.2.1 The character of torts

Anyone who teaches law is certain to be asked 'What does tort mean?' If only there was an easy answer! It seems to be generally accepted that the word itself is a surviving relic of Norman French and means simply 'wrong'. This does not tell us very much. Winfield defines the meaning as follows:

QUOTATION

'Tortious liability arises from the breach of a duty primarily fixed by law; this duty is towards persons generally and its breach is redressible by an action for unliquidated damages.'

W V H Rogers, Winfield and Jolowicz on Tort (16th edn, Sweet & Maxwell, 2002)

The definition is helpful in that it shows that there are three elements:

1. a duty fixed by law – as we shall see this does not necessarily, nor indeed usually, mean fixed by statute but a duty which the courts have recognised

2. the duty must be owed generally – as we shall see individual torts have been developed so that a general duty is owed to any person in a position to bring an action based on that tort

3. the breach of duty must entitle the claimant to general **damages**.

damages

Refers to the compensation awarded by the court in a successful claim

The nature of the duty varies from tort to tort. For example where negligence is alleged, the duty is to take reasonable care; in the case of trespass to the person the duty is to refrain from infringing a person's bodily integrity.

The class of persons to whom a duty is owed may be limited. For example in negligence, a duty is owed only to those who ought reasonably have been foreseen as likely to be affected by failure to take reasonable care; in trespass to the person the duty is owed only to those directly affected by the action.

The injury sustained must be of a type recognised by the law. In negligence for example it took many years for the courts to recognise that psychiatric harm was as much an injury as physical damage. In trespass to the person and other torts which are actionable *per se* it is unnecessary to prove damage, the infringement of the right being regarded as injury enough.

1.2.2 The functions and purposes of torts

defendant

The person against whom a claim in tort is made

The aim of the law of torts is twofold:

1. to compensate someone who has suffered a wrong at the hands of the **defendant** and

2. to deter persons from acting in such a way that another person's rights are infringed.

Compensation

Clearly a person who has suffered injury is entitled to financial compensation which is intended, so far as possible, to put them in the position they would have been in but for the wrongdoing of the defendant. Where the damage is purely to property this may be possible, but real difficulty arises in cases of personal injury. The rules which guide the courts in such matters are discussed in detail in Chapter 20.

The award of damages can also be regarded as ensuring that an injured party receives justice in that loss caused by the tort is compensated. In some cases the 'victim' would not agree that justice has been done. How often does the media report a case where a 'victim' makes it clear that the money is in reality no compensation for the loss which has occurred. While the finding of liability may go some way to satisfy the injured party's desire for vengeance, having 'had their day in court', it is only rarely that a punitive element of damages is payable.

From the defendant's point of view, the concept of justice is also debatable. The amount of damages is assessed purely by the effect on the claimant. A defendant who has caused serious personal injury to the particular victim because of some personal characteristic of that victim will find that the award far exceeds the amount which would have been payable to another, less vulnerable, victim.

The law does not compensate a person for all types of damage. We shall see, for example in Chapter 14, that generally there is no duty to respect another's privacy. A person who publishes something which is true is not liable for defamation no matter how detrimental the publication may be to the 'victim'.

The law does not always regard a person as having a legal claim. In negligence for example a person who suffers psychiatric damage as a result of the defendant having negligently caused harm to someone else, will only be able to bring an action when certain very strict conditions have been complied with (see Chapter 6).

Deterrence

The deterrent effect of torts is debatable. This is illustrated by the decision of certain publishers to go ahead and publish defamatory material in the belief that, if the 'victim' brings an action, the profit will outweigh any possible compensation. In such cases if an action is brought damages can include a punitive element, but such a publisher may also calculate that the 'victim' is unlikely to bring an action. An action for defamation frequently has the effect of ensuring that the material becomes known to many more people, no legal aid is available and the outcome is unpredictable as in many cases the final decision rests with a jury. None of these are matters which a 'victim' is likely to ignore.

Where insurance is required, for example in relation to motor vehicles (Road Traffic Act 1988), the deterrent effect is perhaps more effective. A person who is liable may well find that once the insurance company has paid the compensation, the premium goes up. Defendants may or may not care that their actions have caused injury to someone else, but all are likely to be very concerned about the effect on their pockets!

The deterrent effect is also reinforced in the case of professionals who are subject to strict codes of practice, for example health care professionals, lawyers and accountants. Professional governing bodies usually have powers to prevent future practice where the code is not obeyed thus preventing a wrongdoer from earning a living.

1.2.3 The interests protected by the law of torts

Common law develops incrementally by virtue of the doctrine of precedent but it is possible to classify, in broad terms, the general nature of interests which the law of torts protects:

- personal security
- property
- reputation
- economic interests.

Reference should be made to the various chapters for more detail. The following paragraphs simply draw the reader's attention to the specific torts which may be relevant to the particular interests.

Personal security is most obviously protected by the torts of trespass to the person and trespass to land. When negligence is studied it is clear that this tort also has a part to play in ensuring that an individual does not suffer harm by the unreasonable acts or omissions of others. Nuisance helps to protect an **occupier** of land from activities on neighbouring land which are detrimental to health or comfort. Statutory torts created by the Protection from Harassment Act 1997 and the Consumer Protection Act 1987 also play an important role.

occupier

In liability for damage caused by the state of premises the occupier is the person in actual control of the premises when the damage occurs – so there can be dual occupation

Property is protected by the torts of trespass to land and interference with goods. Nuisance and *Rylands v Fletcher* (1868) LR 1 Exch 265 also help by providing a remedy for wrongful interference with the use of land or damage caused to land, in both cases caused by some activity or omission on the wrongdoer's land. Negligence also has a role to play where property is damaged as a result of failure to take reasonable care.

A person's reputation is protected by the tort of defamation. The equitable remedies available for breach of confidentiality, although not strictly part of tort law, and the growing influence of the European Convention on Human Rights cannot be ignored in this context. These may help to protect privacy by preventing publication of true but detrimental information.

economic loss

Refers to a loss that is purely financial, eg loss of profit – in contrast to personal injury or damage to property

Economic loss is an oddity. Damages are calculated to take account of financial loss sustained by the victim of a tort (see generally Chapter 20) but, as will be seen in Chapter 6, there are restrictions on the availability of a claim in negligence for what is described as 'pure economic loss'. The 'economic' torts of deceit, malicious falsehood, passing off and interference with trade (see Chapter 15), may ensure that a business is protected from unfair competition. Economic loss will also be compensated where the law of contract can be used.

1.2.4 The parties to an action in tort

Capacity generally

The usual principle applies to torts as to any other part of the civil law. In order to bring or defend an action, the party concerned must have legal capacity. A minor can neither bring nor defend an action in their own name but must rely on representation by a suitable adult. Similar rules apply to those of unsound mind. Special rules apply to certain other groups, for example corporations and trade unions. Until the twentieth century, married women were also included as a slightly different case but now they are generally treated as any other person!

The state

As the Crown is traditionally regarded as the fount of all justice, it is not surprising that special rules have evolved as to the liability of the state and its officials. In relation to the monarch the old idea that the 'King can do no wrong' is maintained and no action can be brought against the sovereign personally, nor in respect of certain prerogative and statutory powers.

Until 1947 the only remedy against the Crown was by way of petition of right asking the monarch for redress of a wrong. This anomaly was dealt with by the Crown Proceedings Act 1947. The present position is that the Crown is usually in the same position as any other legal person and can therefore sue or be sued in relation to torts in much the same way as anyone else.

> **vicarious liability**
> Not a tort in itself but a means of imposing liability on somebody who is responsible for the tortfeasor usually an employer

There are some oddities. For example, the doctrine of **vicarious liability** cannot apply to heads of government departments as all servants of the Crown are fellow employees. The head of department cannot therefore be regarded as employing subordinate officials. In practice this was of little importance as the wrongdoer remained personally liable and the Treasury Solicitor would satisfy any judgment. Theoretically, however, it was possible for the Crown to plead immunity when an allegation of tortious behaviour was made. This has been dealt with by the Crown Proceedings Act 1947 which brought Crown immunity in tort to an end in most circumstances.

Foreign sovereigns and their servants have long enjoyed what is popularly known as 'diplomatic immunity' for tortious actions. Such immunity can always be waived but its existence can and does cause problems. By way of example, a person whose vehicle has been damaged by the negligent driving of a chauffeur employed by a foreign embassy will be unable to obtain compensation if the chauffeur can show that the accident occurred in the course of employment by the embassy unless immunity is waived.

The Member States of the European Union may have liability to their citizens where the state has failed to implement EU legislation (*Francovich v Italy* [1991] ECR I–5357). The European Union is liable for the activities of its institutions or servants by virtue of Article 288 EC Treaty.

Minors

A person does not become legally adult until their eighteenth birthday is reached (Family Law Reform Act 1969 s 1). Until that time a minor may only sue or defend an action by a responsible adult known as a 'litigation friend'. Apart from this procedural requirement a minor has exactly the same rights and duties in torts as an adult. We shall see, however, that certain allowances may be made, particularly in relation to the defences of voluntary assumption of risk and contributory negligence, for a less mature understanding.

The general rule is that minors may be liable for their own tortious activities. The fact of immaturity is relevant in some cases. For example in a case of negligence, the actions of the child will not be judged by the usual standard of the reasonable man but by the standard of a reasonable and prudent child of the same age.

Victims of child tortfeasors might well hope that the minor's parents would be liable for the child's wrongdoing. This is not the case unless:

- the parent can be shown to have vicarious liability, or
- the parent has personally been negligent, for example in *Bebee v Sales* (1916) 32 TLR 413 by failing to exercise reasonable control over a 15-year-old who injured another child's eye with an airgun given to him by his father. The father had failed to exercise proper control when he did not remove the gun from the boy's possession after he had smashed a neighbour's window.

There is no general rule that a child may not sue its parent but a child injured while in the womb is subject to special rules. These are found in the Congenital Disabilities (Civil Liability) Act 1976 which provides

1. the child must be born alive and disabled
2. the defendant must have potential tort liability to the child even if the mother was not harmed and has no cause of action
3. the mother herself cannot be liable for any injury to her unborn child.

Married persons

As far as claims by or against third parties are concerned, married people are in the same position as anyone else. Where a claim is made by one spouse against the other, proceedings are not subject to any special rules except that the court has power to stay any proceedings if no substantial benefit is likely to be obtained by either party if the matter continues. This provision, found in the Law Reform (Husband and Wife) Act 1962 s 1(2)(a), is designed to ensure that the courts do not become yet another forum in which husband and wife can fight purely personal battles for the sake of it.

Corporations

A corporation is an artificial person having legal personality by virtue of incorporation. A corporation can sue for any tort which is committed against it save for those where commission of the tort is clearly impossible, for example false imprisonment. Similarly, the corporation is an appropriate defendant, usually by virtue of vicarious liability as the employer of someone who has in fact committed the tort.

Partnerships

Partnerships do not have legal personality and cannot therefore sue or be sued. A right of action vests in the partners who sue as individuals. Where a tort has been committed by the firm, the individual partners have joint and **several liability** to the claimant. The Rules of Court make special provision to ensure that legal actions are not duplicated or unduly prolonged.

It should be noted that a new type of partnership was brought into being by the Limited Liability Partnerships Act 2000. Where a partnership is formed by virtue of the Act, it has its own legal personality and can sue or be sued in the same way as any other corporation.

Persons of unsound mind

A person who is of unsound mind may sue, through the services of a litigation friend, for any tort committed against them. Where such a person has allegedly committed a tort the position is not straightforward.

If a tort requires a particular state of mind, then evidence will be needed that the person had that state of mind.

several liability
Where there are joint tortfeasors each one can be separately liable for the whole damage – so if one lacks funds to pay compensation the claimant can bring the action against the one that can pay

CASE EXAMPLE

Morriss v Marsden [1952] 1 All ER 925

While the defendant did not know that he was doing wrong, he attacked and seriously injured the claimant. The evidence showed that he intended to strike the claimant and he was therefore liable.

Where the actions are involuntary, the person is unlikely to be liable.

1.2.5 Tort and mental state

In torts two mental states are relevant:

- intention
- **malice**.

Intention

In the criminal law, the general principle is that a person must intend to commit the crime if they are to be found guilty (the element of *mens rea*). It is very rarely the case that a person must be shown to have intended to commit a tort although where this can be shown, the claimant may find it easier to establish a case.

Having said this, many torts require the defendant to have intended to do the act which amounts to the tort. In trespass to the person, for example, the defendant must have intended to touch the claimant in order to be liable although they need not have intended to commit battery. A trespass to land cannot be committed by a parachutist who is blown onto land by the wind.

In the tort of negligence, the defendant is liable for unintended consequences of an act. Liability rests on the fact that the defendant failed to foresee the potential consequences and thus failed to guard against them. If the consequences are intended, then some other tort may have been committed. By way of example, if a motorist deliberately rams another vehicle, there may be liability for trespass to the person or trespass to goods, but there will be no liability for negligence.

Malice

In some rare circumstances, the defendant's motive may be relevant. An improper motive is usually referred to as malice and its presence can have the effect of rendering what might otherwise be a reasonable action unreasonable and therefore unlawful. Examples of this are found in the tort of malicious falsehood (see Chapter 15) and in nuisance (see Chapter 9). Malice may also defeat the defence of qualified privilege available in defamation (see Chapter 14).

1.2.6 Alternative methods of obtaining compensation

Alternative Dispute Resolution (ADR)

While a person may be able to bring legal action to seek a remedy for some injury or damage which has been suffered, this can be fraught with difficulty. Despite the recent reforms, the court system is slow and expensive. The availability of legal aid has been substantially curtailed. Perhaps most importantly, there can never be any true certainty as to the outcome. While the victim of wrongdoing may well wish to see the defendant publicly found liable by a judge in a court of law, most will think long and hard before venturing into such uncharted waters.

Over recent years other methods to resolve issues have been developed so that there are now various methods of ADR available. These include

- arbitration
- adjudication
- conciliation and
- mediation.

Each may be relevant in the context of torts; for example conciliation and mediation schemes have been created by a number of local authorities to deal with complaints of statutory nuisance (see Chapter 9).

For full discussion of ADR the reader should consult a text on the English legal system.

Insurance

The purpose of insurance from a defendant's point of view is to protect them from personally having to foot the bill. From the claimant's point of view, the fact that a defendant is insured will mean that there are resources from which any damages will be met.

As the level of damages for personal injury can be very high, insurance is compulsory in certain circumstances. The Road Traffic Act 1988 makes third party insurance compulsory for all motor vehicles while the Employers' Liability (Compulsory Insurance) Act 1969 requires employers to have insurance against liability for injury to employees. Professionals, for example solicitors and doctors, are required to have third party insurance as a condition of practice although they will be covered by their employers' insurance if employed. Insurance against public liability may be required as a term in a standard form contract, for example the 'Standard Form of Building Contract' (commonly known as the JCT contract) which is widely used by the construction industry.

Individuals may choose to obtain no-fault insurance to protect themselves and/or their property in the event of accidental damage. Common examples are household insurance policies which protect the buildings and contents. Other policies protect against redundancy, ill health and death.

The judges are of course aware that many awards of damages will in fact be paid by insurance companies and that individuals may have chosen to protect themselves against misfortune. This may in some cases influence the way in which a case is approached. In the context of road traffic accidents, the courts can impose a very high standard of care.

The availability of insurance may also be relevant. One of the policy reasons influencing the decision on **nervous shock** arising from the Hillsborough cases (see Chapter 6) was the need to ensure that the number of potential claims was limited. This means that insurance companies are in a position to make a realistic assessment of potential liability, an essential first step to setting the amount of a premium!

nervous shock
A recognised psychiatric injury such as clinical depression and Post Traumatic Stress Disorder caused by a single shocking event

1.2.7 Relationships with other areas of law

Crime

In one sense, torts are the civil equivalent of crimes. Each requires a certain standard to be observed and breach of the 'code' leads to consequences. Tortious behaviour may entitle a 'victim' to compensation or some other remedy while criminal behaviour will lead to punishment of the person convicted and may also lead to compensation of the victim by means of a criminal compensation order, or by payment of compensation by the Criminal Injuries Compensation Authority. The distinction between crime and torts is essentially one of degree. A crime is generally regarded by society as wrongdoing of a sufficiently extreme nature that it requires punishment, while tortious behaviour leaves the 'victim' to decide whether or not to pursue a private remedy.

In some circumstances, the two areas of law overlap. This is particularly evident in cases involving trespass to the person which overlaps with criminal assaults and torts such as conversion and trespass to goods. In such cases it may be possible for civil action to be brought using tort even though the wrongdoer has been punished by the criminal law. It was partly to avoid such duplication of actions that the criminal courts have been given power to award compensation to the victim in straightforward cases.

Contract

Both the law of contract and the law of torts are concerned to ensure that a person fulfils a duty whether this is imposed by agreement (contract) or law (torts). For example, for many years the only remedy for a deliberate misrepresentation inducing a party to enter a contract was to be found in the tort of deceit. As can be seen from consultation of a textbook on contract law, tortious principles have to some extent been assimilated into contract law.

Other areas of contract law such as consumer protection demonstrate a close link with torts. The reader is referred to Chapter 12 for more detailed discussion.

Academic writers are divided over the issues raised. Some believe that the separate law is evolving into a new category, a general law of obligations which gives rise to a remedy whenever an obligation is breached. This is so whether the obligation arises from agreement between the parties or from a duty imposed by law. The arguments continue but we are beginning to see textbooks published which are concerned with the 'Law of restitution' or the 'Law of obligations' indicating that evolution is continuing.

Land law

While torts are rarely concerned with rights relating to the title to land, many torts, for example trespass to land and *Rylands v Fletcher*, depend on the legal status of the parties in relation to the occupation of the land affected or from which the problem emanates. The torts lawyer needs to be fully aware of the basic principles of land law. This text generally assumes such knowledge although the reader's attention will be drawn to specific problems where necessary.

1.3 Fault and no-fault liability

1.3.1 Fault liability

'There can be no liability without fault.' This old legal adage was reworded by Lord Atkin in *Donoghue v Stevenson* [1932] AC 562 when he said that the law of tort is:

QUOTATION

'based upon a general public sentiment of moral wrongdoing for which the offender must pay.'

Case law, as readers will see as they progress through this book, upholds Lord Atkin's view. Although not all torts require intention to do wrong, each in reality imposes an expected standard of behaviour and a defendant who fails to meet that standard, whether by being insufficiently careful (negligence) or by doing something which is regarded as an infringement of another's rights (trespass to the person or to land), may find that an aggrieved person has a legal remedy.

The tort of negligence provides perhaps the best example of the problems of torts which require a claimant to prove fault. Among the problems which such a claimant faces are:

- evidential difficulties – it is not always possible to prove that the defendant was at fault even though damage has been suffered
- the need in some cases, for example where the damage suffered is nervous shock, to bring the claimant within a recognised class of 'victim' – failure may mean that although the actual damage is the same, some claimants may succeed while others fail.

Arguments in favour of a fault-based system include:

- the potential deterrent value of a finding of fault (see above section 1.2.2)
- the possibility that the defendant will in fact be punished for the wrongdoing although punitive damages are rarely awarded.

1.3.2 Strict liability

strict liability
Refers to torts where the claimant does not have to show fault on the part of the defendant – the most obvious ones are under the Animals Act 1971 and the Consumer Protection Act 1987

While most torts contain an element of fault in the sense of failure to meet a required stadard or intention to do a particular act, some are described as bearing **strict liability**. In such cases there is no requirement to show that the defendant was at fault. Torts of strict liability include liability under the Consumer Protection Act 1987 and the Animals Act 1971. Where the requirements of the tort have been fulfilled, the defendant will be liable even though in reality there is no fault in the sense of intention or negligence. It would however be wrong to say that a defendant who is in breach of a particular requirement is always liable. While the torts may impose 'strict liability' defences are usually available even if they are limited. Liability is 'strict' not 'absolute'.

For a detailed discussion of the merits and demerits of a fault based system in the context of negligence where it causes most difficulty, see Chapter 3. The reader is also referred to Chapter 11 on *Rylands v Fletcher* for an interesting tort which started life as a tort of strict liability, but now appears to have changed its character to become fault based!

1.3.3 No-fault schemes

The problems faced by claimants who need to prove fault have already been highlighted. The question arises 'Is the law always an appropriate tool to deal with wrongful behaviour which causes damage?'

This question was considered by the Royal Commission on Civil Liability and Compensation for Personal Injury (Cmnd 7054, 1978) which is from now on referred to as the Pearson Committee. The report showed that at that time the number of people suffering serious injury or death was around 3,000,000 each year of whom something under 250,000 made a claim in torts. Taking into account all sources of compensation, this small proportion of the total number of victims actually received about 25 per cent of all monies paid for accidental injury. The Pearson Committee also found that the costs of the torts system were disproportionate to the amount paid to claimants and that administrative costs swallowed up a larger percentage of the budget than the costs of other sources for compensation, for example the social security system. There was no doubt then, nor is there now, that where compensation for a tort is paid, the claimant will in fact receive a greater sum than from other sources. In summary the Pearson Committee found that

- the torts system gives disproportionate benefits to a minority of people suffering accidental injury
- the system is expensive in terms of cost
- court action is slow and complex.

It was recommended that a no-fault system of compensation should be introduced to deal with accident compensation. This has not been done in England but a scheme was set up in New Zealand in 1974 and corresponding rights of action in tort were abolished. Under the scheme the claimant originally received a lump sum for bodily impairment in addition to a weekly payment of a sum equivalent to 80 per cent earnings subject to a statutory maximum amount. The scheme proved too expensive to continue and in 1992 the payment of a lump sum ceased and was replaced by an additional weekly payment in cases of permanent disability. The New Zealand scheme has proved more costly than had been anticipated and is criticised as the focus is still on the cause of the injury, disability resulting from degeneration being excluded. Blindness is blindness whether it is caused by an accidental injury or by a disease, but only the victim of the accident will benefit under the scheme.

The Pearson Committee made many recommendations but most have not been implemented. Some have been partially implemented – the court system has been reformed in recent years and some provisions have been made to recoup at least part of the cost of compensation borne by the social security system. Little else has happened or is likely to happen.

In spite of the failures of torts, people who suffer personal injury may be entitled to compensation from other sources provided they are able to fulfil the relevant criteria applicable to each.

1. More people are now taking out insurance policies which will pay out in the event of ill health, accidental injury or unemployment. Such policies are not inexpensive and tend to be subject to strict conditions making them sometimes less effective than the insured might expect.
2. There is some limited provision for compulsory liability insurance, for example in relation to road traffic accidents and accidents at work.

3. A person injured as a result of a criminal act may be entitled to payment under the Criminal Injuries Compensation Scheme although this is sometimes criticised as inadequate, as awards are made on a 'tariff' basis rather than on the basis of the extent of the victim's actual loss.
4. Social security benefits are payable to all those who qualify and not only to all who suffer injury. The level of such benefits is not generous, the criteria for qualification are rigorously enforced and many benefits are means-tested.

The system is not perfect and many people will continue to receive no compensation at all. The consequences of medical accidents cause particular concern and the British Medical Association advocates a no-fault scheme for the victims of such accidents (No Fault Compensation Working Party Report 1991). The government has contributed to the debate by consultations over the way in which compensation for clinical negligence should be awarded. In 2001 the Department of Health published a paper – *Clinical negligence – what are the issues and options for reform?* – outlining the perceived problems and suggesting that the solution might be found in

- no fault compensation which would save time and costs
- structured settlements which would mean weekly or monthly payments
- fixed tariffs for specific injuries
- more use of mediation or other methods of ADR.

The debate will no doubt continue as it has since the Pearson Committee published its report in 1978.

1.4 Joint and several tortfeasors

1.4.1 Joint and several liability

Injury can be caused by more than one person. Where it results from one act caused by more than one person, the persons responsible are called 'joint' tortfeasors. This will be the case where a person carries out a tortious act on the instructions of another person. In cases where the injury results from the cumulative effect of more than one person acting independently, the wrongdoers are known as 'several concurrent' tortfeasors. Provided the injury results from the combined actions, in other words the claimant has a single, indivisible injury, any or all of the wrongdoers are liable to the claimant for the full extent of the injury.

From the claimant's point of view, this may have advantages as the choice of defendant can be dictated by the extent to which each defendant is likely to be able to meet any award of damages. Defendants on the other hand may take a different view as the one defendant in a position to pay may find that the entire sum has to be found if co-tortfeasors are insolvent.

Not surprisingly defendants may well consider this to be unjust and the rules, while ensuring that the claimant is fully compensated, make provision for allocation of financial liability between defendants.

1.4.2 Contributions between tortfeasors

We have seen that the distinction between joint tortfeasors and several concurrent tortfeasors is in practice of little importance to a claimant. Full compensation is recoverable. This means that if the defendant against whom judgment is given is unable to satisfy the claim, the claimant is free to sue another defendant. Clearly this runs counter to the desire to minimise any potential waste of court time and costs. This problem is dealt with by the provision that costs cannot be obtained by a claimant for a second or subsequent action unless the court is satisfied that the action is reasonable in all the circumstances (Civil Liability (Contribution) Act 1978 s 4).

None of this helps the defendant who may find that a substantial amount is owed in circumstances where others share responsibility. Help is however available by virtue of the Civil Liability (Contribution) Act 1978. This provides in s 1(1) that a person liable for damage can recover a contribution from any other person who is also liable for that damage, whether that other person has joint or several liability. Rules exist to make sure that the claimant can only recover the actual loss – there is no chance of suing more than one defendant and getting damages twice over!

The amount of any contribution should reflect the extent to which each defendant bears responsibility for the damage. The way this works is similar to the basis on which contributory negligence apportions blame between the claimant and the defendants by virtue of the Law Reform (Contributory Negligence) Act 1945 which is discussed in Chapters 5 and 19.

1.5 Tort and human rights

1.5.1 An innovation in English law?

Legal and political influences

To judge by the headlines in the press, one can be forgiven for thinking that the concept of human rights did not exist in England and Wales before 1998 but this is not strictly true. One of the main reasons for resistance to the idea of legislative protection of human rights was the view that the common law, for example through principles enshrined in Magna Carta 1215 and the Bill of Rights 1688, was able to give adequate protection by means such as the prerogative orders (*habeas corpus, mandamus, certiorari*) and the process of judicial review. Each of these could restrain the abuse of a citizen's rights by the state. In addition the doctrine of precedent allows for the incremental development of the law in this area.

The twentieth century saw the growth of powers vested in the state, for example in the areas of social welfare, health and control of the environment, so that the potential for abuse of the individual by the state increased, or was perceived to do so. State control of many aspects of individual life was also perceived to have increased when the United Kingdom joined the European Union in 1972. The current debate over whether or not the United Kingdom can support the proposed European Constitution, which it is suggested will extend European control to national matters such as the provision of health care, serves to fuel concerns as to the extent of state (or European) control over individual rights and freedoms. The argument about state control and individual rights looks likely to continue.

The issue of human rights is therefore a political one as it is for Parliament to decide whether, and if so to what extent, individual rights and freedoms and protection from abuse need to be enshrined in statute rather than relying on the common law.

The Convention and its basis in the law of the United Kingdom

The Convention for the Protection of Human Rights and Fundamental Freedoms (hereafter 'the Convention') is an international treaty which the United Kingdom was the first country to sign as long ago as 1951, but until Parliament acted, the Convention had little effect in the United Kingdom.

From 1966 British citizens were able to petition the European Court of Human Rights (referred to hereafter as ECtHR) to obtain rulings as to whether or not **fundamental rights** had been abrogated by the activities of the state. The problem with this was that the British Government was not bound to have any regard for the decisions of the ECtHR. This meant that whether or not the decisions led to change in the United Kingdom depended largely on political decisions.

From the 1970s onwards debate raged as to the need for a modern Bill of Rights for the United Kingdom and in 1997 the Labour Party won a general election on the basis that the Convention would be incorporated as part of United Kingdom law. The manifesto promise was fulfilled when the Human Rights Act 1998 was passed, bringing most of the Convention into effect as part of the law of the United Kingdom in October 2000.

1.5.2 The Human Rights Act 1998

The Act is said to have incorporated the Convention into national law. While this is true to a substantial extent, some important provisions of the Convention have not been incorporated, for example Article 13 which gives a right to an effective remedy in a national court, and for the time being the incorporation of certain other articles has been delayed. (For full details of these issues, refer to a text on constitutional law and to texts on human rights.)

The main provisions of the Act are as follows:

- Section 2 – requires any court or tribunal hearing any case which involves a question of Convention rights to take into account the jurisprudence (case law) of the ECtHR whenever it is relevant to the issue.
- Section 3 – requires the courts to interpret all legislation in a way which is compatible with the rights enshrined in the Convention, giving the courts the right to make a 'declaration of incompatibility' where a statute is found to be inadequate to uphold a Convention right (a 'fast track' procedure for the amendment of offending legislation is found in s 10 and Sched 2).
- Section 6 – makes it unlawful for a **public authority** to act in a way which is incompatible with Convention rights unless constrained to do so by primary legislation. The term public authority is widely construed and can include bodies carrying out functions on behalf of a public authority and exercising the powers conferred upon such an authority. It is not clear when these 'quasi' public bodies will be treated as public bodies. The following contrasting cases demonstrate the difficulty which at present remains unresolved.

CASE EXAMPLE

R(A) v Partnerships in Care Ltd [2002] 1 WLR 2610

Managers of a private psychiatric hospital altered the care and treatment of a patient. This was held to be an act of a public nature as the managers were acting in accordance with statutory regimes imposed by the Registered Homes Act 1984 and the Mental Health Act 1983.

CASE EXAMPLE

R (Heather) v Leonard Cheshire Foundation [2002] EWCA Civ 366

The Leonard Cheshire Foundation decided to close one of its homes. Despite the fact that it was in part publicly funded and was regulated by the state, it was held that it was not a public body.

- Section 7 – gives a right to challenge decisions or actions by a public authority, the courts having power to declare that decision or action unlawful and, by s 8, to grant appropriate remedies, for example damages.

The Human Rights Act 1998 has introduced what can be regarded as an umbrella over the rights of individuals, enabling them to resist oppression by the state by challenging the legitimacy of acts and omissions by the state and/or failures of the law to give effective protection of those rights which the Convention sets out as fundamental.

While protection from abuse by the state or a public body is perhaps the primary aim of the Convention, indirectly it may be of benefit in disputes between private individuals, as the court has a positive obligation to enforce Convention rights. This can involve

- exercising judicial discretion in a way which gives effect to such rights
- interpreting legislation in accordance with the Convention
- developing the common law so that it is compatible with Convention rights
- creating a remedy in private disputes where it is necessary in order to protect an individual's rights.

CASE EXAMPLE

Venables and Thompson v Newsgroup Newspapers and Associated Newspapers Ltd [2001] 2 WLR 1038

Injunctions were continued to prevent the two boys convicted of the killing of James Bulger from being identified, the court being satisfied that this was necessary to safeguard their rights under Article 2 (the right to life) and Article 8 (the right to respect for private life).

The effect of the Human Rights Act has been huge. It is almost a daily occurrence (at least for those interested in law) to read in the press of cases in which '**human rights**' are raised as an issue and the area of tort law is no exception.

Figure 1.1 Human rights are like an umbrella that provides basic rights that overarch the law.

1.5.3 Incorporation of human rights into the law of tort

The general requirement, set out in s 2 of the Act, takes account of the ECtHR case law. It must be remembered that this has been developed since the early 1950s. This means that modern cases may well be decided in a rather different way than if reliance had been placed only on common law. It is not possible at this time to anticipate the long-term effect of this requirement but in the context of the law of tort, as will be seen, some old ideas have had to be reconsidered and in some cases abandoned. Specific reference to relevant cases will be made as appropriate as individual torts are discussed later in this book. In this chapter, the intention is merely to give a flavour of how the Convention is influencing the development of this particular area of law.

1.5.4 Human rights and trespass to the person

The tort is one of the oldest in the common law and has served to protect individuals from unlawful threats of violence (assault), unlawful violence (battery) and unlawful detention (false imprisonment) (see Chapter 13 of this book). This gives no remedy in English common law to those who are lawfully subjected to what they perceive as unwarranted and unpleasant behaviour. The Convention, in Article 3, imposes an additional requirement by which the lawfulness of behaviour can be judged.

ARTICLE

'No one shall be subjected to torture or to inhuman or degrading treatment or punishment' (Art 3).

This Article has been important in cases involving medical treatment which show that it does not extend as far as some people would like.

CASE EXAMPLE

Pretty v United Kingdom [2002] 2 FLR 45

Diane Pretty suffered from a degenerative disease and wanted her husband to be allowed to help her to take her own life. The DPP refused to give an undertaking that Mr Pretty would not be prosecuted under the Suicide Act 1961 s 2(1), so Mrs Pretty sought judicial review alleging that the decision of the DPP was unlawful and seeking a declaration that the Suicide Act was incompatible with Article 3 and other parts of the Convention. When her case was heard by the House of Lords her appeal was dismissed and she appealed to the ECtHR.

JUDGMENT

'. . . the absolute and unqualified prohibition on a Member State inflicting the proscribed treatment requires that "treatment" should not be given an unrestricted or extravagant meaning. It cannot . . . be plausibly suggested that the [DPP] or any other agent of the United Kingdom is inflicting the proscribed treatment on Mrs Pretty, whose suffering derives from her cruel disease' (para 13).

Diane Pretty's suffering was clearly the result of her disease rather than the result of any treatment. She was left with no legal redress using either the common law or the Convention. However there are other cases in which the treatment itself, while lawful under English law, has been found to be 'inhuman or degrading'. Two cases, which were heard by the ECtHR before the Human Rights Act 1998 became law, give an idea of the way in which such claims will be considered in the future. In both cases, the English courts would now be able to hear the complaints pursuant to s 6 and would have regard to these and other cases in which the compass of Article 3 has been considered.

CASE EXAMPLE

Keenan v United Kingdom (2002) 33 EHRR 38, ECtHR

Mark Keenan committed suicide while in prison. Throughout his detention it was clear that he suffered from a chronic psychiatric problem. Nine days before his expected release date, he received an additional 28 days in prison for an assault on prison officers. He hanged himself the day after he received the sentence which meant that his release would be delayed. His mother complained to the court that among other matters of concern, the way in which his medical care had been delivered and the delay in his discharge amounted to inhuman and degrading treatment.

The court held that there had been a violation of Article 3 stating

JUDGMENT

'The lack of effective monitoring of Mark Keenan's condition and lack of informed psychiatric input into his assessment and treatment disclose significant defects in the medical care provided to a mentally ill person known to be a suicide risk. The belated imposition on him in those circumstances of a serious disciplinary punishment . . . is not compatible with the standard of treatment required in respect of a mentally ill person. It must be regarded as constituting inhuman and degrading treatment and punishment within the meaning of Article 3 of the Convention' (para 115).

CASE EXAMPLE

Price v United Kingdom (2001) 11 BHRC 401

Ms Price, a Thalidomide victim who also had kidney problems, was imprisoned for failure to pay a civil debt. She had to spend the first night at a police station in a cell which was not designed to accommodate those with disability. She was forced to sleep in her wheelchair, was unable to reach the emergency button and unable to use the toilet. Despite her deteriorating condition a doctor was not called for over four hours. Once moved to a prison she stayed in a Health Care Centre where the facilities were better adapted to her needs. However, she complained that she was forced to allow male officers to assist her to clean herself after using the toilet and that a female officer later exposed her to male officers when helping her to the toilet. She complained that her treatment was humiliating and degrading.

The court held that while

JUDGMENT

'there is no evidence in this case of any positive intention to humiliate or debase the applicant . . . the court considers that to detain a severely disabled person in [such] conditions constitutes degrading treatment contrary to Article 3' (para 30).

In both Keenan and Price, the detention was lawful and there could be no remedy for false imprisonment neither had either been assaulted or battered to enable the tort of trespass to the person to be used. It is clear that the way each was treated, while lawful, was wholly inappropriate having regard to their respective needs. The Human Rights Act 1998 can therefore provide a remedy where the common law fails to do so.

1.5.5 Human rights and negligence

To date this area of tort law has been most affected by the requirements of Article 13. Article 13 is not incorporated by the Human Rights Act 1998, the view being taken that a sufficient remedy exists by virtue of ss 7 and 8. Decisions of the ECtHR are however relevant in the United Kingdom by virtue of s 2 which expressly requires ECtHR case law to be taken into account in deciding cases before the English courts and tribunals.

ARTICLE

'Every one whose rights and freedoms as set forth in this Convention are violated shall have an effective remedy before a national authority notwithstanding that the violation has been committed by persons acting in an official capacity' (Art 13).

In the case of *Keenan v United Kingdom* (2002) ECtHR, 33 EHRR 38 described above, it can be suggested that an allegation of negligence could have been made on the basis that, in the light of his psychiatric condition, the way in which he was treated was inappropriate and caused him injury. As can be seen in Chapter 4, he would have had to prove that his treatment caused psychiatric injury and this is not clear. He undoubtedly suffered anguish, fear and even terror but the ECtHR held that 'There is no evidence that this would be regarded as "injury" in the sense recognised by domestic law' (para 128). On this basis the ECtHR held that there had been a violation of Article 13 as there was no effective remedy for violation of his rights under Article 3.

In the context of child care, issues under Article 13 have arisen from the idea that a local authority could not be sued in negligence for decisions made as to the care of children which, with hindsight, proved to be inappropriate and to have caused the children injury (*X and Others v Bedfordshire County Council* [1995] 3 All ER 353). The reason behind this view was that local authorities act for the benefit of society as a whole and would be unduly inhibited by the possibility of being held to account in negligence, unless the circumstances were wholly exceptional. The case came before the ECtHR as *Z and Others v United Kingdom* [2001] 2 FLR 612.

CASE EXAMPLE

Z and Others v United Kingdom [2001] 2 FLR 612; (2001) 34 EHRR 3, ECtHR

Z and her siblings first came to the attention of social services in October 1987. Thereafter there was a string of concerns as to the children's welfare raised by neighbours, the police, teachers, the children's GP and health visitor. In December 1992 the local authority at last applied for and obtained an interim care order. The consultant child psychiatrist who examined the children in January 1993 stated that the case was the worst case of neglect and emotional abuse that she had seen in her professional career. A full care order was made in April 1993. In June of that year, the Official Solicitor started an action on behalf of the children against the local authority for damages for negligence and/or breach of statutory duty. At all stages, right through to the House of Lords, the English courts held that the children's claim must fail. The Children Act 1989 cannot be construed to confer a private law cause of action and the claim in negligence was struck out on the public policy ground that it was not just and reasonable to impose a duty of care on a local authority when dealing with child care cases. The merits of the children's case could not therefore be investigated by the English court.

Having found violation of Articles 3 and 6 (the right to a fair trial), the ECtHR found that:

JUDGMENT

'the applicants did not have available to them an appropriate means of obtaining a determination of their allegations that the local authority failed to protect them from inhuman and degrading treatment and the possibility of obtaining an enforceable award of compensation for the damage suffered thereby . . . [T]here has accordingly been a violation of Article 13 of the Convention' (para 111).

The result of *Z and Others v United Kingdom* has been to change the previously held view that cases of negligence against public authorities should only exceptionally give rise to a right to claim. In effect this meant that such authorities were usually regarded as having immunity from legal action. (For a detailed discussion of this issue, see Chapter 3.)

1.5.6 Human rights and nuisance

Common law nuisance does not always provide a remedy for un-neighbourly behaviour, particularly where the defence of statutory authority can be used or the public interest demands that an activity should continue. By Article 8 the right to privacy and family life is guaranteed subject to legal and necessary interference. The courts have interpreted this very broadly to include problems with night flights into airports, sewage, and low flying military aircraft as interference, but even so a remedy is not always available.

ARTICLE

1. Everyone has the right to respect for his private and family life, his home and his correspondence.

2. There shall be no interference by a public authority with this right except such as is in accordance with the law and is necessary in a democratic society in the interests of national security, public safety or the economic well-being of the country, for the prevention of disorder or crime, for the protection of health or morals, or for the protection of the rights and freedoms of others' (Art 8).

It seemed in 2001 that, as a result of the application of Article 8, night flights into and out of Heathrow Airport might be ended or at the least rigorously curtailed.

CASE EXAMPLE

Hatton v United Kingdom (2001) 11 BHRC 634 (Chambers judgment)

Mrs Hatton and others complained that night flights into and out of Heathrow meant that they all suffered sleep deprivation and consequential health problems. They were unable to bring a case before the English courts against the Civil Aviation Authority as the airport was operated by statutory authority found in the Civil Aviation Act 1982 which, by s 76, specifically excluded civil liability arising from the operation of the airport. Having found that the noise was capable of being an infringement of Article 8, the ECtHR had to consider whether the state had fulfilled its positive duty 'to take reasonable and appropriate measures to secure the applicants' rights under Article 8(1)' (para 95).

The court held

JUDGMENT

'. . . regard must be had to the fair balance that has to be struck between the competing interests of the individual and the community as a whole' (para 96),

and found that

JUDGMENT

'. . . the State failed to strike a fair balance between the United Kingdom's economic well-being and the applicants' effective enjoyment of their right to respect for their homes and their private and family lives' (para 107).

The hope that night flights might be curtailed was short-lived. In *Hatton and Others v United Kingdom* ECtHR 08/07/2003 (Application no 36022/97) the government appealed to the Grand Chamber, arguing that the economic well-being of the country meant that night flights into the airport were necessary and that the interference with the right under Article 8(1) went no further than was necessary for this purpose. The Grand Chamber agreed with the British Government that the interference was justified under the provisions of Article 8(2).

JUDGMENT

'The question is whether . . . a fair balance was struck between the competing interests of the individuals affected by the night noise and the community as a whole.'

The court held that a fair balance had in fact been achieved. The court also found that domestic remedies had been inadequate to review the position and therefore amounted to a breach of Article 13. This meant that the claimants were entitled to costs.

It is interesting to note that five of the judges, in a court of 17, held that the 'concern for environmental protection shares a common ground with the general concern for human rights' and that 'one of the important functions of human rights protection is to protect "small minorities" whose "subjective element" makes them different from the majority.' The five judges held that compensation should be payable to the claimant.

Night flights continue and indeed, at the time of writing, consultation has started about the expansion of London's airports!

Two cases were later decided in which the English courts considered the impact of Article 8.

CASE EXAMPLE

Marcic v Thames Water Utilities [2003] UKHL 66

This was an important test case concerning the potential liability of water service providers for failure to resolve problems experienced by those receiving their services.

Mr Marcic's property was regularly flooded with sewage as the drains provided by Thames Water were inadequate to cope when there was heavy rainfall. The fabric of the house and his gardens were damaged by regular flooding from 1992 onwards. There was no prospect that Thames Water would undertake remedial work in the foreseeable future using the criteria by which priorities were decided.

In the High Court it was held that Thames Water had no liability in nuisance but that Mr Marcic was entitled to a remedy for breach of his Article 8 rights. The Court of Appeal held that Mr Marcic had a valid claim in nuisance at common law but went on to discuss the human rights issue. Although Mr Marcic's rights under Article 8(1) had been violated, the issue turned on Article 8(2) – did the interference go beyond what was necessary in a democratic society? The Court of Appeal held that it did and that Thames Water were liable for infringement of Mr Marcic's Article 8 rights. The matter then went to the House of Lords which held that Mr Marcic could not succeed in his claim using nuisance nor had there been an infringement of his Article 8 rights.

Lord Hoffmann explained

JUDGMENT

'[*Hatton v The United Kingdom*] makes it clear that the Convention does not accord absolute protection to property or even to residential properties. It requires a fair balance to be struck between the interests of persons whose homes and property are affected and the interests of other people, such as customers and the general public' (para 71).

Mr Marcic's action was dismissed. (For further discussion of the nuisance aspect of this case see Chapter 10.)

In the second case, the English court considered the impact of Article 1 First Protocol as well as Article 8.

ARTICLE

'Every . . . person is entitled to the peaceful enjoyment of his possessions. No one shall be deprived of his possessions except in the public interest and subject to the conditions provided for by law and by the general principles of international law' (Art 1 First Protocol).

CASE EXAMPLE

Dennis and Dennis v Ministrs of Defence [2003] EWHC 793 (QB)

The case concerned the effect of noise from RAF Harrier jet fighters which regularly over flew the neighbouring estate. Having found that a nuisance was established, Mr Justice Buckley further held (at para 48) 'that the public interest clearly demands that RAF Wittering should continue to train its pilots.' No remedy of injunction was thus available using the common law.

It was argued that the noise interference was a breach of Article 8 and that the impact on the market value of the estate was a breach of Article 1 First Protocol. Having found that there was interference with Article 8 rights the judge (at para 61), referred to *S v France* (1990) 65 D & R 250 in which it was stated that

JUDGMENT

'Noise nuisance which is particularly severe . . . may seriously affect the value of real property … and thus amount to a partial appropriation.'

On this basis he held

JUDGMENT

'that a fair balance would not be struck in the absence of compensation. I would thus award damages under section 8 in respect of Articles 8 and 1' (para 63).

1.5.7 Human rights and other torts

The fact that only three aspects of the impact of human rights into tort law have been highlighted does not mean that there will be no impact in other torts. As has been seen, the fact that the Convention does not have obvious effect is not relevant (eg who would have thought, prior to 1998, that flooding by sewage would be regarded as a breach of the right to respect for privacy and a family home?).

The rights protected by the Convention are expressed as principles enforced by a duty on the state to ensure that they are protected. This means that where the law of tort fails to provide a remedy but a person's Convention right has been violated, it may be the case that the state is under a duty to rethink the issue in order to provide the required protection. Developments have been rapid and this is likely to continue.

Definition	Case
The Convention	
effective from 1951 but only incorporated into UK law from October 2000	
Human Rights Act 1998	
incorporates most of the Convention but not Article 13 allows reliance on Convention rights in the UK courts	
Human rights and trespass to the person	
Article 3 prohibition of inhuman and degrading treatment	*Keenan v UK* (2002) *Price v UK* (2001)
Human rights and negligence	
although Article 13 right to a remedy not incorporated, public authorities no longer ha~ve blanket immunity from actions for negligence	*Z v UK* (2001)
Human rights and nuisance	
Article 8 capable of wide interpretation night flights – flooding by sewage –	*Hatton v UK* (2003) *Marcic v Thames Water* (2003)
Article 1 First Protocol – peaceful enjoyment of property noise interference from aircraft a breach of Article 8 and loss of value of home a breach of First Protocol – compensation payable	*Dennis v Ministry of Defence* (2003)

Conclusion

This is a fast developing area of the law. The Human Rights Act 1998 will almost certainly have further impact on the law of tort.

SUMMARY

- Tort law concerns civil wrongs and developed out of the old writ system
- Torts involve duties fixed by law
- The main aims of tort are to compensate the victim and to deter wrongdoing
- Tort protects personal security, reputation, property and some economic interests
- Tort interrelates with both Contract Law and Criminal Law but also differs from both
- Tort generally involves fault liability but there are also some strict liability torts
- Human rights can affect torts through the European Convention of Human Rights and the Human Rights Act 1988 which incorporates much of the Convention into English law

2

Negligence: duty of care

AIMS AND OBJECTIVES

After reading this chapter you should be able to:

- Understand the basic origins and character of negligence
- Understand the essential elements of a negligence claim
- Understand the reasons for retreating from the Anns two-part test
- Understand the role of policy in establishing the existence of a duty of care
- Be able to critically analyse the concept of duty of care
- Be able to apply the tests to factual situations to determine the existence of a duty of care

2.1 Duty of care

2.1.1 The origins of negligence and the neighbour principle

The historical background

The origins of negligence lie in other torts in a process known as an action on the case, a method of proving tort through showing negligence or carelessness. Traditionally most torts depended on proof of an intentional and direct interference with the claimant or with his property. Where this was impossible a claimant could make out a special case for liability based on careless deeds.

Long before the twentieth century judges had begun to recognise that many more people suffered loss or injury through careless acts than through intentional ones. Judges towards the end of the eighteenth century established the principle that defendants in certain specific situations might be considered liable for their careless act where they caused foreseeable loss or injury to a claimant. However, there was no general duty of care and there was no means of establishing one. One attempt to establish a formula through which duty situations could be identified came in *Heaven v Pender* (1883) 11 QBD 503.

In the case Brett MR suggested that

JUDGMENT

'wherever one person is . . . placed in such a position with regard to another that everyone of ordinary sense . . . would at once recognise that if he did not use ordinary care and skill . . . he would cause danger or injury to the person or property of the other, a duty arises to use ordinary care and skill to avoid such danger.'

The development of a general test for establishing the existence of a duty of care

The modern tort of negligence begins with Lord Atkin's groundbreaking judgment in *Donoghue v Stevenson* [1932] AC 562. A new approach was necessary in the case because no other action was available.

The judgment is important not just for the decision itself, or only for identifying negligence as a separate tort in its own right, but also for devising the appropriate tests for determining whether negligence has actually occurred.

CASE EXAMPLE

Donoghue v Stevenson [1932] AC 562

The claimant argued that she had suffered shock and gastroenteritis after drinking ginger beer from an opaque bottle out of which a decomposing snail had fallen when the dregs were poured. A friend had bought her the drink and so the claimant was unable to sue in her own right in contract. She nevertheless claimed £500 from the manufacturer for his negligence and was successful. The House of Lords was prepared to accept that there could be liability on the manufacturer. Two major objections were discussed in the case. The first on these is referred to as the 'contract fallacy'. A previous case, *Winterbottom v Wright* (1842) 10 M & W 109, appeared to contain a clear rule preventing a duty of care from being established in the absence of a contractual relationship. The parties to the action were the manufacturer of the ginger beer and the eventual consumer of his product, the ginger beer actually having been bought by the claimant's friend from the owner of a roadside café. The judges rejected the application of this principle in the case. The second potential problem was one raised by Lord Buckminster, who objected to the possibility of a general test for establishing duty of care, and indeed to the specific duty established in the case. He did so on the basis that it would be destructive to commerce and would only harm consumers by the cost of paying damages in successful actions being added to the price of the manufacturer's goods. Again the majority rejected this argument.

Lord Atkin's judgment contained five critical elements:

- Lack of privity of contract did not prevent the claimant from claiming.
- Negligence was accepted as a separate tort in its own right.
- Negligence would be proved by satisfying a three-part test:
  - the existence of a duty of care owed to the claimant by the defendant
  - a breach of that duty by falling below the appropriate standard of care
  - damage caused by the defendant's breach of duty that was not too remote a consequence of the breach.

- The method of determining the existence of a duty of care – the so-called '**neighbour principle**'. This is not the *ratio* of the case but is rather *obiter dicta*. Nevertheless it is a vital guiding principle on which the actual *ratio* was ultimately dependent.

JUDGMENT

'You must take reasonable care to avoid acts or omissions which you can reasonably foresee would be likely to injure your neighbour. Who then in law is my neighbour? . . . persons who are so closely and directly affected by my act that I ought reasonably to have them in my contemplation as being affected so when I am directing my mind to the acts or omissions in question.'

◼ A manufacturer would owe a duty of care towards consumers or users of his/her products not to cause them harm. This is commonly referred to as the 'narrow *ratio*' of the case.

So from the 'neighbour principle' of Lord Atkin the tort of negligence is identified as being based on foreseeability of harm. The case gives us one clear example of a relationship where possible harm is foreseeable and a duty of care then exists – the duty of a manufacturer to the consumers or users of his or her products.

In one sense then the case of *Donoghue v Stevenson* gives us a very simple way of looking at negligence:

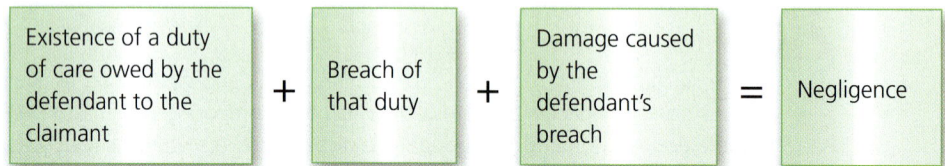

| Existence of a duty of care owed by the defendant to the claimant | **+** | Breach of that duty | **+** | Damage caused by the defendant's breach | **=** | Negligence |

Figure 2.1 The basic elements of an action for negligence

It is important to note that there is a distinction between the duty of care in law (sometimes called the 'notional duty') and the duty of care in fact. In establishing duty the court must be certain that the case involves not just a risk of a type recognised by the law as leading to a duty but that the resulting risk is a type envisaged by the law. In *Bourhill v Young* [1943] AC 92 the court would not accept the existence of a duty in nervous shock because the claimant was not within the area of foreseeable harm. In doing so it approved the judgment of Cardozo J in the American case *Palsgraf v Long Island Railway Co* 284 NY 339 (1928). In imposing a duty then a judge must be certain not just that the circumstances are those where a duty is commonly accepted but that the particular defendant owes a duty in the circumstances to the particular claimant.

ACTIVITY

Quick quiz

In the following situation state which types of loss are recoverable from the manufacturer under the principle in *Donoghue v Stevenson*

Sacha bought a new toaster last week and on the second time of using the toaster it burst into flames. When she bought it the toaster was in a sealed package, and on both occasions that she has used it she has followed the manufacturer's instructions precisely. Sacha is not in any way to blame for the damage that has resulted:

◼ The toaster was completely destroyed and Sacha wants a replacement.

◼ The decorating in the kitchen has suffered smoke damage and needs redecorating.

◼ A cupboard behind the toaster was burnt so badly that it needs replacing.

◼ Sacha's arm was badly burnt as she tried to put out the fire and she would like compensation for the injury.

2.1.2 Development in defining duty and the two-part test in *Anns*

Over many years the tort of negligence developed incrementally, case by case, with a duty of care being established in numerous relationships. Lawyers were able to use the neighbour principle to argue for the extension of negligence into areas previously not covered by the tort where damage was a foreseeable consequence of the defendant's acts or omissions.

At a much later stage in time the test was simplified. The new test did not depend on a duty of care being determined in a given case according to how the case fitted in with past law. Under the new test a duty would be imposed because of the **proximity** of the relationship between the two parties unless there were policy reasons for not doing so. This of course means legal proximity (the extent to which the deeds of one can affect the other), not proximity based on physical closeness.

proximity
Refers to the fact that the defendant should contemplate that his actions may have an effect on potential claimants – rather than physical closeness

CASE EXAMPLE

Anns v Merton London Borough Council [1978] AC 728

The local authority had failed to ensure that building work complied with the plans, and as a result the building had inadequate foundations. The claimant, a tenant who had leased the property after it had changed hands many times, claimed that the damage to the property threatened health and safety and sued successfully. The decision was clearly arrived at on policy grounds.

Lord Wilberforce, in framing the 'two-part' test, suggested that the appropriate method of determining whether or not the defendant owed a duty of care in a given case was as follows.

- First it should be established that there is sufficient proximity between defendant and claimant for damage to be a foreseeable possibility of any careless act or omission.
- If this was established then it was only for the court to decide whether or not there were any policy considerations that might either limit the scope of the duty or remove it altogether.

Lord Wilberforce explained the position in the following terms:

JUDGMENT

'. . . the position has now been reached that in order to establish that a duty of care arises in a particular situation, it is not necessary to bring the facts of that situation within those of previous situations in which a duty of care has been held to exist. Rather the question has to be approached in two stages. First one has to ask whether, as between the alleged wrong-doer and the person who has suffered damage there is a sufficient relationship of proximity or neighbourhood such that, in the reasonable contemplation of the former, carelessness on his part may be likely to cause damage to the latter – in which case a prima facie duty of care arises. Secondly, if the first question is answered affirmatively, it is necessary to consider whether there are any considerations which ought to negative, or to reduce or limit the scope of the duty or the class of person to whom it is owed or the damages to which a breach of it may give rise . . .'

Lord Wilberforce's two-part test led to some significant developments in the law of negligence in the 1980s, particularly in relation to economic loss and nervous shock (see later for instance *Junior Books v Veitchi* [1983] 1 AC 520 in Chapter 6 section 6.2). However, these developments were not always considered appropriate and the 'two-part' test caused distress among many judges.

'The two part test looked deceptively simple. In effect the plaintiff, having established foreseeability, raised a presumption of the existence of a duty which the defendant then had to rebut on policy grounds.'

J Murray, *Street on Torts* (11th edn, Butterworths, 2003)

The clear problem with the two-part test is the amount of discretion given to judges to determine whether or not a duty should exist in a given situation. As a result of a general unease with the test, the judgments in a series of cases in the 1980s display criticism by senior judges of the two-part test.

Lord Keith in *Governors of the Peabody Donation Fund v Sir Lindsay Parkinson & Co Ltd* [1985] AC 210 suggested that whether or not it was just and fair to impose a duty was a more appropriate test than mere policy considerations.

Lord Oliver in *Leigh and Sillavan Ltd v Aliakmon Shipping Co Ltd (The Aliakmon)* [1986] 1 AC 785 considered that the test should not be considered as giving the court a free hand to determine what limits to set in each case.

In *Curran v Northern Ireland Co-ownership Housing Association Ltd* [1987] AC 718 Lord Bridge indicated that the courts should be wary of extending those cases where a statutory body could be under a duty to control the activities of third parties. He also commented that the *Anns* test 'obscured the important distinction between **misfeasance** and **non-feasance**'.

In this last case Lord Bridge approved the judgment of Brennan J in the High Court of Australia in *Sutherland Shire Council v Heyman* (1985) 60 ALR 1. In this case the judge argued that it was 'preferable that the law should develop novel categories of negligence incrementally and by analogy with established categories'.

In *Yuen Kun Yeu v Attorney General of Hong Kong* [1987] 2 All ER 705 Lord Keith also argued that the *Anns* test had been '. . . elevated to a degree of importance greater than its merits', and this he felt was probably not Lord Wilberforce's original intention.

These judgments all show a much more cautious approach in determining the existence of a duty of care than need be the case under the two-part test. As a result of this the two-part test was in fact later discarded and the case of *Anns* also overruled.

misfeasance
This is where the defendant has acted wrongly

non-feasance
This is where the defendant has a duty to act and is liable for a failure to act

CASE EXAMPLE

Murphy v Brentwood District Council [1990] 2 All ER 908

A house had been built on a concrete raft laid on a landfill site. The council had been asked to inspect and had approved the design of the raft. The raft was actually inadequate and cracks later appeared when the house subsided. The claimant sold the house for £35,000 less than its value in good condition would have been and sued the council for negligence in approving the raft. The House of Lords held that the council was not liable on the basis that the council could not owe a greater duty of care to the claimant than the builder. In doing so the court also overruled Anns and the two-part test, preferring instead a new three-part test suggested by Lords Keith, Oliver and Bridge in *Caparo v Dickman* [1990] 1 All ER 568.

2.1.3 The retreat from *Anns* and the three-part test from *Caparo*

In *Caparo v Dickman* the House of Lords had in fact shown some dissatisfaction with the two-part test and preferred a return to the more traditional incremental approach by reference to past cases. The test was able to change in *Murphy* because they had identified an incremental approach with three stages.

CASE EXAMPLE

Caparo v Dickman [1990] 1 All ER 568

Shareholders in a company bought more shares and then made a successful takeover bid for the company after studying the audited accounts prepared by the defendants. They later regretted the move and sued the auditors claiming that they had relied on accounts which had shown a sizeable surplus rather than the deficit that was in fact the case.

The House of Lords decided that the auditors owed no duty of care since company accounts are not prepared for the purposes of people taking over a company and cannot then be relied on by them for such purposes. The court also considered a three-stage test in imposing liability appropriate.

- Firstly it should be considered whether the consequences of the defendant's behaviour was reasonably foreseeable.
- Secondly the court should consider whether there is a sufficient relationship of proximity between the parties for a duty to be imposed.
- Lastly the court should ask the question whether or not it is fair, just and reasonable in all the circumstances to impose a duty of care.

In *Caparo* Lord Bridge explained the flaws in the *Anns* two-part test, the need for the modern three-part test and also for a return to an incremental development in the law of negligence.

JUDGMENT

'. . . since the *Anns* case a series of decisions of the Privy Council and of your Lordship's House have emphasised the inability of any single general principle to provide a practical test which can be applied to every situation to determine whether a duty of care is owed and, if so what is its scope. What emerges is that, in addition to the foreseeability of damage, necessary ingredients in any situation giving rise to a duty of care are that there should exist between the party owing the duty and the party to whom it is owed a relationship characterised by the law as one of "proximity" or "neighbourhood" and that the situation should be one in which the court considers it fair, just and reasonable that the law should impose a duty of a given scope upon the one party for the benefit of the other. We must now, I think, recognise the wisdom of the words of Brennan J in the High Court of Australia in *Sutherland Shire Council v Heyman* (1985) 60 ALR 1 where he said:

QUOTATION

"It is preferable, in my view, that the law should develop novel categories of negligence incrementally and by analogy with established categories, rather than by a massive extension of a prima facie duty of care restrained only by indefinable 'considerations which ought to negative or to reduce or limit the scope of the duty or the class of the person to whom it is owed".'

Reasonable foresight

The basic requirement of foresight is simply that the defendant must have foreseen the risk of harm to the claimant at the time he or she is alleged to have been negligent.

This is slightly confusing given the fact that a claimant must then go on and satisfy the **remoteness of damage** test. It is also confusing because foreseeability of harm is also a necessary ingredient of proximity. However, although the two are quite closely linked they are still distinct concepts.

Foresight is always critical of course in determining whether or not there is a duty of care owed. It should also be remembered that there is no general, all embracing duty of care. The existence of the duty depends on the individual circumstances.

remoteness of damage

Also known as causation in law – refers to damage which is foreseeable and therefore which the courts are prepared to compensate – they would not compensate for damage that was too remote a consequence of the defendant's breach

CASE EXAMPLE

Topp v London Country Bus (South West) Ltd [1993] 1 WLR 976

A bus company did not owe a duty of care when leaving a bus unattended and joy riders stole the bus and injured the claimant.

It is of course possible that attitudes to what is considered reasonably foreseeable can change, as can be seen from comparing the next two cases.

CASE EXAMPLE

Gunn v Wallsend Slipway & Engineering Co Ltd, The Times, 24 November 1989

There was held to be no duty of care to a woman who contracted mesothelioma from inhaling asbestos dust from her husband's overalls. At the time the risk was felt to be unforeseeable.

But a contrary line has since been adopted. This will very often depend on the availability of technical information at a given point in time.

CASE EXAMPLE

Margereson v J W Roberts Ltd [1996] PIQR P358

Here the danger of children playing near an asbestos factory inhaling dust and contracting related illnesses was said to be foreseeable, even though the events in question were in 1933.

Proximity

Proximity was a major part of both the neighbour principle and Lord Wilberforce's two-part test and is still a major factor in identifying the existence of a duty of care. Proximity of course means legal rather than factual proximity, exactly what Lord Atkin's neighbour principle explained.

CASE EXAMPLE

John Munroe (Acrylics) Ltd v London Fire and Civil Defence Authority, The Times, 22 May 1997

Here there was held to be insufficient proximity between a fire brigade and individual owners of property for a duty to respond to calls to be imposed.

Determining whether there is proximity also inevitably seems to be influenced by policy considerations.

CASE EXAMPLE

Hill v Chief Constable of West Yorkshire [1988] 2 All ER 238

There was insufficient proximity between the police and the public for a duty to be imposed to protect individual members of the public from specific crimes. So relatives of victims of the Yorkshire Ripper had no claim against the police for any careless or ineffective handling of the case. The argument that the Ripper's thirteenth victim would not have died but for the negligence of the police investigation was therefore rejected.

The distinction between foreseeability and proximity can be shown when examining the area of liability for nervous shock particularly in the rules relating to secondary victims (see Chapter 6 section 6.1.4). Where physical damage is caused by the defendant's negligence it is not difficult to establish proximity. There is quite clearly physical as well as legal proximity. However, where the damage is nervous shock and the claimant is a secondary victim physical proximity may be much more tenuous. The foreseeability of harm may not be problematic. Nevertheless, the claimant in this situation then needs to go on to establish the relationship with the primary victim, the closeness in time and space and the witnessing of the event or its immediate aftermath with his own unaided senses in order to establish liability.

Fairness and reasonableness

This requirement is in reality identifying that there must be a limit to liability and no duty will be imposed unless it is just in all the circumstances.

CASE EXAMPLE

Hemmens v Wilson Browne [1994] 2 WLR 323

A man had instructed his solicitors to settle a sum of money on a third party. The deed was then negligently drafted so that the gift was unenforceable. There was no duty owed by the solicitors to the third party in question when it was in the power of the man to remedy the situation by instructing the drafting of another document, but he had changed his mind and refused to do so.

But it may be that the requirement that it is just and reasonable to impose a duty is little different in practice to the policy considerations of former times, particularly in respect of duties allegedly owed by public bodies.

CASE EXAMPLE

Ephraim v Newham London Borough Council [1993] PIQR P156

Here the court felt that it would not be fair to impose a duty of care on the defendant council to ensure the existence of a fire escape in rented accommodation. They had advised the claimant on availability of flats and the claimant was then injured in a fire. The flat was without a fire escape.

It is also not fair, just and reasonable to impose a duty where it conflicts with a duty owed by the defendant to another party.

CASE EXAMPLE

Jain v Strategic Health Authority [2009] 2 WLR 248

The claimant's suffered damage to their business, a private nursing home, after the defendant had applied successfully to have the home's registration cancelled. The order cancelling the registration was later overturned when it was found that the inspection of the home had been careless and misrepresented the facts. The claimants were unable to resuscitate their business. However, the court rejected their claim in negligence since to impose a duty on the defendant to the claimants would interfere with the duty it owed to the residents of registered nursing homes and the general public.

There are clearly overlaps between all three parts of the new three-part test. The circumstances in which the courts will accept that it is just and reasonable to impose a duty are inevitably intertwined with the foreseeability of harm and the proximity of the parties.

Besides this there appears to be very little difference between the fair and reasonable requirement and pure policy considerations.

CASE EXAMPLE

Mitchell v Glasgow City Council [2009] 2 WLR 481

Mitchell was killed by his neighbour who had been abusing and threatening him for many years. Both were tenants in council properties. The killing occurred after the neighbour had been informed by the council that it was serving him a notice that he would be evicted if he continued to behave in an anti-social manner. Mitchell's family brought an action against the council claiming that it had negligently failed to warn him about the meeting with his neighbour even though this was likely to aggravate things. They also argued a breach of the Human Rights Act since the council failed to protect Mitchell's right to life. The House of Lords held that, while some harm to Mitchell was foreseeable, it would not be 'fair, just and reasonable' to impose a duty on the council to warn Mitchell about the meeting with his neighbour because the legislation covering eviction for anti-social behaviour made no mention of such a duty, and to impose one would place an unnecessary burden on landlords who would be less likely to intervene to reduce anti-social behaviour.

It is questionable, therefore, whether the courts have merely replaced one uncertain test as to whether a duty exists with another equally uncertain test.

The problems associated with the *Caparo* test are identified in Street on Torts.

QUOTATION

'Judicial conservatism and the adoption by the House of Lords of Brennan J's dictum in *Sutherland Shire Council v Heyman* may not close the categories of negligence. It does of course restrict their growth. First, by demanding that new duty-situations develop incrementally, it becomes harder to establish a new category of negligence significantly different from, or wider in scope, than its predecessors. Second, it may be that where a duty-situation is not entirely novel but analogous to a category or case where earlier authorities refused to recognise a duty, the door is indeed closed to expansion of the classes of duty-situations.'

J Murray, *Street on Torts* (11th edn, Butterworths, 2003)

2.2 The problem of policy

Policy has always been a major consideration in determining liability in negligence. As *Winfield and Jolowicz* put it

'. . . the court must decide not simply whether there is or is not a duty, but whether there should or should not be one.'

2.2.1 Policy factors considered by judges

A great number of factors may be considered by judges in deciding whether or not to impose a duty of care on a defendant in a particular case.

- Loss allocation – inevitably judges are more likely to impose a duty on a party who is able to stand the loss, the role of insurance clearly is a major determining factor also.
- Practical considerations – the courts for instance may be willing to impose vicarious liability on companies that can then plan effective policies for the future avoidance of liability.
- Moral considerations – for instance the public might be more prepared to accept a 'good Samaritan' law than would the judges.
- Protection of professionals – Lord Denning in particular expressed concern here that professionals should not be prevented from working by restrictive rulings.

- Constitutional considerations – the judges are not keen to be seen as law makers, which they acknowledge is Parliament's role.
- The 'floodgates' argument – judges are reluctant to impose liability where to do so might encourage large numbers of claims on the same issue – this does not appear to be a morally justifiable position and it has particularly hampered the development of liability for nervous shock.
- The beneficial effects of imposing a duty for future conduct – in *Smolden v Whitworth and Nolan* [1997] PIQR P133 the court imposed a duty on a rugby referee who failed to properly control a scrum.

2.2.2 Policy and the refusal to impose a duty

Prior to the acceptance of the *Caparo* three-part test judges often in the past identified policy reasons as the justification for refusing to impose liability in certain situations. There are many examples of policy based either on the particular class of defendant or on the circumstances in which the claim arises. These are considered below.

Liability of lawyers for court work

CASE EXAMPLE

Rondel v Worsley [1969] 1 AC 191

The claimant argued that he had only lost his case in court because of the negligent presentation of the case by the barrister. The court refused to impose a duty because fear of a negligence action might prevent the barrister from effectively carrying out his duties in court and in any case could lead to cases being reopened thus ending certainty in litigation.

The Judges have, however, subsequently removed this immunity because there are now better ways of avoiding abuse of process.

CASE EXAMPLE

Hall (Arthur & Co) v Simons [2000] 3 All ER 673

The appeals involved three separate claims against solicitors for negligent handling of proceedings. The solicitors all claimed immunity from a negligence action in respect of advocacy. The Court of Appeal held that none of the claims were covered by the immunity. The House of Lords, in a court of seven judges with three dissenting, decided that there was no longer any need for immunity in civil proceedings as collateral attacks like these would normally be struck out as an abuse of process, so there was no longer any justification.

The removal of the immunity and the reasoning behind it was also accepted by the House of Lords in respect of negligent advice in *Moy v Pettman Smith and Perry* [2005] UKHL 7.

Immunity of judges from legal action

It was declared in *Sirros v Moore* [1975] QB 118 that a judge would not be liable for any negligence done in the performance of judicial office. Although with inferior judges it is possible that there is liability for acts done in excess of jurisdiction.

Liability of the police to the public

As we have already seen in *Hill v Chief Constable of West Yorkshire* one argument here of course is that there is an alternative means of compensating through a claim to the Criminal Injuries Compensation Authority.

But this is not always the case and in certain circumstances the courts are prepared to impose a specific duty on bodies such as the police.

CASE EXAMPLE

Reeves v Commissioner of the Metropolitan Police [1999] 3 WLR 363

Police were holding a prisoner who was a known suicide risk. When the prisoner did commit suicide the court rejected the police defence of novus actus interveniens. The suicide was the very risk that the police should have been guarding against.

The sort of blanket immunity from negligence actions enjoyed by the police has in any case led to the issue being challenged in a human rights context.

CASE EXAMPLE

Osman v United Kingdom (2000) ECtHR, 29 EHRR 245; [1999] Crim LR 82

Osman was killed by one of his teachers who formed an unnatural attachment to the boy. The teacher was convicted and later detained in a mental hospital. In a civil action for negligence against the police, the court rejected the claim on the basis of the immunity in Hill. A subsequent application to the European Court of Human Rights identified that this contravened Article 6. While the court appreciated that the rule was in place to ensure the effectiveness of the police, it had not been balanced with the rights of the public.

In general in any case the courts will not impose a duty on the police to act and therefore impose liability for a failure to act.

CASE EXAMPLE

Cowan v Chief Constable for Avon and Somerset [2001] EWCA Civ 1699

The claimant was being unlawfully evicted and threatened with violence by men acting for the landlord and the police were called to the scene by the claimant. The police were apparently unaware of the provisions of the Protection from Eviction Act 1977 and as a result failed to warn the men that they were committing a crime. The claimant then alleged negligence by the police in failing to protect him. The court held that the police owed no duty to the claimant. Such duties only arise where there is a special relationship and there was none here.

As a result it has been held that the police do not owe any duty to a victim of crime, not only for negligence in the investigation of crime but also in the training of its officers on how to handle racial incidents.

CASE EXAMPLE

Brooks v Commissioner of Police for the Metropolis [2005] UKHL 24; [2005] 1 WLR 1459

This involved the friend of the murdered teenager Stephen Lawrence. He claimed that he had suffered post-traumatic stress disorder both as a result of the handling of the crime investigation and as the result of his own treatment as a witness and as a victim. The House of Lords would not accept that the police owed any duty in these respects. The reasoning is not unlike that in Hill, that to allow potential liability to witnesses and victims of crime would prevent the police from concentrating on their primary functions and would lead to a very defensive approach to tackling crime.

The same line was taken and the principle in *Hill v Chief Constable of West Yorkshire* was followed in joined appeals *Chief Constable of Hertfordshire v Van Colle; Smith v Chief Constable of Sussex* [2008] UKHL 50. Both cases involved prospective witnesses in criminal proceedings who had been attacked and murdered by the accused. In the first, the House of Lords rejected a claim that the police had breached the deceased's right to life under Article 2 of the European Convention of Human Rights because the test in *Osman v UK* was not satisfied. The murderer was a seriously disturbed and unpredictable person and the court concluded that the police could not have anticipated his behaviour. In the second, there were no 'special circumstances', as required by *Hill* to impose a duty on the police.

One other consideration is that the police do not appear either to owe a duty of care towards 'informers', on whose support they rely extensively in the investigation of crime.

CASE EXAMPLE

Marsh v Chief Constable of Lancashire Constabulary [2003] EWCA Civ 284

Here a car dealer who was an informer for the police sought damages when his former business associate assaulted him. The former partner had been arrested but subsequently released by the police. The court held that it would not be 'fair, just and reasonable' to impose a duty on the police to take into account the claimant when considering releasing the business partner on bail. There was a duty to take the safety of the public into account in ordering release but there was no special relationship between the police and informers that would entitle the claimant to be owed a personal duty.

However, this is not to say that the police will be immune from action in all situations.

CASE EXAMPLE

Kuddus v Chief Constable of Leicestershire Constabulary [2001] 2 WLR 1789

Here a police officer had forged the claimant's signature on a statement withdrawing a complaint. The court accepted that this was misfeasance in a public office and that it was possible to make an award of **exemplary damages** in such circumstances.

Liability of public authorities

exemplary damages
A form of damages which is not related to compensation for damage suffered but which the court makes to show its disapproval of the defendant's action

The liability of public authorities has been the subject of a wide range of cases both for misfeasance and more often for non-feasance. Inevitably public authorities in any case act under statutory duties. Since public money is involved in settling such claims it is also inevitable that policy is a major consideration in determining whether or not claims in negligence are possible.

Similar attitudes are often taken to those applied to the police. The decision will very often rest on the fact of whether or not it is fair, just and reasonable in the circumstances to impose a duty. In this way the Court of Appeal would not accept that a health authority could be liable for the murder of a child by a psychiatric outpatient in *Palmer v Tees HA and Hartlepool and East Durham NHS Trust* [1999] Lloyd's Rep Med 351. The reasoning is very close to that in Hill.

In the case of non-feasance the traditional position was that in *Home Office v Dorset Yacht Co* [1970] AC 1004. The reasoning here was that where a public authority exercised discretion there could only be liability if the authority exercised that discretion so carelessly and unreasonably that in effect it could be said that it had not exercised discretion at all.

Again the argument given by judges for not imposing a duty of care on a public body is very often the lack of proximity with the claimant.

CASE EXAMPLE

K v Secretary of State for the Home Department [2002] EWCA Civ 983

Here a Kenyan citizen had been imprisoned for buggery of a minor and also for burglary and a deportation order was issued. For some reason the Home Secretary permitted his release and seven months later he raped the claimant. The court rejected the claim that the Home Office was liable for negligently releasing the man despite it being reasonably foreseeable that he would commit further crimes. There was insufficient proximity between the claimant and the Home Secretary for a duty to be imposed.

Two further connected reasons why a claim may be impossible against a public body are the effects of Crown Immunity and the fact that there is an alternative remedy for the damage suffered.

CASE EXAMPLE

Matthews v Ministry of Defence [2003] 1 All ER 689

The claimant suffered injury after being exposed to asbestos dust while serving in the Royal Navy between 1955 and 1968. Section 10 of the Crown Proceedings Act 1947 gave the Crown immunity from tort actions for such damage. An alternative system of compensation was created in 1983 by statutory instrument. The fact that the 1947 provision was repealed in 1987 would not help the claimant because it operated only in respect of subsequent claims and the claimant was therefore still subject to the provision. The claimant argued that the provision was contrary to Article 6 of the European Convention on Human Rights in that it prevented him from having his rights determined by an independent and impartial tribunal. The trial judge held that the provision was a procedural bar to a substantive claim and infringed the Article 6 rights. The Court of Appeal held that the provision was substantive rather than procedural and that Article 6 did not apply and allowed the Crown's appeal. In the House of Lords it was held that the provision was indeed substantive and meant that the claimant did not have any right to claim under English law. The alternative system of compensation was not incompatible with the Convention and there were no Article 6 rights in the circumstances.

Nevertheless, it may still be possible to identify a duty to act by a public body because of its assumption of responsibility and because of the specialist knowledge the particular body possesses. This in effect represents more than simple non-feasance.

CASE EXAMPLE

Thames Trains Ltd v Health and Safety Executive [2002] EWHC 1415 QB

This case followed the Ladbroke Grove rail crash. The claimants accepted liability and intended to settle with the victims. Here they were seeking a contribution towards that settlement from the Health and Safety Executive (HSE). The argument was that HSE was under a statutory duty to regulate safety on railways and therefore should at least be held partly responsible. For this the claimants needed to show that HSE owed a duty of care also to passengers using the railways. The court held that, even though public regulators owe no specific duty to the public who may be injured if they fail to regulate effectively, the claim should not be struck out. This was because the regulator also possessed detailed knowledge of the dangerous state of the signalling system that led to the accident.

Specific types of claim

The courts have also been reluctant to allow claims in certain circumstances that they feel would otherwise offend a superior principle, for example the action for 'wrongful life' is denied because judges take it that it would to be to interfere with the 'sanctity of life'.

CASE EXAMPLE

McKay v Essex Area Health Authority [1982] QB 1166

A pregnant woman was not advised that she had contracted German measles and that her child would thus be born severely disabled. The claim was obviously made so that the parents would have the means to support such a severely disabled child. The court would not impose a duty on a doctor to advise of the need for an abortion in such circumstances because that would interfere with the idea of the sanctity of life and public policy would not allow that.

Nevertheless, in a long line of cases the courts have accepted that there can be an action for 'wrongful birth'. This type of action is in effect a claim for economic loss, the cost of raising a baby usually where a negligent sterilisation operation has been followed by an actual birth (see *Emeh v Kensington and Chelsea HA* [1985] QB 1012, *Gold v Haringey HA* [1987] 2 All ER 888 and *Udale v Bloomsbury HA* [1983] 1 WLR 1098.

Now it has been accepted that there may be liability on the part of a negligent health authority for the extra costs of coping with a disabled child, although not for the general maintenance of the child.

CASE EXAMPLE

Rand v East Dorset HA (2001) 56 BMLR 39

Here doctors negligently failed to warn a couple of the results of a scan that showed that their baby would be born with Down's syndrome. The court held that this deprived the parents of the opportunity to abort the foetus and that the heath authority should be liable for the increased costs of supporting a child with the disability. *Hedley Byrne* principles applied and damages were awarded for the financial loss that arose directly from the negligence (see *Hedley Byrne v Heller and Partners Ltd* [1964] AC 465).

The courts have also been reluctant to accept the existence of a duty of care in situations where there is traditionally no obvious legal protection in English law, for example privacy.

CASE EXAMPLE

Kaye v Robertson [1991] FSR 62

A famous TV actor suffered severe head injuries in an accident and was in intensive care. A newspaper then sent a photographer to the hospital who took a flash photograph. While the Court of Appeal did allow an injunction to prevent publication of the photograph, they were unable to find that there was any actionable battery or libel and there was no duty that could give rise to an action in negligence. There was no right of privacy.

2.2.3 Policy and the three-part test

One of the major concerns expressed about Lord Wilberforce's test from *Anns* was that it put too much power in the hands of judges to decide cases on policy issues alone.

While the test may have been flawed it is almost inevitable that policy considerations will still have a part to play in determining liability. The major difference is that under *Anns* this was openly done, whereas now there is the danger that it might be done much more secretly through the third part of the *Caparo* test, that it must be fair, just and reasonable in the circumstances to impose a duty. In this disguised manner policy was clearly a consideration in the decision in *Hill* even while that very aspect of the test in *Anns* was subject to wider criticism.

Policy has been an issue then in determining the duty of care owed by public regulatory bodies.

CASE EXAMPLE

Philcox v Civil Aviation Authority, The Times, 8 June, 1995

The Authority here was held not to owe a duty of care to the owner of an aircraft to ensure that he properly maintained that aircraft. Any duty arising out of the Authority's supervisory role was owed to the public.

It has also been a determining factor in the development of the immunity of actions enjoyed by professionals and lawyers in particular.

CASE EXAMPLE

Kelley v Corston [1997] 4 All ER 466

There was no duty of care owed by a barrister for negligent advice to settle prior to a court hearing on ancillary relief in divorce proceedings.

Policy also seems to have operated in protection of the public services.

CASE EXAMPLE

Clunis v Camden and Islington Health Authority [1998] 3 All ER 180

The defendant Health Authority had an obvious duty of care to treat and to provide after care on discharge from hospital for the claimant who had a long history of mental illness. The Court of Appeal would not accept that this duty extended so that the defendants would be liable when the man stabbed another man to death and was convicted of manslaughter.

This seems to be particularly so in the case of breaches of statutory duties by public bodies. If this were not the case then the possible deterrent effects of tort could be fully used.

CASE EXAMPLE

Phelps v London Borough of Hillingdon [2000] 4 All ER 504

Because of breaches of statutory duties under the 1944 and 1981 Education Acts by educational psychiatrists, children were not diagnosed as having learning difficulties. Nevertheless, the House of Lords decided that there was no intention in either Act that there should be a civil action for damages for such breaches.

Lord Slynn said

JUDGMENT

'. . . although the duties were intended to benefit a particular group, mainly children with special educational needs, the 1981 Act is essentially providing a general structure . . . The general nature of the duties imposed on local authorities in the context of a national system of education . . . the remedies available by way of appeal and judicial review indicate that Parliament did not intend to create a statutory remedy by way of damages.'

Again one of the reasons why judges may decide that it is not fair, just or reasonable to impose a duty is the availability of other remedies in disputes with public bodies.

CASE EXAMPLE

R v Cambridge University, ex p Persaud [2001] EWCA Civ 534

This is a case actually involving judicial review rather than a claim for negligence in tort. It concerned unfair treatment by the Board of Graduate Studies of the University and the Court of Appeal quashed the decision taken by the board. The Court held that, since judicial review is available to students in such circumstances, there was no general principle allowing a claim for negligence. Nevertheless, the Court did accept that each case should be judged on its individual facts and therefore it is possible that a duty of care may be identified.

While policy appears to have been a major factor in developing immunity for public bodies, it now appears that this immunity may be under threat because of the human rights implications.

CASE EXAMPLE

X v Bedfordshire County Council [1995] 3 All ER 353

This was a series of appeals for striking out actions against public authorities. One line involved child abuse where the local authority failed to act after the children were referred to them. The argument was that the children suffered long term damage that could have been avoided had the council acted promptly. The other group involved a failure to provide special needs facilities. In the case of the child abuse negligence it was held that it would not be just or reasonable to impose a duty, since it would cut across the council's other statutory obligations and remove resources that could otherwise be used for child protection. The justification given by the judges in the House of Lords was that the statute that the council were allegedly in breach of was for the benefit of the public generally, not only individuals.

The case was later taken to the European Court of Human Rights (under a different name) and a different answer given.

CASE EXAMPLE

Z and others v United Kingdom (2001) 2 FLR 612; [2001] 34 EHRR 3

The European Court of Human Rights accepted that the children had been subjected to inhuman and degrading treatment contrary to Article 3, and also that they had been refused an effective remedy contrary to Article 13. This result may mean that English courts will be forced to rethink the blanket immunity from liability that they have in the past been prepared to offer public bodies.

Over a long period of time then it has been the case that judges have used policy as a means of ensuring that there is not an unrestricted expansion of liability in tort.

In *Stovin v Wise* [1996] AC 923 at 949 Lord Hoffman explained the position in very explicit terms.

JUDGMENT

'The trend of authorities has been to discourage the assumption that anyone who suffers loss is prima facie entitled to compensation from a person (preferably insured or a public authority) whose act or omission can be said to have caused it. The default position is that he is not.'

In *Harris v Perry* [2008] EWCA Civ 907 the Court of Appeal held that it was impractical for parents to keep children under constant supervision and it would not be in the public interest for the law to require them to do so.

Did the defendant owe the claimant a DUTY OF CARE?

The principle in past cases applies because the material facts are analogous to those in past cases

- There is sufficient proximity between the parties in law for the defendant to have the claimant in his/her contemplation when acting or failing to act
- The harm is a reasonably foreseeable consequence of the defendant's act or omission
- In all the circumstances of the case it is fair, just and reasonable for the duty to be imposed on the defendant

— NO →

YES
↓

Did the defendant BREACH the duty?

The defendant fell below the standard of care appropriate to the particular duty owed – measured objectively against the standards of a 'reasonable man'

— NO →

THE DEFENDANT IS NOT LIABLE FOR NEGLIGENCE

YES
↓

Did the defendant's breach of duty CAUSE the claimant's DAMAGE?

- The defendant's act or omission was the factual cause of the damage – 'but for' the act or omission it would not have occurred
- The damage is a reasonably foreseeable consequence of the breach of duty

— NO →

YES
↓

THE DEFENDANT IS LIABLE FOR NEGLIGENCE

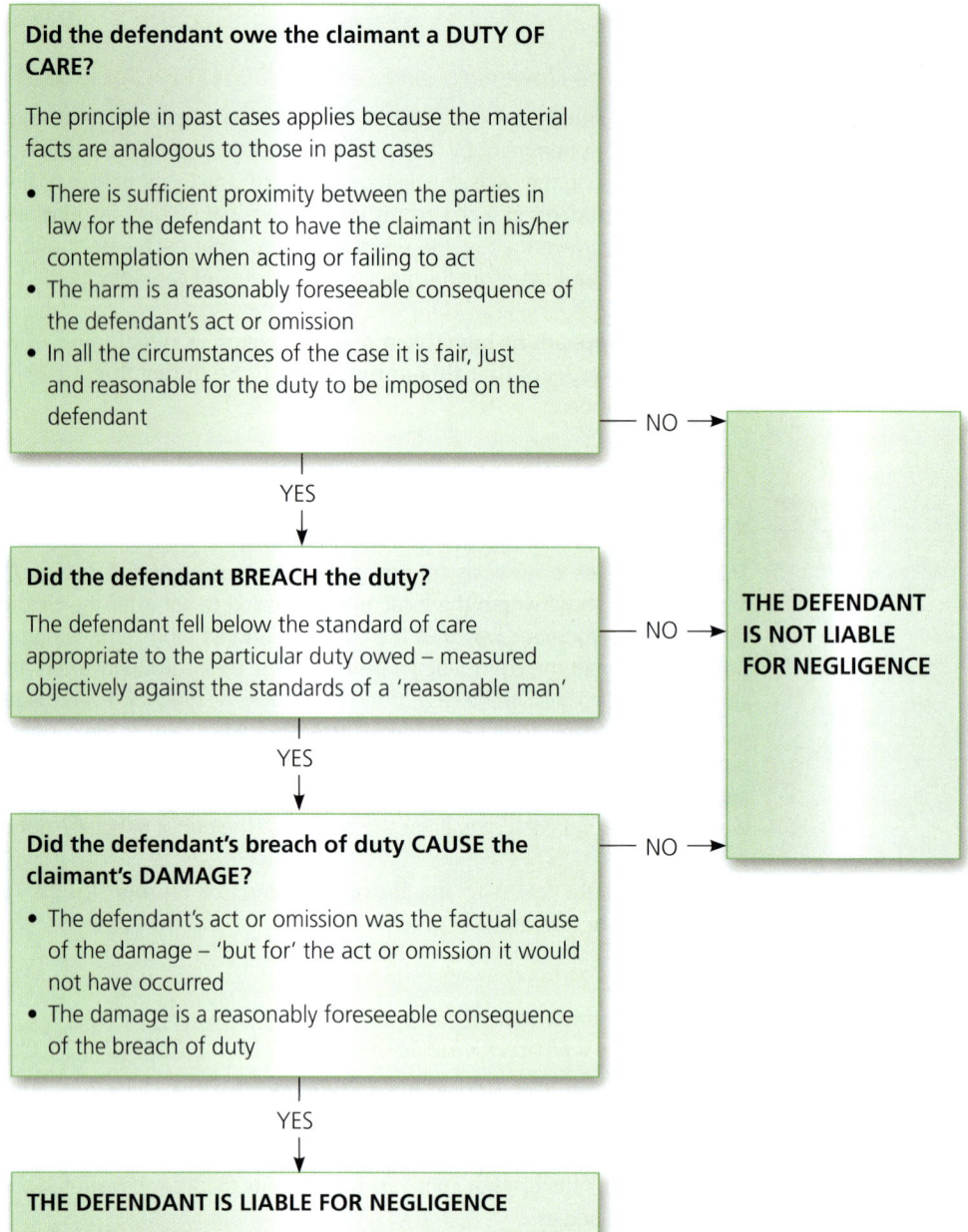

Figure 2.2 The essential elements for proof of negligence with particular emphasis on the establishment of a duty of care

Discuss the extent to which the concept of the duty of care in negligence has developed so that both claimant and defendant are treated fairly.

Outline the essential elements of a negligence claim arising from *Donoghue v Stevenson*

- Duty of care
- Breach of duty
- Foreseeable damage caused by the breach

Discuss the means of establishing duty

- Lord Atkins' neighbour principle
- Involves both foresight of harm and legal proximity of the parties
- Fair to both parties
- Fairer than the privity fallacy that preceded it

Discuss the fairness of the incremental approach

- Based on real situations and relationships
- No general duty of care – so fair

Discuss the fairness of the two-part test from *Anns*

- First part same as neighbour principle
- Second part based on policy – so could work unfairly
- But main criticism was that it gave too much discretion to judges – so overruled

Discuss the fairness of the *Caparo* three-part test

- Based on foreseeable harm, legal proximity, and fair, just and reasonable to impose a duty
- So first two very close to neighbour principle
- Question whether the third is just a secret way of reaching policy decisions which can be unfair

Discuss areas affected by public policy

- Lawyers originally followed *Rondel v Worsley* but this has changed since *Hall v Simonds* – so is fairer
- Police immunity *Hill v Chief Constable of West Yorkshire*
- Local authorities etc

ACTIVITY

Self-assessment questions

1. Why is *Donoghue v Stevenson* such an important case?
2. Exactly who or what in the law of negligence is a 'neighbour'?
3. What are the three main ingredients that must be proved for a successful claim of negligence?
4. In what ways was the test in *Anns* such a radical change from before?
5. Why did the House of Lords discard this test in *Murphy*?
6. What are the three elements of the three-part test from *Caparo v Dickman*?
7. Is the new test actually any better?
8. What factors does a court now take into account in determining whether or not to impose a duty of care?
9. What is the role of policy in establishing a duty of care?
10. To what extent does the duty of care concept act as a control device in negligence claims?

Essay writing

Using the guide in Appendix 1 try the following essay title.

In *McLoughlin v O'Brian* [1982] 2 All ER 298 Lord Wilberforce suggested that 'at the margins, the boundaries of a man's responsibilities for acts of negligence have to be fixed as a matter of policy.'

In the light of subsequent developments consider the extent to which policy is a major factor in determining the existence of a duty of care.

KEY FACTS

The development of the duty of care in negligence	Case
Negligence requires the existence of a duty of care, which is breached by the defendant and causes damage to the claimant that is not too remote a consequence of the breach – Lord Atkin. The existence of a duty is established by reference to Lord Atkin's 'neighbour principle' – neighbours are those people who are so closely affected by our deeds that we should take care to avoid harming them.	*Donoghue v Stevenson* (1932)
A development of the test was Lord Wilberforce's 'two-part' test – firstly see if there is sufficient proximity between claimant and defendant to impose a duty, secondly decide whether policy reasons will prevent a duty being imposed.	*Anns v Merton LBC* (1978)
This test was later overruled.	*Murphy v Brentwood District Council* (1990)

A new 'three-part' test for establishing a duty is now used – is there proximity, is the damage foreseeable, is it just and reasonable to impose a duty?	*Caparo v Dickman* (1990)
Policy has always played a part in deciding whether to impose a duty – eg immunity of the police from negligence actions for failing to prevent a crime.	*Hill v Chief Constable of West Yorkshire* (1988)
– And for refusing to impose a duty on public authorities for non-feasance.	*Phelps v Hillingdon BC* (2000)
– Sometimes judges refuse to impose a duty because to do so would conflict with a superior principle, eg the idea of 'sanctity of life'.	*McKay v Essex AHA* (1982)
– The 'floodgates' argument has been a regular justification for not imposing a duty of care.	
– A dislike for deciding cases purely on policy grounds was one of the reasons for overruling Anns.	
– Now policy may still be a factor, only a more hidden one.	*Hill v Chief Constable of West Yorkshire* (1988)
– However sometimes judges will impose a duty because the public body has assumed a responsibility towards people who might suffer damage if it fails to act.	*Thames Trains v HSE* (2002)

SUMMARY

- Prior to 1932 there was no specific action for negligence available – although there was a similar action called 'on the case'
- *Donoghue v Stevenson* established the elements for a successful claim in negligence: duty of care owed by the defendant to the claimant, breach of that duty, and foreseeable damage caused by the breach
- It also established the neighbour principle (a means of identifying when a duty of care is owed)
- A later two-part test devised by Lord Wilberforce was based on (1) whether there was legal proximity between the parties and (2) whether there were any policy reasons to refuse to impose a duty
- Judges were unhappy with the excess of power this test gave them so it was later overruled and replaced with a three-part test for establishing duty from *Caparo v Dickman*: foreseeable harm, legal proximity of the parties, and that it is fair, just and reasonable to impose a duty
- There are certain situations where the courts are reluctant to impose a duty because of policy reasons

Further reading

Conway, H, 'Negligence claims after *Kelley v Corston*' [2000] NLJ 96.
Denning, Lord, The Discipline of Law (Butterworths, 1979), Part 6 Chapter 1.
von Hagen, D, 'Oral references – careless talk costs money' [2001] DJ Freeman Litigation Review 9.

3

Negligence: breach of duty

AIMS AND OBJECTIVES

After reading this chapter you should be able to:

■ Understand the usual means of measuring the standard of care
■ Understand the different measure applicable to professionals, particularly doctors
■ Understand the factors used in determining whether a defendant has fallen below the standard of care appropriate to the duty owed
■ Be able to critically analyse the concepts of standard of care and breach of duty of care
■ Be able to identify the appropriate standard of care in factual situations
■ Be able to apply the factors for determining breach to factual situations in order to establish if a breach has occurred

3.1 The standard of care and the 'reasonable man' test

3.1.1 The standard of care

We have already seen how negligence occurs where a person owing a duty of care to another person breaches that duty and causes damage which is not too remote a consequence of the breach of duty.

Breach of duty, the second element of negligence, actually refers to the standard of care that is appropriate to the duty owed. A breach of duty simply occurs when the party owing the particular duty falls below the standard of behaviour that is required by the particular duty in question.

The judge in the case will determine the standard of care and whether or not the defendant's behaviour has fallen below that standard according to established tests. While the standard of care in any situation is a question of law, whether or not the defendant has fallen below the standard is a question of fact that will be determined by reference to all of the circumstances of the case.

The standard of care required is generally measured according to an objective method of testing. In this way, while what is the appropriate standard is obviously determined factually according to the circumstances of the case, it is nevertheless the standard that would have been adopted by a 'reasonable man' confronted by the same circumstances that will be taken as the measure by which the defendant's actions will be judged.

3.1.2 The 'reasonable man' test

The objective standard measured according to the standards of the 'reasonable man' was first identified in:

CASE EXAMPLE

Blyth v Proprietors of the Birmingham Waterworks [1856] 11 Exch 781

A water main was laid in which there was a 'fire plug'. This was a wooden plug in the main that would allow water to flow through a cast iron tube up to the street when necessary. A severe frost loosened the plug and water flooded the claimant's house, the cast iron tube being blocked with ice. The frost was beyond normal expectation. There was nothing that the defendants could have reasonably done to prevent the damage and there was no liability.

In explaining how the standard of care is measured and identifying the significance of the 'reasonable man' in objectively measuring the standard Alderson B made the following observation:

JUDGMENT

'Negligence is the omission to do something which a reasonable man, guided upon those considerations which ordinarily regulate human affairs, would do, or doing something which a prudent and reasonable man would not do.'

The test on the face of it seems simple enough. The question is who is the reasonable man by whose standards we are supposed to judge our behaviour?

Judges have over time attempted to define the character of the reasonable man in order that the objective standard can be more closely understood.

In *Hall v Brooklands Auto-Racing Club* [1933] 1 KB 205 Greer LJ defined the reasonable man as follows.

JUDGMENT

'The person concerned is sometimes described as "the man on the street", or as the "man on the Clapham Omnibus", or, as I recently read in an American author, the "man who takes the magazines at home and in the evening pushes the lawnmower in his shirt sleeves".'

The use of the 'reasonable man' is an objective measure but it is also a means of placing that test in the context of human characteristics. Precise characteristics that can be associated with the reasonable man have also been considered in judgments.

CASE EXAMPLE

Glasgow Corporation v Muir [1943] AC 448

Here small children were scalded when a tea urn was dropped. The urn was being carried through a narrow passage where the children were buying ice creams when the corporation allowed a church picnic to come inside on a rainy day. Liability was assessed according to the 'reasonable man' test.

In establishing on what to base an objective standard Lord Macmillan concluded that:

JUDGMENT

'The standard of foresight of the reasonable man is an impersonal test. It eliminates the personal equation and is independent of the idiosyncrasies of the particular person whose conduct is in question. Some persons are by nature unduly timorous and imagine every path beset by lions; others, of more robust temperament, fail to foresee or nonchalantly disregard even the most obvious dangers. The reasonable man is presumed to be free from both over-apprehension and from over-confidence.'

In fact the breach of duty is another way of saying that the defendant is at fault and is therefore liable for the damage caused. The issue of whether liability should always be based on fault or whether there should be a no-fault liability system is a controversial question and one that we will return to.

Certainly in practice who or what is the reasonable man and what constitutes an objective standard, are concepts determined by the judges in a case. Judges in reaching a decision will also base their judgment on either policy or expediency as the need arises.

Policy considerations that can influence a judge include:

■ Who can best stand the loss – clearly a claimant needs to claim from a party who can afford to pay. The key rule in deciding whether or not to bring a case is 'Never sue a man of straw' (a person of no means).
■ Whether or not the defendant is insured – in most circumstances in the modern day it will be an insurance company rather than the actual defendant who will pay the compensation. This would be the case for instance of motorists, employers, professional bodies, manufacturers, etc.
■ The extent to which the decision will prevent similar behaviour in the future – the tort system is mainly about compensating for loss and damage suffered but it should also have a deterrent element.
■ Whether or not the decision would 'open the floodgates' to further cases.
■ Whether or not particular types of actions should be discouraged – for instance against the police or administrators of the law.
■ Whether or not there are alternative means of gaining a remedy.

3.2 Determining the standard of care

Through the cases judges have developed a number of rules concerning those things that should be taken into account in determining the standard by which the defendant's behaviour should be measured.

3.2.1 Foreseeability of risk

There is no obligation on the defendant to guard against risks other than those that are within his/her reasonable contemplation. It would be unfair to make a defendant responsible for the unforeseeable.

CASE EXAMPLE

Roe v Minister of Health [1954] 2 QB 66

A patient became paralysed after being injected with nupercaine, a spinal anaesthetic. This had been stored inside glass ampoules themselves stored in a sterilising fluid, phenol. Evidence at the trial showed that the phenol solution had entered the anaesthetic through hairline cracks in the ampoules, contaminating it and causing the paralysis. There was no liability because such an event had not previously occurred and was unforeseeable as a result.

Nevertheless, if the defendant is aware of the possibility of harm he must guard against it, and it will be a breach of the duty of care to fail to.

CASE EXAMPLE

Walker v Northumberland County Council [1995] 1 All ER 737

Here a senior social worker had suffered a nervous breakdown. His employers knew that he might suffer another breakdown when he returned to work if the pressures of his work were too severe and stressful. They took insufficient steps to reduce the pressures of his workload and, when he was again made ill, they were in breach of their duty to take reasonable steps to avoid psychiatric injury knowing of his state of health.

3.2.2 The magnitude of the risk

Wherever we owe a duty to another person we must all guard against the risk of doing harm. This is only reasonable. The degree of caution that we must exercise will obviously be dictated by the likelihood of the risk. The magnitude of the risk then can be balanced against the extremes that must be taken in order to avoid it.

CASE EXAMPLE

Bolton v Stone [1951] AC 850 HL

Miss Stone was standing outside a cricket ground and was hit by a cricket ball that had been hit out of the ground. She was actually 100 yards from where the batsman had struck the ball. The batsman was 78 yards from a 17 foot high fence over which the ball had travelled. This was quite incredible and it was shown that balls had only been struck out of the ground six times in 28 years. There was no negligence. The cricket ground had done everything reasonably possible to avoid risks of people being hit.

Lord Radcliffe identified the connection with the basic 'reasonable man' test:

JUDGMENT

'the fact remains that, unless there has been something which a reasonable man would blame as falling beneath the standard of conduct that he would set for himself and require of his neighbour, there has been no breach of legal duty.'

The defendant though must take into account any factors that might increase the risk of harm occurring.

CASE EXAMPLE

Haley v London Electricity Board [1965] AC 778

Here a hole was being dug along a pavement and a hammer was left propped up on the pavement to warn passers by of the presence of the hole. A blind man was passing and his stick failed to touch the hammer and he tripped and fell which left him deaf. It was held that there was a sufficiently large proportion of blind people in the community for precautions to be taken that would protect them also and the cost would be very low. The defendants were liable for negligence.

Statutory health and safety law means that formal risk assessment is now a common requirement in all industries and this creates an obligation in relation to specific incidents as well as in general terms.

CASE EXAMPLE

Davis v Stena Line [2005] EWHC 420 (QB)

A passenger on a ferry fell overboard. The likelihood of such accidents was high and well known to the company which had failed to provide adequate training for the crew in such events. The captain of the ferry attempted a risky rescue, involving throwing the man a rope and pulling him up the high sided vessel and through a door. Weather conditions were very bad and the man died in the swell created by the ferry. A passing ship which had previously spotted the man alive in the water had been in a position to launch its fast rescue boat. The court held that (1) the rescue attempted by the ferry captain would have had very little chance of success and it was negligent of the captain not to consider the better alternative option and (2) negligent on the part of the company not to have provided the captain with the training that would have enabled him to make that decision.

thin skull rule
Also known as the 'eggshell skull rule' – means that the defendant has to take extra care of a claimant who is susceptible to a certain type of harm

3.2.3 The extent of the possible harm (the 'thin skull' rule)

The court will not only be concerned with the likelihood that harm will occur but the risk that the harm will be great if it does occur. In this sense the defendant must 'take the claimant how he finds him', the so-called '**thin skull**' rule.

CASE EXAMPLE

Paris v Stepney Borough Council [1951] AC 367

The claimant here who was a mechanic was already blind in one eye. He was then blinded in the other eye in an accident at work when his employers had failed to supply him with safety goggles that they were actually legally required to do. They were then liable to the defendant to the extent of causing his total blindness rather than merely for the loss of the sight in the one eye. The claimant's partial sight meant that the duty towards him was necessarily greater than normal.

The same principle can apply even though the foreseeable harm is psychiatric rather than physical.

CASE EXAMPLE

Walker v Northumberland County Council [1995] 1 All ER 737

An area social services officer had particularly onerous and stressful responsibilities and suffered a nervous breakdown. He returned to work after three months on the understanding that there would be a lighter workload and less pressure. He was nevertheless expected to clear up the backlog and suffered a further breakdown leading to eventual dismissal on ill health. The employers were held to have breached their duty to protect his psychiatric well being and health.

It is also possible for the characteristic in question to be something other than the claimant's health or physical characteristics.

CASE EXAMPLE

Mattocks v Mann [1993] RTR 13 CA

Here the claimant was able to recover the cost of hiring a replacement vehicle used during a delay caused by the insurers' negligent failure to pay for repairs to her vehicle. She was unable to pay for the repair costs herself and it was foreseeable that she would hope that the insurers would meet those costs.

3.2.4 The social utility of the activity

A defendant can sometimes escape liability in a case because it is possible to show that there was a justification for taking the risk in question. This might be so for instance where the defendant acts to avoid a potentially worse event.

CASE EXAMPLE

Watt v Hertfordshire County Council [1954] 1 WLR 835

A woman was trapped in a car crash. The fire station summoned to the incident had a special heavy jack for using in such circumstances. It would normally be taken to the scene properly secured in its own vehicle, but the vehicle was elsewhere. The jack was taken unsecured in another vehicle because of the emergency and when the driver was forced to brake sharply the jack moved injuring a fireman. There was no negligence because the situation was an emergency and justified the risk.

However, this will not mean that the taking of any risk at all can be justified. Only the precise circumstances can justify the taking of the risk.

CASE EXAMPLE

Griffin v Mersey Regional Ambulance [1998] PIQR P34

There was liability when an ambulance crossing a light on red crashed. However, the other motorist was held to be 60 per cent contributorily negligent.

3.2.5 The practicability of precautions

The reasonable man only has to do what is reasonable in order to avoid risks of harm. This means that there is no obligation to go to extraordinary lengths, particularly if the risk is slight.

CASE EXAMPLE

Latimer v AEC Ltd [1953] AC 643

A factory became flooded after a torrential rainstorm. The water mixed with oil and grease on the floor making the surface very slippery and dangerous. When the water subsided sawdust was spread over the floors in order to make them secure. There was not enough to cover the whole floor and Latimer slipped on an uncovered patch and was injured. The House of Lords held that everything reasonable had been done in the circumstances and, balancing out the possible risks, it was unreasonable to expect the factory to be closed. It was held that there was no negligence.

The context in which the damage occurs may very often dictate that the defendant has little chance to protect against it. In this way there was no liability when an inmate in a young offenders' institution was injured in a knife attack by another inmate: *Thompson v Home Office* [2001] EWCA Civ 331.

Generally though where the defendant has sufficient control of circumstances to be able to avoid the harm, he would be obliged to act. This is particularly so where the welfare of the claimant is entrusted to the defendant.

CASE EXAMPLE

Bradford-Smart v West Sussex County Council, The Times, 29th January, 2002

The Court of Appeal accepted that a school would be in breach of its duty of care to its pupils if it failed to take steps that were within its power to put a stop to bullying. The Court accepted that this could apply even to incidents that arose off the school premises, although in general it was accepted that only rare exceptions would give rise to a breach of duty, and that the present case was not such an occasion.

3.2.6 Common practice

A negligent activity cannot be excused merely because it is common practice. Nevertheless, the fact that something is generally practised may be strong evidence that it is not negligent, otherwise it would not normally be carried out.

This of course is not an absolute principle and it will not necessarily be negligent merely to fail to follow common practice.

CASE EXAMPLE

Brown v Rolls-Royce Ltd [1960] 1 WLR 210

An employee contracted dermatitis. The employers provided adequate washing facilities but they did not provide a barrier cream that was commonly used in the industry. They were not negligent in not providing the barrier cream because it could not be shown in the case that using the cream was guaranteed to prevent the condition.

3.3 The standard of care and different classes of defendant

The standard of care is measured objectively but the courts have often looked at whether the standard may differ according to the type of person who owes the duty.

3.3.1 Children

Traditionally there was little case law involving the standard of care owed by children. Case law from other jurisdictions indicated that a child was not expected to have the same skill or understanding as an adult and therefore the standard of care owed was that appropriate to the age of the child in question.

CASE EXAMPLE

McHale v Watson (1966) 115 CLR 199

A 12-year-old boy injured a girl in the eye when he threw a steel rod at a post. There was held to be no negligence.

This seems to be more of a subjective than an objective test but the English courts have tended to follow it.

CASE EXAMPLE

Mullin v Richards [1998] 1 All ER 920

Here two 15-year-old schoolgirls were 'fencing' with plastic rulers. One ruler broke and one of the girls was injured in the eye. The Court of Appeal held that since such games were commonplace and would normally not lead to injury then the injury was unforeseeable to girls of that age and there was no negligence.

In *Orchard v Lee* [2009] EWCA Civ 295 it was held that the mere fact that a risk of harm was insufficient on its own to make a 13-year-old boy liable for injuries he caused to a lunch break supervisor when he was running backwards in a school playground. The reasoning was that the school did not prohibit running in the playground so that the defendant was merely doing what any boy of the same age would do in a designated play area.

However, the judges have been willing on occasions to make awards of contributory negligence against child claimants.

CASE EXAMPLE

Armstrong v Cottrell [1993] PIQR P109 CA

The judge in this case was prepared to reduce damages for a 12-year-old by a third because he felt that children of that age should know the Highway Code.

And this can even be to a high level of reduction with quite young children.

CASE EXAMPLE

Morales v Eccleston [1991] RTR 151

Damages were reduced by 75 per cent when an 11-year-old ran into the road to recover his football.

One further aspect of the standard expected of children is that the law expects that young children should be supervised. This can be seen as a precise aspect of the duty owed to young children in the case of occupiers' liability (see *Phipps v Rochester Corporation* [1995] 1 QB 450 (section 8.2.3)).

CASE EXAMPLE

Jenny v North Lincolnshire CC [2000] LGR 269

The Court of Appeal held that the local authority was liable for the injuries to a young school pupil who was injured as the result of being on a major road during school hours.

3.3.2 The disabled

Where a person is sick or suffering from a disability it is likely that the standard of care owed is what would be appropriate in the case of the reasonable man suffering the same illness or disability. It is inevitable that the same degree of care will not be expected as would for a person in normal health.

A person suffering from a disability of the mind may be liable for the torts he commits if sufficiently aware of the quality of the act.

CASE EXAMPLE

Morriss v Marsden [1952] 1 All ER 925

Here the defendant was a schizophrenic who attacked a claimant and was thus accused of battery. It was held that persons suffering from a mental illness could be liable for intentional torts even if unaware that their actions were wrong if they knew the quality of the act they committed.

3.3.3 Motorists

In general the same standard of care is expected of all motorists regardless of their age or experience, and even of learner drivers.

CASE EXAMPLE

Nettleship v Weston [1971] 2 QB 691

A learner driver on her third lesson crashed into a lamp post injuring the person teaching her to drive. The Court of Appeal found that she was liable despite being a learner driver.

In identifying that the standard of care of all motorists is the same and that there is no reduction in the standard because of inexperience Lord Denning commented as follows.

JUDGMENT

'[The law] requires of him the same standard of care as of any other driver. The learner driver may be doing his best, but his incompetent best is not good enough. He must drive in as good a manner as a driver of skill, experience and care, who is sound in mind and limb, who makes no errors of judgment, has good eyesight and hearing, and is free from any infirmity . . .'

Lord Denning identified in the case that this is probably to do with the fact that motorists are obliged to carry compulsory insurance and therefore the degree of risk associated with the particular class of driver can be reflected in the insurance premium they are expected to pay.

The principle might even extend to a motorist who becomes physically incapable of controlling the vehicle because of a physical impairment.

CASE EXAMPLE

Roberts v Ramsbottom [1980] 1 All ER 7

A driver crashed into a stationary vehicle after suffering a cerebral haemorrhage (a stroke). He continued to drive after the seizure and the court felt that he was negligent for doing so. The court accepted that a defendant would have a defence if his actions were entirely beyond his control, but that here the driver should have stopped driving immediately.

However, a motorist will not be liable if he is unaware of the disabling condition that causes the loss of control.

CASE EXAMPLE

Mansfield v Weetabix Ltd [1997] PIQR P526

Here it was held that the driver could not have reasonably known of the infirmity that led to his loss of control and the subsequent accident so there was no fault. The previous case was said to be wrongly decided on this point but was still correct in that the driver continued to drive when he should have known that he was unfit to do so.

3.3.4 People engaged in sport

The standard of care appropriate to participants in sport is the ordinary standard of reasonable care. The level of care required will depend on the circumstances of the case including whether the player is a professional or an amateur.

CASE EXAMPLE

Condon v Basi [1985] 2 All ER 453

Here the ordinary standard of reasonable care was applied when a footballer was injured in a dangerous and unacceptable tackle during an amateur football match. Sir John Donaldson MR suggested in the case that a much higher degree of care would be expected of a professional footballer.

Professional players are assumed to be more knowledgeable of the potential risks and consequences of injury and are thus more likely to be found in breach of their duty of care to fellow professionals.

CASE EXAMPLE

McCord v Swansea City AFC Ltd and another, The Times, 11th February, 1997

Here a tackle by a player of the defendant football club ended the claimant's career. While the judge was not prepared to consider the tackle as reckless, it was a serious mistake of judgement that amounted to a breach of his duty of care to fellow players.

However, the level of care required is always taken in the context of the individual circumstances because of the inherent risk of injury of which each player is aware.

CASE EXAMPLE

Pitcher v Huddersfield Town Football Club Ltd [2001] All ER (D) 223

The claimant, a professional football player, suffered a knee injury ending his career after a rash tackle. The judge did not accept that the defendant player had fallen below an appropriate standard. He had mistimed his tackle but such errors of judgement were commonplace in the sport.

While participants in sport are inevitably aware of the risks of engaging in sporting activities, particularly contact sports of any kind, they are nevertheless to be protected from unnecessary harm by the officials in the game. In this way a referee in a sporting contest owes a duty of care to the players.

CASE EXAMPLE

Smolden v Whitworth [1997] PIQR P133

In a colts rugby match, that is one involving young and inexperienced players, the referee had been approached by the coaches about repeated collapsing of the scrum by players on the other side. He failed to properly control the scrums and eventually one player was seriously injured, leading to paralysis, when the scrum collapsed. The Court of Appeal agreed that the referee had fallen below the standard of care that he owed to the players. They were, however, eager to emphasise that the judgment was appropriate to the colts but not to the senior game where the players would be more experienced. (The existence of this duty and the appropriate standard have been recently affirmed in *Vowles v Evans and Another* [2003] EWCA Civ 318.)

Sporting authorities may also fall below the appropriate standard of care when they fail to provide the proper facilities to deal with sporting injuries.

CASE EXAMPLE

Watson v British Boxing Board of Control [2001] QB 1134

The claimant suffered severe head injuries after a blow to the head during a boxing match as a result of which he also suffered brain damage. The organisers were held to be in breach of their duty of care by failing to provide adequate medical facilities at the ringside that could have reduced the extent of the damage.

A spectator at a sporting contest is generally said to consent to the risks associated with being present at the sport. A person engaged in the sport, then, will not be liable in negligence to a spectator for any injuries or damage caused in the normal course of the sport unless the sportsman has shown a blatant and reckless disregard for the safety of the spectator.

CASE EXAMPLE

Wooldridge v Sumner [1963] 2 QB 43

A photographer stood behind a line of shrubs marking the perimeter of the arena at the National Horse Show at White City Stadium. The defendant tried to take a corner too fast on his horse with the result that the horse plunged through the shrubs and injured the claimant. The Court of Appeal held that the defendant was not liable for negligence, but had merely made an error of judgement in how fast he should be going at the time.

In *Mountford v Newlands School and Another* [2007] EWCA Civ 21 the Court of Appeal held that a school would be liable for injury sustained in a seven-a-side under-15 rugby game because the referee did not prevent a boy over 15 from playing in breach of the rules.

The duty of care owed to a disabled participant in sporting events will be greater than that owed to an able bodied sportsman, simply because the disability will require a greater degree of care.

CASE EXAMPLE

Morrell v Owen, The Times, 14th December, 1993

Here athletics coaches were held to be in breach of their duty of care to a paraplegic archer. The disabled athlete was hit on the head by a discus and suffered brain damage as a result.

3.3.5 People lacking specialist skills

If a person carries out a task requiring a specialist skill he will be judged according to the standard of a person reasonably competent in the exercise of that skill. This does not mean that an amateur will be expected to show the same degree of skill as a professional.

CASE EXAMPLE

Wells v Cooper [1958] 2 QB 265

A tradesman delivering fish was injured when a door handle fitted by the householder came off in his hand. The Court of Appeal held that the appropriate standard of care was that of a reasonably competent carpenter. The claimant's complaint was that the handle was fixed to the door with three-quarter-inch screws that he claimed were inadequate. Since these were the screws that a carpenter would have used there could be no negligence.

Nevertheless, a person not possessing specialist skills will not be expected to exercise the same standard of care as a skilled person unless that standard is appropriate to the circumstances.

CASE EXAMPLE

Phillips v Whiteley [1938] 1 All ER 566

A jeweller pierced ears in a whitewashed room using sterilised equipment. When the claimant contracted a blood disorder the jeweller was not negligent. He had taken all reasonable steps in the circumstances to avoid the risk of harm and could not be fixed with the same standard of care as a surgeon performing an operation. The appropriate standard of care was the degree of care that should be taken by a jeweller carrying out the procedure, not that which would be appropriate to a surgeon.

3.3.6 People using equipment

In general where people use equipment they are taken to know how to use it properly, unless it is very specialist equipment requiring specialist skills. So where a person suffers injury, loss or damage while using the equipment there is no requirement by the other party to check that they are able to use it properly, and so no breach.

CASE EXAMPLE

Makepeace v Evans, The Times, 13th June, 2000, CA

The claimant was a decorator hired by the first defendant sub-contractors, who in turn were hired by the second defendant main contractors. The claimant used a scaffolding tower provided by the second defendants. Their site agent did not enquire whether the claimant was competent to use it. When the claimant was injured his action against the second defendants failed. It was a standard piece of equipment in the trade, and they were entitled to assume that he was able to use it, or seek advice. The court held that to say otherwise would be to 'extend the nursemaid school of negligence too far'.

ACTIVITY

Quick quiz

Consider how it will be decided whether there has been a breach of a duty of care in the following situations

1. Jamie is an eleven-year-old boy who has caused a crash by running out in front of cars while playing 'chicken'.
2. Tom has been injured when stones from a quarry have hit him on his head after blasting. He was walking on a pavement a mile away from the quarry. The quarry face is shielded by a high hill, and no previous explosions from the quarry have ever caused this to happen before.
3. Tan, an acupuncturist has been treating Rachel for pains in her shoulders. Tan has followed normal methods precisely but Rachel has suffered a rare infection.
4. During a forest fire Tristram used explosives to blow up his neighbour Ali's trees in order to prevent the fire from spreading to his own farm and also to the nearby village of Trumpton.

ACTIVITY

Self-assessment questions

1. Who exactly is a 'reasonable man'?
2. In what ways does a 'reasonable man' differ from an average man?
3. How big a part does policy play in determining the standard of care in negligence?
4. To what extent must a person owing a duty weigh up the risks associated with his acts and omissions?

5. What exactly is the 'thin skull' rule?
6. When will a standard of care be lowered due to inexperience of the person owing the duty?
7. What standard of care does a child usually owe?
8. What effect does the fact that the acts leading to the damage were common practice have on deciding whether there is a breach of duty?

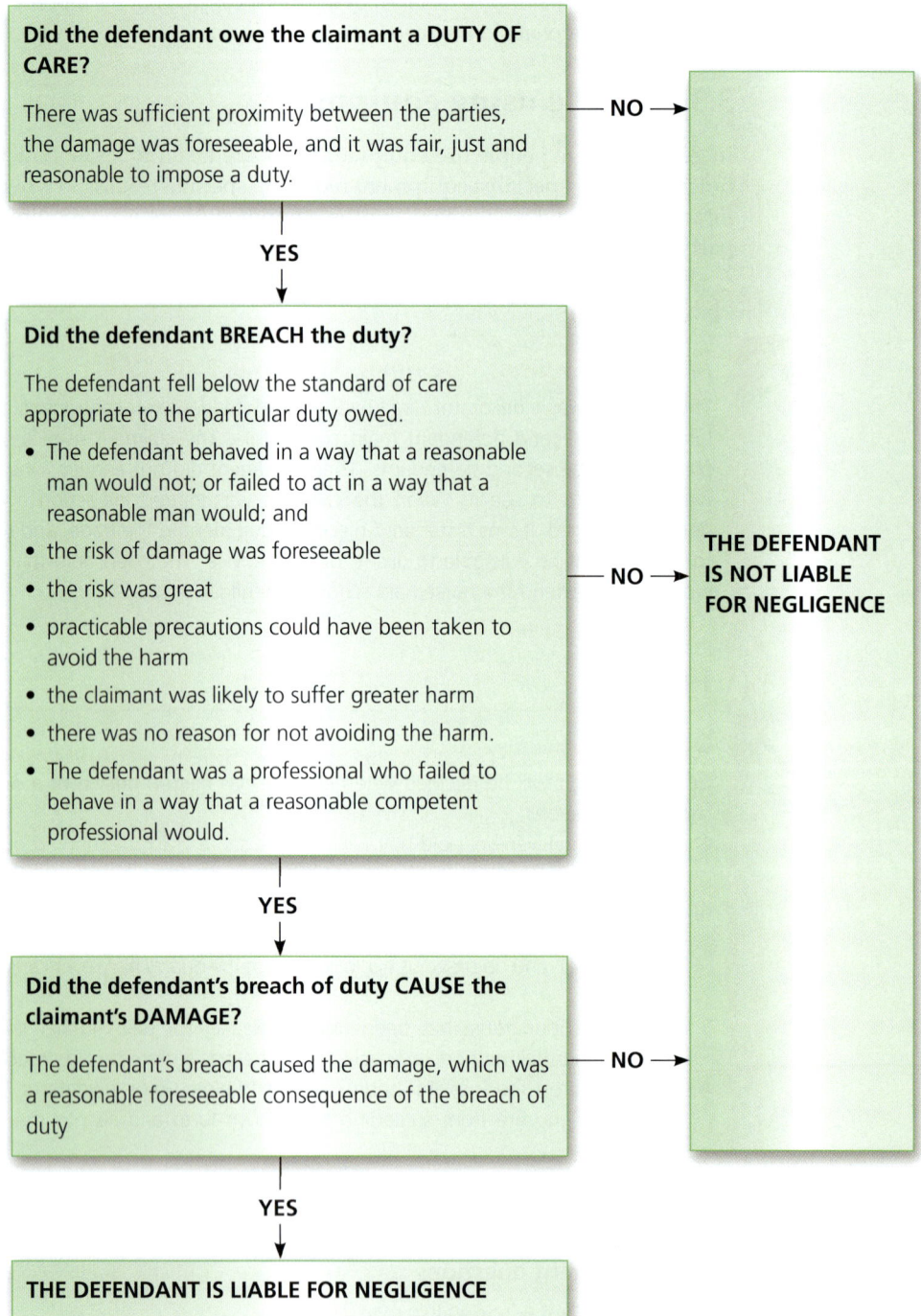

Did the defendant owe the claimant a DUTY OF CARE?

There was sufficient proximity between the parties, the damage was foreseeable, and it was fair, just and reasonable to impose a duty.

— NO →

YES

Did the defendant BREACH the duty?

The defendant fell below the standard of care appropriate to the particular duty owed.

- The defendant behaved in a way that a reasonable man would not; or failed to act in a way that a reasonable man would; and
- the risk of damage was foreseeable
- the risk was great
- practicable precautions could have been taken to avoid the harm
- the claimant was likely to suffer greater harm
- there was no reason for not avoiding the harm.
- The defendant was a professional who failed to behave in a way that a reasonable competent professional would.

— NO →

THE DEFENDANT IS NOT LIABLE FOR NEGLIGENCE

YES

Did the defendant's breach of duty CAUSE the claimant's DAMAGE?

The defendant's breach caused the damage, which was a reasonable foreseeable consequence of the breach of duty

— NO →

YES

THE DEFENDANT IS LIABLE FOR NEGLIGENCE

Figure 3.1 The essential elements for proof of negligence with particular emphasis on the breach of the duty of care

The standard of care and testing breach of duty	Case
A breach of duty occurs where a person falls below the standard of care appropriate to the duty he owes.	
The standard of care is that appropriate to the 'reasonable man'.	*Blyth v Birmingham Waterworks* (1856)
The reasonable man is free from both over-apprehension and over-confidence.	*Glasgow Corporation v Muir* (1943)
Policy considerations often govern what the standard will be, eg the floodgates argument.	
Factors to be taken into consideration	**Case**
Many factors are taken into account in determining whether the duty is breached:	
• foreseeability of harm	*Roe v Minister of Health* (1954)
• the magnitude of the risk	*Bolton v Stone* (1951)
• the 'thin skull rule'	*Paris v Stepney BC* (1951)
• the social utility of the act	*Watt v Herts CC* (1954)
• the practicability of precautions.	*Latimer v AEC* (1953)
Different types of defendant	**Case**
Consideration will be made for different types of defendant, eg	
• children – are expected to be less cautious	*Mullin v Richards* (1998)
• the disabled	*Morriss v Marsden* (1952)
• motorists – all owe the same duty even if inexperienced	*Nettleship v Weston* (1971)
• sportsmen – will depend on rules of sport being observed	*Smolden v Whitworth* (1997)
• people lacking specialist skills	*Wells v Cooper* (1958)
• people using equipment.	*Makepeace v Evans* (2000)

3.4 The standard of care appropriate to experts and professionals

3.4.1 Breach of the duty of care and medical negligence claims

Medical negligence is in many ways a specialist type of negligence action and is important because recent years have seen a dramatic increase in the numbers of claims against doctors and health authorities. This has also led to the worry that the UK will follow the USA, where medical malpractice claims and the so-called 'ambulance chasing' by lawyers is commonplace.

However, it is still quite difficult in England and Wales to bring successful medical negligence claims. The major reasons for this are twofold:

- the difficulties that are experienced when trying to prove both breach of the duty of care (the subject of this chapter), and
- the problem of causation (an area subject to its own particular problems and considered in detail in Chapter 4).

Doctors are not exempt from the law and, just as with anybody, if they fall below the standard of care that is appropriate to them, they may be found liable in negligence for a breach of their well established duty of care to their patients. Professionals, and in particular doctors, who are a very specific 'body of professionals', do not conform to the usual rules on the breach of duty in negligence and therefore are more appropriately considered as a special category on their own.

As McNair J identified in *Bolam v Friern Hospital Management Committee* [1957] 1 WLR 582 atp 582:

JUDGMENT

'In the ordinary case which does not involve any special skill . . . negligence . . . means a failure to do some act which a reasonable man in the circumstances would do, or the doing of some act which a reasonable man in the circumstances would not do . . . But where you get a situation which involves the use of some special skill or competence, then the test as to whether there has been negligence or not is not the test of the man on the top of a Clapham omnibus, because he has not got this skill.'

The standard of care appropriate to professionals then is not judged according to the reasonable man test, so his actions are not compared with those of the 'man on the Clapham omnibus'. Rather they are compared against the accepted standards of members of their own profession. This in itself complicates the objective measure that is normally used to determine negligence and leads on also to many criticisms.

3.4.2 The '*Bolam* test'

The standard of care appropriate to professionals is not then judged according to the reasonable man test, so their actions are not compared with those of the 'man on the Clapham omnibus'.

On the contrary a person exercising such specialist skills will be judged instead by comparison with his natural peer group, in other words other people who exercise the same skill and who have the same expertise. The standard test originates in a case alleging medical negligence but it is equally appropriate to all professionals.

CASE EXAMPLE

Bolam v Friern Hospital Management Committee [1957] 1 WLR 582

Mr Bolam suffered from depression and entered hospital to undergo electro-convulsive therapy. The practice, as the name suggests, causes possibly quite severe muscular spasms. The doctor giving the treatment failed to provide either relaxant drugs or any means of restraint during the treatment. The claimant suffered a fractured pelvis and the question for the court was whether there was negligence in the practice of providing neither restraint nor relaxants. The court received evidence that a number of different practitioners carrying out the type of treatment took different views on the use of restraints or relaxant drugs. McNair J, established the standard of care appropriate to doctors as '. . . the standard of the ordinary skilled man exercising and professing to have that special skill'. Since there were doctors who would have carried out the therapy in the same manner the doctor here had acted in accordance with a competent body of medical opinion and there could be no negligence.

So a doctor will be considered negligent when he has failed to act in a way that would be accepted as being appropriate by a 'competent body of medical opinion'. Taking the situation in *Bolam* as an example, since there were a number of different practices that were adopted and accepted as appropriate by different doctors, then the role of the court was to listen to the expert evidence of other doctors and to determine on the basis of that evidence whether or not the practice conformed to that acceptable to a 'competent body of medical opinion'.

Of course this in itself is a source of potential criticism. The test has been criticised to an extent by judges in decided cases. It has been a wider source of criticism for academic commentators.

As Sally Sheldon points out the test is very different to cases involving non-professionals where, having heard evidence from experts the court will reach its own conclusions on whether or not the duty of care has been breached by falling below the acceptable standard. The situation is somewhat different for doctors:

QUOTATION

'Once the court is convinced that two (or more) different schools of thought exist within the profession, it seems that all the defendant must do is to show that he has acted in accordance with one of them, subject to the caveat that such a school must constitute a "responsible body of opinion".'

'"A responsible body of medical men skilled in that particular art . . .": Rethinking the *Bolam* test', *Feminist Perspectives on Health Care Law* S Sheldon and M Thompson (eds) (Cavendish Publishing, 1998), p 16

3.4.3 Applying the test

The test not surprisingly has caused controversy. Nevertheless, the House of Lords has subsequently approved it in relation to various aspects of medical treatment and responsibility, even where they might also have criticised the rule.

Consent

It has, for instance, been accepted as appropriate in determining the level of information a doctor should give when obtaining consent from a patient. In doing so the House of Lords also dismissed the doctrine of 'informed consent' as having application in English law.

CASE EXAMPLE

Sidaway v Governors of the Bethlem Royal & Maudsley Hospitals [1985] AC 871

Mrs Sidaway had suffered persistent pain in her right arm and shoulder and had on advice of her surgeon consented to a spinal operation to relieve the pain. On obtaining consent, the doctor had accurately informed her that there was a less than 1 per cent risk of something going wrong. What Mrs Sidaway claimed the doctor had not told her was the potentially catastrophic consequences if something did go wrong. In the event, while the operation was carried out without negligence, the damage did occur and she was left paralysed. She sued on the grounds that the surgeon had been negligent in failing to properly warn of the possible extent of the damage. The House of Lords held that the degree of information given by the doctor conformed to '. . . a practice accepted as proper by a responsible body of neuro-surgical opinion . . .' so that there was no negligence. They also rejected the idea that there should be a doctrine of 'informed consent' as there is in other jurisdictions because this would make operation of the *Bolam* test impossible.

Lord Diplock explained the reasoning behind the decision.

JUDGMENT

The only effect that mention of risks can have on the patient's mind, if it has any at all, can be in the direction of deterring the patient from undergoing the treatment which in the expert opinion of the doctor it is in the patient's best interests to undergo. To decide what risks the existence of which a patient should be voluntarily warned . . . is as much an exercise of professional skill and judgement as any other part of the doctor's comprehensive duty of care.'

In a much earlier judgment, *Hatcher v Black, The Times*, 2nd July, 1954, Lord Denning had taken a much firmer stance in identifying that the level of information given by a doctor was indeed a clinical decision. In the case he complained that the rise in medical negligence claims was in effect 'a "dagger" at the doctor's back'.

One of the difficult areas for judges to determine is the degree of information that should be given to a patient in advance of any form of intrusive medical treatment.

CASE EXAMPLE

Chapman v Oxford Radcliffe Hospital NHS Trust (Unreported, May 29, 2002)

Here the patient suffered meningitis and then underwent a series of operations and different treatment including the insertion of a titanium plate in his skull to replace infected bone that had needed to be removed. This was then removed when an infection developed. Following the treatment the patient claimed to suffer various neurological disorders. He then claimed that he had not been properly advised about the potential risks involved in the treatment, particularly the risk of infection from the plate. It was held that sufficient information had been given to the claimant who, in the light of the serious nature of his illness would probably have consented anyway, and the health authority was not negligent in the circumstances.

However, the courts appear now to be prepared to take a more active view in determining what level of information is appropriate to give a patient in advance of treatment.

CASE EXAMPLE

Chester v Afshar [2004] UKHL 41; [2004] 4 All ER 587

The claimant, who suffered from back pain, consulted a well-known neurosurgeon who recommended an operation. The claimant did not wish to undergo an operation but was persuaded by the surgeon. In fact there was a small risk, between 1 per cent and 2 per cent, of nerve damage resulting from the operation that might range from minor effects to paralysis. The court accepted that the doctor had failed to warn of these risks and in fact the claimant did suffer fairly serious nerve damage, although there was no question of negligence in the operation. The Court of Appeal held that the surgeon had fallen below the appropriate standard in failing to give full information which, if it had been given, would have meant that the claimant would not have had the operation at that time. Thus she would not have suffered the nerve damage at that time either. The Court felt that if it did not establish liability in the case then it would be to undermine the duty on doctors to warn of risks that no reasonable patient would refuse even after advice of risks was given. Doctors would be given the discretion in that instance not to inform at all. The House of Lords agreed despite the obvious problem in relation to the standard means of proving causation.

Where consent is required in respect of children who are incapable of giving a valid consent it is customary for doctors to seek the consent of the parents of the child. If this is withheld doctors commonly seek the consent of the courts either through care proceedings or through the inherent jurisdiction of the High Court. A failure to do so could result in a breach of Article 8 of the European Convention of Human Rights. This was the case in *Glass v UK* (2004) 39 EHRR 15.

Examination and diagnosis

The original test in *Bolam* had its context in situations where the medical professionals had a range of potential clinical practices to choose from. It was quite rightly used to determine whether or not the choice was legitimate according to the standards accepted by doctors. The rule, however, has been extended well beyond this simple context and has also been accepted and held to apply to the diagnosis of illness.

CASE EXAMPLE

Maynard v West Midlands Regional Health Authority [1985] 1 All ER 635

Here consultants operated before the results of certain tests they had ordered became available. They both considered that the patient had pulmonary tuberculosis, but also felt that she might have Hodgkin's disease and decided to operate immediately without benefit of the information from the tests. She claimed that the operation damaged her vocal cords unnecessarily. The court determined that there was no negligence because the doctors had followed a practice approved by a responsible body of medical opinion, even if it was true that quite conflicting practices were possible at the time.

In the above case Lord Scarman stated that:

JUDGMENT

'There is seldom any one answer exclusive of all others to problems of professional judgement. A court may prefer one body of opinion to the other; but that is no basis for a conclusion of negligence.'

The application of the test to diagnosis may be critical. This is because one potential result of misdiagnosis is that the wrong treatment may be given or wrong operation carried out, leading to even further problems.

CASE EXAMPLE

Ryan v East London and City HA [2001] WL 1890334

Here a child suffered a permanent spinal disability following an operation that had been carried out after a misdiagnosis of a spinal tumour. The court accepted that if the diagnosis had not been negligent the child would have had the correct treatment and not suffered the disability.

In this way failing to take proper account of technical information which then leads on to mistreatment is also falling below the appropriate standard of care if a competent body of medical opinion would have reacted to the information differently.

CASE EXAMPLE

Hunt v NHS Litigation Authority [2002] WL 1480071

Here the doctor failed to fully realise the implications of a cardiotocograph and gave a woman in labour drugs to speed up her labour, then left her in the care of midwifes, attending periodically. In fact the doctor should have noticed that the baby had an irregular heartbeat and that something was wrong. The baby suffered brain damage when it was born with the cord tight around its neck. The doctor should have carried out a forceps delivery at a much earlier stage if she had reacted correctly to the information from the tests.

The test will inevitably be appropriate in terms of the examination given by a doctor as well as the diagnosis resulting from it.

CASE EXAMPLE

Reynolds v North Tyneside HA [2002] Lloyd's Rep Med 459

A baby suffered injury and it was shown that a vaginal examination of the mother by the midwife at an appropriate time would have lessened the chance of injury. The judge accepted evidence that a reasonably prompt examination would have been expected of midwives at the time of the case and the health authority thus fell below the appropriate standard of care in failing to provide one.

Choice of treatment

It is also long since accepted that the test applies to medical treatment, so that all aspects of medicine fall within the scope of the rule.

CASE EXAMPLE

Whitehouse v Jordan [1981] 1 All ER 267

A senior registrar had carried out a forceps delivery of a baby. The baby had become wedged and suffered asphyxia and brain damage. The allegation was that the doctor had used the forceps with too much force and that was the cause of the damage. In fact the mother gave evidence that she had been lifted off the bed when the forceps were applied to the baby's head. In the House of Lords, Lord Edmund-Davis rejected the view put forward by Lord Denning in the Court of Appeal that an error of clinical judgement should not necessarily be treated the same as negligence.

Lord Denning considered that

JUDGMENT

'. . . while some errors may be completely consistent with the due exercise of professional skill, other acts or omissions . . . may be so glaringly below proper standards as to make a finding of negligence inevitable.'

Nevertheless, he confirmed that the *Bolam* test was the appropriate test by which to measure standards of professional activity.

Level of expertise

Of course the standard will not necessarily reduce because of the lack of expertise of the doctor. The standard is that appropriate to the doctor or professional exercising and professing to possess the skill in question. It is not, therefore, possible to argue that the standard is reduced because the defendant lacks experience. So the junior doctor must exercise the same degree of skill as the experienced doctor.

CASE EXAMPLE

Wilsher v Essex Area Health Authority [1988] 1 All ER 871

A baby was born prematurely and with an oxygen deficiency. A junior doctor then administered excess oxygen by mistake. The junior doctor inserted a catheter in an artery rather than a vein and a registrar failed to spot the mistake. The baby was later found to be nearly blind. A possible cause of the blindness was the excess oxygen. The House of Lords rejected the health authority's argument that the standard of care expected should be reduced because it was a junior doctor. Accepting such an argument would then mean that the care a patient was entitled to would depend on the experience of the doctor who treated them. This was unacceptable and negligence was held to have occurred in the case.

While the same standard of skill is expected of the doctor (professional) regardless of his level of experience, in circumstances where the defendant lacks the resources that might generally be available the court will recognise that the same standard of care cannot be expected. However, this is recognition of the resource implications.

CASE EXAMPLE

Knight v Home Office [1990] 3 All ER 237

A prisoner had committed suicide while in a prison hospital. In NHS hospitals there would be a general duty of care to protect suicide risks from harm. The court recognised that because of the greater difficulty of supervising prisoners who might attempt suicide and the lack of resources available to deal with the problem, the same standard of care could not be expected of the prison doctors.

However, this principle may depend on the type of care in question. For instance a prisoner might expect the same standard of obstetric care as would generally be available (see *Brooks v Home Office* [1999] 2 FLR 33).

3.4.4 The *Bolam* principle and professionals generally

The rule that the appropriate standard of care in relation to professionals is measured against the standard held by a reasonable, competent body of professional opinion is not a rule exclusive to doctors. It can be applied to professionals generally.

A person professing to exercise a particular professional skill will be expected to act in accordance with the standards accepted by a competent body of opinion, expert in the particular skill in question, and again it will be measured against the practices accepted as competent within that profession.

CASE EXAMPLE

Luxmoore-May v Messenger May and Baverstock [1990] 1 All ER 1067

Auctioneers sold paintings at auction for £840. Some months later the paintings were then resold for £88,000. It was alleged that the auctioneers were negligent in failing to recognise that the paintings were the work of a famous artist. The Court of Appeal held that the auctioneers should be judged according to the standards of a competent body of opinion skilled in the profession of the auctioneers. In the event they were not negligent because it was shown that there could be divergence of opinion on the origins of the paintings.

The *Bolam* test may in any case apply even though the defendant lacks the appropriate professional qualifications and is not applying the same reasoning that a professional would apply.

CASE EXAMPLE

Adams and another v Rhymney Valley District Council, *The Times*, 11th August, 2000, CA

The defendant council fitted double glazed windows in the claimant's council flat. The windows had removable keys and the council did not fit smoke alarms in the flat. The keys were not kept in the windows. During a fire one of the claimants was badly injured breaking the windows trying to get out and three of the claimant's children died in the fire. The trial judge rejected the claim on the basis that the council had exercised the skill of a competent window designer in fitting windows with removable keys. The Court of Appeal dismissed the appeal and rejected the argument that *Bolam* had been wrongly applied. Even though the council had not consulted the police or the fire brigade they had not produced a negligent design for the windows.

The standard expected of the professional is that of a competent body of professional opinion, not of professional opinion generally. So that it is possible for the practice of the professional in question to be accepted in fact by only a minority of professionals.

CASE EXAMPLE

Defreitas v O'Brien and Connolly [1995] 6 Med LR 108

A doctor specialising in spinal surgery considered an intricate exploratory operation necessary. The argument that there was negligence because as it was shown only 11 out of over 1,000 surgeons who regularly performed the operation would have operated in this case was rejected. The Court of Appeal held that the number involved was capable of being seen as a competent body of medical opinion in the circumstances.

This might include even unorthodox or unusual practices.

CASE EXAMPLE

Shakoor v Situ (t/a Eternal Health Co) [2001] 1 WLR 410

The claimant, who suffered from a skin condition, went to a Chinese herbalist who prescribed a remedy. The claimant later died of acute liver failure that was found to be a rare and unpredictable reaction to the remedy. S's widow brought proceedings alleging negligence in prescribing the remedy, or alternatively, in failing to provide warning of the risks. The court held that it was necessary to consider the standard of care of a practitioner of alternative medicine. It was implied that (1) he was presenting himself as competent to practice within the system of law and medicine under which his standard of care would be judged; (2) he knew, rather than believed, that the remedy was not harmful; and (3) if a patient reacted adversely to the remedy and as a result sought orthodox medical help then this would be discussed in an orthodox medical journal. In the instant case, the actions of the herbalist were consistent with the standard of care appropriate to traditional Chinese herbal medicine in accordance with established requirements. So there was no breach of duty.

Common practice among a profession is often cited as indicating that the practice is acceptable and not negligent. There are of course some practices that can be seen as negligent regardless of whether they are commonly carried out or not.

CASE EXAMPLE

Re Herald of Free Enterprise, The Independent, 18th December, 1987

It was argued that it was standard practice for the bow doors of roll-on roll-off ferries to be left open on leaving ports. It was still, however, seen as being a dangerous practice and negligent on the part of the master of the ferry.

One final aspect of the standard of care expected of professionals is that they should keep reasonably abreast of changes and developments in their profession. They would not, however, be expected to be immediately aware of all new ideas.

CASE EXAMPLE

Crawford v Board of Governors of Charing Cross Hospital, The Times, 8th December, 1983

Here a patient suffered brachial palsy following an operation. It was argued that this was due to the position of his arm during a blood transfusion and that the anaesthetist should have been aware of the risk because of a recent article in The Lancet, a journal for doctors. The court rejected the argument. There was no negligence because the reasonable doctor cannot be expected to keep up with every new development.

However, it is important that where guidelines are issued by government or by the professional bodies governing the professions that indicate best practice, then professionals should act according to those guidelines.

CASE EXAMPLE

Thomson v James and Others (1996) 31 BMLR 1

A GP failed to follow government guidelines in advising parents on vaccinations for rubella, measles and mumps. A child was then not vaccinated following the advice of the GP and contracted first measles and later meningitis and was brain damaged as a result. The doctor was negligent in failing to issue proper advice.

ACTIVITY

Quick quiz

Using *Bolam* criteria in each of the following situations consider whether or not the doctor defendant is likely to have breached his duty of care, giving reasons for your answers

1. A patient has suffered paralysis when the doctor carried out a treatment which on statistical evidence available to the court is only generally carried out by 11 out of 1,000 doctors, although the 11 contain many very experienced and well-respected doctors.
2. A patient has suffered paralysis when a doctor carried out experimental treatment which has not previously been performed. The doctor is an eminent surgeon.
3. A patient has suffered paralysis when he received what he alleged to be negligent treatment and the defence was that the doctor carrying out the treatment was a junior and very inexperienced doctor.
4. A patient has suffered paralysis following an operation carried out by a doctor carrying out a standard procedure and where there were known risks of paralysis. However, the claimant is arguing that the doctor was negligent because an article in an American journal in the month the operation was carried out explained a new procedure which tests showed reduced the risk of paralysis to very low proportions.

3.4.5 Criticism of the *'Bolam* test'

Although the test is the appropriate method of determining whether a professional has fallen below an appropriate standard of care and is therefore negligent in a given case it has not been without consistent criticism.

QUOTATION

'Many academic commentators and organisations campaigning for victims of medical accidents perceive [that] the *Bolam* test . . . has been used by the courts to abdicate responsibility for defining and enforcing patient rights . . . *Bolam* out of control came close to acquiring demonic status in some quarters.'

M Brazier and J Miola 'Bye-bye Bolam: A Medical Litigation Revolution?', [2000] *Medical Law Review* 8, pp 85-114 at p 85.

Over time commentators have identified numerous problems with the rule:

■ The test allows professionals to set their own standard in negligence actions – in the case of people other than professionals the standard is an objective one, measured against the 'reasonable man'. In this case the court will decide what the appropriate standard is. In the case of professionals, however, the standard is measured subjectively according to what other professionals, brought to court as expert witnesses, say it is.

- As such it protects professionals to a greater degree than is the case for anyone else – it is sufficient for a professional to bring to court a fellow professional to say that he would have done the same in the circumstances for the allegation of negligence to fail.
- Practices that are only marginal may be accepted as a result – the danger is that the test can legitimise practices that are highly experimental without real credibility, or at the least practices that few other responsible practitioners would carry out.
- There is a danger that professionals will close ranks – even if this is not the case the criticism will certainly be made and this can have the obvious effect of undermining confidence in the profession.
- It is impossible to say what a reasonable, competent body of professional opinion is – in some cases this can just amount to a question of numbers. The judges in any case are in effect leaving the definition to be made by those accused of the negligence.

There have in fact been a number of cases where doubt has been cast on how appropriate the test is and where judges have preferred to take a more objective view.

CASE EXAMPLE

Lybert v Warrington Health Authority, The Times, 17th May, 1996

Evidence was introduced to show that a warning given by a gynaecologist concerning the possibility of a sterilisation operation failing conformed to established practice. Nevertheless, the Court of Appeal was prepared to declare that the warning was inadequate and therefore negligent.

Most recently the House of Lords has suggested that it is for the court in each individual case to determine what is the standard of care appropriate to the professional against whom the negligence is alleged, and not for professional opinion.

CASE EXAMPLE

Bolitho v City and Hackney Health Authority [1997] 4 All ER 771

A two-year-old boy was in hospital being treated for croup. His airways became blocked and, despite being summoned on more than one occasion by nursing staff, a doctor failed to attend. The boy suffered a cardiac arrest and brain damage as a result. This could have been avoided if a doctor had intubated and cleared the obstruction. The hospital admitted that the doctor was negligent in failing to attend. Nevertheless, they claimed that they were not liable because the doctor stated that even if she had attended she would not have intubated and so the cardiac arrest and brain damage would in any case have occurred. Evidence was introduced to show that there were at the time two schools of thought as to whether or not to intubate in such circumstances. The case is ultimately one of causation and whether the *Bolam* test applies at that point, but the House of Lords rejected the view that because certain medical opinion accepted the practice of the doctor in question that they were bound to accept it because of Bolam.

In *Bolitho v City and Hackney Health Authority* the House of Lords rejected the idea that a doctor should escape liability for negligence merely because of evidence put forward by a number of experts on medical practices who claimed to represent a 'reasonable' or 'responsible' or 'respectable' body of opinion. Lord Browne-Wilkinson explained their rejection in this way:

JUDGMENT

'The use of these adjectives – responsible, reasonable and respectable – all show that the court has to be satisfied that the exponents of the body of medical opinion relied upon can demonstrate that such opinion has a logical basis . . .'

He also suggested that:

JUDGMENT

'. . . if, in a rare case, it can be demonstrated that the professional opinion is not capable of withstanding logical analysis, the judge is entitled to hold that the body of opinion is not reasonable or responsible.'

But he still accepted the significance of using *Bolam* in stating that:

JUDGMENT

'It is only where a judge can be satisfied that the body of expert opinion cannot be logically supported at all that such opinion will not provide the bench mark by reference to which the defendant's conduct falls to be assessed.'

The same criticisms as expressed in *Bolitho* have been raised in subsequent cases. Judges have been prepared to ignore the expert evidence of doctors where they feel that there is no real basis for the medical opinion.

CASE EXAMPLE

Marriott v West Midlands AHA and Others [1999] Lloyd's Rep Med 23

A claimant became seriously ill after his GP failed to respond to the claimant's wife's call for help. The claimant had been injured in a fall down stairs and had been admitted to hospital but released the following day, despite his protests that he was feeling unwell. When his condition deteriorated his wife contacted the GP who said that there was no need to attend, after which the claimant became seriously unwell. The Court of Appeal rejected the claim that the doctor was not negligent based on the evidence of other doctors. The court felt that the *Bolam* test could only apply where there was a logical basis for the arguments of the expert witnesses.

While certain academics will argue that *Bolitho* 'is likely to change the face of health care law in this country' (M Brazier and J Miola, 'Bye-bye Bolam: A Medical Litigation Revolution?' at p 86) perhaps caution is still necessary:

QUOTATION

'The decision in this case is potentially of major significance in that it is the first in which the House of Lords has expressed reservations about the *Bolam* test.
. . .
Although the departure from *Bolam* is somewhat guarded, it does permit the court to choose in appropriate cases between two bodies of opinion.
. . .
According to the House of Lords this can only happen when the judge is unable "as a matter of logic" to accept one of the professional opinions. Such cases are likely to be rare, according to the House of Lords, as experts are selected for their eminence and are not likely to present opinions which are insupportable in logic.'

V Harpwood, 'The End of the *Bolam* Test?' *Medical Law Monitor*, Volume 4, Issue No 10

One comment on the significance of *Bolitho* to the application of the *Bolam* test is also finally worth noting.

QUOTATION

'A very important point has emerged from the House of Lords decision with regard to the position of defending doctors. Their Lordships focused on the words used in earlier medical negligence judgments and found the adjectives "responsible", "reasonable" and "respectable" being used to describe a body of opinion which would act as a successful defence. They held that this "showed that the court had to be satisfied that the exponents of the body of opinion relied upon could demonstrate that such opinion had a logical basis". This means that it will become increasingly difficult for doctors to justify their actions on the basis of producing colleagues who will say that they would have done the same. To escape liability they will have to present a convincing and logical argument to a judge who has little or no medical knowledge.'

W Scott, '*Bolam* and *Bolitho*: A new standard of care for doctors?' [1998] NL

ACTIVITY

Self-assessment questions

1. How does the test used for measuring the standard of care appropriate to a professional differ from the normal test?
2. What justifications does McNair J give for departing from the principles that are generally used to determine what the standard of care is and whether or not it has been breached?
3. How widely has the application of the *Bolam* test spread in the context of the original case?
4. What is the value of expert witness evidence in determining whether or not a professional has breached his duty of care?
5. What do you think that Lord Scarman meant in *Maynard* when he said that 'A court may prefer one body of opinion to the other; but that is no basis for a conclusion of negligence'?
6. Why do you think that the judges were not prepared to reduce the standard of care for inexperience in *Wilsher*?
7. In what ways do you think that Brazier and Miola are correct to say that the *Bolam* test 'has been used by the courts to abdicate responsibility for defining and enforcing patient rights'?
8. What is the value of expert witness evidence in determining whether or not a professional has breached his duty of care?
9. In what ways has *Bolitho* not really made any inroad on the *Bolam* test?
10. What criticisms can be made of the test used for establishing the standard of care owed by professionals?

ACTIVITY

Applying the law

Consider how the courts would determine whether there was a breach in the following situations:

1. Harold is a gynaecologist who when called by midwives because of a difficult birth nevertheless persuades the midwives to continue. The baby dies during delivery. Certain doctors suggest that only a Caesarean section delivery was appropriate in the case but Harold states that, even if he had attended he would not have carried out a Caesarean and other doctors say that they would have reacted similarly.
2. During a forceps delivery of Martha's baby, Harold, an inexperienced doctor who has never performed a forceps delivery before, damages the baby's head so badly that the baby suffers almost total brain damage and dies.

SAMPLE ESSAY QUESTION

'The rules governing breach of duty are inconsistently applied so that they have the potential to be unfair to either party.' Discuss the accuracy of the above statement.

Explain breach and describe how the standard of care is measured

- Breach is falling below the standard that is appropriate to the duty owed
- Based on the reasonable man test *Blyth v Birmingham Waterworks* So is an objective test
- And the standard does not reduce merely because of, eg, inexperience *Nettleship v Weston*

Explain the factors that the court will take into account in assessing breach

- Foreseeability of the risk of harm *Roe v Minister of Health*
- The magnitude of harm *Bolton v Stone, Haley v London Electricity Board*
- The effects of the 'thin skull' rule *Paris v Stepney BC, Page v Smith*
- The practicability of any possible precautions *Latimer v AEC, Bolton v Stone*
- Possible effect of common practice *Brown v Rolls Royce, Re Herald of Free Enterprise*

Discuss whether these cause inconsistency or injustice

- Objective measure should lead to consistency and justice
- Inexperience will not excuse – the same standard is expected so creates consistency and is fairer to claimant but could appear unfair to defendant
- Recovery only possible for foreseeable damage so fair
- The 'thin skull rule' may cause inconsistency or appear unfair
- And common practice may apply inconsistently

Explain the different approach applied to professionals, particularly doctors

- Measured against 'a competent body of professional opinion' *Bolam v Friern Hospital Management Committee*
- So more subjective than objective

Discuss whether this leads to inconsistency or injustice

- Allows them in effect to set their own standards which may mean that claims are easier to defeat
- Definitely inconsistent with reasonable man standard
- Risky practices may still be accepted
- A danger of professionals 'closing ranks' to defeat claims
- Harder to determine what 'a competent body of professional opinion' actually is until it is tested

The standard of care of professionals	Case
A breach of duty occurs where a person falls below the standard of care appropriate to the duty he owes.	
The standard of care is usually that appropriate to the 'reasonable man'.	*Blyth v Birmingham Waterworks* (1856)
But the standard appropriate to professionals is judged according to the standards of a competent body of professional opinion.	*Bolam v Friern Hospital Management Committee* (1957)
This is because the 'reasonable man' does not share those skills.	
And all aspects of medicine are tested against this rule, including even complementary medicine.	*Whitehouse v Jordan* (1981) *Shakoor v Situ* (2001)
Though there is no lowering of standard to take account of inexperience.	*Wilsher v Essex AHA* (1988)
The rule is criticised for allowing doctors to set their own standards while standards generally are measured according to an objective standard.	
It is felt that the standard should not be applied to hypothetical situations.	*Bolitho v City & Hackney HA* (1997)

3.5 Fault liability and the need for reform

Fault liability, particularly in the case of medical negligence as we have seen, seems unfair to claimants because of the problems associated both with amassing evidence and of actually proving fault.

It seems obviously wrong to impose liability on a body such as a health authority unless that body can be shown to have done wrong. The fact that the defendant satisfies legal tests on fault is nevertheless scant comfort to a person who places his safety in the hands of professional people and finds himself later to have suffered irreversible and disabling damage.

Fault liability can also be seen as unfair to victims who have suffered harm because the degree to which a person can easily gather evidence and therefore present a winnable case may depend on the degree of publicity that the case has produced. Inevitably people involved in an event gaining media attention or involving a number of claimants may be in a better position to find suitable evidence.

In this way fault liability can also be unfair to society generally in not providing an adequate means of remedying wrongs since the fault based system can create classes of victims who can be compensated and classes who cannot. This can be particularly true of the victims of pure accidents and those suffering from genetic disorders.

It can also be seen as unfair to defendants since there are no identified degrees of culpability. This in turn means that a defendant will not be penalised according to the degree of negligence shown.

The rules concerning the standard of care as well as the imposing of duties mean that very often a claimant's ability to recover for the wrong suffered is determined according to the whims of policy and therefore can be subject to arbitrary and often inconsistent reasoning.

In fairness to the fault based system its major justification is that it does punish the wrongdoer and so is said to have some deterrent value.

However, no-fault systems have been advocated on a number of occasions. The Pearson Committee in 1978 suggested such a system in the case of personal injury claims, though this has never been accepted or implemented. Two no-fault based medical negligence bills have also been introduced unsuccessfully. The principle is not without precedent since such a system has operated in New Zealand (see Chapter 1, section 1.3.3).

In the case of health care professionals it is interesting to note that the Chief Medical Officer has proposed a new system for claims against NHS Trusts in a June 2003 report 'Making amends'. The system advocated is an attempt to avoid the delays and costs of pursuing claims through the courts, although of course it will not prevent a claimant from pursuing a claim in this way. The substance of the proposals is for a 'right of redress' where investigation of a patient's complaint reveals 'serious shortcomings' and which result in 'harm which could have been avoided'. The proposed result would include appropriate care and rehabilitation and compensation up to £30,000. There are more complex provisions in the case of severely neurologically damaged babies.

For additional discussion of fault-based liability, see Chapter 1 section 1.3.

ACTIVITY

Essay writing

Using the guide in Appendix 1, try the following essay title.

Consider the extent to which the rules by which the courts determine whether there is a breach of a duty of care actually discourage people from engaging in activities that may harm or damage others.

SUMMARY

- A breach occurs when the defendant falls below the standard of care appropriate to the duty owed
- Measured against the standard of the 'reasonable man'
- So is an objective standard, eg the reasonable motorist
- There is no lowering of the standard for those who lack experience
- Judges take many factors into account
  - the foreseeability of the risk of harm
  - the magnitude of the risk
  - the effects of the 'thin skull' rule
  - the practicability of any possible precautions
  - the possible effect of common practice
- Measured differently in the case of professionals
  - measured against 'a competent body of professional opinion'
  - the *Bolam* test
  - which causes controversy

Further reading

Elvin, J, 'Liability for negligent refereeing of a rugby match' (2003) 119 LQR 560.

Stein, R and Swaine, F, 'Ms B v an NHS Trust: The patient's right to choose' [2002] NLJ 642.

Toczek, L, 'A case of foul play' [2002] NLJ 868.

4

Negligence: causation

AIMS AND OBJECTIVES

After reading this chapter you should be able to:

- Understand the usual means of establishing causation in fact, the 'but for' test
- Understand the problems that arise in proving causation in fact where there are multiple causes of the damage
- Understand the possible effects on the liability of the original defendant of a plea of *novus actus interveniens*, where the chain of causation has been broken
- Understand the test for establishing causation in law, reasonable foreseeability of harm, so that the damage is not too remote a consequence of the defendant's breach of duty
- Understand the requirements for a plea of *res ipsa loquitur*, and the effects of a successful plea
- Be able to critically analyse the concepts of causation in law and causation in fact
- Be able to apply the tests to factual situations to determine whether the defendant has caused the damage suffered by the claimant

4.1 Introduction

Once the claimant has shown the existence of a duty of care and proved that it has been breached by falling below the appropriate standard of care he must still prove that the defendant's negligent act or omission actually caused the damage.

As with the other two elements of negligence, the burden is on the claimant to prove the causal link on a balance of probabilities. This may actually be quite difficult to do, particularly where the incident leading to the damage has been the result of multiple causes or where the damage suffered is of an unusual type.

Causation is also clearly appropriate to other torts, not just negligence. Even in those torts that are strict liability and where the claimant as a result is relieved only of the burden of proving fault causation is still an issue and the claimant must still show a direct link between the defendant's acts or omissions and the damage suffered.

Causation is necessarily measured against the facts of the individual cases. Nevertheless, as in the other areas, policy can still play a big part in decisions.

In establishing negligence the courts will measure causation in two different ways:

- According to the **'but for' test**, that the defendant's negligent act or omission did in fact cause the claimant's damage (causation in fact).

'but for' test
The main test for establishing factual causation in an action for negligence – but for the defendant's breach of duty the damage would not have occurred

■ By establishing that the damage is still sufficiently proximate in law to hold the defendant liable to compensate the victim (causation in law – more commonly referred to as remoteness of damage). (This latter area is the subject of section 4.5.)

4.2 Causation in fact and the 'but for' test

The simplest proposition, and the effective starting point in establishing causation, is to say that the defendant will only be liable in negligence if the claimant would not have suffered the damage 'but for' the defendant's negligent act or omission.

The test was explained simply and precisely by Lord Denning in *Cork v Kirby MacLean Ltd* [1952] 2 All ER 402

In many cases where the negligence of the defendant is obvious the facts allow the test to operate simply and straightforwardly. The negligence either was the cause of the damage or there was some alternative cause and the defendant is not liable.

JUDGMENT

'. . . if the damage would not have happened but for a particular fault, then that fault is the cause of the damage; if it would have happened just the same, fault or no fault, the fault is not the cause of the damage.'

CASE EXAMPLE

Barnett v Chelsea & Kensington Hospital Management Committee [1969] 1 QB 428

Three night watchmen from a college went to the casualty ward of the hospital at around 5.00 am on the morning of New Year's Day complaining of vomiting and stomach pains after drinking tea. The doctor on duty, in clear breach of his duty towards the men, then refused to attend to them or examine them and told them to call on their own doctors in the morning. A few hours later one of the men died, as it was discovered later, through arsenic poisoning. The court found that the hospital was not liable for the failure to treat, even though this was a clear breach of their duty, because it was shown that the man would not have recovered even if he had received treatment. The failure to treat was not the cause of death.

However, the facts of a case will not necessarily always be as straightforward as this. In consequence there can be difficulties in establishing causation. For instance, the test may have to be applied to an omission rather than to an act itself, in which case the court has to determine what would have happened if the defendant had chosen to act rather than to do nothing. Only then can the court be sure that the defendant's omission is in fact the cause of the damage suffered by the claimant.

CASE EXAMPLE

Brock v Frenchay Healthcare Trust (Unreported, 1998)

Here a 16-year-old boy suffered irreversible brain damage after a fall from a bicycle when he had not been wearing a crash helmet. He had been taken immediately to hospital but the doctors had failed to discover that he had a fractured skull, although it was accepted that there was no negligence involved. The boy was discharged but was readmitted after it became apparent that he was seriously ill. Doctors prepared for an emergency operation and to give the boy a drug, Mannitol, used to relieve pressure on the brain. In the event the anaesthetist did not use the drug until the surgeon arrived and the issue before the court was whether the eventual damage could have been averted if it had been administered earlier. The Court of Appeal, applying the principles in *Bolitho v City and Hackney HA* [1997] 4 All ER 771 (see later in section 4.3.1), held that there was nothing in the evidence to suggest that the drug, if used earlier, would have had any significant impact on the actual injuries.

It is of course possible that the defendant's injury follows naturally from the negligent omission, because the events leading to the damage would not have occurred but for the negligent omission.

CASE EXAMPLE

Chester v Afshar [2004] UKHL 41; [2004] 4 All ER 587

Here as we have already seen (see Chapter 3 section 3.4.3), the Court of Appeal held that the surgeon had fallen below the appropriate standard by failing to give full information on the risks of neurological damage from an operation. The Court accepted that there was evidence to show that the claimant would not have undergone the operation but for the failure to advise of the risks, even though she admitted that she may have been prepared to have the operation at a later stage. It was a simple logic for the Court to accept that the injuries arose directly from the operation, which, even though not carried out negligently, would not have taken place but for the omission to warn of the risks. The House of Lords acknowledged that the problem facing the claimant was that she had admitted that she would have had the operation at some point in the future but not at that time so that it is hard to say that the negligent omission to reveal the full extent of the risks by the doctor could be said to be the direct cause of the injury suffered. Nevertheless, the House, as in Fairchild (see later 4.3.1), was prepared to avoid the problems associated with applying the 'but for' test in order to give a just result.

Their Lordships appear to be inconsistent in their reasoning. Lord Steyn stated:

JUDGMENT

'… it is a distinctive feature of the present case that but for the surgeon's negligent failure to warn the claimant of the small risk of serious injury the actual injury would not have occurred when it did and the chance of it occurring on a subsequent occasion was very small. It could therefore be said that the breach by the surgeon resulted in the very injury about which the claimant was entitled to be warned.'

Lord Hoffman dissenting, on the other hand stated:

JUDGMENT

'… this argument is about as logical as saying that if one had been told, on entering a casino, that the odds on number 7 coming up at roulette were only 1 in 37, one would have gone away and come back next week or gone to a different casino. The question is whether one would have taken the opportunity to avoid or reduce the risk, not whether one would have changed the scenario in some irrelevant detail.'

4.3 Problems in proving causation

Very often the problem is not purely one of fact and the process of establishing cause is not so much scientific enquiry as attributing blame. Inevitably interpretation of the factual evidence may still depend on the value judgements used by the court. For instance a pedestrian runs onto the road into the path of an oncoming vehicle that is travelling over the speed limit for the area and the pedestrian is injured. In purest scientific terms the actual cause of the accident is that both parties were present on the road at the same time. It is possible in the circumstances to feel that the pedestrian has done as much as, if not more than, the motorist in causing his own injuries. Inevitably however, even allowing for a successful claim of contributory negligence, the motorist would be held to have caused the victim's injuries, because he is blameworthy by exceeding the speed limit.

Even greater problems may occur where the level of knowledge available to the court makes it impossible to pinpoint the precise cause. This may be particularly appropriate where medicine and medical technology is concerned.

4.3.1 The problem of multiple causes

The problem of proving a causal link between the defendant's negligent act and the damage is always made more difficult where there is the possibility of more than one cause. In such instances the court is forced into the position of trying to determine which of the possibilities is the actual cause of the damage suffered. Very often the court will find that it is impossible to do this with accuracy and the claimant may be left without compensation at all.

CASE EXAMPLE

Wilsher v Essex Area Health Authority [1986] 3 All ER 801 CA

Here a baby after being delivered was given excess oxygen as a result of the admitted error of the doctor and the baby then suffered blindness through retrolental fibroplasia. The House of Lords identified that the excess oxygen was just one of six possible causes of the condition and therefore it could not be said to fall squarely within the risk created by the defendants. The court would not impose liability on the defendant in these circumstances although this seems very unfair.

The difficulty of identifying precise cause means that the case law is often inconsistent. The risk then is that the decision will appear on the surface to be unfair to the claimant. This again is all too common where the chance of recovery may have been lost through negligence in medical treatment or diagnosis.

CASE EXAMPLE

Hotson v East Berkshire Area Health Authority [1987] 1 All ER 210

A young boy suffered a fractured hip when he fell out of a tree. The hospital negligently failed to make a correct early diagnosis so that he later developed avascular necrosis, a deformity of the hip. Expert evidence confirmed that he would have had a 75 per cent chance of the deformity even without the failure to diagnose promptly. On this basis the trial judge, and later the Court of Appeal, awarded him 25 per cent of the damages they would have considered appropriate for the condition for the loss of a chance of recovery. The trial judge commented that the hospital had translated the probability of the disability developing into a certainty by negligence in their failure to diagnose. However, the House of Lords allowed the Health Authority's appeal and would not consider the slim chance of recovery an issue of causation.

Lord Ackner summed up the issue of causation in the case quite succinctly.

JUDGMENT

'. . . the deformed hip . . . was not caused by the admitted breach by the defendants . . . but was caused by the separation of the left femoral epiphysis when he fell . . . I have sought to stress that this case was a relatively simple case concerned with the proof of causation, upon which the plaintiff failed, because he was unable to prove on the balance of probabilities that his deformed hip was caused by the defendant's breach of duty in delaying over a period of five days a proper diagnosis and treatment.'

However unfair the position of the House of Lords may appear there is nevertheless no disputing its legal logic.

QUOTATION

'The emotive speech and obvious feelings for a "lost chance" plaintiff must not let us colour or obscure the real issue – the existence of an "evidentiary gap". Proof of causation should not be accepted on anything less than the balance of probabilities, as is common with all civil actions.'

T Hill 'A lost chance for compensation in the tort of negligence by the House of Lords' (1991) 54 MLR 511

The House of Lords has had a more recent opportunity to review the law on 'loss of a chance'.

CASE EXAMPLE

Gregg v Scott [2005] UKHL 2; [2005] 2 WLR 268

The claimant was concerned about a lump under his arm but his GP failed to refer him to a hospital for tests, dismissing the lump as harmless fatty tissue. When the claimant saw another GP nine months later, by which time he was in considerable pain, he was referred to hospital for tests and cancer of the lymph glands was diagnosed which it was established had spread considerably during the delay. The claimant argued negligence on the part of the original doctor and it was shown that if his condition had been diagnosed on the first visit and treatment had started at that point he would have had a 42 per cent chance of being alive and disease free in ten years, whereas as a result of the delay in treatment his chances of being alive and disease free after ten years had reduced to 25 per cent. The House of Lords, on a split decision 3:2, was unwilling to depart from the principle in Hotson by awarding the claimant a proportion of what he would have recovered if the doctor's negligence had in fact caused his premature death. Interestingly the House added that, had the claimant sought damages for the pain and suffering experienced during the delay in treatment these might have been awarded.

The majority judges and the dissenting judges were clearly unconvinced by each other's irreconcilable reasoning.

Lord Hoffman, delivering the leading judgment held that:

JUDGMENT

'Academic writers have suggested that in cases of clinical negligence, the need to prove causation is too restrictive … In the present case it is urged that Mr Gregg has suffered a wrong and ought to have a remedy [and that] the exceptional rule in Fairchild should be generalised and damages awarded in all cases in which the defendant may have caused an injury and has increased the likelihood of the injury … It should be first noted that adopting such a rule would involve abandoning a good deal of authority.'

Lord Nicholls dissenting, on the other hand stated:

JUDGMENT

'Given the uncertainty of outcome, the appropriate characterisation of a patient's loss in this type of case must surely be that it comprises the loss of a chance of a favourable outcome, rather than the loss of the outcome itself. Justice so requires … And this analysis of a patient's loss accords with the purpose of the legal duty … to promote the patient's prospects of recovery by exercising due skill and care in diagnosing and treating the patient's condition. This approach also achieves a basic object of the law of tort. The common law imposes duties and seeks to provide appropriate remedies in the event of a breach of duty. If negligent diagnosis … diminishes a patient's prospects of recovery, a law which does not recognise this as a wrong calling for redress would be seriously deficient …'

Ultimately the legal justification for failing to provide a remedy in the 'loss of a chance' cases lies in the fact that the claimant's arguments on causation rests on a possibility rather than a probability of harm occurring, and on a simple balance of probabilities test the claims fail.

The reverse possibility of course is that the court chooses to accept the chance of a causative link between the defendant's acts and the damage. However, in this instance it may risk the possibility of unfairly penalising the defendant.

CASE EXAMPLE

McGhee v National Coal Board [1973] 3 All ER 1008

Here the claimant worked in a brick kiln where he was exposed to brick dust, a possible cause of the dermatitis that he in fact contracted. The Board was not liable for exposure during working hours. They were held liable for materially increasing the risk of the claimant contracting the disease because of their failure to provide washing facilities, even though it could not be shown that he would have avoided the disease if there had been facilities. The reasoning of the court was that, since the employer was clearly negligent in failing to provide basic health and safety the burden should shift on to them to disprove the causal link. This type of test is clearly more advantageous to a claimant than the basic 'but for' test applied so rigidly in *Hotson v East Berkshire AHA* [1987] 1 All ER 210.

The problems that the courts have in determining cause are further added to in circumstances where they are also asked to decide the possible outcomes of hypothetical situations.

CASE EXAMPLE

Bolitho v City and Hackney Health Authority [1997] 4 All ER 771

Here the doctor had been negligent in failing to attend a child with severe respiratory difficulties despite the requests of the nursing staff for her attendance. The doctor claimed that this fact was irrelevant in relation to the cardiac arrest and eventual death of the child. Her argument was that, even if she had attended the child with the breathing difficulties she would not in any case have intubated and thus the same damage would have occurred and that there was responsible medical opinion that would support the practice in the circumstances of the case. The House of Lords rejected the idea that the *Bolam* test should be applied to the issue of causation in order that the Health Authority should escape liability.

Nevertheless, there are occasions where the courts appear to take a pragmatic approach where proof of causation is difficult.

CASE EXAMPLE

Bonnington Castings Ltd v Wardlaw [1956] AC 613

The claimant contracted pneumoconiosis after years of working in dusty conditions and without adequate washing facilities. There were two principal causes of dust, the one requiring no extraction system and the other which did, but no extractor was provided. It was impossible to prove accurately which dust the claimant had inhaled most of. Since the dust which should have been extracted legally was at least a partial cause of his illness the court were prepared to award compensation.

The courts are also at times prepared to accept the chance of a causal connection with the damage or the chance of damage being avoided without the defendant's negligent act or omission.

CASE EXAMPLE

Stovold v Barlows, The Times, 30th October, 1995

It was claimed that a house sale was lost through the negligence of the solicitors. The Court of Appeal felt that there was at least a 50 per cent chance that the deal would otherwise have gone through and so awarded half damages.

But equally courts have been prepared to place too much emphasis on a single cause out of a number of possibilities, leading to unfair treatment of the claimant.

C ASE EXAMPLE

Fairchild v Glenhaven Funeral Services Ltd and others [2001] All ER (D) 125 (Dec), CA

This case involved a number of appeals. The claimants suffered mesothelioma after exposure to asbestos dust over many years working for a number of different employees. The medical evidence identified that the inhaling of asbestos fibres was the cause of the disease. Nevertheless, it was impossible to identify in which particular employment the disease was actually contracted. The Court of Appeal accepted that medical evidence could not identify a single cause of the disease, which might be caused by contact with even a single asbestos fibre, or may involve cumulative exposure to fibres. As a result the Court held that the precise employer responsible could not be identified and so the claim should be rejected. It is impossible to say with certainty how the disease begins, but it is possible to identify that prolonged exposure worsens the risk. It seems then that the Court of Appeal applied *Wilsher v Essex AHA* [1986] 3 All ER 801 inappropriately where *McGhee v NCB* [1973] 3 All ER 1008 might have been more fairly applied in the circumstances. The House of Lords has in any case subsequently reversed the Court of Appeal decision (see later in section 4.3.3).

The decision in the Court of Appeal inevitably led to criticism.

QUOTATION

'The "single hit" theory that one asbestos fibre alone is capable of initiating mesothelioma has been the source of incalculable harm . . . The key point is that the "single hit" theory presupposes a deterministic view which is not supported by science. It encourages a mindset much closer to criminal law – equating the "guilty" fibre with the knife or bullet which severs the victim's aorta. Of course, lawyers, like most non-scientists, find it hard to resist reducing a complex process to an easily visualised analogy. But they must not forget that the notion of the "guilty" fibre has no basis in the epidemiological evidence . . . The counter-argument that it is unjust to impose liability upon those not responsible for the "guilty" fibre . . . overlooks the role of tort in deterring all negligent behaviour not simply that which can be shown to result in actual injury.'

C Miller, 'Why the House of Lords must overturn the Fairchild decision' [2002] NLJ 319

Multiple causes can arise generally in one of two ways:

- the multiple causes are concurrent or
- the multiple causes are consecutive.

Inevitably the role of the court is to determine and apportion liability and the result may be different in either case.

4.3.2 Multiple concurrent causes

If the damage is caused by multiple causes that are acting concurrently, or at the same time, then the 'but for' test appears to be incapable of providing an absolute test of causation. The case law demonstrates the difficulties faced by the courts in trying to identify the precise cause.

On the one hand the court may decide that the negligence has '. . . materially increased the risk . . .' of damage and that the defendant should therefore be liable for damages.

CASE EXAMPLE

McGhee v National Coal Board [1973] 3 All ER 1008

Here, as we have already seen, the court was prepared to make the employer liable for the dermatitis suffered by the worker in the brick kiln. The court did so because it considered that the risk of the particular damage occurring had been materially increased by the defendant's negligent failure to provide adequate washing facilities, even though it was impossible to pinpoint the lack of washing facilities as the precise cause of the condition.

Where the courts use this 'material contribution test' it can be difficult in any case to determine the exact extent of the defendant's contribution and this naturally leads to some strange and apparently arbitrary decisions.

CASE EXAMPLE

Holtby v Brigham & Cowan (Hull) Ltd [2000] 3 All ER 421

Here, the claimant had been exposed to asbestos dust for more than 40 years while working for different employers. When he contracted asbestosis he sued the defendants, for whom he had only worked for half of that time. The trial judge reduced damages by 25 per cent. The claimant appealed and tried to argue for application of the principle in *McGhee*, that once having established a material contribution by the defendants he was entitled to full damages. The Court of Appeal rejected his argument and upheld the trial judge's award, even though 50 per cent deduction would have seemed more accurate. McGhee was distinguished.

In comparison, where there is a number of possible concurrent causes of the damage and it is impossible to identify one specific cause responsible for the damage, then it is unlikely that the court will hold that a single cause is ultimately responsible. The consequence of this of course could be that the claimant is left without an action at all, even though the damage must have resulted from one of the causes. While perhaps technically accurate it also seems potentially unfair.

CASE EXAMPLE

Wilsher v Essex Area Health Authority [1986] 3 All ER 801, CA

Here the court identified that there were at least five other possible causes of the baby's blindness and the claimant thus could not establish the necessary causal link with the defendant's negligence and was without a remedy.

4.3.3 Multiple consecutive causes

Where causes leading to the loss or damage suffered are consecutive, or come one after the other, then ordinarily the liability will remain with the first event unless subsequent events have added to the damage. The 'but for' test will be applied to the original defendant.

CASE EXAMPLE

Performance Cars Ltd v Abraham [1962] 1 QB 33

The defendant negligently drove his vehicle so that it collided with a Rolls Royce car. When the Rolls Royce was also later negligently struck by another car the court held that this did not relieve the original defendant of liability for a re-spray that had in any case been made necessary by the first collision.

In this way where a pre-existing condition of the claimant has contributed to the eventual damage it has been held that this may affect the extent of the liability of the defendant.

CASE EXAMPLE

Cutler v Vauxhall Motors [1971] 1 QB 418

The claimant suffered a grazed ankle following his employer's negligence. The claimant already suffered a varicose condition and when an ulcer formed on the area of the graze he required an operation. While the defendant was held liable for the negligence the court identified that the liability applied only in respect of the graze, not the operation.

However, a court when it is trying to determine where liability lies in the case of consecutive causes has inevitably at times been influenced by the desire to avoid in any way under-compensating the victim.

CASE EXAMPLE

Baker v Willoughby [1970] AC 467

The claimant was knocked down by a car and suffered a permanent stiff leg as a result. He was then forced to take work on a reduced income. At a later time he was shot in the injured leg during an armed robbery and this resulted in the leg having to be amputated. The House of Lords rejected the driver's claim that he was then only liable for damages up to the point of the amputation. The court identified that the loss of earnings was a permanent state of affairs and had resulted from the original injury. The armed robbery and amputation of the leg had not altered this fact even though the eventual damage was different and worse.

Lord Reid explained why in his judgment.

JUDGMENT

'A man is not compensated for the physical injury; he is compensated for the loss which he suffers as a result of that injury. His loss is not in having a stiff leg; it is in his inability to lead a full life, his inability to enjoy those amenities which depend on freedom of movement and his inability to earn as much as he used to earn or could have earned if there had been no accident. In this case the second injury did not diminish any of these. So why should it be regarded as having obliterated or superseded them?'

Nevertheless, the picture is even less straightforward because the courts have also at times been keen to ensure that the victim is not over-compensated at the expense of the defendant. Again the principle is that the defendant should only be liable for the extent of the damage actually caused by him.

CASE EXAMPLE

Jobling v Associated Dairies [1982] AC 794

In 1973, and as a result of his employer's negligence, the claimant slipped on the floor of a refrigerator in his employer's butcher's shop and injured his back losing 50 per cent of his earning capacity as a result. Then in 1976 he later developed spondylotic myelopathy, a crippling back disorder which was in fact unrelated to the fall. The court held that the defendant employer was liable for damages only up to the condition developing in 1976, since the condition, and therefore any further loss of earnings, would have occurred anyway despite the original negligence. The court, while not overruling *Baker v Willoughby*, was nevertheless very critical of the case.

The two cases taken together demonstrate the important relationship between causation where there are multiple causes and the principles on which damages should be awarded.

- Where a claimant suffers damage from two separate consecutive causes the second tortfeasor should only be liable for any additional damage caused over that suffered as a result of the first tort.
- Where a claimant suffers from a condition that is unconnected with a tort that has also caused him to suffer injury or damage of a similar type then the damages imposed on the tortfeasor must be reduced to take into account the effect of the condition.

Interestingly the points that can be taken from the two cases are not necessarily mutually exclusive.

CASE EXAMPLE

Murrell v Healey [2001] 4 All ER 345

The claimant had been injured in two car accidents six months apart, both caused by the negligence of separate defendants. He was paid a settlement in respect of the first claim during which he alleged that it was possible he would be unable to work again. In the second claim, and prior to the actual settlement for the first, he claimed that he did in fact expect to return to work in two months but that the second incident had damaged his knees and hips and that would prevent him from returning to work. This fact was disputed by other evidence in the case of either claim. The trial judge in the second claim held that damages should be reduced by the amount that the settlement from the first covered the same damage. He also held that no post trial loss of earnings should be allowed since the injuries to the knees and hips was not the cause of the second accident. The Court of Appeal held that the judge should have considered any additional damage caused by the second accident. In this way, if the claimant could have done light work after the first accident but that this was prevented by the second then damages should have been based on that. As the claimant had in effect removed this possibility by his evidence in the first claim, no further damages were awarded.

The fact that the courts are prepared to consider the impact that future foreseeable tortious acts may have on termination of the claimant's employment is yet another source of complication to establishing cause.

CASE EXAMPLE

Heil v Rankin [2000] 2 WLR 1173

Here a police officer who suffered post traumatic stress disorder following a car crash was discharged from the police force. The court held that it was a foreseeable consequence of such employment that he would at some point suffer another event that might cause his retirement from the force and that they were entitled to take this into account when assessing damages.

The House of Lords has recently accepted that in certain circumstances where there are a number of defendants all contributing to the same basic injury, then a modified approach to causation has to be taken.

CASE EXAMPLE

Fairchild v Glenhaven Funeral Services Ltd and others [2002] 3 WLR 89

This is a major case involving three joined appeals. They all concerned employees who had contracted mesothelioma as a result of prolonged exposure to asbestos dust with a number of different employers. Because of the difficulty of identifying during which employment the disease was actually contracted the Court of Appeal in fact rejected the claims. The House of Lords accepted the expert evidence that it is scientifically uncertain whether inhaling a single fibre or inhalation of many fibres causes the disease, so it is impossible to say accurately which employer caused the disease. However, the House of Lords held that, because it is evident that the greater the exposure to the dust the greater are the chances of the disease occurring, then each employer has a duty to take reasonable care to prevent employees from inhaling the dust. Besides this the House felt that any other cause of developing the diseases could be ignored in the case. On the basis that the claimants suffered the very injuries that the defendants were supposed to guard against, the House of Lords were prepared to impose liability on all employers. The House chose to apply the 'material risk' test from *McGhee*. In doing so the House held that because all of the defendants had contributed to a risk of mesothelioma, then no distinction should be drawn between the making of a material risk of causing the disease and a course of action that would materially increase the risk of the disease. Because the employers in the case never argued that they should only be liable for a proportion of the damages then each employer should be liable to compensate its employee in full, even though the employee may have inhaled more asbestos fibres while working for another employee.

At first sight it is quite difficult to see the precise differences between the three very significant cases of *Wilsher*, *McGhee v National Coal Board*, and *Fairchild v Glenhaven Funeral Services Ltd and others* itself, all of which still stand as leading authorities. A number of points can be made:

- The judges in the House of Lords in *Fairchild* accepted that the sufferers of diseases such as mesothelioma, while inevitably deserving of compensation, are unable to satisfy the normal tests for causation because they will invariably be unable to point to a single party who is responsible.
- The Court was prepared to accept the possibility of a claim for three connected reasons:
  - Because claimants in such actions were unable to satisfy the normal tests for causation only because of the current state of medical knowledge on the disease, although there could be no doubt that exposure to the asbestos fibres in whatever volume was at the root of the disease.
  - As a result of this it was fairer to give the defendants the burden of proving that their negligence could not be the actual cause rather than make the claimants prove the precise cause.

- And if the House did not take this approach then it would be almost impossible for such claimants to ever make successful claims for the disease in which case the employer's duty of care would be made meaningless as they could almost never be made liable.
- The majority of the judges were therefore prepared to accept an exceptional principle that where there was proof that a defendant's negligence materially increased the risk of a claimant suffering from a particular disease then this would be sufficient basis for a claim against that defendant. This was said to be based on the principle in *McGhee*.
- The Court was not prepared to extend the principle in *McGhee* to factual circumstances such as those in *Wilsher* where the problem for causation was in fact that there were a number of very different potential causes of the injury other than the defendant's negligence, and evidence would be needed to show that the negligence was the actual cause.

As Lord Bingham stated:

JUDGMENT

'It is one thing to treat an increase in risk as equivalent to the making of a material contribution where a single noxious agent is involved, but quite another where any one of a number of noxious agents may equally probably have caused the damage.'

- The House of Lords appear to have engaged in a policy decision in order to ensure that there is compensation for asbestos related diseases contracted in the course of employment.

QUOTATION

'[J]urisdictions worldwide have grappled with concerns regarding an effective formulation for determining causation, and, as far as authorities selected by Lord Bingham illustrate, they have concluded that effectively throwing one's hands into the air and retreating behind the convenient barrier of scientific uncertainty to deny a single remedy when there are multiple possible causes cannot be an effective or just solution as far as the injured third party is concerned.'

J Lowther, 'Fairchild clarifying rules on causation' (2002) 14 ELM 4

- Nevertheless, while the Law Lords have claimed to have created an exceptional principle the extent of its application is not really clear and may depend on arbitrary considerations.

QUOTATION

'The dense and closely argued judgments in Fairchild will keep legal scholars engaged for some time. Their Lordships . . . have tried to limit the scope. Lord Bingham's judgment, for instance, relates purely to mesothelioma claims. However, it is hard to see how this principle could not apply to all 'indivisible' diseases . . . Can we expect argument that the balance weighs less in favour of the defendant when the disease is less ferocious than mesothelioma? That would be a difficult argument to run, given that McGhee itself related to a claim for dermatitis . . . [what] is clear [is] that insurers cannot resist claims on the basis that the claimant cannot identify who was responsible for allowing exposure to the guilty fibre or fibres.'

A Morgan, 'Inference, principle and the proof of causation' (2002) NLJ 1060

- Establishing liability in a case may depend on how broadly or how narrowly the particular duty is expressed.

Case	Wilsher v Essex AHA [1986]	McGhee v National Coal Board [1973]	Fairchild v Glenhaven Funeral Services and Others [2001]	Hotson v East Berkshire AHA [1987]
The damage suffered by the claimant	The baby suffered blindness through retrolental fibroplasia	The employee contracted dermatitis, a painful skin disease	Various employees contracted mesothelioma, a cancer affecting the lungs caused by exposure to asbestos fibres	The boy suffered avuncular necrosis, a permanent deformity of the hip
The breach of duty by the defendant	A junior doctor employed by the defendant health authority administered excess oxygen after a difficult birth	The employer failed to provide adequate washing facilities in the workplace so the employee could not wash till he got home	All of the employers had exposed the claimants to asbestos fibres, although some were no longer in business	The doctor employed by the health authority failed to diagnose the greenstick fracture at the appropriate time
Liability for harm	No liability	Liability	Liability	No liability
The reason for the decision	Scientific evidence showed that there were six possible causes of the condition suffered by the baby – so on a balance of probabilities it could not be proved that the doctor's breach of duty was the factual cause of the harm	Even though it could not be shown that the employee would not have contracted the disease but for the employer's breach of basic health and safety duties, the employer had materially increased the risk of the employee catching the disease, and it was for the employer to disprove causation	Although it is currently scientifically impossible to identify which particular asbestos fibre caused the disease or even whether it was more than one fibre, exposing the employee to asbestos by any of the employers was material contribution to the risk of harm so any could be liable	Scientific evidence showed that there was a 75% chance that the boy would have suffered the deformity as a result of his injury even if the fracture had been immediately diagnosed – on a balance of probabilities it could not be proved that the doctor's breach of duty was the factual cause of the deformity
'But for' test applied	Yes	No	No	Yes

Table 4.1 Chart explaining the relationship between key cases on multiple consecutive causes

The area has subsequently been the cause of even more argument and even more confusion.

CASE EXAMPLE

Barker v Corus (UK) (formerly Saint Gobain Pipelines plc); Murray v British Shipbuilders (Hydromatics) Ltd; Patterson v Smiths Dock Ltd and Others [2006] UKHL 20; [2006] All ER (D) 23

This involved three appeals concerning questions left unanswered in Fairchild. Barker had died as a result of mesothelioma. He had been exposed to asbestos fibres during three different periods, once in the employment of the defendant, once during different employment and once during a period of self-employment. The defendant argued that causation could not be proved since the disease could have been contracted solely during the period of self-employment, and alternatively that, although mesothelioma was an indivisible injury that damages should be apportioned between the different possible causes so that the defendant should not be bound to pay full damages. The trial judge allowed a claim under Fairchild subject to a 20 per cent reduction for contributory negligence for a failure by Barker to protect himself during his self-employment. The Court of Appeal also applied *Fairchild*, accepted that the defendant was jointly and severally liable and rejected the possibility of apportionment. The House of Lords held that in such circumstances a defendant could only be liable for the share of damages equivalent to the share of the risk of contracting mesothelioma created by his breach of duty, and therefore apportioned damages accordingly.

Lady Hale commenting on the potential injustice caused by the relaxation of standard rules of causation in *Fairchild* stated:

JUDGMENT

'... for the first time in our legal history, persons are made liable for damage even though they may not have caused it at all, simply because they have materially contributed to the risk ...'

Lord Hoffman explaining the position taken by the court stated:

JUDGMENT

'... since this is a case in which science can only deal with probabilities the law should accept that position and attribute liability according to probability.'

The decision was praised in certain quarters:

QUOTATION

'The pragmatic decision . . . reflects a desire not only to ensure that the traditional causation tests remain the cornerstones for Tort based compensation claims but to redress the inequities thrown up by . . . Fairchild.'

Joe McManus, 'Playing it fair', New Law Journal, 26 May 2006, p 871

However, the decision was regretted by the Prime Minister and in effect, in the case of mesothelioma claims only, was reversed by a hastily included provision in the Compensation Act 2006. Undoubtedly the law is left in a state of some uncertainty. As Alison McAdams suggests:

QUOTATION

'… it is difficult for any party to be confident how this area of law will develop, since the rationale being adopted seems to be one of proceeding by way of compromise …' and 'It is also uncertain whether the "single agent" rule will be interpreted narrowly or widely in the future.'

ACTIVITY

Self-assessment questions

1. What is the difference between causation in fact and causation in law?
2. How does the 'but for' test work?
3. In what ways is causation a problem to a claimant trying to prove medical negligence?
4. What exactly is the effect of the judgment in *Hotson v East Berkshire Area Health Authority*?
5. What is the difference in the judgments in *McGhee* and in *Wilsher*?
6. What effect has the case of *Fairchild v Glenhaven Funeral Services* had on proving causation in fact?
7. How do courts react when there are multiple causes for the damage suffered?
8. How do the courts react when the claimant has a pre-existing condition?
9. What is the justification for the decision in *Performance Cars v Abraham*?
10. Why exactly are *Baker v Willoughby* and *Jobling v Associated Dairies* decided differently?
11. Do these two judgments represent fair results to both claimants and defendants?
12. In what ways does the case of *Heil v Rankin* cause complications?

KEY FACTS

Causation in fact	Case
A defendant may be liable in negligence if 'but for' his act or omission the damage would not have occurred	*Barnett v Chelsea & Kensington Hospital Management Committee* (1969)
Multiple causes	**Case**
It may be difficult at times to prove causation and courts will not impose liability where the cause is uncertain.	*Wilsher v Essex AHA* (1986)
Courts are very reluctant to base liability on loss of a chance.	*Hotson v East Berks AHA* (1987)
Where there are multiple causes the court may feel that the defendant's act has materially increased the risk.	*McGhee v National Coal Board* (1973)
Where there are multiple consecutive causes the liability remains with the first defendant unless the later cause increased the damage.	*Performance Cars v Abraham* (1962)
Though they are careful not to undercompensate or to overcompensate.	*Baker v Willoughby* (1970); *Jobling v Associated Dairies* (1982)
But where a number of defendants all contribute to the risk of harm no distinction should be drawn between creating a material risk of causing the disease and materially increasing the risk of the disease in determining liability.	*Fairchild v Glenhaven Funeral Services and Others* (2001)

4.4 *Novus actus interveniens*

4.4.1 Breaking the chain of causation

novus actus interveniens

Means 'a new act intervenes' – refers to situations where the defendant is excused liability because another intervening act has broken the chain of causation

Even though the defendant can be identified as negligent and the 'but for' test satisfied in some senses, the chain of causation may be broken by a subsequent, intervening act. If the court accepts that this intervening act is the true cause of the damage suffered then the defendant may not be liable despite his breach of duty.

Such a plea by the defendant is known as *novus actus interveniens*. Translated it means 'a new act intervenes', and it is an effective defence. If, however, the intervening act is not accepted by the court as being the true cause of the damage then the chain is unbroken and the defendant remains liable for his breach.

CASE EXAMPLE

Kirkham v Chief Constable of Greater Manchester [1990] 3 All ER 882

Police who had transferred a prisoner to Risley remand centre had failed to inform the authorities there that the prisoner was a known suicide risk. When the prisoner did in fact commit suicide the police were held liable for their failure to warn the prison authorities. Their plea of *novus actus interveniens* by the prisoner failed, since he was suffering from clinical depression, not in full control, and therefore the suicide was not as such a voluntary act.

The effects of an intervening act can easily be illustrated in diagram form.

An unbroken chain of causation where the defendant is liable

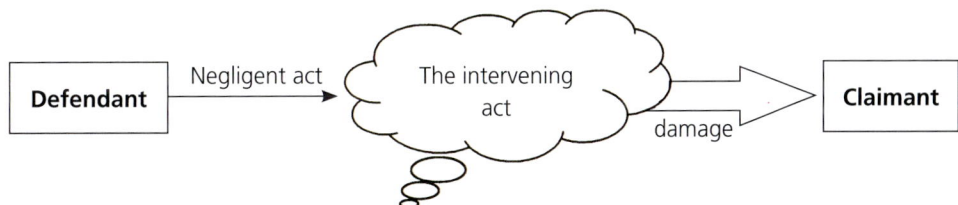

A chain of causation broken *by a novus actus interveniens* so the defendant is not liable

Figure 4.1 The effect of a break in the chain of causation

The area is full of difficulties and the possibility of the plea succeeding is entirely dependent on the facts of the individual case. The case law seems, however, to fall into three easily definable categories:

- where the intervening act is caused by the claimant himself
- where the intervening act is an act of nature
- where the intervening act is the cause of a third party in which case a new defendant may in effect be introduced into the case.

4.4.2 An intervening act of the claimant

This is very closely connected with contributory negligence. Unlike contributory negligence, however, where the defendant is liable but damages are reduced by the extent to which the claimant is responsible for the harm he suffers, the plea here is that the claimant is actually responsible for his own damage. Therefore the chain of causation is broken and the defendant has no liability at all.

CASE EXAMPLE

McKew v Holland & Hannen & Cubitts (Scotland) Ltd [1969] 3 All ER 1621

The claimant suffered an injury to his leg leaving it seriously weakened as a result of the defendants' negligence. When he later tried to climb a steep flight of steps with no handrail without asking for help he fell and suffered further serious injuries. The court held that the defendants were not liable for this fall. The claimant's act was a *novus actus interveniens*.

Lord Reid identified that:

JUDGMENT

'A defender is not liable for a consequence of a kind which is not foreseeable. But it does not follow that he is liable for every consequence that a reasonable man could foresee.'

However, if the defendant's original breach is still the operating cause of the later damage and the claimant was not acting unreasonably, then the plea that the chain of causation is broken will fail.

CASE EXAMPLE

Wieland v Cyril Lord Carpets Ltd [1969] 3 All ER 1006

Mrs Wieland suffered an injury following the defendant's negligence causing her to have to wear a surgical collar. She wore bifocals and wearing the collar restricted her head movement and meant her use of her spectacles was also seriously impaired. When she then fell down a flight of stairs and sustained further injuries the defendants were liable for those injuries. The court held that there was no break in the chain of causation. The risk to Mrs Wieland in the circumstances was said to be foreseeable. The obvious difference with the last case was that the claimant did nothing unreasonable.

So providing the claimant's actions are reasonable there will not necessarily be a break in the chain of causation.

CASE EXAMPLE

Lord v Pacific Steam Navigation Co. Ltd (The Oropesa) [1943] 1 All ER 211

Here through the negligence of those sailing a ship, The Oropesa, another ship was damaged in a collision between the two. The captain of the other ship together with some crew members then put to sea in a lifeboat in order to consult with the captain of The Oropesa as to what to do to save their own ship. Some of the sailors drowned. The Court of Appeal held that the decision to take out the lifeboat was a perfectly reasonable one to make in the circumstances and so there was no break in the chain of causation.

It will not, however, be a *novus actus interveniens* by the claimant himself if the alleged intervening act is one that the defendant was under a duty to prevent.

CASE EXAMPLE

Reeves v Commissioner of the Metropolitan Police [1999] 3 WLR 363

Here police were holding a prisoner who was a known suicide risk. The prisoner did in fact commit suicide. While the police accepted that they owed the claimant a duty of care, they nevertheless denied liability, arguing a *novus actus interveniens* by the claimant himself. The court rejected the argument, as the suicide was the specific act that the police should have been seeking to prevent.

4.4.3 An intervening act of nature

A plea that an act of nature has broken the chain of causation will rarely succeed. The reason for this is that the claimant in this instance is then left without any means of gaining a remedy for the wrong suffered.

However, the defendant may well be relieved of liability in those situations where he can show that the act of nature that he argues is breaking the chain of causation is unforeseeable and independent of his own negligence.

CASE EXAMPLE

Carslogie Steamship Co. v Royal Norwegian Government [1952] AC 292

The claimant's ship was damaged following a collision with a vessel of the defendant's navy and through the defendant's fault. After a delay for repairs the ship then embarked on a voyage it would not otherwise have taken. On that voyage the ship suffered further damage during a heavy storm. The argument that the defendant should be liable for both the original damage and the damage caused by the storm failed. The House of Lords accepted that the storm was a genuine break in the chain of causation and the defendant could not be held liable for the full extent of the damage. The storm damage was not a consequence of the collision but was a quite separate occurrence that might have happened on any voyage.

4.4.4 An intervening act of a third party

In order to succeed with a plea of *novus actus interveniens* in these circumstances the defendant must show that the act of the third party was also negligent and was of such magnitude that it did in fact break the chain of causation. Furthermore, the defendant must not be under any duty to guard against the act of the third party.

CASE EXAMPLE

Knightley v Johns [1982] 1 All ER 851

The defendant, through his negligent driving, crashed and blocked a tunnel. The police officer in charge at the scene then negligently sent a police officer against the flow of traffic to block off the tunnel at the other end. There was a second accident and the police officer was injured as a result. The court held that the defendant was not liable for the injuries sustained by this policeman. They were the fault of the other police officer and his action amounted to a *novus actus interveniens*.

Stephenson LJ identified that:

JUDGMENT

'the original tortfeasor, whose negligence created the danger which invites rescuers, will be responsible for injury and damage which are the natural and probable results of the wrongful act' but in accepting that the chain of causation had been broken he also commented that

JUDGMENT

'Negligent conduct is more likely to break the chain of causation than conduct which is not.'

Furthermore, for the act of the third party to break the chain of causation, the consequences of the third party's act must be foreseeable.

CASE EXAMPLE

Lamb v Camden London Borough Council [1981] QB 625

Here the defendant council negligently broke a water main as a result of which the claimants' house suffered water damage and the claimants had to move out. While the claimants were out of the house squatters moved in and caused much more damage. The council was held not liable for the further damage. The actions of the squatters were a *novus actus interveniens*. It was not foreseeable.

As already mentioned above, for the chain of causation to be broken, the defendant must not have any duty to guard against the third party's act.

CASE EXAMPLE

Ward v Cannock Chase District Council [1986] 3 All ER 537

Here the defendant council negligently allowed a house to fall into general disrepair. The house adjoined the claimants' house. When the claimants were forced to move out of their house while the repairs to the adjoining house were carried out vandals and thieves who broke in damaged it. The council had failed to make proper repairs and act quickly enough in repairing the house next door. The court held that this meant that acts of vandalism were almost inevitable. There was no *novus actus interveniens* and the council was held liable.

Nevertheless, it is also possible that in such circumstances both the defendant and the third party have in fact contributed to the damage caused. In such circumstances both parties will be held individually liable accordingly.

CASE EXAMPLE

Rouse v Squires [1973] QB 889

The defendant drove negligently, causing his lorry to jack-knife on a motorway, as a result of which an accident occurred in which many vehicles were involved, including the claimant. Another driver because he was driving much too fast then negligently collided with some of the stationary vehicles from the first incident, killing the claimant. Despite the obvious responsibility of the later driver, the chain of causation was held not to be broken. The damage in the second incident was held to be a foreseeable consequence of the first and the first driver was held to be 25 per cent responsible for the death of the claimant. The remaining liability was with the driver of the vehicle involved in the second collision. The court identified that the negligence of the lorry driver was an operative cause of the claimant's death and that the chain of causation could not be broken by the effect of a later driver driving too fast or not keeping a proper lookout for hazards ahead. It did accept that someone deliberately or recklessly driving into the crashed vehicles could break the causal chain.

So the effects of a successful plea of *novus actus interveniens* in simple terms would appear to be as follows:

■ Where it is the claimant's own act that intervenes – the defendant is relieved of liability and the claimant has no possible remedy for the damage suffered.

■ Where there is an intervening act of nature – it is likely that the claimant will have no defendant to sue and no remedy.

■ Where a third party is responsible for the intervening act – the claimant will have no action against the original defendant – whether or not the claimant still has a possible action and a remedy will depend on whether the third party is also negligent.

ACTIVITY

Self-assessment questions

1. What exactly does the phrase *novus actus interveniens* mean?
2. What are the necessary requirements for a successful claim of *novus actus interveniens* by a defendant?
3. What is the difference between a plea of *novus actus interveniens* and one of contributory negligence?
4. What are the three types of *novus actus*?
5. Which is the least likely to be successful?
6. Which is the most likely to still give the claimant a remedy?
7. What happens to the claimant's claim when the defence proves successful?

KEY FACTS

Novus actus interveniens	Case
A defendant will not be liable where there is a *novus actus interveniens* (a new act intervening).	
This is because the 'chain of causation' is broken by the intervening act.	
An intervening act could be of three types:	
• an intervening act of the claimant	*McKew v Holland & Hannen & Cubitts* (1969)
• an intervening act of nature	*Carslogie Steamship Co v Royal Norwegian Government* (1952)
• an intervening act of a third party.	*Knightley v Johns* (1982)
But there will be no break in the chain of causation where the intervening event is reasonable and foreseeable.	*Lord v Pacific Steam Navigation Co Ltd (The Oropesa)* (1943)
Or where the defendant was under a duty to prevent the act that is alleged to break the chain of causation.	*Reeves v Commissioner of the Metropolitan Police* (1999)

ACTIVITY

Quick quiz

In the following situations consider which type of *novus actus interveniens* is involved and whether or not the defendant in the case is likely to be held liable.

1. During a very severe storm Atmar is driving well over the speed limit, loses control of his car, and crashes into Jacquie's car causing some damage to the bumper and left side

wing. The storm causes a large tree to uproot. This then falls onto Jacquie's car destroying it completely.

2. During a very severe storm Jacquie is driving well over the speed limit, loses control of her car and crashes into Sukhy's car causing the radiator to burst and leak water. Sukhy then drives home, a distance of 30 miles. The radiator leaks on the way and boils dry causing the engine to seize. The engine is completely destroyed as a result.

3. During a very severe storm Sukhy is driving well over the speed limit, loses control of his car and crashes into Chris's car which stalls and will not start. In fact only minimal damage was done to the front bumper of Chris's car. Chris pushes his car safely into the side of the road, calls the AA and waits for them to attend to restart his car. Norman, who is driving well above the speed limit, loses control of his car, skids violently across the road and crashes into Chris's car. Chris's car is a write off and Chris is killed in the collision.

4.5 Causation in law and testing remoteness of damage

4.5.1 The tests of remoteness

The final element of proof in negligence is whether there is causation in law, otherwise known as remoteness of damage. Even though a causal link can be proved factually according to the 'but for' test the claimant may still be prevented from winning the case if the damage suffered is too remote a consequence of the defendant's breach of duty.

The test is a matter of law rather than fact and like other aspects of negligence is much influenced by policy considerations. The principle justification for the rule is that the defendant should not be overburdened by compensating for damage linked to the breach that is of a kind that is unlikely or unforeseeable.

The original test of remoteness, however, was that the claimant could recover in respect of a loss that was a direct consequence of the defendant's breach regardless of how foreseeable this loss was.

CASE EXAMPLE

Re Polemis and Furness, Withy & Co [1921] 3 KB 560

Charterers of a ship filled the hold with containers of benzene that then leaked during the voyage, filling the hold with vapour. In port the ship was being unloaded when a stevedore negligently dropped a plank into the hold. A spark then ignited the vapours and the ship was destroyed. The arbitrator held that this was too unlikely a consequence of dropping the plank, though some damage was of course foreseeable. The Court of Appeal held that the charterers, as employers of the stevedores, were liable.

Scrutton LJ stated that

JUDGMENT

'. . . if the act would or might probably cause damage, the fact that the damage it in fact causes is not the exact kind of damage one would expect is immaterial, so long as the damage is in fact directly traceable to the negligent act.'

The test was not without its difficulties and it was criticised for its failure to distinguish between degrees of negligence.

In *Overseas Tankship (UK) Ltd v Morts Dock & Engineering Co (The Wagon Mound (No 1))* [1961] AC 388 Viscount Simmonds explained the deficiencies in the traditional 'direct consequence' rule.

JUDGMENT

'It does not seem consonant with current ideas of justice or morality, that for an act of negligence, however slight or venial, which results in some trivial foreseeable damage, the actor should be liable for all the consequences, however unforeseeable and however grave, so long as they can be said to be direct.'

As a result the test was later changed to one of liability for damage only that was a reasonably foreseeable consequence of the breach.

CASE EXAMPLE

Overseas Tankship (UK) Ltd v Morts Dock & Engineering Co (The Wagon Mound (No 1)) [1961] AC 388

Due to the defendant's negligence, bunkering oil was leaked into Sydney harbour from a tanker. The oil floated on the water to the claimant's wharf, mixing with various flotsam and jetsam, including patches of cotton wadding. Welding was taking place in the wharf and the claimant's manager enquired whether there was a risk of the oil igniting. This was considered unlikely since the oil had an extremely high flash point. Welding then continued and sparks did in fact ignite the oil-soaked wadding and then set fire to ships being repaired in the wharf. The oil also caused fouling to the wharf. The trial judge held that since some damage, the fouling, was foreseeable, the defendants were liable also for the fire damage which was a direct consequence of their breach of duty in allowing the spillage. The Privy Council reversed this decision, holding that the defendant could not be liable for the fire damage since the correct test for remoteness was reasonable foreseeability and, because of the improbability of the oil igniting, the fire damage was unforeseeable.

Viscount Simonds explained the principle and the reason for the change to the former test in *Re Polemis and Furness, Withy & Co* [1921] 3 KB 560.

JUDGMENT

'. . . if it is asked why a man should be responsible for the natural or necessary or probable consequences of his act the answer is that it is not because they are natural or necessary or probable, but because, since they have this quality, it is judged by the standard of the reasonable man that he ought to have foreseen them.'

Of course, while the reasoning in the case is in keeping with other aspects of negligence it still raises questions.

QUOTATION

'Although the Wagon Mound principle has clearly been accepted by English law the reasoning on which it is based is not unassailable. As a matter of policy it is not immediately apparent why the law should opt for a rule which limits the liability of a defendant who has broken a legally recognised duty at the expense of an innocent victim of this act. If it is an important part of the deterrent role of tort that the costs of accidents should fall on the least cost avoider it is presumably the case that it is the real rather than the notional costs which should be placed in the equation.'

K M Stanton, *The Modern Law of Tort* (Sweet & Maxwell, 1994), p 96

4.5.2 Applying the reasonable foreseeability test

The critical element of the test in *The Wagon Mound* is foreseeability of the general rather than the specific type of damage. It is not therefore necessary for the full extent of the damage to be foreseen in order for there to be liability.

CASE EXAMPLE

Bradford v Robinson Rentals [1967] 1 All ER 267

The claimant suffered frostbite when sent on a long journey from Exeter to Bedford by his employers in severe winter weather, being sent in a van without a working heater. The defendants argued that in England this type of damage was too remote and unforeseeable for them to be held liable. The court, however, disagreed. The court identified that it was certainly foreseeable that some cold-related illness was a possibility in the circumstances. As a result the court felt that it was immaterial that the actual damage was frostbite, and the defendant was held liable.

It is not therefore necessary for the defendant to have contemplated or to have foreseen the precise consequences of the negligent act or omission, provided that he is aware of the possibility of damage resulting.

CASE EXAMPLE

Margereson v J W Roberts Ltd [1996] PIQR P358

The court in this case considered that the owner of an asbestos works should have been aware of the dangers of people inhaling the asbestos dust, even in 1933. In consequence the court was prepared to impose liability on the defendant in respect of mesothelioma contracted by children who played in dust from the factory that collected in the streets around the entrance to the factory and the surrounding area.

If damage is foreseeable then neither is it necessary, when the defendant is negligent, for the precise consequences of the act or omission to be foreseen when some damage is a foreseeable consequence.

CASE EXAMPLE

Hughes v The Lord Advocate [1963] AC 837

Post Office employees working in a hole in the road negligently left a manhole uncovered inside a tent and then left the tent unattended. As a safety precaution the workmen left four lit paraffin lamps at the corners of the tent at night. A boy entered the tent with one of the lamps and when it fell into the hole there was an explosion, the boy fell in also and was burnt. This was an unlikely chain of events but the court nevertheless held the defendants liable since some fire-related damage was a foreseeable consequence of leaving the scene unattended.

If damage is foreseeable it will not matter that the damage is actually more extensive than might have been foreseeable, provided that the kind of damage itself is foreseeable.

CASE EXAMPLE

Vacwell Engineering Co Ltd v BDH Chemicals Ltd [1971] 1 QB 88

Here the defendants were the suppliers of a chemical product to the claimants. The defendants negligently failed to warn the claimants that the chemical would explode if it came into contact with water. When one of the claimant's scientists did expose the chemical to water there was an alarming explosion, causing very extensive damage. The court held that the defendants were liable even though the resultant damage to property was far more severe than might have been foreseen.

The court will not only be concerned with the likelihood of harm resulting from the defendant's negligence. It will also take account of the risk that the harm will be greater if it involves a claimant with a particular sensitivity. In this way the defendant is said to have to 'take the claimant how he finds him'. This is the so-called 'thin skull' rule.

CASE EXAMPLE

Paris v Stepney Borough Council [1951] AC 367

The claimant was a mechanic who was already blind in one eye. He was working under a vehicle and trying to undo a tight nut but had not been supplied with safety goggles by his employer, the defendants, as they were legally required to do. The claimant was then injured in his good eye, causing him total blindness. The court held that the defendants were liable for the full extent of the claimant's blindness, rather than for causing blindness in one eye. The court identified that the claimant's condition meant that the defendants owed him a higher duty of care than would normally be the case and were in effect responsible for and therefore liable for his total blindness.

The 'thin skull' rule operates then so that the defendant will be liable for the full extent of the damage if damage of the type caused is in fact foreseeable.

CASE EXAMPLE

Smith v Leech Brain & Co Ltd [1962] 2 QB 405

An employee suffered a burnt lip as a result of being splashed by molten metal following his employers' negligence. The burn activated a cancer from which the claimant later died. His lip had actually been in a pre-malignant state at the time of the burn. Some form of harm from the burn was foreseeable. The court held that even though the death from cancer was not immediately foreseeable, harm resulting from the negligence was, and the defendants were held liable as a result.

The same principle can apply even where the harm is psychiatric damage and this is particularly important in employment relationships where employers subject employees to unnecessary stress.

CASE EXAMPLE

Walker v Northumberland CC [1995] 1 All ER 737

A senior social worker had already suffered one nervous breakdown and was allowed to return to work by his doctor on the understanding that his work schedule would not be too excessive or stressful. When in fact the employer subjected the claimant to even more stress this resulted in a second nervous breakdown. The court held that the employer was liable. This was because after the first breakdown they were aware of his susceptibility to stress and did nothing to reduce his workload or the pressure associated with it.

The principle can also apply where the expected damage is physical injury but the claimant suffers shock instead and has a particular sensitivity.

The test of reasonable foreseeability and claims for personal injury

In general the cases above seem to indicate that the courts will take a fairly broad view of what is reasonably foreseeable in the event that the damage suffered is personal injury.

CASE EXAMPLE

Jolley v London Borough of Sutton [2000] 3 All ER 409, HL

A council failed to move an abandoned boat for two years. It was well known that children played in the boat and it was a clear danger. A boy of 14 was then hurt when he and a friend jacked up the boat in order to try to repair it. The Court of Appeal felt that the activities engaged in by the boys and therefore the specific type of damage caused were not at all foreseeable. The House of Lords, however, disagreed with this reasoning. The House acknowledged that the boat was dangerous, and as a result that it was quite foreseeable that children coming into contact with the boat might suffer some kind of harm. The precise manner in which the injuries occurred was not important. It was sufficient that some harm was foreseeable for the defendant council to be liable for its negligence.

Nevertheless, there have been occasions on which courts have taken a much narrower view of what is foreseeable. As a result the decisions appear on the surface to work unfairly on the claimant.

CASE EXAMPLE

Tremain v Pike [1969] 3 All ER 1303

The claimant was a herdsman who contracted Weil's disease during the course of his work. This is a rare disease and is only contracted through contact with rats' urine. The claimant argued that this in fact happened when he worked with hay and washed with water that was contaminated with rats' urine. The court did accept that the defendant had negligently allowed the rat population on his farm to grow too large and that there was some inevitable risk of damage from rats. Nevertheless, the court held that the defendant was not liable since the court considered that the disease was so rare in humans that it was an unforeseeable consequence of the negligence.

On occasions it also appears that the test in *Hughes v Lord Advocate* [1963] AC 837 can be contradicted if the court focuses too closely on the circumstances in which the damage occurs, rather than on the mere fact that some damage is foreseeable.

CASE EXAMPLE

Doughty v Turner Manufacturing Co Ltd [1964] 1 QB 518

Here, due to negligence, a cover over a cauldron of heated sodium cyanide was allowed to slide into the liquid in the tank. The cover was made of asbestos compound. There was a chemical explosion and the claimant who was working on the tank was badly burned. The Court of Appeal accepted that it was previously unknown that there would be such a chemical reaction between the asbestos and the sodium cyanide and the court held that the defendants were not liable as a result. The chemical reaction was unforeseeable and the damage was thus too remote. However, there certainly seems to be merit in the claimant's argument that damage from the liquid if splashed would be foreseeable. In deciding the case the Court of Appeal chose to apply the persuasive precedent of the Privy Council in *The Wagon Mound* rather than its own previous precedent in *Re Polemis*.

The judges will also apply policy reasons in determining whether an outcome is reasonably foreseeable.

CASE EXAMPLE

Corr v IBC Vehicles Ltd [2008] UKHL 13

An employee was badly injured as a result of his employer's negligence. He also developed post-traumatic stress disorder as a result and eventually committed suicide. The Court of Appeal accepted that depression was a foreseeable consequence of the original negligence. On this basis, since suicide is not uncommon in cases of depression, unless any evidence was introduced to the contrary, there was nothing to prevent recovery. The Court commented that to treat the chain of causation as being broken by the suicide would be unjustified and awarded the man's widow damages under the Fatal Accidents Act 1976. The House of Lords subsequently upheld this ruling. The view had already been confirmed in *Rothwell v Chemical and Insulating Co Ltd* [2007] UKHL 39 where the House of Lords rejected a similar claim because the employee could not show that his employer should have foreseen the risk of psychiatric injury and the claim did not fall within the exception identified in *Page v Smith* [1996] AC 155.

In contrast in *Grieves v FT Everard and Sons Ltd* [2006] EWCA Civ 27 the Court of Appeal was not prepared to accept a causal link between asbestos exposure and the development of pleural plaques (which could lead to subsequent asbestos related diseases) and a depressive illness based on the fear of contracting such an illness.

The test of reasonable foreseeability and claims for property damage

With few exceptions the courts in general appear to adopt a much narrower approach to what might be considered foreseeable when the damage in question is to property rather than personal injury.

CASE EXAMPLE

Overseas Tankship (UK) Ltd v Morts Dock & Engineering Co (The Wagon Mound (No 1)) [1961] AC 388

The trial judge acknowledged that some damage was foreseeable in the circumstances. The judge, however, felt that the type of damage that was foreseeable would be fouling of the harbour and ships moored in it by the oil. He did not feel that fire damage was foreseeable in the circumstances. But since he believed fouling was foreseeable he held that the fire damage was also a direct consequence of the defendant's negligence. Inevitably the Privy Council could only consider the appeal on this basis.

Even the degree of risk of the type of damage actually caused has been considered narrowly thus avoiding imposing liability.

CASE EXAMPLE

Overseas Tankship (UK) Ltd v Miller Steamship Co Pty (The Wagon Mound (No 2)) [1967] 1 AC 617

The owners of the two ships that were being repaired in the wharf and were damaged in the fire brought this case. The trial judge showed a very narrow approach to foreseeability in relation to an action for property damage. While he accepted, unlike the trial judge in *Wagon Mound (No 1)*, that fire was a foreseeable consequence of the defendant's negligence, he nevertheless felt that it was so remote as to not give rise to any liability. He was reversed by the Privy Council which held that provided the type of damage was foreseeable, then liability must result and the degree of likelihood was irrelevant. The Privy Council was able to reach this result in the appeal because the trial judge had actually accepted fire damage as a remote but foreseeable consequence of the negligence.

4.5.3 Points for discussion

It is difficult in some ways to see a real difference between the test based on direct consequences and the test based on reasonable foreseeability. In many instances certainly damage that is reasonably foreseeable will also be a direct consequence of the defendant's negligent acts or omissions. It is similarly difficult to contemplate situations that are totally unforeseeable and yet are still a direct consequence.

Besides this the difference may well be unimportant for a number of reasons, including:

■ The effect of the 'thin skull' rule is that many victims may be compensated for damage that the defendant will probably not have contemplated at all.
■ Many areas of quite remote damage are in any case within the scope of insurance and so a claimant may still gain some form of compensation even though this cannot be gained from the potential defendant.

ACTIVITY

Self-assessment questions

1. What are judges trying to achieve with the rule on remoteness of damage?
2. When precisely will damage be too remote to be compensated?
3. How does the *Wagon Mound* test differ from that in *Re Polemis*?
4. How exactly is reasonable foreseeability measured, in other words what has to be foreseen?
5. Do the attitudes of the courts generally vary according to the type of damage caused?
6. To what extent are the judgments in *Doughty v Turner Manufacturing* and *Hughes v Lord Advocate* consistent?
7. What is the effect of a claimant's peculiar sensitivities on the issue of remoteness of damage?
8. Is there any justification for adopting a narrower approach to remoteness in cases involving property damage than in those involving personal injury?

KEY FACTS

Remoteness of damage	Case
At one time a defendant was liable for all damage that was a direct consequence of his negligent act or omission.	*Re Polemis and Furness, Withy & Co* (1921)
Now the modern test is one of liability for reasonable foreseeable damage.	*The Wagon Mound (No 2)* (1967)
Only the general, not the actual type of damage needs to be foreseen.	*Bradford v Robinson Rentals* (1967)
Nor do the precise consequences of the negligent act or omission have to be foreseen.	*Hughes v Lord Advocate* (1963)
The 'thin skull' rule applies means that the defendant will be liable for the full extent of injuries suffered by a claimant with particular sensitivities.	*Smith v Leech Brain* (1962)
The courts generally, but not always, seem to take a broader view of remoteness in personal injury cases than they do with property damage.	Compare *The Wagon Mound (No 1)* (1961) with *Bradford* (1967) or *Doughty* (1964)

Did the defendant owe the claimant a DUTY OF CARE?

There was sufficient proximity between the parties, the damage was foreseeable and it was fair, just and reasonable to impose a duty.

— NO →

YES
↓

Did the defendant BREACH the duty?

The defendant fell below the standard of care appropriate to the particular duty owed – measured objectively against the standards of a 'reasonable man'.

— NO →

THE DEFENDANT IS NOT LIABLE FOR NEGLIGENCE

YES
↓

Did the defendant's breach of duty CAUSE the claimant's DAMAGE?

— NO →

- The breach was the factual cause of the damage
- The damage would not have occurred but for the defendant's breach of duty.
- If there was more than one cause then the defendant's breach was the substantial cause, or
- the breach of duty materially increased the risk that damage would occur.
- There was no break in the chain of causation.
- The damage was not too remote a consequence of the defendant's breach of duty.
- The damage was a foreseeable consequence of the defendant's breach of duty.
- The damage was of a type that was reasonably foreseeable.

YES
↓

THE DEFENDANT IS LIABLE FOR NEGLIGENCE

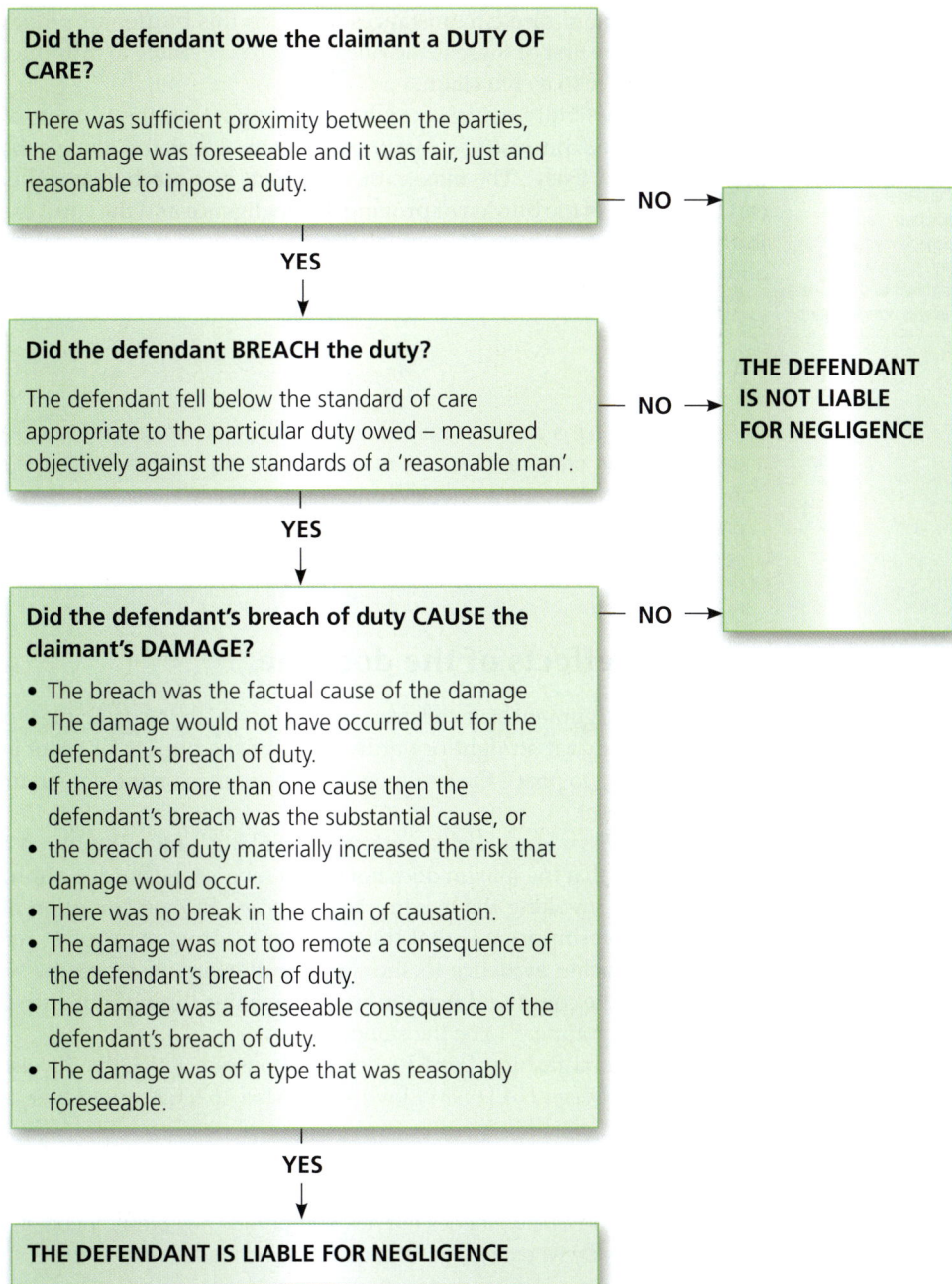

Figure 4.2 The essential elements for proof of negligence with particular emphasis on the cause of damage

4.6 Proving negligence

4.6.1 Pleading *res ipsa loquitur*

One of the common threads throughout all law is the general maxim that 'he who accuses must prove'. In this way the party claiming the negligence has the burden of proof and must show the defendant's breach of the duty of care.

The burden of proof can work very harshly on a claimant who is bound to collect all of the necessary evidence in order to show that there is negligence. This can be particularly difficult for instance in a medical negligence claim where a mass of highly technical evidence may need to be produced in order to satisfy the burden.

res ipsa loquitur
Literally: 'the thing speaks for itself' – where the claimant is unable to show details of the negligence but the damage was obviously caused negligently the defendant will be required to show that he was not negligent

There are certain rare circumstances in which this burden of proof can be made less demanding. The first of these is the rule of that it is possible to introduce criminal convictions as evidence in a civil claim.

A second possibility, which may have an impact on the burden of proof, is an old common law maxim *res ipsa loquitur*. Literally translated *res ipsa loquitur* means 'the thing speaks for itself'. The maxim therefore acts as a mechanism whereby the claimant can be relieved of the burden of proving the negligence and the court can infer negligence in those situations where the factual circumstances of the case would make proving it almost impossible.

The rule is easily justified.

QUOTATION

'*Res ipsa loquitur* is an immensely important vehicle for importing strict liability into negligence cases. In practice, there are many cases where res ipsa loquitur is properly invoked in which the defendant is unable to show affirmatively either that he took all reasonable precautions to avoid injury or that the particular cause of the injury was not associated with negligence on his part.'

M A Milner, *Negligence in Modern Law* (Butterworths, 1967), pp 89–93

4.6.2 The effects of the doctrine

There is some argument as to the exact means by which the principle works. The simplest explanation is that it straightforwardly reverses the burden of proof and instead of the claimant having to prove the negligence, the burden is on the defendant to prove that he was not negligent.

In *Wilsher v Essex Area Health Authority* [1986] 3 All ER 801, CA, on the other hand, it was suggested that the maxim does not in fact reverse the burden of proof. Instead it was suggested that invoking the maxim raises a *prima facie* presumption of negligence. The result of this presumption is that the defendant is then required to rebut the presumption by introducing evidence to show that in the circumstances he was not negligent. Nevertheless, the court held that the burden remains throughout with the claimant. This though does not appear to be the standard view.

In more general fashion Lord Justice Hobhouse in *Ratcliffe v Plymouth & Torbay HA, Exeter & North Devon HA* [1998] Lloyd's Rep Med 162, CA stated that the doctrine:

JUDGMENT

'is not a principle of law; it does not relate to or raise any presumption. It is merely a guide to help to identify when a *prima facie* case is being made out.'

Whatever the precise mechanism is, it does at least give a claimant who alleges negligence the opportunity to demand some contrary proof from the defendant in circumstances where the collection of evidence would prove difficult if not impossible.

CASE EXAMPLE

Henderson v H E Jenkins & Sons [1970] AC 282

The claimant's husband was killed when the brakes of a lorry failed while it was on a steep hill. The defendants argued that this was to do with a latent defect which caused corrosion in the brake pipes. This defect could only be detected once the pipes were removed, which was a practice not recommended by the manufacturers. The court would not accept this as sufficient to rebut the claimant's argument that there was negligence involved. The court held that the defendants should have gone on to show that there was nothing else in the vehicle's history that could account for the corrosion of the brakes. The defendants were required to prove that they were not negligent, had failed to do so and so were held liable.

Because the maxim can be equally harsh on the defendant the maxim is very narrowly construed by the courts and it will only be accepted as an appropriate plea if the facts of the case fit specific criteria that have been laid down by the courts.

CASE EXAMPLE

Scott v London and St Katherine's Dock Co (1865) 3 H & C 596

Here the claimant was standing outside the defendant's warehouse when several large bags of sugar fell on him. There was little or no explanation for the incident and no evidence that could be introduced that would show that any particular person had been negligent. The trial judge initially found for the defendant since there was no proof of negligence. However, on appeal this was reversed and the criteria for dealing with such claims were established.

Erle CJ explained the application of the maxim.

JUDGMENT

'where the thing is shewn to be under the management of the defendant or his servants, and the accident is such that in the ordinary course of things could not happen if those who have the management use proper care, it affords reasonable evidence, in the absence of explanation by the defendants that the accident arose from want of care.'

4.6.3 The criteria for claiming *res ipsa loquitur*

The criteria arising from the judgment in the last case are quite clear and give a systematic means of applying the maxim and determining the circumstances in which it can be used.

There are then three specific criteria for successfully pleading *res ipsa loquitur*:

■ At all material times the thing causing the harm must have been in the control of the defendant.
■ The incident must be of a type that could only have been caused by negligence.
■ The cause of the incident is not known and there is no other obvious explanation for the incident.

The incident was in the control of the defendant

The basis of the plea is that there is no explanation available for proof of negligence but that the defendant caused the damage. Inevitably the defendant must be in control of the situation that has led to the damage, or there can be no liability.

What does actually fall within the defendant's control is a question of fact in each case for the court to decide.

CASE EXAMPLE

Gee v Metropolitan Railway Co (1873) LR 8 QB 161

A passenger leaned on a train door shortly after it left the station. The door opened and the passenger fell out and was injured. The defendants were responsible for ensuring that all doors were properly closed before the train left the station. There was no reasonable explanation for why the door opened. However, the defendants were in control at the material time and the court thus held that they were liable.

Actual control is a question of fact. As a result it is possible to show from the circumstances that it would be unfair to suggest that the defendant had actual control. In the absence of control then the defendant cannot be said to be the cause without proof.

CASE EXAMPLE

Easson v London and North Eastern Railway [1944] KB 421

Here a boy passenger fell through the door of a train when it was a long way from its last stop. There may well have been other reasons why the door was open or not secure. For instance it was possible that another passenger had opened the door. The court certainly felt that it was impossible to say that the doors were under the control of the railway company throughout the entire journey and as a result res ipsa could not apply.

It seems only fair that if the defendant is in control of the circumstances in which the damage occurred he should be called on to give some explanation of the incident.

The incident is of a type usually associated with negligence

It is also obviously of critical importance to show also that the incident causing the damage is of a type that would not normally occur if proper care were taken. If this is so then the incident can be seen as one of a type that would commonly be caused only by negligence. The absence of a reasonable explanation by the defendant means that it is reasonable to assume that the event occurred because of lack of care.

CASE EXAMPLE

Scott v London and St Katherine's Dock Co (1865) 3 H & C 596

Here the facts really do speak for themselves. Large bags of sugar are inanimate objects and it is unlikely that they could fall from a hoist without a lack of care being taken. They may well have been stacked carelessly and too close to the opening. It could be that a careless employee brushed against them causing them to fall. What is certain is that, if they had been stacked safely, they would not have fallen and injured the claimant.

Res ipsa is often pleaded in medical negligence cases because the claimant is entitled to an explanation of how the damage occurred if not by negligence.

CASE EXAMPLE

Glass v Cambridge Health Authority [1995] 6 Med LR 91

A man who was shown to have a normal healthy heart nevertheless went into cardiac arrest while under a general anaesthetic. The maxim was held to have been appropriately pleaded in the case although the Health Authority was able to introduce evidence to show why they had not been negligent.

In medical negligence cases the plea is common because of the difficulties of showing the precise negligence and the plea may often be used because the precise party responsible for the damage is unknown.

CASE EXAMPLE

Mahon v Osborne [1939] 2 KB 14

Here after an operation a patient later died. It was discovered that a swab was inside him. It was clear that the swab must have been left in the patient during an operation and that it could not have been there but for negligence, although the precise member of the medical staff who was actually responsible could not be identified. Scott LJ, however, felt that some positive evidence of neglect of duty in the operation was needed in such cases.

The maxim in such cases may be used when the claim is that a particular body is vicariously liable for the acts of the tortfeasor.

CASE EXAMPLE

Ward v Tesco Stores Ltd [1976] 1 WLR 810

A customer slipped on yoghurt that had been spilt onto the supermarket's floor. Tesco claimed that they had a procedure in place whereby the floors were cleaned regularly throughout the day and staff were instructed to stay with such spillages when they were found until they were cleaned. Nevertheless the customer was also able to show evidence of other spillages that were not immediately cleaned up. The court accepted that such occurrences could only result from negligence.

There is no other explanation for the incident causing damage

The third and final criterion for the plea to have effect is that it is impossible for the claimant to introduce evidence to give any explanation of the incident. If the circumstances of the incident are capable of explanation by the claimant then the usual burden applies and the claimant should show how the facts prove negligence.

A plea of *res ipsa loquitur* can only apply because there are no other means available to explain the true cause of the incident. It is thus fairer in the circumstances to ask the defendant to introduce some evidence to rebut the presumption that negligence has occurred.

CASE EXAMPLE

Barkway v South Wales Transport Co Ltd [1950] 1 All ER 392

Without apparent reason a bus mounted a pavement and this resulted in injury to the claimant. In fact it was discovered that a tyre had burst because of a defect in the wall of the tyre that could not have been discovered earlier. *Res ipsa* was shown to be inappropriate, however, when it was discovered that the bus company gave no instructions to drivers to report heavy blows suffered by the tyres. As a result the court held that it was possible for negligence to be shown and the defendants were liable.

Comment

We have already seen that there is debate among the judiciary as to the proper role of the maxim in relation to medical negligence cases.

It has been argued at different points that the maxim should always apply because the three criteria will generally be satisfied and because the claimant may otherwise face a very difficult time collecting the appropriate evidence.

The courts, nevertheless, have been reluctant to accept such widespread application of the maxim. The Pearson Report in 1978 also rejected general application because of the fear of an escalating number of claims resulting and the consequent rise in insurance premiums for medical staff.

4.6.4 Strict liability in negligence

Res ipsa was formerly very often used in cases involving foreign bodies in foodstuffs. Clearly while it may be difficult to show how the material got there it is nevertheless something that should not happen if proper care is taken.

EC law is fairly explicit on such issues and has traditionally imposed stricter standards than English law. English law is now very much in line with European law since the passing of the Consumer Protection Act 1987, enacted to comply with EC directives. The Product Safety Directive has also subsequently been implemented in the form of regulations.

The Consumer Protection Act allows that any person within the chain of distribution of a product is strictly liable if a consumer suffers harm as the result of defects

At all material times was the thing causing harm to the claimant in the control of the defendant?	NO →	*Res ipsa loquitur* will not apply • The claimant would have to prove the defendant was responsible • It is unlikely that the claimant could do so successfully

YES

Was the incident one that could only have occurred through negligence?	NO →	*Res ipsa loquitur* will not apply • A claim in negligence would not be possible

YES

Was there any other explanation for the event causing damage to the claimant?	YES →	If the event was caused by the defendant's negligence and there is proof of negligence then that proof should be raised in the claim – a plea of *res ipsa loquitur* is not appropriate

NO

The defendant must prove that he was not negligent, and not responsible for the damage suffered by the claimant

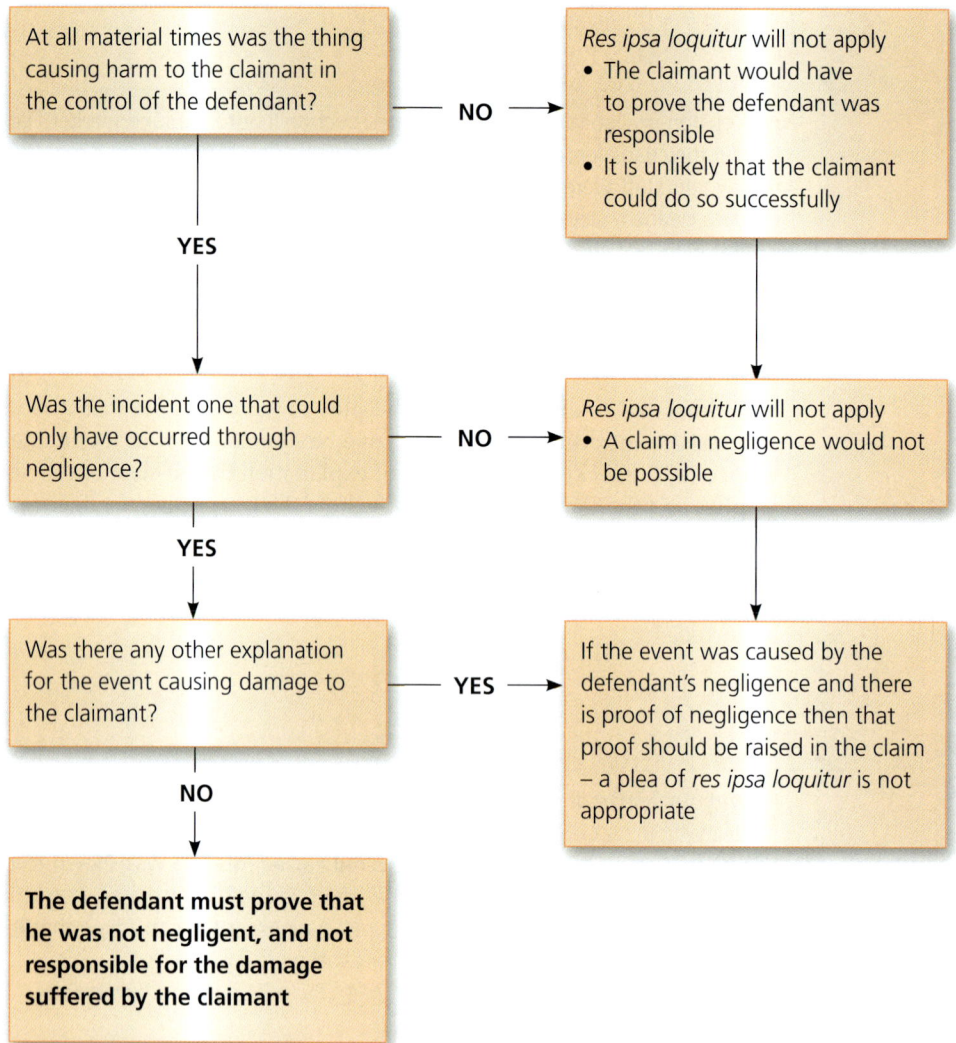

Figure 4.3 Diagram illustrating the requirements for making a plea of *res ipsa loquitur*

in the product. The customer has the option to sue without showing fault but merely proving the defect and the existence of the defendant in the chain of distribution (see later Chapter 12, section 12.1).

While fault is in a sense abolished in the Act causation is still an issue.

ACTIVITY

Self-assessment questions

1. *Res ipsa loquitur* means the thing speaks for itself, but what does this mean precisely in relation to the incident in question?
2. What three elements must always be present for a judge to accept that the doctrine applies in the case?
3. To what extent is it accurate to speak of a reversal of the burden of proof?
4. What sorts of things indicate that the loss or damage suffered could only have been the result of negligence?
5. Why has the doctrine regularly been pleaded in medical negligence cases?
6. What is the effect of the doctrine in consumer protection law?

SAMPLE ESSAY QUESTION

'The two main aims of tort are to compensate the victims of wrongdoing and to deter wrongdoing.' Discuss whether the rules on causation and remoteness of damage achieve these aims.

Explain the basic rules on causation in fact and remoteness of damage

- The but for test generally applies – but for the defendant's negligence the damage would not have occurred
- Courts will not compensate for loss that is too remote a consequence of the defendant's breach – so will only compensate foreseeable loss

---

Discuss the problems associated with multiple causes and how the courts have overcome them

- With consecutive causes the first defendant is liable unless the second defendant has increased the damage – fair as claimant should only be compensated once but may not deter effectively
- With concurrent multiple causes – can be harsh and not deter if 'but for' test is applied where there are many possible causes
- But if there is a single cause but more than one defendant courts may accept that that cause materially increased the risk of harm or was a material contribution to the harm – ensures the claimant is compensated and is a deterrent but may be unfair on defendant
- Problem, too, of overcompensating or undercompensating victim

---

Discuss the problems associated with loss of a chance

- Defendant not liable on a balance of probabilities
- So defendant goes uncompensated
- And no deterrent to a defendant who has breached his duty

Discuss the problems associated with *novus actus interveniens*

- Three types – act of claimant, of nature, of a third party
- Breaks chain of causation – so usually no compensation and not much deterrent

---

Explain the problems associated with remoteness of damage

- Legal test based on foreseeable harm
- There has been inconsistent application
- If court tests against precise circumstances and damage then little chance of compensation or deterrent
- But if takes more liberal view then provides compensation and deterrent
- Different approach – direct consequences rule – when thin skull rule applies

Res ipsa loquitur	Case
Res ipsa loquitur means the thing speaks for itself – it is a means of establishing negligence where proof is hard to come by.	
The doctrine in effect means that the defendant has to prove that he was not negligent if the plea is raised successfully.	
There are three essential aspects to the plea:	
• At all material times events leading to the damage were under the control of the defendant.	*Gee v Metropolitan Railway* (1873)
• The incident is of a type usually associated with negligence.	*Scott v London and St Katherine's Dock* (1865)
• There is no other explanation.	*Barkway v South Wales Transport* (1950)
It can be particularly appropriate to medical negligence claims.	

SUMMARY

■ There are two types of causation: causation in fact and causation in law (remoteness of damage)

■ Causation in fact is usually measured by the 'but for' test – damage would not have occurred 'but for' the defendant's breach of duty

■ But different approaches are taken when there are multiple causes: possibly no liability where there is a pre-existing condition – if there are several different concurrent causes then 'but for' test applies – but if defendant materially increases the risk of harm or materially contributes then any defendant may be liable – but sometimes judges prefer to apportion damages

■ A *novus actus interveniens* by the claimant or an act of nature or an act of a third party breaks the chain of causation and the first defendant is not liable

■ Remoteness of damage, causation in law is a legal test – the defendant is only liable for foreseeable damage

■ Judges sometimes take a broad application where there is personal injury so it is the general circumstances and general type of damage rather than precise circumstances and specific damage that must be foreseen

■ Often judges take a narrow application where there is property damage

Further reading

Hill, T, 'A lost chance for compensation in the tort of negligence by the House of Lords' (1991) 54 MLR 511.

Morgan, A, 'Inference, principle and the proof of causation' [2002] NLJ 1060.

Owen, R F, 'Causation and apportionment' [2000] NLJ 1116.

5

Negligence: defences

AIMS AND OBJECTIVES

After reading this chapter you should be able to:

▪ Understand the criteria for establishing the defences of *Volenti non fit injuria* (voluntary assumption of risk) and contributory negligence
▪ Understand that *Volenti* is a complete defence removing liability while contributory negligence is only a partial defence with the effect of reducing damages
▪ Be able to critically analyse the two defences
▪ Be able to apply the two defences to factual situations

5.1 Introduction

Causation also needs to be considered when determining whether or not the claimant has either accepted a risk of harm and voluntarily taken it, or indeed has otherwise contributed to his own damage by taking insufficient care for his own safety. In this way a claimant who takes part in sporting activities, particularly in the case of a contact sport, may have voluntarily assumed the risk of injury by taking part and being aware of the nature of the sport. Similarly in the case of road traffic accidents there may be contributory negligence, for instance where the claimant has failed to wear a seat belt, or in the case of an accident involving a motorbike where the claimant failed to wear a crash helmet.

If on the other hand the claimant has contributed so much to the damage suffered as to be entirely responsible, then this will probably result in a successful plea of *novus actus interveniens*.

There are two specific defences that are particularly appropriate here, *volenti non fit injuria* (voluntary assumption of a risk) and contributory negligence. The distinction between volenti and contributory negligence is clearly important. *Volenti* is a complete defence and so defeats the claim, whereas contributory negligence is a partial defence only reducing the claimant's damages. Besides this, statutory provisions such as the Unfair Contract Terms Act 1977 s 2(3) suggest that *volenti* might succeed even without an agreement between the two parties.

However, it is not easy to succeed in a defence of *volenti* since use of contributory negligence and apportionment of responsibility is more fair than denying any redress to a claimant where a defendant has been in breach of a duty of care.

5.2 *Volenti non fit injuria*

Volenti non fit injuria is a complete defence, unlike contributory negligence which only reduces damages, and if it is successful then a claimant will recover no damages. The defence succeeds because there is a voluntary assumption of the risk of harm by the claimant and a simple translation would be that no injury is done to one who freely consents to the risk.

Distinction must be drawn between:

- an intentional infliction of harm – which is negatived by consent, for example where a patient signs a consent form in respect of an operation there is no battery, and
- a negligent infliction of harm – in which for the defendant to avoid liability for his otherwise negligent act the claimant must voluntarily accept the risk of injury.

It must be remembered of course that before the defence can be applied successfully it must be shown that the defendant did in fact commit a tort.

CASE EXAMPLE

Wooldridge v Sumner [1963] 2 QB 43

The claimant attended a horse show as a professional photographer. A rider who was riding too fast lost control of his horse which then injured the claimant. The Court of Appeal recognised that the rider owed spectators a duty of care. Nevertheless, they considered that he had been guilty of an error of judgement in his riding of the horse but not negligence. He had not breached his duty so *volenti* was not an issue.

Some judges take the view that the defence succeeds because there is an express or implied agreement between the defendant and the claimant. However, certain judges believe that the defence can still succeed where the claimant has come upon a danger that has already been created by the defendant.

To succeed, the defendant will in any case have to show three things:

- knowledge of the precise risk involved
- exercise of free choice by the claimant
- a voluntary acceptance of the risk.

Knowledge of the precise risk

The test of *volenti* is a subjective one, not an objective one. It will not help the defendant to argue that the claimant ought to have been aware of the risk. The defence only applies where the claimant does actually know of the risk and freely accepts it.

Nevertheless, where a defence of *volenti* may fail for just such a reason, the defendant may still be able to successfully claim contributory negligence and at least reduce the amount of damages that are payable.

It is not sufficient then merely that the claimant has knowledge of the existence of the risk. The defence is *volenti non fit injuria* and not *scienti non fit injuria*. The claimant must fully understand the precise nature of the actual risk and be prepared to run it.

CASE EXAMPLE

Stermer v Lawson (1977) 79 DLR (3d) 366

The claimant borrowed the defendant's motorbike but was not shown how to use it so he could not and did not appreciate the risks involved. The defendant's claim of *volenti* failed as a result. The court held that he was unaware of the precise risk and therefore was not personally responsible.

Exercise of free choice by the claimant

Similarly the risk must be freely taken for the defence to succeed. There will be no defence where the claimant had no choice but to accept the risk.

CASE EXAMPLE

Smith v Baker [1891] AC 325

The claimant drilled rock in a quarry bottom. He was injured when a crane moved rocks over his head and some fell on him. *Volenti* failed in the case because, as the court explained, the worker was given no proper warning of when the crane was in use and so was unaware of the danger. He was aware of the risk of stones falling but there was no voluntary assumption of risk in the circumstances.

Lord Halsbury LC explained why the defence could not apply.

JUDGMENT

'I think that a person who relies on the maxim must shew a consent to the particular thing done . . . in order to defeat a plaintiff's right by the maxim relied on . . . the jury ought to be able to affirm that he consented to the particular thing being done which would involve the risk, and consented to take the risk upon himself.'

If the claimant's behaviour is such that he need not have been in any danger but for his own actions then *volenti* is clearly a possibility.

CASE EXAMPLE

ICI Ltd v Shatwell [1965] AC 656

The claimant and his brother were working in the defendants' quarry. They disregarded the defendants' orders and also statutory regulations by testing detonators without taking appropriate precautions. The claimant was injured in an explosion and maintained that the defendants were vicariously liable on the basis of the claimant's brother, who instructed him not to follow the instructions, having been negligent and in breach of statutory duty. The court held against him. By ignoring his employers and listening to his brother's unauthorised comments he had assumed the risk of injury by exercising his own free choice.

A voluntary acceptance of the risk

For a defendant to successfully raise the defence, the claimant must have had a genuine free choice, freedom of will and no feeling of constraint.

As Scott LJ put it in *Bowater v Rowley Regis Corporation* [1944] KB 476

JUDGMENT

'A man cannot be said to be truly willing unless he is in a position to choose freely.'

CASE EXAMPLE

Smith v Baker [1891] AC 325

Here while the employers pleaded *volenti* it could not apply because there had been no warning of the moment of a recurring danger. Although the claimant knew of the risk, there was no evidence that he had voluntarily accepted the risk. Merely continuing to work in the circumstances was not voluntary acceptance of the risk.

However, if an employee is not in a predicament actually imposed upon him by the defendant, but instead by pursuing a dangerous method of work through personal choice he injures himself, then *volenti* may well apply and the defence might succeed.

CASE EXAMPLE

ICI v Shatwell [1965] AC 656

Here the court held that if the claimant had sued his brother, the action would have failed on the basis of *volenti* and, as a result, the defendants were not vicariously liable. The claimant had consented to the conduct that had caused his injury. He had voluntarily accepted the risk of harm and was responsible for his own injury.

The fact that the claimant has engaged in or attempted a rescue does not mean that he has voluntarily accepted the risk.

CASE EXAMPLE

Haynes v Harwood [1935] 1 KB 146

Here the claimant, a policeman, was injured when he attempted to stop a runaway horse. He was under a duty because of his employment to try to stop the horse and protect the public so he had not acted voluntarily. The court would not accept the defence.

However, if there is no actual danger then a claimant in such circumstances may indeed have voluntarily accepted the risk of harm.

CASE EXAMPLE

Cutler v United Dairies [1933] 2 KB 297

A horse bolted into an empty field. Nobody was in actual danger. The claimant tried to calm the horse but was injured. The court held that the claimant was indeed *volenti* and had exercised free choice. The defence succeeded.

In the case of sporting events as Barwick CJ identified in *Rootes v Shelton* [1968] ALR 33

JUDGMENT

'By engaging in a sport . . . the participants may be held to have accepted risks which are inherent in that sport . . . but this does not eliminate all duty of care of the one participant to the other.'

Lord Diplock has explained the position regarding spectators in *Wooldridge v Sumner* [1963] 2 QB 43

JUDGMENT

'A person attending a game or competition takes the risk of any damage caused to him by any act of a participant done in the course of and for the purposes of the game or competition notwithstanding that such an act may involve an error of judgement or a lapse of skill, unless the participant's conduct is such as to evince a reckless disregard for the spectator's safety.'

Nevertheless, a spectator does not consent to the negligence of a competitor merely by being present at the sporting event.

Agreement

In some cases judges have indicated that for the defence to succeed there must be either an express or implied agreement that the claimant would waive any claim against the defendant. This may for instance be as a result of an exclusion clause. Even then it would be subject to s 2(1) of the Unfair Contract Terms Act 1977.

The courts are more reluctant to imply that there is an agreement that a claimant will accept the risk of injury.

CASE EXAMPLE

Dann v Hamilton [1939] 1 KB 509

Hamilton drove the claimant and her mother to London to see the Coronation decorations. Hamilton drank alcohol during the evening. They met a man who was given a lift but who left the car shortly before it was involved in an accident when the claimant was injured and Hamilton was killed. The man had said to the claimant and her mother 'You two have more pluck than I have'. The claimant said, 'You should be like me. If anything is going to happen, it will happen'. The court held that *volenti* could not apply. The claimant had not consented to the defendant's negligence.

Asquith J indicated that the defence was only applicable when the claimant came to a situation where the defendant's negligence had already created the danger. He also stated

JUDGMENT

'There may be cases in which the drunkenness of the driver at the material time is so extreme and so glaring that to accept a lift from him is like engaging in an intrinsically and obviously dangerous occupation, intermeddling with an unexploded bomb or walking on the edge of an unfenced cliff.'

In *Nettleship v Weston* [1971] 2 QB 691 Lord Denning commented:

JUDGMENT

'Nothing will suffice short of an agreement to waive any claim for negligence. The claimant must agree, expressly or impliedly, to waive any claim for any injury that may befall him due to the lack of reasonable care by the defendant.'

Where a defendant tries to rely on an exclusion clause if the damage is death or personal injury the defence of *volenti* may fail because of s 2(1) Unfair Contract Terms Act 1977 which states:

SECTION

's 2(1) A person cannot by reference to any contract term or to a notice given to persons generally or to particular persons exclude or restrict his liability for death or personal injury resulting from negligence.'

In the case of other damage s 2(2) may apply. This states that:

SECTION

's 2(2) In the case of other loss or damage, a person cannot so exclude or restrict his liability for negligence except in so far as the term or notice satisfies the requirement of reasonableness.'

In cases where there is no agreement and the claimant comes upon an already existing risk then s 2(3) may apply:

SECTION

's 2(3) Where a contract term or notice purports to exclude or restrict liability for negligence a person's agreement to or awareness of it is not of itself to be taken as indicating his voluntary acceptance of any risk.'

5.3 Contributory negligence

In cases where a claimant suffers damage partly though his own negligence as well as through the negligence of the defendant then contributory negligence may be used to reduce damages by the extent to which the claimant was responsible for his own loss or injury.

Contributory negligence was originally a complete defence so that no damages at all were payable if the defence succeeded.

CASE EXAMPLE

Butterfield v Forester (1809) 11 East 60

Here the defendant obstructed a road by placing a pole across it. The claimant was injured when his horse collided with the pole while he was violently riding the horse. It was held that the claimant had contributed to his own harm. Taking proper care would have avoided the accident and he was unable to claim any damages.

In the nineteenth century this was particularly harsh on people sustaining injuries while at work. Such a rule was hardly fair where a claimant's negligence was only slight in comparison to the defendant's negligence.

Where, however, a defendant had the last opportunity to avoid the damage to the claimant then the claimant, despite his own contributory negligence, could recover from the defendant. This was known as the rule of last opportunity.

CASE EXAMPLE

Davies v Mann (1842) 10 M & W 546

The claimant fettered a donkey's feet and the donkey was then negligently turned loose on the highway. The defendant drove his wagon and horses too fast and the donkey was killed in the ensuing collision. It was held that the defendant was liable. He could have avoided the accident if he had driven more slowly.

The last opportunity rule was extended to cases of 'constructive' last opportunity. If the defendant would have had the last opportunity but for his own negligence, he would then be in the same position as if they had actually had the last opportunity. The claimant again recovered in full. So there were arguments as to who, in fact, had had the last opportunity to avoid the damage. A claimant either recovered damages or could recover nothing at all. Apportionment of damages was not available at common law.

The Law Reform (Contributory Negligence) Act 1945 changed the nature of the rule so that damages could be altered according to the extent to which the claimant had contributed to his own harm. Damages will then be reduced proportionately accordingly.

CASE EXAMPLE

Sayers v Harlow Urban District Council [1958] 1 WLR 623

A lady became trapped in a public lavatory when through negligent maintenance the door lock became jammed. She then stood on the toilet roll holder in an effort to climb out of the cubicle. She had to catch a bus so it was reasonable for her to try to get out in the circumstances, and so her act did not break the chain of causation. The council was liable but the damages were reduced by 25 per cent because of the careless manner in which she tried to get out.

The Act states at s 1(1) that:

SECTION

's 1(1) Where any person suffers damage as the result partly of his own fault and partly of the fault of any other person or persons, a claim in respect of that damage shall not be defeated by reason of the fault of the person suffering the damage, but the damage recoverable in respect thereof shall be reduced to such extent as the court thinks just and equitable having regard to the claimant's share in the responsibility for the damage.'

The Act only applies where the damage was caused partly by the fault of the defendant and partly by the fault of the claimant.

Section 4 – 'Damage' includes 'loss of life and personal injury' and also, it seems, property damage.

Also by s 4 –

SECTION

's 4 "Fault" means "negligence, breach of statutory duty or other act or omission which gives rise to liability in tort or would, apart from this Act, give rise to the defence of contributory negligence".'

The defence has become a common aspect of claims for injuries or damage sustained in road traffic accidents, so that damages can be reduced where a motor cycle passenger fails to take the precaution of wearing a crash helmet.

CASE EXAMPLE

O'Connell v Jackson [1972] 1 QB 270

Here it was acknowledged that the passenger received much greater injuries because of not wearing a crash helmet. So damages were reduced accordingly.

The defence is also commonly applied to passengers of motor cars who fail to wear seat belts as required by law.

CASE EXAMPLE

Froom v Butcher [1976] QB 286

Again the passenger here suffered greater injuries than would have been the case if he had been wearing a seat belt. The court reduced the damages as a result of this.

As Lord Denning explained in the Court of Appeal:

JUDGMENT

'Contributory negligence is a man's carelessness in looking after his own safety. He is guilty of contributory negligence if he ought reasonably to have foreseen that, if he did not act as a reasonable prudent man, he might hurt himself.'

A successful claim of contributory negligence depends on the defendant showing that the claimant has been negligent himself and is therefore partly to blame. This will mean that use of the defence, just as in negligence, depends on showing that the behaviour of the claimant meant that harm was foreseeable.

CASE EXAMPLE

Jones v Livox Quarries Ltd [1952] 2 QB 608

The claimant was employed in a quarry and, in defiance of his employer's express instructions, rode on the rear tow bar of a 'traxcavator'. The driver was unaware of the claimant and when another vehicle collided with the traxcavator the claimant was injured. The court reduced his damages by 5 per cent.

Lord Denning stated that:

JUDGMENT

'A person is guilty of contributory negligence if he ought reasonably to have foreseen that, if he did not act as a reasonable, prudent man, he might be hurt himself; and in his reckonings he must take into account the possibility of others being careless.'

So for a successful claim a defendant must prove:

- fault on the part of the claimant (that he failed to take reasonable care for his own safety), and
- that negligence by the claimant (ie a failure to take reasonable care) was a cause of the damage suffered.

Fault on the part of the claimant

A claimant is under a duty to take care for himself. The appropriate standard of care is the same as that generally applied in negligence and is basically objective.

A failure, by the claimant, to take care for his own safety may be a cause of the damage. For example, where the claimant is injured in an accident but both the claimant and defendant are equally to blame.

Alternatively a claimant may be injured in an accident where he has placed himself in a dangerous position and therefore at risk of injury.

CASE EXAMPLE

Davies v Swan Motor Co (Swansea) Ltd [1949] 2 KB 291

The claimant's husband had ridden on the step of a dustcart and was well aware of the dangers involved in doing so. One of the defendant's buses overtook the dustcart and the husband was killed in a collision. Both drivers were held to be negligent by the court but there was contributory negligence by the husband because of the dangerous manner in which he had ridden on the dustcart.

This inevitably applies even though the defendant has been negligent because the claimant has increased the risk of injury or suffered a worse injury as a result.

CASE EXAMPLE

Jones v Livox Quarries Ltd [1952] 2 QB 608

A vehicle was driven negligently into the back of a traxcavator. The claimant was riding on the traxcavator's tow bar. The claimant was injured but he had exposed himself to the risk of injury from the traxcavator being run into from behind. The court reduced his damages because of his contributory negligence.

A claimant might also place himself in a position that is not dangerous but which involves circumstances making it more likely that he will suffer harm. An example is where a claimant knows that a driver is drunk but nevertheless accepts a lift. *Volenti* will not apply but there will be contributory negligence as in *Owens v Brimmell* [1977] 2 WLR 943.

Also a claimant might place himself in a position which is not dangerous in itself but then fails to take precautions to avoid danger and in doing so increases the amount of harm suffered.

CASE EXAMPLE

Froom v Butcher [1976] QB 286

A car accident was caused by the defendant's negligence but the claimant was not wearing a seat belt as a result of which he suffered worse injuries. The court applied an objective standard of care. A prudent person would have worn a seat belt, so damages were reduced by 20 per cent.

Contributory negligence can also be applied to children even though we would expect a child to be less careful than an adult. However, it would be very difficult to show that a very young child was guilty of contributory negligence.

CASE EXAMPLE

Gough v Thorne [1966] 1 WLR 1387

A lorry driver signalled to the claimant, who was 13 years old, to cross a road. She did so but did not stop to see if the road was clear. A car, being driven negligently, injured the claimant, who was held not to be guilty of contributory negligence. The outcome would have been different if she had been an adult (see: the words of Lord Denning).

In the case of people at work there is legislation for their general protection and it appears that the courts consider that the prevention or reduction of an employee's damages due to contributory negligence should not undermine such protection.

The courts are reluctant in any case to find contributory negligence where an employee pursues an action for breach of statutory duty and possibly where there is an action for negligence.

In assessing contributory negligence the court will take into account the influence, upon an employee, of long hours and fatigue, repetition leading to a slackening of attention, noise and pre- occupation in a task sometimes at the expense of personal safety.

Nevertheless it is possible to succeed in claiming contributory negligence against employees.

CASE EXAMPLE

Jayes v IMI (Kynoch) Ltd [1985] ICR 155

The claimant, who was an experienced workman, lost the tip of a finger when his hand was pulled into a machine while he was cleaning it after removing the safety guard. He accepted that what he had done was very foolish and, because of the claimant's failure to take care of his own safety, the court held that he was 100 per cent contributorily negligent.

Where a rescuer is negligent in carrying out a rescue, then damages may also be reduced on the basis of contributory negligence.

CASE EXAMPLE

Harrison v British Railways Board [1981] 3 All ER 679

The defendant tried to board a moving train. The claimant guard saw the defendant but gave an incorrect signal to the train driver, to accelerate rather than to stop. The claimant guard then tried to pull the defendant onto the train but both fell and the claimant was injured. The court held that where someone places himself in danger and it is foreseeable that someone else will attempt a rescue then the rescued person owes a duty of care to the rescuer. As a result of the wrong signal the claimant was contributorily negligent and the court reduced his damages by 20 per cent. However, the court did point out that it would be rare for contributory negligence to be used against a rescuer.

Sometimes the defendant's negligence causes a claimant to be in imminent danger. If the claimant acts to avoid a reasonably perceived greater danger but makes a wrong decision, then the court may well have sympathy.

CASE EXAMPLE

Jones v Boyce (1816) 1 Stark 492

The claimant thought that the defendant's coach was going to crash and so he jumped out of it and in doing so broke his leg. As the coach did not crash he would have suffered no harm if he had remained where he was. However, the court accepted that he acted as a prudent and reasonable person would in the circumstances and so there was no contributory negligence.

Negligence by the claimant contributing to the damage

A claimant's contributory negligence must be a legal and factual cause of the harm to the claimant although it does not have to be a cause of the accident itself. An example of this is not wearing a seatbelt which may well cause more damage but not have been the cause of the accident itself, as in *Froom v Butcher* [1976] QB 286.

Factual causation involves the 'but for' test – would the alleged consequence have occurred but for the negligent cause?

CASE EXAMPLE

Jones v Livox Quarries Ltd [1952] 2 QB 608

Here the claimant riding on the towbar was one of the causes of his injury. Factual causation was established and the damage was not too remote. The court rejected an argument that the claimant's negligence had not caused damage to himself because the only foreseeable injury was by falling off the traxcavator, as opposed to being struck from behind.

It should also be remembered that proving a claimant has contributed to his harm is not the same as proving fault but is to do with his relative blameworthiness.

CASE EXAMPLE

Badger v Ministry of Defence [2005] EWHC 2941 (QB); [2005] All ER (D) 248

The claimant died of lung cancer at age 63. The defendant admitted that it had breached a statutory duty in exposing the claimant to asbestos dust but argued that damages should be reduced because if the claimant had not smoked cigarettes he would also have been unlikely to die of lung cancer at such a young age. The facts were complex since the claimant died of lung cancer, attributable to both exposure to asbestos and to smoking, but also had asbestosis, attributable to the exposure and also had heart disease and emphysema, attributable in part at least to his smoking. The claimant should have been aware by 1971 when the first health warnings appeared on cigarette packets of the risk of smoking to his health. He was also warned by doctors in 1968, 1991, 1992, and 1995 and advised to give up smoking. The court was satisfied that the claimant contributed to his harm and reduced damages by 20 per cent.

Apportioning damages

In deciding what apportionment is 'just and equitable' the courts consider the extent to which the claimant's and defendant's respective negligence caused the damage to the claimant and will also determine where blame lies.

On causation the courts will generally adopt a commonsense approach in order to reach an apportionment.

CASE EXAMPLE

Stapley v Gypsum Mines Ltd [1953] AC 663

Two miners disobeyed instructions and continued to work when they should have dealt with an unsafe part of the roof which was a danger to them. One of the miners died when the roof collapsed and his widow sued the defendants for negligence. The House of Lords took a commonsense approach and held that both miners were causes of the harm. The claimant's action succeeded but damages were reduced by 80 per cent because of the contributory negligence.

In the case of blameworthiness the test is objective and is measured against the standard of behaviour of the reasonable man.

In claims where there are multiple defendants and the claimant is not at fault then the loss may be recovered from any of the defendants. That defendant will then seek a contribution from the others under the Civil Liability (Contribution) Act 1978. However, if there was contributory negligence by the claimant then the court must consider:

- the amount by which the claimant's damages should be reduced as a result of his own contributory negligence; but also
- the amount of contribution recoverable from each defendant.

CASE EXAMPLE

Fitzgerald v Lane and Patel [1988] 2 All ER 961

The claimant stepped out onto a busy road and was then struck by the first defendant's vehicle. This impact pushed the claimant into the path of the second defendant's vehicle. Both defendants were found to be negligent but there was also contributory negligence by the claimant. Initially all three parties were held equally to blame and damages were reduced by one third. However, the House of Lords indicated that this was the wrong approach. They suggested that there was a direct comparison between the negligence of both defendants and the negligence in the claimant's conduct. As a result damages were reduced by 50 per cent because the claimant's blame was equal to that of the defendants.

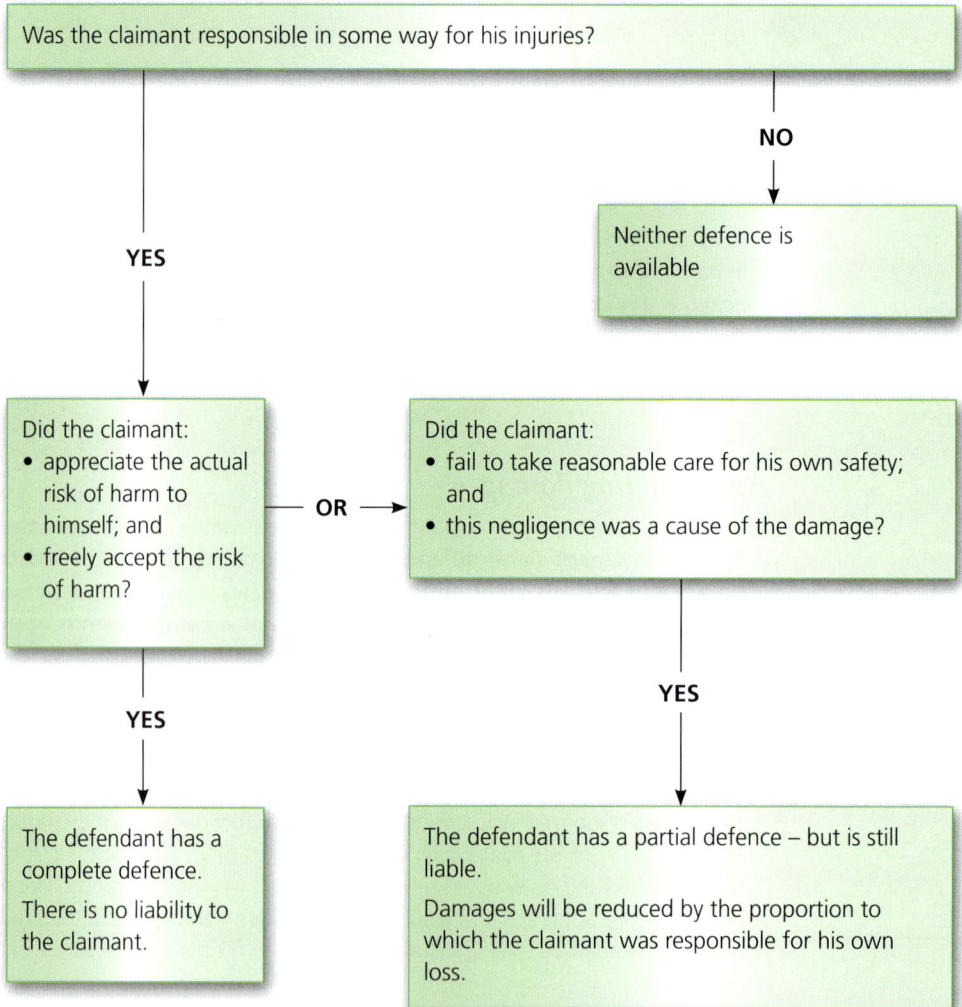

Figure 5.1 The availability of defences of *volenti non fit injuria* and contributory negligence and contrasting their effects

ACTIVITY

Self-assessment questions

1. What would a defendant have to prove about a claimant for a defence of *volenti* to succeed?
2. Why was the case of *ICI v Shatwell* decided how it was?
3. Is the test for *volenti* to succeed objective or subjective?

4. When will a claimant injured during a sporting event be deemed to have consented to the risk of injury?
5. What are the basic differences between the defences of *volenti* and contributory negligence?
6. What is the effect of a successful plea of contributory negligence?
7. What is the claimant's standard of care in relation to contributory negligence?
8. Why exactly did the claimant fail in *Livox*?
9. Why is the defence of contributory negligence so commonplace in road traffic accidents?

ACTIVITY

Quick quiz

In the following situations say which defence a defendant might seek to apply, if at all, and why, and comment on the chances of using the defence successfully.

1. Morris was injured when he went for a flight in a light aeroplane with Peter, who Morris knows does not have a pilot's licence.
2. Lee was injured when he was elbowed in the face by Danny during a professional football match.
3. Manjit lost a hand while trying to free a blockage in the machine that he works on. His foreman had told him not to turn the machine off at any time.
4. Marion fell off a horse and was badly injured during a show jumping contest when the horse pulled up at a large fence.
5. Derek was injured when he was a passenger in his friend Ali's open top sports car. Derek was thrown out of the car when Ali, who Derek knew was almost too drunk to stand up, skidded and collided with a lamp post.

SAMPLE ESSAY QUESTION

'There is very little difference in the defences of *volenti non fit injuria* and contributory negligence when applied to a claim in negligence so that at least one of then is superfluous and unnecessary.' Discuss the accuracy of the above statement.

Explain the defence of *volenti non fit injuria*

It is a complete defence when
- defendant is negligent and causes damage to the claimant
- but the claimant has voluntarily exposed himself to the risk of harm

---

Explain the essential elements of the defence
- The claimant exercised free choice in accepting the risk
- The claimant understood the exact nature of the risk
- The claimant voluntarily accepted the risk

Explain the application of the defence to sport and medical treatment

- In sport the injury must have occurred within the rules of the game
- In medicine the patient must consent to all treatment
- And must be made aware of risk in broad terms
- Although emergency treatment may be an exception

Explain the defence of contributory negligence

- A partial defence under Law Reform (Contributory Negligence) Act 1945
- Damages are reduced to the extent to which the claimant is responsible for his own harm

Explain the essential elements of the defence

- The claimant failed to take reasonable care for his own safety
- This failure to take care was a cause of the harm suffered

Compare the effects of the defences

- *Volenti* is a complete defence, contributory negligence is only partial
- *Volenti* removes liability contributory negligence reduces damages
- Before the 1945 Act the effects were the same
- *Volenti* is the free acceptance of a known risk, whereas contributory negligence merely means that the claimant failed to take care of his own safety and partially caused the harm
- Similar approach when claimant is a child
- But existence of two defences has caused confusion, eg sometimes both defences are referred to as consent to harm
- Harder to succeed under *volenti* than under contributory negligence
- In contributory negligence there is an apportioning of blame, whereas with *volenti* no blame is attached to the defendant
- There are obvious difficulties in accurately apportioning blame, so *volenti* simpler
- *Volenti* not available under the Road Traffic Act because of the availability of compulsory third party insurance, whereas contributory negligence is commonly used in road traffic accidents

KEY FACTS

Volenti non fit injuria (voluntary acceptance of risk)	Case
A defendant will not be liable where there is a voluntary assumption of risk.	
So for the defence to succeed there must be:	
• knowledge of the precise risk involved	*Stermer v Lawson* (1977)
• exercise of free choice by claimant	*Smith v Baker* (1891)
• voluntary acceptance of the risk.	*ICI v Shatwell* (1965)
Engaging in a rescue need not mean that there is voluntary conduct.	*Haynes v Harwood* (1935)
A lack of actual danger may lead to a successful claim.	*Cutler v United Dairies* (1933)
Contributory negligence	**Case**
Originally a complete defence removing all liability.	*Butterfield v Forester* (1809)
Now the Law Reform (Contributory Negligence) Act 1945 means that damages may be reduced where there is contributory negligence.	
The defendant must show that:	
• the claimant has failed to take reasonable care of himself; and	*Sayers v Harlow UDC* (1958)
• this caused the injury or damage.	*Jones v Livox Quarries* (1952)
The defence is common in motoring accidents where claimants fail to wear seat belts.	*Froom v Butcher* (1976)
Or where motor cycle passengers fail to wear crash helmets.	*O'Connell v Jackson* (1972)
Even 100% reduction is possible in the case of breaches of statutory duties.	*Jayes v IMI (Kynoch) Ltd* (1985)

119

NEGLIGENCE: DEFENCES

SUMMARY

- Both are defences to a claim in negligence
- *Volenti* is a complete defence when the defendant is negligent and causes damage to the claimant but the claimant has voluntarily exposed himself to the risk of harm
- The claimant must have understood the exact nature of the risk and voluntarily accepted the risk
- The defence is particularly appropriate in the case of sport and medical treatment
- Contributory negligence is a partial defence under Law Reform (Contributory Negligence) Act 1945 where damages are reduced to the extent to which the claimant is responsible for his own harm
- The claimant must have failed to take reasonable care for his own safety and his failure to take care was a cause of the harm suffered

Further reading

Harvey, B and Marston, J, 'Intoxication and claimants in negligence' [1999] NLJ 1004.
Murray, J, Street on Torts (11th edn, Butterworths, 2003), Chapter 15.

6

Negligence and novel duty situations

AIMS AND OBJECTIVES

After reading this chapter you should be able to:

- Understand the criteria for establishing the existence of a duty of care in relation to nervous shock (psychiatric damage)
- Understand the restrictions on the scope of the duty
- Understand the criteria for imposing pure economic loss
- Understand the reasons for the reluctance for imposing liability for pure economic loss
- Understand the criteria for imposing liability for economic loss caused by a negligent misstatement
- Understand the limited circumstances in which the law is prepared to impose liability for a failure to act
- Be able to critically analyse each of these novel duty situations
- Be able to apply the law on each duty to factual situations and reach conclusions as to liability

We have already seen how the tort of negligence is based on the existence firstly of a duty of care owed by the defendant to the claimant. The law has developed over time to include many instances where a duty of care exists.

There are numerous straightforward relationships where we might naturally expect a duty of care to exist. These would include such relationships as those between fellow motorists; between doctor and patient; between employer and employee; between manufacturers of products and their consumers; and, of course, there are many others. We have already seen examples in the case law of all of these.

There are also certain situations that are less obvious that have had to be considered by the courts where the duty arises more from specific circumstances than because of the relationship between the parties. They have proved to be more controversial but in some of them the courts have held that a duty of care does in fact exist. They include the following four major examples.

6.1 Nervous shock (psychiatric injury)

6.1.1 The historical background

This is another area of negligence that has been the subject of uncertain development. The extent to which liability has been imposed has expanded or contracted according to:

- The state of medical knowledge, ie psychiatric medicine and the recognition of psychiatric disorders has developed dramatically over the past 100 years; the great concern expressed in recent years over soldiers who were executed in the First World War is an interesting example of that.

- Policy considerations on the part of judges, particularly the 'floodgates' argument, that to impose liability in a particular situation may lead to a rush of claims and so should be avoided whatever the justice of the case; this has had the effect of operating particularly harshly on secondary victims.

Actions failed in the last century for three specific reasons:

- Because of the state of medical knowledge, psychiatric illness or injury was not properly recognised so there could be no duty if the type of damage concerned was not recognised.
- Another problem of course was the fear that a person making such a claim could actually be faking the symptoms.
- Finally there was the 'floodgates' argument, that once one claim was accepted it would lead to a multitude of claims.

CASE EXAMPLE

Victoria Railway Commissioners v Coultas (1888) 13 App Cas 222

Nervous shock resulting from involvement in a train crash did not give rise to liability, not least because of the 'floodgates' argument.

Even from the start there were two aspects to determining whether liability should be imposed:

- Firstly the injury alleged must conform to judicial attitudes of what constitutes nervous shock, a recognised psychiatric disorder.
- Secondly the person claiming to have suffered nervous shock must fall into a category accepted by the courts as being entitled to claim.

6.1.2 Nervous shock, psychiatric injury and the type of recoverable damage

The claim must then involve an actual, recognised psychiatric condition capable of resulting from the shock of the incident and recognised as having long-term effects.

CASE EXAMPLE

Reilly v Merseyside Regional Health Authority (1994) 23 BMLR 26

The court would not impose liability when a couple became trapped in a lift as the result of negligence and suffered insomnia and claustrophobia after they were rescued. These could not be classed as recognised psychiatric illnesses.

Psychiatry is now well advanced and in modern times conditions such as Post Traumatic Stress Disorder, Depression and Acute Anxiety Syndrome would be recognised. However, the courts would be reluctant to allow a claim purely for a temporary upset such as grief or distress or fright because it is accepted that these are common problems that periodically we all suffer from.

CASE EXAMPLE

Tredget v Bexley Health Authority [1994] 5 Med LR 178

The parents of a child born with serious injuries following medical negligence and then dying two days later successfully claimed for nervous shock. The result of the case is perhaps surprising but the court held that they did indeed suffer from psychiatric injuries despite the defendants' argument that their condition was no more than profound grief.

The courts in recent times have been prepared to accept a claim that is partly caused by grief and partly by the severe shock of the event.

CASE EXAMPLE

Vernon v Bosely (No. 1) [1997] 1 All ER 577

Here a father had witnessed his children being drowned in a car negligently driven by their nanny. His claim was successful and he recovered damages for nervous shock that was held to be partly the result of pathological grief and bereavement, but partly also the consequence of the trauma of witnessing the events.

6.1.3 The development of a test of liability

Originally claims were first allowed purely on the basis of foreseeability of a real and immediate fear of personal danger (the so-called 'Kennedy' test) so that the class of possible claimants was at first very limited.

CASE EXAMPLE

Dulieu v White & Sons [1901] 2 KB 669

The court accepted a claim when a woman suffered nervous shock after a horse and van that had been negligently driven burst through the window of a pub where she was washing glasses. She was able to recover because she had been put in fear for her own safety.

This limitation was later extended to include a claim for nervous shock suffered as the result of witnessing traumatic events involving close family members and therefore fearing for their safety.

CASE EXAMPLE

Hambrook v Stokes Bros [1925] 1 KB 141

A woman recovered damages for nervous shock when she saw a runaway lorry going downhill towards where she had left her three children, and then heard that there had indeed been an accident involving a child. The court disapproved the 'Kennedy' test and considered that it would be unfair not to compensate a mother who had feared for the safety of her children when she could have claimed if she only feared for her own safety.

This principle was even extended at one point to include shock suffered from witnessing events involving close but not related people and fearing for the safety of the victim.

CASE EXAMPLE

Dooley v Cammell Laird & Co [1951] 1 Lloyd's Rep 271

A crane driver claimed successfully for nervous shock when he saw a load fall and thought that workmates underneath would have been injured.

Indeed claims have even been allowed where harm to the person with whom the close tie exists would be impossible.

CASE EXAMPLE

Owens v Liverpool Corporation [1933] 1 KB 394

Here relatives of a deceased person recovered damages for nervous shock when the coffin fell out of the hearse that they were following.

One restriction on this development was to prevent a party from recovering who was not within the 'area of impact' of the event.

CASE EXAMPLE

King v Phillips [1953] 1 QB 429

A mother suffered nervous shock when from 70 yards away she saw a taxi reverse into her small child's bicycle and presumed him to be injured. Her claim failed because the court said she was too far away from the incident and outside of the range of foresight of the defendant.

An alternative measure to the area of impact test is whether the claimant falls within the 'area of shock'.

CASE EXAMPLE

Bourhill v Young [1943] AC 92

A pregnant Edinburgh fishwife claimed to have suffered nervous shock after getting off a tram, hearing the impact of a crash involving a motorcyclist, and later seeing blood on the road, after which she gave birth to a still-born child. The House of Lords held that, as a stranger to the motorcyclist, she was outside the area of foreseeable shock and her claim failed.

Successful claims for nervous shock have also been made even where the traumatic event is not an accident of some kind, as is usually the case in such claims. The same principle of reasonable foresight has therefore allowed for recovery in nervous shock claims even where the principal damage was to property rather than involving injury to or the safety of a person.

CASE EXAMPLE

Attia v British Gas [1987] 3 All ER 455

A woman who witnessed her house burning down when she arrived home was able to claim successfully for nervous shock. She was within the area of impact. The claim was said to be within the reasonable foresight of the contractors who negligently installed her central heating, causing the fire.

Traditionally it was well established in the case law that a rescuer was able to recover when suffering nervous shock.

CASE EXAMPLE

Chadwick v British Railways Board [1967] 1 WLR 912

When two trains crashed in a tunnel a man who lived nearby was asked because of his small size to crawl into the wreckage to give injections to trapped passengers. He was able to claim successfully for the anxiety neurosis he suffered as a result. This was largely explained on the basis that he was a primary victim, at risk himself in the circumstances.

Usually only professional rescuers will be able to claim or those present at the scene or the immediate aftermath.

CASE EXAMPLE

Hale v London Underground (1992) 11 BMLR 81

A fireman claimed successfully for Post Traumatic Stress Disorder that he suffered following the King's Cross fire.

However claims for shock suffered at the scene of disasters will not be successful in the case of those people considered only to be bystanders.

CASE EXAMPLE

McFarlane v E E Caledonia [1994] 2 All ER 1

A person who was helping to receive casualties from the *Piper Alpha* oilrig failed in his claim because he was classed as a mere bystander rather than a rescuer at the scene.

As we have seen the tests developed above involve the proximity of the claimant in time and space to the negligent incident or the closeness of the relationship with the party who is present. The widest point of expansion of liability came under the two-part test from *Anns* (see *Anns v Merton LBC* [1978] AC 728, at section 6.2.2 below), and allowed for recovery when the claimant was not present at the scene but was at the 'immediate aftermath'. Inevitably ' the meaning of immediate aftermath' was open to an interpretation based on policy.

CASE EXAMPLE

McLoughlin v O'Brian [1982] 2 All ER 298, HL

A woman was summoned to a hospital about an hour after her children and husband were involved in a car crash. One child was dead, two were badly injured, all were in shock and they had not yet been cleaned up. The House of Lords held that since the relationship with the victims was sufficiently close and the woman was present at the 'immediate aftermath' she could claim. Lord Wilberforce identified a three-part test for secondary victims that was approved later in *Alcock v Chief Constable of South Yorkshire* [1992] 4 All ER 907 (see section 6.1.4 below).

6.1.4 Restrictions on the scope of the duty

In the very important and controversial case following the Hillsborough disaster the House of Lords reviewed all aspects of the duty. The 'floodgates argument' was clearly an important feature of their deliberations and the House identified a fairly restrictive set of circumstances in which a claim for nervous shock might succeed.

CASE EXAMPLE

Alcock v Chief Constable of South Yorkshire [1992] 4 All ER 907

At the start of a football match police allowed a large crowd of supporters into a caged pen as the result of which 95 people in the stand suffered crush injuries and were killed. Since the match was being televised much of the disaster was shown on live television. A number of claims for nervous shock were made. These varied between those present or not present at the scene, those with close family ties to the dead and those who were merely friends. The House of Lords refused all of the claims and identified the factors important to consider in determining whether a party might recover. These were:

■ The proximity of the relationship with a party who was a victim of the incident – a successful claim would depend on the existence of a close tie of love and affection with the victim, or presence at the scene as a rescuer.

■ The proximity in time and space to the negligent incident – there could be a claim in respect of an incident or the immediate aftermath that was witnessed or experienced directly, there could be none where the incident was merely reported.

■ The cause of the nervous shock – the court accepted that this must be the result of witnessing or hearing the horrifying event or the immediate aftermath.

Lord Ackner identified these restrictions as follows.

JUDGMENT

'Because "shock" in its nature is capable of affecting such a wide range of persons, Lord Wilberforce in *McLoughlin v O'Brian* (1983) concluded that there was a real need for the law to place some limitation upon the extent of admissible claims and in this context he considered that there were three elements inherent in any claim.

1. The class of persons whose claims should be recognised.

Lord Wilberforce . . . contrasted the closest of family ties – parent and child and husband and wife – with that of the ordinary bystander. As regards [the former] the justifications for admitting such claims is the presumption, which I would accept as being rebuttable, that the love and affection normally associated with persons in those relationships is such that a defendant ought reasonably contemplate that they may be so closely and directly affected by his conduct as to suffer shock resulting in psychiatric illness. While as a generalisation more remote relatives and friends can reasonably be expected not to suffer illness from the shock, there can well be relatives and friends whose relationship is so close and intimate that their love and affection for the victim is comparable . . .

2. The proximity of the plaintiff to the accident.

It is accepted that the proximity to the accident must be close both in time and space. Direct and immediate sight or hearing of the accident is not required. It is reasonably foreseeable that injury by shock can be caused to a plaintiff, not only through the sight or hearing of the event, but of its immediate aftermath.

3. The means by which the shock is caused.

Lord Wilberforce concluded that the shock must come through sight or hearing of the event or its immediate aftermath.'

The case then identifies for the future the classes of claimants who will be successful and those who will not:

■ Primary victims – present at the scene of the shocking event and either injured or at risk of injury.

■ Secondary victims – present at the scene or its immediate aftermath and with a close tie of love and affection to the primary victim and having witnessed or heard the traumatic events with their own unaided senses.

■ It was also considered that secondary victims watching an event on live television that contravened broadcasting standards in relation to close up shots, etc might claim from the broadcasting authority.

Primary victims

Primary victims traditionally included those who were present at the scene and may suffer physical injury or their own safety was threatened. This was the situation in the landmark case of *Dulieu v White* [1901] 2 KB 669 where the woman could have been hurt by the horse coming through the glass window, and did in fact suffer a miscarriage as a result of the defendant's negligence.

The primary victim need not suffer any physical injury. It is sufficient that he is present at the event causing the shock and is at risk of harm. Neither will it matter that the primary victim is more susceptible to shock. This contrasts with secondary victims who are compared with 'a man of ordinary phlegm' and will not be compensated if they are more likely to suffer psychiatric illness.

CASE EXAMPLE

Page v Smith [1996] 3 All ER 272

Here Page was involved in a car accident caused by the defendant's negligence. Although he actually suffered no physical injury he suffered a recurrence of 'chronic fatigue syndrome' which he had suffered some years before. The House of Lords held that the defendant was liable for the psychiatric injury caused to the claimant.

Lord Lloyd identified the clear distinctions between primary victims and secondary victims.

JUDGMENT

'In claims by secondary victims the law insists on certain control mechanisms, in order as a matter of policy to limit the number of potential victims. Thus the defendant will not be liable unless psychiatric injury is foreseeable in a person of normal fortitude. These control mechanisms have no place where the plaintiff is the primary victim.'

One consequence of the application of the 'thin skull' rule in *Page v Smith* is that a psychiatric injury that follows a physical injury will rarely be considered unforeseeable and therefore too remote a consequence of the breach.

CASE EXAMPLE

Simmons v British Steel [2004] UKHL 20

Following an industrial injury caused by his employer's negligence the claimant suffered a worsening of his psoriasis, a stress related skin disease, and of a depressive illness, also leading to a personality change. This resulted from his anger at his employer's lack of apology and lack of support, rather than from the injury itself. However, the court imposed liability for both types of injury even though, as the court admitted, the psychological injuries were not reasonably foreseeable, because the claimant was a primary victim.

Secondary victims

These are people who are not primary victims of the incident but who are able to show a close enough tie of love and affection to a victim of the incident and who witnessed the incident or its 'immediate aftermath' at close hand. The probable limit of this is in *McLoughlin v O'Brian*. In *Alcock* the judges were reluctant to allow claims because of lack of both proximity in time and space to the incidents at Hillsborough and turned down claims from people who had identified bodies in the morgue some time after the events of the match.

Indeed the courts have engaged in some fairly fine distinctions as to what can acceptably be called 'the immediate aftermath' in later cases.

CASE EXAMPLE

Taylor v Somerset HA [1993] 4 Med LR 34

The claimant's husband suffered a fatal heart attack while at work. She was told only that he had been taken to hospital and when she arrived at the hospital she was told that he was dead. She was so shocked that she would not believe he was dead until she identified his body in the mortuary. She later suffered a psychiatric illness and claimed against the hospital. Even though she was at the hospital within an hour her action failed. The court held that the actual purpose for her visit was to identify the body so that it was not to do with the cause of his death.

Rescuers

These may well of course be primary victims and at risk in the circumstances of the incident causing the nervous shock. Traditionally in any case courts tended to treat professional rescuers as primary victims.

CASE EXAMPLE

Hale v London Underground (1992) 11 BMLR 81

A fireman who had been involved in the rescue of victims at the King's Cross fire suffered Post Traumatic Stress Disorder and recovered damages for nervous shock.

However, the question of who qualifies as a rescuer and will be able to recover damages has been subject to some uncertain development.

CASE EXAMPLE

Duncan v British Coal [1990] 1 All ER 540

There was surprisingly no liability where a miner saw a close colleague crushed in a roof fall that was the fault of the employers, and tried unsuccessfully to resuscitate him.

The House of Lords appear to now be taking a more restrictive attitude to claims by members of the emergency services for psychiatric injury suffered while dealing with the aftermath of a disaster in the course of their duties. A rescuer will only be able to claim where he is a genuine 'primary victim'.

CASE EXAMPLE

White v Chief Constable of South Yorkshire [1998] 1 All ER 1, HL

Police officers who claimed to have suffered Post Traumatic Stress Disorder following their part in the rescue operation at the Hillsborough disaster were denied a remedy by the House of Lords. The reasoning seems to be that they did not actually put themselves at risk, and that public policy prevented them from recovering when the relatives of the deceased in the disaster could not.

Figure 6.1 The means of determining liability for nervous shock

As a more recent alternative the courts have been willing to accept that a rescuer can also claim as a secondary victim. However, this will only be possible where the rescuer conforms to all of the requirements for secondary victims laid out in *Alcock*.

CASE EXAMPLE

Greatorex v Greatorex [2000] 4 All ER 769

Here a fire officer attended the scene of an accident caused by the negligence of his son. When he was required to attend to his son he claimed afterwards to suffer nervous shock. The court would not accept the claim because of the conflict that it would cause between family members, but had the son not been the cause of the accident a claim may have been possible in the circumstances.

So the fact that a person can prove that they are a rescuer is insufficient on its own to claim unless they can also prove that they are either a genuine primary victim or a genuine secondary victim.

CASE EXAMPLE

Stephen Monk v PC Harrington UK Ltd [2008] EWHC 1879 (QB)

The claimant helped two workers who were injured when a platform fell on them during the building of the new Wembley Stadium. The court denied him damages for psychiatric injury. While the court accepted that the man did act as a rescuer, it would not accept his argument that he was a primary victim because he felt that he had caused the accident as he was responsible for supervision of the platform that fell. The court felt that he was unlikely to have believed at any time that he was in danger.

Those unable to claim

The tests developed by the courts have meant that different classes of victims of nervous shock are unable to claim even though their injury and their right to a claim may seem legitimate. These can be classified in specific groups.

Bystanders

The law has always made a distinction between rescuers or people who are at risk in the incident and those who are merely bystanders and have no claim. This point goes back as far as *Bourhill v Young* [1943] AC 92.

CASE EXAMPLE

McFarlane v EE Caledonia Ltd [1994] 2 All ER 1

A person on shore receiving survivors from the *Piper Alpha* oilrig disaster was not classed as a rescuer and therefore had no valid claim despite suffering nervous shock.

Secondary victims with no close tie of love and affection to the victim

Alcock identified that in some relationships a close tie can be presumed. These might include parents and children and spouses. In all other cases a claimant would need to prove the tie and this led to claims failing in *Alcock* even where the primary victim was a close relation.

Workmates who witness accidents involving their colleagues will not be able to claim because any ties are not close enough to involve foreseeable harm.

CASE EXAMPLE

Robertson and Rough v Forth Road Bridge Joint Board [1995] IRLR 251

Three workmates had been repairing the Forth Road Bridge during a gale. One of them was sitting on a piece of metal on a truck when a gust of wind blew him off the bridge and he was killed. His colleagues who witnessed this were unable to claim. They were held not to be primary victims and had insufficient ties with the dead worker for injury to be foreseeable.

Secondary victims not present at the event or its immediate aftermath

A major control mechanism from both *McLoughlin* and *Alcock* in restricting claims by secondary victims is that the shock must result from being present at the scene of the event or its immediate aftermath. The mechanism has been used to defeat many claims but a range of recent decisions appear to have given a broader definition to the term 'immediate aftermath'.

While *Alcock* claims were defeated because they exceeded the two hours accepted as immediate aftermath in *McLoughlin*, a period of 24 hours has subsequently been accepted as falling within the criteria and giving rise to liability.

CASE EXAMPLE

Farrell v Merton, Sutton and Wandsworth HA (2000) 57 BMLR 158

A woman recovered damages for nervous shock when doctors had negligently caused damage to her new-born baby. The shock she suffered on witnessing the child fell within the immediate aftermath because doctors had prevented her from seeing the child until the day after the birth.

There has even been some stretching of the meaning of witnessing the event or its immediate aftermath.

CASE EXAMPLE

Froggatt v Chesterfield and North Derbyshire Royal Hospital NHS Trust [2002] WL 3167323

A woman had a breast surgically removed after she was negligently diagnosed as suffering from breast cancer and obviously recovered damages. Her husband successfully claimed for nervous shock even though this actually occurred the first time that he saw her undressed afterwards. Her son also claimed successfully for the shock caused when he heard a telephone conversation in which his mother had identified that she had cancer and might die.

It has even recently proved possible for a claim to succeed where the psychiatric injury has resulted from another form of inconvenience or distress that itself has resulted from the traumatic event.

CASE EXAMPLE

McLoughlin v Jones [2001] EWCA Civ 1743

The claimant here was wrongly convicted and also imprisoned as a result of his solicitor's negligence. The claimant suffered psychiatric injury as a result of the trauma involved and the solicitor was held liable.

Besides this the traumatic event may in any case be something that in other circumstances might appear to lack the horror associated with accidents but nevertheless can result in the claimant still being traumatised.

CASE EXAMPLE

Howarth v Green [2001] EWHC 2687 (QB)

The claimant suffered nervous shock after being hypnotised in front of the audience. The court held that a psychiatric injury was a foreseeable consequence of the activity and held the hypnotist liable.

Perhaps the most remarkable development is that the courts now seem prepared to accept that the shocking event itself can last over a considerable period of time.

CASE EXAMPLE

North Glamorgan NHS Trust v Walters [2002] EWCA Civ 1792

Doctors negligently failed to diagnose that a 10-month-old baby suffering from hepatitis required a liver transplant. His mother was reassured that he would be unlucky not to recover; however, he suffered a major fit in front of her. They were both then taken to a London hospital for the child to have a liver transplant and on arrival it was discovered that the child had irreversible and severe brain damage. The parents' permission was gained to switch off life support and the baby died minutes later in its mother's arms. The whole episode took 36 hours and the mother suffered pathological grief, recognised as a psychiatric illness, as a result, and sued successfully. The defendants appealed on the grounds that the psychiatric injury was not brought about as a result of witnessing a single shocking event. The Court of Appeal rejected this argument and held that the whole period from when the baby suffered the fit to when it died was 'a single horrifying event'. The trial judge was correct to conclude that the appreciation of the horror was sudden because seeing the fit, hearing that the baby was irreversibly brain damaged, and the recommendation to end life support all had an immediate impact and were part of a continuous chain of events. The case could therefore be distinguished from those cases involving a gradual realisation of shocking consequences over a period of time.

Walters was referred to in *Atkins v Seghal* [2003] EWCA Civ 697 where a mother was told of her daughter's death by a police officer but did not see the body until two hours later. The Court of Appeal accepted that this still represented the immediate aftermath.

The House of Lords has also shown its willingness to develop the area of nervous shock in quite dramatic fashion. Recent case law suggests that the House will even be prepared to accept a claim for negligence causing nervous shock in circumstances where the claimant is a secondary victim, but the last two controls under *Alcock*, present at the event or its immediate aftermath and witnessing the event with own unaided senses, are arguably not satisfied.

CASE EXAMPLE

W v Essex and Another [2000] 2 All ER 237

The claimants were parents who also acted as specialist foster parents for a local authority. They agreed to foster a 15-year-old boy, having stated beforehand that they were not prepared to take a child with a record of or suspected of being a child abuser. In fact the boy had been cautioned in the past for indecent assault and was currently under investigation for rape. The boy then committed serious acts of sexual abuse against the claimants' children. The children bought negligence claims and the parents bought claims for psychiatric injury caused through the shock of discovering the abuse. The marriage eventually broke up and both parents suffered from depression. The Court of Appeal struck out the parents' claim on the ground that it would not be fair and reasonable on policy grounds to impose such a duty on the authority because of its implication for fostering arrangements. On eventual appeal, the House of Lords rejected the council's arguments that the parents were secondary victims who were neither near in time or space nor witnessed the shocking event, the abuse of their children. Lord Slynn left open the question of whether the parents could be classed as primary victims. He also considered that it was arguable whether or not the shock of learning of the abuse fell within the immediate aftermath or not, and that it was impossible to say that the psychiatric injuries in question fell outside of that which the law considers deserving of compensation. As a result the House was not prepared to strike out the claims of the parents.

Those suffering a gradual rather than a sudden shock

Successful claims for nervous shock have traditionally been associated with a single traumatic event. In the case of secondary victims where the psychiatric injury is the result of a gradual appreciation of events rather than a sudden shock then there will be no liability.

CASE EXAMPLE

Sion v Hampstead Health Authority [1994] 5 Med LR 170

A father claimed to have suffered psychiatric injury as the result of watching his son gradually deteriorate and then die over the space of 14 days, with the gradual realisation that death might result from medical negligence. The court would not accept that there could be a claim because there was no sudden appreciation of a horrifying event.

This contrasts with recent decisions involving primary victims where the slow realisation of possibly being infected with a potentially deadly and frightening disease caused the injury. See the litigation involving CJD (the human form of so-called 'mad cow disease' – *Schedule 2 Claimants v Medical Research Council and Secretary of State for Health* (2000) 54 BMLR 1 and *Andrews and Others v Secretary of State for Health* (2000) 54 BMLR 111.

Those where there is no causal link between the incident and the damage

If the psychiatric injury can be attributed to an event other than the horrifying incident in question then there is no causal link and no possible claim. Indeed we have already seen the effect of this in *Taylor v Somerset HA* [1993] 4 Med LR 34.

CASE EXAMPLE

Calascione v Dixon (1994) 19 BMLR 97

The defendant was responsible for the death of a 20-year-old in a motorcycle accident. He was not liable however for the psychiatric injuries suffered by the mother of the young man. It was shown that the psychiatric illness was more the result of the stress of the inquest and a private prosecution rather than the incident itself.

6.1.5 The problem of policy

Clearly the area of recovery for psychiatric injury (nervous shock) has been subject to an erratic development. There is no doubt that secondary victims have been treated harshly by comparison to primary victims, although taken the kind of harm suffered, they are just as likely to suffer harm. Even in the case of bystanders it seems that it is policy reasons rather than the foreseeability of harm that has led to a denial of liability.

QUOTATION

'[I]t is generally recognised that the rules governing recovery for damages for nervous shock lack coherence, logic, justice and even plain common sense.'

F A Trindade, 'Reformulation of the Nervous Shock Rules' (2003) 179 LQR 204

The need for reform in the area has been identified by the Law Commission in its Report, *Liability for Psychiatric Illness*, (Law Com No 249) in 1998. Their chief recommendations are:

■ To retain the requirement of a close tie of love and affection to the primary victim in the case of secondary victims.
■ To remove the requirements for secondary victims to show proximity in time and space, and that the event has been witnessed by the claimant's own unaided senses.
■ That the injury should be accepted even where not caused by a sudden traumatic event.

The proposals seem to be much fairer. However, it is not clear whether or not there is any likelihood of them becoming law. In the light of recent response to Law Commission proposals it may be unlikely, at least in the near future.

ACTIVITY

Self-assessment questions

1. What exactly is meant by the term 'nervous shock'?
2. Why were courts originally reluctant to allow a claimant to recover for nervous shock, and why has this changed?
3. How broad is the definition of 'psychiatric injury'?
4. Has there been any logical kind of development to nervous shock?
5. What is the 'area of impact' and what is the 'area of shock'?
6. What is the difference between a 'primary victim' and a 'secondary victim'?
7. In what specific ways is a primary victim in a better position to claim than a secondary victim?
8. What are the three essential features of a successful claim by a secondary victim?

9. How did the courts originally define the meaning of 'immediate aftermath' in the decisions of cases?

10. To what extent is policy a determining factor in deciding whether or not a claim will succeed?

11. To what extent does *McLoughlin v O'Brian* fit in with other cases?

12. In what way is *Attia v British Gas* such a strange case?

13. In what ways do the cases of *N Glamorgan NHS Trust v Walters* and *W v Essex CC* demonstrate major developments in the law on nervous shock?

14. What improvements would the Law Commission proposals make to the law?

ACTIVITY

Multiple choice questions

In the following series of situations, in each case suggest which of the statements may raise a successful claim of nervous shock.

1. (a) Rajinder is present when his dog is run over by Andrew's negligent driving and suffers nervous shock.
   (b) Rajinder hears his mother has been run over by Andrew's negligent driving three weeks ago and he suffers nervous shock.
   (c) Rajinder is a passenger in a car when his friend Parminder, the driver, is killed by Andrew's negligent driving and Rajinder suffers nervous shock.
   (d) Rajinder hears screams when Andrew crashes his car and Rajinder suffers nervous shock.

2. (a) Sally hears that a friend has died in a car crash caused by negligence and suffers from profound grief.
   (b) Sally sees her friend killed in an accident at work caused by the employer's negligence and cannot sleep.
   (c) Sally is called to the hospital to identify her mother's body after a car driver has negligently run her over and it makes her very angry.
   (d) Sally is with her father when he drowns as a result of negligence when a ferry sinks and she suffers post traumatic stress disorder.

KEY FACTS

The development of a claim for psychiatric injury	Case
Originally courts were unwilling to allow actions for nervous shock.	*Victoria Railway Commissioners v Coultas* (1888)
This was because of the primitive state of psychiatric medicine.	
So the key requirement is always that the illness amounts to a recognised psychiatric disorder.	*Vernon v Bosely* (1997)
An action was at first only possible if the claimant was also in physical danger.	*Dulieu v White* (1901)
But this was then extended to include a person who was in the area of shock, ie witnessed the accident and had some close tie with the victim.	*Hambrook v Stokes* (1925)
The widest extent of the duty was to include witnessing the immediate aftermath of the accident.	*McLoughlin v O'Brian* (1982)
The event causing shock may be made up of a series of events lasting over quite a prolonged period of time.	*North Glamorgan NHS Trust v Walters* (2002)
A claim has even been allowed for nervous shock on witnessing property damage.	*Attia v British Gas* (1987)

Those who can claim for nervous shock	Case
Now basic rules identify a restricted range of people who can claim – which include: • Primary victims – present and either injured or at risk • Secondary victims – close tie of love and affection to the victim, and a witness of the incident or its immediate aftermath – here the meaning of immediate aftermath has been expressed very narrowly (no more than two hours) – but recently the court accepted that the shocking event itself lasted 36 hours) • Rescuers – where the rescuer is either a genuine primary victim; or a genuine secondary victim – but there is now no general category of liability to a rescuer (Those witnessing it on live TV in contravention of broadcasting requirements – possibly)	*Alcock v Chief Constable of South Yorkshire* (1992) *Page v Smith* (1996) *McLoughlin v O'Brian* (1982) *N Glamorgan NHS Trust v Walters* (2002) *White v Chief Constable of South Yorkshire* (1998) *Greatorex v Greatorex* (2000)
Those who cannot claim for nervous shock	**Case**
There are a number of classes of people who could not claim: • Mere bystanders • Secondary victims without close ties to the victim • Secondary victims not present at the scene or the immediate aftermath – but see the decision in • Those not suffering a recognised psychiatric injury • Those outside of the area of foreseeable shock of the accident The Law Commission has suggested relaxing the rules for claims by secondary victims, so that they should only need to prove the close tie of love and affection with the primary victim	 *McFarlane v E E Caledonia* (1994) *Robertson and Rough v Forth Road Bridge Joint Board* (1995) *Alcock v Chief Constable of South Yorkshire* (1992) *W v Essex CC* (2000) *Reilly v Merseyside Regional Health Authority* (1994) *Bourhill v Young* (1943)

6.2 Pure economic loss

6.2.1 The traditional position

The *Hedley Byrne* case (see *Hedley Byrne v Heller and Partners Ltd* [1964] AC 465 at section 6.3.1) introduced the concept that a claimant could recover for economic loss arising from negligently made statements. However, the courts have always distinguished such an action from 'pure economic loss' arising out of negligent acts. The position here was traditionally very clear; there was no liability for a 'pure economic loss'.

In the past this was based on policy and the idea that 'economic loss', for instance a loss of profit, was a concept applicable to contract law rather than tort. The principle has been quite clearly stated and illustrated in past cases.

CASE EXAMPLE

Spartan Steel v Martin & Co (Contractors) Ltd [1973] 1 QB 27

An electric power cable was negligently cut by the defendants, resulting in loss of power to the claimants, who manufactured steel alloys. A 'melt' in the claimant's furnace at the time of the power cuts had to be destroyed to stop it from solidifying and wrecking the furnace. The claimants were able to claim for physical damage and the loss of profit on the 'melt' in the furnace. The court refused to allow their claim for lost profits for four further 'melts' they argued they could have completed while the power was still off. The loss was foreseeable. Nevertheless, Lord Denning held that a line must be drawn as a matter of policy, and that the loss was better borne by the insurers than by the defendants alone.

In the case Lord Denning explained the basis of the rule as follows:

JUDGMENT

'It seems to me better to consider the particular relationship in hand, and see whether or not, as a matter of policy, economic loss should be recoverable or not.'

There appears to be an artificial distinction here created for policy reasons purely for the purpose of restricting any extension of liability. The distinction has the obvious potential to create unfair anomalies in the law. For instance it might mean that an architect giving negligent advice leading to the construction of a defective building could be liable where the builder whose negligence leads to a defect in a building may not be.

Nevertheless other cases have confirmed the principle that a pure economic loss arising from a negligent act is unrecoverable.

CASE EXAMPLE

Weller & Co v Foot and Mouth Disease Research Institute [1966] 1 QB 569

Auctioneers' regular income from sale of cattle was disrupted as the result of a ban on the movement of livestock following an escape of a virus from the defendant's premises. No liability could be accepted for their loss of profit.

However, there have also been situations where an economic loss was recovered, although in less clear-cut situations where the difference between a negligent statement and a negligent act was less obvious.

CASE EXAMPLE

Dutton v Bognor Regis Urban District Council [1972] 1 QB 373

A local authority was responsible for a negligently carried out building inspection that resulted in defective foundations having to be repaired at great financial cost to the owner of the building. The Court of Appeal held that, since a local authority were under no duty to carry out an inspection then they could not be held liable for a negligent inspection. Nevertheless they were prepared to impose liability on the basis of physical damage, that the defective foundations were a risk to the health and safety of the occupants. The claimant as a result was awarded damages to restore the building to a state where it was no longer a danger. Clearly it is difficult to distinguish between a negligent inspection (an act) and a satisfactory report based on the inspection (a statement). The case did not fit easily under either *Hedley Byrne or Donoghue v Stevenson* ([1932] AC 562), which perhaps explains the court's reasoning.

6.2.2 Pure economic loss under *Anns*

Further erosion of the basic principle that pure economic loss is unrecoverable came as a result of Lord Wilberforce's 'two-part' test.

CASE EXAMPLE

Anns v Merton London Borough Council [1978] AC 728

Here the negligent building inspection had failed to reveal that the foundations were too shallow. On the basis of the two-part test and that there were no policy grounds to avoid imposing a duty, the tenant was able to recover the cost of making the flat safe: economic loss in other words.

Because of the availability of the *Anns* two-part test, the so-called 'high water mark' was then reached in respect of recovery for a pure economic loss.

CASE EXAMPLE

Junior Books Ltd v Veitchi Co Ltd [1983] 1 AC 520

The claimants' architects nominated the defendants to lay the floor in the claimants' new print works. As a result they sub-contracted to the main builders to complete the work. In the event the defendants laid a thoroughly unusable floor which then had to be re-laid. The claimants could not sue the builders who had hired the floor layers at the claimant's request, and they had no contractual relationship with the floor layers. Nevertheless they succeeded in winning damages not just for the cost of re-laying the floor, but also for their loss of profit during the delay. There were said to be three key issues:
- The claimant had nominated the defendants and so they relied on the defendants' skill and judgement.
- The defendants were aware of this reliance at all material times.
- The damage caused was a direct and foreseeable consequence of the defendants' negligence.

Lord Fraser's explanation of the reasons for liability was that:

JUDGMENT

'The proximity of the parties is extremely close, falling only just short of a direct contractual relationship.'

Lord Brandon dissented and criticised the other judges for creating obligations in a non-contractual relationship only appropriate as between contracting parties.

6.2.3 Pure economic loss after *Anns*

Almost immediately judges considered that the relaxation of the principle concerning recovery for economic loss had now gone too far. A long line of cases followed which tried to limit the scope the above cases.

CASE EXAMPLE

Governors of the Peabody Donation Fund v Sir Lindsay Parkinson & Co Ltd [1985] 3 All ER 529

The court would not accept that there was liability owed for a negligent council inspection that resulted in a drain having to be re-laid because it did not conform to regulations. The council's duty in inspecting was to protect the health and safety of the public.

The cases had often arisen because an action in contract was not available and the reliance test from *Junior Books Ltd v Veitchi Co Ltd* [1983] 1 AC 520 was argued.

CASE EXAMPLE

Muirhead v Industrial Tank Specialists Ltd [1985] 3 All ER 705

Fish merchandisers bought lobsters while they were cheap, to sell on when their price increased. They bought storage tanks in which to hold the lobsters and lost money when the French built pumps in the tanks were defective and the lobsters could not be stored. They originally succeeded against the supplier of the tanks in contract but when they went into liquidation bought an action in tort against the manufacturers of the pumps. Their claim that the test of proximity and reliance in Junior Books applied failed. The court held that reliance had only been possible in that case because the claimants nominated the defendants. The case was therefore distinguished.

The argument that costs of repairing defects in property that could lead to a danger to health or safety, approved in *Anns*, was also gradually rejected.

CASE EXAMPLE

D & F Estates v Church Commissioners [1989] 2 All ER 992

Liability against builders was rejected when plaster cracked, fell off walls, and had to be replaced as the result of the negligence of sub-contractors. The builders had satisfied their duty by hiring competent tradesmen and, in the absence of injury or an actual risk to health, any loss was purely economic and not recoverable.

These represent only a few of the cases where *Anns* was argued to allow economic loss and was rejected or the case distinguished. The general unease that was felt at Lord Wilberforce's test in *Anns* and at the extension of liability for economic loss led eventually to the over-ruling of *Anns*, and thus back to a more restrictive attitude towards economic loss.

CASE EXAMPLE

Murphy v Brentwood District Council [1990] 2 All ER 908

The House of Lords would not impose liability on a council that had approved plans for a concrete raft on which properties were built and which then moved causing cracks in the walls. The claimant was forced to sell the house for £35,000 under the value if there had been no defects, but in the absence of any injury, loss was purely economic. So the ratio in Anns was overruled and the principle of law now is that a local authority will not be liable for the cost of repairing dangerous defects (in the case gas pipes had broken during the settlement of the property) until physical injury is actually caused. Junior Books v Veitchi was not overruled but was allowed to stand on its own facts. It is unlikely, however, to have much impact on future cases.

In his judgment Lord Bridge explained the basis for denying liability.

JUDGMENT

'If a dangerous defect in a chattel is discovered before it causes any personal injury or damage to property, because the danger is now known and the chattel cannot safely be used unless the defect is repaired, the defect becomes merely a defect in quality. The chattel is either capable of repair at economic cost or it is worthless and must be scrapped. In either case the loss sustained by the owner or hirer of the chattel is purely economic. It is recoverable against any party who owes the loser a relevant contractual duty. But it is not recoverable in tort in the absence of a special relationship of proximity imposing on the tortfeasor a duty of care to safeguard the plaintiff from economic loss.'

The principles in *Murphy v Brentwood DC* [1990] 2 All ER 908 have subsequently been accepted and followed by the courts.

CASE EXAMPLE

Department of the Environment v Thomas Bates & Sons Ltd [1990] 2 All ER 943

Here the claimant failed to recover the cost of repairing a building that had been built of concrete that was of insufficient strength to support its intended load, although it was not dangerous to carry its existing load. The court held that such cost was purely economic and thus unrecoverable.

As a result it would appear that the present policy of the courts in relation to economic loss is that recovery for such loss should be through the normal insurance of the injured party rather than through the courts by using an action for negligence.

CASE EXAMPLE

Marc Rich & Co v Bishop Rock Marine Co. Ltd [1995] 1 WLR 1071

A vessel was negligently classed as seaworthy, and then sank. The classification society did not owe a duty of care to the owners of a cargo that sank with the ship. This was economic loss. The House of Lords applied the three-part test from *Caparo v Dickman* [1990] 1 All ER 568 (see section 6.3.2 below) and determined that it was not just and reasonable in the circumstances of the case to impose a duty.

ACTIVITY

Self-assessment questions

1. What exactly is a 'pure economic loss'?
2. Why are the courts more willing to accept an economic loss caused by a negligently made statement than one resulting from a negligent act or omission?
3. Why were judges in later cases nervous about the judgment in *Junior Books*?
4. What is the difference between physical damage to property and the cost of repairing defects in property?
5. How would the courts now prefer a claimant to recover compensation for an economic loss?
6. Why did the judges in *Murphy* decide not to overrule *Junior Books*?

KEY FACTS

Pure economic loss	Case
The courts have always been reluctant to allow liability for 'pure economic loss', since it is felt that it is more to do with contract.	*Spartan Steel v Martin* (1973)
Although claims have been successful where there has been a risk also to health.	*Dutton v Bognor Regis UDC* (1972)
And the position on economic loss was drastically relaxed as the result of Lord Wilberforce's two-part test.	*Anns v Merton LBC* (1978)

And in a 'near contractual' relationship between the two parties.	*Junior Books v Veitchi* (1983)
Later judges were unhappy with Anns and the two-part test and these were eventually over-ruled (but not Junior Books).	*Murphy v Brentwood DC* (1990)
The principle in Murphy has been followed in subsequent cases.	*Department of the Environment v Thomas Bates & Sons Ltd* (1990)
It appears that the more appropriate remedy for the damage is a claim against the claimant's own insurance.	*Marc Rich & Co v Bishop Rock Marine Co Ltd* (1995)

6.3 Negligent misstatement

6.3.1 The origins of liability

The law of torts is concerned mainly with compensating for physical damage or personal injury, not for loss that is only economic. The obvious justification for this stance is that economic loss, or for instance loss of a profit or bargain is more traditionally associated with contract law and the judges have always been eager to separate out the two.

An action for an economic loss caused by a statement was traditionally available in tort, but in the tort of deceit and only in the case of fraudulently made statements.

CASE EXAMPLE

Derry v Peek (1889) 14 App Cas 337

A representation in a share prospectus that a tram company could use motive power led to loss when the Board of Trade refused the company a licence to use motorised trams. The company had fully expected to be granted the licence, so their misstatement was not considered to be fraudulent.

That action for economic loss caused by reliance on a negligently made statement should be available was reaffirmed even more recently, although not without some fundamental disagreement being expressed.

CASE EXAMPLE

Candler v Crane Christmas & Co [1951] 2 KB 164

Accountants negligently prepared a company's accounts and investors then lost money. In the absence of a contractual relationship or fraud the court was not prepared to declare the existence of a duty of care.

Lord Denning, dissenting, felt that there should be a duty of care to the investor and to

JUDGMENT

'. . . any third party to whom they themselves show the accounts, or to whom they know their employer is going to show the accounts so as to induce them to invest money . . .'

The House of Lords eventually accepted this dissenting judgment a long time afterwards, and initially only in obiter.

CASE EXAMPLE

Hedley Byrne v Heller and Partners Ltd [1964] AC 465

An advertising company was approached with a view to preparing a campaign for a small company, Easipower, with whom they had not previously dealt. The advertisers then did the most sensible thing in the circumstances and approached Easipower's bank for a credit reference. The bank gave a satisfactory reference without checking on their current financial standing and the advertisers produced the campaign. They then lost money when Easipower went into liquidation. They sued the bank for their negligently prepared advice. They failed, because the bank had included a disclaimer of liability in the credit reference. Nevertheless, the House of Lords, approving Lord Denning's dissenting judgment in the last case, held that such an action should be possible, and this has subsequently been accepted as law.

Lord Reid explained the basis for imposing liability.

JUDGMENT

'A reasonable man, knowing that he was being trusted or that his skill and judgement were being relied on, would, I think, have three courses open to him. He could keep silent or decline to give the information or advice sought: or he could give an answer with a clear qualification that he accepted no responsibility for it or that it was given without that reflection or inquiry which a careful answer would require: or he could simply answer without any such qualification. If he chooses to adopt the last course he must, I think, be held to have accepted some responsibility for his answer being given carefully, or to have accepted a relationship with the inquirer which requires him to exercise such care as the circumstances require.'

The interesting point of the court's approval of the principle in the case is that they were holding that such a duty could apply despite there being no contractual relationship, and despite the fact that, in effect, they were accepting that they could impose liability for an economic loss.

As a result the House of Lords laid down strict guidelines for when the principle could apply.

(i)   There must be a special relationship between the two parties – based on the skill and judgement of the defendant and the reliance placed upon it.

(ii)   The person giving the advice must be possessed of special skill relating to the type of advice given – so the defendant ought to have realised that the claimant would rely on that skill.

(iii) The party receiving the advice has acted in reliance on it – and in the circumstances it was reasonable for the claimant to rely on the advice.

The subsequent case law has in general followed, but also in some cases added to, these requirements.

The basis of the specific duty has also been identified in the case law.

In *Smith v Eric S Bush* [1990] 1 AC 831 HL Lord Templeman identified that

JUDGMENT

'The duty of professional men "is not merely a duty to use care in their reports. They have also a duty to use care in their work which results in their reports".'

6.3.2 The criteria for imposing liability

A special relationship

The precise meaning of 'special relationship' was never really examined in *Hedley Byrne* and so it has become an area for judicial policy making. The original leaning was towards a narrow interpretation that would then only include a relationship where the party giving the advice was in the business of giving advice of the sort in question.

However, it has since been suggested that a business or professional relationship might in general give rise to the duty if the claimant is genuinely seeking professional advice.

CASE EXAMPLE

Howard Marine & Dredging Co Ltd v Ogden & Sons Ltd [1978] QB 574

Dredging took a lot longer because the hirers of the barges had misstated the payload weight to the party hiring them. It was accepted that the relationship, while a standard business one, could give rise to a special relationship for the purposes of imposing a duty.

A purely social relationship should not normally give rise to a duty of care, but has done when it has been established that carefully considered advice was being sought from a party with some expertise.

CASE EXAMPLE

Chaudry v Prabhaker [1988] 3 All ER 718

A woman asked her friend, who, while not a mechanic, had some experience of cars, to find her a good second-hand car that had not been in an accident. When it was later discovered that the car advised on had been in an accident and was not completely roadworthy, the friend advising on its purchase was successfully sued.

Common relationships where a duty will be identified though are those where valuers or accountants are providing the advice. Even though there may not be a contractual relationship between a building society surveyor and the house purchaser, it might still be possible to identify a special relationship.

CASE EXAMPLE

Yianni v Edwin Evans & Sons [1982] 2 QB 438

A building society surveyor was held to owe a duty to purchasers of a property valued at £12,000 where it was later discovered that repairs worth £18,000 were required. The court was prepared to impose the duty here because it was shown that at the time less than 15 per cent of purchasers would have their own independent survey carried out, and therefore it was foreseeable that they would rely on the standard building society survey.

The test is whether there is sufficient proximity between the parties for there to be the possibility of reliance and therefore for the duty to arise.

CASE EXAMPLE

Raja v Gray (2002) 33 EG 98 (CS)

Here the question was whether there was a duty of care owed by valuers appointed by receivers. The Court of Appeal accepted that the case law showed that there was a duty owed by valuers to parties with an interest in mortgaged property. Nevertheless, it was not prepared to accept that the same duty was owed where a receiver appointed the valuer because there would be insufficient proximity between the parties. The valuers would be purely acting for the receivers and it would be unfair to hold that their advice could be generally relied upon.

Simple policy reasons can be used to determine that there is insufficient proximity between parties to impose liability.

CASE EXAMPLE

West Bromwich Albion Football Club Ltd v El-Safty [2005] EWHC 2866 (QB)

A professional footballer suffered a knee injury and, on the advice of the club physiotherapist, was sent for consultation with the defendant specialist. The defendant advised reconstructive surgery which failed and the player had to retire. It was later accepted that the advice was negligent and that other treatment should have been considered first. The football club then sued the doctor for the economic loss that it had suffered as a result of the player's premature retirement from the game, arguing that because the club had referred the player and had paid for his treatment there was a special relationship over and above that normally relating to employers. The court held that there was insufficient proximity between the club and the doctor, the person really taking the advice was the player, and it would be unfair to impose a duty in the circumstances. It is easy to see why. If such a duty was imposed then there could be a flood of claims by employers in general in respect of the costs of replacing workers injured in negligent events.

The issue of exactly who is owed a duty of care by an accountant has proved to add its own complexities in determining the existence of a special relationship. Originally, for instance it was held that there was no duty held to persons who might in general terms rely on the accounts since there was no contractual relationship. This was precisely the position taken in *Candler v Crane Christmas & Co* [1951] 2 KB 164.

Nevertheless, following *Hedley Byrne* the possibility of such a duty arising has been considered by the courts. In *JEB Fasteners v Marks Bloom & Co* [1983] 3 All ER 289 the court accepted this possibility in certain circumstances even though it did not apply in the case because the accounts had no actual effect on the take-over since that had been undergone for other more specific reasons (see later).

More recently the courts have examined in detail the reasons why a duty will not be imposed upon an accountant in relation to the audited accounts of companies.

CASE EXAMPLE

Caparo Industries plc v Dickman [1990] 1 All ER 568

The case concerned the annual audit of a company required under the Companies Act 1985. The House of Lords held that the purposes of such audits was to enable the members of the company to exercise control over the officers in the administration of the company. As a result there could be no duty owed to the claimant in the case who was a shareholder purchasing further shares and who claimed to have suffered economic loss as a result of the negligently prepared accounts.

The possession of special skill or expertise

Ordinarily then a claim is only possible if the party giving the advice is a specialist in the field which the advice concerns.

CASE EXAMPLE

Mutual Life and Citizens Assurance Co Ltd v Evatt [1971] AC 793

A representative of an insurance company gave advice about the products of another company. The court held that there could only be a duty in such circumstances if the party giving the advice had held himself out as being in the business of giving the advice in question.

So advice given in a purely social context could not usually give rise to liability. In this way the defendant in *Chaudry v Prabhaker* might be considered unfortunate, although the result was justified since he should have applied the same caution in advising that he would have if he had been buying it himself.

Reasonable reliance on the advice

It is only fair and logical that if there has been no reliance placed on the advice given then there cannot be liability on the defendant for giving it.

CASE EXAMPLE

JEB Fasteners Ltd v Marks Bloom & Co [1983] 3 All ER 289

A negligent statement of the value of a company's stock did not give rise to a duty. This was because the party buying the company was doing so only to secure the services of two directors, and so placed no reliance on the stock.

In consequence it will not be foreseeable reliance if the claimant belongs to a group of potential claimants that is too large for the claimant to have fairly within his contemplation when giving the advice.

CASE EXAMPLE

Goodwill v British Pregnancy Advisory Service [1996] 2 All ER 161

Here a man had not been properly advised of the possibility that his vasectomy could automatically reverse itself. It was held that there could be no duty of care owed to a future girlfriend of the man.

Furthermore, a court will not automatically accept that a special relationship exists merely because the relationship is one of trust.

CASE EXAMPLE

Jones v Wright [1991] 2 WLR 814

There was no liability in favour of investors when auditors should have discovered that there had been a misuse of trust funds.

Although it is much more likely that there will be genuine reliance in contractual situations or those that are near contractual such as pre-contractual arrangements. In *Commissioner of Police for the Metropolis v Lennon* [2004] EWCA Civ 130, for instance, acting on advice the claimant took time off before moving to a new force and as a result lost his housing allowance. The police were held liable under *Hedley Byrne*.

However, whenever there is foreseeable reliance on advice that has been given then there will be a duty of care owed.

CASE EXAMPLE

Smith v Eric S Bush [1990] 2 WLR 790

A building society valuation had identified that chimney breasts had been removed, but the valuer had failed to check whether the brickwork above was properly secured. It was not, and after the purchase it collapsed. The court determined that there was a duty of care because, as in *Yianni v Edwin Evans and Sons* ([1982] 2 QB 438), even though the contract was between building society and valuer, it was reasonably foreseeable that the purchaser would rely on it.

Inevitably for a claim to succeed it must be shown that reliance on the negligently given advice was indeed reasonable.

CASE EXAMPLE

Lambert v West Devon BC (1997) 96 LGR 45

The council was held liable when the claimant relied on its advice that he could begin building even though planning permission had not yet been obtained. Since the defendant was the body from which permission was being sought, it was perfectly reasonable that the claimant would rely on the advice given as being accurate.

The test is obviously whether the defendant knew or ought reasonably to be expected to know of the reliance on the advice given (see *Yianni v Edwin Evans & Sons*). In this way foreseeable reliance by the party seeking the advice might also prevent an exclusion of liability clause in a contract from operating successfully.

CASE EXAMPLE

Harris v Wyre Forest District Council [1989] 1 All ER 691

Here in the sale of a council house a negligent survey had been carried out for the local authority. Even though the purchaser did not see the valuation he could rely on it and a disclaimer of liability inserted in the valuation was ineffective because it was not reasonable within the terms of the Unfair Contract Terms Act 1977.

Policy considerations have been as important in identifying when reasonable reliance occurs as in determining when a special relationship exists between the parties. This was clear in *Caparo*. As a result the range of claimants that might be covered by *Hedley Byrne* principles is limited. The courts are not prepared to extend the range at the expense of holding to the principle that it is fair, just and reasonable to impose a duty as is required by the *Caparo* three-part test for liability in negligence.

CASE EXAMPLE

Newell v Ministry of Defence [2002] EWHC 1006 (QB)

An army officer made an application for early release and then waited for what he alleged was an unreasonable time for a reply and claimed negligence on the part of his employers. While waiting to hear, he had turned down a civilian job and claimed to have lost financially as a result. The court was not prepared to accept that the employer had undertaken any responsibility for his affairs in seeking civilian employment and rejected the argument that he could bring himself within the scope of the duty. It would not be fair to impose a duty in circumstances where the employer was in no way involved in the officer's applications for civilian employment.

Where a duty to act is imposed by statute a civil action is only usually available to a party when the type of harm suffered was that anticipated by the statute. This was one of the reasons why the action failed in *Caparo v Dickman*. However, a duty may apply where the public would generally benefit.

CASE EXAMPLE

Law Society v KPMG Peat Marwick [2000] 4 All ER 540

Here the Law Society was owed a duty of care by a firm of accountants hired by solicitors to prepare annual accounts for the Law Society because Law Society compensation to clients of firms would be possible on a bad report.

6.3.3 The current state of the law

In *Caparo v Dickman* the House of Lords had the opportunity to consider the principles involved in liability under *Hedley Byrne*. The financial booms and rapid development in property markets had not only led to a greater increase in home ownership and share ownership, it had also led on to a great number of claims for negligent misstatement, particularly against property surveyors and accountants.

The House of Lords preferred an incremental approach to establishing the duty of care, as we have already seen. They also made a number of observations regarding the circumstances in which the *Hedley Byrne* type duty will be owed.

- The advice must be required for a purpose described at the time to the defendant at least in general terms.
- This purpose must be made known actually or by inference to the party giving the advice at the time it is given.
- If the advice will subsequently be communicated to the party relying on it, this fact must be known by the advisor.
- The advisor must be aware that the advice will be acted upon without benefit of any further independent advice.
- The person alleging to have relied on the advice must show actual reliance and consequent detriment suffered.

So the significant feature of this development of the duty is the express or implied knowledge of the purpose for which the claimant acted in reliance of the statement.

Guidance on the factors to be taken into account in deciding whether a duty of care in fact exists have subsequently been provided by the Court of Appeal.

CASE EXAMPLE

James McNaughten Paper Group Ltd v Hicks Anderson & Co [1991] 1 All ER 134

Here accountants who drew up accounts at very short notice for the Chairman of a company had no duty of care to the person who acquired the company in a take-over bid, having inspected the accounts. The Court of Appeal identified the factors that should be taken into account in establishing a duty of care as follows:
1. the purpose for which the statement was made
2. the purpose for which the statement was communicated
3. the relationship between the person giving the advice, the person receiving the advice, and any relevant third party
4. the size of any class that the person receiving the advice belonged to
5. the degree of knowledge of the person giving the advice.
As a result of this final point *Caparo* has been distinguished in some later cases.

This is a very narrow approach to the duty and subsequent cases have tended to take a more relaxed view. In *Henderson v Merrett Syndicates* [1994] 3 All ER 506, for instance, the court added a fifth factor for determining that a duty exists under *Hedley Byrne* principles. The requirement is that there is an assumption of responsibility by the party giving the advice.

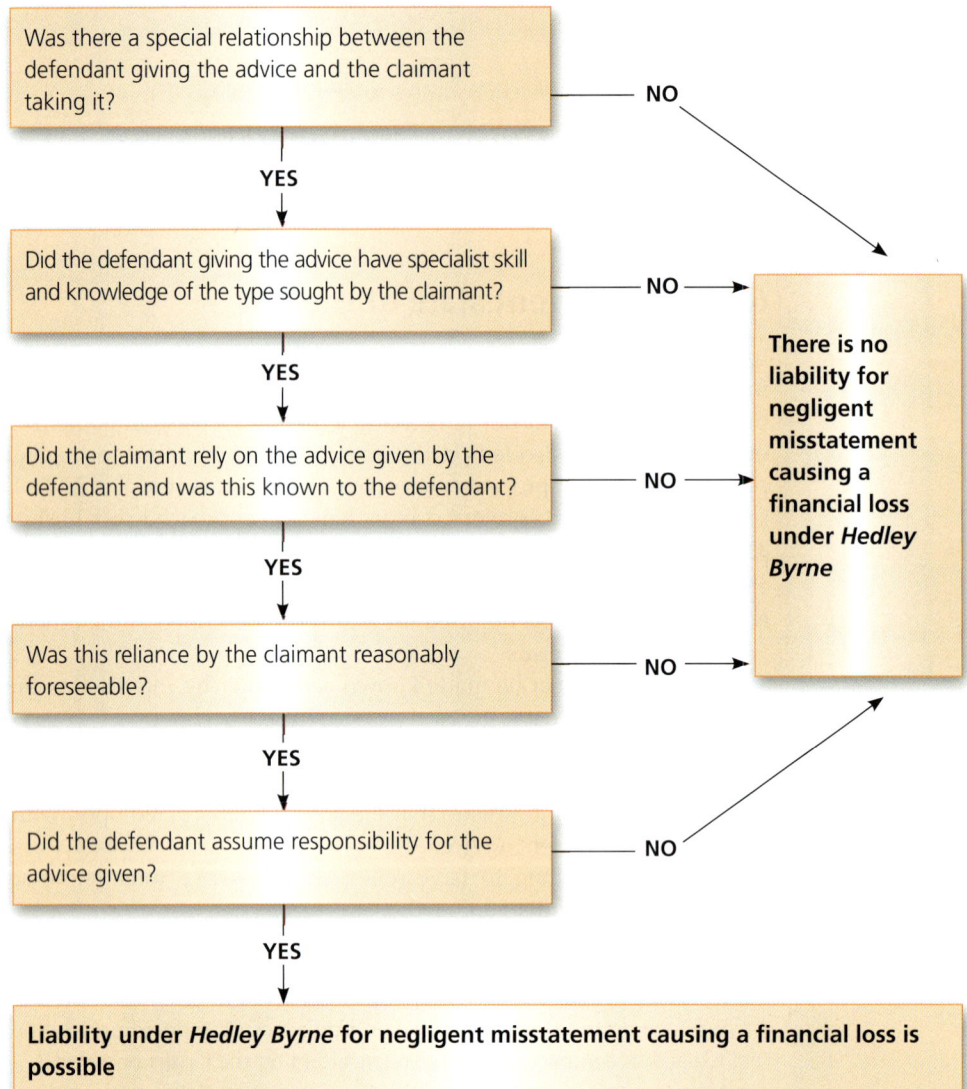

Figure 6.2 Diagram illustrating the essential elements for a successful claim under *Hedley Byrne*

Some cases certainly seem to be at odds with the general principle and liability has been imposed apparently to prevent a party being without any remedy.

CASE EXAMPLE

White v Jones [1995] 1 All ER 691

Solicitors who negligently failed to draw up a will before the testator's death were held to owe a duty to the intended beneficiaries who consequently lost their inheritance. Any contractual relationship was with the testator and since a will can be changed a beneficiary is not necessarily ensured the inheritance. Nevertheless, the House of Lords were prepared to identify both a special relationship in the circumstances and reliance.

Certain cases appear not to fit easily within the *Hedley Byrne* principle because the person relying on the advice is not the person who actually suffers the loss.

CASE EXAMPLE

Ross v Caunters [1980] Ch 297

Here solicitors were held to be liable to the beneficiaries under a will for failing to warn the testator not to allow the spouse of a beneficiary to witness the will. The court decided that the duty existed because there was sufficient proximity between the defendant and the beneficiaries who in effect relied on their expertise.

As a result it sometimes appears that a court will impose liability simply because it is foreseeable that a party will rely on the negligent advice.

CASE EXAMPLE

Ministry of Housing and Local Government v Sharp [1971] 2 QB 223

The court held the ministry liable when a land registry clerk negligently gave a clean certificate to land that was actually subject to a charge, as a result of which the ministry lost compensation that it would otherwise have been entitled to. Any reliance, and indeed any special relationship, was by the purchaser of the property. Nevertheless this reliance in effect led only to a loss by the ministry.

However, in some instances the case seems out of context because the court is uncertain whether it is the principle in *Hedley Byrne* or that in *Donoghue v Stevenson* which is the appropriate one to apply. The latter is certainly less restrictive.

CASE EXAMPLE

Spring v Guardian Assurance plc [1995] 3 WLR 354

An employee of an insurance company was dismissed and then prevented from gaining a position with another company because of a negligently prepared and highly unfavourable reference provided by the first company. The House of Lords held that the first employers were liable because of the reference, but the House was split on whether *Hedley Byrne* should apply.

The approach to dealing with negligently prepared references has since been developed by the Court of Appeal. In *Bartholomew v London Borough of Hackney* [1999] IRLR 246 the Court increased the duty to ensuring that information provided is accurate and that the reference does not create any unfair impression.

This test has now been developed further.

CASE EXAMPLE

Cox v Sun Alliance Life Ltd [2001] IRLR 448

The claimant was a branch manager who was suspended for reasons not related to dishonesty. An allegation of dishonesty was made during negotiations for a termination agreement. However, the investigation that followed was abandoned and Sun Life agreed that in any references they would make no mention of the allegation. However, they did so in one reference which cost the claimant a job and he sued successfully for negligence. Lord Justice Mummery stated that: before divulging information that is unfavourable to an ex-employee in a reference, the employer must believe in the truth of the information, have reasonable grounds for that belief and make a reasonably thorough investigation before making the statement.

What is clear is that policy remains an important fact in determining whether or not a duty is imposed in particular circumstances.

CASE EXAMPLE

Gorham v British Telecommunications plc [2000] 1 WLR 2129

The claimant had asked the defendants to sell him a pension that would provide benefits not only for himself but also for his dependants in the event of his death. Standard Life sold him a pension, but one which did not fulfil this requirement. In fact the company should have advised him to remain with his existing employee pension scheme in the circumstances. The court held that the claimant was owed a duty to be advised in a way that would achieve his stated purpose. This duty had been breached because the pension that he was sold on the contrary affected him detrimentally.

ACTIVITY

Self-assessment questions

1. Why did the House of Lords in *Hedley Byrne* alter the previous rule in *Candler v Crane Christmas & Co*?
2. What exactly is a special relationship?
3. How can the decision in *Chaudry v Prabhaker* be justified?
4. What level of specialist expertise is required for liability under *Hedley Byrne*?
5. Against what standards is reasonable reliance measured?
6. How can the *Goodwill v BPAS* case be distinguished from other cases on reasonable reliance?
7. Why was the decision in *Yianni v Edwin Evans* greeted with such shock by building society surveyors?
8. To what extent does the case of *Caparo v Dickman* limit liability under *Hedley Byrne*?
9. What elements have been added to the test for liability by *Caparo*?
10. What further aspect of the test has been added by the case of *Henderson v Merrett Syndicates*?
11. How do cases like *White v Jones* and *Spring v Guardian Assurance* fit in with the normal rule?

KEY FACTS

The origins of the duty	Case
Originally there was only an action available for misrepresentations if they were made fraudulently.	*Derry v Peek* (1889)
And an action for negligence was originally specifically rejected.	*Candler v Crane, Christmas & Co* (1951)
But the House of Lords eventually accepted in obiter that such an action was possible.	*Hedley Byrne v Heller & Partners* (1964)
The essential elements of the duty	**Case**
But only subject to certain requirements: • the existence of a special relationship	*Yianni v Edwin Evans* (1982)
• where the party giving the advice has specialist skill and knowledge of the type sought	*Mutual Life & Citizens Assurance v Evatt* (1971)
• the other party acts in reliance of the advice which is known to the other party	*Smith v Eric S Bush* (1990)
• limitations on these requirements have since been made – the principal one being that the reliance is reasonably foreseeable to the defendant	*Caparo v Dickman* (1990)

• and a list of import factors to be considered has been identified including:
  • the purpose for which the statement was made and communicated
  • the relationship between all relevant parties
  • the degree of knowledge of the defendant
	James McNaughten Paper Group v Hicks Anderson (1991)

• a requirement that the defendant has assumed responsibility for the advice has been added.	*Henderson v Merrett Syndicates (1994)*
But there are also cases that do not fit the principle neatly.	*White v Jones (1995); Spring v Guardian Assurance (1995)*

6.4 Liability for omissions

The law of England distinguishes two ways of establishing tortious liability:

■ misfeasance – the infliction of damage or injury by a positive act; and
■ non-feasance – causing harm by failing to prevent it or allowing it to happen.

The law does not include any general liability for non-feasance, or failing to act. There are of course those that believe that the law should include a 'good neighbour' principle, but this idea has generally not been accepted and in any case would be very difficult and unfair to enforce in most circumstances.

There are two fairly obvious historical reasons for the courts taking this position:

■ The problem of showing causation – showing that somebody failed to prevent harm is much more difficult than showing that they caused it.
■ The problem of imposing onerous burdens – it is hard to define the situations in which it could be said that a defendant should act and there is a distinct possibility of unfairness in doing so. For instance, should a person who sees someone drowning be obliged to jump in to attempt a rescue even if he cannot swim himself?

The law has, however, recognised a number of exceptions where there will be a duty to act and liability resulting where a party then fails to act. These have all been identified and categorised.

CASE EXAMPLE

Smith v Littlewoods Organisation Ltd [1987] 1 All ER 710

The defendants bought a cinema to demolish and rebuild as a supermarket. It was then left empty and vandals broke in and set fire to it, the fire spread and caused damage to adjoining property. There was no liability since the defendant was not responsible for the acts of strangers.

As Goff LJ in the House of Lords stated

JUDGMENT

'In such a case it is not possible to invoke a general duty of care; for it is well recognised that there is no general duty of care to prevent third parties from causing such damage.'

Further than this he discussed the situations in which the law will impose a duty for a failure to act.

The defendant owes a duty by a contractual or other undertaking

The defendant may owe a contractual duty to act.

CASE EXAMPLE

Stansbie v Troman [1948] 2 KB 48

A decorator was given the key to the premises he was decorating and told to lock the door when he left. He failed to do so and a thief entered the house and stole property. The decorator was held liable for a breach of duty in failing to lock the door.

In general, liability in this instance will arise as a result of non-feasance rather than misfeasance, the failure to act according to the terms of the contract.

CASE EXAMPLE

Bailey v HSS Alarms, The Times, 20th June, 2000, CA

The defendants had entered into a contract with the installers of an alarm system to monitor the system and report activated alarms to the police. When one alarm was activated and the defendants failed to report it to the police, burglars entered the premises and valuable property was taken. The contract did not exclude such a duty being owed, the damage was not too remote a consequence of the defendants' breach and they were held liable.

The duty might also arise from the specific character of an actual undertaking.

CASE EXAMPLE

Barnett v Chelsea & Kensington Hospital Management Committee [1969] 1 QB 428

Here the hospital casualty department undertook to diagnose ailments and injuries and treat their patients. They were therefore in breach of their duty of care when the doctor negligently failed to diagnose the condition of a patient who later died of arsenic poisoning. However, there was no liability since there was in fact nothing that could have been done to save the patient.

However, policy considerations may still prevent a duty from being imposed at all.

CASE EXAMPLE

Hill v Chief Constable of West Yorkshire [1988] 2 All ER 238

The court here rejected a powerful argument by the mother of the Yorkshire Ripper's last victim that her murder might have been avoided with adequate policing. It was held that the police have no duty to the victims of crime to prevent the crime, or to catch the criminal according to any set time scale.

Lord Keith expressed the reasoning of the House of Lords.

JUDGMENT

'The general sense of public duty which motivates police forces is unlikely to be appreciably reinforced by the imposition of such liability . . . The result would be a significant diversion of police manpower and attention from their most important function, that of the suppression of crime.'

The defendant owes a duty because of a special relationship with the claimant

Clearly in certain situations the nature of the defendant's duty arises because of the potential danger to the public presented by the activity carried out by the defendant.

This duty is particularly appropriate to public bodies. In such cases the defendant may have a duty to act and the failure to act will lead to liability.

CASE EXAMPLE

Home Office v Dorset Yacht Co Ltd [1970] AC 1004

Borstal boys who had been taken on a residential outing escaped due to the negligence of the warders. These young offenders then did considerable damage to neighbouring property. The Home Office was held liable for its employees' failure to control the offenders in their charge.

There can still be a duty in such a relationship leading to liability for its breach despite the fact that the claimant has contributed to his own harm.

CASE EXAMPLE

Barrett v Ministry of Defence [1995] 3 All ER 87 CA

Employers were liable for the death of a naval airman who became so drunk on cheap alcohol provided in the mess that he fell into a coma and drowned in his own vomit. The Court of Appeal would not impose liability for supplying the drink since the claimant had a responsibility for his own safety. The defendants were held liable, however, for a failure to call a doctor or to look after him properly when he had collapsed. Damages were reduced by two thirds to account for the man's contributory negligence.

As we have already seen there is generally not considered to be any special relationship between the police and the public (see Chapter 2, section 2.2.2 *Cowan v Chief Constable for Avon and Somerset* [2001] EWCA Civ 1699).

However, there are clear circumstances in which public authorities are in a special relationship with parties affected by their failures to act and where liability may be imposed (see section 6.1.4 above *W v Essex and Another* [2000] 2 All ER 237).

There is now a developing law on the failure of public bodies to act in respect of statutory duties to children including education cases and abuse cases. An interesting aspect of this is whether public bodies owe a common law duty of care to parents when they are acting in respect of a statutory duty to their children.

CASE EXAMPLE

D v East Berkshire Community Health NHS Trust [2005] UKHL 23; [2005] 2 WLR 993

Three joined appeals involved either doctors or social workers who had carried out investigations of parents where there was a suspicion of child abuse. The investigations revealed that the suspicions were unfounded. The parents then claimed that the original suspicion was unfounded and negligent and sought damages for psychiatric injury. The House of Lords held that there was no duty owed to the parents since this would conflict with the statutory duties owed to the children to investigate.

The defendant owes a duty because of damage caused by a third party who is within his control

If the defendant can in fact be said to be responsible for a third party then there may be liability for a failure to properly exercise that control.

CASE EXAMPLE

Haynes v Harwood [1935] 1 KB 146

A driver left his horse-drawn van unattended in a street. Boys then threw stones at the horses, which bolted. A policeman was then injured while trying to prevent harm to pedestrians. The driver was held liable. He had failed to leave the horses in a secure state and the boys' act was entirely foreseeable.

As we have already seen, officials in sporting events owe a duty to the participants (see Chapter 3, section 3.3.4 *Smolden v Whitworth and Nolan* [1997] PIQR P133). On this basis the officials can be said to be in control of the participants. A failure to enforce the rules of the sport properly by that official leading to injury of a participant will then be seen as a breach of duty and liability may result.

CASE EXAMPLE

Vowles v Evans and Another [2003] EWCA Civ 318

The claimant was playing in an amateur rugby match refereed by the defendant and for whom the Welsh Rugby Union Ltd was therefore also vicariously liable. In a very fast moving game he suffered serious injuries during a scrummage. The referee failed to operate according to the rules and allowed the substitution of a front row forward, even though in the circumstances he should have been considering insisting on non-contestable scrummages. As play was stopped at the time and the referee had plenty of time to deliberate on the issue he was in breach of his duty to care for the safety of the players.

Again this principle might operate in relation to public officials, such as the duty a prison officer has to control prisoners. So the damage done by the Borstal boys in *Home Office v Dorset Yacht Co* [1970] AC 1004 is an example of a failure to exercise proper control. The case of *W v Essex and Another* is another more recent and more dramatic example (see section 6.1.4).

Another obvious example where the duty might arise is in an employer's duty to his employees to hire competent staff for them to work with.

CASE EXAMPLE

Hudson v Ridge Manufacturing Co Ltd [1957] 2 QB 348

Here an employee was injured following an incident involving a fellow employee who was a known practical joker. The employer had failed to deal with this employee's activities in the past and so was held liable on this occasion.

Again the police are generally immune from such actions in relation to the investigation of crime where it is held that they do not owe a duty of care to prevent crime (see *Hill v Chief Constable of West Yorkshire* [1988] 2 All ER 238).

visitor
Usually refers to somebody who enters premises lawfully

The defendant owes a duty because of control over land or some other dangerous thing

If the defendant is in control of premises then there is a duty to ensure that **visitors** to the premises use them safely without risk to others.

CASE EXAMPLE

Cunningham v Reading Football Club Ltd [1992] PIQR P141

Here the football club was held liable for the injuries caused by football hooligans who broke up lumps of concrete off the premises and used them as missiles. The club had failed to exercise proper control over these visitors and was liable.

In this way a defendant might owe a duty even for damage caused by acts of nature where he has failed to properly deal with the hazard arising.

CASE EXAMPLE

Goldman v Hargrave [1967] 1 AC 645

Here a tree was struck by lightning on the defendant's land and ignited. Clearly the occupier was not responsible for the fire. However, when the defendant failed to deal with the fire and it spread to neighbouring property he was held liable.

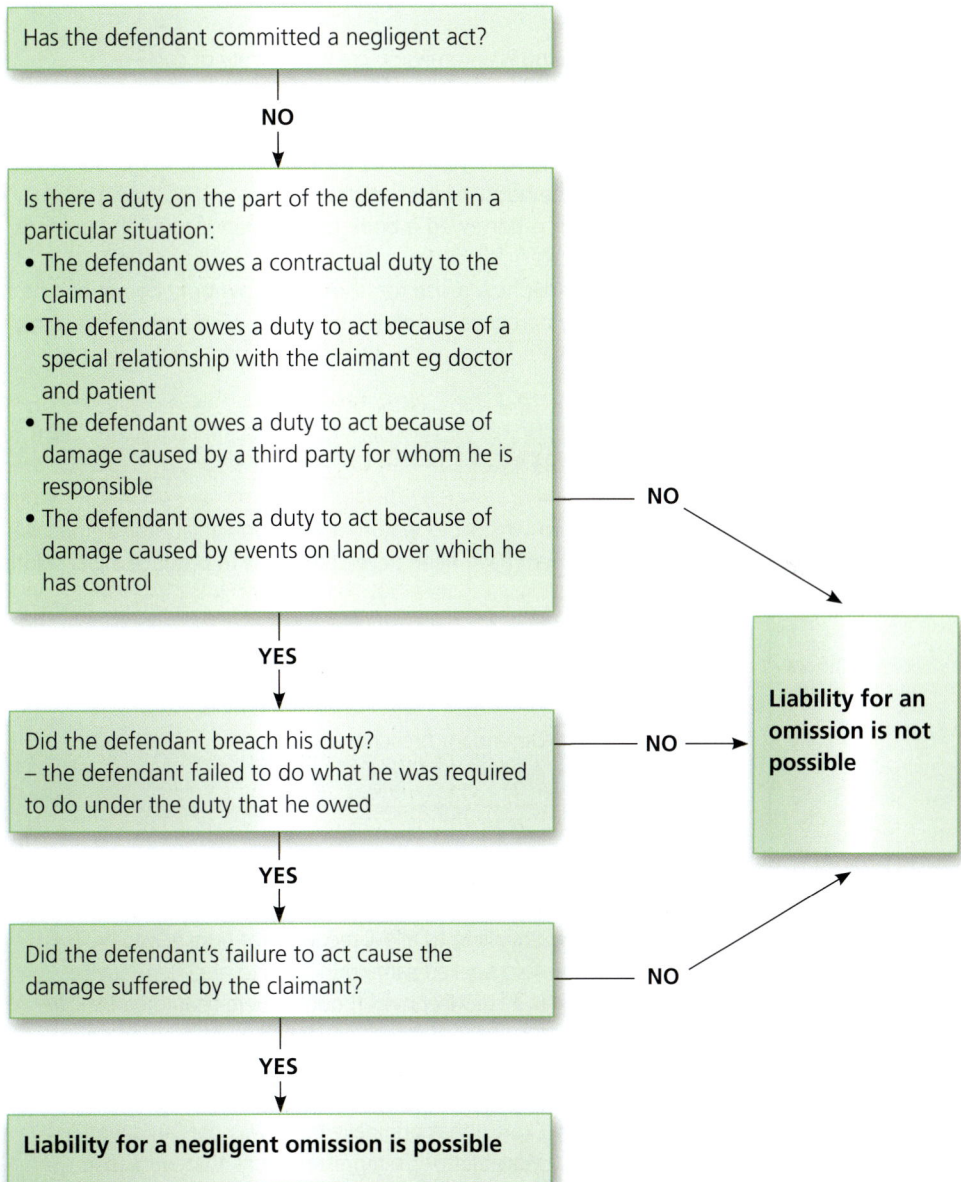

```
┌─────────────────────────────────────────────┐
│ Has the defendant committed a negligent act? │
└─────────────────────────────────────────────┘
                        │
                       NO
                        │
┌─────────────────────────────────────────────┐
│ Is there a duty on the part of the defendant  │
│ in a particular situation:                     │
│ • The defendant owes a contractual duty to     │
│   the claimant                                 │
│ • The defendant owes a duty to act because of  │
│   a special relationship with the claimant eg  │
│   doctor and patient                           │
│ • The defendant owes a duty to act because of  │
│   damage caused by a third party for whom he   │
│   is responsible                               │      NO
│ • The defendant owes a duty to act because of  │
│   damage caused by events on land over which   │
│   he has control                               │
└─────────────────────────────────────────────┘
                       YES
                        │
┌─────────────────────────────────────────────┐
│ Did the defendant breach his duty?            │      NO
│ – the defendant failed to do what he was       │
│ required to do under the duty that he owed     │
└─────────────────────────────────────────────┘
                       YES
                        │
┌─────────────────────────────────────────────┐
│ Did the defendant's failure to act cause the  │      NO
│ damage suffered by the claimant?              │
└─────────────────────────────────────────────┘
                       YES
                        │
┌─────────────────────────────────────────────┐
│ Liability for a negligent omission is possible │
└─────────────────────────────────────────────┘

            Liability for an omission is not possible
```

Figure 6.3 Diagram illustrating the essential elements for a successful claim under *Hedley Byrne*

ACTIVITY

Self-assessment questions

1. What exactly is 'non-feasance'?
2. Why did English law traditionally reject the idea of liability for a failure to act?
3. In which situations will courts impose liability where there has only been an omission to act?
4. What is the common factor in those situations where the courts will impose such liability?
5. What significant warning does the case of *Hudson v Ridge Manufacturing* [1957] 2 QB 348 provide for employers?

ACTIVITY

Quick quiz

Which of the following is an omission creating a duty of care?

1. A man sees another man bleeding to death in the street and walks past.
2. A doctor refuses to attend to a sick patient who then dies.
3. An electrician paid to fit new lights for a householder leaves some bare wires overnight and a child of the house is electrocuted.
4. A person who has borrowed a book from a friend leaves the book on the bus and it is lost.
5. I could help my nephew revise for his A Level Law but I do not and he fails.
6. Sparks from my barbecue are blown by a high wind and set fire to my next door neighbour's shed.

SAMPLE ESSAY QUESTION

Discuss the extent to which the way that rules on liability for a financial loss caused by a negligent misstatement have been developed so as to produce a just solution to a dispute.

Explain the basis of a claim in negligence

- Defendant owes claimant a duty of care
- Defendant breaches the duty
- And causes foreseeable harm

Discuss the original attitude of the courts

- Unwilling to allow recovery for pure economic loss
- Also applied same principles to negligent advice
- But Lord Denning thought there should be liability
- Consider that this reluctance was based on policy grounds so was probably unjust to potential claimants
- Explain that originally there was only an action available for misrepresentations that were made fraudulently

Explain the original basis of a claim for negligent misstatement causing a pecuniary loss

- Existence of a special relationship
- Possession of specialist skill by the person giving the advice
- Reasonable reliance on the defendant's skill and judgment

Discuss the later developments of the tort

- The widest point of liability came with liability owed for advice given by a friend – potentially unfair to possible defendants
- And the tort has impacted upon valuers and auditors particularly
- But courts have since rejected a test of foreseeability and the narrower test of knowledge of the purpose for which the advice is now needed – harder to bring an action
- The test of knowledge includes the purpose for which the statement was made and communicated, the relationship between all relevant parties, and the degree of knowledge of the defendant
- A later development requires assumption of responsibility for the advice given – so again makes an action harder to bring

Discuss potential future development

- Courts have gradually rejected the early expansion and have narrowed the basis for the test clearly aiming to be fair to defendants, but comes at the expense of claimants
- Further expansion is unlikely

KEY FACTS

Liability for omissions	Case
There is no general liability for a failure to act. But there can be liability where there is a positive duty to act which will arise only in specific situations – where	*Smith v Littlewoods Organisation Ltd* (1987)
• there is a contractual duty to act	*Stansbie v Troman* (1948)
• there is a duty based on a special relationship	*Home Office v Dorset Yacht Co* (1970)
• the defendant has a duty to control another person's acts for whom he is responsible	*Haynes v Harwood* (1935)
• the defendant has a duty to control events causing danger on his land.	*Goldman v Hargrave* (1967)

Nervous shock (psychiatric damage)

- Originally no claim possible because of inadequate psychiatric knowledge, fear of fraudulent claims and floodgates opening
- But was later accepted as a recognised psychiatric injury caused by a single traumatic event to defined classes of victim
- Primary victims are those present at the scene and at risk of foreseeable injury or present at the scene and suffering injury *Dulieu v White*
- Secondary victims are those with a close tie of love and affection to the person injured in the accident, with sufficient proximity in time and space to the event or its immediate aftermath and who saw or heard the accident or its immediate aftermath with their own unaided senses
- Rescuers may also claim if they are genuine primary or secondary victims
- There are many potential claimants who cannot claim including: those not suffering a recognisable injury; people not within the area of impact; people not within the area of shock; bystanders; people without close ties to a primary victim; people falling outside of the event or its immediate aftermath; people who are told of the event rather than witnessing it; slow burn victims
- But the development of the law has been inconsistent and there are a number of anomalous cases

Pure economic loss

- Courts have always been unwilling to allow recovery for 'pure economic loss'
- This is because contract law is more appropriate for loss of profit
- Some claims have been successful where there has been a risk also to health
- And also in a 'near contractual' relationship between the two parties

Negligent misstatement

- Originally an action was only available for advice given fraudulently
- Then it was accepted that an action was possible if:
  - there was a special relationship between the parties
  - the party giving the advice had specialist knowledge of the type needed by the other party, and
  - there was reasonable reliance on the advice
- These requirements have since been limited to include:
  - that the reliance is reasonably foreseeable to the defendant
  - that the defendant has knowledge of the purpose for which the advice is needed, and
  - that the defendant has assumed responsibility for the advice given
- There are also some anomalous cases

Liability for omissions

- There is no general liability for a failure to act – usually a defendant must act negligently rather than fail to act
- But there can be liability where there is a positive duty to act
- This arises only in four specific situations:
  - where there is a contractual duty to act
  - where there is a duty based on a special relationship such as doctor and patient
  - where the defendant has a duty to control another person's acts for whom he is responsible, and
  - where the defendant has a duty to control events causing danger on his land

Further reading

Brooman, S, 'Back to basics' [1995] LEJ 23.
Denning, Lord, *The Discipline of Law* (Butterworths, 1979), Part 6, Chapters 3 and 4.
Trindade, F A, 'Reformulation of the nervous shock rules' (2003) 119 LQR 204.

7

Occupiers' liability and liability for defective premises

AIMS AND OBJECTIVES

After reading this chapter you should be able to:

- Understand the nature of liability under the Occupiers' Liability Acts
- Understand the definitions of occupier and premises
- Understand the different types of visitor and the Act appropriate to each
- Understand the scope of the different duties under the two Acts
- Understand the different standard of care appropriate to children
- Understand the means of occupiers avoiding liability in respect of tradesmen, where independent contractors have caused the harm, and the effect of warnings, exclusion clauses and defences
- Be able to critically analyse the Acts
- Be able to apply the law to factual situations and reach conclusions as to liability

7.1 Origins and general character

7.1.1 Introduction and origins

Occupiers' liability concerns the liability of an 'occupier' of land or premises for the injury or loss or damage to property suffered by claimants while on the occupier's 'premises'. Therefore it must immediately be distinguished from damage caused by the defendant's use of his land, which is suffered by the claimant outside of the occupier's land. If this were on the claimant's own land then it might lead to an action in nuisance (see Chapter 9) or possibly *Rylands v Fletcher* (1868) LR 1 Exch 265 (see Chapter 10), or there may in any case be an action in negligence available.

Liability for land and premises falls into two distinct areas:

- Liability by an occupier of premises for loss or injury caused by the state of the premises – such liability can also be divided according to whom has suffered the loss or injury.
- Liability by a person other than an occupier of land for defects in the premises themselves – this involves landlords and builders.

Occupiers' liability is a fairly recent tort and is found in two statutes:

- the Occupiers' Liability Act 1957 – which is concerned with the duty of care owed to all lawful visitors and
- the Occupiers' Liability Act 1984 – which is concerned with the duty owed to people other than lawful visitors, the major group here being **trespassers**.

Both areas then are statutory in form, but certainly in the case of occupiers' liability have developed out of negligence. As a result much of the terminology and many of the principles are the same or similar to basic negligence principles. Indeed, though the Acts do contain extensive definition, where definitions are not supplied in the Acts these are to be found in the common law.

Inevitably there is some overlap with negligence. The basic liability arises from the loss or injury caused by the 'state of the premises'. Loss or damage that arises other than because of the state of the premises then should be claimed for under negligence where this is possible.

CASE EXAMPLE

Ogwo v Taylor [1987] 2 WLR 988

Here there was no liability under the Act when a fireman was injured in a fire on the defendant's premises. As Brown LJ commented in the case the fire did not result from defects in the state of the premises, so liability was in negligence.

Nevertheless academics have argued that the Act should still apply in the case of damage caused other than by the state of the premises since s 1(1) of the 1957 Act states that the Act should apply '. . . in respect of dangers due to the state of the premises or to things done or omitted to be done on them.'

The law on occupiers' liability is generally accepted as being very straightforward:

QUOTATION

'the 1957 Occupiers' Liability Act . . . has always been regarded as a particularly well drafted statute, partly because it is one of the few statutes which attempts to give illustrations and examples of the way in which it is to operate, and partly because there has been little litigation which involves its interpretation.'

V Harpwood, *Principles of Tort* (Cavendish Publishing, 2000)

On the other hand the law on defective premises has never been considered to be particularly straightforward:

QUOTATION

'few areas of tort have fallen into greater confusion than the liability of those who build and sell premises.'

W Rogers, *The Law of Tort* (Sweet & Maxwell, 1989)

Although the 1957 Act has been described as a particularly well drafted statute it still suffers from under-use. The Pearson Report in 1978 for instance recognised that as many as 27 per cent of reported accidents occur in the home. Nevertheless apparently very few claims are made following domestic accidents. There can obviously be many reasons for this. These include ignorance of the possibility of making a claim, a natural reluctance to sue friends or family, and sometimes even a lack of household insurance might prevent a claim.

7.1.2 Definition of occupier – potential defendants

In the case of both the 1957 Act and the 1984 Act potential defendants are identified as being occupiers of premises.

There is in fact no statutory definition of 'occupier' in either Act. Section 1(2) of the 1957 Act merely states that the rules apply '. . . in consequence of a person's occupation or control of premises . . .'. In the absence of a statutory test the established test for determining occupation then is found in the common law.

CASE EXAMPLE

Wheat v E Lacon & Co Ltd [1966] AC 552

A manager of a public house was given the right to rent out rooms in his private quarters even though he had no proprietary interest in the premises. When a paying guest fell on an unlit staircase, the House of Lords held that both the manager and his employers could be occupiers for the purposes of the Act. In the event neither had actually breached their duty since it was a stranger who had removed the light bulb and therefore there was no liability to the manager.

Earlier in the Court of Appeal Lord Denning had commented:

JUDGMENT

'There is no difficulty in having more than one occupier at one and the same time, each of which is under a duty of care to visitors.'

Identifying the occupier will depend then on various considerations, including the nature of the interest held and therefore the particular duty owed. For instance, in a case like the above the brewery might very obviously be responsible for ensuring that there were no defects in the wiring, while the publican himself might be responsible for ensuring that light bulbs were changed.

So there can be dual or multiple simultaneous occupation of premises and the identity of the defendant, which party was in control of the premises, may depend on the circumstances in which the damage or injury was suffered.

CASE EXAMPLE

Collier v Anglian Water Authority, *The Times*, 26th March, 1983

Here a promenade formed part of the sea defences for which the water authority was responsible. The local authority owned the land, and was responsible for cleaning the promenade. Both could therefore be classed as occupiers for the purposes of the Act. When the claimant was injured as a result of disrepair to the promenade, it was the water authority rather than the local authority which was liable, though both were occupiers.

Control and therefore occupation of premises does not require either proprietary interest or possession, so the position is quite different to trespass to land (see later Chapter 8). All that is required for liability is that the defendant has sufficient control of the premises at the time that the damage was caused to be responsible for it.

CASE EXAMPLE

Harris v Birkenhead Corporation [1976] 1 All ER 341

Here a four-year-old child had been injured in an empty house which was not boarded up or secured in any way. The child had entered the premises and fallen from a second floor window. Even though the council had not yet taken possession of the house they were liable since they had served notice of a compulsory purchase order and were effectively in control of the premises. They were held to be occupiers and liable even though they had not yet taken physical control because in effect they had legal control of the premises and were the best placed in that sense to avoid accidents of the sort that occurred.

In the final analysis the court in applying the control test to determine the identity of the defendant will be influenced by the ability of the party to meet a successful claim, whether through insurance or by other means.

7.1.3 Definition of 'premises'

The Acts are again relatively silent on the meaning of premises and there is no fixed definition. Some limited reference is given in s 1(3)(a) which refers to a person having occupation or control of any '. . . fixed or moveable structure, including any vessel, vehicle and aircraft . . .'

As a result the common law again applies and besides the obvious, such as houses, buildings and the land itself, premises have also been held to include:

- ships in dry dock – *London Graving Dock v Horton* [1951] AC 737
- vehicles – *Hartwell v Grayson* [1947] KB 901
- aircraft – *Fosbroke-Hobbes v Airwork Ltd* [1937] 1 All ER 108
- lifts – *Haseldine v Daw & Son Ltd* [1941] 2 KB 343
- and even a ladder – *Wheeler v Copas* [1981] 3 All ER 405.

7.2 Liability to lawful visitors under the 1957 Act

7.2.1 Potential claimants

The 1957 Act was passed in order to simplify a fairly complex common law, whereby the duty owed to a person entering premises varied according to the capacity in which that person entered. The Act introduced a common duty to be applied to all lawful visitors.

By s 1(2) the classes of people to whom the occupier owes a duty remains as it was under common law. These are called visitors under the Act and as a result of s 1(2) will include:

- Invitees – these are people who not only have permission to enter but whose entry is in the material interest of the occupier – it can include, for example, friends making a social call, but also people invited onto land for a specific purpose, for example to give a quote for work.
- Licensees – these are people whose entry is to the material interest of the occupier, for example customers, they can include anyone with permission to be on the premises for whatever purpose (there was a very unfair distinction drawn between invitees and licensees at common law – the latter were treated somewhat harshly by the common law, being entitled to no more than warnings of danger of which the occupier was aware – it was indeed criticism of this unfairness by the Law Reform Committee in 1954 that in part led to the passing of the 1957 Act) – visitors under an implied license will need to prove that the conduct of the occupier amounted to a grant of a licence.

CASE EXAMPLE

Lowery v Walker [1911] AC 10

Ten members of the public had used a short cut across the defendant's land for many years. While the defendant objected, he took no legal steps to stop it. When he set loose a wild horse onto the land, which savaged the claimant, he was liable. The House of Lords concluded that the defendant's conduct had created an implied licence in favour of the claimant.

An implied licence can be created in the following situations, for example:

- Those entering under a contractual agreement which could occur in one of two situations:
    - where the person has a direct contract with the occupier, for example a painter and decorator, plumber, etc – in this case the express terms of the contract will determine the extent of the duty or there may be an implied duty to keep the premises safe – by s 5(1) the common duty of care will apply unless the contract actually provides for a greater level of care
    - where the person entering has a contract with a third party, for example a sub-contractor – in this case that person ranks as a licensee and the question is whether or not they could be subject to the exclusion clauses imposed by the occupier.
- Those not requiring any permission to enter because of a legal right to enter, for example meter readers, police officers in execution of a warrant, etc – s 6(2) provides that such persons are 'visitors for that purpose whether or not the occupier has given permission'. Persons entering under this category traditionally would have included those exercising either public or private rights of way – specific rules covered these parties at common law but neither is covered by the 1957 Act.

The 1957 Act imposes no duty of care towards trespassers. A more limited duty is owed to trespassers under the Occupiers' Liability Act 1984. Certain other categories of entrants are also not covered by the 1957 Act. These include:

- Those using a private right of way – here the 1984 Act now applies but prior to that there would have been no liability.

CASE EXAMPLE

Holden v White [1982] 2 WLR 1030

Here a milkman was injured because of a defective manhole cover on the defendant's premises while using a private right of way. It was held that he was not a visitor for the purposes of the 1957 Act and his claim was unsuccessful.

- Those entering under an access agreement or order under the National Parks and Access to the Countryside Act 1949 (which is specifically excluded by s 1(4) of the 1957 Act but is also now dealt with under the 1984 Act).
- Those using a public right of way – these are excluded by both the 1957 Act and the 1984 Act and will fall under common law with the tortfeasor being liable for misfeasance but not nonfeasance unlike either Act.

CASE EXAMPLE

McGeown v Northern Ireland Housing Executive [1994] 3 All ER 53

The claimant lived in a cul-de-sac on a housing estate owned by the defendants. She was injured on a footpath belonging to the defendants but which had become a public right of way. The reason for the injury was a failure to maintain the footpath and her action failed.

ACTIVITY

Quick quiz

Consider which of the following potential claimants would be able to class themselves as visitors for the purposes of the OLA 1957 and why.

1. Trevor is a milkman delivering milk to Archie's door.
2. Kurt is a milkman who picks flowers in Archie's garden after delivering the milk.
3. Gordon, a football fan with a season ticket for the Wanderers, arrives at the ground on Wednesday night for the match with United.

4. Hannah regularly crosses Farmer Giles' field using a well-known public path.
5. Greg is at Mavis's house on Monday morning as agreed to paint the outside.
6. Ali is a police officer who has called at Brian's house for some routine enquiries.
7. Tom regularly climbs over his neighbour's back fence and comes through his back garden on his way home, knowing that his neighbour works later so will be out.
8. Parminder calls at her friend Baljinder's house as arranged to enjoy a meal together.
9. Baljinder is at her friend Parminder's house for a meal and enters Parminder's bedroom and takes a valuable ring.
10. Yuri is an employee of British Gas and has called at Ojukwu's house to read the gas meter.

7.2.2 The scope of the Act – the common duty of care

The extent of the duty of care is set out in s 2(1)

SECTION

's 2(1) An occupier owes the same duty, the common duty of care, to all his visitors except insofar as he is free to do and does extend, restrict, modify or exclude his duty to any visitors by agreement or otherwise.'

'Common' here is obviously used to signify that the Act applies to all types of lawful visitors by comparison with the more disparate range of duties that were formerly held under the common law.

The nature of the duty is found in s 2(2). The duty is to

SECTION

's 2(2) . . . take such care as in all the circumstances of the case is reasonable to see that the visitor will be reasonably safe for the purpose for which he is invited or permitted by the occupier to be there.'

Three key points need to be made straight away:

■ Firstly, the standard of care is that generally applied in negligence, the standard of the 'reasonable man'. As a result the occupier is merely obliged to guard against foreseeable risks, not unexpected risks.

CASE EXAMPLE

Fryer v Pearson, *The Times*, 4th April, 2000

A family visitor was injured by a needle while kneeling on the floor. The court held that the occupiers, the house owners, had not breached the duty. There was nothing to suggest that they knew the needle was on the floor or had created the danger. The Court of Appeal distinguished *Ward v Tesco Stores* [1976] 1 WLR 810 where a greater duty might be owed by a shopkeeper towards customers slipping on spilled yoghurt.

It is certainly true that an occupier will not have to go to extraordinary lengths to protect a visitor from harm.

CASE EXAMPLE

Cole v Davis-Gilbert and the Royal British Legion [2007] All ER (D) 20 (Mar)

A woman broke her leg when she stepped on a hole hidden by grass while she was crossing a village green. The hole was used for inserting a maypole during annual fetes. She sued the owner of the village green arguing that, as an occupier, he had a duty to keep visitors safe.

She also sued the British Legion which had erected the maypole and filled the hole after the fete, some 21 months before the woman's injuries. At first instance she failed against the owner but succeeded against the Royal British Legion. The Court of Appeal held that there could be no duty on the owner to inspect the green for holes. Even a daily inspection could not guarantee that there would be no holes as the green was used by many people for many different purposes. Even if the British Legion owed a duty to see that the hole was properly filled in, this duty could not last indefinitely, and certainly not for 21 months after it last filled it. As Lord Justice Scott Baker observed in his judgment, sometimes accidents are just pure accidents.

- Secondly, the duty in the 1957 Act only applies so long as the visitor is carrying out activities that are authorised within the terms of the visit. So if the visitor strays he may lose protection under the 1957 Act, although an action might still be possible since the 1984 Act might still apply.
- Thirdly, the duty is to keep the visitor safe, and not necessarily to maintain safe premises. If the latter were the case it would make industry unworkable, so it is possible to cordon off unsafe parts as long as the visitor is still made safe in those parts to which he lawfully has access.

CASE EXAMPLE

Searson v Brioland [2005] EWCA Civ 26

The claimant was injured entering a hotel to attend a wedding because the threshold was higher than the floor level. The occupier was liable and should have placed a warning notice.

However, because of the scope and potential limitations of the duty the Act sensibly makes some different rules for particular classes of visitor.

7.2.3 Liability to children

Under s 2(3) the occupier

SECTION

's 2(3) . . . must be prepared for children to be less careful than adults . . . the premises must be reasonably safe for a child of that age . . .'

This demonstrates again that it is the visitor that must be kept safe and that in the case of children the standard of care is measured subjectively rather than objectively.

The reasoning is perfectly logical, what may pose no threat to an adult may nevertheless be very dangerous to a child.

CASE EXAMPLE

Moloney v Lambeth LBC (1966) 64 LGR 440

Here a four-year-old fell through a gap in railings guarding a stairwell and was injured. An adult could not have fallen through the gap so such an injury would have been impossible. Nevertheless it was dangerous to a child and a child in any case may have been incapable of appreciating the risk involved. The occupier was held to be liable by the court.

Children in any case are taken to be unlikely to appreciate risks in a way that an adult would and indeed might even be attracted to the danger. As a result an occupier should do nothing to attract the child to the danger and must guard against any kind of 'allurement' which places a child visitor at risk of harm.

CASE EXAMPLE

Glasgow Corporation v Taylor [1922] 1 AC 44

Here a seven-year-old child ate poisonous berries in a botanical gardens and died as a result. The shrub on which the berries grew was not fenced off in any way. The court held that the occupier should have expected that the berries might naturally attract a young child's interest and the occupier was liable.

Nevertheless, the mere existence of an allurement on its own is not sufficient ground for liability.

CASE EXAMPLE

Liddle v Yorkshire (North Riding) CC [1944] 2 KB 101

A child was injured when he jumped off a soil bank while showing off to his friends. The court held that, despite the obvious allurement, the defendant was not liable since the occupier had warned the child away from the bank on numerous previous occasions.

In fact, even though an allurement exists there will be no liability on the occupier if the damage or injury suffered is not foreseeable. As with negligence generally it is the general type of damage that must be foreseen rather than the specific circumstances in which the damage occurs.

CASE EXAMPLE

Jolley v London Borough of Sutton [2000] 3 All ER 409, HL; [1998] 3 All ER 559, CA

The council failed to move an abandoned boat from an estuary shore for two years. Children regularly played in the boat and it was clearly a potential danger. When two young boys of 14 jacked the boat up to repair it, the boat fell on one, injuring him. In the Court of Appeal the action for compensation failed, since it was held that, while the boat was an obvious allurement, the course of action taken by the boys and therefore the specific type of damage were not foreseeable. The House of Lords reversed this. The House felt that it was an obvious risk that children playing on or near the boat might be injured. It was sufficient for liability that some injury was foreseeable.

As Lord Hoffmann said in the House of Lords in the case:

JUDGMENT

'. . . the [trial] judge's broad description of the risk as being that children would "meddle with the boat at the risk of some physical injury" was the correct one to adopt . . .'

So the House of Lords applied the principle of causation from *The Wagon Mound*.

Obviously the decision can seem harsh since it would be quite difficult to argue that the council could in fact have foreseen the very unusual way in which the injuries occurred. Nevertheless, the Act imposes a duty on an occupier to recognise that children may behave in very different ways to adults. It is possible therefore to see the judgment as a very practical application of the law.

QUOTATION

'In essence, the House of Lords has conformed in case law what all parents knew already: the only predictable attribute of children is that they are unpredictable, and society (including councils) should protect them accordingly.'

S Brooman, 'Expect the Unexpected', L Ex, November 2000, p 34

In any case the courts will sometimes take the view that very young children should be under the supervision of a parent or other adult. In this case the occupier might find that he is relieved of liability.

CASE EXAMPLE

Phipps v Rochester Corporation [1955] 1 QB 450

A five-year-old child was injured having fallen down a trench dug by the defendant council where the child frequently played. The defendant was not liable because the court concluded that the parents should have had a child of that age under proper control.

In his judgment Devlin J explained the position

JUDGMENT

'. . . the responsibility for the safety of little children must rest primarily upon the parents; it is their duty to see that such children are not allowed to wander about by themselves, or at the least to satisfy themselves that the places to which they do allow their children to go unaccompanied are safe for them to go. It would not be socially desirable if parents were, as a matter of course, able to shift the burden of looking after their children from their own shoulders to those persons who happen to have accessible bits of land.'

7.2.4 Liability to persons entering to exercise a calling

Sensibly the Act also has a more particular attitude to professional visitors, taking the view that, by s 2(3)(b), in relation to activities carried on within their trade, the occupier is entitled to expect that '. . . a person in the exercise of his calling, will appreciate and guard against any special risks ordinarily incident to it . . .'.

So whereas an occupier must accept child visitors to be less capable, in the case of visitors exercising their calling the occupier will not be liable where tradesmen fail to guard against risks which they should know about.

CASE EXAMPLE

Roles v Nathan [1963] 1 WLR 1117

The Court of Appeal refused to impose liability on the occupiers when chimney sweeps died after inhaling carbon monoxide fumes while cleaning flues in an industrial chimney. The sweeps should have accepted the advice of the occupiers to complete the work with the boilers off rather than leaving them lit.

However, tradesmen might still have an action against their employer if the latter has agreed to an unsafe system of work.

CASE EXAMPLE

General Cleaning Contractors v Christmas [1953] AC 180

Occupiers were not liable for an injury sustained when a window cleaner fell after a window closed on him, but the employers were.

However, the existence of a skill is not proof *per se* that the occupier is not liable to the skilled visitor. It depends on whether the normal safeguards associated with the trade would have been sufficient to avert the loss or injury.

CASE EXAMPLE

Salmon v Seafarers Restaurants Ltd [1983] 1 WLR 1264

Owners of a chip shop were liable for the injuries caused to a fireman which were unavoidable because of the character of the fire. The fireman was obviously bound to take the normal risks associated with fire fighting. However, he had exercised all of the normal skills of a fireman and it was only the character of the fire that caused his injuries, not anything that he could have guarded against himself. As a result of this the court held the occupier liable.

7.2.5 Liability for the torts of independent contractors

Generally the occupier will be able to avoid liability for loss or injuries suffered by his visitors when the cause of damage is the negligence of an independent contractor hired by the occupier. Unders 2(4) the occupier is not liable for 'damage caused to a visitor by a danger due to the faulty execution of any work or construction, maintenance or repair by an independent contractor employed by the occupier'.

It is a sensible rule because reputable contractors will in any case be covered by their own insurance and so the claimant will still be able to recover compensation.

However, three requirements will apply:

- Firstly, it must be reasonable for the occupier to have entrusted the work to the independent contractor.
- Secondly, the contractor hired must be competent to carry out the task.
- Thirdly, if possible the occupier must inspect the work.

It is reasonable to hire a contractor

It must be reasonable for the occupier to have entrusted the work to the independent contractor in the first place. This in itself depends on the character of the occupier and also on the nature of the work done. For example, much less might be expected of a private householder than of a business which might already employ its own specialists.

CASE EXAMPLE

Haseldine v Daw & Son Ltd [1941] 2 KB 343

Here the issue was the death of the claimant following the negligent repair of a lift by the independent contractors. The occupier was not liable because repair of a lift is a highly specialist activity and could not be expected of the occupier. The court accepted that the occupier had discharged his duty by hiring a supposedly competent contractor to carry out the work.

The contractor must be competent to carry out the work

For the occupier to avoid liability, the contractor that he hired must be competent to carry out the actual task required. Again there is little adequate check that somebody like a householder can make. They might improve their chance of avoiding liability as an occupier by using contractors recommended by a trade association etc.

CASE EXAMPLE

Ferguson v Welsh [1987] 3 All ER 777

Demolition contractors were hired by the local authority and also employed the claimant to complete the work. When the claimant was injured as a result of their unsafe working systems the court held that the local authority was liable.

As Goff LJ explained, the local authority has a duty not to

JUDGMENT

'countenance the unsafe working methods of cowboy operators.'

The fact that the contractor fails to carry insurance for the activity should be a fair indication to the occupier that the contractor is not competent.

CASE EXAMPLE

Bottomley v Todmorden Cricket Club [2003] EWCA Civ 1575

The club hired a stunt team to carry out a 'firework display'. The team chose to use ordinary gunpowder, petrol and propane gas rather than the more traditional fireworks and also then enlisted the help of the claimant, an unpaid amateur with no experience of pyrotechnics, for the stunt. The claimant was burnt and broke an arm when the stunt went wrong. The stunt team had no insurance and the court held that this was sufficient to impose liability on the cricket club.

Although this will not always apply if there are other accepted means of assessing the independent contractor's competence to carry out the work.

CASE EXAMPLE

Naylor (t/a Mainstream) v Payling [2004] EWCA Civ 560

The claimant was injured while being thrown out of a nightclub owing to the negligence of the door attendant. The door attendant was supplied by an independent contractor. The claimant successfully sued on the basis that the nightclub had negligently failed to check whether the independent contractor had insurance and for negligently failing to ascertain whether the independent contractor was competent. The nightclub appealed and the Court of Appeal upheld that appeal. It held that there was no obligation to check whether the independent contractor was insured since the nightclub had complied with a local scheme supported by both the local authority and the police for establishing whether door attendants were suitably qualified for the work.

The occupier may be expected to inspect the work

Thirdly, and only if it is in fact possible, the occupier must inspect the work to ensure that it has been carried out to an appropriate standard.

Inevitably the more complex and technical the work and the less expert the occupier, then the less reasonable it is to impose this obligation. It may be sufficient that a competent contractor was hired. Although where an inspection is straightforward then the requirement still exists.

CASE EXAMPLE

Woodward v Mayor of Hastings [1945] KB 174

Occupiers were liable when a child was injured on school steps which were negligently left in an icy state after they had been cleared of snow. The danger should have been obvious to the occupiers and the court held them liable.

In the case it was identified that there was

JUDGMENT

'no esoteric quality in the nature of the work which the cleaning of a snow covered step demands.'

However, it may be that in certain circumstances the occupier is obliged to delegate supervision of the work to a suitable professional, for example an architect, in order to ultimately avoid liability for any damage or injury.

CASE EXAMPLE

A M F International Ltd v Magnet Bowling Ltd [1968] 2 All ER 789

The company AMF International were contracted to install bowling equipment in a centre that was being built by contractors hired by Magnet. The contractors gave the go ahead for the equipment to be installed but then AMF's equipment was destroyed when the partially built building was flooded during torrential rainfall. Magnet were held to be liable for failing to check on the state that the contractors had left the building in before AMF were instructed to enter it.

One interesting aspect of the occupier's duty to inspect is the duty to inspect also that the independent contractor is insured so that he may stand the loss if found liable. This in itself is also another example of the occupier's duty to ensure that a competent contractor is chosen, since it can be assumed that a competent contractor would not engage in work without public liability insurance cover.

CASE EXAMPLE

Gwillam v West Hertfordshire NHS Trust [2002] 3 WLR 1425

The hospital trust was responsible for a fund raising fair held on its premises for which it hired a 'splat-wall' from a firm called Club Entertainments who were also responsible for operating it. (A 'splat wall' is a wall that a person wearing a Velcro suit will stick to after bouncing from a trampoline.) The claimant was injured when she fell because the wall had been negligently assembled. As part of the contract between the trust and Club Entertainments the wall was to be covered by the latter's public liability insurance. However, this had expired four days before the fair and the claimant sought damages from the trust. Both Lord Woolf CJ and Lord Justice Waller in the Court of Appeal held that there was a duty to ensure that the contractor had insurance cover, but that the trust had not breached this duty. Lord Woolf CJ in any case felt that the trust had not breached the duty to keep the woman safe while on its premises.

ACTIVITY

Quick quiz

Consider whether or not a duty would be owed under the Occupiers' Liability Act 1957 in the following circumstances and suggest whether an action is likely to succeed

1. Ted, a burglar, has been injured when he broke into Melanie's house and fell downstairs in the dark because the handrail was broken and had not been repaired.
2. Ted, a postman, was injured while delivering letters to Melanie's house when the chimney pot fell on him.
3. Ted, an electrician, was injured when he was electrocuted by a live wire while he was fitting new lights for Melanie.
4. Ted, a four-year-old child, was very ill after he ate berries from a bush overhanging from Melanie's garden. Ted was on his own on the pavement outside Melanie's house at 7 pm at night when he ate the berries. Melanie had shouted to Ted on several occasions before when she had seen him going to pick the berries.

7.2.6 Avoiding the duty

As we have already seen, according to s 2(1) the occupier is free to extend, restrict, modify or exclude his duty to visitors. This can be achieved by the occupier in one of three ways.

Warnings

Under s 2(4)(a) a warning will not absolve the occupier of liability unless '. . . in all the circumstances it was enough to enable the visitor to be reasonably safe.'

What amounts to a sufficient warning then will be a question of fact in each case. In *Roles v Nathan* ([1963] 1 WLR 1117) for instance Lord Denning used the example of a warning that the only access to the premises over a rotting footbridge was unsafe. This he said could not absolve the occupier because the visitor had no other means of access and so would have no choice but to use the unsafe bridge. Presumably this means that if there were another means of access which was safe, then the warning not to use the footbridge may well be sufficient.

Sometimes in any case even a very precise warning may be insufficient to safeguard the visitor and the occupier may be obliged to set up barriers instead to ensure the visitor's safety.

CASE EXAMPLE

Rae v Mars (UK) Ltd (1990) 3 EG 80

Here a warning notice was used in respect of a deep pit inside the entrance of a dark shed with no artificial lighting. The occupier was held liable because the pit was immediately inside the entrance and so the warning was insufficient to safeguard the visitor from the danger.

However, the occupier will not be obliged to take excessive steps to avoid danger when the danger is obvious and sufficient steps have been taken to prevent harm.

CASE EXAMPLE

Beaton v Devon County Council [2002] EWCA Civ 1675

The claimant was injured while riding through a cycle tunnel. The tunnel was in good condition and the defendant council had supplied good lighting throughout it. There were two gullies in the tunnel but this was well known. The Court of Appeal held that the council had done everything practicable to keep cyclists safe.

The actual wording of warning signs can be critical in determining whether liability is avoided. A distinction must be made between a proper warning, for example 'Danger steps slippery when wet' and mere attempts to set up a defence of *volenti*, for example 'Persons enter at their own risk', which will not absolve liability and even ones that are attempts to exclude liability, for example 'No liability will be accepted for any injury howsoever caused' will be subject to the limitations in the Unfair Contracts Terms Act 1977, particularly s 2(1) in this case.

Nevertheless, there are certain risks that are possibly so obvious to all that a court will decide that no additional warning is needed in the circumstances.

CASE EXAMPLE

Staples v West Dorset DC (1995) 93 LGR 536

Danger of wet algae on a high wall at Lyme Regis should have been obvious. Therefore there was no additional duty to warn of the danger and no liability on the council when a visitor slipped on the wall and was injured.

Exclusion clauses

Section 2(1) of the 1957 Act specifically refers to the right of the occupier to exclude liability 'by agreement or otherwise'. Therefore they can be included as a term in a contractual licence and may be alternatively communicated in an effective notice.

CASE EXAMPLE

Ashdown v Samuel Williams & Sons Ltd [1957] 1 QB 409

The claimant was injured by the negligent shunting of railway trucks while on the occupier's land. She was unable to recover for injuries sustained in a shunting yard because notices excluding liability were sufficiently bought to her attention and she was no more than a contractual licensee when she entered.

The use of exclusion clauses, however, will be subject to various restrictions:

- They are apparently unavailable in the case of persons entering under a legal right.
- They will not apply in the case of strangers, for example a tenant's visitors, because they will not have had any chance in advance to agree to the exclusion – this is under s 3(1) – however, such visitors will be able to take advantage of any additional protections identified in the contract.
- They will most probably fail against children, who may be unable to read and who may not fully understand their implications.
- They will not be allowed in respect of death or personal injury caused by the occupier's negligence because this will be prevented by s 2(1) Unfair Contract Terms Act 1977.
- There is also an additional argument that, since the Occupiers' Liability Act 1984 imposes a minimum standard of care owed to trespassers, then this minimum standard should be beyond exclusion, or trespassers would have better rights than lawful visitors.

General defences

There are two possible defences:

a The claimant's contributory negligence. Under the Law Reform (Contributory Negligence) Act 1945 this has the effect of reducing awards of damages according to the extent to which the court believes that the visitor is responsible for his own injuries or loss.

b *Volenti non fit injuria* – consent. Section 2(5) allows that the occupier '. . . has no liability to a visitor in respect of risks willingly accepted as his by the visitor . . .'. However, a number of basic requirements apply:

■ The risk must be fully understood by the visitor.

CASE EXAMPLE

Simms v Leigh RFC [1960] 2 All ER 923

There was no liability to a rugby football player when the injury was sustained within the normal rules of the game.

■ Mere knowledge of the risk is also insufficient, it must actually be accepted by the visitor and the knowledge must be sufficient to make the visitor safe.

CASE EXAMPLE

White v Blackmore [1972] 2 QB 651

General knowledge that 'jalopy racing' was a dangerous activity did not mean that the claimant had accepted inadequate safety arrangements. The court held the occupier liable.

■ If the claimant has no choice but to enter the premises then he cannot be taken to have accepted the risk and the defence will be unavailable.

CASE EXAMPLE

Burnett v British Waterways Board [1973] 2 All ER 631

A claimant entering the defendant's dry dock on a barge had no choice but to be there and so volenti was unavailable as a defence.

■ Express warnings that the claimant enters at his own risk may well be caught by the Unfair Contract Terms Act 1977.

ACTIVITY

Self-assessment questions

1. Who exactly is a visitor?
2. What sorts of people are non-visitors?
3. What decides whether a person is an occupier?
4. Why is the duty called 'the common duty of care'?
5. What exactly is the duty owed by the occupier?
6. Why should children have a different duty of care applied to them?
7. What exactly is 'allurement'?
8. What protection does the case of *Phipps v Rochester Corporation* give to an occupier?
9. When will a tradesman be able to successfully sue an occupier?
10. When will an occupier be liable for the negligent acts or omissions of people who have carried out work on his premises?
11. How can an occupier avoid being liable to a lawful visitor?
12. When will a warning sign protect an occupier from liability and when will it not?
13. When is an exclusion clause likely to be used and what will prevent it from succeeding?

Is the Defendant an OCCUPIER of PREMISES?

• D has sole control of premises at time harm caused to C
• D is one of many people with interest in premises but was in control at material times

NO

NO LIABILITY

YES

Is the Claimant a VISITOR?

• Invited onto premises by D
• Enters to pursue a contract
• Enters under a licence granted by D
• Enters with legal authority

NO

Is the Claimant:

• A trespasser
• Entering under the National Parks and Access to the Countryside Act 1949
• Using a private right of way

YES

YES

OLA 1984 MAY APPLY

Has D BREACHED his DUTY?

D failed to keep C safe for the legitimate purposes of C's visit

NO

NO LIABILITY UNDER OLA 1957

YES

Can D AVOID LIABILITY?

• D provided an effective warning
• D can rely on a valid exclusion
• C consented or is contributorily negligent

YES

NO

D LIABLE UNDER 1957 ACT

Figure 7.1 The assessment of liability under the Occupiers' Liability Act 1957

Occupiers' liability – general	Case
Occupiers' liability is covered by two Acts: the Occupiers' Liability Act 1957 in the case of lawful 'visitors', and the Occupiers' Liability Act 1984 in the case of trespassers.	
An 'occupier' is anybody in actual control of the land.	*Wheat v Lacon* (1966)
Premises is widely defined and has included even a ladder.	*Wheeler v Copas* (1981)

The duty and the standard of care in the 1957 Act	Case/statute
A 'common duty of care' is owed to all lawful visitors.	s 2(1)
The duty is to ensure that the visitor is safe for the purposes of the visit.	s 2(2)
Must take extra care for children, who are less careful than adults and not put extra danger or 'allurements' in their path.	s 2(3) *Glasgow Corporation v Taylor* (1922)
Applies to any foreseeable danger to the child regardless of what injury is actually caused.	*Jolley v London Borough of Sutton* (2000)
Although it is assumed that parents should keep control of young children.	*Phipps v Rochester Corporation* (1955)
A person carrying out a trade or calling on the occupier's premises must prepare for the risks associated with the trade.	*Roles v Nathan* (1963)
The occupier will not be liable for damage which is the result of work done by independent contractors if:	
• it is reasonable to entrust the work	*Haseldine v Daw* (1941)
• a reputable contractor is chosen	*Ferguson v Welsh* (1987)
• the occupier is not obliged to inspect the work.	*Woodward v Mayor of Hastings* (1945)

Avoiding the duty	Case
Possible to avoid liability where:	
• adequate warnings are given	*Rae v Mars* (1990)
• exclusion clauses can be relied on – subject to the Unfair Contract Terms Act	
• defences of consent or contributory negligence apply.	

7.3 Liability to trespassers and non-visitors under the 1984 Act

7.3.1 Common law and the duty of common humanity

The 1984 Act was introduced to provide a limited duty of care mainly towards trespassers. The Act came about because traditionally at common law trespassers were treated rather harshly and an occupier owed such entrants no duty at all, other than possibly to refrain from deliberately or recklessly inflicting damage or injury.

CASE EXAMPLE

Bird v Holbreck (1828) 4 Bing 628

This case did not particularly create any duty to protect a trespasser from harm but it finally made the use of mantraps illegal.

However, an occupier was still entitled to take reasonable steps in his own protection or in the protection of his property.

CASE EXAMPLE

Clayton v Deane (1817) Taunt 489

The court here accepted that an occupier was entitled to use reasonable deterrents to keep trespassers out, in this case broken glass on top of a wall. The requirement was that the deterrent should be reasonably visible to the trespasser.

The common law could be particularly harsh when it was applied to child trespassers who might have limited understanding, either of the risks confronting them, or indeed the nature of trespass itself.

CASE EXAMPLE

Addie v Dumbreck [1929] AC 358

Children frequently played on colliery premises and near to dangerous machinery and were turned away by the owners. When one child was injured the court held that there was no liability on the occupier since the child was a trespasser.

Because of the growth of more dangerous premises and taking into account the difficulties of making children appreciate danger many attempts were made to change the law and this was finally achieved with the establishment of the so-called 'common duty of humanity'.

CASE EXAMPLE

British Railways Board v Herrington [1972] AC 877

A six-year-old was badly burned when straying onto an electrified railway line, through vandalised fencing. It was well known that the fences were often broken and that small children played near the line and the railway board regularly repaired it. The House of Lords, using the *Practice Statement*, established the 'common duty of humanity'. This was a limited duty owed to child trespassers when the occupier knew of the danger and of the likelihood of the trespass, and had the skill, knowledge and resources to avoid an accident.

This duty would obviously operate in fairly limited circumstances and was not without criticism or difficulties. Because of some of the impracticalities of the rule the 1984 Act was passed.

7.3.2 When the Act applies

By s 1(1)(a) a duty applies in respect of people other than visitors (who are covered by the 1957 Act) for

SECTION

's 1(1)(a) . . . injury on the premises by reason of any danger due to the state of the premises or things done or omitted to be done on them.'

Thus the 1984 Act provides compensation for injuries only. Damage to property is not covered, reflecting an understandable view that trespassers are deserving of less protection than are lawful visitors.

The occupier will only owe a duty under s1(3) if:

SECTION

's 1(3)(a) he is aware of the danger or has reasonable grounds to believe it exists;
   (b) he knows or has reasonable grounds to believe that the other is in the vicinity of the danger (in either case whether the other has lawful authority for being in that vicinity or not); and
   (c) the risk is one against which, in all the circumstances of the case, he may reasonably be expected to offer the other some protection.'

So the first part of the test is subjective and based on the occupier's actual knowledge, but the final part is objective and based on what a reasonable occupier should do.

7.3.3 The nature of the duty

The character of the duty is identified in the Act. According to s 1(4) the duty is to '. . . take such care as is reasonable in all the circumstances' to prevent injury to the non-visitor 'by reason of the danger concerned'.

So the standard of care is clearly an objective standard based on negligence. What is required of the occupier depends on the circumstances of each case. The greater the degree of risk the more precautions the occupier will have to take. Factors to be taken into account include the nature of the premises, the degree of danger, the practicality of taking precautions and of course the age of the trespasser.

CASE EXAMPLE

Tomlinson v Congleton Borough Council [2003] 3 WLR 705

The local authority owned a park including a lake. Warning signs were posted prohibiting swimming and diving because the water was dangerous, but the council knew that these were generally ignored. The council decided to make the lake inaccessible to the public but delayed start on this work because of lack of funds. The claimant, aged 18, dived into the lake, struck his head and suffered paralysis as a result of a severe spinal injury. His claim under the 1984 Act was initially rejected by the trial judge but succeeded in the Court of Appeal. The Court of Appeal was satisfied that all three aspects of s 1(3) were satisfied. The Court felt that the gravity of the risk of injury, the frequency with which people were exposed to the risk and the fact that the lake acted as an allurement, all meant that the scheme to make the lake inaccessible should have been completed with greater urgency. However, the Court reduced damages by two-thirds because of the contributory negligence of the claimant. The House of Lords, however, accepted the council's appeal. It based its decision on three reasons. Firstly, that the danger was not due to the state of the premises (although Lord Hutton felt that because the water was so dark and murky it was). Secondly, the House felt that it was not the sort of risk that a defendant should have to guard against but one that the trespasser in fact chose to run. Finally, the House felt that the council would not have breached its duty even in the case of a lawful visitor since the practicality and financial cost of avoiding the danger was not such that a reasonable occupier ought to be obliged to go to such ends.

The mere fact that the occupier has taken precautions or fenced the premises does not in itself indicate that the occupier knew or ought to have known of the existence of a danger.

CASE EXAMPLE

White v St Albans City Council, The Times, 12th March, 1990

Here the claimant had taken an unauthorised short cut over the council's land. He fell from a narrow bridge that had been fenced. The court did not feel that this was sufficient to make the council liable.

In assessing whether s 1(3) applies the court must take into account all of the circumstances at the time the injury occurred.

CASE EXAMPLE

Donoghue v Folkestone Properties [2003] EWCA Civ 231

The claimant was injured when he was trespassing on a slipway in a harbour and dived into the sea. The injury happened in the middle of winter and it was around midnight when the injury was caused. The court held that the occupier did not owe a duty of care. A reasonable occupier would not expect that a trespasser might be present or engage in such a foolhardy escapade.

So there can be no liability if the occupier had no reason to suspect the presence of a trespasser.

CASE EXAMPLE

Higgs v Foster [2004] EWCA Civ 843

A police officer investigating a crime entered the occupier's premises for surveillance purposes and fell into an uncovered inspection pit behind some coaches and suffered severe injuries causing him to retire from the police force. The police officer was a trespasser and the occupier could not have anticipated the presence of the trespasser or that he would have gone behind the coaches for any reason so there was no liability.

Similarly there can be no liability if the occupier was unaware of the danger or had no reason to suspect the danger.

CASE EXAMPLE

Rhind v Astbury Water Park [2004] EWCA Civ 756

The claimant had ignored a notice stating 'Private Property. Strictly no Swimming' and jumped into a lake, being injured by objects below the surface of the water. The claimant was a trespasser and the occupier had no reason to know that there were dangerous objects below the surface so there was no liability.

7.3.4 Avoiding liability under the 1984 Act

Again, as with the 1957 Act, it is possible for the occupier to avoid liability and warnings. The defence of *volenti* and the possibility of exclusion of liability all need to be considered.

Warnings

Under s 1(5) in an appropriate case the occupier could do so by taking '. . . such steps as are reasonable in all the circumstances . . .'. This might, in the case of adult trespassers, be achieved by use of effective warnings or by discouraging people from entering.

CASE EXAMPLE

Westwood v The Post Office [1973] 1 QB 591

A notice posted on a motor room door that 'Only the authorised attendant is permitted to enter' was held as sufficient warning for an intelligent adult. The occupier was not liable.

However, once again, it is unlikely that such warnings will succeed in the case of children, who may not be able to read or may not understand the warning. It is possible that in certain circumstances even physical barriers may be insufficient to discharge the occupier's duty.

Volenti

Section 1(6) also preserves the defence of *volenti*. Again the claimant must appreciate the nature and degree of the risk, not merely be aware of its existence for the defence to apply.

CASE EXAMPLE

Ratcliffe v McConnell [1999] 1 WLR 670

A warning notice at the shallow end of a swimming pool read: 'Deep end shallow dive'. The pool was always kept locked after hours and the claimant knew that entry was prohibited at this time. He was a trespasser and when he was injured while diving into the shallow end his claim failed. The court held that he was aware of the risk and had freely accepted it.

Exclusion of liability

There is no reference to exclusion clauses in the Act unlike the 1957 Act. It has been argued that exclusion should be impossible since the Act creates a minimum standard of care that would then be thwarted. However, this does then create the uneasy situation where a trespasser may well be entitled to more care than a lawful visitor.

ACTIVITY

Self-assessment questions

1. What protections, if any, did the law traditionally offer to trespassers?
2. Is it possible for an occupier to legitimately protect against intruders?
3. What type of damage is compensated under the 1984 Act?
4. Do the 'duty of common humanity' and the duty owed to trespassers under the 1984 Act differ at all?
5. What factors must be present in order to impose a duty on the occupier under the 1984 Act?
6. What difficulties are created by the minimum standard of care in the 1984 Act?

ACTIVITY

Quick quiz

Consider the following problem on occupiers' liability:

Alsopp Towers is a large pleasure theme park. At the entrance gate there is a sign which reads

'All of the rides are dangerous and customers enter entirely at their own risk'.

Consider any liability that Alsopp Towers may incur for the following customers

(a) Jasbir catches her heel in a gap between the boards while getting off 'The Screw', falls several feet, and injures herself badly.

(b) Sean, who is a delivery driver, leaves his lorry to pick flowers from one of the ornamental borders and tears his shoe and sock and cuts his foot quite badly on broken glass.

(c) Pedro, an electrical contractor who is repairing one of the rides, is electrocuted and badly burnt when Daisy, who operates the ride, carelessly plugs it in.

(d) Tom and Jerry, two ten-year-old boys, have sneaked in by climbing over a fence. They are both injured when they walk across the rails on one of the rides and are hit by one of the cars.

Is the Defendant an OCCUPIER of PREMISES?

- D has sole control of premises at time harm caused to C
- D is one of many people with interest in premises but was in control at material times

NO

YES

NO LIABILITY

Is the Claimant a VISITOR?

- Invited onto premises by D
- Enters to pursue a contract
- Enters under a licence granted by D
- Enters with legal authority

NO

Is C:

- A trespasser?
- Entering under the National Parks and Access to the Countryside Act 1949?
- Using a private right of way?

YES

Is D AWARE of DANGER and:

- Knows or believes C is in danger; or
- The risk is one against which D should guard?

YES

YES

OLA 1957 MAY APPLY

OLA 1984 MAY APPLY

If D not taking care to avoid risk of injury

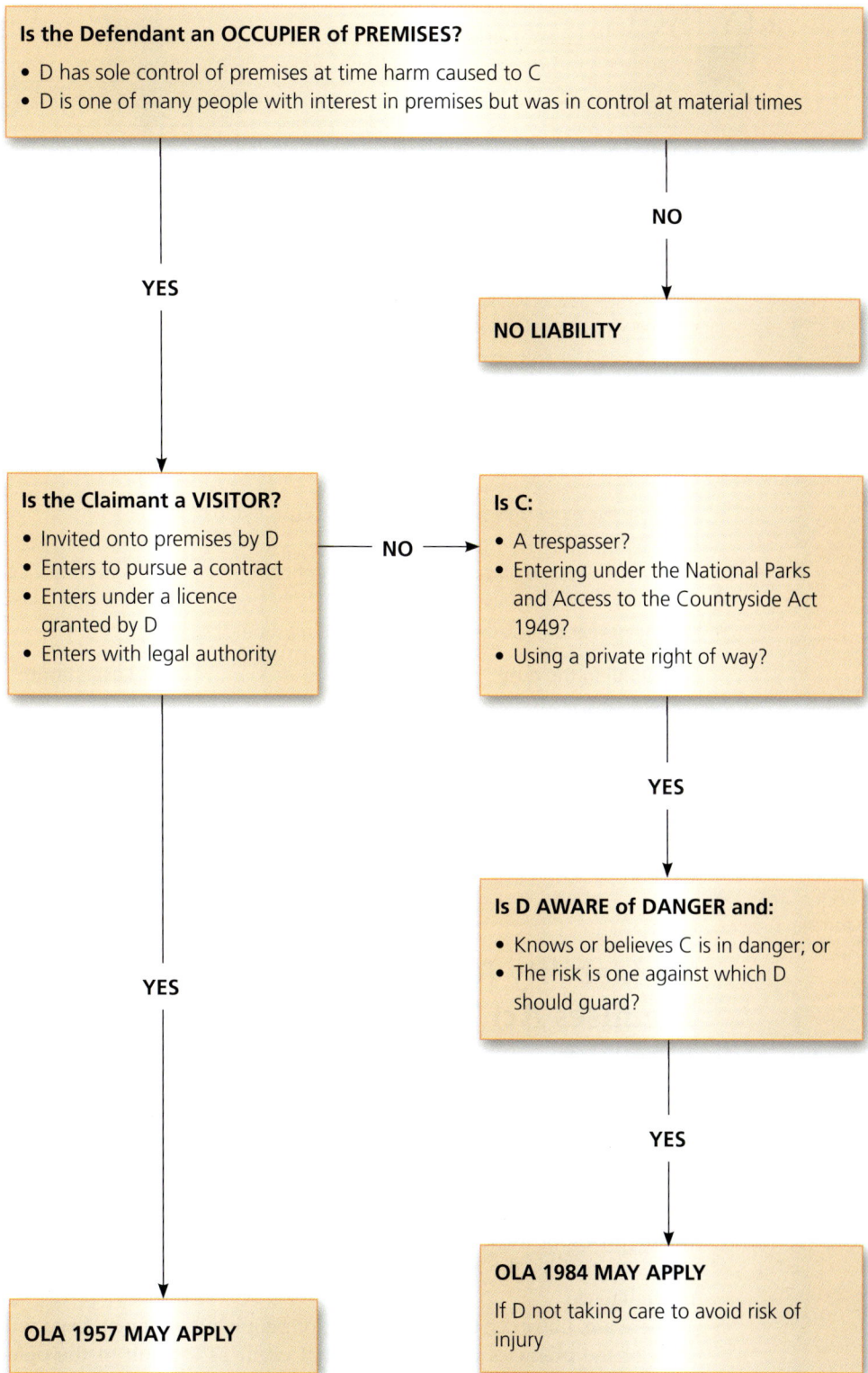

Figure 7.2 The assessment of liability under the Occupiers' Liability Act 1984

The common law	Case
The law was originally merely not to deliberately cause harm.	*Bird v Holbreck* (1828)
Because of the harshness of the rule as it applied to children a common duty of humanity to trespassers was introduced.	*BR Board v Herrington* (1972)

The scope of the duty under the 1984 Act	Case/statute
This was given statutory force in the 1984 Act.	
The occupier only owes a duty if he:	s 1(3)
• is aware of the danger or has reasonable grounds to believe it exists	
• knows or believes the other is in the vicinity of the danger and	
• the risk is one against which he may be expected to offer some protection.	
Compensation is only available in respect of personal injury or death, not personal property.	*Tomlinson v Congleton Borough Council* (2003)
The greater the risk the more precautions must be taken.	

Avoiding the duty	Case/statute
The occupier can defend if he has taken reasonable steps to avoid harm.	s 1(5)
So warnings may succeed – but not against children.	*Westwood v The Post Office* (1973)
Volenti is also possible if the trespasser is fully aware of the risk.	s 1(6)
	Ratcliffe v McConnell (1999)

7.4 Liability for defective premises and the Defective Premises Act 1972

We have already seen that it is possible for persons other than the occupier of land to be responsible for damage that is caused by the state of the premises. The obvious example of this is that identified in section 7.2.5 regarding independent contractors. If the usual occupier of the land can satisfy the tests in s 2(4) of the 1957 Act and show that an independent contractor who has worked on the land was in fact the cause of the damage then, provided the independent contractor can also be shown to have control of the premises for those purposes, the independent contractor may be liable. If, however, this last test fails, the independent contractor may still be liable under the normal rules of negligence.

There are, however, other categories of people who may be fixed with liability for the state of the premises and damages that occur as a result of the defective state of the premises. There are generally two classes of person to whom this will apply and such liability falls under the Defective Premises Act 1972. The two classes are landlords and builders.

Landlords

It is possible that a landlord might retain control of certain parts of premises. If the test in *Wheat v Lacon* is satisfied then the landlord may be classed as an occupier and may be subject to the duties in either the 1957 or the 1984 Acts.

In other cases where the landlord no longer has control over the premises then liability may still be possible either under the Defective Premises Act 1972 or under some often inconsistent common law.

The early common law was based on the contract between landlord and tenant and the maxim *caveat emptor* was applied so that there was general immunity from negligence actions. This has been reaffirmed.

CASE EXAMPLE

Rimmer v Liverpool Corporation [1984] 2 WLR 426

Here there was held to be no duty of care owed by a landlord to ensure the safety of the premises at the time of letting. The claimant was injured when he put his hand through a glass panel but there was no liability on the landlord.

The Act was passed at a time when it was generally felt that tenants were badly treated not just by their landlords but also by the existing law.

The basic duty is found in s 4 of the Act.

■ By s 4(1) where the landlord has the obligation of maintenance and repair then he has a duty to all those likely to be affected 'to take such care as is reasonable in all the circumstances [to prevent] personal injury or damage . . . caused by a relevant defect'.
■ By s 4(2) the duty is owed if the landlord knows or ought to know of the defect.
■ By s 4(3) a relevant defect is identified as 'one arising from or continuing from an act or omission . . . which constituted . . . a failure to carry out the obligation of "maintenance or repair".'

The duties can neither be restricted nor excluded by virtue of the Act.

Further duties also exist in the Landlord and Tenant Act 1985, in respect of the structure, the exterior and services in leases under seven years; and in the Housing Act 1988 in respect of basements and roofs.

Builders

The expression 'builder' has been used in the widest sense to include all persons involved in the construction or sale of a building. In this way the term might arguably include surveyors, architects and others. However, it is not certain whether this would actually apply in the case of the Defective Premises Act 1972.

Obviously one of the major problems facing potential claimants will usually involve latent defects in the property. With modern properties this may in part be covered by the NHBC scheme where builders are covered by it. Where a builder merely worked on premises he may in any case face liability under straightforward *Donoghue v Stevenson* [1932] AC 562 principles. However, where the builder was also owner and sold on, then traditionally there was no liability because of the doctrine of privity of contract.

The Defective Premises Act 1972 removed this anomaly by s 3 and allowed that there would be no reduction or removal of liability merely because of the 'subsequent disposal of the premises'.

A number of cases in the 1970s, *Dutton v Bognor Regis UDC* [1972] 1 QB 373, *Anns v Merton LBC* [1978] AC 728 included, attempted to remove various of the builders' immunities. However, these were for the most part overruled in *Murphy v Brentwood DC* [1990] 2 All ER 908. This case accepted that 'In the case of a building . . . a careless builder is liable on the principle in *Donoghue v Stevenson* where a latent defect results in physical injury to anyone, or damage to the property of any such person'. The builder will not, however, be liable for damage to the building itself because this is pure economic loss (the case has been criticised).

For the claimant who wishes to recover for damage to the building itself the appropriate action is through the Defective Premises Act 1972.

student
mentor tip

"Understand and know your case law, especially *Donoghue v Stephenson*."
Anthony, London South Bank University

OCCUPIERS' LIABILITY AND LIABILITY FOR DEFECTIVE PREMISES

The duty is identified in s 1 and this imposes three obligations:

- ■ that the work is carried out in workmanlike manner
- ■ that proper materials are used
- ■ that the house is fit for human habitation.

The Act does have a number of limitations:

- ■ it only applies to dwellings, not commercial premises
- ■ the limitation period is only six years from completion
- ■ it excludes approved schemes such as the NHBC scheme
- ■ the definition of pure economic loss is uncertain – and it is possible that the Act goes no further than the common law
- ■ it is also uncertain to whom the Act applies.

SAMPLE ESSAY QUESTION

'The Occupiers' Liability Act 1957 modifies the common law to the extent that the safety of lawful visitors is ensured.' Discuss how the law on occupiers' liability has developed in the light of the above statement.

Explain the basis of the 1957 Act

- The Act is a statutory form of negligence
- But was introduced to create a common duty of care where different visitors were formerly owed a different duty
- But breach and causation still apply

Explain the scope of the duty under the Act

- Basic duty in s 2(1) – the common duty of care owed to all lawful visitors
- But s 2(1) also allows the occupier to extend, restrict, modify or exclude his duty
- Duty under s 2(2) is to take reasonable care to keep the visitor safe for the purposes for which the visitor is permitted entry onto the premises

Discuss how many aspects of the common law are incorporated in the Act, eg:

- Definitions of occupier and premises
- Extra care taken over children – but allurement and parental responsibility for young children is common law
- The position on those entering to exercise a trade

Discuss how an occupier can avoid liability

- Where the damage is caused by the negligence of an independent contractor and it is appropriate to hire one
- Where appropriate warning notices are used, sometimes exclusion clauses are possible, and where consent or contributory negligence apply
- These are more extensive than under common law so possibly fail to ensure safety of visitor

- Discuss the common features of the common law and the Act
- Discuss the ways in which the Act improves upon the common law – if any – the Act was mainly introduced to standardise the duty owed to different types of lawful visitor

SUMMARY

- Occupiers' liability is covered by two Acts: The Occupiers' Liability Act 1957 for lawful 'visitors', and the Occupiers' Liability Act 1984 for trespassers
- An 'occupier' is anybody in actual control of the land and premises is broadly defined
- By s 2(1) of the 1957 Act a 'common duty of care' is owed to all lawful visitors
- By s 2(2) the duty is to ensure that the visitor is safe for the purposes of the visit
- Under s 2(3) an occupier must take extra care for children, who are less cautious, and not allure them – although parents are responsible for young children
- A person carrying out a trade or calling on the occupier's premises must guard against the risks associated with the trade
- The occupier is not liable for damage which is the result of work done by independent contractors if:
  - it is reasonable to entrust the work
  - a reputable contractor is chosen, and
  - the occupier inspects the work if necessary
- Adequate warnings; exclusion clauses and the defences of consent or contributory negligence can also be used to avoid liability
- Trespassers are protected by the 1984 Act under s 1(3) if the occupier:
  - is aware of the danger
  - knows of the trespass, and
  - the risk is one against which he may be expected to offer some protection but only covers personal injury

Further reading

Farrelly, M, 'Dangerous premises and liability to trespassers' [2001] NLJ 309.
Harvey, B and Marston, J, *Cases and Commentary on Tort* (4th edn, Longman, 2000), Chapter 7.
Wilkinson, H, 'Boys will be boys' [2000] NLJ 870.

8

Trespass to land

AIMS AND OBJECTIVES

After reading this chapter you should be able to:

■ Understand the definition of land
■ Understand the nature of trespass
■ Understand who can be a party to an action in trespass
■ Understand the available defences
■ Understand the different remedies
■ Be able to critically analyse the tort
■ Be able to apply the law to factual situations and reach conclusions as to liability

8.1 The origins and character of trespass to land

'Trespassers will be prosecuted' is a phrase which appears on notices throughout England. Most people do not realise that it is rarely possible to prosecute. Originally trespass to land was a crime as well as a civil offence. This is generally no longer the case, the only remedy being available through the civil courts. Trespass to land is one of the oldest torts originating from the old action for trespass (see Chapter 1).

English common law has always gone to great lengths to protect interests in land. In the early days, a landowner was entitled to place man-traps or other devices on his land and would not be liable for any injury caused. This is no longer the case. People are entitled to say who can come onto their land and to take steps to keep unwanted visitors (trespassers) out, but the steps must be not be likely to cause injury. As has been seen, in Chapter 8, in certain circumstances landowners can be liable for injuries caused to unlawful visitors resulting from a danger on the land. (Occupiers' Liability Act 1984.)

The tort retains some original characteristics. It is actionable *per se*, so that no actual damage need be caused. It is enough that the trespasser has crossed the boundary intentionally for liability to arise. Trespass will occur when even a small part of the trespasser's anatomy has crossed the boundary. Thus in *Franklin v Jeffries*, *The Times*, 11th March, 1985 there was a trespass when an unwanted arm came through an open window. Obviously the level of compensation where no actual damage has occurred will in most cases be limited. It will be seen however that it is not unusual for the remedy of choice to be an injunction, preventing a repeat of the tort.

The interference with the owner's rights must be direct and intentional. Indirect interference may give rise to a cause of action in nuisance (see Chapter 9). The issue of intention can cause some problems. The action itself must be deliberate but there is no requirement that there should be any intention to trespass. A drunkard who staggers up the path to what he mistakenly believes to be his own front door intentionally trespasses on the neighbour's land. They intended to go along that path although they did not intend to trespass. In *Conway v George Wimpey & Co Ltd* [1951] 2 KB 266 it was held that it was irrelevant that the person was unaware that they were trespassing or even honestly believed that the land was theirs. Conversely, a parachutist who gets blown onto land by the wind does not commit trespass as the entry was not intended. In *Smith v Stone* (1647) Style 65 a person who was pushed onto land by someone else was not liable for trespass.

It is sometimes argued that the tort protects a right of privacy. As will be seen, this is unlikely to happen in most cases. Photographs taken with a long lens may infringe privacy and be actionable as breach of confidentiality or nuisance, but without the crossing of the boundary there is no trespass.

8.2 Definition

A simple definition is

QUOTATION

'a direct physical and unlawful interference with land which is in the possession of another person.'

Trespass to land can occur in a number of ways, the most common being by way of entry onto land. It can also occur by remaining on land having been asked to leave and after a reasonable time has been allowed for that purpose.

CASE EXAMPLE

Robson v Hallett [1967] 2 All ER 407

A police officer was invited into a house to pursue enquiries. The consent to his being there was withdrawn and he tried to leave. Before he could do so he was assaulted. The issue was whether or not at the time of the assault he was a lawful or unlawful visitor.

Once permission is withdrawn a reasonable time must be allowed for the visitor to leave and Lord Diplock stated that

JUDGMENT

'provided he did so with reasonable expedition, he would not be a trespasser while he was doing so.'

Placing an object on or against land will also amount to trespass. This can extend to the placing of a human being on land. In *Smith v Stone* it was held

JUDGMENT

'that it is the trespasse of the party that carryed the defendant upon the land, and not the trespasses of the defendant: as he that drives my cattel into another man's land is the trespassor against him, and not I who am the owner of the cattel.'

More usually cases are concerned with objects. An example of the more usual case is found in *Westripp v Baldock* [1938] 2 All ER 799, when it was held that a ladder leaning against the claimant's wall was a trespass.

8.3 What is 'land'?

The word 'land' sounds simple – we all know what it means but for legal purposes it can mean vastly more than the soil itself. The term includes the surface of the soil, any buildings erected on it, the air space above it and the subsoil beneath it. In theory therefore 'land' includes airspace out to infinity and the subsoil through to Australia! Clearly in the modern world this is nonsense. Limits have to be drawn.

In *Bernstein v Skyviews and General Ltd* [1977] 2 All ER 902 Mr Justice Griffiths said that he could find 'no support in authority for the view that a landowner's rights in the air space above his property extend to an unlimited height.' As the Judge observed, this would mean that every time an aircraft or a satellite passed over the land a trespass would be committed. In trying to balance the rights of the landowner with those of the general public to take advantage of modern technology, the Judge concluded

JUDGMENT

'The balance is in my judgment best struck in our present society by restricting the rights of an owner in the air space … to such height as is necessary for the ordinary use and enjoyment of his land and the structures on it, and declaring that above that height he has no greater rights in the air space than any other member of the public.'

CASE EXAMPLE

Bernstein v Skyviews and General Ltd [1977] 2 All ER 902

The defendants' business was taking aerial photographs of premises which were then sold to the owners of the premises. They took pictures of the claimant's house. He claimed that the defendants were liable for trespass. Mr Justice Griffiths found that the defendants had flown over the land without permission but, in the light of the reasoning set out above, held that there had been no trespass.

Bernstein is in reality more concerned with the issue of privacy. The position of commercial airlines has been dealt with by the Civil Aviation Act 1982 which provides

SECTION

's 76(1) No action shall lie in respect of trespass . . . , by reason of the flight of an aircraft over any property at a height . . . which, having regard to wind, weather and all the circumstances of the case is reasonable, or the ordinary incidents of such flight . . .'

If property or persons are damaged by things falling from the aircraft, including a person, then by

SECTION

s 76(2) there is strict liability for the damage. The Convention on Liability for Space Objects 1972 deals with damage caused by spacecraft.

An owner's rights in relation to the subsoil are restricted in various ways but the fact that ownership vests in him has been used to advantage in the context of problems arising from the use of the highway (see section 8.5.2).

8.4 Parties to the action

8.4.1 Who can sue?

So far, the person whose rights have allegedly been infringed has been referred to as the owner of the land. This implies that ownership is necessary to maintain an action for trespass. This is not in fact the case. As a general rule, the person in possession of land has the right to sue, thus proving that there is some truth in the saying that 'possession is nine-tenths of the law'. Rejecting the proposition that legal title is necessary before an action can be brought, Lord Kenyon CJ in *Graham v Peat* (1801) 1 East 244 said 'Any possession is a legal possession against a wrongdoer'. As a consequence, even a squatter has enforceable rights against anyone who enters that land other than a person with a better legal title.

In contrast an action attempted against a party with superior rights of occupation is bound to fail.

CASE EXAMPLE

Delaney v T P Smith & Co [1946] KB 393

The claimant and the defendant had reached an oral agreement under which the claimant would acquire a tenancy of the defendant's property. However, the claimant then secretly entered the property before the lease was actually executed. When the defendant then ejected the claimant he sued in trespass but failed. The agreement on the lease had not been put in writing as required, as a result of which the defendant still had superior rights of occupation and was entitled to eject the claimant.

It would also of course be possible for a tenant to bring an action in trespass against the freehold owner of the property because a leaseholder has rights of exclusive possession. However, it would not be possible for a lodger to sue in trespass against a landlord because a lodger only has a license.

CASE EXAMPLE

White v Bayley (1861) 142 ER 438

The claimant was paid £75 a year for managing and living in premises rented by his employers. When the defendants gave the claimant notice to quit and took possession the claimant forcibly re-entered. The defendants sought an injunction. The claimant then brought a counter claim in trespass but failed. As the court identified he was entitled to '... the use but not the occupation of the premises ...'

8.4.2 Who can be sued?

The general and obvious rule is that the person who commits a trespass will be liable for it. This simple statement is modified in some ways.

A person with a better legal title is able to enter land and eject the trespasser from it without being liable in their turn for trespass. It should be noted that where there is an issue of residential occupancy, even a better legal title will not protect the person from liability under the Protection from Eviction Act 1977 which requires that a court order for possession be obtained prior to any eviction.

It will be seen that certain defences will protect someone who clearly enters land without authority to do so in order to deal with an emergency (see section 8.6.3).

8.5 Actions amounting to trespass

The various ways in which a trespass may occur have already been discussed but it is useful to consider the principles which have emerged from case law in order to 'put flesh on the bones' of the basic rules.

8.5.1 Airspace

It has already been seen that claimants are only entitled to limited protection against infringement of the airspace above their land (*Bernstein v Skyways and General Ltd*). Protection will be given by the courts against something which occurs at a lower level and has a more immediate impact than an over-flying aircraft. In *Kelson v Imperial Tobacco Co* [1957] 2 QB 334 it was held that an advertising sign which overhung the claimant's land amounted to a trespass.

The construction industry is particularly vulnerable in this regard as the use of very tall cranes is common. Such cranes have wide booms which are likely to travel through another's airspace. In *Woolerton & Wilson v Richard Costain Ltd* [1970] 1 WLR 411 the defendants' crane swung over the claimant's land. The defendants were liable for trespass. More recently, in *Anchor Brewhouse Developments Ltd and Others v Berkley House (Docklands Developments) Ltd* (1987) 38 BLR 82 the matter was further considered.

CASE EXAMPLE

Anchor Brewhouse Developments Ltd and Others v Berkley House (Docklands Developments) Ltd [1987] 38 BLR 82

A site was being developed which involved the use of very tall cranes. When the cranes were not being used they were left so that the booms were free to swing with the wind to avoid them being blown over. As they swung, the cranes travelled over adjoining property.

The over-swinging cranes amounted to a trespass. Drawing a distinction with over-flying aircraft Mr Justice Scott rejected the concept of the balancing of rights propounded in *Bernstein*. He took the view that by erecting a structure on land, the landowner takes the airspace into his possession.

JUDGMENT

'If an adjoining owner places a structure on his (the adjoining owner's) land that overhangs his neighbour's land, he thereby takes into his possession air space to which his neighbour is entitled.'

8.5.2 Highways

It has been accepted for many years that the public has a right of passage along a highway. This includes other activities

JUDGMENT

'[p]rovided these activities are reasonable, do not involve the commission of a public or private nuisance, and do not amount to an obstruction of the highway unreasonably impeding the primary right of the general public to pass and repass . . .'

Lord Irvine LC in *DPP v Jones* [1999] 2 All ER 257

In *DPP v Jones* the House of Lords accepted that reasonable activity could include a peaceful non-obstructive assembly of people.

The soil of the highway is deemed to belong up to the mid-point to those who own the land on either side. By the Highways Act 1980 a highways authority is the owner of the surface of a public highway to the depth of two spits, that is the depth of two spades and is responsible for maintenance and operation of the highway. The subsoil remains vested in the adjoining owners. This can have some odd consequences. In *Harrison v Duke of Rutland* [1893] 1 QB 142 it was held to be a trespass to the adjoining owner's land when the defendant used the road for the purpose of disturbing the claimant's exercise of shooting rights over his land. In *Hickman v Maisey* [1900] 1 QB 752 the defendant was a racing tout who had used a public highway passing across the claimant's land to observe the progress of race horses being trained on that land. The defendant was liable in trespass. In both these cases, the defendant was held to have abused the general public right of passage and thus to have committed an unlawful act.

8.5.3 Trespass *ab initio*

The old rule of **trespass *ab initio*** states that a person who enters land lawfully but subsequently abuses that right of entry will be liable for the entire transaction, not merely that portion of it which follows the abuse. The rule is illustrated by *The Six Carpenters' Case* (1610) 8 Co Rep 146a.

CASE EXAMPLE

The Six Carpenters' Case (1610) 8 Co Rep 146a

Six carpenters entered a public house, the Queen's Head, Cripplegate, where they consumed a quart of wine worth 7d and bread worth 1d. They refused to pay. The issue was whether the refusal to pay made their entry into the public house tortious.

It was held that when a person has permission or authority to enter premises, he will be a trespasser *ab initio* if that purpose is abused, for example by a theft. The courts deem that the entry was in fact for that unlawful purpose and therefore a trespass. However, refusing to pay for wine and bread does not make the original entry tortious; it does not take away the entire reason for the entry.

It all seems very complicated but a more recent case has helped to shed some light on how the principle might be applied today. In *Elias v Passmore* [1934] 2 KB 164 documents were seized by police officers executing a warrant. Some documents were seized unlawfully. It was held that they were trespassers as to the documents unlawfully seized. They were not trespassers *ab initio*, which would have made them liable for damage done to the front door when entry was effected, as the entry was by virtue of an independent ground, namely the warrant.

More recently still, Lord Denning MR described the doctrine as 'a by-product of the old forms of action. Now that they are buried, it can be interred with their bones.' (*Chic Fashions (West Wales) Ltd v Jones* [1968] 1 All ER 229.) Lord Denning was not however entirely consistent. In *Cinnamond v British Airports Authority* [1980] 2 All ER 368 he referred to the doctrine without criticism and indeed commenting on its potential usefulness.

The doctrine is unusual in that the legality of an act is judged by what happens subsequently. The entry may become unlawful by virtue of what the defendant has done after the entry. It can be argued that it is still important that this can happen in the area of the protection of one's person, goods and land against abuse of official power (*Winfield and Jolowicz*, p 498).

8.6 Defences

8.6.1 Consent

A person who enters land with consent of the person in possession is not liable for trespass.

Consent may be express, for example an invitation to 'Come in' when a caller knocks at the door. Express consent may be more formally granted by the creation of a legal agreement granting a licence, for example a theatre ticket grants a licence to enter the theatre on that occasion. In the realms of land law licences granting rights over land are of crucial importance but these are not considered here.

Consent may also be implied. A shopping centre gives implied consent to shoppers to enter the centre; a householder gives implied consent to those delivering post. An unlocked front gate allows anyone to go as far as the front door to enquire whether or not the householder is interested in whatever the caller is peddling, for example religion or a political party.

Withdrawal of consent can occur at any time although in the case of property licences notice is usually required. Shopping centres plagued by persistent shop-lifters are more frequently turning to the civil law of trespass for assistance. Provided the civil action is successful, the centre can hope to obtain an injunction to restrain the shop-lifter from returning with an effective sanction should they in fact do so. Breach of injunction is of course punishable as a contempt of court and can lead to imprisonment. A householder can withdraw implied consent to callers by simply locking the gate.

8.6.2 Lawful authority

The police and others may have authority to enter property by virtue of statute. The provisions of the relevant Act must be fully adhered to. The police are governed by the provisions of the Police and Criminal Evidence Act 1984. Other statutes also grant powers of entry. Examples include

- the Children Act 1989 which gives social workers the right to enter premises to seek a child at risk provided a warrant has been granted by a magistrate
- the Environment Act 1995 which gives the Environment Agency and local authorities power to enter premises to deal with environmental protection issues.

8.6.3 Necessity

A trespass to land may be excused if it occurs as a result of necessity. Necessity is a defence if action is taken in an emergency to deal with a genuinely perceived danger. The fact that with hindsight the danger did not in fact materialise is irrelevant.

The danger may be to property as well as people.

CASE EXAMPLE

Cope v Sharp (No 2) [1912] 1 KB 496

The defendant entered the claimant's land and burned a strip of heather in order to protect the defendant's own land. Although the action proved to have been unnecessary, the fire not spreading as feared, the court held that the action was motivated by a genuine perception of danger and was therefore necessary.

This has been subjected to some comment in later cases. In *Esso Petroleum Co Ltd v Southport Corporation* [1955] 3 All ER 864 (a case involving the discharge of oil from a stricken tanker to save not just the ship but also the crew) Mr Justice Devlin (as he then was) said at first instance

JUDGMENT

'The safety of human lives belongs to a different scale of values from the safety of property. The two are beyond comparison and the necessity for saving life has at all times been considered a proper ground for inflicting such damage as may be necessary upon another's property.'

The courts have been concerned to limit the defence. In *London Borough of Southwark v Williams* [1971] 2 All ER 175 the issue was whether homeless squatters could use the defence when they had taken possession of empty property belonging to the claimant. Lord Denning MR commented

JUDGMENT

'If homelessness were once admitted as a defence to trespass, no one's house would be safe. Necessity would open a door which no man could shut.'

While the decision in *London Borough of Southwark v Williams* may be questioned on moral grounds, the law apparently putting property rights before the needs of people, the reasoning can be understood. It is difficult not to agree with the sentiments expressed by Lord Denning that to hold otherwise would be to open the floodgates, which the courts try to avoid doing.

The defence was however held to apply to damage to property in *Rigby v Chief Constable of Northamptonshire* [1985] 2 All ER 985.

CASE EXAMPLE

Rigby v Chief Constable of Northamptonshire [1985] 2 All ER 985

During a strike by the fire service there was a siege of a gun shop in which a dangerous armed psychopath was hiding. The police fired a tear-gas canister into the shop which ignited powder causing a serious fire. The shop-owners claimed damages for trespass to land.

JUDGMENT

' . . . a defence of necessity is available in the absence of negligence on the part of the defendant creating or contributing to the necessity. In this case there was a dangerous armed psychopath whom it was urgently necessary to arrest.'

Taylor J

The defence of necessity was upheld. Had the defendant been negligent, that tort would have provided an appropriate remedy.

8.7 Remedies

8.7.1 Damages or injunction?

In a simple case the claimant may seek compensation for the injury done to his land, whether this relates to physical damage or the sum lost by reason of being out of possession. The latter takes the form of *mesne profits* equating to the rent which would have been recoverable had there been a proper letting. Where there is a likelihood that a trespass will be repeated, an injunction will usually be the remedy of choice.

Difficulties arise when the trespass is a continuing problem as with the erection of a building which encroaches onto the claimant's land. An injunction could be granted whereby the encroaching building would be demolished, or the defendant can in effect, purchase the right to continue the trespass by payment of damages. The latter will not always be sufficient to convince the claimant that they have received justice. The courts are reluctant to allow the defendant to 'get away with it' in this way.

In *Shelfer v City of London Electric Lighting Co* [1895] 1 Ch 287 it was held that where the appropriate remedy would usually be the grant of an injunction, damages could be awarded in lieu only:

(i) if the injury to the claimant's rights is small

(ii) is capable of being estimated in money

(iii) can be adequately compensated by a small money payment and

(iv) the case is one in which it would be oppressive to the defendant to grant an injunction.

These rules were recently considered in a case where the defendant had built a house in breach of a restrictive covenant prohibiting any building on that part of the land.

CASE EXAMPLE

Jaggard v Sawyer [1995] 2 All ER 189

At first instance, the judge refused an injunction, granting damages in lieu. The claimant appealed. Holding that the decision at first instance was correct, Sir Thomas Bingham LJ accepted that the first three requirements of Shelfer were satisfied. He then turned to consider the issue of oppression of the defendant.

JUDGMENT

'The oppression must be judged as at the date the court is asked to grant an injunction and . . . the court cannot ignore the reality with which it is then confronted.'

On the facts the grant of an injunction to demolish the house would be oppressive and the award of damages in lieu was appropriate.

The Court of Appeal was undoubtedly influenced by the fact that no application to the court was made until the building work was at an advanced stage. In the absence of blatant and calculated disregard for the law by the defendant the courts are reluctant to order the demolition of a building.

In other cases, the situation is easier to deal with. For example, a trespass into airspace may well be remedied by injunction, as will a frequent incursion on foot or by car into the claimant's land.

8.7.2 Re-entry

By the Criminal Law Act 1977 it is an offence for anyone other than a displaced residential occupier, to use or threaten violence for the purpose of securing entry to land occupied by another. Peaceable re-entry is lawful. Case law indicates that a land-owner may not have civil liability if no more force than is necessary is used to remove a trespasser (*Hemmings v Stoke Poges Golf Club* [1920] 1 KB 720). It is not clear whether this rule survives the Criminal Law Act 1977. Lord Clarke in *Ropaigealach v Barclays Bank plc* [2000] 1 QB 263 took the view that the rule does survive but as yet there is no case law on the specific point.

A displaced residential occupier may not be prosecuted pursuant to the Criminal Law Act 1977 but needs to be wary of the Protection from Eviction Act 1977 (see the next section) and the Protection from Harassment Act 1997 (discussed in section 13.6.2).

8.7.3 Action for the recovery of land

A person may bring an action to recover possession of land (formerly known as an action for ejectment). The action can be brought against any person without a better legal title than the claimant. Thus someone who has been 'squatting' on land for six months would be able to bring an action against a later squatter.

Someone seeking to recover possession from a residential occupier, even if the occupier is a squatter, will generally require a court order before eviction can take place. Unlawful eviction or other conduct calculated to 'persuade' an occupier to leave a dwelling is punishable as a crime (Protection from Eviction Act 1977).

Anyone seeking to recover possession of land should also be wary of the provisions of the Protection from Harassment Act 1997 the terms of which are broad enough to encompass behaviour which might not fall within the definitions to be found in the Protection from Eviction Act.

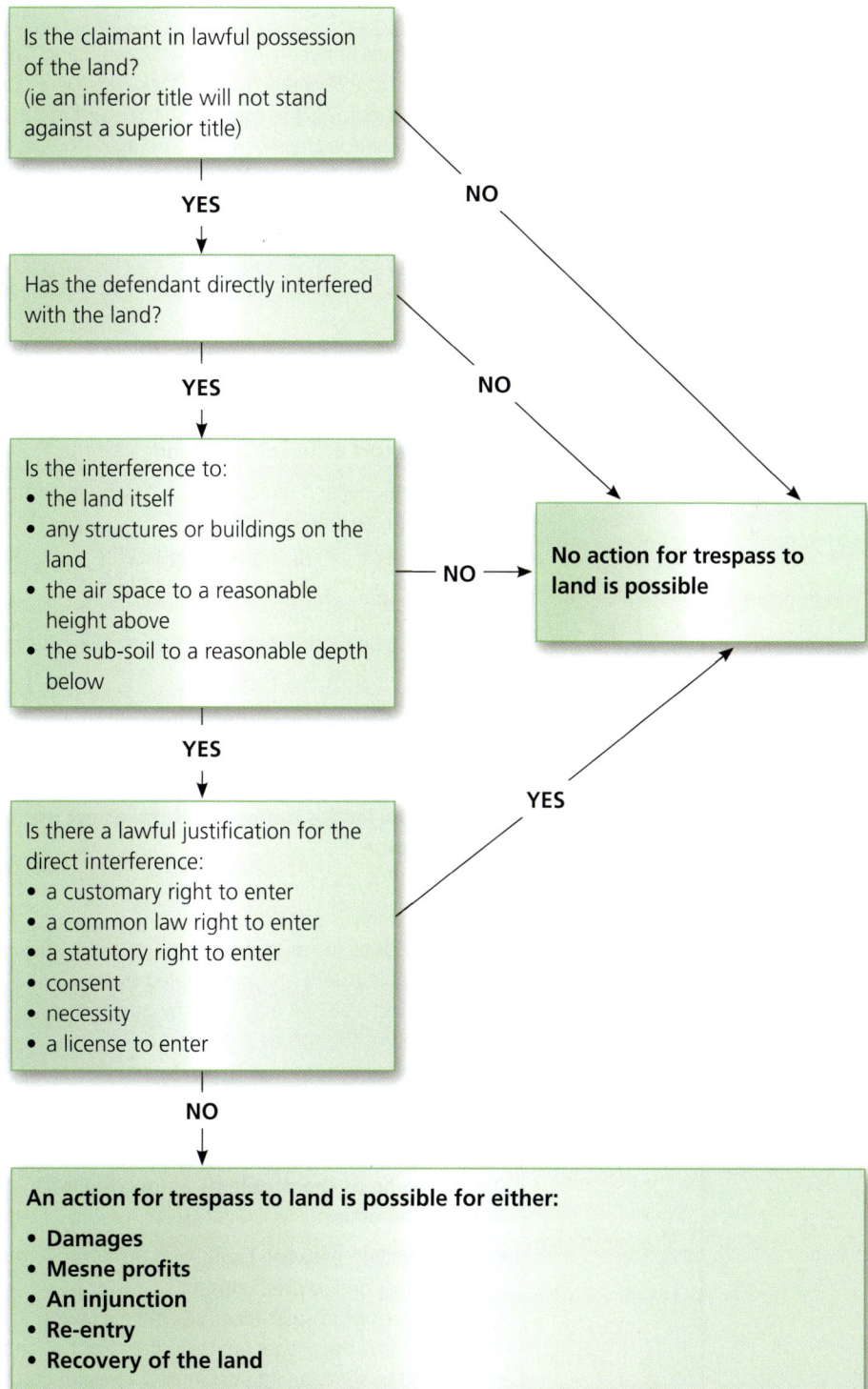

Figure 8.1 Diagram illustrating the essential elements for a claim in trespass to land, including the possible remediesSelf-assessment questions

ACTIVITY

Self-assessment questions

1. What is meant by the word 'land' for the purposes of this tort?
2. In what circumstances can a person who does not have legal title to land bring an action for trespass to land?
3. Explain the essential difference between *Bernstein v Skyways and General Ltd* and *Anchor Brewhouse Developments Ltd v Berkeley House (Docklands Developments) Ltd*.
4. What, exactly, is trespass ab initio? Is the concept still relevant in the twenty-first century?
5. How does *Shelfer v City of London Electric Lighting Co* assist the courts to decide whether or not the grant of an injunction is an appropriate remedy?

SAMPLE ESSAY QUESTION

'The two principal aims of tort law are to compensate the victims of wrongs and to deter wrong-doing.' Discuss the extent to which the tort of trespass to land succeeds in achieving these aims.

Define the tort of trespass to land

- Any intentional and direct entry onto land in another person's possession
- Can involve entering land voluntarily and intentionally or remaining on the land after permission is withdrawn
- Could also be placing things on the land or taking things away from the land
- And can include even the merest contact

Discuss how land is defined and the effect on compensation

- Obviously covers the land itself and anything built on it – so possibly is effective
- But extends to the airspace above – but only to a reasonable extent and is regulated by the Civil Aviation Act 1982 so may limit the effectiveness of protection of the tort as a deterrent
- Also extends to subsoil with similar problems

Discuss some of the problems associated with bringing an action

- The distinction between lawful and unlawful entry and express and implied consent
- The concept of trespass *ab initio* where a lawful visitor abuses the proper limits on their right to enter
- The need to show an interest in land to claim and the need to have a superior right of possession to the defendant

Discuss the available remedies and whether they adequately remedy or deter

- Damages – but only if some damage to the land – and mesne profits possible
- Injunctions
- Removal of trespasser by reasonable force

Discuss the effectiveness as a deterrent or means of compensation

- The tort is actionable *per se* so may act as a deterrent
- Compensation is only relevant if damage has been caused
- Entry by mistake will not necessarily remove liability increasing the possibility of both compensation and deterrence
- Only available to people with a superior interest in land so does not protect lodgers or deter bad behaviour by landlords
- Statutory right to enter may deny compensation for harm
- Damages are difficult to assess, limits on granting injunctions, requirement of reasonable force in removing trespassers – so limits effectiveness of both compensation and deterrence

KEY FACTS

Definition	Case
Actionable *per se*	
Direct and unlawful interference with land in possession of another	*Franklin v Jeffries* (1985); *Conway v George Wimpey & Co Ltd* (1951)
Must be intentional	
'Land' includes surface and everything on the surface, the subsoil and airspace	
'Subsoil' can extend beneath highway	*Harrison v Duke of Rutland* (1893); *Hickman v Maisey* (1900)
'Airspace' extends only to height necessary for ordinary use and enjoyment of land	*Kelson v Imperial Tobacco* (1957); *Bernstein v Skyviews* (1977);
Usually occurs with entry but can include placing object onto land	*Anchor Brewhouse Development v Berkley House (Docklands Developments)* (1987)
a person	*Smith v Stone* (1647)
a ladder against a wall	*Westripp v Baldock* (1938)
Can include remaining on land after permission to be there is withdrawn	

Claimant	Case
Must be in possession of the land Possession does not necessarily mean legal right – in some circumstances a squatter can sue	*Graham v Peat* (1801)

Trespass *ab initio*	Case
Subsequent actions can cause lawful entry to be regarded as unlawful making entry a trespass For modern potential see	*Six Carpenters' Case* (1610) *Elias v Passmore* (1934)

Defences	Case/statute
Consent – can be express, for example by invitation, or implied, for example delivery of mail – can be withdrawn Lawful authority – statutory examples include:	*Police and Criminal Evidence Act* 1984; *Children Act* 1989; *Environment Act* 1995
Necessity – limited to entry to deal with genuinely perceived danger	*Cope v Sharp (No 2)* (1912) *Esso Petroleum v Southport Corp* (1956)

Remedies	Case/statute
Damages – for actual damage but can extend to compensation for loss caused by being out of possession (*mesne profits*)	
Injunction – where trespass is continuing problem or likely to recur unless damages would adequately compensate claimant or injunction would be unduly oppressive to defendant	*Shelfer v City of London Electric Lighting* (1895); *Jaggard v Sawyer* (1995)
Re-entry – must be peaceable – note special rules relating to eviction of residential occupier	
Action for recovery of land – can be used by anyone with better legal title than defendant – note importance where residential premises involved	*Protection from Eviction Act* 1977

SUMMARY

- Trespass involves direct interference with another person's land
- A person with an interest in the land can sue anyone with a lesser interest in the land but not someone with a superior interest
- Must involve direct entry onto the land although can be merely temporary
- Trespass is actionable *per se* so no damage has to be caused
- Land includes the subsoil below and the air space above to some extent
- A legal entry can become a trespass where the legitimate purpose of the visit is exceeded
- Defences include: a customary or a common law or a statutory right to enter, consent, necessity, and licenses
- And remedies include: ejectment, repossession, and damages

9

Nuisance

AIMS AND OBJECTIVES

After reading this chapter you should be able to:

■ Understand the differences between private nuisance, public nuisance and statutory nuisance
■ Understand what determines who the potential parties are in each action
■ Understand the essential elements for proving private nuisance
■ Understand the essential elements for proving public nuisance
■ Understand the scope of statutory nuisance
■ Understand the defences available to a claim of nuisance
■ Be able to critically analyse the tort of nuisance
■ Be able to apply the law to factual situations and reach conclusions as to liability

9.1 Nuisance generally

Nuisance is perhaps the part of tort law which is most closely connected to protection of the environment. As will be seen, action in nuisance can lie for oil spills, nasty smells, noise and anything else which affects nearby land or the comfort and convenience of the occupiers of that land.

The problem of pollution, whatever form it takes, is also the subject of statutory regulation, much of which stems from regulations and directives coming from the European Union. More recently, as seen in Chapter 1, the European Convention on Human Rights and the Human Rights Act 1998 are also having an impact, providing a remedy where either the common law or statute fails to do so.

Nuisance may take three forms:

■ private nuisance
■ public nuisance
■ statutory nuisance.

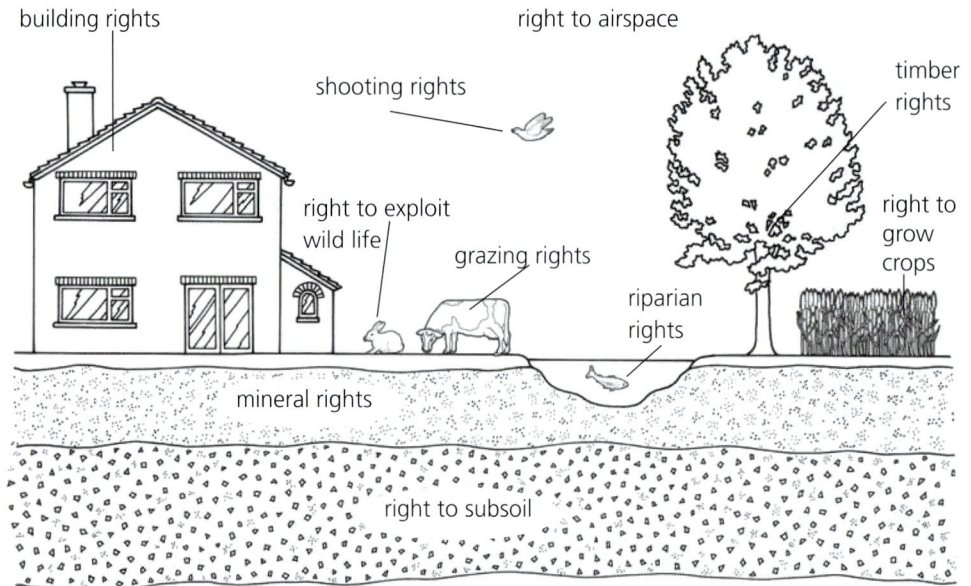

Figure 9.1 Land

As will be seen these are not necessarily mutually exclusive of each other but the traditional method of discussing each separately will be followed.

Nuisance is concerned with the use of land. We have already seen that the word 'land' has an extended meaning in law (Chapter 8 section 8.3). For the purposes of nuisance a wider meaning is given. Nuisance is concerned with all aspects of land use. This can include:

- the right to grow crops and graze animals
- shooting rights
- riparian rights
- rights of support from neighbouring land
- timber rights
- leisure and domestic activity
- mineral rights
- etc.

(For a full discussion of the meaning of 'land', reference should be made to a text on land law.)

It is essential that the interest being interfered with is one recognised by law. In *Hunter and Others v Canary Wharf* [1997] 2 WLR 684 a tower block interfered with television signals. The House of Lords held that this amounted to interference with a 'purely recreational facility as opposed to interference with the health or physical comfort or well-being' of the claimant. This may seem odd in the twenty-first century but the judges did take into account the wide-spread availability of cable and satellite television. The judges also considered whether the fact that a building blocked television signals was capable of amounting to a nuisance. Referring to an old principle Goff LJ said:

JUDGMENT

' . . . [I]n the absence of an easement, more is required than the mere presence of a neighbouring building to give rise to an actionable private nuisance. . . . [I]t will generally arise from something emanating from the defendant's land.'

A building clearly cannot 'emanate' from land and is therefore unlikely to amount to an actionable nuisance. The defendant has a legal right to use the airspace above his land provided such use is reasonable. Building on that land is a reasonable use in the absence of malice. It is difficult to see how a building can be a malicious use of land but perhaps a hoarding or a screen would suffice.

9.2 Private nuisance

9.2.1 Definition

An actionable private nuisance occurs where a person's use or enjoyment of their land is unlawfully interfered with by activities carried on by another person on their land. In most cases, the two areas of land are likely to be close together. The activities complained of must generally be continuous but it is possible, in rare circumstances, for a 'one off' activity to amount to a nuisance.

9.2.2 Interference

The interference must be indirect. A simple example to illustrate this arises from a garden bonfire. The bonfire itself is not a nuisance but the smoke arising from it can mean that neighbours have to take in washing and shut windows. The activity is lighting the bonfire, the indirect consequence of that activity is the smoke. Direct interference may amount to trespass to land (see Chapter 8).

9.2.3 A balancing act between competing interests

The tort is essentially concerned with balancing the competing interests of neighbours to make lawful use of their own land. The difficulty is that what may be reasonable to the person carrying out the activity, may be perceived as wholly unreasonable by a neighbour because of the way it interferes with what the neighbours want to do on their land. The courts are left to conduct a balancing act. Only interference which is found by the court to be unreasonable can amount to a private nuisance. In considering whether or not the interference is reasonable, the courts will have regard to

- the extent of the harm
- the nature of the use interfered with.

The extent of the harm is judged on the basis of the impact on the claimant. This is judged subjectively. *Street* gives a good example. A defendant who plays a trumpet very loudly objectively causes a nuisance to a neighbour. It will not be perceived subjectively as a nuisance by a neighbour who is deaf and who is therefore unlikely to hear the noise.

The use to which the claimant puts their land is relevant. In *Smith v Giddy* [1904] 2 KB 448 a defendant was liable in nuisance for the branches of trees on his property which overhung the claimant's land. While this would normally have been an unactionable blockage of light, the fact that the claimant ran a fruit orchard and the interference meant that the fruit trees did not grow properly was decisive in the decision that the defendant was liable.

It will be seen later that the social utility of the defendant's use of land is only relevant to the remedy which may be awarded.

9.3 The parties to an action in private nuisance

9.3.1 Who can sue?

Private nuisance protects interests in and the enjoyment of land. In order to bring an action, the claimant must have a legal interest in the land. This will normally mean a right to exclusive possession by way of freehold or leasehold title. A licensee, for example a lodger or a member of the owner's family, has no interest in land and cannot therefore bring an action.

CASE EXAMPLE

Malone v Laskey [1907] 2 KB 141

The claimant lived with her husband who occupied a house as licensee. Vibrations from the use of an engine on the defendant's adjoining land caused a bracket to fall onto the claimant causing her injury. Her claim in nuisance was dismissed by the Court of Appeal as she had no interest in the land on which to found a claim.

In 1993 it was believed that the apparent injustice suffered by a person in Mrs Malone's situation had been remedied. In *Khorasandjian v Bush* [1993] 3 WLR 476 a claim by a daughter living with her parents succeeded when the majority of the Court of Appeal recognised that an injunction on the ground of private nuisance could be granted despite the fact that she had no interest in the land. The case concerned harassment by way of telephone calls and was heard prior to the Protection from Harassment Act 1997. It may be that the judges were influenced by the need to find a remedy for what was, on the facts, serious harassment.

The apparent easing of the requirement for the claimant to have a legal interest was reversed when *Hunter and Others v Canary Wharf Ltd* and *Hunter and Others v London Docklands Corporation* [1997] AC 655 were heard together by the House of Lords.

The first case concerned interference with television reception, the second damage caused by dust during the construction of a road. The House of Lords certainly took the view that the Court of Appeal in *Khorasandjian* had been trying to create 'by the back door a tort of harassment'. Pointing out that the decision was inconsistent with that in *Malone v Laskey* [1907] 2 QB 141, Goff LJ stated very clearly

JUDGMENT

'. . . an action in private nuisance will only lie at the suit of a person who has a right to the land affected. Ordinarily, such a person can only sue if he has the right of exclusive possession . . .'

The position now appears to be clear but the fact is that the injustice suffered by a lodger or some other person without a right to exclusive possession remains. The Protection from Harassment Act 1997 will help some claimants, for example the daughter in *Khoras-andjian*, but not someone who cannot meet the criteria of the statute. It may be that in the future we may see an action under the Human Rights Act 1998 for breach of Article 8 of the European Convention on Human Rights.

A reversioner is the person to whom the land will return after the expiration of the current occupier's interest, for example at the end of a lease. Such a person can sue if it can be shown that the reversion, ie the value of the land after its return, will be diminished by the present nuisance. This tends to mean that the nuisance will be permanent. In *Tucker v Newman* (1839) 11 Ad & El 40 a reversioner was successful when a house had been built on adjoining land. The eaves of the house over-hung his land and allowed rainwater to fall onto it.

9.3.2 Who can be sued?

The creator of the nuisance

The obvious answer, and the one which is usually correct, is the person who causes the nuisance. Unlike the claimant, it seems that the defendant need not have an interest in the land on which the activity takes place. In *Esso Petroleum Co Ltd v Southport Corporation* [1956] AC 218 (for facts see Chapter 8, section 8.6.4) Mr Justice Devlin (as he then was) said

JUDGMENT

> 'I can see no reason why if the defendant as licensee or trespasser misuses someone else's land, he should not be liable in nuisance in the same way as an adjoining occupier would be.'

This simple statement is not as straight-forward as it might appear. In *Thomas v National Union of Mineworkers* [1985] 2 All ER 1 (for facts see Chapter 13, section 13.2.2) it was said by Mr Justice Scott, at first instance, that an activity on the highway which unduly interferes with the right of citizens to enjoy the highway could amount to a 'species of private nuisance, namely unreasonable interferences with the claimant's right to use the highway.' This statement is apparently contradicted in *Hussain v Lancaster City Council* [2000] QB 1 where the claimants were the victims of extreme racial harassment by persons using the highway. It was held by the Court of Appeal that there was no nuisance because the wrong-doing did not involve the defendants' use of their land. The wrongdoers, who were not the defendants, had no legal interest in the highway.

If *Hussain* is correct the implications for the law relating to private nuisance are substantial as those in temporary possession of land but with no legal interest in that land, such as independent contractors, may be able to escape liability. The decision in *Hussain* may have resulted from policy influences. To hold a local authority liable in nuisance for the activities of those using the highway who are responsible for racial harassment would indeed be to open the floodgates. It may be therefore that we shall see in future cases that *Hussain* is held to apply only to its own very specific facts.

The occupier

Generally the occupier of the premises from which the nuisance emanates will be liable for that nuisance. This is subject to qualification where the nuisance is caused by

- independent contractors
- trespassers
- an act of nature.

Independent contractors

An independent contractor's activities may be the cause of a nuisance. An obvious example is the problems caused to neighbours by building works. In such cases, there are certain 'non-delegable' duties which fall on the occupier notwithstanding that the nuisance arises from the activities of the contractor. Such duties relate to activities which carry with them particular danger. In *Bower v Peate* (1876) 1 QBD 321 the defendant employed a contractor to demolish his house. The adjoining house was damaged as a result of the work. The occupier was held liable.

The courts have refined this principle to cover only those activities by the contractor which are extra-hazardous, for instance those acts which 'in their very nature, involve in the eyes of the law special danger to others' (per Slesser LJ in *Honeywill and Stein v Larkin Brothers Ltd* [1934] 1 KB 191). The essence of 'special danger' seems to be that the activity carries with it a special risk that a nuisance may be caused to neighbours. (For a fuller discussion of the potential liability for the activities of an independent contractor see Chapter 7, section 7.2.5.)

Trespassers

An occupier may well feel that if the nuisance is caused by a trespasser, then there ought to be no liability on their part for a resulting nuisance. Life is not that simple. The occupier will be liable if the 'nuisance' is adopted by using the state of affairs for the occupier's own purpose or where the nuisance is 'continued'. This point is illustrated by *Sedleigh-Denfield v O'Callaghan (Trustees for St Joseph's Society for Foreign Missions)* [1940] AC 880.

CASE EXAMPLE

Sedleigh-Denfield v O'Callaghan (Trustees for St Joseph's Society for Foreign Missions) [1940] AC 880

A ditch on the boundary of the claimant's land belonged to the defendants. A trespasser laid a culvert in the ditch and no grid was put in place to prevent rubbish etc from blocking it. A grid was in fact placed on top of the culvert where it served no useful purpose. This was known to the defendants. Thereafter, over a three-year period, the ditch was cleaned out twice a year by the defendants. After a heavy storm the culvert became blocked and the claimant's land was flooded.

JUDGMENT

'After the lapse of nearly three years, [the defendants] must be taken to have suffered the nuisance to continue, for they neglected to take the very simple step of placing the grid in the proper place, which would have removed the danger to their neighbour's land. They adopted the nuisance, for they continued during all that time to use the artificial contrivance . . . for the purpose of getting rid of water from their property without taking the proper means for rendering it safe.'

Viscount Maugham LJ

It seems that an occupier who knows, or is deemed to know, that the potential for the creation of a nuisance exists, will be held liable even though the original act which created the nuisance was not the present occupier's act.

CASE EXAMPLE

Anthony and others v The Coal Authority [2005] EWHC 1654 (QB)

Between 1957 and 1995, first the National Coal Board and as it became the British Coal Corporation, tipped waste from mining onto a tip on its land. In 1995 the tip was partly landscaped and passed into private hands. In 1996 spontaneous combustion of the coal created a fire which continued for three years. The claimant sued the Coal Authority, the body taking over responsibility of the former two bodies, for the interference caused by the fumes and smoke. The defendant was held liable under the principle in *Sedleigh-Denfield v O'Callaghan* that it became aware of the problem while the tip was still under its control and failed to prevent the nuisance.

An act of nature

Until recently, a nuisance resulting from an act of nature, for example a severe storm which washed topsoil onto a neighbour's land, would not impose liability on the occupier of the land from which the soil had been washed. This, at first sight, appears to be very reasonable as it may well be impossible to foretell the consequences of an unusual and extreme event. But what about the situation where an occupier is aware, or ought to be aware, of the potential for the nuisance to occur? It would be unjust if the occupier could escape liability in such circumstances.

The matter was first considered by the Privy Council in *Goldman v Hargrave* [1967] 1 AC 645 when Lord Wilberforce explained that the occupier's duty is in reality more positive, resulting in liability for failure to take positive steps to abate a nuisance of which the occupier is aware.

CASE EXAMPLE

Goldman v Hargrave [1967] 1 AC 645

The defendant dealt with a fire caused by lightning hitting a gum-tree. The tree was felled, cut into sections, and left to burn itself out. The weather deteriorated and the fire reignited causing damage to the claimant's land.

It was held that on the facts the defendant owed the claimant a duty to abate the nuisance which he was, or ought to have been, aware arose from the natural state of affairs on his land.

The principle set out in *Goldman v Hargrave* has been enshrined in English law in the case of *Leakey v National Trust* [1980] QB 485:

CASE EXAMPLE

Leakey v National Trust [1980] QB 485

The defendants owned a hill known as Barrow Mump; the claimants' homes were at the foot of the hill. The homes were threatened by the possibility that the hill would slip as a result of the action of the weather on the type of clay. From time to time small slips occurred onto the claimants' land. The defendants had been aware of the problem for more than eight years and had taken no steps to minimise the risk.

Developing the dicta from *Sedleigh-Denfield* Megaw LJ held that where a potential nuisance exists resulting from an act of nature and the defendant was aware of the danger, it would be an injustice were the occupier not to be under a duty to ameliorate the nuisance. Explaining the scope of the duty, the Judge went on to say

JUDGMENT

'the duty is a duty to do that which is reasonable in the circumstances . . . to prevent or minimise the known risk of damage or injury to one's neighbour or his property.'

In considering what can reasonably be done, the court should have regard to what the particular defendant could have reasonably been expected to do. This is not the standard of the 'reasonable man' whom we meet in the context of negligence. It takes account of matters such as cost in relation to the defendant's means; the need for physical exertion in the context of the defendant's age and state of health. Alongside this the court will have regard to what if anything, the neighbour could reasonably have been expected to do to protect his own land.

The issue of what is reasonable was further considered in *Holbeck Hall Hotel Ltd v Scarborough Borough Council* [2000] 2 All ER 705.

CASE EXAMPLE

Holbeck Hall Hotel Ltd v Scarborough Borough Council [2000] 2 All ER 705

The hotel stood at the top of a cliff. On 6th June 1993 the lawn between the hotel and the edge of the cliff fell into the sea and the land collapsed beneath the hotel so that it became unsafe and had to be demolished. The coastline was owned by the defendants. It had been known since 1893 that cliff falls occurred along that part of the coastline. Some remedial work was carried out in 1989 but was ineffective in preventing further erosion and collapse. At first instance it was held that the defendants were liable. The matter came before the Court of Appeal.

Holding that a duty to ameliorate the potential nuisance arises when 'the defect is known and the hazard or danger to the claimants' land is reasonably foreseeable' Stuart-Smith LJ explained

JUDGMENT

'It is the existence of the defect coupled with the danger that constitutes the nuisance; it is knowledge or presumed knowledge of the nuisance that involves liability for continuing it when it could reasonably be abated.'

The important point at issue was what knowledge of the risk could be imputed to the defendants? It was clear that without further substantial geological investigation, the extent of the risk could not be anticipated although it was known that gradual erosion would be likely to continue. Lord Justice Stuart-Smith concluded that the scope of the defendants' duty was limited to what ought to have been foreseen without further investigation.

Pointing out that *Goldman* and *Leakey* were decided prior to *Caparo Industries Ltd v Dickman* [1990] 2 AC 605, Lord Justice Stuart-Smith reminded the Court that the three stage test of

- foreseeability
- proximity and
- the need for it to be fair just and reasonable

applies whatever the nature of the damage. He stated

JUDGMENT

'. . . I do not think it is just and reasonable in a case like the present to impose liability for damage which is greater in extent than anything that was foreseen or foreseeable . . .'

So where does all this leave the potential for liability arising from natural causes? It seems that occupiers who know or ought to know of the potential for a nuisance arising from the state of affairs on their land owe what the judges have described as a 'measured duty of care' to do what can reasonably be done having regard to such matters as their resources etc. It is clear that imputed knowledge will not extend to knowledge which could only be obtained by further investigation.

The nuisance must be a foreseeable result of the activity, whether it arises from an activity or from natural causes. *The Wagon Mound (No 2) (Overseas Tankship (UK) Ltd v the Miller Steam Ship Co Pty Ltd)* [1967] 1 AC 617 involved allegations of nuisance as well as negligence. On the nuisance point, the rules as to foreseeability of damage were held to be the same in both negligence and nuisance. Lord Reid put it simply saying

JUDGMENT

'It is not sufficient that the injury suffered . . . was the direct consequence of the nuisance, if that injury was in the relevant sense unforeseeable . . .'

(For a full discussion of the principles of *The Wagon Mound* see Chapter 4 section 4.5.1.)

The issue of foreseeability has been further considered by the House of Lords in *Cambridge Water Co Ltd v Eastern Counties Leather plc* [1994] 2 WLR 53. (For the facts of this case, see Chapter 10 section 10.3.2.) Goff LJ explained that the fact that defendants have taken all reasonable care to avoid the nuisance will not exonerate them from liability but he went on to say

QUOTATION

'. . . it by no means follows that the defendant should be held liable for damage of a type which he could not reasonably foresee . . . foreseeability of harm is indeed a prerequisite of the recovery of damages in . . . nuisance.'

Landlords

While a tenant who creates a nuisance will be liable, in certain circumstances the landlord may also have liability. A landlord who authorises the activity which creates the nuisance will be liable, if the nuisance is an inevitable result of the permitted activity.

CASE EXAMPLE

Tetley and others v Chitty and others [1986] 1 All ER 663

Premises were leased for the purpose of a go-karting club. The landlord, a local authority, were well aware of the potential problems such use would cause in the way of noise. It was held that as noise was a natural and necessary consequence of the use of go-karts, the landlord was liable for the nuisance which had been authorised.

ACTIVITY

Self-assessment questions

1. What is the essential purpose of the judges when deciding a claim using the tort of private nuisance?
2. Does the decision in *Hunter v Canary Wharf* mean that some classes of occupiers may be unable to bring an action for private nuisance thereby suffering injustice?
3. When is a person liable for a nuisance arising from
   (a) the activities of someone else
   (b) an act of nature?

9.4 The essential elements of private nuisance

9.4.1 Introduction

It is clear from the definition (above section 9.2.1) that there are three elements which must be proved:

(i) an unlawful, in the sense of unreasonable, use of land
(ii) which causes indirect interference
(iii) with another's land.

9.4.2 Unlawful use of land

Everyone has the right to use their land for their own purposes. While this may be subject to other parts of the law, for example town planning legislation, the general right exists and cannot be interfered with by others. Difficulties arise only when the use to which one person puts the land interferes with what a nearby occupier wishes to do on their land. It is always a question of fact but the general rule is that if the use causes interference which is unreasonable, then it is likely to be regarded by the courts as unlawful and a private nuisance.

The essence of unlawfulness for the purpose of this tort is therefore that the use is unreasonable. The judges need the wisdom of Solomon to untangle the respective claims of neighbours. What neighbour A regards as perfectly reasonable use of '*Blackacre*' may be regarded as totally unreasonable by B when it interferes with B's use of 'Whiteacre'.

The activity complained of must result in interference which is more than the inevitable result of ordinary life.

CASE EXAMPLE

Southwark London Borough Council v Mills and Others, Baxter v Camden London Borough Council [1999] 2 WLR 742

Cases were brought by tenants who lived in blocks of flats owned by the councils. The flats were badly soundproofed and the tenants complained that their lives were made miserable by everyday noises coming from next door.

As the noises complained of were part and parcel of everyday life, the behaviour of those causing the noise could not be unreasonable. It was not unreasonable activity which was causing the tenants' problems but lack of sound-proofing.

There are no hard and fast rules as to when use will be regarded as unreasonable but past cases give a good indication of how the courts will approach the task and the issues which will be taken into account. The basic question to ask is whether the defendant's act is foreseeably likely to cause the nuisance. If the answer to this question is in the affirmative, the defendant is liable. Matters which will be considered by the courts include

- locality
- duration
- malice
- sensitivity of the claimant

but none of these matters is decisive nor is the list exhaustive.

Locality

No one reasonably expects the same levels of peace and quiet in urban and industrial areas which are to be found in rural areas. Each has its own characteristics. This means that where the activity occurs is important. As Thesiger LJ said in *Sturges v Bridgman* (1879) 11 Ch D 852

JUDGMENT

'What would be a nuisance in Belgrave Square would not necessarily be so in Bermondsey.'

It is clear that where actual physical damage is caused as a result of the activity, the issue of locality is not relevant. In *St Helen's Smelting Co v Tipping* (1865) 11 HL Cas 642 the fact that the industrial use which caused physical damage occurred in an industrial area was held to be irrelevant.

Where however the interference is with a person's comfort, peace or personal freedom, locality is important. In *Laws v Florinplace Ltd* [1981] 1 All ER 659 an injunction was granted to prevent the use of a shop converted to a sex shop and cinema club in a residential area.

Duration

It is said that for an activity to amount to a nuisance, it must be continuous. This requirement may be satisfied by an activity which recurs regularly; there is no requirement that it should continue day and night over a period of time!

The fact that an activity is temporary, does not mean that it cannot amount to a nuisance. Examples can be most easily found in the context of building work. Such work almost invariably causes annoyance and inconvenience to the neighbours but it would be wholly unreasonable to prevent such work taking place. It must however be carried out in a way which is sensitive to the needs of the neighbours.

The extent of the interference is very relevant.

CASE EXAMPLE

Andreae v Selfridge & Co Ltd [1937] 3 All ER 255

Demolition work created an excessive amount of noise and dust which interfered with the business of a hotel. No injunction was granted, as building work is not in itself an unreasonable use of land, but the excessive interference with the business meant that damages were payable.

An injunction will however be granted where the temporary interference can reasonably be avoided.

CASE EXAMPLE

De Keyser's Royal Hotel Ltd v Spicer Bros Ltd (1914) 30 TLR 257

Pile driving at night meant that the sleep of the owner of the next door hotel was disturbed. An injunction was granted to prevent the work at night.

A 'one off' or isolated incident can be a nuisance. Thus in *Spicer v Smee* [1946] 1 All ER 489 a fire was caused by defective wiring in the defendant's property resulting in the claimant's property being burned to the ground. The defendant was held liable in nuisance, the damage resulting from a dangerous state of affairs on the defendant's premises. The position was explained by Mr Justice Potter in *Crown River Cruises Ltd v Kimbolton Fireworks Ltd* [1996] 2 Lloyds Rep 533 when debris from a 20 minute firework display set fire to one of the claimant's barges. The judge said

JUDGMENT

'Where an activity creates a state of affairs which gives rise to risk of escape of physically dangerous or damaging material . . . then the law of nuisance is . . . available to give a remedy for that state of affairs, albeit brief in duration.'

Malice

It is rare for the motive behind a defendant's act to be relevant in the law of tort save in those torts based on intention. In nuisance, the defendant's motive, if it can be characterised as ill-will or spite, may well result in the court regarding what would otherwise be a reasonable activity as unreasonable and therefore a nuisance.

CASE EXAMPLE

Christie v Davey [1893] 1 Ch 316

The claimant taught music and had a musical family. Music was frequently played and could be heard by the defendant who lived in the adjoining house. In retaliation, the defendant banged trays and beat on the wall to disturb the claimant.

JUDGMENT

Finding that the defendant had acted deliberately and maliciously to interfere with the claimant, Mr Justice North explained that had the defendant not acted maliciously, he would have taken a different view of the case. The malicious nature of the behaviour meant that it 'was not a legitimate use of the defendant's house to use it for the purpose of vexing and annoying his neighbours'.

CASE EXAMPLE

Hollywood Silver Fox Farm Ltd v Emmett [1936] 2 KB 468

The claimant ran a farm on which silver foxes were bred for the fur trade. At the time this was morally acceptable. The defendant, who owned the next-door farm wanted to sell land for development and believed that the presence of the fox farm reduced the value of the site. He arranged for gun shots to be fired near to the fox enclosures so that their breeding would be interrupted. It was held that the defendant's motive amounted to malice and he was liable in nuisance.

These examples are easily understood but the rules are complicated by an apparently contradictory case heard in 1895.

CASE EXAMPLE

Bradford Corporation v Pickles [1895] AC 587

Water percolated under the defendant's land eventually reaching the claimant's land from beneath which it was extracted by the claimant to maintain the municipal water supply. The defendant began to pump out the water from his own land in order to reach mineral deposits. As a result, the quantity and quality of the water reaching the claimant's land was diminished. The claimant asked for an injunction to stop the defendant from damaging the water supply to their land.

Holding that a landowner had an absolute right to extract water from undefined channels beneath his own land, Lord Macnaghton said that an act which gives rise to no legal injury cannot be made tortious no matter what the defendant's motive. It had been suggested that the defendant's motive in the case was to force the claimant to purchase either his land or the water. Even if this was morally wrong, the motive could not make the lawful act unlawful.

This at first sight appears totally to contradict the later cases on malice. However, it must be borne in mind that the court found that the factual interference in *Bradford Corporation v Pickles* was minimal. It can be suggested that the decision was reached on the principle *'de minimis non curat lex'* (the law will not correct a trivial injury). Had the damage been substantial, the outcome may have been different (*Street*, p 373).

Sensitivity of the claimant

Nuisance only operates to protect the claimant's **reasonable** use of their land. Where the use to which the claimant puts the land is unusually sensitive to things such as heat or fumes the defendant will not be liable.

CASE EXAMPLE

Robinson v Kilvert (1889) 41 Ch D 88

The claimant stored brown paper on the ground floor of a warehouse. The paper needed particular conditions for storage if it was not to deteriorate. Heat from the basement, used by the defendant, seeped into the ground floor and caused damage to the paper. It was held that there was no nuisance. The heating would not have caused problems for ordinary use of the premises. It was the particular character of the paper being stored that led to the damage.

Where however ordinary uses of land are also interfered with, there will be a remedy for that interference and for the interference with the sensitive use. This is understood if a simple example is used. If fumes cause damage to roses, a quintessentially English flower, then the claimant will be entitled to a remedy, not only for the damage to the rose bushes but also for any damage which has been caused to exotic and sensitive plants (*McKinnon Industries Ltd v Walker* (1951) 3 DLR 577).

In general the law is now moving away from the concept of 'abnormal sensitivity' and more towards a general test of foreseeability in line with negligence.

CASE EXAMPLE

Network Rail Infrastructure v Morris [2004] EWCA Civ 172

The claimant ran a recording studio close to a railway line. The defendant then installed new track circuits which interfered with the claimant's amplification system and caused the claimant to lose business as a result. The Court of Appeal held that the defendant was not liable, not because the recording studio represented an abnormally sensitive use of land, but because it was not foreseeable that the installation would interfere with the claimant's use of land in such a way.

The case also runs in line with the line of cases (eg *Hunter v Canary Wharf* and *Bridlington Relay Ltd v Yorkshire Electricity Board*) which prevent claims for interference with recreational activities.

9.4.3 Indirect interference

The cases referred to all demonstrate that the consequences suffered by the claimant are the indirect result of the defendant's activity or the state of affairs on the defendant's land.

9.4.4 The use and enjoyment of land

Nuisance is not actionable *per se* thus the claimant must prove damage. Where physical damage has been caused to the land itself, the claimant will not usually face undue difficulty in establishing a case. Interference with use and enjoyment of land is more complex. It has already been seen that the issue is judged subjectively, the courts asking the question 'What effect does this activity have on this claimant?' It is obviously not enough for a claimant living in a town to complain that a neighbour keeps chickens in the garden. Something more is needed. For example if a cockerel is also kept which welcomes the dawn (and wakes the neighbours) with a 'cock-a-doodle-doo' every morning, the neighbours are likely to have a valid cause of action. Simply taking a dislike to a neighbour's activity will not suffice.

The interference, although it is intangible, must still be substantial. Lord Knight Bruce VC explained that it must interfere with 'the ordinary comfort physically of human existence.' He discounted 'elegant or dainty modes and habits of living' preferring to judge comfort 'according to plain and simple notions' (*Walter v Selfe* (1851) 4 De G & Sm 315).

Interests which are regarded as aesthetic are not usually protected. Thus the courts have refused to recognise

- The right to a view (*A-G v Doughty* (1752) 2 Ves Sen 453).
- The right to an unrestricted flow of air in the absence of an easement (*Bland v Moseley* (1587) 9 Co Rep 58; *Chastey v Ackland* [1895] 2 Ch 389).
- In the absence of an easement, the right to light (*Dalton v Angus* (1881) 6 App Cas 740).

Reviewing these cases in *Hunter and Others v Canary Wharf Ltd*, the House of Lords held that there could be no right to freedom from interference with television reception. (For a fuller discussion of this case see above section 9.1.)

9.5 Defences

This section deals with the accepted defences of

prescription
A defence in private nuisance where the thing complained of had been active for 20 years or more and the claimant had known about it and not complained before

- **prescription**
- statutory authority
- planning consent.

It also deals with matters which are commonly thought of as defences but which are not in fact effective

- coming to the nuisance
- social utility
- acts of others.

It can be argued that the last three matters could be morally justified as defences but the courts have not given any indication that the position may change.

9.5.1 Prescription

While the fact that the claimant moved to the nuisance is not a defence, it is possible for a person to obtain a prescriptive right to carry on an activity that in the eyes of some amounts to a private nuisance. The activity complained of must have been continuously carried on for at least 20 years. Throughout that time it must have been actionable as a private nuisance but nobody has in fact taken action.

Care should be taken in relation to this defence. It does not matter how long an activity has been carried on for unless, for the last 20 years at least, someone has been in occupation of nearby land and would have been able to establish a nuisance affecting that land. The occupiers of a new housing development built next to an isolated church in which bells have been rung for centuries may be able to silence the bells. The basis of this is that until the new houses were built no-one had been in a position to establish a nuisance.

The leading case on this issue is *Sturges v Bridgman* (1879) 11 ChD 852.

CASE EXAMPLE

Sturges v Bridgman (1879) 11 ChD 852

For more than 20 years a confectioner had carried on his business which included the use of an industrial pestle and mortar to grind sugar. The premises abutted onto the garden of premises occupied by a doctor. The doctor built a new consulting room at the bottom of his garden but found that it could not be used because of the noise and vibration coming from the confectioner's premises. The doctor was able to obtain an injunction against the confectioner despite the fact that the business had been in operation for more than 20 years. It had only become an actionable nuisance once the new consulting room was built therefore no prescriptive right could exist.

This defence, if established, is a species of easement. For more detailed discussion of the acquisition of easements by prescription, reference should be made to a text on land law.

9.5.2 Statutory authority

In the modern world many activities are undertaken by public utilities and large commercial enterprises, some of which require the assistance of specific legislation to be established. Examples of recent projects requiring legislation include the re-development of Docklands, the construction of the Channel Tunnel and the creation of the high-speed rail link between the Tunnel and London.

When an actionable nuisance arises as a result of the activity permitted by the statute, the statute must be interpreted by the courts to ascertain whether or not the nuisance itself has been authorised and what, if any, remedy may be available. (For a discussion on how the courts approach this task, see Chapter 16 Breach of a Statutory Duty.)

Some statutes contain a 'nuisance' clause which specifically states that the common law of nuisance shall continue to apply to the activity. In such a case the parties adversely affected need only satisfy the usual rules. Occasionally statutes make it explicitly clear that carrying out the permitted activity will not give rise to a civil claim. We have already seen that the Civil Aviation Act 1982 contains specific provision that over-flying aircraft cannot give rise to a claim in nuisance or trespass to land (see Chapter 8 section 8.3).

Other statutes may prescribe a remedy while not specifically stating that there shall be no remedy in nuisance. An example of this is found in the Water Industry Act 1991 which gives individuals the right to complain to the Director-General of Water Services who has enforcement powers. In the recent case of *Marcic v Thames Water Utilities Ltd* [2003] UKHL 66 (for facts see Chapter 1 section 1.5.6) it was held that the common law of nuisance could 'not impose on Thames Water obligations inconsistent with the statutory scheme' (per Lord Nicholls at para 33), leaving the claimant no remedy for what was in reality a nuisance even if it was not one in law.

Other statutes are silent on the issue. The question then to be answered is whether the activity is within the scope of that authorised by the statute. If it is, and is the inevitable consequence of that activity, there will be no redress. It is for the organisation carrying out the activity to prove that it is within the scope of the statute and that all reasonable care has been taken to minimise the problems.

The basis of this approach was explained by Lord Wilberforce in *Allen v Gulf Oil Refining Ltd* [1980] QB 156 when he said

JUDGMENT

'It is now well settled that where Parliament by express direction or by necessary implication has authorised [an activity], that carries with it an authority to do what is authorised with immunity from any action based on nuisance.'

It may be that the provisions of the Human Rights Act 1998 have altered the position somewhat. This is discussed in section 9.9.3.

9.5.3 Planning permission

Planning permission is granted by local authorities using delegated statutory powers. Those making the decisions are the elected representatives of the local community and among the issues they must take into account is the suitability of the proposals for the particular area. It can be argued therefore that the issue of locality has been considered by the local authority which has decided that the proposal is in fact likely to be a reasonable use of land in that locality. This could mean that the grant of planning permission should be regarded as a defence working in a similar way to statutory authority. This is not in fact the case although as we shall see, there is some movement in the courts towards this idea.

In *Allen v Gulf Oil Refining Ltd* Lord Cumming-Bruce said

JUDGMENT

'the planning authority has no jurisdiction to authorise nuisance save (if at all) in so far as it has … power to permit the change of the character of the neighbourhood . . .'

This comment proved to be important when *Gillingham Borough Council v Medway (Chatham) Dock Co Ltd* [1993] QB 343 came before the courts.

CASE EXAMPLE

Gillingham Borough Council v Medway (Chatham) Dock Co Ltd [1993] QB 343

The Council alleged a public nuisance was being caused by the operation of a former naval dockyard as a commercial enterprise. Heavy goods vehicles were using local residential roads by night disturbing the local population. Planning permission had been given for the development despite acknowledged concerns about the extensive use of one particular entrance to the area. It was this which caused the eventual problem.

Mr Justice Buckley stated that he must

JUDGMENT

'judge the present claim in nuisance by reference to the present character of the neighbourhood pursuant to the planning permission . . .'

He took the view that

JUDGMENT

'The [defendant] could not operate a commercial port . . . without disturbing nearby residents'

and that it was that operation which was specifically authorised. In conclusion the Judge stated that

JUDGMENT

'. . . where planning consent is given for a development or change of use, the question of nuisance will . . . fall to be decided by reference to a neighbourhood with that development or use and not as it was previously . . .'

These two cases seem to indicate that the grant of planning permission can indeed have the same effect as statutory authority. Following *Gillingham* the view was taken that the grant of planning permission of itself meant that no nuisance could arise from the authorised activity.

This proved to be inaccurate when the matter was considered further by the Court of Appeal in *Wheeler and Another v J J Saunders Ltd and Others* [1996] Ch 19:

CASE EXAMPLE

Wheeler and Another v J J Saunders Ltd and Others [1996] Ch 19

The claimants bought a farmhouse on land next to farmland and obtained planning permission to convert outbuildings into holiday homes. This was the only permitted use of the outbuildings by virtue of a restrictive covenant in the title deeds of the premises. The defendants obtained planning permission to build two pig housing units on the farmland but very close to the holiday homes. At first instance it was held that the smell coming from the pig units amounted to a nuisance. The defendants appealed arguing that as they had planning permission for the units, no nuisance could be actionable.

Considering the judgments in *Allen v Gulf Oil* and in *Gillingham v Medway*, Lord Justice Peter Gibson held that planning permission can only amount to a defence where as a result of the permitted activity

JUDGMENT

'there will be a change in the character of the neighbourhood.'

On the facts this had not happened in this case as the farmland remained farmland with an intensified use and the nuisance caused by the smell was not inevitable.

JUDGMENT

'[T]he judge was entitled to conclude that the planning consents did not prevent the [claimants] from succeeding in their claim in nuisance.'

So where does this leave the law? The rules can be summarised as follows:

■ Where planning consent is granted for a development which will inevitably mean a change in the nature of the locality, an actionable nuisance will not arise provided the operation is undertaken with reasonable care.

In other cases, the grant of planning consent will simply be one of the factors taken into account by the court but will not of itself afford a defence to a nuisance.

A different problem occurs for instance where sporting venues are involved.

CASE EXAMPLE

Watson v Croft Promo-sport [2009] EWCA Civ 15

Planning permission was gained in 1963 to use a former aerodrome as a motor racing track. After a while racing ceased for a few years, but in 1995 new owners reopened it and it became a very popular circuit. The new owners reapplied for planning permission for 210 days per year and following a public inquiry this was again granted. The claimant who lived about 300 metres from the circuit brought an action in private nuisance. The planning authority had accepted that the planning permission in 1998 had changed the character of the area and so the defendant's use of the circuit was reasonable. However, the Court of Appeal granted an injunction restraining the defendant from using the race track for more than 40 days per year.

9.5.4 Coming to the nuisance

This section considers the first of three issues which are commonly thought to raise a defence but which do not in fact do so!

Unless the defence of prescription applies (see above section 9.5.1) the fact that an activity has continued for some time without anyone complaining about it will make no difference to the validity of a claim. In *Bliss v Hall* (1838) 4 Bing NC 183 the claimant who had just moved to the area was granted an injunction to prevent a nuisance caused by a tallow-chandlery. The chandlery had been emitting 'divers noisome, noxious, and offensive vapours, fumes, smells and stenches' for three years prior to the claimant's action but this could not be a defence.

Modern cases such as *Miller v Jackson* [1977] QB 966 and *Kennaway v Thompson* [1980] 3 WLR 361 make it clear that the issue may be relevant to the remedy granted to the claimant. It will not however enable the court to conclude that a nuisance does not exist where the relevant criteria are satisfied (see section 9.6 for full discussion of remedies).

9.5.5 Social utility

The fact that the defendant's activity is of social utility and benefit to the general community does not amount to a defence. This can have some results which may be devastating for the local community and the economy. In *Adams v Ursell* [1913] 1 Ch 269 a fried-fish shop was closed as it was a nuisance to the residents in the part of the street where it was situated. The fact that its closure would cause great hardship to the defendant and the poor people who were his customers was irrelevant. Similarly in *Bellew v Cement Co* [1948] Ir R 61 the only cement factory in Ireland was closed despite the urgent need for building at that time.

The modern cases indicate that social utility may be taken into account in considering the remedy but it will not be regarded as a defence.

9.5.6 The nuisance results from the acts of many people

Defendants may well feel very hard done by when they are found liable for a nuisance emanating from their land which results from the actions of others. It has already been seen that a defendant can be liable for the acts of a trespasser (*Sedleigh-Denfield v O'Callagan*). Where the nuisance is caused by many individuals each doing something which is not in itself unlawful, the occupier may well find that they are liable because of the cumulative effect (*Thorpe v Brumfitt* (1873) LR 8 Ch App 650).

This may perhaps be relevant where a landowner permits discarded goods to be placed on land. The situation would be partly governed by environmental protection legislation but the potential for civil liability for nuisance remains.

9.6 Remedies

9.6.1 Injunction

An injunction is the remedy of choice where a nuisance is continuing or is likely to recur. The principles which govern injunctions generally are discussed in Chapter 20. For the moment it is enough to state that an injunction should be granted unless the injury suffered by the claimant is trivial or temporary in nature or the activity is an isolated incident or so irregular that any injury can be compensated with damages.

CASE EXAMPLE

Swaine v Great Northern Railway (1864) 4 De GJ & S 211

Manure heaps generally caused no trouble but intermittently became offensive when removal was delayed and occasionally when dead dogs and cats were found in the heap. It was held that an injunction would be inappropriate as the problem was occasional but those who were inconvenienced were entitled to damages.

We have already seen in *Bliss v Hall* and *Sturges v Bridgman* that the fact that the claimant moved to the nuisance is irrelevant. Lord Denning took a very different view in *Miller v Jackson* [1977] QB 966.

CASE EXAMPLE

Miller v Jackson [1977] QB 966

A cricket ground had been used for more than 70 years when a new housing estate was built. The houses were so close to the ground that balls regularly came into the garden meaning that using the garden during a match was dangerous. The claimants alleged nuisance and negligence. The majority of the Court of Appeal held that both torts were established (Lord Denning dissenting) and the majority also held that no injunction should be granted (Lord Lane dissenting).

Lord Denning's judgment is interesting in the view he took as to whether or not the use of the cricket ground could be regarded as unreasonable use of that land. Rejecting the precedent set by *Sturges v Bridgman* he argued that the case should be approached 'on principles applicable to modern conditions'. There was a conflict between the interest of the public at large and the private interest. The public interest would be served by preservation of playing fields in the face of mounting development and thus allow people to enjoy the benefit of outdoor games. The private interest is to secure privacy of home and garden without interference.

Taking account of the fact that the claimants bought the house in mid-summer when the cricket season was at its height, Lord Denning took the view that the risk of balls coming into the property should have been obvious. On this basis, he held

JUDGMENT

'As between [these] conflicting interests, I am of the opinion that the public interest should prevail over the private interest.'

The majority of the court having found a nuisance, an injunction was refused although damages were awarded.

The case has since been criticised but not over-ruled. The judgment seems to have contributed to the more recent tendency to tailor an injunction to try to give a fair balance between competing interests. A good example of this is found in *Kennaway v Thompson* [1980] 3 WLR 361.

CASE EXAMPLE

Kennaway v Thompson [1980] 3 WLR 361

The claimant had built and occupied a house next to a lake on which, as she knew at that time, there had been water sports for the last 10 years. Over the years the use of the lake increased as it became a centre for world-class events involving much larger and noisier boats. The court found that the increased use, which attracted large numbers of spectators, had gone beyond the point at which the claimant could reasonably be expected to tolerate it. At first instance the claimant was refused an injunction but the Court of Appeal took a different view.

The Court held that it was bound by the principles expounded in *Shelfer v City of London Electric Lighting Co* [1895] 1 Ch 287 in which the principle was laid down that unless the injury to the claimant was small, an injunction should be the appropriate remedy. In this case, the injury was not small and the claimant was entitled to an injunction. The judges were concerned to balance the interests of claimant and defendant. They concluded that an injunction allowing one annual international event over three days plus three club events each year of one day each but separated by at least four weeks would achieve this. A limit was also imposed on the power of the boats used and the number of water-skiing boats at other times.

While it is likely that neither of the parties was completely happy with the outcome, the case illustrates the extent to which the courts are now prepared to go to try to achieve a true balance between the competing interests of neighbours.

9.6.2 Damages

The claimant will be able to recover damages for any loss which has occurred to the value of the land and for any physical consequences of the nuisance or business loss. There has been some doubt about whether damages for personal injury which has resulted from the nuisance can be recovered. The doubt has been raised by the judgment in *Hunter v Canary Wharf* where it was held by three of the judges that damages for personal injury could not be recovered in the tort of private nuisance. The view that such damages cannot be awarded has been confirmed obiter in *Transco plc v Stockport Metropolitan Borough Council* [2003] UKHL 61, a case about *Rylands v Fletcher* (1868) LR 1 Exch 265 which is discussed in detail in Chapter 10.

Does the claimant have a proprietary interest in the land affected by the nuisance?

YES

Is there an indirect interference with the land?
- The interference involves eg noise, vibrations, smell, smoke, fumes etc
- But not direct interference

YES

NO

NO

Has the nuisance caused damage to property?

NO

Has the nuisance interfered with the claimant's use or enjoyment of his land?

NO

YES

YES

Is there an unreasonable use of land?
- The locality is such that the nuisance is not acceptable
- The nuisance is continuous
- The claimant is not over sensitive
- There may be malice
- The interference is not with a purely recreational use of land

NO

No action in private nuisance is possible

YES

YES

Is there an available defence?
- Statutory authority
- Planning permission (if the character of the land has been changed by statute)
- Prescription (20 years uninterrupted)
- Act of a stranger
- Act of God
- Consent
- Public policy

YES

NO

An action in private nuisance is possible

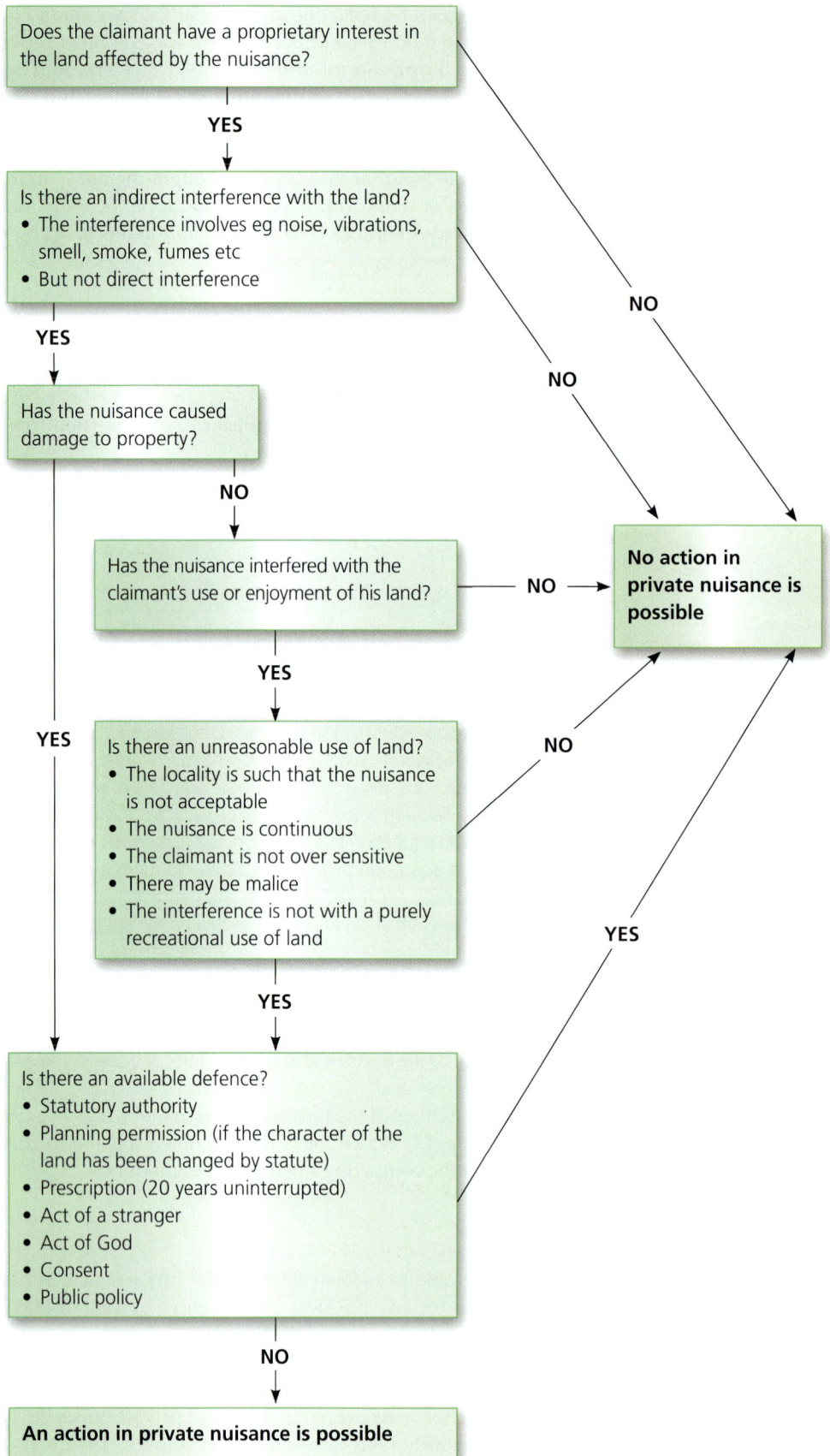

Figure 9.2 Diagram illustrating the essential elements for a claim in private nuisance

9.6.3 Abatement

A person affected by a nuisance has the right to take action to reduce or eliminate the nuisance. This self-help remedy is not as straight forward as it would seem. Where tree branches overhang the claimant's land, for example, the offending branches can be lopped without entering the defendant's land. Care must be taken not to cause unnecessary damage to the trees and the branches must be returned to the defendant.

Where entry onto the defendant's land is necessary the claimant needs to alert the defendant to the problem and give enough time for the necessary remedial action to be taken. If the claimant then needs to take action, care must be taken to do only that which is necessary and not to cause unnecessary damage.

Where the situation is such that there is a serious risk of damage to people or property, action can be taken without notice.

The remedy looks attractive at first sight but has one major drawback. In many cases the existence of the nuisance may well have caused a deterioration of the relationship between neighbours. It is unlikely that exercising the right to abate the nuisance will improve the relationship!

ACTIVITY

Self-assessment questions

1. What is meant by the word 'unlawful' in the context of private nuisance?
2. Explain the matters which may be relevant to the court's decision.
3. Consider the extent to which the defendant's motive for the activity may be relevant.
4. How does the defence of prescription contradict the principle that coming to the nuisance is no defence?
5. Explain the circumstances in which the grant of planning consent by a local planning authority may serve as a defence.

KEY FACTS

Key facts on private nuisance

Definition	Case
One person's use of their land unlawfully interferes with another's use of their land.	
Requires balancing of interests of parties concerned.	
Interference is unlawful if it is unreasonable.	
Claimant	**Case**
Must have a legal interest – usually right to exclusive possession.	
Others, eg lodgers, have no remedy.	*Malone v Laskey* (1907)
Note – HL over-ruling	*Hunter v Canary Wharf* (1997)
CA attempt to widen categories of claimant in	*Khorasandjian v Bush* (1993)

Defendant	Case
Person who creates nuisance usually occupier.	
Independent contractors liable for their activities unless extra-hazardous when occupier remains liable.	*Honeywill and Stein v Larkin Brothers* (1934)
Occupier who 'adopts' nuisance created by trespasser liable for that nuisance.	*Sedleigh-Denfield v O'Callaghan* (1940)
Occupier liable for act of nature where they are or ought to be aware of the potential for nuisance	*Goldman v Hargrave* (1967)
but note requirement of reasonable foreseeability.	*Leakey v National Trust* (1980)
	Cambridge Water v Eastern Counties Leather (1994)
	Holbeck Hall Hotel v Scarborough BC (2000)
Landlords not generally liable unless nuisance inevitable result of activity permitted by terms of letting.	*Tetley v Chitty* (1986)

Unlawful	Case
If interference is unreasonable it is likely to be unlawful.	
Problem for courts as 'unreasonable' cannot be defined.	
Ordinary every-day activities cannot be unreasonable.	*Southwark LBC v Mills* (1999)
Relevant factors depend on facts of particular case but include:	
locality	*Sturges v Bridgman* (1879);
but note locality irrelevant where physical damage caused	*Laws v Florinplace Ltd* (1981)
duration in sense of continuous or regular – can be temporary as in case of building work which is insensitive to needs of neighbours.	*St Helen's v Tipping* (1865); *Andreae v Selfridge* (1937);
Exceptionally can be 'one off' incident.	*De Keyser's Royal Hotel v Spicer Bros* (1914)
	Spicer v Smee (1946);
	Crown River Cruises v Kimbolton Fireworks (1996)
Note effect of malice which can make activity unreasonable.	*Christie v Davey* (1893);
	Hollywood Silver Fox Farm v Emmett (1936)
No remedy if only damage caused results from unusual sensitivity of claimant or claimant's property.	*Robinson v Kilvert* (1889);
	McKinnon Industries v Walker (1951)

Damage	Case
Must be proved – not usually difficult in case of physical damage.	
Court must consider effect of the particular activity on the particular claimant – subjective assessment.	
Interference must be with interest recognised thus, eg no right to a view	*A-G v Doughty* (1752)
nor to freedom of interference with TV reception.	*Hunter v Canary Wharf* (1997)
Must be reasonably foreseeable.	*Cambridge Water v Eastern Counties Leather* (1994)

Defences	Case
Prescription – activity has amounted to actionable nuisance for at least 20 years without anyone in position to do so taking action.	*Sturges v Bridgman* (1879)
Statutory authority – statute may give remedy or specifically provide that the common law shall not apply – possible action for breach of statutory duty – if statute does not say no remedy for activity permitted by statute which inevitably creates nuisance.	*Allen v Gulf Oil* (1980)
Planning consent – full defence if nuisance inevitable consequence of change in nature of locality authorised by the consent.	*Gillingham BC v Medway (Chatham) Dock* (1993)
No defence in other circumstances.	*Wheeler v J J Saunders* (1996)

Oddities	Case
Fact that claimant moved to the area of the nuisance and even knew about it is no defence.	*Bliss v Hall* (1838)
but see Lord Denning's comments in	*Miller v Jackson* (1977)
Activity which has social utility may be prohibited.	*Adams v Ursell* (1913); *Bellew v Cement Co* (1948)
Nuisance can result from acts of many people none of which is in itself unlawful.	*Thorpe v Brumfitt* (1873)

Remedies	Case
Injunction – must be granted unless injury is trivial or can be adequately compensated by damages – can be tailored to strike balance between interests of claimant and defendant.	*Kennaway v Thompson* (1980)
Damages – recoverable for loss to value of the land and any physical damage to land – not available for personal injury.	*Hunter v Canary Wharf* (1997); *Transco v Stockport MBC* (2003)
Abatement or self-help.	

9.7 Public nuisance

9.7.1 Definition

The most commonly used definition is that given by Lord Justice Romer in *Attorney-General (on the relation of Glamorgan County Council and Pontardawe Rural District Council) v PYA Quarries Ltd* [1957] 2 QB 169:

JUDGMENT

'Any nuisance is "public" which materially affects the reasonable comfort and convenience of life of a class of Her Majesty's subjects.'

It is clear from this definition that in reality it is impossible to state precisely what a public nuisance is! Some things are however certain.

Public nuisance is a crime as well as a tort and can lead to prosecution and punishment. Apart from noting this fact, this book does not concern itself with the criminal aspect.

An action for public nuisance is brought by the Attorney-General on behalf of all those affected. The civil action is known as a 'relator action'. This enables an injunction to be obtained prohibiting nuisance behaviour when it would be unreasonable to expect each individual affected to bring their own separate action, saving time and costs. Local authorities may also apply on behalf of the local community (Local Government Act 1972 s 222).

Damages cannot be awarded to any individual for injuries caused by a public nuisance unless that individual can prove that they have suffered special damage beyond that generally arising from the nuisance. Where an individual has suffered such additional injury, the action may be brought by the Attorney-General or by the individual.

9.7.2 Elements of the tort

A class of people

The question can be asked – what is a class of people? How many people need to be affected before an action can be brought? This is in reality simply a question of fact in each case.

Special damage

If an individual is to succeed, damage which is 'particular, direct and substantial' beyond that suffered by others affected must be proved (per Brett J in *Benjamin v Storr* (1874) LR 9 CP 400).

CASE EXAMPLE

Benjamin v Storr (1874) LR 9 CP 400

The claimant ran a coffee house. The light to the windows was obstructed by the defendant's horse-drawn vans which stood outside the coffee-house. As a result the claimant had to use gas lamps all day, his customers had problems reaching the coffee house and they complained about the smell from the horses. The court had little difficulty in finding that the claimant had suffered in excess of others affected by the defendant's actions.

special damage
This occurs in slander where the claimant usually has to prove that he has suffered damage as a result – also occurs in public nuisance where the claimant has to show that he has suffered damage over that suffered by the public generally

Unless **special damage** can be established, there is no cause of action available to individuals. In *Thomas v National Union of Mineworkers* working miners claimed that they had suffered special damage by reason of the pickets who were obstructing the highway. As their entrance into the mine was not physically prevented, it was held that the obstruction of the highway did not cause the working miners special damage.

Where public nuisance is concerned, there is no requirement that the claimant has an interest in land. The following case example concerns rights of navigation over a river bed.

CASE EXAMPLE

Tate & Lyle Industries Ltd v Greater London Council and another [1983] 2 AC 509

The claimants operated a jetty that they had built on the bank of the Thames from which refined sugar could be loaded onto boats. They obtained a licence from the Port of London Authority (PLA) to build a new jetty for the off-loading of raw sugar. At the same time the PLA granted a licence to the GLC to build two ferry terminals. The new 'sugar' jetty was rendered very expensive to operate because of silting caused by the ferry terminals. The claimants sued the GLC and the PLA in public nuisance

JUDGMENT

'[The] interference with the public right of navigation caused particular damage to [the claimants] because vessels of the requisite dimensions were unable to pass and repass over the bed and foreshore between the main channel and the [jetties].'

A particular set of facts may give rise to claims in both public and private nuisance. *Halsey v Esso Petroleum Co Ltd* [1961] 1 WLR 683 illustrates this very clearly.

CASE EXAMPLE

Halsey v Esso Petroleum Co Ltd [1961] 1 WLR 683

The claimant lived on a house adjoining the Fulham Road in London, a very busy area, and near to a depot owned and operated by the defendants. The claimant and his neighbours all suffered from the use of the depot but the claimant alleged that he suffered more than most. Washing, hung out to dry, and his car, parked on the road outside his house, was damaged by acid smuts; the noise of tankers turning into and out of the depot kept him awake at night; finally there was a dreadful smell. The smuts were disgorged from the chimneys in the depot, the noise from the tankers came from the use of the highway.

It was held that the damage to the washing and the consequences of the smell interfered with the claimant's use and enjoyment of his land and arose from the defendant's use of their land. This gave rise to liability for private nuisance. The damage to the car occurred on the highway and did not affect the claimant's use and enjoyment of his land; the sleepless nights also resulted from use of the highway. These were held to give rise to liability in public nuisance and the claimant was able to recover damages as he had suffered more than other residents who were affected by the defendant's activities.

Highways

Many public nuisances occur as a result of abuse of the right of passage over a highway. A temporary obstruction is unlikely to amount to a public nuisance unless it is also unreasonable. This is illustrated by *Trevett v Lee* [1955] 1 All ER 406. Unlike in private nuisance it appears that a claimant can recover for personal injury *Corby Group Litigation v Corby BC* [2008] EWCA Civ 463.

CASE EXAMPLE

Trevett v Lee [1955] 1 All ER 406

The claimant tripped over a hosepipe laid across the highway by the defendant who had no mains connection to his premises. The claimant's action failed as the use by the defendant was regarded as reasonable.

Where premises adjoin the highway and damage is caused by something falling onto the highway there may be liability for public nuisance on the part of the land owner. The evidence must show that the owner knew or ought to have known of the danger. Thus in *Noble v Harrison* [1926] 2 KB 332 the defendant was not liable when a branch fell from a tree onto the claimant's vehicle. The defect which caused the fall of the branch was latent and could not have been found on reasonable examination of the tree.

Dangerous premises which collapse onto a highway will amount to a public nuisance if the collapse is caused by lack of maintenance. In *Wringe v Cohen* [1940] 1 KB 229 it was made clear that knowledge or imputed knowledge of the dangerous state of the premises is not required. It is enough that want of repair has led to the consequence which has occurred.

Local authorities and the Highways Authority face a never-ending battle to maintain the highway in a safe condition. Following the Highways Act 1980 s 41(1) a highway authority is under a duty to maintain the highway and is liable for any damage resulting from lack of repair unless reasonable care has been taken to maintain the highway in a safe condition (s 58). A person who trips over uneven paving stones will probably be able to obtain compensation. However, the duty has limitations. In *Sandhar v Department of Transport* [2004] EWCA Civ 1440 there was held to be no general common law duty to salt roads to prevent the build-up of ice.

9.7.3 Remedies

The individual who can establish a case will be entitled to damages. It was thought that these could include compensation for personal injury but doubt has now been cast on this by *Hunter v Canary Wharf and Transco v Stockport* (see section 9.6.2).

An injunction will usually be granted on the application of the Attorney-General or a local authority but there is theoretically no reason why an individual should not obtain such an order in an appropriate case.

KEY FACTS

Public nuisance	Case
Defined as something which affects the comfort and convenience of a class of people.	
Crime as well as tort.	
Action taken on behalf of those affected by Attorney-General or local authority.	
Individual can bring action only if they have suffered special damage above and beyond that suffered by the other members of the class.	*Benjamin v Storr* (1874)
Individual affected need not have any interest in land	*Tate & Lyle v GLC* (1983)
facts of particular case can amount to both public and private nuisance.	*Halsey v Esso Petroleum* (1961)
Abuse of right of passage over highway can be public nuisance – damage caused by something falling onto highway can be nuisance.	*Noble v Harrison* (1926) *Wringe v Cohen* (1940)

ACTIVITY

Self-assessment questions

1. What are the significant differences between private nuisance and public nuisance?
2. Explain the extent to which an individual affected by public nuisance can hope to receive damages for special damage.

9.8 Statutory nuisance

9.8.1 Introduction

Statutory nuisance is not generally dealt with in a book on tort law. It is however useful to include some brief detail. A statutory nuisance will often also amount to a private nuisance. Where this is the case, the claimant has the choice of a simple, cheap and effective course of action available by virtue of powers vested in the local authority.

9.8.2 Definition

A statutory nuisance is defined by Environmental Protection Act 1990 s 79. The definition includes

- premises prejudicial to health or a nuisance
- smoke from premises prejudicial to health or a nuisance
- fumes or gases from premises
- dust, steam, smell or other effluvia arising on industrial, trade or business premises
- accumulations or deposits

- animals
- noise emitted from premises or from or caused by a vehicle, machinery or equipment in a street
- any other matter declared by statute to be a statutory nuisance, provided in each case the matter is prejudicial to health or a nuisance.

'Prejudicial to health' in this context means actually injurious or likely to cause injury to health. The reference appears to be to physical rather than mental health. 'Nuisance' has the same meaning as for the common law tort.

9.8.3 What action can be taken?

The local authority has a duty to investigate complaints from local inhabitants in respect of statutory nuisance. Once the authority is satisfied that a nuisance exists, or is likely to occur or to recur, an abatement notice must be served which tells the person on whom it is served what is wrong, what needs to be done to put matters right (abatement) and imposes a time limit for compliance.

There is a right of appeal to the magistrates' court against the notice. Non-compliance means that the local authority will take enforcement action through the magistrates' court which has power to require the work to be done within a specified time limit. Thereafter, for every day that the work remains outstanding, a fine will be imposed.

The advantage of local authority action is that it does not cost the complainant anything, beyond the usual payment of Council Tax, and the sanction available through the courts tends to mean that abatement notices are not ignored.

For a full discussion of statutory nuisance, reference should be made to a text on environmental law.

9.9 Nuisance in relation to other parts of the law

9.9.1 Nuisance in relation to negligence

It has been seen that nuisance and negligence have at least two things in common:

(i) a duty of care
(ii) foreseeability of damage.

The duty of care is in fact dissimilar. In negligence the duty of care is to avoid acts or omissions which the reasonable person would foresee as likely to cause injury or damage. Provided reasonable care is taken to avoid those risks, the defendant will not be liable. In nuisance, the duty of care is to take reasonable care in carrying out the activity complained of. In *Sedleigh-Denfield v O'Callagan* the defendants failed to take reasonable care having 'adopted' a defective culvert; in *Goldman v Hargrave* and in *Leakey v National Trust* the defendants failed to take reasonable care to deal with the consequences of an act of nature. The fact that a defendant has taken all reasonable care to avoid a nuisance will not of itself mean that the defendant is not liable (*Cambridge Water v Eastern Counties Leather*).

In relation to damage, in both torts the rules in *The Wagon Mound* apply so that the defendant will be liable for damage which is of the type or kind which is a reasonably foreseeable consequence of the act.

9.9.2 Nuisance in relation to *Rylands v Fletcher*

In reality the torts have much in common. This is hardly surprising when it is remembered that *Rylands v Fletcher* is rooted in nuisance. As we have seen, nuisance will generally only be established where an activity has continued for some time. This leaves a gap where the claimant's land has been damaged as a result of a non-negligent escape of something from the defendant's land. As will be seen in Chapter 10, *Rylands v Fletcher* goes some way to fill the gap by setting out circumstances in which defendants will be liable for the escape of something dangerous from their land.

9.9.3 Nuisance in relation to human rights

The general issue of human rights is considered in Chapter 1 and reference should be made to that Chapter for detail. We have seen that in a number of cases, notably in *Hatton and Others v UK* (2003) ECtHR 37 EHRR 28 and *Dennis and Dennis v Ministry of Defence* [2003] EWHC 793 (QB), that a nuisance which is not actionable, in both cases because of the wider public interest, may nonetheless be recognised as a breach of Article 8. In *Hatton* it was held that no compensation should be awarded but in *Dennis* the High Court held that the claimants were entitled to compensation for the reduced value of their land.

This is a very recent development in English law. The true extent of the impact of human rights on the law of nuisance is not yet clear but it can be suggested that further developments are very likely to occur.

9.10 Other remedies for nuisance behaviour

It is easy to see that the tort of nuisance in all its various guises cannot deal with all forms of nuisance behaviour. Stories of the 'neighbours from hell' are common. Problems between neighbours can have a serious effect on both individuals and their communities. People are not always reasonable nor are they always prepared to accept that their behaviour is causing problems for others. Nuisance does not provide a remedy where, for example, children are running riot or where abusive and aggressive behaviour regularly occurs.

In some cases the criminal law may be of some help. Vandalism, for example, may amount to criminal damage and the perpetrator can be punished. It is easy to see that this is not often a very effective remedy.

Anti-social behaviour orders

The anti-social behaviour order, introduced by the Crime and Disorder Act 1998, enables the magistrates' court to tailor an order to the particular circumstances. This can include imposing a curfew, excluding a person from a particular area or forbidding a person to contact named individuals. The order can only be made on the application of the police or a local authority. The basic requirements are

■ the person against whom the order is sought is aged 10 or more
■ the behaviour complained of has caused or is likely to cause harassment, alarm or distress to one or more persons not in the same household.

The best indication of the type of behaviour with which the orders are intended to deal is found in a Consultation Paper published in 1995:

QUOTATION

'Such behaviour manifests itself in many different ways and at varying levels of intensity. This can include vandalism, noise, verbal and physical abuse, threats of violence, racial harassment, damage to property, trespass, nuisance from dogs, car repairs on the street, joyriding, domestic violence, drugs and other criminal activities such as burglary.'

Consultation Paper on Probationary Tenancies, Dept of the Environment (1995)

Examples of orders which have been imposed include one on teenagers who were prevented from entering a particular area following disturbances (see for example *R v Manchester Crown Court, ex p McCann* [2001] Legal Action Group Journal February p 27) and against tenants using their home for the purposes of drug-dealing and prostitution (see for example *Leicester CC v Lewis* [2000] Legal Action Group Journal November p 21).

Breach of the order is a criminal offence and can be punished by up to five years' imprisonment and/or an unlimited fine where the breach is serious enough to be tried in the Crown Court.

Protection from Harassment Act 1997

This is discussed in some detail in Chapter 13 section 13.6.2 in the context of trespass to the person. It will also be useful where nuisance fails to provide a remedy because the person subjected to the nuisance does not have the necessary interest in land.

Alternative dispute resolution, etc

In many cases taking legal action is likely to exacerbate an already difficult situation. It is clear that lack of effective communication between neighbours can mean that nothing is said about the problem until matters have reached the point where there is a major argument or worse. Some local authorities have introduced mediation or conciliation schemes to try to take the confrontational aspect out of the situation and to reach an acceptable solution.

Given the drive to reduce the number of cases coming before the courts where an alternative way can be appropriately used, it is likely that such schemes will proliferate. Could it be that the use of such schemes where they are available may become a condition precedent to the taking of court action?

SAMPLE ESSAY QUESTION

'The torts of private and public nuisance achieve different ends but are equally effective'. Discuss the accuracy of the above statement.

Outline the basic elements of a claim in private nuisance

- Defined as unlawful, indirect interference with another person's use or enjoyment of land
- Claimants have to show an interest in the land
- There is a difference between nuisance causing damage and one causing interference with comfort or the enjoyment of land
- Unlawful means unreasonable behaviour

Discuss factors courts use to determine whether there is unreasonable use of land

- Locality – what is a nuisance in one area may not be in another
- Duration – a nuisance must be continuous interference
- Abnormal sensitivity of the claimant may relieve liability
- The presence of malice by either party

Outline the basic elements of a claim in public nuisance

- Defined as something which affects the comfort and convenience of a class of people
- But a claimant must suffer special damage over that suffered by the class
- Most actions involve the highway, eg obstruction to the highway and condition of the highway

Discuss the effectiveness of private nuisance

- The limitation on potential claimants
- Difficult to establish use of land is unreasonable
- Easier to claim nuisance where damage occurs
- Liability dependent on locality is unfair
- Statutory authority makes it harder to claim
- The effect of the other defences

Discuss the effectiveness of public nuisance

- The definition lacks clarity
- Not having to show an interest in the land makes the action less restrictive than private nuisance
- The meaning of class of people may be uncertain
- Is a crime as well as a tort so may have more deterrent value
- Brought by the Attorney-General so may be harder to bring but more likely to be successful
- If special damage cannot be shown then no action is possible

SUMMARY

- There are three types of nuisance: private nuisance, public nuisance, and now statutory nuisance also (eg Clean Air Act 1993, Environment Act 1995, Environmental Protection Act 1990)
- A private nuisance is defined as an unlawful indirect interference with a person's use or enjoyment of his land (but not a purely recreational use)
- Unlawful means unreasonable, and what is unreasonable can depend on: locality, whether the nuisance is continuous, the sensitivity of the claimant, whether damage is caused or merely inconvenience, the presence of malice
- The interference must be indirect; direct interference would be a trespass
- Defences include: statutory authority, prescription, act of a stranger, consent and public policy
- A public nuisance is one that interferes with the material comfort of a class of Her Majesty's subjects but involves damage to the claimant over and above that caused to the public generally
- It usually involves the highway: ie damage caused by obstructions to the highway, projections over the highway, and the condition of the highway

10

Strict liability and land – Rylands v Fletcher

AIMS AND OBJECTIVES

After reading this chapter you should be able to:

- Understand the unique purposes behind the creation of the rule
- Understand the essential elements that must be proved for a successful claim
- Understand the wide range of available defences
- Understand the limitations on bringing a claim
- Be able to critically analyse the tort and identify the wide range of difficulties associated with it
- Be able to apply the law to factual situations and reach conclusions as to liability

10.1 Purpose and character of the tort

Trespass to land protects landowners from infringement of their boundaries. The tort of negligence gives a right of action where damage is caused as a result of a 'careless' act. We have also seen that the tort of nuisance comes to the assistance of a person whose use of land is interfered with indirectly by activities of the defendant on their land. It might appear that all possible eventualities have been catered for but this is not the case.

Trespass to land depends on direct and intentional interference while negligence will fail if it can be shown that the defendant did all that was reasonable to minimise the risk of damage. Nuisance will generally only be established if the activity is continuing over a period of time even though there can be liability for a 'one off' incident in rare cases.

Where does this leave occupiers whose land is damaged by a non-negligent escape of something from another's land?

The rule in *Rylands v Fletcher* ((1865) 3 H & C 774 (Court of Exchequer)) came about to fill this gap. It has its roots in nuisance and in reality most claimants are likely to plead nuisance as an alternative to Rylands v Fletcher. For many years it has been argued that Rylands v Fletcher is a tort of strict liability. It is questionable whether this has been an accurate view since the early part of the twentieth century. From that time, as will be seen, the judges have gradually changed the rules so that it has long been a favourite question of examiners – 'To what extent can the tort of *Rylands v Fletcher* be truly described as a tort of strict liability?' The issue will be returned to later in this Chapter.

10.2 Definition

The definition most commonly used is found in the judgment of Mr Justice Blackburn in *Rylands v Fletcher* as modified in the House of Lords judgment in the same case by Lord Cairns LC, (1868) LR 3 HL 330.

JUDGMENT

'A person who for his own purpose brings onto his land and collects and keeps there anything likely to do mischief if it escapes, must keep it in at his peril, and if he does not do so, is . . . answerable for all the damage which is the natural consequence of its escape. The use of the land must amount to a non-natural use.'

On the face of it, there is no requirement of fault on the part of the person who accumulates the thing nor need the escape nor the likelihood of damage be foreseeable. It is these facts which for many years led lawyers to argue that the tort imposed strict liability. As we shall see, the judges have refined these basic principles over the years.

10.3 Elements of the tort

10.3.1 Bringing onto land and keeping there

The first requirement is that the thing must be brought onto the land. Anything which is naturally there will not suffice. In *Giles v Walker* (1890) 24 QBD 656 the defendant was not liable for the spread of thistledown from his land and in *Ellison v Ministry of Defence* (1997) 81 BLR 101 it was held that at Greenham Common (the scene of a very long-running protest against nuclear weapons) a natural accumulation of rainwater which escaped and caused flooding to neighbouring land did not give rise to liability.

The fact that something naturally on the land has escaped will not suffice for liability under *Rylands v Fletcher* but we have already seen in Chapter 9, section 9.3.2, there may be liability in nuisance (*Leakey v National Trust* [1980] QB 485).

It is not essential that the thing be brought onto the land by an owner or occupier. In *Charing Cross Electric Supply Co v Hydraulic Power Co* [1914] 3 KB 772, CA water mains were placed above electric cables. When the water main burst, the cables were flooded and a large part of London was blacked out. The water company, a mere licensee with no interest in the land, was liable for the escape of the water.

The thing has to be accumulated for the purposes of the defendant but this does not necessarily mean that it is also for the defendant's benefit. The accumulation of sewage by a local authority is done for the purpose of exercising statutory powers. It cannot be said that the local authority benefits from the accumulation (*Smeaton v Ilford Corporation* [1954] Ch 450).

10.3.2 Something likely to do mischief if it escapes

The thing need not be dangerous in itself but it must be likely to cause damage should an escape occur. This point is illustrated by the facts of *Rylands v Fletcher*.

CASE EXAMPLE

Rylands v Fletcher (1868) LR 1 Exch 265; LR 3 HL 330

The defendants used reputable engineers to build a reservoir on their land to accumulate water. While the reservoir was under construction, the engineers came across old mine shafts which they failed to seal properly. When the reservoir became full of water, it escaped along the old shafts into the mine owned by the claimant. Water is not intrinsically dangerous but a large accumulation of water will be likely to cause damage if it escapes. The defendant was held liable and the tort of *Rylands v Fletcher* came into being.

Over the years a wide variety of things have been held to be likely to cause damage if they escape and for this reason have been categorised as dangerous. Examples include:

- The owners of a cemetery were liable when branches from yew trees spread across the boundary into an adjoining field where they were eaten and poisoned animals pastured in the field (*Crowhurst v Amersham Burial Board* (1879) 4 Ex D 5).
- A motor car, which was then regarded as a 'new fangled thing', was stored in a garage with petrol in the tank. The car caught fire and a neighbour's house was damaged. The owner of the car was held liable under *Rylands v Fletcher* (*Musgrove v Pandelis* [1919] 2 KB 43).
- A flag pole 'escaped' from a building by falling and causing damage. It was held to be a dangerous thing (*Shiffman v Order of the Hospital of St John of Jerusalem* [1936] 1 All ER 557).
- A fairground was liable when a chair flew from a 'chair-o-plane' roundabout causing injury to a neighbouring stall-holder (*Hale v Jennings Bros* [1938] 1 All ER 579).
- Electricity stored in high voltage cables which 'leaked' from under the claimant's land and electrocuted his cows meant that the defendant was liable (*Hillier v Air Ministry* (1962) CLY 2084).

The list could go on but what is clear is that anything can be regarded as dangerous in particular circumstances. The courts have avoided giving a definition of 'dangerous' and have decided each case on its own particular facts.

Recent case law has added another dimension to what will be regarded as 'dangerous.' In *Cambridge Water v Eastern Counties Leather* [1994] 2 WLR 53 Goff LJ explained that

JUDGMENT

'. . . foreseeability of damage of the relevant type should be regarded as a prerequisite of liability in damages under the rule.'

He added that it must be possible to foresee the potential for damage at the time the accumulation occurs. The facts of the case illustrate the point.

CASE EXAMPLE

Cambridge Water v Eastern Counties Leather [1994] 2 WLR 53

Chemicals which were stored by the defendants seeped into the underground water supply used by the claimant. At the time the chemicals were accumulated the amount of contamination caused to the water supply was within acceptable standards. Some time later, the law was changed and the level of contamination could no longer be tolerated. The change in the law could not have been foreseen by the defendants who were found not to be liable.

The issue of foreseeability has been discussed in the later case of *Transco plc v Stockport Metropolitan Council* [2003] UKHL 61 which enabled the House of Lords to review the scope and application of the tort.

CASE EXAMPLE

Transco plc v Stockport Metropolitan Council [2003] UKHL 61

A multi-story block of flats, built by the defendants, was supplied with water for domestic use. A large pipe from the water mains led to tanks in the bottom of the buildings to supply the needs of 66 households. Without negligence, the pipe failed and water escaped. Without negligence the leak was undiscovered for some time by which time sufficient water had escaped to cause an embankment beneath the claimant's gas mains to collapse. As a result, the gas main posed an immediate and serious risk. The claimants took prompt action and sought to recover the cost from the defendants on the basis that the defendants were strictly liable under *Rylands v Fletcher*.

Lord Bingham acknowledged that

JUDGMENT

'many things not ordinarily regarded as sources of mischief or danger may nonetheless prove to be such if they escape.'

Having reviewed cases since *Rylands v Fletcher* itself, he concluded

JUDGMENT

'It must be shown that the defendant has done something which he recognised, or judged by the standards appropriate at the relevant place and time, he ought reasonably to have recognised, as giving rise to an exceptionally high risk of danger or mischief if there should be an escape, however unlikely an escape may have been thought to be.'

It is clear from this judgment that the issue of foreseeability is closely linked to the concept of 'non-natural user' discussed below in section 10.3.4.

The rules for foreseeability of the type of damage are those which have previously been discussed coming from *The Wagon Mound (No 1)* (see *Overseas Tankship (UK) Ltd v Morts Dock & Engineering Co (The Wagon Mound)* [1961] AC 388).

When considering the nature of damage caused, it is clear that there will be other factors being satisfied as well as liability for damage to property. For many years it was not clear whether there could also be liability for personal injury. In *Read v Lyons* [1947] AC 156 the damage caused was personal injury. While the case was decided upon the issue of escape, the judges discussed, obiter, whether or not the tort could enable such damages to be paid. Lord Macmillan suggested that there could not be liability for personal injury in the absence of negligence, stating that the basis of *Rylands v Fletcher* is a mutual duty owed between landowners. 'It has nothing to do with personal injury'. Lord Simonds stated that he could not support the view that liability under the tort 'extends to purely personal injuries . . .'. The point was discussed obiter and it should be remembered that damages had in fact been awarded for personal injury in *Hale v Jennings Bros*. In *Hunter v Canary Wharf* [1997] 2 All ER 426 the judges, in holding that a claimant must have an interest in the land affected by the nuisance, appear to have ruled out the possibility of a claim for purely personal injury arising from nuisance.

In *Transco v Stockport*, two of the judges took the opportunity to debate this issue further. Although the comments are obiter as the case did not involve any claim for personal injury, they are informative. Lord Bingham stated

JUDGMENT

'. . . the claim cannot include a claim for death or personal injury, since such claim does not relate to any right in or enjoyment of land.'

Lord Bingham acknowledged that his view, given the close relationship between *Rylands v Fletcher* and nuisance, was based on *Hunter v Canary Wharf*. Lord Hoffmann referred to the fact that claims for personal injury had been admitted in the past but stated that

JUDGMENT

'. . . the point is now settled by [Cambridge Water] which decided that *Rylands v Fletcher* is a special form of nuisance and *Hunter v Canary Wharf* . . . which decided that nuisance is a tort against land. It must, I think, follow that damages for personal injuries are not recoverable under the rule.'

10.3.3 The thing must escape

This means precisely what it says – the thing must move from the land controlled by the defendant to land controlled by the claimant. This is clear from the facts of *Rylands v Fletcher* but it was explained in *Read v J Lyons & Co Ltd*.

CASE EXAMPLE

Read v J Lyons & Co Ltd [1947] AC 156

In 1942, munitions were manufactured by the defendants. The claimant was a munitions inspector in the shell-filling shop when an explosion occurred. One person was killed and the claimant was injured. There was no negligence involved in the explosion.

Viscount Simon LC held that the claimant could not succeed in her claim under *Rylands v Fletcher*, explaining

JUDGMENT

'Escape, for the purpose of . . . *Rylands v Fletcher* means escape from a place which the defendant has occupation of, or control over, to a place which is outside his occupation or control.'

It is also clear that the 'thing' itself need not escape. In *Miles v Forest Rock Granite Co (Leicestershire) Ltd* (1918) 34 TLR 500 the use of explosives on the defendants' land caused rocks to fall on the highway. There had been an escape – the blast.

It is sometimes difficult to see how the courts have enforced this requirement. In *Hale v Jennings* both the roundabout and the injured stall-holder were in fact on the same land while in *Crown River Cruises v Kimbolton Fireworks* [1996] 2 Lloyd's Rep 533 both parties occupied the same stretch of river.

The different approaches perhaps anticipate or reflect the view expressed by Mr Justice Lawton in *British Celanese v A H Hunt (Capacitors) Ltd* [1969] 1 WLR 959 when he said the escape should be

JUDGMENT

'from a set of circumstances over which the defendant has control to a set of circumstances where he does not.'

We shall see that the identity of the defendant in some cases will depend on whether the judges follow the approach set out in *Read v Lyons* or in *British Celanese v Hunt*.

10.3.4 Non-natural use

It is always difficult to decide where the discussion of non-natural use should appear. It is arguable that all the above essential elements of the tort are involved therefore it has been decided to include this very important issue at this point.

The House of Lords in *Rylands v Fletcher* stated that the escape must be of something which is brought onto the land and does not naturally occur there. This view is potentially extremely wide and the flood-gates were at risk of being opened to extremes. Over the years the courts have guarded against this risk by refusing to give a specific definition of what will be regarded as 'non-natural use' preferring instead to deal with the issue on a case by case basis.

In *Read v J Lyons & Co Ltd* Viscount Simons LC said *obiter* that he would question

JUDGMENT

'whether the making of munitions in a factory at the government's request in time of war for the purpose of helping to defeat the enemy'

was a non-natural use of land. In the same case Lord Porter said that the court should take into account

JUDGMENT

'all the circumstances of time and practice of mankind … so that what may be regarded as dangerous or non-natural may vary according to the circumstances.'

While Viscount Simon's view can be understood in the context of the times, it is Lord Porter's view which appears to have influenced later decisions.

Lord Porter's view appears to have been based in an earlier view expressed by the Privy Council *Rickards v Lothian* [1913] AC 280. In that case Lord Moulton held that the issue of non-natural use could be explained as follows:

JUDGMENT

'It is not every use . . . that brings into play that principle. . . . It must be some special use bringing with it increased danger to others and must not merely be the ordinary use of the land or such a use as is proper for the benefit of the community.'

The issue of benefit to the community was an obvious element taken into account in *Read v Lyons*. It was also a factor in *British Celanese v Hunt* when the problem was caused by the manufacture of goods of a common type needed 'for the benefit of the community' (per Lawton J). Mr Justice Lawton was also influenced by the fact that the defendant's factory was an industrial use of premises which were situated on an industrial estate. The use of the premises for a non-industrial use would have been non-natural in that locality.

The issue was considered by Goff LJ in his minority judgment in *Cambridge Water v Eastern Counties Leather*. Goff LJ argued that to accept the view stated by Lord Moulton (quoted above) would be to extend the concept of natural use beyond 'reasonable bounds'. In *Cambridge Water v Eastern Counties Leather* it had been accepted at first instance that the creation of employment was a proper consideration in deciding the issue of natural use. Goff LJ said that he could not accept that the creation of employment is

JUDGMENT

'sufficient of itself to establish a particular use as constituting a natural or ordinary use of land.'

While acknowledging that this issue was not relevant to the decision in the case, he went on to say that

JUDGMENT

'the storage of substantial quantities of chemicals on industrial premises should be regarded as an almost classic case of non-natural use.'

The issue has apparently now been resolved in *Transco v Stockport*. Citing Lord Moulton's statement in *Rickards v Lothian*, Lord Bingham said

JUDGMENT

'I think it clear that ordinary user is a preferable test to natural user, making it clear that the rule in *Rylands v Fletcher* is engaged only where the defendant's use is shown to be extraordinary and unusual.'

Tying this point with that of foreseeability, Lord Bingham said

JUDGMENT

'The question is whether the defendant has done something which he recognises, or ought to recognise, as being quite out of the ordinary in the place and at the time when he does it.'

Lord Hoffmann suggested that

JUDGMENT

'A useful guide in deciding whether the risk has been created by a "non-natural" user of land is … to ask whether the damage was something against which the occupier could reasonably be expected to have insured himself.'

On the facts in *Transco v Stockport* the judges were unanimous in finding that the supply of water for domestic purposes in large pipes which were not maintained at high pressure did not amount to non-natural use.

10.4 Parties to the action

10.4.1 Potential claimants

Judges have expressed different views as to who can claim. In *Rylands v Fletcher* no indication is given that a claimant needs to have a proprietary interest in the land affected by the escape.

In *Read v Lyons* Lord Macmillan expressed the view that the tort

JUDGMENT

'derives from a conception of the mutual duties of adjoining or neighbouring landowners.'

When it is remembered that the tort has its roots in nuisance, decisions relating to that tort are seen to be relevant. In this context, *Hunter v Canary Wharf* is helpful. As we have seen, the House of Lords held that in order to bring an action in nuisance, the claimant must have a legal interest in the land affected by the nuisance.

There would be no reason to believe that a different approach would be taken in *Rylands v Fletcher* were it not for *Crown River Cruises v Kimbolton Fireworks*. The claimant in that case had no interest in land and, although claims in *Rylands v Fletcher* were rejected, the logical outcome of the 'control' approach stated in *British Celanese v Hunt* allowed the claimant to establish liability for nuisance.

The debate will no doubt continue but in the meantime it is likely that the close link to nuisance will be maintained and that the decision in *Hunter v Canary Wharf* will prevail. There is much other law which protects the environment and, as we shall see, the tort is likely to be restricted to situations where the problems are indeed concerned only with damage relating to an escape onto land in which the claimant has an interest.

10.4.2 Potential defendants

We have seen that in *Read v Lyons* the court took the view that the defendant would be the person, even if it were only as a mere licensee, from whose land the 'thing' had escaped onto another's land while in *British Celanese v Hunt* liability could lie on the person from whose control the 'thing' had escaped.

The issue is still unclear. In *Rigby v Chief Constable of Northants* [1985] 2 All ER 985 the claimant alleged that the tear gas had 'escaped' from the defendant's control onto the claimant's property and therefore the defendant was liable under *Rylands v Fletcher*. The claim was rejected but in the course of his judgment Mr Justice Taylor appeared to accept the 'control' approach. He said:

JUDGMENT

'I can see no difference in principle between allowing a man-eating tiger to escape from your land on to that of another and allowing it to escape from the back of your wagon parked on the highway.'

10.5 Defences

10.5.1 Statutory authority

A statute may impose a duty on the defendant to accumulate the thing which has escaped. In such a case, the defendant will not be liable for the escape, in the absence of negligence, provided the damage is the inevitable consequence of any escape. This is illustrated by two contrasting cases:

CASE EXAMPLE

Charing Cross Electricity Co v Hydraulic Power Co [1914] 3 KB 772

The claimant's land was damaged by the escape of water maintained at high pressure in the defendant's mains. The statute enabling the provision of water for industrial purposes was permissive only. There was no duty to maintain water under high pressure. Had the water not been maintained under high pressure it would not have escaped. As the escape was not the inevitable consequence of the exercise of the statutory power, the defendants were liable.

CASE EXAMPLE

Green v Chelsea Waterworks Co (1894) 70 LT 547

The defendant was under a duty to maintain pressure in its water mains. Damage would inevitably be caused by any escape of water thus the defendants were not liable when an escape happened.

10.5.2 Consent

A person who consents to the accumulation cannot later complain when the thing escapes and damages the land. This is commonly seen in the case of buildings in multiple occupation where a tenant will be taken to have consented to the accumulation of a thing from which that land benefits.

CASE EXAMPLE

Peters v Prince of Wales Theatre (Birmingham) Ltd [1943] KB 73

The defendant employed a sprinkler system to protect the building from fire. The claimant also occupied the building and complained when stock was damaged by water from the sprinklers. It was held that the water supply benefited both claimant and defendant. There could be no liability.

10.5.3 Act of a stranger

A defendant will not be liable for the consequences of an escape which has been caused by the act of a person over whom the defendant has no control.

CASE EXAMPLE

Perry v Kendricks Transport Ltd [1956] 1 WLR 85

The defendants stored motor coaches on their land. The petrol tanks of the coaches were empty. Children took off the fuel cap and threw in a lighted match. The claimant was injured in the resulting explosion.

Holding that the defendants were not liable to the claimant, Lord Jenkins explained that to establish liability it would be necessary to show that

JUDGMENT

' . . . in the circumstances . . . the dangerous thing was left in such a condition that it was a reasonable and probable consequence of their action, which they ought to have foreseen, that children might meddle with the dangerous thing and cause it to escape.'

Had the children's actions been foreseeable, the claimant would have been able to claim in negligence. As it was, on the facts, the defendants were not liable.

It seems therefore that a defendant may be liable in negligence for the foreseeable act of a stranger.

10.5.4 Act of God

An act of God is an unforeseeable natural phenomenon. This was explained by Lord Hobhouse in *Transco v Stockport* as describing events

(i)   which involve no human agency

(ii)   which it is not realistically possible to guard against

(iii) which is due directly and exclusively to natural causes and

(iv)   which could not be prevented by any amount of foresight, pains and care.

Two contrasting cases are instructive, both dealing with damage caused by flooding after exceptional rainfall.

CASE EXAMPLE

Nichols v Marsland (1876) 2 ExD 1

Four bridges were washed away when artificial lakes overflowed following rain 'greater and more violent than any within the memory of witnesses'.

It was held that the defendant could not reasonably have anticipated such an act of nature and she was not liable.

CASE EXAMPLE

Greenock Corporation v Caledonian Railway [1917] AC 556

The defendants constructed an artificial paddling pool by diverting a stream. There was a rainfall of extraordinary violence which caused the pool to overflow. This resulted in damage to the claimants' property.

It was held that the defendants were liable. Rainfall, even if exceptionally heavy, was not an Act of God.

The issue seems to be not whether the event could be anticipated but whether human prudence should have foreseen the possibility of the event and guarded against it. Thus the possibility of heavy rainfall or exceptionally strong winds which occur, even if rarely, within England can be anticipated. A person who accumulates something which may cause damage if it escapes as a result of such occurrence is unlikely to escape liability. Even an escape caused by an earthquake might be said to be capable of being anticipated when it is remembered that 25 earthquakes measuring 4.5 or greater occurred in Britain during the twentieth century (British Geological Survey, accessed at www.quakes.bgs. ac.uk/hazard/eqlst.htm).

The reasoning of the courts seems to point to the possibility of liability in negligence for failure to prevent a reasonably foreseeable risk.

10.5.5 Default of the claimant

A person who causes the damage cannot complain nor can the defendant be liable in such circumstances.

CASE EXAMPLE

Ponting v Noakes [1894] 2 QB 281

The claimant's horse leant across a boundary fence to reach and eat from a poisonous tree. The horse died.

It was held the damage had been caused by the horse's intrusion into the defendant's land. The defendant could not be liable (additionally there had been no escape).

10.6 Problems with the rule

At first sight *Rylands v Fletcher* may be thought to have potential to ensure that dangerous things are properly controlled. The definition of the tort seems quite clear – people who accumulate something which is potentially dangerous will be liable if damage is caused as a result of an escape even in the absence of negligence. The potential for dealing with the effects of pollution is clear. However, when the tort is looked at in depth, its effectiveness in dealing with anything other than a local, individual problem is questionable.

10.6.1 Strict liability?

Over the years, the courts have refined the requirements so that what appeared to be a tort of strict liability has gradually become one where some element of fault is required. We see this in the requirement that the potential for damage, should an escape occur, must be foreseen at the time the thing is accumulated (*Cambridge Water v Eastern Counties Leather*). It can perhaps be suggested that this, when taken into account with the restrictions on the defences of act of a stranger and Act of God, mean that the tort is now fault based.

Lord Hobhouse endeavoured to explain the present position in *Transco v Stockport*:

JUDGMENT

'It is . . . the creation of a recognisable risk to other landowners which is an essential constituent of the tort and the liability of the defendant. But, once such a risk has been established, the liability for the foreseeable consequences of failure to control and confine it is strict.'

The matter continues to be confused – the likelihood is that examiners will continue to ask questions based on this issue!

10.6.2 Effective to protect the environment?

It is obvious that as the tort was originally envisaged, it could serve as a potent protection against pollution of the environment. By way of the various arguments concerning natural and non-natural use it can be argued that the potential has been substantially eroded if not completely eliminated. Elements such as benefit to society (*British Celanese v Hunt*) or to society generally (*Read v Lyons*) have been held to be sufficient to protect the defendant from liability. The question can be asked – does it really matter in the twenty-first century?

A statement by Goff LJ in *Cambridge Water v Eastern Counties Leather* may provide a clue. He took the view that while the preservation of the environment was an issue of

JUDGMENT

'crucial importance to mankind . . . it does not follow . . . that a common law principle . . . should be developed or rendered more strict to provide for liability in respect of such pollution.'

He went on to argue that

JUDGMENT

'given so much well-informed and carefully structured legislation is now being put in place for this purpose, there is less need for the courts to develop a common law principle to achieve the same end . . .'

Goff LJ's view is supported by the legislation coming from the European Union which is gradually ensuring that development must be sustainable and that any polluter should pay for damage to the environment. These principles are seen to be upheld by the regime governing planning decisions, which now requires an environmental impact assessment for major development proposals and by legislation governing industries which create an especial risk, for example the Nuclear Installations Act 1965 which governs liability caused by the escape of ionising radiations and the Merchant Shipping Act 1995 which governs liability for oil pollution caused by ships. Goff LJ is clearly of the view that the tort should be restricted to 'private' issues as he said 'it is more appropriate for strict liability in respect of operations of high risk to be imposed by Parliament.'

It has been decided in Australia that *Rylands v Fletcher* serves no useful purpose and should be subsumed into negligence (*Burnie Port Authority v General Jones Pty Ltd* (1994) 179 CLR 520). The tort is no longer part of Australian law.

The Australian approach was considered by the House of Lords in *Transco v Stockport*. Lord Hoffmann suggested that the tort has a residuary role to play despite the extension of statutory regulation and control over hazardous activities. Lord Hobhouse discussed this in more detail when he said that the tort is still useful despite the ever-increasing amount of statutory regulation:

JUDGMENT

'The area of regulation is not exhaustive; it does not necessarily give the third party . . . an adequate or, even, any say; the Government decision may give priority to some . . . need which it considers must over-ride . . . individual interests; it will not normally deal with civil liability for damage to property; it does not provide . . . adequate knowledge and control to [enable a person] to evaluate and protect himself from the consequent risk.'

In *Transco v Stockport* the judges were unanimous in their opinion that the tort continues to exist and in its way continues to provide an element of protection of the environment.

It seems therefore that *Rylands v Fletcher* may continue to develop but only in connection with what can be described as 'local' or 'individual' problems, wider issues remaining the province of Parliament and the EU.

ACTIVITY

Self-assessment questions

1. Explain the key elements in *Rylands v Fletcher*.
2. What must 'reasonably be foreseen' in order to establish liability for the tort?
3. Explain the current position in respect of liability for personal injury in relation to the tort.
4. What distinctions can be drawn between the concepts of 'natural' and 'non-natural' use of land?
5. What useful purpose if any does the tort serve in the twenty-first century?
6. Describe the defence of 'Act of God' and give examples of when it may apply.

10.7 Liability for fire

10.7.1 Fires Prevention (Metropolis) Act 1774

The Act, despite its title, does not apply only in the metropolis but is of general application.

SECTION

's 86 No action shall lie against a person where a fire accidentally begins . . . no action suit or process whatever shall be [taken] against any person in whose [buildings] or on whose estate, any fire . . . shall accidentally begin . . .'

The issue for the courts has been the meaning of 'accidentally' as it is unlikely in the extreme that any person other than an arsonist will deliberately light a fire intending to damage another person's property.

It was held in *Filliter v Phippard* (1847) 11 QB 347 that the Act does not give protection where the fire is started intentionally nor where it is started negligently. As Lord Denman CJ explained, the words used in the statute could only cover 'a fire produced by mere chance or incapable of being traced to any cause'. It may seem odd that these rules should still apply when forensic investigation is usually able to trace the cause of a fire but the effect of the rules is illustrated in *Collingwood v Home and Colonial Stores Ltd* (1936) 155 LT 550.

CASE EXAMPLE

Collingwood v Home and Colonial Stores Ltd (1936) 155 LT 550

A fire spread from the defendants' premises to those of the claimant. It was caused by the defective wiring on the defendants' premises. However there was no negligence on the defendants' part and the wiring of premises was a reasonable and ordinary use of land. The defendants were protected by the Act. They could not be liable under negligence nor *Rylands v Fletcher*.

10.7.2 At common law

We have seen that the Fires Prevention (Metropolis) Act 1774 only gives a defence in the absence of negligence. This is explained in *Musgrove v Pandalis* [1919] 2 KB 43.

CASE EXAMPLE

Musgrove v Pandalis [1919] 2 KB 43

The claimant's flat was over a garage let to the defendant in which he stored his car. The defendant's chauffeur accidentally started a fire when he started the engine. Had he been competent in his duties, the chauffeur would have turned off the tap connecting the petrol tank to the carburettor. He did not do so and the fire spread to the claimant's flat.

The first fire, in the engine, had started accidentally but the later fire, resulting from the first fire, was caused by the chauffeur's negligence. The two fires were distinguished from each other. The later fire was caused by negligence and therefore the statutory immunity could not apply. This Court of Appeal decision was accepted as providing a proper approach in the later case of *Goldman v Hargrave* [1967] 1 AC 645.

The courts have also considered the potential for liability under *Rylands v Fletcher* for the spread of fire. In *Musgrove v Pandalis* the Court of Appeal had indicated that the statutory defence could not apply if liability were based on the principles of *Rylands v Fletcher*. This issue was further considered in *Mason v Levy Auto Parts of England Ltd* [1967] 2 QB 530.

CASE EXAMPLE

Mason v Levy Auto Parts of England Ltd [1967] 2 QB 530

Large quantities of scrap tyres were stored on the defendants' land. They were ignited and the resulting fire spread, damaging the claimant's premises.

Considering the possibility of liability under *Rylands v Fletcher*, Mr Justice Romer decided that the basis of liability depended on whether the defendant

JUDGMENT

'(a) . . . brought onto his land things likely to catch fire, and kept them there in such circumstances that, if they did ignite, the fire would be likely to spread to the [claimant's] land;
(b) he did so in the course of some non-natural use; and
(c) the thing ignited and the fire spread.'

The Judge went on to say that, having regard to the quantities of the material and the way in which it was stored, this amounted to non-natural use. The defendant was liable under *Rylands v Fletcher*.

The Judge also acknowledged that the considerations which he had taken into account might justify a finding of negligence. This immediately raises the question of whether an act of a stranger can be an effective defence should the claim be in relation to *Rylands v Fletcher*. In *Perry v Kendricks Transport Ltd* we have seen that the courts accepted that the defendants had no control over the strangers who threw the match into the petrol tank causing the explosion which injured the claimant. Holding that there could be no liability under *Rylands v Fletcher*, Lord Justice Jenkins stated that were the criteria for negligence made out, that is had it been found to be reasonably foreseeable 'that children might meddle with the dangerous thing and cause it so escape' then there might be liability for negligence. He went on to say that in such a case, *Rylands v Fletcher* would no longer be needed as the claimant would rely on negligence.

The question of whether an act of a stranger could be available as a defence was considered by Lord Denning MR in *H & E Emmanuel Ltd v Greater London Council* [1971] 2 All ER 835. Workmen clearing demolition debris lit a bonfire the sparks from which set fire to the claimant's adjoining property. Lord Denning stated

JUDGMENT

'I think a "stranger" is anyone who in lighting a fire or allowing it to escape acts contrary to anything which the occupier could anticipate that he would do.'

In the same case, Lord Justice Phillimore quoted with approval from the fifteenth-century case, *Beaulieu v Fingham* (1401) YB 2 Hen 4 fo 18 pl 6, when the judge in that case said

JUDGMENT

'I shall answer to my neighbour for him who enters my house by my leave or knowledge . . . if [he] acts in such a way with a candle or other things that my neighbour's house is burned.'

Lord Phillimore suggested that the word 'negligently' should be inserted before 'acts' to ensure that an occupier would be liable for the acts of those who were invitees or licensees even though the specific act were unforeseeable.

CASE EXAMPLE

Balfour v Barty-King [1957] 1 QB 496

An independent contractor was employed by the defendant to thaw frozen pipes in an attic containing a lot of flammable material. The contractor did the job by using a blowlamp. Not surprisingly a fire was started which spread and destroyed the claimant's house next door. It was held that the defendant was liable.

It is clear from the cases that an independent contractor cannot be a 'stranger' as the contractor is under the control of the employer.

Work which involves the risk of fire is regarded as a hazardous activity which imposes a non-delegable duty to ensure that the fire is kept safe (for detailed discussion of the issue of liability for hazardous activities see Chapter 18, section 18.3.5).

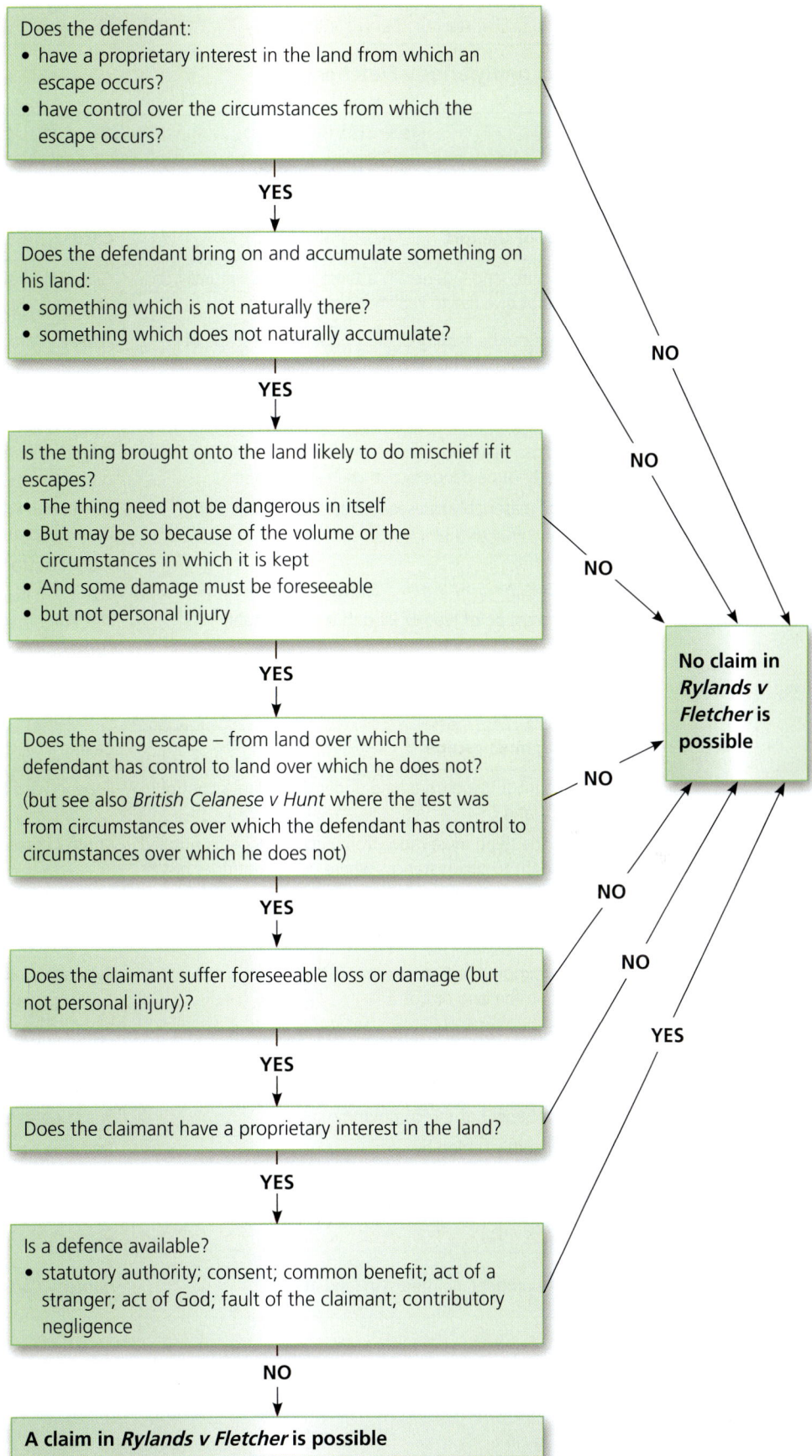

Figure 10.1 Diagram illustrating the essential elements of a claim in *Rylands v Fletcher*

Key facts on *Rylands v Fletcher*

Definition	Case
Bringing onto land and keeping there anything which it is foreseeably likely may cause damage if it escapes.	
Elements of the tort	**Case**
Bringing onto land – generally a thing which is naturally on land will not give rise to liability. Note there can be liability under nuisance for escape of something naturally on land.	*Giles v Walker* (1890) *Ellison v MOD* (1997) *Leakey v National Trust* (1980)
Something likely to cause damage if it escapes	**Case**
Anything can be dangerous in certain circumstances – the thing need not be dangerous in itself – eg water. It must be reasonably foreseeable that should the thing escape, damage may be caused.	*Rylands v Fletcher* (1868) *Cambridge Water v Eastern Counties Leather* (1994) *Transco v Stockport MC* (2003)
Damage must be of type or kind that is reasonably foreseeable. No claim is possible for personal injury.	*The Wagon Mound (No 1)* (1961) *Hunter v Canary Wharf* (1997) *Transco v Stockport MC* (2003)
The thing must escape	**Case**
The thing must move from land under defendant's control to claimant's land. Contrast the thing must move from circumstances controlled by defendant to circumstances where defendant does not have control.	*Read v Lyons* (1947) *British Celanese v Hunt* (1969)
Defendant's use of land must be 'non-natural'	**Case**
Originally simply a test of whether the thing occurred naturally on the land or not. Could vary according to circumstances at the time – eg making munitions in time of war a natural use. Must be more than ordinary use. Proper for benefit of the community. Now apparently settled by Use must be extraordinary and unusual, something quite out of the ordinary in that place and at that time.	*Rylands v Fletcher* (1868) *Read v Lyons* (1947) *Rickards v Lothian* (1913) *British Celanese v Hunt* (1969) *Transco v Stockport MC* (2003)
Claimant	**Case**
Must have proprietary interest in land affected.	*Hunter v Canary Wharf* (1997)

Defendant	Case
Unclear whether legal interest in land is necessary.	*Read v Lyons* (1947)
	British Celanese v Hunt (1969)
	Rigby v Chief Constable of Northants (1985)

Defences	Case
Statutory authority – if duty to accumulate imposed, no liability in the event of escape in the absence of negligence.	*Charing Cross Electricity v Hydraulic Power Co* (1914)
	Green v Chelsea Waterworks (1894)
Consent – can be implied if claimant benefits from the accumulation.	*Peters v Prince of Wales Theatre* (1943)
Act of a stranger – no liability for action by person over whom defendant has no control.	*Perry v Kendricks Transport Ltd* (1956)
Act of God – no liability if escape caused by unforeseeable natural phenomenon which cannot realistically be guarded against.	*Transco v Stockport MC* (2003)
Default of claimant.	

Problems with the Rule	Case
Usefulness diminished by development from strict liability to requirement of foreseeability.	*Rylands v Fletcher* (1868)
Environment better protected generally by legislation specific to particular problems.	
Note Australian abolition of Rule but held in	*Transco v Stockport MC* (2003)
Rule has residuary role in England.	

Fires Prevention (Metropolis) Act 1774	Case
No liability for fire which begins accidentally.	*Collingwood v Home and Colonial Stores* (1936)
	Filliter v Phippard (1847)
No protection where fire started deliberately or negligently.	*Musgrove v Pandelis* (1919)
	Mason v Levy Auto Parts (1967)

	Trespass to land	Private nuisance	Public nuisance	*Rylands v Fletcher*
Claimants	A person in possession of land	A person with a proprietary interest in land	A member of a class of Her Majesty's citizens	A person harmed by the escape of the dangerous thing
Defendants	Any person carrying out the trespass	A landowner, or a person creating or adopting nuisance	A person creating nuisance	A person in control of land from which thing escapes
Duration of interference	A single trespass is enough	Must be continuous	A single interference is enough	A single escape is enough
Directness	Must be direct	Must be indirect	Could be direct or indirect	Could be direct or indirect
Need to prove fault	Actionable *per se* – so no need to prove fault	Requires unreasonable use of land – which is similar to fault	Fault need not be proved	Cambridge Water says foreseeability is required – so suggest fault
Locality of interference	Not relevant	Relevant unless damage is caused	Could be relevant, eg to losing client connection	Could be relevant in deciding what is non-natural
Availability of damages	Any damage related to the trespass – and no need to show damage	Physical harm, economic loss	Physical harm, personal injury, economic loss	Physical loss
Defences	Customary right to enter, common law right, statutory right, consent, necessity, license	Statutory authority, prescription, consent, act of stranger, public policy, over sensitivity of claimant	General defences	Consent, common benefit, act of a stranger, or God, statutory authority, contributory negligence
Whether also a crime	Yes – possible under some statute	No – unless statutory	Yes – can be	No

Figure 10.2 The similarities and differences between the torts relating to land

SAMPLE ESSAY QUESTION

Discuss the extent to which it is accurate to still refer to *Rylands v Fletcher* as a tort of strict liability.

Explain the original basis of the rule

- Defendant brings onto land and accumulates
- a thing likely to cause 'mischief' if it escapes
- and it does escape causing damage

Discuss how other requirements have been added

- Lord Cairns added non-natural use of land
- Things stored in large quantities are commonly non-natural while truly domestic uses are not
- Lord Macmillan narrowed the concept of escape – from land to land rather than circumstances to circumstances
- Goff LJ in *Cambridge Water* added foreseeability of harm

Consider the wide range of potential defences

- *Volenti non fit injuria*
- Common benefit – where the parties share the same premises
- Act of God – extreme weather
- Act of a stranger
- Statutory authority
- Damage caused through the fault of the claimant himself
- Contributory negligence under the Law Reform (Contributory Negligence) Act 1945 which reduces damages

Explain how the tort has developed

- The debate over the escape – may make it harder to claim
- The thing accumulated does not have to be what escapes – makes it easier top claim
- Things that naturally accumulate cannot lead to liability – may be unfair on a claimant
- The problem of identifying what amounts to a non-natural use of land – changes over time

Discuss the issue of whether the tort is still strict liability

- The effectiveness of the tort was limited straightaway by Lord Cairns by adding the requirement of non-natural use of land – which appears to vary according to the context in which the thing escapes
- Certain activities by their nature have been identified as always a non-natural use of land
- The meaning given to accumulation is not unlike fault liability
- The requirement of foreseeability makes it little different from negligence – rather than strict liability
- The tort has been described as a more specific type of nuisance – but again an action is harder to succeed in
- There is an unusually wide range of available defences for something described as strict liability

SUMMARY

- The basic rule according to Blackburn J was that a person should be liable for the damage caused by things brought onto and accumulated on the land which then escape – so concerned liability for dangerous things
- There were originally three essential ingredients to the tort: a bringing onto and accumulating on the land (something not naturally there), of a thing likely to cause mischief if it escapes, and the thing does escape and causes damage
- In the House of Lords in the case Lord Cairns added another requirement – that it must involve a 'non-natural' use of land
- Later Goff LJ added the requirement of foreseeable damage – and the tort is now generally seen as a type of nuisance
- Who will be a defendant and who can claim as a claimant will depend on whether the escape has to be from one person's land to another's or from the defendant's control to a situation outside of his control
- Although the tort is described as strict liability it clearly now requires proof of fault and there are also many defences including: act of God, act of a stranger, consent, common benefit and statutory authority

11

Liability for animals

11.1 Introduction

By the middle of the twentieth century, the law relating to liability for damage or injury done by animals was confused. An owner could be liable under various torts on the requirements of those torts being established (see section 11.3). There were also other common law actions which imposed strict liability for harm done by animals. It was acknowledged that animals are by their nature unpredictable and that owners kept animals at their peril. Strict liability depended on whether the animals were 'ferae naturae' (loosely translated as wild animals) or 'mansuetae naturae' (loosely translated as tame animals). In the case of wild animals, the owner was presumed to know that they were dangerous and would be liable without fault, while in the case of tame animals, knowledge of the animal's dangerous tendency had to be proved before liability would be imposed. This is perhaps the origin of the saying 'Every dog is allowed one bite'.

It was hoped that there would be a thorough and wide-ranging reform of this area of law with liability being based either on the principles of negligence or strictly imposed for damage done by all animals. The opportunity was not taken, the Animals Act 1971 continuing a distinction between liability for dangerous and non-dangerous species alongside liability under various torts.

11.2 Statutory liability

11.2.1 Generally

The basic principle of the Animals Act 1971 is that a person who keeps a dangerous animal has strict liability for any damage which the animal may cause. A person who keeps an animal which is domesticated and is usually regarded as harmless will only be liable if the animal has given cause to fear that it has unusual characteristics which make it potentially dangerous.

11.2.2 Who is liable

Liability is imposed on the 'keeper' of the animal. A person is a keeper of the animal if

SECTION

's 6(3) (a) he owns the animal or has it in his possession; or
　　　(b) he is the head of a household of which a member under the age of sixteen owns the
　　　　　animal or has it in his possession.'

If an animal strays, the original keeper remains liable unless and until another person fulfils the requirements of s 6(3). A person who takes a stray into safe-keeping to prevent it from causing damage or until it can be returned will not be regarded as the keeper (s 6(4)).

11.2.3 Which animals are dangerous?

The definition is provided by s 6(2)

SECTION

's 6(2) A dangerous species is a species
　　(a) which is not commonly domesticated in the British Islands; and
　　(b) whose fully grown animals normally have such characteristics that they are likely,
　　　　unless restrained, to cause severe damage or that any damage they may cause is likely
　　　　to be severe.'

Potentially ferocious animals such as tigers clearly fall within the definition. Other animals, not known for ferocity, are also caught if any damage is likely to be severe. This would apply, for example, to elephants which rarely attack but whose sheer size means that any damage would be likely to be severe.

CASE EXAMPLE

Behrens v Bertram Mills [1957] 2 QB 1

The claimants ran a booth in a fun fair operated by the defendants who were the owners of a circus. The defendant's troop of elephants had to pass the booth on their way to the circus ring. One, Bullu, was frightened by a small dog and in its fright trampled the booth injuring the claimants. Although Bullu was described as 'no more dangerous than a cow' the defendants were liable.

Although the case was decided before the Animals Act was passed, it is illustrative of the severity of damage which can be caused by a tame but very large animal.

CASE EXAMPLE

Tutin v Chipperfield Promotions Ltd (1980) 130 NLJ 807

The claimant agreed to take part in a camel race at the Horse of the Year Show. As the race started she was thrown off the camel by its awkward gait. It was held that the camel was a member of a dangerous species although the claimant did not succeed in this claim as on the facts the defence of voluntary assumption of risk applied. (She had also pleaded negligence on the part of the defendant and was successful on that basis.)

It is clear that whether or not an animal is a member of a dangerous species is a question of law and not one of fact. Neither the elephant in *Behrens v Bertram Mills* nor the camel in *Tutin v Chipperfield Promotions* was dangerous in the ordinary sense of the word but both species satisfied the legal test.

Any animal which is not covered by the definition is termed 'non-dangerous'.

11.2.4 Liability for dangerous animals

By s 2(1)

SECTION

's 2(1) Where any damage is caused by an animal which belongs to a dangerous species, any person who is a keeper of the animal is liable for the damage . . .'

This was explained by Lord Nicholls in *Mirvahedy (FC) v Henley and another* [2003] UKHL 16 when he said

JUDGMENT

'If you choose to keep a dangerous animal not commonly domesticated in this country, you are liable for damage done by the animal. It matters not that you take every precaution to prevent the animal escaping. You may not realise that the animal is dangerous. Liability is independent of fault. Liability is independent of knowledge of the animal's dangerous characteristics.'

By s 5 the only defences available are that the damage was caused by the claimant's fault or occurred when the claimant had voluntarily assumed the risk (see section 11.2.5 for a full discussion of s 5).

11.2.5 Liability for non-dangerous animals

The basis for liability is set out in s 2(2)

SECTION

's 2(2) Where damage is caused by an animal which does not belong to a dangerous species, a keeper of the animal is liable for the damage . . . if

(a) the damage is of a kind which the animal, unless restrained, was likely to cause or which, if caused by the animal, was likely to be severe; and

(b) the likelihood of the damage or of its being severe was due to characteristics of the animal which are not normally found in animals of the same species or are not normally so found except at particular times or in particular circumstances; and

(c) those characteristics were known to the keeper [or his servant having charge of the animal or to a member of his household who is the keeper but aged under sixteen].'

This sub-section is not a model of clear parliamentary draftsmanship. It has been described in various uncomplimentary ways by the judges who have had to try to interpret and apply it, s 2(2)(b) in particular causing great difficulty. There have been a number of different approaches taken over the years but the section has recently come before the House of Lords for the first time in *Mirvahedy (FC) v Henley and Another*. To some extent the law has been clarified although no doubt problems will still arise in future cases. All three parts of s 2(2) must be satisfied but for convenience, each will be considered separately. The facts of *Mirvahedy* are given at this point for the sake of convenience. Relevant parts of the judgments are discussed later where appropriate.

CASE EXAMPLE

Mirvahedy (FC) v Henley and Another [2003] UKHL 16

Three horses were kept by the defendants in a field next to their house. Something fright-ened the horses and they bolted out of the field. They pushed over an electric fence and a surrounding wooden fence and then stampeded along a track onto a road. They ran for more than a mile onto a main dual-carriageway road where one of the horses collided with the car driven by the claimant. The claimant was seriously injured and the horse was killed. The claimant alleged that the defendants were liable under the Animals Act.

Section 2(2)(a) The nature of the damage

The damage must be 'of a kind which the animal unless restrained was likely to cause' or 'of a kind . . . which, if caused by the animal, was likely to be severe.' What does the word 'likely' mean? This has exercised judicial minds on several occasions.

CASE EXAMPLE

Smith v Ainger, The Times, 5th June, 1990

The defendant's dog, an Alsatian cross, had a history of attacking other dogs. When it attacked the claimant's dog, the claimant was knocked over, breaking his leg. The Court of Appeal had to consider whether the injury was one which was 'likely' to occur unless the dog was restrained.

At first sight, the nature of the injury was unlikely – a bite would be more likely. The court held however that the words 'was likely' meant 'such as might well happen' rather than 'probable'. On this basis, on the facts, it was likely that the dog would attack another dog and that the owner of the other dog would intervene or, as in this case, get in the way. Were this to happen, there was a material risk that the owner would be bitten or buffeted and suffer injury. No distinction needed to be drawn between a bite and a buffet. The damage caused to the claimant was of a kind which the dog was likely to cause.

In many cases the severity of the damage can clearly be anticipated.

CASE EXAMPLE

Curtis v Betts [1990] 1 WLR 459

The claimant, aged 11, was attacked and bitten by Max, a bull mastiff weighing 70 kg. The child knew the dog and as he cycled past he called to Max who was being put into a car. The dog leapt at the child and bit him on the face. It was held that s 2(2)(a) was satisfied.

Slade LJ said

JUDGMENT

'Max was a dog of the bull mastiff breed. If he did bite anyone, the damage was likely to be severe.'

As with dangerous animals, the damage need not be the result of anything other than the size and weight of the animal. Thus in *Jaundrill v Gillett, The Times*, 30th January, 1996 the Court of Appeal accepted that horses were likely to cause damage by virtue of their weight.

While Lord Scott in *Mirvahedy* stated, obiter, that he had doubts as to earlier interpreta-tions of s 2(2)(a), the issue was not further considered and the Court of Appeal decisions continue to provide guidance.

Section 2(2)(b) Is the behaviour normal or abnormal?

Once s 2(2)(a) is satisfied, the cause of the animal's dangerousness must be established. This can be done in two ways:

(i) the danger was caused by characteristics 'which are not normally found in animals of the same species'; or

(ii) it was caused by characteristics which are not normally found in animals of the same species 'except at particular times or in particular circumstances.'

If the first approach is to be used, the characteristic which causes the danger must result from some abnormality. Lord Nicholls in *Mirvahedy* explained that this deals with 'a case where animals of the same species are normally docile but the particular animal is not.' The second approach covers animals which are not normally vicious but which may be dangerous at certain times. An example of this can be found in the case of a bitch with a litter who bites to defend her pups. While this is normal behaviour for a bitch in such circumstances, the second limb of s 2(2)(b) means that there can be liability on the part of the keeper even though at other times the bitch is completely docile.

The judges have not been in agreement as to how s 2(2)(b) should be interpreted.

CASE EXAMPLE

Cummings v Grainger [1977] QB 397

An Alsatian was loose in a scrap-yard to guard against intruders. The claimant went into the yard and was seriously injured by the dog. The Court of Appeal held that the dog had characteristics not normally found in an Alsatian dog except when it is being used as a guard dog. The second limb of s 2(2)(b) was therefore satisfied.

In *Curtis v Betts* above, discussing whether the dog's behaviour fell within s 2(2)(b), the Court of Appeal agreed with the trial judge that

JUDGMENT

'bull mastiffs have a tendency to react fiercely at particular times and in particular circumstances, namely when defending the boundaries of what they regard as their own territory . . .' On the facts it was held that the accident occurred when the dog was defending its territory and therefore fell within the second limb of s 2(2)(b).

These cases seem to make a clear statement that an owner cannot escape liability merely because the animal is potentially dangerous only at certain times and that all animals of that species share the same characteristic.

Other judges have argued that if all animals of the same species share the same characteristic at specific times then that cannot be termed an abnormal characteristic. This argument is based on the assumption that the requirement of abnormality in the first limb of the sub-section also applies to the second limb when the sub-section is read as a whole.

CASE EXAMPLE

Breedon v Lampard (21 March 1985, CA unreported)

The claimant was injured when a horse (Raffles) kicked out when the claimant approached either too quickly or too closely from behind. Raffles was wearing a red ribbon on his tail, a traditional warning to others that the horse is prone to kick. Accepting that it is normal for all horses to kick in some circumstances, the judges took the view that s 2(2)(b) should be construed as imposing a single test, namely that the characteristic which led to the injury was abnormal.

Taking this view, the second limb merely serves to avoid attempts at escaping liability by arguing, for example, that all bitches bite sometimes.

The conflict has been partially resolved by the House of Lords in *Mirvahedy*. Each of the judges accepted that it is normal for horses to bolt when they are badly frightened. Three members of the court, Lords Nicholls, Hobhouse and Walker, held that the second limb of the sub-section applied. Although the horses were behaving normally for frightened horses, Lord Nicholls noted

JUDGMENT

'it was precisely because they were behaving in [an] unusual way caused by their panic that the road accident took place.'

This sufficed to bring their behaviour within the second limb of the sub-section. The minority judgments of Lords Slynn and Scott argue that the correct interpretation of the sub-section meant that liability could not be imposed when the behaviour was normal at the particular time. Only if it was abnormal at that time would the sub-section be satisfied.

Section 2(2)(b) What is a 'characteristic?'

While *Mirvahedy* seems to have settled the arguments about abnormality, another argument remains – what constitutes a 'characteristic' for the purposes of the sub-section? This question was considered by the Court of Appeal in *Gloster v Chief Constable of Greater Manchester* [2000] PIQR P114.

CASE EXAMPLE

Gloster v Chief Constable of Greater Manchester [2000] PIQR P114

A German shepherd dog (Jack) was a trained police dog rated as 'satisfactory' and 'not over-aggressive'. His handler was about to release the dog to chase a car thief when he fell. Jack slipped his collar and set off after the innocent claimant who had not heard any warning not to run as the dog was about to be loosed. The claimant was bitten twice in the leg before Jack was called off. The issue was whether a dog which had been trained to be aggressive in certain circumstances had a 'characteristic' which would be caught by the sub-section. The defendant was not held liable as the requirement of s 2 was not satisfied.

JUDGMENT

Lord Justice Pill argued that the relevant characteristic was the dog's ability to be trained, a normal characteristic for the breed and therefore not caught by the sub-section. The damage was due to the training and not to the dog's characteristic.

This approach was criticised in *Mirvahedy* by Lord Scott in his minority judgment when he referred to *Gloster* while discussing the meaning of s 2(2)(b)

'The damage complained of was the bite. The likelihood of being chased and bitten was due to a characteristic of the police dog not normally found in German Shepherd dogs. There was, in my opinion, no more to be said about paragraph b [of the sub-section] than that.'

The other judges in *Mirvahedy* did not comment on this aspect of the *Gloster* judgment so that the issue of what amounts to a characteristic remains open.

It is clear that the characteristic need not be one which indicates a possibility that the animal will attack humans but it must be one which is not usually found in the particular species.

CASE EXAMPLE

Wallace v Newton [1982] 1 WLR 375

A horse which was known to be unpredictable lashed out and injured the claimant when being loaded into a trailer. It was held that this was a characteristic peculiar to the animal. The defendant was liable as he was aware of the characteristic which is not usually found in horses.

CASE EXAMPLE

Freeman v Higher Park Farm [2008] EWCA Civ 1185

The court had to consider whether s 2(2)(b) included a horse that bucked when beginning to canter injuring an experienced rider. The court held that bucking was a normal characteristic of a horse and horses do not buck at any particular time. Liability was also denied because *volenti* under s 5(2) applied.

Section 2(2)(c) Does the keeper know?

The sub-section makes it clear that there will only be liability for damage caused by a non-dangerous animal if the dangerous tendency is known to the keeper. In the case of an animal's owner who is under 16, the child's knowledge will be imputed to the head of the household for this purpose. Apart from this exception, the requirement is of 'actual' rather than 'constructive' knowledge. Where a keeper 'should have' known, but did not know, of the likely consequences in particular circumstances, although there may be no liability under the Animals Act, there may be liability in negligence (see section 11.3.5).

11.2.6 Statutory defences

While liability under the Act is strict, it is not absolute. The Act sets out defences which can absolve the keeper from liability for injury or damage caused by either dangerous or non-dangerous animals.

Fault of claimant and voluntary assumption of risk

By s 5(1)

SECTION

's 5(1) 'a person is not liable . . . for any damage which is wholly the fault of the person suffering it.'

By s 5(2) there is no liability to a person who 'has voluntarily accepted the risk' of damage.

The cases show that people can be very stupid at times. In *Marlor v Bell* (1900) 16 TLR 239 the claimant was injured when he stroked a zebra; in *Sylvester v Chapman Ltd* (1935) 79 SJ 777 the claimant went into a leopard's pen to remove a lighted cigarette.

More recently, in *Dhesi v Chief Constable of West Midlands Police*, *The Times*, 9th May, 2000, both defences were held to apply.

CASE EXAMPLE

Dhesi v Chief Constable of West Midlands Police, The Times, 9th May, 2000

The claimant and some other youths were involved in a confrontation with the police. The claimant was carrying a hockey stick which he was swinging from side to side in an angry and aggressive manner. He ran off and hid in some brambles. Having been tracked by a police dog and its handler, he was warned three times that the dog would be loosed if he did not surrender. He did not do so and the dog was loosed. In his struggle to get away from the dog, the claimant was bitten several times.

It was held that he had voluntarily accepted the risk of being injured and that the resulting damage was entirely his own fault.

Liability to trespassers

By s 5(3)(a) a person is not liable if a trespasser is injured by an animal which is not being kept for the purpose of protection. Where an animal is being kept on premises for the purpose of protection of persons or property, a keeper will not be liable to a trespasser 'if keeping [the animal] there for that purpose was not unreasonable' (s 5(3)(b)).

CASE EXAMPLE

Cummings v Grainger [1977] QB 397

The defendant ran a breaker's yard and at night a German shepherd dog was allowed to run free for security purposes. The claimant knew about the dog when she entered the yard one night with a friend who also knew about the dog. The claimant, who had no right of entry and was a trespasser, was attacked and bitten by the dog.

The issue was whether the keeping of the dog for protection was reasonable. Lord Denning MR held

JUDGMENT

'The only reasonable way of protecting the place was to have a guard dog. True it was a fierce dog. But why not? A gentle dog would be no good. The thieves would soon make friends with him. It seems to me that it was very reasonable – or at least not unreasonable – for the defendant to keep this dog there.'

The claimant was also held to have voluntarily accepted the risk when she entered the yard.

It must be remembered that the Guard Dogs Act 1975 has since come into effect setting stringent conditions for the use of guard dogs and making it a criminal offence to allow a guard dog to run freely unless it is under the control of a handler.

11.2.7 Liability for livestock

The term 'livestock' is defined by s 11 as

SECTION

's 11 cattle, horses, asses, mules, hinnies, sheep, pigs, goats and poultry, and also deer not in the wild state.'

A keeper of livestock will be liable for damage caused by the animals to land or property belonging to someone else onto which the animals have strayed (s 4). Additional rights of the person whose land or property has been damaged are set out in s 7:

SECTION

's 7 (i) a right to detain straying livestock which are not under someone's control but subject to notifying the police within 48 hours and giving the owner (if known) notice;
(ii) after 14 days, the right to sell the livestock to recoup losses unless an appropriate amount has earlier been offered by the owner. This includes the right to recoup the cost of keeping the livestock safely and with proper care.'

The issue of fencing land has caused problems but the position is now reasonably clear. There is generally a duty to prevent livestock from straying onto the highway (s 8) except in those areas such as some national parks where local people have a lawful right to graze animals on the highway. In such a case, adjoining land owners have no claim for any damage done by the animals straying onto their land from the highway (s 5(5)).

11.2.8 Liability for injury to livestock caused by dogs

The keeper of a dog which causes damage to livestock is liable for that damage (s 3). For the purpose of s 3, the term 'livestock' includes 'pheasants, partridges and grouse' if these are in captivity. Further, by s 9(1), a person who kills or injures a dog is not liable for that damage provided:

SECTION

's 9(1) (a) that person acts to protect livestock and is entitled to do so;
 (b) notice is given to the police within 48 hours.'

A person is entitled to act provided the livestock is on their land or that of a person for whom they act, s 9(2)(a), and at that time they reasonably believe that:

SECTION

's 9(3)(i) the dog is worrying or about to worry the livestock and there is no other reasonable means to end or prevent the worrying; or
 (ii) the dog has been worrying the livestock, is still in the area and not under anyone's control and there is no practicable way to find out to whom the dog belongs.'

11.3 Liability at common law

11.3.1 Trespass to land

The owner of animals which stray onto another's land may be liable in trespass to land. Examples are found in relation to fox-hunting.

CASE EXAMPLE

Paul v Summerhayes (1878) 4 QBD 9

The claimant had frequently informed the defendant, the local hunt, that it was not permitted to cross his land. The defendant persisted in doing so and was found to be liable for trespass.

CASE EXAMPLE

League against Cruel Sports Ltd v Scott [1986] QB 240

The defendant was liable for allowing fox hounds to run onto land owned by the claimant without the claimant's consent.

```
┌────────────────────────────────────────────────────────────────────┐
│ Has animal caused damage?                                            │
└────────────────────────────────────────────────────────────────────┘
                                  │
                                 YES
                                  ↓
┌────────────────────────────────────────────────────────────────────┐
│ Is animal a dangerous species?                                       │
│ • Not normally domesticated in the UK                                │
│ • Fully grown animals normally have such characteristics that they   │
│   are likely unless restrained to cause severe damage, or any        │
│   damage they cause is likely to be severe                           │
└────────────────────────────────────────────────────────────────────┘
              │                                      │
             YES                                    NO
              ↓                                      │
┌──────────────────────────────┐                    │
│ KEEPER STRICTLY LIABLE        │                    │
└──────────────────────────────┘                    ↓
┌────────────────────────────────────────────────────────────────────┐
│ Is animal a non-dangerous species?                                   │
│ • Normally domesticated in the UK                                    │
│ • Not classed as dangerous under s 6(2)                              │
└────────────────────────────────────────────────────────────────────┘
                                  │
                                 YES
                                  ↓
┌────────────────────────────────────────────────────────────────────┐
│ • Was damage of a kind that the animal unless restrained is likely   │
│   to cause, or damage caused is likely to be severe? and             │
│ • Was the likelihood of damage or severity of damage because of      │
│   characteristics unusual in that species except at certain times    │
│   or in certain circumstances? and                                   │
│ • Did the keeper (or the keeper's servant or a person of the         │
│   household under aged 16) know of those characteristics or          │
│   circumstances?                                                     │
└────────────────────────────────────────────────────────────────────┘
                                  │
                                 YES
                                  ↓
┌────────────────────────────────────────────────────────────────────┐
│ Is there an available defence?                                       │
│ • Damage is wholly the fault of the claimant                         │
│ • Victim voluntarily undertook risk of damage                        │
│ • Animal is not kept for protection, or if it is this is reasonable  │
│   and the animal is not left free                                    │
│ • Contributory negligence                                            │
└────────────────────────────────────────────────────────────────────┘
                                  │
                                 NO
                                  ↓
┌────────────────────────────────────────────────────────────────────┐
│ KEEPER liable under act                                              │
└────────────────────────────────────────────────────────────────────┘
```

Figure 11.1 Liability under the Animals Act 1971

11.3.2 Trespass to goods

It may seem improbable but in *Manton v Brocklebank* [1923] 2 KB 212 a person who had trained his dog to steal golf balls was held liable for trespass to goods.

11.3.3 Trespass to the person

An animal can be used against another person in the same way as any other weapon. It is likely that someone who deliberately sets an animal on a person will be liable for assault and/or battery.

11.3.4 Defamation

It has been suggested that a person who teaches a talking bird, for example a parrot, to say something which is defamatory of another will be liable for defamation.

11.3.5 Negligence

It is clear that there can be no liability under the Animals Act for damage caused by a non-dangerous species which has never previously shown evidence of potentially dangerous characteristics. This is of little comfort to the victim. It may be possible for the victim to obtain compensation by way of negligence. The usual rules as to duty, breach and causation must be satisfied (see Chapter 2).

CASE EXAMPLE

Fardon v Harcourt Rivington (1932) 146 LT 391

A dog had been left in a car during very hot weather. Trying to escape, the dog broke a window and a splinter of glass injured the claimant's eye.

JUDGMENT

'Quite apart from the liability imposed upon the owner of animals . . . by reason of knowledge of their propensities, there is . . . the ordinary duty to take care in the cases put upon negligence.'

On the facts the defendant was not liable as he could not guard against a 'fantastic possibility'.

An action in negligence is possible where the defendant's failure to control an animal leads to a foreseeable risk that it may cause harm.

CASE EXAMPLE

Birch v Mills (1995) 9 CL 354

The claimant was walking dogs on leads along a public road when a herd of cows in an unfenced field chased the dogs and hurt the claimant. It was held that as the cattle were known to be frisky and to chase dogs, it was reasonably foreseeable that a person leading the dog was likely to get hurt.

CASE EXAMPLE

Draper v Hodder [1972] 2 QB 556

A pack of Jack Russell dogs owned by the defendant got into his neighbour's garden and savaged a child playing there. It was impossible to identify which dog or dogs had actually injured the child. Knowledge by the defendant that any individual dog had dangerous propensities could not be proved.

JUDGMENT

The defendant was found liable for negligence. A pack of terriers is liable to attack any moving target and the defendant, an experienced dog breeder, knew this. The risk of injury if the animals were not sufficiently controlled was foreseeable.

However, there will be no liability where there is only a remote possibility of an injury and a claim has already failed under s 2 of the Act, *Whippey v Jones* [2009] EWCA Civ 452.

11.3.6 Nuisance

Keeping animals on land can lead to a nuisance. Examples include offensive smells and/or noise. In *Leeman v Montague* [1936] 2 All ER 1677 the crowing of cockerels was held to amount to a nuisance. Today it is likely that such complaints would be dealt with as statutory nuisances but the possibility of using the common law still exists.

11.4 Other statutory provision

The Guard Dogs Act 1975 has already been mentioned (see section 11.2.6 above). Other statutes are intended to ensure that animals are not kept in such a way as to present a threat to people. The Dangerous Dogs Act 1991, for example, contains detailed provisions requiring proper control of certain breeds of dogs which are enforced by criminal sanction. The issue of control is addressed by the Dangerous Wild Animals Act 1976 and the Zoo Licensing Act 1981 requiring licences if such animals are to be kept and providing for compulsory insurance against liability for any damage such animals might cause.

SAMPLE ESSAY QUESTION

Discuss the argument that the Animals Act 1971 ensures that the keeper of an animal, whether of a dangerous or non-dangerous species, is fully liable for all the damage done by the animal.

Define keeper

- The owner of the animal or the head of a household in which a person under 16 is the owner of the animal

Explain the basis of liability for a dangerous species

- Defined in s 6(2) – an animal not commonly domesticated in UK and with characteristics that, unless restricted are likely to cause severe damage or any damage caused is likely to be severe
- Dangerous is a question of fact in each case
- The keeper is strictly liable

Explain where there is liability for non-dangerous species under the Act

- The damage is of a kind animal is likely to cause unless restrained or if caused by animal is likely to be severe; and
- The likelihood or severity of damage is due to characteristics of individual animal or species or of species at specific times; and
- The keeper knows of the characteristics

Discuss whether the provisions do ensure that the keeper is fully liable

- The definition of keeper is very broad
- For 'dangerous' animals liability is strict– so it does ensure liability
- It may even include animals that are not actually dangerous
- Rules on non-dangerous species – dependent on specific characteristics and knowledge of those characteristics so that, eg 'the dog always gets the first bite free' – so this may limit liability and be unfair in certain circumstances
- The court in *Mirhavedy* appears to have created a form of strict liability in the case of non-dangerous species
- There is no need for a link between characteristics and damage
- It is hard to distinguish between permanent and temporary characteristics

Discuss the possible impact of the defences on claims

- S 5(1) - Damage due entirely to fault of victim
- S 5(2) - Victim voluntarily accepted risk
- S 5(3) – Animal was either not kept for protection or if so then it was reasonable to do so
- S 10 – Contributory negligence
- May reduce the possibility of a successful claim even though the animal has caused damage

KEY FACTS

Key facts on liability for animals

Animals Act 1971	Case/statute
Who is liable?	
A person who owns the animal or has it in their possession. In the case of an owner under 16, the head of that household.	s 6(3)
Dangerous animals	**Case/statute**
Not commonly domesticated in the British Islands which when fully grown have characteristics which mean that any damage they cause is likely to be severe. Damage can be due to any characteristic including natural ferocity or size and weight.	s 6(2) *Behrens v Bertram Mills* (1957); *Tutin v Chipperfield* (1980)
Non-dangerous animals	**Case/statute**
Any animal not included in definition of a dangerous animal. Liability for dangerous animals Keeper has strict liability for any damage caused.	s 2(1)

Note liability independent of fault or knowledge of animal's dangerous characteristics.	*Mirvahedy v Henley* (2003)
Liability for non-dangerous animals	
Governed by	s 2(2)
Keeper is liable if damage is of kind which animal likely to cause unless restrained or if caused is likely to be severe or the likelihood of damage being caused or likely to be severe is due to abnormal characteristics for the species or to characteristics only found at particular times and if the keeper or servant or child owner knows about the characteristics.	
Damage can be likely even if not an obvious risk.	
No need to distinguish between a bite and a buffet;	*Smith v Ainger* (1990)
damage caused by a large dog which bites is likely to be severe.	*Curtis v Betts* (1990)
Likelihood can be attributed to animal's size and weight.	*Jaundrill v Gillett* (1996)
Normal or abnormal behaviour	**Case/statute**
A characteristic is abnormal where it is not possessed by other animals of same species or only present at certain times.	*Cummings v Grainger* (1977) *Curtis v Betts* (1990)
Note – majority view that horses responding normally to fright was unusual behaviour and enough to make behaviour abnormal.	*Mirvahedy* (2003)
Meaning of 'characteristic'	**Case/statute**
Ability of animal to be trained is a characteristic, not the taught aggressive behaviour in limited circumstances which results.	*Gloster v Chief Constable of Greater Manchester* (2000)
But note criticism by Lord Scott.	*Mirvahedy* (2003)
Does not have to show risk that animal will attack humans.	*Wallace v Newton* (1982)
Keeper's knowledge	**Case/statute**
Must be actual knowledge.	
Knowledge imputed to keeper when child under 16 is aware.	
Defences	**Case/statute**
Fault of claimant and/or voluntary assumption of risk.	*Dhesi v Chief Constable of West Midlands Police* (2000)
No liability if person injured is a trespasser and animal is not kept for the purpose of protection or it is reasonable to keep the animal for protection.	*Cummings v Grainger* (1977)
Livestock	**Case/statute**
Keeper liable for damage to land or property caused by livestock which strays – except where lawful right to graze animals on unfenced land, eg in some national parks.	s 4
Occupier of land onto which the animals have strayed has right to detain animals which are not under someone's control and to sell the animals to recoup losses.	s 7

Liability for dogs	Case/statute
Keeper of dog liable for damage caused to livestock.	s 3
Person responsible for livestock not liable if they kill or injure a dog which is worrying the livestock and there is no other reasonable means to stop the dog or if the dog has been worrying, is still in the area and not under anyone's control.	s 9
Liability at common law	**Case/statute**
Owner may be liable for:	
trespass to land	*Paul v Summerhayes* (1878)
trespass to goods	*Manton v Brocklebank* (1923)
trespass to person if animal 'set on' a person	
defamation but unlikely	
negligence	*Fardon v Harcourt Rivington* (1932); *Birch v Mills* (1995); *Draper v Hodder* (1972)
nuisance.	*Leeman v Montague* (1936)
	Other statutory provision
	Guard Dogs Act 1975
	Dangerous Dogs Act 1991
	Dangerous Wild Animals Act 1976
	Zoo Licensing Act 1981

SUMMARY

- Common law originally provided strict liability actions for damage caused by dangerous species of animals and for damage caused by straying livestock
- These were replaced by the Animals Act 1971 although it is still possible to bring actions under other torts, eg negligence, trespass to the person etc
- The Animals Act 1971 distinguishes between 'dangerous species' and 'non-dangerous' species
- A dangerous species is one not domesticated in the UK and which is likely to cause severe damage unless restrained – and a keeper of such an animal is liable for all the damage it causes – so liability is strict
- A keeper of a non-dangerous animal is liable if: damage is likely if the animal is unrestrained, or damage is likely to be severe; because of characteristics not normally associated with the species, or only at specific times or in specific circumstances; and these characteristics were known to the keeper
- A keeper is somebody who is responsible for the animal or who is the head of the household where the actual keeper is a person under the age of 16
- Possible defences are: consent, damage caused wholly by the claimant's own fault and contributory negligence
- The Act also provides an action for damage caused by straying livestock and there is also an action for livestock killed by dogs, including the right to kill the dog in some circumstances to protect the livestock
- There is a limited duty to prevent livestock from straying on the highway
- Remoteness of damage is likely to be measured against the direct consequence test rather than the reasonably foreseeable test

12

Torts relating to goods

AIMS AND OBJECTIVES

After reading this chapter you should be able to:

■ Understand the common law basis for liability for defective products
■ Understand the statutory basis for liability for defective products
■ Understand the bases of liability for interference with goods
■ Be able to critically analyse each tort
■ Be able to apply the law to factual situations and reach conclusions as to liability

This chapter is divided into two parts. The first part deals with liability for defective products while the second part deals with liability for torts committed against goods.

12.1 Common law liability for defective products

12.1.1 Introduction

This area of law is partly dealt with by contract and consumer law and partly by torts, with a substantial contribution from statute. It is not appropriate to consider contract and consumer law in depth in a book on torts but it will be considered briefly. For detailed discussion reference should be made to texts relevant to the specific area such as C Turner, *Unlocking Contract Law* 2nd Edition (Hodder Education, 2007).

12.1.2 Liability in contract and consumer law

From the nineteenth century onwards, the courts have been concerned to prevent large businesses from taking advantage of their strength to 'bully' consumers. Consumers were first protected by the Sale of Goods Act 1893. Protection is now found in the Sale of Goods Act 1979 as amended by the Sale and Supply of Goods Act 1994. The Act works by implying certain terms into all contracts for the sale of goods. An example is the requirement that the goods be 'fit for their purpose' (s 14) which is not however implied into a private sale. Fitness for purpose includes a requirement that the goods should be free of defects and safe in normal use. People who are injured by goods which they have purchased have a remedy for breach of the term implied into the contract. Protection was extended by the Unfair Contract Terms Act 1977 which imposed strict limitations on the extent to which a business could exclude liability for defective products by means of an exclusion or limitation clause.

Where there is liability under the Sale of Goods Act, it is strict liability so far as the seller of the product is concerned. The buyer is entitled to be repaid the purchase price of the goods and to be compensated for further damage (but see a text on contract law for the rules relating to remoteness of damage).

It sounds as if all situations are covered but there is one fundamental flaw – only a party to a contract can generally sue for breach of that contract. This means that a person injured by a product received as a gift cannot claim using the Sale of Goods Act. This is the doctrine of privity of contract. The Contracts (Rights of Third Parties) Act 1999 has recently come into effect whereby a third party can have rights under the contract between the buyer and seller of the products but only provided certain conditions are fulfilled. It is not likely that this will provide an effective remedy in many cases.

What then are the rights of a person injured by a defective product who is not the buyer of that product?

12.1.3 Liability in negligence

Liability for loss or damage caused by defective products is usually accepted as starting in 1932. However, in more limited form there are much older examples.

CASE EXAMPLE

Dixon v Bell (1816) 5 M&S 198

A master handed a gun to his young servant who had no experience of handling guns. The boy was injured when the gun went off. It was accepted that the goods were potentially dangerous and 'capable of doing mischief' so there was held to be liability for the injuries caused by putting dangerous and defective goods in circulation.

As was seen in Chapter 2, the case of *Donoghue v Stevenson* [1932] AC 562 gave rise to two rules:

(i) the neighbour test which was intended to apply in all cases (the so-called 'wide-rule') and

(ii) the principle that a manufacturer owes a duty of care to the consumer (the so-called 'narrow rule').

The narrow rule was explained by Lord Macmillan when he said

QUOTATION

'. . . a person who engages in . . . manufacturing articles of food and drink intended for consumption by a member of the public in the form in which he issues them is under a duty to take care in the manufacture of those articles. That duty . . . he owes to those whom he intends to consume his products.'

It has been clear since 1932 that a manufacturer owes a duty of care to the ultimate consumer where products reach the consumer in much the same form as they left the factory.

As Lord Atkin identified in the case:

QUOTATION

'… a manufacturer of products which he sells in such form as to show that he intends them to reach the ultimate consumer in the form in which they left him with no reasonable possibility of intermediate examination, and with the knowledge that the absence of reasonable care in the preparation or putting up of the products will result in an injury to the consumer's life or property, owes a duty to the consumer to take reasonable care …'

So essentially there are three key elements that must be proved for a successful claim for product liability in negligence:

- the goods must reach the consumer and be intended to reach the consumer in the same form in which they left the manufacturer
- there is no possibility of an examination of or interference with the goods between leaving the manufacturer and reaching the end consumer
- the manufacturer knows that failing to take sufficient care of the goods may put the consumer at risk of foreseeable harm.

12.1.4 The scope of liability

Product liability in negligence concerns damage caused by or losses arising from the defect in the goods. Claims for replacement goods are made in contract law usually under the Sale of Goods Act 1979.

Originally product liability in negligence was restricted to foodstuffs but this has subsequently been extended to cover the full range of products. For instance it has included:

- a range of manufactured consumer durables – in *Grant v Australian Knitting Mills Ltd* [1936] AC 85 woollen underpants contained a chemical which caused the consumer to develop dermatitis, a painful skin disease; in *Herschtal v Stewart and Arden Ltd* [1940] 1 KB 155 it included a defective motor car
- defects in a house, which can also include the fixtures and fittings (*Batty v Metropolitan Property Realisations Ltd* [1978] QB 554)
- defective repair to a lift which then caused injury (*Haseldine v Daw & Son Ltd* [1941] 2 KB 343)
- more recently it has included computer software (*St Albans City and District Council v International Computers Ltd* [1996] 4 All ER 481).

12.1.5 Bringing a claim in negligence for damage caused by defective products

Product liability in negligence relies on proving the same essential elements as for claims in negligence generally: the existence of a duty of care owed by the manufacturer to the 'ultimate consumer' of the product; breach of duty by the manufacturer; foreseeable damage caused by the defendant's breach of duty.

Duty of care

The duty of care only applies in respect of goods reaching the consumer in the same form that they left the manufacturer where there is no chance of an intermediate examination.

Breach of duty

A breach of the duty by the manufacturer will generally involve a failure in the production process or alternatively a failure to rectify a known defect before the product reaches the consumer. So this may include:

- failing to check products that have been exposed to chemicals during the manufacturing process that then may cause harm (*Grant v Australian Knitting Mills Ltd* [1936])
- failing to remedy a known fault, which may include failing to recall defective products in sufficient time to avoid harm to the consumer (*Walton v British Leyland UK Ltd* [1978] Times 13th July)

Foreseeable damage caused by the defendant's breach of duty

The consumer can only recover compensation by proving that the damage was actually caused by the defect in the goods. If there is another possible cause of the damage then the consumer is unlikely to gain compensation.

12.1.6 Potential claimants

The original description in *Donoghue v Stevenson* given to those able to sue a manufacturer for damage caused by defective goods was 'ultimate consumers' or 'end users'. On the basis that the case exploded the so-called 'privity fallacy' of *Winterbottom v Wright* (1842) 10 M & W 109 it was inevitable that Lord Atkin would produce a description that was sufficiently broad to cover people who had not bought the goods themselves.

In any case, applying the neighbour principle, a claimant is anybody that the manufacturer 'should have in his contemplation' as being likely to be harmed if the goods are defective. So over time the definition has been broadened to include other situations involving foreseeable harm:

- suppliers that are injured because of the defect in the goods – in *Barnett v H and J Packer & Co* [1940] 3 All ER 575 sharp metal protruding from a sweet injured a shopkeeper who was storing the sweets and the manufacturer was liable for the injury
- bystanders – in *Stennet v Hancock and Peters* [1939] 2 All ER 578 a pedestrian was injured by a component that had been negligently reassembled by a garage and which then fell off a lorry.

12.1.7 Potential defendants

The original defendant in common law product liability was limited to the manufacturer of the defective goods. However, over time the law has expanded to include a wider range of potential defendants, including a number in the chain of production and distribution where they have a potential impact on the safety of the goods:

- wholesalers (*Watson v Buckley, Osborne Garrett & Co Ltd* [1940] 1 All ER 174)
- retailers (*Kubach v Hollands* [1937] 3 All ER 907)
- other suppliers of goods (eg through mail order) (*Herschtal v Stewart and Arden Ltd* [1940] 1 KB 155) – but only when the duty owed by the supplier goes beyond distributing the goods and requires that the goods are inspected
- people who repair goods (*Haseldine v CA Daw & Son Ltd* [1941] 2 KB 343)
- people who assemble goods (*Malfroot v Noxal Ltd* (1935) 51 TLR 551).

The consumer has a reasonable range of potential defendants to sue as a result. However, it is a more limited range than under the Consumer Protection Act 1987.

The problem for a consumer who seeks to rely on negligence arises from the need to prove fault, ie breach of the duty of care. It will be remembered that a person will not be liable for negligence if they have taken all reasonable steps to avoid injuring someone else. In some cases it is clear that there must have been fault and the courts have to be able to draw an inference of fault from the facts. This rather difficult concept is illustrated by two cases.

CASE EXAMPLE

Grant v Australian Knitting Mills Ltd [1936] AC 85

The claimant purchased some woollen underwear manufactured by the defendants. The garment was contaminated by sulphites which would not normally be present. This caused the claimant to suffer severely from dermatitis.

Finding the defendant liable, Lord Wright said

JUDGMENT

'According to the evidence, the method of manufacture was correct, the danger of excess sulphites being left was recognised and guarded against. . . . If excess sulphites were left in the garment, that could only be because someone was at fault. . . . Negligence is found as a matter of inference from the existence of the defects taken in connection with all the known circumstances.'

CASE EXAMPLE

Evans v Triplex Safety Glass Co Ltd [1938] 1 All ER 283

The claimant bought a car fitted by the makers with a windscreen of 'Triplex Toughened Safety Glass'. While he was driving the car the windscreen shattered injuring the claimant and his passengers.

JUDGMENT

Holding that the defendant was not liable Mr Justice Porter explained that an inference of fault on the part of the manufacturers could not be drawn for several reasons:
(i) the windscreen had been in place for more than a year before the accident
(ii) the disintegration could have resulted from another cause during the course of use of the car
(iii) it could have been badly fitted in the first place.

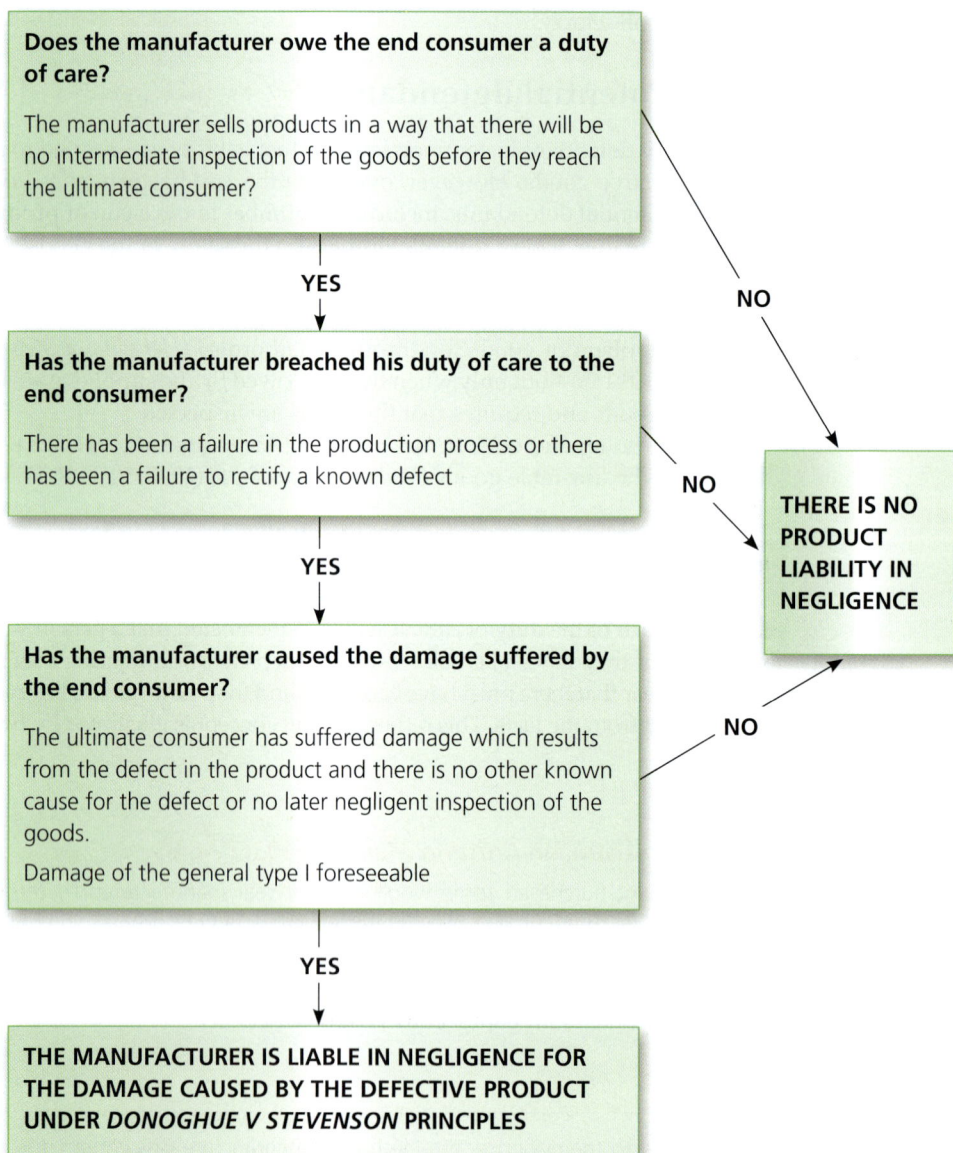

Does the manufacturer owe the end consumer a duty of care?

The manufacturer sells products in a way that there will be no intermediate inspection of the goods before they reach the ultimate consumer?

YES ↓   NO →

Has the manufacturer breached his duty of care to the end consumer?

There has been a failure in the production process or there has been a failure to rectify a known defect

YES ↓   NO →

Has the manufacturer caused the damage suffered by the end consumer?

The ultimate consumer has suffered damage which results from the defect in the product and there is no other known cause for the defect or no later negligent inspection of the goods.

Damage of the general type I foreseeable

YES ↓   NO →

THERE IS NO PRODUCT LIABILITY IN NEGLIGENCE

THE MANUFACTURER IS LIABLE IN NEGLIGENCE FOR THE DAMAGE CAUSED BY THE DEFECTIVE PRODUCT UNDER *DONOGHUE V STEVENSON* PRINCIPLES

Figure 12.1 Diagram illustrating the requirements for a claim in product liability in negligence under *Donoghue v Stevenson*

Unlike the cases of *Donoghue v Stevenson* and *Grant v Australian Knitting Mills* [1936] AC 85 where the cause of the problem was clear, in this case there were a number of potential causes thus fault could not be inferred.

These cases illustrate the difficulties faced by a claimant in bringing a successful action. There can be no certainty that the court will find that the defect has arisen by virtue of the defendant's fault as it seems that the claimant has to show that all other possible causes have been eliminated.

Additional problems faced by a claimant arise from the globalisation of trade. Products are imported from all over the world. While in some cases it is theoretically possible to bring an action in negligence against a foreign manufacturer, the matter is fraught with difficulty.

12.2 Statutory liability – the Consumer Protection Act 1987

12.2.1 Background

The tort of negligence is not of much practical help in many cases. In the 1970s a number of babies were born in the United Kingdom who were seriously damaged by a drug taken by their mothers in the early stages of pregnancy for severe morning sickness. The drug, Thalidomide, was suspected of causing birth defects and was, at the time it was prescribed in the United Kingdom, banned in many countries including the United States of America. Although eventually a compensation fund for the victims was created, it took many years during which time the victims had enormous difficulty in establishing the facts of the case. This and other concerns prompted the European Union to consider creating a system which would allow consumers injured by defective products to obtain compensation more easily. Eventually Directive 85/374/EEC was created. The Preamble to the Directive states 'liability without fault on the part of the producer is the sole means of adequately solving the problem, peculiar to our age of increasing technicality, of a fair apportionment of the risks inherent in modern technological production.'

The Directive was eventually passed into UK law by the Consumer Protection Act 1987 Part I.

12.2.2 Potential defendants under the Act

Section 2(1) of the Act states that there shall be liability 'where any damage is caused wholly or partly by a defect in a product.'

The class of those who may be liable is spelled out in s 2(2) which provides that s 2(1) applies to

SECTION

's 2(2) (a) the producer of the product;
    (b) any person who, by putting his name on the product or using a trade mark or other distinguishing mark in relation to the product, has held himself out to be the producer . . . ;
    (c) any person who has imported the product into a member State from a place outside the member States in order, in the course of . . . business . . . to supply it to another.'

The producer of the product

A 'producer' is obviously the manufacturer of the product but the term is expanded to include those who win or abstract non-manufactured substances, for example coal and other mined substances. It also includes those who have subjected a non-manufactured product, for example food crops, to an industrial process which has created essential characteristics of the product, for example corn flakes from corn or frozen vegetables (s 1(2)).

SECTION

's 1(3) Where an essential component fails and damage is caused, both the manufacturer of the part and the manufacturer of the defective component will be liable.'

The 'own-brander'

The term is amplified in the Directive to include he who 'presents himself as the producer'. The effect of this description may mean that an own-brander who clearly states that the goods are produced 'for' that business rather than 'by' that business will escape liability. It will probably apply, for example to the supermarket chain which markets it 'own brands' even though the goods are produced by a manufacturer.

The importer

When goods have been imported into the European Union from outside that area, the importer will be liable provided it has been imported with intent 'to supply it to another' (s 2(2)(c)). For example if goods have been imported from China into France and from there exported into the United Kingdom for sale to consumers, the original French importer will have liability.

CASE EXAMPLE

G v Fry Surgical International Ltd (unreported – cited in *Oughton and Lowry Textbook on Consumer Law* (2nd ed, Blackstone Press, 2000) at p 221)

The claimant was injured in an operation when a pair of surgical scissors broke. The scissors had been manufactured in Sweden, at that time not a member of the EU, and imported into the UK. The case was in fact settled without a judgment but the importer paid compensation.

Anonymous producers

While the mere fact that a supplier has supplied the goods in question is not of itself enough to make the supplier liable (unlike the Sale of Goods Act which imposes liability on the supplier), a supplier has a duty to provide information which identifies the producer on request by a consumer (s 2(3)). This is intended to enable a consumer to trace the goods back to the person who will have liability under the Act. The requirement is strengthened by the fact that should the supplier fail to provide the necessary information within a reasonable time, liability will rest on the supplier. As Winfield and Jolowicz suggest (p 355) 'the importance of adequate record keeping can hardly be overemphasised', as the supplier could find that a substantial bill has to be met if those earlier in the chain of supply cannot be identified.

12.2.3 Products covered by the Act

Product is defined in s 2(1) as '… any goods or electricity and (subject to subs (3)) includes a product which is comprised in another product, whether by virtue of being a component part, raw material or otherwise …'

Goods are defined in s 45(1) as '… substances, growing crops, and things comprised in land by virtue of being attached to it and any ship, aircraft or vehicle …'

Buildings, nuclear power, and agricultural produce which has not undergone an industrial process are all exempted from the scope of the Act.

12.2.4 The nature of the damage

By s 5 damage means death or personal injury in all circumstances. While damage to property is also recoverable, this is limited. There is no liability for loss or damage to the product itself or to any product of which the defective product forms part (s 5(2)).

Where damage to property has occurred, liability is restricted to those cases where the value of the claim exceeds £275 (s 5(4)) and where the property which has been damaged is 'ordinarily intended for private use, occupation or consumption' and the claimant intended to use the property for such purposes (s 5(3)).

The meaning of 'defect'

For the producer to be liable, the injury or damage must be caused 'wholly or partly by a defect in a product'. The meaning of 'defect' is accordingly of crucial importance.

The Act defines a product as being defective 'if the safety of the product is not such as persons generally are entitled to expect' (s 3(1)). In deciding whether or not a product is defective the court must take into account all the circumstances and in particular:

SECTION

's 3(1) (a) the way in which, and the purposes for which, it has been marketed, its get-up, the use of any mark in relation to the product and any instructions for, or warnings with respect to, doing or refraining from doing anything with or in relation to the product;

(b) what might reasonably be expected to be done with or in relation to the product; and

(c) the time when the product was supplied . . .'

Nothing is to be inferred from the fact that a product supplied at a later date is safer than the product in question.

While the Act (and the Directive from which it is derived) appears to impose a standard of safety, it is not in fact clearly explained what that standard is. The standard seems to be closely related to the tests in negligence, ie what standard would a reasonable producer maintain, but this disregards the requirement of the Directive that the producer should have strict liability for the defective product. The Directive provides some additional guidance by providing that

'A product is defective when it does not provide the safety which a person is entitled to expect, taking all circumstances into account including

(a) the presentation of the product;

(b) the use to which it could reasonably be expected that the product would be put;

(c) the time when the product was put into circulation.'

The issue was considered by the Court of Appeal in 2000:

CASE EXAMPLE

Abouzaid v Mothercare (UK) Ltd [2000] EWCA Civ 348

The claimant sustained a serious injury to his eye when attempting to fasten elastic straps to secure a sleeping-bag to a pushchair. As he was trying to fasten the buckle, the elastic slipped through his fingers and the buckle hit him in the eye. He claimed damages under the Consumer Protection Act.

Considering the meaning of 'defective' Lord Justice Pill concluded

JUDGMENT

'the product was defective within the meaning of the Act . . . The product was defective because it was supplied with a design that permitted the risk [of an eye injury] to arise and without giving a warning that the user should not so position himself that the risk arose. Members of the public were entitled to expect better from the [defendants].'

12.2.5 Defences

Compliance with legal requirements

A producer will not be liable for damage caused by goods which conform to mandatory statutory requirements, whether under UK legislation or EU law (s 4(1)(a)).

Goods not supplied in the course of business.

The Act only applies where goods have been supplied in the course of business. Home-made goods on sale at charitable fairs are not covered by the Act although other law, such as the tort of negligence, may apply.

Defects arising after the date of supply

Common sense suggests that the producer should only be liable for defects in the goods at the time they are put into circulation. The Act reflects this in s 4(1)(d). The defence is limited to defects arising after the date of supply so that there will be liability for defects existing at that time, even though the producer was unaware of them.

The 'state of the art' defence

By s 4(1)(e) it is a defence to show

SECTION

's 4(1)(e) that the state of scientific and technical knowledge at the relevant time was not such that a producer of products of the same description as the product in question might be expected to have discovered the defect if it had existed in his products while they were under his control.'

This mirrors the 'state of the art' defence to allegations of negligence (Chapter 3).

It was thought by some that the defence went further than permitted by the Directive but these fears were allayed by *European Commission v United Kingdom* (Case C-300/95 [1997] All ER (EC) 481. The European Court of Justice found that although the wording of the Act could be read to permit a subjective judgment, the issue of the state of scientific knowledge and its availability to the producer at the relevant time was capable of being decided objectively.

This does not mean that simply because there is some evidence available somewhere in the world that the producer will be expected to be aware of it. In many cases it will take time for research findings to circulate outside the country of origin and to be translated into an accessible language.

In essence, what the Act requires is that a producer is required to guard against foreseeable risks identified by the scientific and technical knowledge available at the relevant time.

CASE EXAMPLE

A v National Blood Authority [2001] EWHC 446 (QB)

The action was brought by 114 claimants who had been infected with hepatitis C when given blood transfusions or blood products produced by the defendants. The infection was caused by the use of infected blood after 1988. The virus was not identifiable until 1988 and a screening test was not generally available until 1991. Nonetheless the risk was known from 1988.

The defendant argued that there could be no liability as although the risk was known, the state of scientific knowledge at the time meant that there was no means of identifying whether or not blood was infected. The court rejected the argument holding that the 'state of the art' defence could not apply. The defendants knew of the risk and chose to supply the product in spite of it. The defendants must therefore take the consequences when injury resulted.

It is unnecessary to show that previous accidents had occurred. In *Abouzaid v Mothercare (UK) Ltd* [2000] EWCA Civ 348 Lord Justice Pill explained that a defect can be found to be 'present whether or not previous accidents had occurred'. He went on to say that 'Knowledge of previous accidents is not an ingredient necessary to a finding that a defect . . . is present.' It is in any event doubtful that 'a record of accidents comes within the category of "scientific and technical knowledge".'

Contributory negligence

By s 6(4) the Law Reform (Contributory Negligence) Act 1945 applies so blame can be apportioned between the producer and the person suffering damage.

12.2.6 Limitation of actions

The general rules discussed in Chapter 20 apply but are modified by the Consumer Protection Act 1987 which inserted a new section into the Limitation Act 1980. By s 11A of the Limitation Act the limitation period for claims under the Consumer Protection Act for personal injury or damage to property runs for three years from the date of the damage or from the date on which it could reasonably have been discovered. In the case of latent damage, there is a long stop of 10 years from the date the product was put into circulation. This means that if damage is not discovered until more than 10 years have elapsed, no remedy can be obtained using the Consumer Protection Act. The usual discretion to extend the limitation period in the case of personal injury (Limitation Act 1980 s 33) cannot be exercised to allow a claim after the end of the 10-year period.

12.2.7 A problem

We have seen that the European Directive was prompted in part by the Thalidomide tragedy. It was hoped that the new law would enable people damaged by drugs to have a simple and effective remedy without the need to prove negligence. It has not worked out that way. There have been a number of multi-party actions brought when a drug has allegedly caused damage to a number of people. Cases have been brought against the manufacturers of benzodiazepine tranquillisers, the manufacturers of Seroxat and most recently the manufacturers of the MMR vaccine. All have foundered but not because the legal case has been lost. None of the cases has come to trial because legal aid, although initially granted, has been withdrawn. There appear to be two reasons why this has happened:

■ the spiralling costs and the uncertain prospects of success in what would amount to test cases
■ the requirement that the action be launched within 10 years of the goods coming onto the market which has meant that there may well be cause for suspicion as to the safety of the product but little actual evidence of any link between the product and the damage.

It seems that without reform of the funding for large multi-group actions and an easing of the limitation period, at least one of the groups intended to benefit from the law has in reality seen no benefit at all.

(For an interesting article on this issue, see 'Why have they let us down' by Jon Robins, Independent Review, 23 September 2003, p 12.)

Is the defendant:
- A producer – a manufacturer – a manufacturer of the final product, an assembler of the final product, a person abstracting minerals from the ground, a person carrying out another industrial process to the goods, eg freezing them
- An importer, eg importing from outside the EU
- An 'own brander'
- A supplier, eg the retailer/wholesaler

YES ↓   **NO** ↘

Are the goods:
- anything growing or any ship, aircraft, vehicle or electricity or a product which is otherwise '… comprised in another product, whether by virtue of being a component part, raw material or otherwise …'
- substances, growing crops, and things comprised in land by virtue of being attached to it and any ship, aircraft or vehicle
- but not buildings and nuclear power
- or agricultural produce which has not undergone an industrial process

YES ↓   ← **NO**

There is no liability under the Consumer Protection Act 1987

Is: the safety of the product not such as persons generally are entitled to expect, taking into account all the circumstances …

YES ↓   **NO** ↗

Is the type of damage:
- death and personal injury,
- loss or damage to property
- but not damage under £275, business property, damage to defective property itself?

YES ↓   **NO**

Does one of the following defences apply?
- The product complies with statute or EC
- The defect did not exist when the goods were supplied
- The goods were not supplied in the course of a business
- The defendant did not supply the product
- The state of technological or scientific knowledge when the goods were supplied were not such that the defect would be apparent

YES ↗

NO ↓

The defendant may be liable under s 1 of the Consumer Protection Act 1987

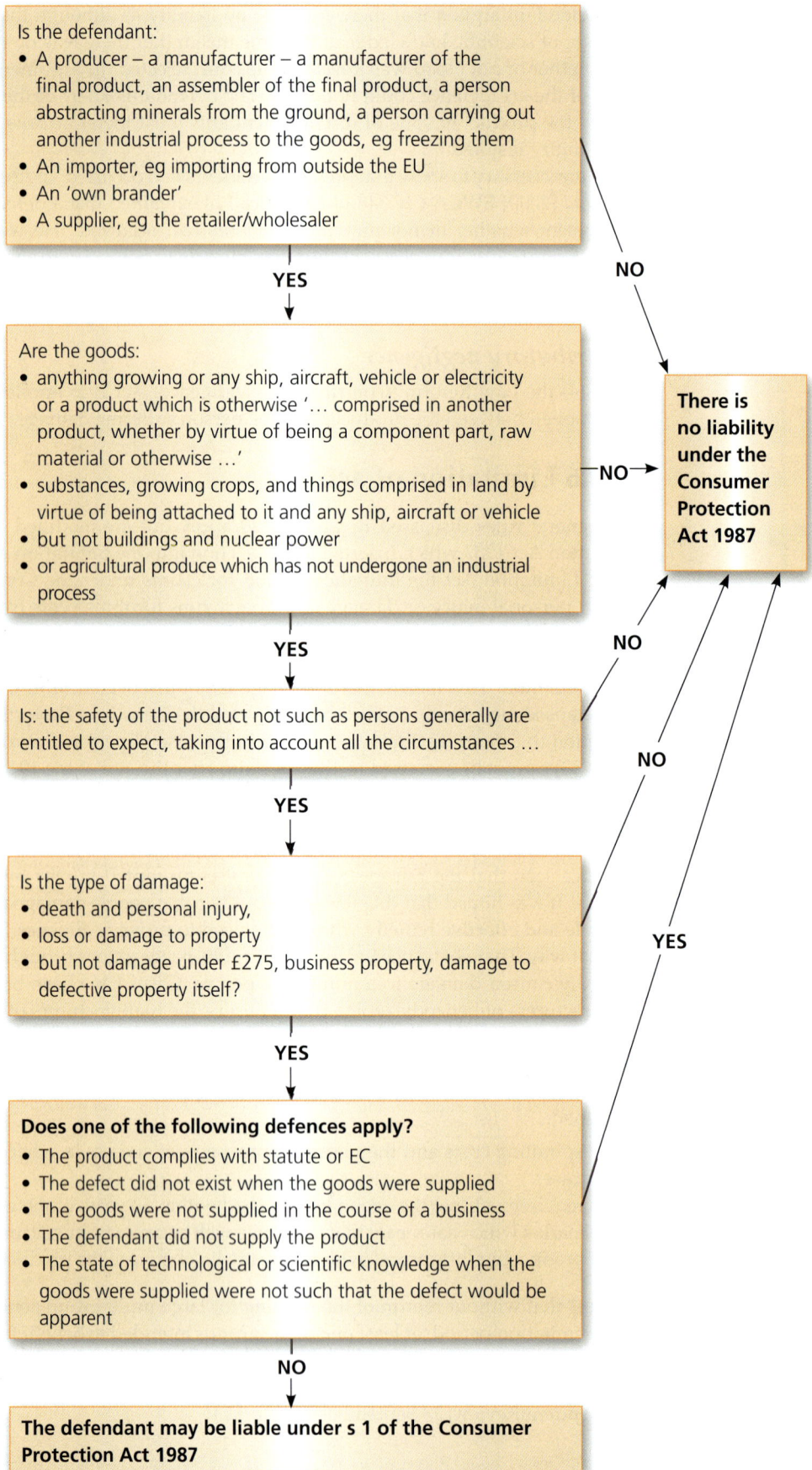

Figure 12.2 Diagram illustrating product liability under s 1 of the Consumer Protection Act 1987

ACTIVITY

Self-assessment questions

1. What precisely is the 'narrow rule' derived from *Donoghue v Stevenson*?
2. Explain the difficulties faced by a claimant who seeks to rely on negligence for damages in respect of injuries caused by defective goods.
3. What is the purpose of Directive 85/374/EEC?
4. Explain precisely who may have liability for damage caused by defective products under the Consumer Protection Act 1987.
5. State the distinction drawn by the Act between compensation for personal injury and compensation for damage to property.
6. When will a product be regarded as 'defective' under the terms of the Act?
7. In the context of the 'state of the art' defence, what is the importance of *A v National Blood Authority*?

12.3 Interference with goods

12.3.1 Trespass to goods

Trespass to goods can be defined as

Any direct and intentional interference with goods in the possession of another without lawful authority.

Like other forms of trespass, the tort is actionable *per se* so that it is unnecessary to show that the goods have been damaged in any way or even that the owner has been permanently deprived of them.

Elements of the tort: Direct and intentional

The act must be intentional in the sense that the person intended to do it. If this is the case, then the fact that the person mistakenly believed that he had the right to do so is irrelevant. In this sense the tort can be described as one of strict liability although damages are usually only nominal if no actual damage is done. Accidental interference will not amount to trespass but may amount to negligence. A person whose car or other property is damaged by the defendant's vehicle has to sue using negligence with its need to prove fault.

The act must also be direct; indirect damage may be actionable under some other tort for example private nuisance or negligence.

Possession of goods

The essence of the tort is that there has been interference with a person's right to possess the goods. A person in actual possession, whether the owner or someone who has borrowed them, is able to bring an action against anyone who does not have a better legal title.

Interference

It has been seen that actual damage is not an essential element of the tort.

CASE EXAMPLE

Kirk v Gregory (1876) 1 ExD 55

Following the death of her brother-in-law the defendant moved jewellery belonging to the deceased to what she believed was a safer place. The jewellery was in fact stolen. It was held that the defendant was liable for trespass to goods by virtue of her act in moving the property.

There has been some debate as to whether or not a mere touching will suffice. Academic consensus appears to be that it will. The example given is that of a person who gently touches a museum exhibit without causing damage. To hold that mere touching is not enough would deprive the museum of any remedy.

Remedies

The remedies for trespass to goods are similar to those for the tort of conversion which is the subject matter of the next part of this chapter. For convenience, all remedies are dealt with later in section 12.3.4.

12.3.2 Conversion

Conversion (formerly known as 'trover') is now governed by the Torts (Interference with Goods) Act 1977 but the old common law rules are still very relevant.

Definition

The essence of the tort is

QUOTATION

'any dealing with another's property in a way which amounts to a denial of his right over it, or an assertion of a right inconsistent with his right, by wrongfully taking, detaining or disposing of it.'

S Deakin, A Johnston and B Markesinis, *Markesinis and Deakin's Tort Law* (5th edn, OUP, 2003), p 438

Elements of the tort: The claimant's rights

The claimant must have title in the sense of:

- ownership
- possession
- an immediate right to possess
- a lien or other equitable title.

Possession alone may be enough to found an action. An example occurs where goods are found. In such case, the finder will have an enforceable right to possession against everyone except someone with a better right.

CASE EXAMPLE

Armory v Delamirie (1721) 1 Stra 505

A chimney sweep's boy found a jewel. He took it to a jeweller for valuation and the jeweller refused to return it. The jeweller was liable for conversion.

CASE EXAMPLE

Parker v British Airways Board [1982] QB 1004

The claimant found a gold brooch on the floor of the executive lounge at Heathrow Airport. The Court of Appeal explained that the occupier of land upon which goods are found will have a better title than the finder if:

- the finder is a trespasser on the land
- the property is in or attached to the land
- the occupier of the land on which the property is found has prior to the finding 'manifested an intention to exercise control over the [land] and things which may be upon or in it'.

Although the defendants had a procedure for dealing with lost property and access to the lounge was restricted, this was not enough to establish intention to control the premises and things found on it. It was held that the claimant was entitled to the brooch.

Intention

The defendant must intend to do the act in question. As with trespass, it is not necessary for the defendant to intend to commit the tort. The fact that the defendant is unaware of the true facts will be no defence. An example occurs when an innocent person has acquired goods from a rogue who has no title to them. The true owner can sue the innocent party in conversion.

The act of conversion

An omission will not be enough, there must be an act of some sort which is inconsistent with the rights of the person in possession (from now on called the owner for the sake of brevity). The act must amount to a denial of title and may take many forms, for example

- taking the goods
- refusal to restore goods by a bailee on demand
- wrongful delivery of goods to a third party
- abuse of possession (for example a bailee who delivers goods to the consignee after notice of stoppage in transit or changing a thing's character by making bread out of flour)
- destroying or disposing of the goods.

12.3.3 Defences to trespass and to conversion

Lawful authority

People who borrow books from a library have lawful authority for possession of that book provided they are a member. A person who takes possession of goods with the consent of the owner, for example as security for a debt, or pursuant to a court order has lawful authority and is not liable for trespass. There will be liability for conversion if an act inconsistent with the extent of the authority is done.

Jus tertii

It is no defence for the defendant to show that another person has a better legal right to possession of the goods than the claimant. This caused problems where in fact this was the case and could leave the defendant facing two legal actions, one by the claimant and one by the person with a better title. To mitigate this difficulty the Torts (Interference with Goods) Act 1977 s 8 enables a defendant to show that a named third party has a better right than the claimant. The rules of court enable directions to be given as to whether or not the third party should be joined as a party to the action.

12.3.4 Remedies

Retaking the goods

The owner can retake the goods from a person without a better title. This simple remedy may be helpful in some cases but the owner needs to be wary of committing trespass to land in his efforts to retake the goods! The owner must act peaceably and use no more force than is reasonable in the particular circumstances.

It should be noted that a person onto whose land the goods have come is entitled to keep those goods until the owner pays for any damage done. A possible remedy where cricket balls are hit onto land causing broken windows or other damage?

Damages: Defendant no longer in possession

Where the defendant no longer has possession of the goods, damages will be for the value of the goods and any consequential loss which is not too remote.

CASE EXAMPLE

Bodley v Reynolds (1846) 8 QBD 779

A carpenter's tools were converted. He was awarded the value of the tools and an additional sum of £10 for his loss of earnings.

CASE EXAMPLE

Saleslease Ltd v Davis [1999] 1 WLR 1644

The test for remoteness of damage is whether or not the loss is reasonably foreseeable. The loss incurred by the claimant's inability to deliver the converted goods under a contract already concluded with a third party will be recoverable only if the defendant is aware of that contract.

Recently the courts have appeared to make a distinction in relation to consequential loss between those cases where the defendant acted dishonestly and those where he did not. In the former case, the defendant would be held liable for all the consequences which flowed directly and naturally from the wrongful conduct (*Kuwait Airways v Iraqi Airways (Nos 4 and 5)* [2002] 2 AC 883, HL).

Defendant in possession of the goods

By the Torts (Interference with Goods) Act 1977 s 3 three orders are possible:
1. delivery of the goods and payment of any consequential damage
2. delivery of the goods with the option for the defendant to pay damages made up of the value of the goods, in either case with the additional payment of damages for consequential loss
3. damages.

While (1) will be ordered at the discretion of the court, the claimant can choose between (2) and (3). Generally the court will only order delivery of goods (specific restitution) where the goods are unique or of particular personal value to the claimant.

In some cases the value of the goods has been increased by the actions of the defendant. Where the defendant has acted honestly, believing that they have good title, the courts will generally allow the cost of improvements to be set against the value of the goods (s 6 Torts (Interference with Goods) Act 1977).

ACTIVITY

Self-assessment questions

1. Define the tort of trespass to goods.
2. What precisely is meant by 'possession' in the context of the tort?
3. What is the essence of the tort of conversion?
4. Explain the principles which will guide the court in assessing damages for trespass to goods or conversion.

SAMPLE ESSAY QUESTION

Discuss the argument that the enactment of the Consumer Protection Act 1987 renders an action for product liability in negligence obsolete.

Identify the existence of a negligence action for defective products

- Derives from *Donoghue v Stevenson*
- A manufacturer of a product owes a duty of care to an end user or consumer of his products not to cause them harm

---

Discuss the essential elements for a successful claim

- The manufacturer owes the consumer a duty of care when the goods are received in the state that they left the manufacturer and there is no chance of an intermediate inspection of the goods
- The manufacturer has breached the duty of care by a failure in the manufacturing process or a failure to remedy a known defect in the goods
- The defect has caused foreseeable damage and there is no other possible cause of the damage

---

Identify the wider range of potential defendants under the Consumer Protection Act

- The consumer can sue producers – which includes manufacturers, people who assemble components, people who abstract minerals from the ground that go into making the product, people who carry out an industrial process etc
- Suppliers
- Importers
- Own branders
- So can sue virtually anyone in the production and supply chain
- Which makes it more effective than negligence where the manufacturer was overseas

Discuss the range of defects and damage covered by the Act

- The consumer can sue for a defect in any goods which also includes a product comprised in another product
- Defect is defined as 'if the safety of the product is not such as persons generally are entitled to expect, taking into account all the circumstances …'
- The Act covers death and personal injury and damage to property – but not small losses under £275, damage to business property, damage to the defective product
- So the Act is the same as negligence on the last but more restrictive on the first two

Discuss the range of available defences

- The product complies with EC or statutory requirements
- The defect did not exist when the product was supplied
- The product was not supplied in the course of a business
- The defendant did not supply the product
- The state of technological knowledge when the product was supplied
- So is possibly broader than that for negligence

KEY FACTS

Key facts on liability for defective goods

Liability for goods	Case/statute
Potential liability under Act as amended – generally remedy only available to buyer of goods.	Sale of Goods Act 1979
Liability in negligence dependent on ability to prove fault.	*Donoghue v Stevenson* (1932)
	Grant v Australian Knitting Mills (1936)
	Evans v Triplex Safety Glass (1938)
Consumer Protection Act 1987	**Case/statute**
Imposes liability where person injured by defective product.	s 2(1)

Who may be liable	Case
Producer. Own brander holding themselves out as producers of the goods. When goods imported into the EU with intent to supply them to another, the importer. Supplier who fails to respond to request for information about producer or importer within reasonable time.	*G v Fry Surgical International Ltd* (unreported)

Damage	Case
Includes death or personal injury. Damage to property where claim exceeds £275. Damage to the product excluded.	

Meaning of 'defect'	Case/statute
Product is defective if its safety is not what people generally are entitled to expect. In deciding, all circumstances relevant but in particular: marketing and instructions with product what is reasonably likely to be done with the product. the time when it was supplied. Can be a design fault.	s 3(1) *Abouzaid v Mothercare (UK)* (2000)

Defences	Case
Compliance with legal requirements. Goods not supplied in the course of business. Defects arose after the date of supply. At the time the goods were put in circulation, scientific and technical knowledge was such that the producer could not be aware of the defect.	*A v National Blood Authority* (2001)

Limitation period	Case
Generally three years from the date of damage or date when it could reasonablly have been discovered. Long stop of 10 years from date product was put into circulation.	

Key facts on interference with goods

Trespass to goods	Case
Direct and intentional interference with goods in possession of another. Actionable per se actual damage by defendant not necessary. If act intended, it is no defence that defendant believed they had a right to the goods. Person in actual possession can sue all except someone with better legal right.	*Kirk v Gregory* (1876)
Conversion	**Case**
Governed by Torts (Interference with Goods) Act 1977. Any dealing with another's property in such a way as to deny that person's rights in respect of the property. Person in actual possession can sue all except someone with better legal right. Dealing must be intended – no defence that defendant mistaken as to their rights.	*Armory v Delamirie* (1721); *Parker v British Airways Board* (1982)
Defences to trespass and conversion	**Case**
Lawful authority. Jus tertii – right of a third party who has better title – court may direct third party to be joined to the action.	
Remedies	**Case**
Self-help by retaking the goods – acting peaceably and with no more force than necessary. Damages – value of goods if defendant no longer in possession together with consequential loss. Where defendant in possession court may order delivery of the goods and damages, claimant may ask for order for delivery with option for defendant to pay damages to make up value and to cover consequential loss or claimant may ask for damages alone. Where honest defendant has increased value of the goods cost of improvement generally allowed against value.	*Bodley v Reynolds* (1846); *Saleslease v Davis* (1999)

SUMMARY

Liability for defective goods

- Consumers can recover compensation for damage caused by defective products through either negligence or the Consumer Protection Act 1987
- In negligence the manufacturer of the goods owes a consumer a duty of care for defective goods that reach a consumer in the state that they left the manufacturer and there is no chance of any intermediate inspection
- The Consumer Protection Act allows consumers to sue a wider range of defendants: producers, suppliers, importers, own-branders
- The consumer can sue for a defect in any goods where 'the safety of the product is not such as persons generally are entitled to expect, taking into account all the circumstances'
- Damages are possible for death and personal injury and damage to property but not: small losses under £275; damage to business property; damage to the defective product
- There are fixed defences: the goods comply with EC/statutory requirements; the defect did not exist when the product was supplied; the goods were not supplied in the course of a business; the defendant did not supply the product; the state of technological knowledge when the product was supplied was not such that the defendant could know of the defect

Interference with goods

- Trespass to goods is the direct, immediate, intentional interference with personal property belonging to another
- Conversion is now under the Torts (Interference with Goods) Act 1977 and involves ownership as well as possession – and it is the intentional, wrongful interference of a substantial nature with the claimant's possession or rights to possession, or dealing with the goods in a manner inconsistent with the rights of the owner

13

Trespass to the person

AIMS AND OBJECTIVES

After reading this chapter you should be able to:

■ Understand the basic origins and character of trespass to the person
■ Understand the elements that are common to all forms of the tort
■ Understand the definition of and essential elements for proving assault
■ Understand the definition of and essential elements for proving battery
■ Understand the definition of and essential elements for proving false imprisonment
■ Understand the definition of and essential elements for proving an action for intentional indirect harm under *Wilkinson v Downton*
■ Understand the basis of liability under the Protection from Harassment Act 1997
■ Be able to critically analyse each tort
■ Be able to apply the law to factual situations and reach conclusions

13.1 The origins and character of trespass

13.1.1 Historical origins

Trespass was one of the two original forms of action (see Chapter 1 section 1.1). The term has survived to the present day in the context of specific torts, one being trespass to the person. The essence of all modern forms of trespass can be found in the old idea that trespass was the appropriate remedy for any direct and forcible injury. As will be seen, trespass to the person relates to direct and forcible injury to the person. Before turning to the tort itself it is necessary to consider the legal meaning of

■ direct
■ forcible and
■ injury.

13.1.2 Direct

The traditional explanation of this word is that the injury must follow so closely on the act that it can be seen as part of the act. This is still true but perhaps implies that injuries caused by a car accident are also direct which is not legally the case. Such injuries are regarded as consequential. (For a more detailed discussion of this point see Chapter 4 section 4.2.) As Lord Denning explained

QUOTATION

'. . . we divide the causes of action now according as the defendant did the injury intentionally or unintentionally. If one man intentionally applies force directly to another, the plaintiff has a cause of action in . . . trespass to the person. . . . If he does not inflict injury intentionally, but only unintentionally, the plaintiff has no cause of action today in trespass. His only cause of action is in negligence.'

Letang v Cooper [1964] 2 All ER 929, CA

This difficult proposition is easier to understand when the facts of the case are considered

CASE EXAMPLE

Letang v Cooper [1964] 2 All ER 929, CA

While on holiday in Cornwall, Mrs Letang was sunbathing on a piece of grass where cars were parked. While she was lying there, Mr Cooper drove into the car park. He did not see her. The car went over Mrs Letang's legs injuring her. She claimed damages on the basis of both negligence and trespass to the person. It was agreed by both sides that the action in negligence was statute-barred, ie the action had not been commenced within the requisite three-year time limit. The question was therefore whether or not her claim could succeed in trespass to the person where the time limit of six years had not expired?

JUDGMENT

'If [the action] is intentional, it is the tort of assault and battery. If negligent and causing damage, it is the tort of negligence . . . [The plaintiff's] only cause of action here . . . (where the damage was unintentional), was negligence and not trespass to the person.'

Lord Denning

The definitions of each of the three component parts of trespass to the person incorporate the word intentional as well as direct. The old meaning must however be understood if the rest of the law is to make any sense! These issues are discussed in more depth in Chapter 1.

13.1.3 Forcible

While the word itself conjures up a picture of force which causes or is capable of causing physical injury, in reality the law uses the term to describe any kind of threatened or actual physical interference with the person of another. An unwanted kiss can be a trespass to the person (*R v Chief Constable of Devon & Cornwall, ex p CEGB* [1981] 3 All ER 826).

13.1.4 Injury

Given the explanation of forcible it comes as no surprise to learn that injury is interpreted widely and can include any infringement of personal dignity or bodily integrity. Actual physical harm is not an essential ingredient of trespass to the person although in many cases it may have occurred. The tort is actionable *per se*. In other words it is not necessary to prove actual damage. It is only necessary to prove that the actions of the defendant fulfil the requisite criteria.

13.1.5 The tort

Trespass to the person has three components which may occur together or separately. Each of itself gives rise to a cause of action. The components are

- assault
- battery
- false imprisonment.

Assault and battery will each be defined and explained, the defences applicable to both these torts being considered together. False imprisonment will then be considered separately.

Trespass to the person can be committed in one of three ways:

D Intentionally and directly causes anticipation of imminent threat of battery to:	→ C =	**ASSAULT**
D Intentionally and directly applies unlawful contact to the body of:	→C =	**BATTERY**
D Intentionally and directly applies a total bodily constraint to the liberty of:	—(C) =	**FALSE IMPRISONMENT**

Figure 13.1 How liability is established in the different types of trespass to the person

13.2 Assault

13.2.1 Definition

The tort can be defined in various ways. For example:

- 'The act of putting another person in reasonable fear or apprehension of an immediate battery by means of an act amounting to an attempt or threat to commit a battery amounts to an actionable assault' (R E V Heuston and R A Buckley, *Salmond and Heuston on the Law of Torts* (20th edn, Sweet & Maxwell, 1992), p 127).
- 'Assault is an act of the defendant which causes the claimant reasonable apprehension of the infliction of a battery on him by the defendant' (*Winfield and Jolowicz*, p 71).
- 'An assault is an act which causes another person to apprehend the infliction of immediate, unlawful, force on his person' (Goff LJ in *Collins v Wilcock* [1984] 3 All ER 374).

As will be seen, none of these definitions covers all the essential elements of the tort. A better definition is perhaps

QUOTATION

An assault is some direct and intentional conduct by the defendant which causes the victim reasonably to fear that unlawful force is about to be used upon their person.

Figure 13.2 Assault

13.2.2 Ingredients of the tort

Direct and intentional

The words direct and intentional have the meaning discussed in section 13.1 above.

Conduct

Conduct in this context amounts to something which threatens the use of unlawful force. An obvious example is shaking a fist under someone's nose causing them to fear that they are about to be punched. In most cases it may be true that the assailant's actions clearly convey the necessary threat, but this is not always so.

In the modern world threats can be conveyed in many ways. Apart from physical action, the most obvious way is by means of a verbal threat. Traditionally, the use of threatening words alone could not amount to an assault (*R v Meade and Belt* (1823) 1 Lew CC 184). This may have been satisfactory in 1823 but in the twenty-first century there are other means of communication, for example by telephone and email. To the victim a verbal threat by these means may be just as credible as a gesture supported by threatening words. In criminal cases there has been recognition that words alone can indeed amount to an assault. In *R v Ireland* [1997] 4 All ER 225 the House of Lords held that silent telephone calls, sometimes accompanied by heavy breathing, could amount to a criminal assault. Lord Steyn, rejecting the proposition in *R v Meade and Belt*, said

JUDGMENT

'The proposition . . . that words can never suffice, is unrealistic and indefensible. There is no reason why something said should be incapable of causing an apprehension of immediate personal violence . . . Take now the case of the silent caller. He intends by his silence to cause fear and he is so understood. The victim is assailed by uncertainty about his intentions. Fear may dominate her emotions . . . She may fear the possibility of immediate personal violence. As a matter of law the caller may be guilty of an assault.'

R v Ireland is of course a criminal case but it is very likely that if a civil action for assault based on words alone were to be brought, the decision would be that an assault had potentially been committed. Whether or not this would be the actual decision would depend on whether or not the other elements of the tort were satisfied.

Words can have the opposite effect by making it clear that the assailant does not intend to carry out the threat.

CASE EXAMPLE

Turberville v Savage (1669) 1 Mod Rep 3

The assailant put his hand on his sword and said 'If it were not assize-time, I would not take such language from you.' The victim alleged that he had been in fear that he was about to be attacked.

The statement was in fact a declaration by the assailant that he did not intend to attack the victim because the judges were in town.

QUOTATION

'The intention as well as the act makes an assault.'

Reasonable fear

The victim's fear that the threat is likely to be carried out must be reasonable. In part this depends on a subjective test which looks at the victim's perception of the situation. In *R v St George* (1840) 9 C&P 483 the judge said

JUDGMENT

'It is an assault to point a weapon at a person, though not loaded, but so near, that if loaded, it might do injury.'

Parke B

The victim in such a case fears perfectly reasonably that he is about to be shot. If, however, the victim knew that the gun was unloaded, any fear would likely be held to be unreasonable.

It follows that the threat must be capable of being carried out at the time it is made. (In the case of telephone threats, the House of Lords in *R v Ireland* indicated that the fear should be that the assailant would be likely to turn up 'within a minute or two'.) What however would be the position if the defendant were to be prevented from carrying out the threat?

CASE EXAMPLE

Stephens v Myers (1830) 4 C&P 349

The claimant was acting as chair at a parish meeting and was seated at some distance from the defendant with other people seated between them. The meeting became angry and a majority decision was taken to expel the defendant. He said that he would rather pull the claimant out of the chair than be expelled and went towards him with a clenched fist. The defendant was stopped by other people before he was close enough actually to hit the claimant. The general opinion of others present was that the defendant would have hit the claimant had he not been stopped before he could do so.

When a person was advancing in a threatening way so that had he not been stopped he would have hit his victim.

It is clear that Mr Stephens' perception that he was about to be hit was reasonable; at the time it was made, Mr Myers was in a position to carry it out. Where the assailant is not in such a position, the outcome may be different.

JUDGMENT

'if he was advancing with that intent, I think it amounts to an assault in law. If he was so advancing, that, within a second or two of time, he would have reached the plaintiff, it seems to me that it is an assault in law.'

Tindal CJ

CASE EXAMPLE

Thomas v National Union of Mineworkers (South Wales Area) [1985] 2 All ER 1

The claimant was a miner who continued to work during a particularly bitter strike by members of the NUM. The claimant and colleagues were bussed into work through a large crowd of striking miners who made threatening gestures and shouted threats at those on the bus.

For liability for assault to occur, there had to be the ability to carry out the threat at the time it was made. The crowd was kept away from the claimant and the others by a large number of police officers. They were also protected by being on a moving bus.

It seems therefore that ability to carry out the threat must exist at the time the threat is made. It has been seen however that this rule has been somewhat relaxed in the area of criminal law (*R v Ireland*). Whether this will enable the courts to devise an effective remedy for threats conveyed via email or the use of other technology remains to be seen. Abusive and threatening emails and text messages are being reported by the media as part of the growing problem of bullying in schools and the workplace. Perhaps it will not be long before this area of the law is reconsidered.

13.3 Battery

13.3.1 Definitions

Different definitions can be found in different sources. Thus

- 'Battery is the intentional and direct application of force to another person' (*Winfield and Jolowicz*, p 71).
- 'The application of force to the person of another without lawful justification' (*Salmond and Heuston*, p 125).
- 'Battery is the actual infliction of unlawful force on another person' (Goff LJ in *Collins v Wilcock*).

The problem is that none of these definitions covers all the requisite elements for liability. A better definition is

QUOTATION

'Where the defendant, intending the result and without lawful justification or the consent of the claimant, does an act which directly and physically affects the person of the claimant.'

13.3.2 Ingredients of the tort

Intention

Life would be intolerable and the courts would be overloaded if every touch we received while going about our daily business was actionable. It is clear that the touching must be intentional if there is to be liability for battery, while non-intentional touching may amount to negligence. (See *Letang v Cooper* above in section 13.1.2.) It must be remembered that it is the touching which must be intentional; it does not matter whether or not the defendant intended to cause injury although this may be relevant to the element of hostility discussed later in this section.

A problem can arise where the defendant intends to hit one person but misses and hits someone else. In such cases the doctrine of 'transferred malice' comes into play. The intention was to hit someone; the fact that the actual person hit was not the intended target is irrelevant.

CASE EXAMPLE

Livingstone v Ministry of Defence [1984] NI 356, NICA

A soldier in Northern Ireland fired a baton round targeting a rioter. He missed and hit the claimant instead. It was held that the soldier had intentionally applied force to the claimant.

Direct

The battery must be the direct result of the defendant's intentional act. This is easily seen when a punch or other form of physical touching occurs.

Case law dating back over the centuries shows just how widely the courts are prepared to stretch the meaning of direct.

CASE EXAMPLE

Gibbons v Pepper (1695) 1 Ld Raym 38

The defendant whipped a horse so that it bolted and ran down the claimant. The defendant was liable in battery for the claimant's injuries.

CASE EXAMPLE

Scott v Shepherd (1773) 2 Wm Bl 892

Shepherd threw a lighted squib into a market house. It landed on the stall of a ginger bread seller. To prevent damage to the stall, Willis picked it up and threw it across the market. Ryal, to save his own stall, picked it up and threw it away. It struck the claimant in the face and exploded, blinding him in one eye.

The defendant intended to scare someone although he did not intend to hurt the particular person who was actually injured. He was liable in battery, Willis and Ryal being held to be Shepherd's 'instruments'.

QUOTATION

'. . . the law insists, and insists quite rightly, that fools and mischievous persons must answer for consequences which common sense would unhesitatingly attribute to their wrongdoing'

Winfield and Jolowicz, p 235

CASE EXAMPLE

Pursell v Horn [1838] 8 A&E 602

The defendant threw water over the claimant. The force applied does not have to be personal contact and the defendant was liable in battery.

CASE EXAMPLE

Nash v Sheen [1955] CLY 3726

The claimant had gone to the defendant's hairdressing salon where she was to receive a 'permanent wave'. A tone rinse was applied to her hair, without her agreement, causing a skin reaction. The defendant was liable in battery.

Although, as the cases illustrate, the courts have been prepared to take a fairly wide view of what amounts to a direct touching, the one thing that does appear to be clear is that only a positive act will suffice. There is unlikely to be liability in battery for an omission.

CASE EXAMPLE

Innes v Wylie [1844] 1 Car & Kir 257

A policeman stood and blocked the claimant's entrance to a meeting of a Society from which the claimant had been banned.

JUDGMENT

'If the policeman was entirely passive like a door or a wall put to prevent the [claimant] from entering the room, and simply obstructing the entrance of the claimant, no assault has been committed on the claimant . . .'.

Denman CJ

Touching

Originally any touch however slight would amount to a battery. In *Cole v Turner* (1704) 6 Mod Rep 149 this appeared to have been qualified by Lord Holt when he said that 'the least touching in anger is a battery.' Does this mean that the touching, in addition to being intentional, must also be hostile?

Goff LJ, in *Collins v Wilcock* [1984] 3 All ER 374 (for facts see section 13.4.1), stated that 'the fundamental principle, plain and incontestable, is that every person's body is inviolate'. He went on to expound this by quoting from Blackstone's Commentaries in which Blackstone explained

QUOTATION

'the law cannot draw the line between different degrees of violence, and therefore totally prohibits the first and lowest stage of it; every man's person being sacred, and no other having a right to meddle with it, in any the slightest manner.'

Goff LJ explained that 'a broader exception has been created . . . embracing all physical contact which is generally acceptable in the ordinary conduct of daily life.' While it may be a matter of personal opinion as to what constitutes generally acceptable conduct, it is clear from the judgment that actions such as tapping someone on the shoulder to gain their attention would not amount to a battery.

These relatively clear ideas were thrown into confusion in 1986 when the Court of Appeal seemed to prefer Lord Holt's explanation in *Cole v Turner*.

CASE EXAMPLE

Wilson v Pringle [1986] 2 All ER 440

A schoolboy admitted that he had pulled a bag which was over the shoulder of another boy. The other boy fell over and was injured. Summary judgment on the basis of battery was entered for the claimant, the defendant eventually appealing to the Court of Appeal.

JUDGMENT

'. . . it is not practicable to define a battery as "physical contact which is not generally acceptable in the ordinary conduct of daily life." In our view . . . there must be an intentional touching or contact in one form or another of the [claimant] by the defendant. That touching must be proved to be a hostile touching . . . Hostility cannot be equated with ill-will or malevolence. It cannot be governed by the obvious intention shown in acts like punching, stabbing or shooting. It cannot be solely governed by an expressed intention, although that may be strong evidence. But the element of hostility . . . must be a question of fact . . . It may be imported from the circumstances'.

Croom-Johnson LJ

In the event, the schoolboy's act of pulling the bag was merely a prank, the necessary element of hostility was lacking.

Wilson v Pringle created more questions than answers. The explanation given is not entirely helpful. It is still necessary to ask 'what does hostility mean?' The question was partially answered in *R v Brown* [1994] 2 All ER 75.

CASE EXAMPLE

R v Brown [1994] 2 All ER 75

The case concerned a group of sado-masochistic homosexuals who willingly co-operated in the commission of acts of violence against each other for sexual pleasure. The men were prosecuted for malicious wounding contrary to s 20 Offences Against the Person Act 1861. The equivalent civil action would be based in battery. Following their conviction, the case reached the House of Lords where one of the issues considered was whether or not hostility on the part of the inflictor of an injury was an essential ingredient for battery.

Having seemingly approved the view in *Collins v Wilcock* that hostility could not be equated with ill will or malevolence, Lord Jauncey went on to say that if the appellants' actions

JUDGMENT

'were unlawful they were also hostile and a necessary ingredient of [malicious wounding] was present.'

It seems therefore that if the touching is unlawful, then it is hostile. As will be seen in the next part of this Chapter, lawful authority in a variety of forms is a full defence to the tort. *R v Brown*, although a criminal case, appears to be go some way to providing an explanation of when a touching will be regarded as hostile.

The question remains however – is a hostile intent necessary in order to establish liability? Where does this leave medical treatment which has been given against the wishes of a patient – doctors after all act with the intention of doing good for their patients. The issues raised by medical cases will be discussed in the next part of this Chapter.

13.4 Defences to assault and battery

These are dealt with in one section as the same defences are available to each tort.

13.4.1 Lawful authority

If a person committing assault and/or battery has legal authority for the action, there can be no liability for that act. Statute gives two groups such authority.

Police officers

The powers of police officers are found in statute and provided an officer acts within the scope of those powers, there can be no complaint for trespass to the person. If however the action goes beyond what is permitted, a police officer may be liable in the civil courts in the same way as any other person.

CASE EXAMPLE

Collins v Wilcock [1984] 3 All ER 374

A police officer needed to obtain a woman's name and address in order to caution her for soliciting for the purpose of prostitution. The officer detained the woman by holding her by the elbow. The woman scratched the police officer and was charged with assaulting a constable in the execution of her duty. The question was whether the police officer was acting lawfully when she held the woman's elbow to detain her.

JUDGMENT

'The fact is that the [police officer] took hold of the [woman] by the left arm in order to restrain her. In so acting she was not proceeding to arrest the [woman]; and since her action went beyond the generally acceptable conduct of touching a person to engage his or her attention, it must follow . . . that her action constituted a battery on the [woman], and was therefore unlawful.'

Goff LJ

Reasonable force may be used to make an arrest (Criminal Justice Act 1967 s 3). What is reasonable depends on the facts. The general rule is that the force must be proportionate to the crime being prevented. The use of lethal force will seldom be necessary and might be thought to be a breach of Article 2 of the European Convention on Human Rights. In *McCann, Farrell and Savage v UK* (1995) 21 EHRR 97, ECtHR, arising from the deaths of three IRA suspects killed by members of the SAS in Gibraltar, it was accepted that lethal force can be used provided it is reasonably justifiable.

Health professionals treating people with mental illness

The Mental Health Act 1983 permits treatment for mental disorder to be given to patients who have been compulsorily detained using powers granted by the Act. By s 63 treatment may be given without the consent of the patient, the Act including additional safeguards for extreme treatment such as psychosurgery and electro-convulsive therapy. Treatment otherwise than for the mental disorder is governed by the same rules which protect people who do not suffer from mental disorder.

13.4.2 Consent

If the claimant consents to the actions of the defendant, the claimant has no cause of action. Consent may be express or implied. It can be argued that there is implied consent to the jostling which occurs in a packed train during the rush-hour.

Sport

A person who takes part in a contact sport such as soccer, rugby or boxing, consents to the touching which occurs when the sport is played according to the rules.

CASE EXAMPLE

Simms v Leigh Rugby Football Club [1969] 2 All ER 923

A broken leg resulted from a tackle during a rugby game.
By voluntarily taking part in a contact sport, players consent to touching which occurs provided it is within the rules of the game. In this case the tackle had been lawful therefore no battery had occurred.

If the touching is not permitted within the rules of the sport, then it is unlawful. The victim has not consented and the assailant may be liable for trespass to the person.

Medical treatment

For consent to be effective in relieving the defendant of liability, it must be real. The victim must understand what it is they are consenting to and the consent must be freely given.

QUOTATION

'Every human being of adult years and sound mind has a right to determine what shall be done with his own body; and a surgeon who performs an operation without his patient's consent, commits an assault . . .'

J Cardoza Schloendorff v Society of New York Hospital (1914) 211 NY 125 at 126

A person with capacity has an absolute right to give or withhold consent to treatment. In *Re T (Adult: Refusal of Treatment)* [1992] 4 All ER 649 Lord Donaldson MR said

JUDGMENT

'. . . the patient's right of choice exists whether the reasons for making that choice are rational, irrational, unknown or even non-existent. That his choice is contrary to what is to be expected of the vast majority of adults is only relevant if there are other reasons for doubting his capacity to decide.'

This can give rise to some very difficult questions for health professionals as is shown in the case of Ms B.

CASE EXAMPLE

Ms B v An NHS Hospital Trust [2002] EWHC 429 (Fam)

Ms B was completely paralysed, able to move her head very slightly and to speak. She was being kept alive on a ventilator and had no hope of any recovery. She faced the rest of her life like this and informed those caring for her that she wanted the ventilator turned off. She was effectively saying that she withdrew her consent to the treatment. The doctors who had been caring for her for over a year found it impossible to accept her decision and argued that she lacked capacity to make her own decisions. Ms B sued for a declaration that she had the necessary capacity and that her continued treatment was a trespass to her person.

Having heard detailed evidence from the medical point of view and from psychiatrists who had examined Ms B as to her mental capacity, the judge, Dame Elizabeth Butler-Sloss P, said

JUDGMENT

'I am . . . entirely satisfied that Ms B is competent to make all relevant decisions about her medical treatment including the decision whether to seek to withdraw from artificial ventilation. Her mental competence is commensurate with the gravity of the decision she may wish to make.'

The defendants were therefore liable for trespass during the time Ms B had been treated against her will and a small sum by way of damages for battery was awarded. (Ms B was transferred to another hospital where her decision was respected and she died a few weeks later.)

On reading the facts of this case, there must be some sympathy for the doctors who knew that Ms B would die if they respected her refusal of treatment. This is an extreme example of the dilemma which is frequently faced by health professionals. Every case will depend on its own particular facts but some principles to assist in making decisions can be found in case law.

The fact that a person is suffering from mental disorder does not of itself mean that they lack capacity. The Mental Health Act 1983 only permits treatment without consent for the actual mental illness.

CASE EXAMPLE

Re C (Adult: Refusal of Treatment) [1994] 1 WLR 290

Mr C, suffering paranoid schizophrenia, was a patient in Broadmoor and unlikely to be well enough to be released from hospital. He developed gangrene in 1993 and the doctors believed that unless his foot was amputated, he would die. He applied for an injunction to prevent amputation then or at any time in the future.

Mr Justice Thorpe was satisfied that despite his illness, Mr C

JUDGMENT

'sufficiently understands the nature, purpose and effects of the proffered operation'.

The judge approved the test set out by the Law Commission (para 2.20 Law Commission Consultation Paper No 129 Mentally Incapacitated Adults and Decisions Making) namely

- does the patient understand and retain treatment information?
- does the patient believe it?
- can the patient weigh the information in the balance to make a choice?

The injunction was granted. Mr C in fact survived as the gangrene was successfully treated by other means.

Where a person genuinely lacks capacity to make their own decisions treatment will be lawful if it is in that person's best interests.

CASE EXAMPLE

Airedale NHS Trust v Bland [1993] 1 All ER 821

Tony Bland was in a persistent vegetative state and unlikely ever to improve. His brain stem continued to function but he had to be fed by artificial means. His parents and those caring for him wished to discontinue artificial feeding which had the inevitable consequence that he would die.

Goff LJ explained

JUDGMENT

'The question is whether it is in the best interests of the patient that his life should be prolonged by the continuance of this form of medical treatment or care.'

Lord Lowry took the view that

JUDGMENT

'if it is not in the interests of an insentient patient to continue the life supporting care and treatment, the doctor would be acting unlawfully if he continued the care and treatment.'

Lord Browne Wilkinson argued

JUDGMENT

'the initial question is "whether it is in the best interests of Antony Bland to continue the invasive medical care." . . . This is a question for the doctor.'

The unanimous decision of the House of Lords was that the treatment, which was not in the best interests of Tony Bland, could lawfully be withdrawn.

Once capacity is established, then the patient must be given the information need to make the decision, whether it is to have travel immunisation or to undergo major surgery. In the case of *Chatterton v Gerson* [1981] 1 All ER 257, Bristow J said

JUDGMENT

'In my judgment once the patient is informed in broad terms of the nature of the procedure which is intended, and gives her consent, that consent is real.'

It must be remembered that an action will only lie in assault or battery where there has been no consent, whether from the patient, the court or a person authorised by the patient to make decisions on their behalf. Failure to ensure that the patient is given sufficient information does not negate the consent which may have been given but may give rise to an action in negligence.

Consent can only be valid if it results from the exercise of free will. Coercion, whether by a relative or a health professional, will mean that the decision is invalid.

CASE EXAMPLE

Re T (Adult: refusal of medical treatment) [1992] 4 All ER 649

T had been seriously injured and required a Caesarean section. She signed a form refusing a blood transfusion. Her condition deteriorated and a transfusion became necessary.

JUDGMENT

'. . . the patient is . . . entitled to receive and indeed invite advice and assistance from others in reaching a decision . . . It is wholly acceptable that the patient should have been persuaded by others of the merits of such a decision . . . It matters not how strong the persuasion was, so long as it did not overbear the independence of the patient's decision.'

Lord Donaldson MR

On the facts, the court held that T's decision was the result of over-persuasion by her mother. Her refusal of a transfusion was invalid.

13.4.3 Necessity

Trespass to the person may be justified where it is essential to prevent harm to others, for example pulling someone back from the path of a speeding car. It may also be used in medical cases to justify treatment of a person without capacity. A health professional is entitled to do all that is necessary to deal with an emergency if a person is, for example, unconscious and there is nothing to indicate that the proposed treatment would be refused.

It is clear that this defence may overlap with the 'best interests' approach described in section 13.4.2 where the patient permanently lacks capacity.

CASE EXAMPLE

F v West Berkshire Health Authority [1989] 2 All ER 545

F, aged 36, had serious mental disability and the mental capacity of a child of four. She had formed a sexual relationship with another patient. The concern was that pregnancy would be disastrous for her and contraception was out of the question. Her doctors sought a declaration from the court that an operation for her sterilisation would be lawful.

JUDGMENT

'. . . to fall within the principle [of necessity] not only (1) must there be a necessity to act when it is not practicable to communicate with the assisted person, but also (2) the action taken must be such as a reasonable person would in all the circumstances take, acting in the best interests of the assisted person . . . [I]n the case of a mentally disordered person . . . action properly taken . . . may extend to include such humdrum matters as routine medical or dental treatment, even simple care such as dressing and undressing and putting to bed.'

Goff LJ

It was held that it was in F's best interests to be able to maintain the sexual relationship and thus, under the doctrine of necessity, the operation for sterilisation should take place to protect her from a possible pregnancy.

13.4.4 Parental authority

Despite the continuing debate over whether or not corporal punishment ought ever to be inflicted on a child, a parent will not be liable for assault or battery if the force used is by way of reasonable chastisement. The child must understand the purpose of the punishment, which must be proportionate to the wrong committed by the child.

The defence is only available to a parent. In *A v United Kingdom*, *The Times*, 1st October 1998 it was held by the Court of Human Rights that Article 3 of the Convention on Human Rights prohibited caning of a child by a step-parent on the basis that it amounted to 'inhuman and degrading treatment'.

As the debate about corporal punishment continues, it will be interesting to see whether the protection of Article 3 is extended to corporal punishment by parents. The Scottish Parliament has debated a Bill to outlaw smacking of young children by their parents but this foundered in part on the difficulty of defining what amounts to 'smacking' and on difficulties of enforcement.

13.4.5 Self-defence

The use of reasonable force to effect an arrest has been discussed above at section 13.4.1 and the rules are similar. Anyone is entitled to use reasonable force in self-defence or to protect others. The force used must be proportionate to the danger.

CASE EXAMPLE

Cockcroft v Smith (1705) 11 Mod 43

There was a scuffle in court between a lawyer and a clerk. The clerk thrust his fingers towards the lawyer's eyes so the lawyer promptly bit off one of the clerk's fingers. This was held not to be a proportionate response to the threat!

Whether or not the force used is proportionate is a question of fact. A recent criminal case has aroused a lot of discussion after a farmer, Tony Martin, was found guilty of manslaughter when he shot a burglar in the back from the top of the stairs. The jury was satisfied that this was a disproportionate response to the threat. In a similar case, *Revill v Newbery* [1996] 1 All ER 291, an allotment holder, fed up with frequent thefts from his allotment, was found to have used disproportionate force when he shot a thief through a hole which he had drilled in a shed.

The use of force in response to words is unlikely to be reasonable unless the words convey an immediate and real threat of the use of force.

CASE EXAMPLE

Lane v Holloway [1967] 3 All ER 129

A poor relationship existed between neighbours and when one came home drunk and rowdy, the woman next door told him to be quiet. He replied 'Shut up you monkey-faced tart'. This led to an argument between the neighbour and the woman's husband. The neighbour made a friendly and ineffectual shove at the husband who responded by beating him so badly that he needed 18 stitches for facial injuries. The beating was not a proportionate response to the drunken neighbour's gestures.

ACTIVITY

Self-assessment questions

1. Explain the importance of the judgment in *Letang v Cooper*.
2. Give a definition of
   (a) assault
   (b) battery.
3. State precisely what is meant by the requirement of 'intention.'
4. Is hostile intent necessary to establish liability for battery?
5. Explain the criteria by which the courts will decide whether or not a person has capacity to give consent to medical treatment.

13.5 False imprisonment

13.5.1 Definition

False imprisonment occurs when a person is unlawfully restrained (whether by arrest, confinement or otherwise) or prevented from leaving any place.

13.5.2 Ingredients of the tort

Restraint

The restraint must be total. If there is a reasonable means of escape, the restraint cannot amount to false imprisonment.

CASE EXAMPLE

Bird v Jones (1845) 7 QB 742

Part of Hammersmith Bridge was closed off for seating to watch a regatta. Mr Bird insisted on walking on that part of the Bridge and climbed into the enclosure. He was prevented from getting out at the other end. There was nothing to stop him from going back the way he had come and crossing the Bridge on the other side which had not been closed off.

JUDGMENT

'A prison may have its boundary large or narrow, visible and tangible, or, though real, still in the conception only; it may be moveable or fixed: but a boundary it must have; and that boundary the party imprisoned must be prevented from passing . . .'

Coleridge J

The claimant was not imprisoned as he was free to leave by the way he had entered.

It can be seen from this judgment that imprisonment need not be supported by physical barriers. A police officer who unlawfully tells someone that they are under arrest may be liable even if he does not touch the victim. The victim is not expected to risk being arrested should they try to escape. The detention in such circumstances is in 'conception only' but is nonetheless real. In fact a police cordon was held to be false imprisonment in *Austin v Commissioner of Police for the Metropolis* [2005] EWHC 480 (QB) (although in the case it was justified for the protection of others).

Surprisingly, false imprisonment can occur even if the victim is unaware of it at the time.

CASE EXAMPLE

Meering v Grahame-White Aviation Co Ltd (1919) 122 LT 44

The claimant was suspected of stealing paint. He was taken to a waiting room where he was told that he was needed to give evidence. He agreed to stay. Unknown to him, the works police had been told not to let him leave and waited outside the room to prevent him from doing so. The Metropolitan Police arrived and he was arrested. He claimed that he had been falsely imprisoned for the hour he had waited.

JUDGMENT

'. . . it appears to me that a person could be imprisoned without his knowing it. I think a person can be imprisoned while he is asleep, while he is in a state of drunkenness, while he is unconscious, and while he is a lunatic.'

Lord Atkin

The issue of knowledge was also considered in *Murray v Ministry of Defence* [1988] 2 All ER 521.

CASE EXAMPLE

Murray v Ministry of Defence [1988] 2 All ER 521

A woman's home was entered and searched in connection with terrorist matters. She knew the purpose of the visit but was not actually arrested until she left the house 30 minutes later. It was unclear whether or not she was aware that she was being detained throughout the period before the arrest.

Lord Griffiths, while accepting that she was probably aware of her detention, said that it is not

JUDGMENT

'an essential element of the tort of false imprisonment that the victim should be aware of the fact of denial of liberty . . . If a person is unaware that he has been falsely imprisoned and has suffered no harm, he can normally expect to recover no more than nominal damages . . .'

It is clear that the judges place great importance on the protection of the liberty of an individual. *Murray v MOD* was a case concerning terrorism in Northern Ireland. The Northern Irish Court of Appeal had been happy to conclude that there had been no false imprisonment, the House of Lords disagreed.

Intentional act

Until recently there was some doubt as to whether the detention had to be intentional or if negligence would suffice. In *Sayers v Harlow Urban District Council* [1958] 1 WLR 623 a woman who was accidentally locked into a cubicle in a ladies' toilet was held not to have been falsely imprisoned. However this view has changed, the House of Lords holding that false imprisonment is a tort of strict liability, thus intention is immaterial.

R v Governor of Brockhill Prison, ex p Evans (No 2) [2000] 4 All ER 15

Ms Evans was sentenced to two years' imprisonment but had spent time in custody prior to sentence. This time entitled her to a reduction of the actual period spent in prison. Using Home Office guidelines, her release date was calculated as 18th November 1996. Judicial review established that the guidelines were wrong and her release date should have been 17th September 1996. The House of Lords held that she had been falsely imprisoned between those dates as false imprisonment is a tort of strict liability. Its consequences cannot be escaped even when, as in this case, the defendant had acted in line with law accepted as correct at that time.

13.5.3 Defences

Reasonable condition for release

A person is entitled to impose a reasonable condition for the release of the claimant. This may be a question of fact, as in *Robinson v Balmain New Ferry Co Ltd* [1910] AC 295 when the Privy Council held it was reasonable for a charge of 1d to be made when a passenger changed his mind about waiting for a ferry and wanted to leave. He would have had to pay a similar sum had he completed his journey.

The facts of *Robinson v Balmain* are perhaps unlikely to recur with any frequency. A more likely scenario in *Herd v Weardale Steel, Coal and Coke Co Ltd* [1915] AC 67 held that reasonable contractual provision could amount to a defence.

CASE EXAMPLE

Herd v Weardale Steel, Coal and Coke Co Ltd [1915] AC 67

A miner went underground at 9.30 am for a shift ending at 4 pm. After a dispute he demanded to be raised to the surface at about 11 am. He was in fact raised at about 1.30 pm.

The House of Lords held his only right to be raised was at the end of his shift or in emergency. It mattered not that the cage could have been used before then as indeed happened.

JUDGMENT

'There were facilities [to raise him] but they were facilities which, in accordance with the conditions that he had accepted by going down, were not available to him until the end of his shift . . .'

Lawful arrest

A lawful arrest made in accordance with the Police and Criminal Evidence Act 1984 s 24(4), as amended by the Serious Organised Crime and Police Act 2005 s 110, cannot amount to false imprisonment. A police officer or private citizen who acts within the provisions will not be liable. A private citizen making a citizen's arrest should be wary as a private citizen only has protection if an arrestable offence has actually been or is being committed by the person arrested and the police have been speedily involved. Store detectives are particularly vulnerable.

CASE EXAMPLE

White v W P Brown [1983] CLY 972

A woman was locked up for 15 minutes by a store detective. This amounted to false imprisonment.

A police officer does not lose the protection if the arrest is mistaken, provided the arrest was reasonable in all the circumstances.

Detention for medical purposes

The Mental Health Act 1983 provides for the lawful detention of persons suffering from mental disorder. The provisions of the Act must be scrupulously followed as breach can mean that false imprisonment has occurred. This has caused difficulties where a person has been clearly ill and in need of treatment which can only be provided in hospital but whose illness does not meet the necessary criteria for compulsory detention. In *R v Bournewood Community and Mental Health NHS Trust, ex p L* [1999] AC 458 the House of Lords held that in such a case, the common law doctrine of necessity would apply to render the detention lawful. The case was then taken to the European Court of Human Rights as *HL v United Kingdom* (Application no 45508/99) [2004]. The court found that the reasoning of the House of Lords could not stand and this provision of the Mental Health Act 1983 breached the applicant's rights under Article 5(1) of the European Convention on Human Rights.

The Mental Incapacity Act 2005 contains a provision that will ensure that all patients detained in a psychiatric hospital will have the right to challenge the legality of their detention by application to a Mental Health Review Tribunal.

Powers to detain persons suffering from physical disease also exist. The Public Health (Control of Disease) Act 1984, subject to strict safeguards, permits the removal to and detention in hospital of a person suffering from a notifiable disease.

Montgomery refers to a case where a person suffering from AIDS and 'bleeding copiously' was prevented, by court order under powers in the 1984 Act, from discharging himself from hospital. By the time the appeal was heard, the danger was past and the order was no longer needed, but the initial order was not criticised by the appeal court (J Montgomery, *Healthcare Law* (2nd edn, OUP, 2003), p 35).

ACTIVITY

Self-assessment questions

1. Give a definition of 'false imprisonment'.
2. Consider whether the judgment in *R v Governor of Brockhill Prison, ex p Evans* means that false imprisonment should be regarded as a tort of strict liability.

13.6 Intentional indirect harm and protection from harassment

Trespass to the person deals with direct harm which is intentionally caused while negligence deals with direct harm which is caused unintentionally. This leaves a gap. What about the situation where harm is caused intentionally but indirectly? Nothing discussed so far in this chapter covers this situation. It would be wrong if a person were able to escape liability for harm which is caused intentionally but indirectly. The gap is partly filled by old law relating to wrongful interference and by the modern statute, the Protection from Harassment Act 1997.

13.6.1 Acts intended to cause harm

The law in this area is not very clear but it seems that a person who acts intentionally with the result that injury is indirectly caused, whether or not the injury is intentional, may be liable.

CASE EXAMPLE

Wilkinson v Downton [1897] 2 QB 57

The defendant, as a practical joke, told the claimant that he had been sent to tell her that her husband had been involved in an accident. Her husband as a result was lying in a public house with two broken legs. She was told that she was to take a cab to bring him home. As a result of this 'prank' the claimant suffered a violent shock causing serious physical consequences which threatened her reason. Her illness involved her husband, who was in reality at all times in the best of health, in substantial expense.

JUDGMENT

A person who 'wilfully [does] an act calculated to cause physical harm to the [claimant] ie to infringe her right to personal safety and has thereby in fact caused physical harm' is liable if there is no justification for the act. 'This wilful injury is in law malicious, although no malicious purpose to cause the harm which was caused, nor any motive of spite, is imputed to the defendant'.

Wright J

It must be noted that there was an acceptance by the judges that the defendant very probably had no intention of causing anything other than a laugh by his actions. The consequences were not intended by him nor could there be any liability for negligence. Despite its lack of clarity, the judgment was approved in the later case of *Janvier v Sweeney* [1919] 2 KB 316.

CASE EXAMPLE

Janvier v Sweeney [1919] 2 KB 316

During the First World War, a woman was told by a caller that he was a detective representing the military authorities and that she was the woman they wanted as she was suspected of corresponding with a German spy. She was extremely frightened and as a result suffered nervous shock, being ill for a prolonged period of time.

JUDGMENT

In the Court of Appeal it was held that the defendant was liable. Stating that this was a much stronger case than *Wilkinson v Downton*, Duke LJ acknowledged that in this case the defendant's intention was to terrify the victim for the purpose of obtaining an unlawful object.

The law was nonetheless left in a state of some confusion. Does the defendant's act have to be calculated to cause harm? Does actual physical or psychiatric harm need to result from the act? The issue has been further considered by the Court of Appeal in *Wong v Parkside Health NHS Trust and another* [2001] EWCA Civ 1721.

CASE EXAMPLE

Wong v Parkside Health NHS Trust and another [2001] EWCA Civ 1721

The claimant alleged harassment against her by three fellow employees and an inadequate response by the employer. One of the issues considered was the precise scope of the tort of intentionally causing harm.

Reviewing the authorities Lady Justice Hale considered whether actual injury needed to be established and whether there needed to be intention to cause injury. She stated

JUDGMENT

'for the tort to be committed . . . there has to be actual damage. The damage is physical harm or recognised psychiatric illness. The defendant must have intended to violate the claimant's interest in his freedom from harm. The conduct complained of has to be such that that degree of harm is sufficiently likely to result so that the defendant cannot be heard to say that he did not 'mean' it to do so. He is taken to have meant it to do so by the combination of the likelihood of such harm being suffered as a result of his behaviour and his deliberately engaging in that behaviour.'

It seems therefore that for the tort to be established it must be proved

1. that the defendant intended to infringe the claimant's 'right to personal safety' (*Wilkinson v Downton*) or 'interest in his freedom from harm' (*Wong v Parkside Health NHS Trust*), and

2. that actual injury, physical or psychiatric, occurred as a result.

This has subsequently been confirmed by the House of Lords.

CASE EXAMPLE

Wainright v Home Office [2004] AC 406; [2003] UKHL 53

The claimants, a mother and her son (who suffered from cerebral palsy and arrested development), went to prison to visit her other son who was on remand. The prison had a drug problem and the son on remand was suspected of supplying drugs so the governor had instructed that his visitors should be strip searched and denied their visiting rights if they refused, though the claimants were unaware of this order in advance of the visit. They were taken to separate rooms. The mother's naked upper body was first examined and then her sexual organs and anus were visually examined, causing her great and visible distress. The son was at first reluctant to take off his underwear, suffered fits of sobbing and shaking, and when the officer examined his naked body that officer also lifted up his penis and pulled back his foreskin. The trial judge held that there was liability in battery and that the strip search was a course of action intended to cause physical or psychiatric harm for which the defendant was also liable. The Court of Appeal disagreed with this latter point, doubted the existence of the tort of *Wilkinson v Downton* in the modern context, and upheld the defendant's appeal. The claimants appealed to the House of Lords on the basis that, firstly there was a tort of invasion of privacy (this was rejected by the House of Lords – see 14.6.2.) and alternatively that damages could be awarded for emotional distress falling short of psychiatric harm where it was intentionally inflicted. The House of Lords accepted the continued existence of the tort in *Wilkinson v Downton* but held that there could be no liability for distress falling short of a recognised psychiatric injury and that, on the facts of the case, the intention essential for proving the tort could not be proved. The appeal was dismissed.

On the requirements for an action in *Wilkinson v Downton* Lord Hoffman stated

JUDGMENT

'Commentators and counsel have been … unwilling to allow *Wilkinson v Downton* to disappear beneath the surface of the law of negligence … I do not resile from the proposition that the policy considerations which limit the heads of recoverable damage in negligence do not apply equally to torts of intention. If someone actually intends to cause harm by a wrongful act and does so, there is ordinarily no reason why he should not have to pay compensation. But I think that … you have to be very careful about what you mean by intend … imputed intention will not do. The defendant must actually have acted in a way which he knew to be unjustifiable and intended to cause harm or at least acted without caring whether he caused harm or not.'

Despite the attempts of the Court of Appeal in Wainright to abolish the tort, *Wilkinson v Downton* has been used even more recently as the sole basis of a successful claim.

CASE EXAMPLE

C v D [2006] EWHC 166 (QB); [2006] All ER (D) 329 (Feb)

A school headmaster was alleged to have sexually abused a pupil. The abuse took various forms, two of which could not be brought under trespass to the person. One was a video made by the defendant of the claimant in the school showers, the second involved the defendant pulling down the claimant's trousers and underwear in the school infirmary and staring at the claimant's genitals. While the trial judge did not feel that psychiatric injury was foreseeable as a likely consequence, he nevertheless did feel that the defendant was reckless as to whether he caused psychiatric harm to the claimant, conforming to the House of Lords in Wainright, and on this basis he held the defendant liable.

13.6.2 Protection from Harassment Act 1997

The problem faced by those who suffer harassment where there is no resulting injury is now dealt with by statute.

The Act provides that a person who pursues a course of conduct which he knows or ought to know amounts to harassment of another person may be guilty of the criminal offence of harassment. By s 3 the Act gives the victim a remedy in civil law.

Conduct will amount to harassment if the course of conduct is such that 'a reasonable person in possession of the same information [as the defendant] would think the course of conduct would amount to harassment of the other' (s 1(2)). The conduct can include causing the claimant to fear violence (s 4(1)) or to cause the claimant alarm or distress (s 7(2)). A 'course of conduct' means that the behaviour must occur more than once but it is clear that the defendant's intention is irrelevant as the judgment is that of the 'reasonable person'.

No actual physical or psychiatric harm need result from the harassment. Alarm or distress will suffice.

There is no remedy under the Act for a 'one off' incident thus the defendant in *Wilkinson v Downton* would not be liable under the Act. The Act does however 'fill a gap' by providing a remedy for many situations where distress is caused, for example by means of 'stalking', telephone calls, e-mails or text messages.

13.6.3 A developing tort of harassment?

As the concept of harassment is gradually more closely defined, remedies are becoming available where the claimant has been subjected to conduct which does not amount to a threat but which nonetheless causes the claimant real harm. It may be that the Act will be enough to fill the gap but it is not yet clear that this will prove to be the case.

There has been much recent case law with quite different results. The best publicised of these cases is *Green*.

CASE EXAMPLE

Green v DB Group Services (UK) Ltd [2006] EWHC 1898

The claimant worked as an assistant company secretary for Deutsche Bank. She was subjected to constant abuse by a group of female staff, was constantly undermined by a male colleague and despite reporting this to her manager and seeking help the company did nothing to support or help her. She suffered a period of sickness with depression as a result and on returning to work suffered a relapse and was unable to return to work. The judge awarded her £800,000 for personal injury and loss of future earnings for the mental illness resulting from the bullying. The award was based on both negligence and breach of the 1997 Act.

In *Howlett v Holding* [2006] EWHC 41 (QB) the Act was used to grant an injunction to put a stop to a campaign of victimisation waged against a former mayor by a disgruntled constituent. However, in *Merilie v Newcastle PCT* [2006] EWHC 1433 (QB) a dentist failed in a claim for harassment against her former employers because she suffered a lifelong personality disorder making her evidence unreliable since it was based only on her own perceptions.

Tort	Required state of mind	Whether direct or indirect	Whether contact required	Frequency	Whether damage needed
Assault	Intention	Must be direct	No contact	Can be a single threat	No – only apprehension
Battery	Intention	Must be direct	Must have contact	Can be a single unlawful contact	No – can be harmless contact
False imprisonment	Question whether it always has to be intentional	Must be direct	Contact not necessary	Can be a single total restraint	No – need not even be aware
Wilkinson v Downton	Intention	Must be indirect	No contact	Can be a single infliction	Yes must suffer from physical or psychiatric harm
Harassment under the Protection from Harassment Act 1997	Intention	Can be either	Can be either	Must be more than one act of harassment (a course of conduct)	Only needs fear, alarm or distress – but could include psychiatric harm

Figure 13.3 Chart identifying the differences between the different torts making up trespass to the person

Courts have accepted that the course of conduct must be sufficiently serious for a claim of harassment to succeed.

CASE EXAMPLE

Ferguson v British Gas Trading Ltd [2009] EWCA Civ 46

The claimant had been a customer of the defendant. After she changed to a different supplier British Gas continued to send her bills for gas that they had not supplied her with and later sent her several letters threatening to cut off her gas supply, to start legal proceedings against her and to inform a credit rating agency. Despite the claimant contacting the company several times, the sending of the bills and threatening letters continued. They were in fact generated by a computer rather than by an individual. The claimant alleged harassment by the company. It argued that, since the claimant knew that the correspondence was unjustified and that it was generated by a computer she should not have taken it as seriously as if it came from an individual employee. The Court of Appeal held that, while the course of conduct must be serious for a claim under s 3 of the Protection from Harassment Act, the fact of there being parallel criminal and civil liability was not generally significant in determining civil liability. The court considered that the conduct of the company was sufficiently serious to amount to harassment, and that there was no apparent policy reason why a corporation should be treated differently to an individual.

ACTIVITY

Self-assessment questions

1. Explain how the principle of *Wilkinson v Downton* differs from trespass to the person.
2. Consider how the principle of *Wilkinson v Downton* has been developed in later cases.
3. What are the basic requirements of the statutory tort created by s 3 Protection from Harassment Act 1997?
4. Explain whether or not the principle of *Wilkinson v Downton* still has a role in protecting an individual from harm.

CHAPTER 13 TRESPASS TO THE PERSON

SAMPLE ESSAY QUESTION

Discuss the effectiveness of the tort of trespass to the person in protecting people's bodily integrity.

Outline the basis of an action in trespass to the person

- Three types – assault, battery and false imprisonment
- All are actionable *per se* so a remedy is available without proof of damage
- *Wilkinson v Downton* covers intentional indirect harm
- And also an action for harassment under the Protection from Harassment Act 1997

Explain the essential elements for assault

- Directly and intentionally causing the claimant to apprehend an imminent battery
- Involve threatening behaviour and the threat must be real and imminent
- And create a feeling of being threatened in the claimant
- Words can negate the fear of assault
- But words alone were traditionally insufficient
- Silent telephone calls have been accepted in criminal law

Explain the essential elements for battery

- Directly and intentionally applying unlawful force
- Judges have given direct a broad interpretation
- Hostility was identified as a requirement and has been said 'the least touching of another in anger is battery'
- But this could not apply in medical battery

Explain the essential elements of false imprisonment

- A total bodily restraint without safe means of escape
- But need not be physical
- And the claimant need not be aware of the restraint
- And the restraint may be justified by a contractual relationship or legitimate expectation

Discuss the range of available defences

- Defences to assault and battery include statutory authority, lawful arrest, Mental Health Act, consent, necessity parental authority, self-defence using reasonable force
- Defences include lawful arrest and detention under PACEA (as amended) (but note different rules for citizen's arrest), Mental Health Act, and consent

Discuss the effectiveness of the tort

- Fact that the tort is actionable per se
- In assault damages are difficult to assess
- Difficulties associated with use of words
- Assault may be ineffective for threats of future harm
- In battery no need for actual harm to be proved
- And a broad view is applied to 'direct'
- Requirement of hostility is problematic
- Consent in sporting context and medical context
- Discuss how the defences may limit the effectiveness, particularly in relation to complaints about the police

KEY FACTS

Key facts on trespass to the person

Assault	Case/statute
Threat to use force against person of someone else.	
Actual harm need not be intended – intention to touch will suffice.	
Words alone traditionally not an assault	*R v Meade and Belt* (1823)
but following verbal threat will suffice for criminal assault. Will this suffice for the tort?	*R v Ireland* (1997)
Words can negate threat.	*Turberville v Savage* (1669)
Victim must believe threat	*R v St George* (1840)
It must be possible to carry out the threat –	*Stephens v Myers* (1830)
contrast with	*Thomas v NUM* (1985)

Battery	Case/statute
Use of force against another person.	
Actual harm need not be caused –	*R v Chief Constable of Devon & Cornwall* (1981)
an unwanted kiss will suffice.	
Use of force must be direct but this is widely	*Scott v Shepherd* (1773);
interpreted.	*Pursell v Horn* (1838);
There must be a touching – is hostility required?	*Nash v Sheen* (1955)
– no in	*Collins v Wilcock* (1984)
but yes in	*Cole v Turner* (1704)
and	*Wilson v Pringle* (1986)
(Note when HL held that if action is unlawful it is also hostile.)	*R v Brown* (1994)
Problem of medical cases – no hostile intent – does this case help?	*R v Brown* (1994)

Defences to assault and battery	Case/statute
Lawful authority – statutory powers given to police officers but any force used must be proportionate.	Police and Criminal Evidence Act 1984
	Collins v Wilcock (1984); *McCann, Farrell and Savage v UK* (1995)
Statutory powers given to those treating people with mental illness.	*Mental Health Act 1983*
Consent: sport – consent extends only to play within the rules of the game.	*Simms v Leigh RFC* (1969)
Medical treatment – every adult with capacity has right to consent to or refuse treatment.	*Re T (Adult: Refusal of Treatment)* (1992); *Ms B v An NHS Hospital Trust* (2002)
Where person lacks capacity, treatment lawful if in the person's best interests.	*Airedale NHS Trust v Bland* (1993)
Necessity – act must be essential to prevent harm.	*F v West Berks HA* (1989)
Parental authority provided child understands why it is being punished and the punishment is proportionate; applies only to a parent.	*A v UK* (1998)
Self-defence – reasonable force proportionate to the threat may be used.	*Cockcroft v Smith* (1705); *Revill v Newbery* (1996); *Lane v Holloway* (1967)

False imprisonment	Case/statute
Total restraint preventing a person from leaving any place; not total if safe means of escape.	*Bird v Jones* (1845)
Restraint need not be physical; can occur even if claimant unaware.	*Meering v Grahame-White Aviation Co Ltd* (1919); *Murray v Ministry of Defence* (1988)
Tort of strict liability.	*R v Governor of Brockhill Prison, ex p Evans (No 2)* (2000)

Defences to false imprisonment	Case/statute
Reasonable condition for release.	*Robinson v Balmain New Ferry* (1910); *Herd v Weardale Steel* (1915)
Lawful arrest in accordance with Police and Criminal Evidence Act 1984 but note risk for private citizen if no crime actually committed by the arrested person.	*White v W P Brown* (1983)
Detention of people with mental illness under Mental Health Act 1983 or under common law doctrine of necessity.	*R v Bournewood Community and Mental Health Trust, ex p L* (1999)

Intentional harm	Case/statute
Provided act intended to cause harm, there can be liability even when elements of trespass to the person cannot be proved.	*Wilkinson v Downton* (1897); *Janvier v Sweeney* (1919)
Actual injury, physical or psychiatric must occur.	*Wong v Parkside Health NHS Trust* (2001)
No liability for distress falling short of a recognised psychiatric injury.	*Wainright v Home Office* (2004)

Protection from Harassment Act 1997	Case/statute
Criminal offence to pursue a course of conduct which perpetrator knows or ought to know amounts to harassment of another.	s 1
Statutory tort entitling victim to damages.	s 3
Conduct can be anything which a reasonable person in the circumstances would think amounts to harassment.	s 1(2)
Course of conduct means it happens more than once.	*Green v DB Group Services (UK) Ltd* (2006)
Defendant's intention is irrelevant.	
No actual harm need be caused.	

Conclusion

Trespass is an old tort which has to some extent been developed to deal with modern life. The gaps are partly filled by liability for intentional harm and by statute. It is likely that further developments will occur, partly resulting from the wide-spread use of information technology.

SUMMARY

- Trespass involves a direct interference with the claimant's person
- It is actionable *per se* so there is no requirement to show that damage occurred
- There are three types: assault, battery, and false imprisonment

Assault
- Intentionally and directly causing another to fear imminent unlawful contact
- No contact is required but there must be threatening actions
- Words alone are insufficient but can be a criminal assault – although words can negate an assault
- The victim must believe the threat and it must be possible to carry it out
- Consent, self-defence and necessity are all possible defences

Battery
- Intentionally and directly applying unlawful force to a person
- Courts have taken a broad view of what is direct
- There is dispute over whether hostility is also a requirement

■ Battery is important in medical treatment – medical treatment in the absence of consent is generally a battery except where there is some justification for not obtaining consent – and it also has a context in sport where players act outside of the rules

■ Consent, necessity and self-defence are all possible defences

False imprisonment

■ Involves total bodily restraint – with no safe means of escape

■ Can occur even where the claimant is unaware of the restraint

■ But it is not possible when the defendant has legitimate expectations that the claimant will remain for a set period of time

■ Consent; mistaken arrest (in the case of police officers); and lawful arrest are all possible defences

Intentional indirect harm

■ Possible where an action in trespass is impossible – but there must be personal injury whether physical or psychiatric

Harassment

■ Under the Protection from Harassment Act 1997 – but there must be a 'course of conduct' – so at least two events

14

Defamation

AIMS AND OBJECTIVES

After reading this chapter you should be able to:

- Understand the essential elements required in proving a claim in defamation
- Understand the available defences
- Understand the reasons for denying a general law of privacy
- Understand the basis of a claim for breach of confidentiality
- Be able to critically analyse each tort
- Be able to apply the law to factual situations and reach conclusions as to liability

14.1 Introduction

Defamation is one of the most technical of torts. The question of whether defamation has occurred is decided by

(i) the judge who decides whether or not the words complained of are capable of being defamatory and

(ii) the jury which, in many cases, decides whether or not the words are actually defamatory.

As will be seen, the question of what can amount to defamatory words is complex. Once this has been decided and it has then been decided that in the particular case the words of the claimant are defamatory, further complications arise from the application of Article 10 European Convention on Human Rights which protects the right to freedom of expression. In *Steel and Morris v UK* [2005] (Application no 68416/01) ECHR two environmental campaigners who had lost a defamation action made against them by McDonalds and were ordered to pay extensive damages successfully proved that the trial had infringed their human rights under Articles 6 and 10 of the Convention. This was because the nature of English defamation law and the absence of any form of legal aid meant that the campaigners had to run their own defence against a large corporate body.

The balance between an individual's right to protect their reputation and the right to freedom of expression is a delicate one, involving the rights of individuals and the right of freedom of the press and other media to report on and draw attention to matters of public interest. This in turn involves consideration of what should constitute a matter of public interest in the sense of matters which are of public concern and in the sense of matters in which the public is interested. The latter may be simply because of the involvement of public figures in some type of allegedly scandalous situation. As a result of this conflict, the tort is one of those evolving most rapidly in present times. A particular focus of attention is the ability or otherwise of the tort to protect privacy. This chapter will first consider the technical aspects of the tort, returning to the discussion of the right to freedom of opinion and the issue of privacy by way of a conclusion.

14.2 The distinction between libel and slander

Defamation can take two forms

(i) libel
(ii) slander.

Libel is usually written or takes some other permanent form. In *Monson v Tussauds Ltd* [1894] 1 QB 671 the 'statement' consisted of a waxwork of the claimant. He had been charged with murder in Scotland and the verdict of 'not proven' had been given. Nonetheless the waxwork was placed near the entrance to the Chamber of Horrors. It was held that this amounted to a libel.

While libel is usually written, statute creates certain other forms. By the Defamation Act 1952, s 1 broadcasts and television performances are to be treated as libel. Cable programmes are to be treated similarly (Cable and Broadcasting Act 1984) as are performances of a play (Theatres Act 1968). The issue of material in a film soundtrack was decided in *Youssoupoff v Metro-Goldwyn-Mayer Pictures Ltd* (1934) 50 TLR 581 when it was held that this could amount to libel.

Slander is a statement in some non-permanent form, usually in the form of words although a gesture may suffice.

Other differences between libel and slander reflect the view that defamation in a permanent form is potentially more serious. Libel is actionable *per se* and general damages can be recovered without evidence that any actual loss has occurred. It can also amount to a crime, although criminal prosecution is very rare.

By contrast, in the case of slander 'special damage' must be shown. A claimant who seeks a remedy for slander must show that some disadvantage or loss which is capable of being measured in money has resulted. This is not always easy to establish. In *Allsop v Allsop* (1865) 5 H&N 534 illness caused by the worry resulting from a slander was held to be too remote. Similarly in *Lynch v Knight* (1861) 9 HLC 597 the fact that a husband turned his wife out after hearing about a pre-marital relationship was also held to be too remote.

Slander is actionable *per se* in very specific circumstances:

(i) where the imputation is that the claimant has committed a criminal offence punishable with imprisonment on the first conviction
(ii) where the imputation is of un-chastity or adultery on the part of a woman or girl (Slander of Women Act 1891)
(iii) where it is imputed that the claimant is infected with a contagious or infectious disease likely to prevent others associating with the claimant
(iv) where the words impute unfitness, dishonesty or incompetence on the part of the claimant in relation to any office, profession, calling, trade or business.

Of these exceptions, it is unclear how the second would be applied in the twenty-first century bearing in mind that men and women are today treated as equals. Unlike her Victorian sister, a modern woman (at least in theory) suffers no worse consequences from un-chastity or adultery than a man. The third exception is also problematic. Venereal disease, plague and leprosy are included as 'contagious or infectious disease' but it is not clear whether or not an imputation of AIDS/HIV would be included. Victims of this disease may become outcasts in certain parts of society as did those suffering venereal disease in the past, but whether they would have any remedy for defamation for a false allegation is uncertain.

It is difficult to understand why the distinction between libel and slander remains even after reforms of the law by the Defamation Acts 1952 and 1996. The position is further complicated by the Human Rights Act 1998 making Article 10, guaranteeing the right to freedom of expression, part of English law. As will be seen, the balance between the tort, whichever form it takes, and Article 10 is difficult to draw.

	Libel	Slander
How made	In permanent form	In transient or temporary form
Examples	• A written statement • Film • Statements broadcast on radio or television	• A spoken statement • Gestures • Tape recordings of live performances
Classification of law	• Tort • Crime (in certain cases)	• Tort only
When actionable	• Is actionable *per se* (without need to prove damage)	Is not actionable *per se* Damage must be proved except false allegations of: • a criminal offence involving imprisonment • a contagious or socially undesirable disease • unchastity of women • unfitness for any trade, profession or employment

Figure 14.1 Chart illustrating the differences between libel and slander

14.3 The elements of defamation

In all cases, the claimant must prove:

(a) that the statement is defamatory
(b) that the statement refers to the claimant and
(c) that it has been published.

Most allegations of slander will also require the claimant to prove damage.

14.3.1 The statement must be defamatory

Generally

It is difficult to reach a simple definition as the case law is less than helpful. In *Cassell & Co Ltd v Broome* [1972] AC 1027 Lord Reid said that it was not for the judges to

JUDGMENT

'frame definitions or to lay down hard and fast rules. It is their function to enunciate principles and much that they say is intended to be illustrative or explanatory and not to be definitive.'

Despite Lord Reid's view, a commonly accepted definition is that given by *Winfield and Jolowicz*:

QUOTATION

'Defamation is the publication of a statement which reflects on a person's reputation and tends to lower him in the estimation of right-thinking members of society generally or tends to make them shun or avoid him.'

Winfield and Jolowicz, p 405

What the definition does not make clear is that the statement must be untrue. Truth is generally a defence to any action for defamation.

The essence of the tort is that a person's reputation is damaged by the statement. The difficulty is how this is to be decided. In *Parmiter v Coupland* (1840) 6 M&W 105 it was stated that the publication needed to

QUOTATION

'be calculated to injure the reputation of another, by exposing them to hatred, contempt or ridicule.'

This narrow definition clearly does not cover all situations. The owner of a business can suffer loss if he is described as dishonest or unreliable. It is unlikely that such allegations would excite 'hatred, contempt or ridicule'.

In *Sim v Stretch* (1936) 52 TLR 669 Lord Atkin suggested that the test should be

QUOTATION

'. . . would the words tend to lower the [claimant] in the estimation of right-thinking members of society generally?'

This in turn raises the question of who are 'right-thinking members of society?' In some circles of society behaviour is admired which in other circles would be condemned.

CASE EXAMPLE

Byrne v Deane [1937] 2 All ER 204

A golf club kept illegal gambling machines, known as 'diddlers', in the club house. The police were told by someone that the machines were there and the club was ordered to remove them. The next day the following piece of doggerel was found on the wall

'For many years upon this spot
You heard the sound of a merry bell
Those who were rash and those who were not
Lost and made a spot of cash
But he who gave the game away
May he byrnne in hell and rue the day.'

Diddleramus

The claimant alleged that the defendants meant and were understood by others to mean that he had 'grassed' to the police and was consequently unfit to remain a member of the golf club.

Holding that it could not be defamatory to say that a person had reported a crime to the police Lord Justice Slesser said

JUDGMENT

'We have to consider . . . the view which would be taken by the ordinary good and worthy subject of the King . . . [who] would not consider such an allegation in itself to be defamatory.'

It seems that the decision will reflect what the judges believe that an ordinary person would understand by the words used.

CASE EXAMPLE

Lewis v Daily Telegraph Ltd [1964] AC 234

The published statement said that the claimant's company was being investigated by the Fraud Squad. The claimant alleged that this would mean, to the ordinary reader, that the business was being carried on fraudulently. It was held that a reasonable person would not believe the business to be guilty merely on the basis of a police inquiry.

In the later case of *Hartt v Newspaper Publishing plc, The Independent,* 27th October, 1989 the ordinary reader was described as being one

QUOTATION

'who is not unduly suspicious, but who can read between the lines. He might think loosely, but is not avid for scandal, and will not select one bad meaning where other non-defamatory meanings are available.'

Add humorous intent to the situation and it is difficult to know where to draw the line. Where the imputation is that the claimant has done something unlawful, the judgment of the ordinary citizen will probably be sufficient. *Byrne v Deane* [1937] 2 All ER 204 provides an example of this. In other cases the position may not be so clear.

CASE EXAMPLE

Berkoff v Burchill [1996] 4 All ER 1008

The claimant, an actor, was described by the defendant as 'hideously ugly'. He alleged that this comment held him up to ridicule or meant that other people would shun or avoid him.

The majority in the Court of Appeal held that the words were capable of being defamatory, Lord Justice Neill saying

JUDGMENT

'. . . it would . . . be open to a jury to conclude that in the context the remarks about Mr Berkoff gave the impression that he was not merely physically unattractive in appearance but actually repulsive . . . to say this of someone in the public eye who makes his living . . . as an actor, is capable of lowering his standing in the estimation of the public and of making him the object of ridicule.'

Lord Justice Millett in his dissenting judgment said

JUDGMENT

'. . . mere chaff and banter are not defamatory, and even serious imputations are not actionable if no one would take them to be meant seriously . . . People must be allowed to poke fun at one another without fear of litigation.'

Lord Millett found that the words complained of were only a cheap joke at the claimant's expense.

The differing views of the judges in *Berkoff v Burchill* only serve to emphasise how difficult it is to decide how words may be seen by ordinary people.

The position is further complicated by the alternative basis of the tort – that the statement makes society 'shun or avoid' the victim.

CASE EXAMPLE

Youssoupoff v Metro-Goldwyn-Mayer Pictures Ltd [1934] 50 TLR 581

A film imputed that the claimant, a Russian princess, had been raped by Rasputin, the so-called 'mad monk' who was a figure of great and allegedly evil influence in pre-revolutionary Russia.

While the claimant was probably pitied, and certainly there was no suggestion that she was in any way to blame for the incident, the court held that the statement could tend to make people 'shun and avoid' her.

At the end of the day, the only certainty appears to be that the decision as to whether or not words are capable of being defamatory depends on what the judges in the particular case believe would be the reaction of those they believe to be ordinary citizens. A complicated sentence but one which reflects the complexity of the problem!

14.3.2 Innuendo

In many cases, the words used are clear and will be defamatory unless true, for example calling someone a thief. It is however possible for words to be inoffensive on the face of it and it is only with particular knowledge of other facts that the reader may reach a conclusion that is defamatory of the claimant. One example of this has already been given in *Byrne v Deane*. The following cases illustrate different outcomes which reflect, in the first case, individual knowledge of the claimant and, in the second, general knowledge available to all.

CASE EXAMPLE

Cassidy v Daily Mirror Group Newspapers Ltd [1929] 2 KB 331

A picture was published which showed Mr Cassidy with a young lady under a heading which stated that she and Mr Cassidy had just announced their engagement to be married. The claimant was Mr Cassidy's wife and this was generally known to be the case even though they led separate lives. She was able to prove that several people believed, as a result of the publication, that she was 'living in sin' with Mr Cassidy, a serious social problem for her in the 1920s. It was held that the words were capable of being defamatory and, once a jury considered the issue, it was decided that the defendant was liable.

CASE EXAMPLE

Tolley v Fry & Sons Ltd [1931] All ER Rep 131

The claimant was a well-known amateur golfer in the days when amateur status was regarded as very important. The defendant had published an advertisement for 'Fry's Chocolate Cream' which showed a sketch of the claimant in golfing gear with a packet of chocolate cream protruding from a pocket. The advertisement included a piece of verse:

'The caddie to Tolley said; 'Oh, Sir!
Good shot, Sir! That ball, see it go, Sir.
My word, how it flies,
Like a Cartet of Fry's.
They're handy, they're good, and priced low, Sir.'

The words were not defamatory in themselves but implied that the claimant had been paid for letting his name be used in the advertisement. This was a serious matter which would have prevented him from taking part in golf competitions as an amateur. It was held that the meaning of the sketch and words combined was capable of being defamatory and indeed a jury found that he had been defamed.

Tolley indicates that in some cases, it is the perception of the ordinary reader, or the right-thinking member of society, which is important. This is illustrated by a modern case:

CASE EXAMPLE

Norman v Future Publishing [1999] EMLR 325

The claimant, a famous opera singer, complained that a passage in an article which said that she had told a joke using an Afro-American dialect, was defamatory because it appeared to show that she had used a derogatory stereotype or that she had mocked people of Afro-American heritage. Taking the comments in the context of the article as a whole, which appeared in a classical music magazine and which was generally complimentary to her talent, the court held that a reasonable reader could not have understood the words in the way alleged. The fact that the claimant denied ever using the words attributed to her was irrelevant, the relevant issue being whether or not the words used in the article were defamatory.

Norman also reiterates the point that an article must be read as a whole.

14.3.3 The statement must refer to the claimant

Claimants must prove that the words referred to them. The most straight-forward way is obviously to show that they are named and sufficient other information is included so that the identity of the person referred to is clear. However, it is not always so straightforward. We have already seen, in *Cassidy v Daily Mirror Newspapers Ltd* that it will suffice that those who know the claimant believe that the claimant is the person referred to. Problems arise where the defendant either did not know of the claimant's existence or intended to refer to someone else. A person can be defamed 'by accident' if they happen to have the same or a similar name to a person referred to in the statement.

CASE EXAMPLE

E Hulton & Co v Jones [1910] AC 20

A Sunday newspaper published a fictitious article about 'Artemus Jones, a churchwarden from Peckham' who had spent a weekend in Dieppe with a lady who was not his wife. The real Artemus Jones was a barrister, unmarried and did not live in Peckham but he was able to bring witnesses who said that on reading the article they had believed it referred to him.

Giving judgment in the House of Lords, Lord Shaw quoted a passage from *Bourke v Warren* (1826) 2 C&P 307 with approval

JUDGMENT

'It is not necessary that all the world should understand the libel; it is sufficient if those who knew the [claimant] can make out that he is the person meant.'

On this basis the claimant received damages of £1,750.

Newspapers and other parts of the media face particular risks. A news report may indeed be true of the person named. What about other people with the same name whose friends and associates believe that the report refers to them?

CASE EXAMPLE

Newstead v London Express Newspaper Ltd [1940] 1 KB 377

The newspaper carried a report of a case before the local court in which it stated that 'Harold Newstead, thirty-year old Camberwell man' had been convicted of bigamy. This was true but there was another Harold Newstead of about the same age who also came from Camberwell of whom it was not true.

The issue was whether or not the words were defamatory of the innocent man. The jury were asked

QUOTATION

'Would reasonable persons understand the words complained of to refer to the [claimant]?'

The jury having decided that the answer to the question was 'Yes' and that the claimant had been defamed, the matter went to the Court of Appeal. Dismissing the appeal, Sir Wilfred Greene MR said

JUDGMENT

'If there is a risk of coincidence, it ought I think, in reason to be borne, not by the innocent party to whom the words are held to refer, but by the party who puts them into circulation.'

The claimant can simply rely on the fact that others, reading an article in which the claimant is not named, may come across some fact or phrase which they connect to the claimant making it clear in their minds that the allegation is about that person.

CASE EXAMPLE

Morgan v Odhams Press Ltd [1971] 1 WLR 1239

The *Sun* newspaper contained an article in which it described how a Miss Murray, likely to be a major witness in a dog-doping trial, had gone into hiding after being kidnapped a week earlier by members of the dog-doping gang. A week earlier she had in fact been staying with the claimant. The claimant said that ordinary readers would assume that he was a member of the gang and witnesses who had seen the claimant with Miss Murray gave evidence that this was in fact what they believed.

The question to be decided was

QUOTATION

'Would readers having knowledge of the circumstances reasonably have understood that the article referred to Mr Morgan?'

If the answer to this question was 'Yes' then Lord Reid observed

JUDGMENT

'It does not matter whether the publisher intended to refer to the [claimant] or not. It does not even matter if he knew of the [claimant's] existence. And it does not matter that he did not know or could not have known the facts which caused the readers with special knowledge to connect the statement with the [claimant].'

As will be seen, the Defamation Act 1996, amending and replacing earlier legislation, now provides a defence of 'offer of amends', to alleviate the consequences of accidental defamation (see section 14.4.7).

14.3.4 The statement must be published

No action can be brought where the statement, no matter how untrue or offensive, is made only to the person about whom the allegation is being made. At least one other person must hear or read the statement and understand it. A deaf person who cannot lip-read would not 'hear' a slander, a foreigner who cannot read English would not understand an article in English.

Publication can be defined as communication of the material to someone other than the person allegedly defamed. Newspapers and books are published so that any defamatory material they contain is published to the readers. A letter is published when it is dictated to a secretary and also when it is opened by someone other than the person defamed.

An exception to the rule concerns publication between spouses. A husband cannot make a publication to his wife, nor a wife to her husband. As was said in *Wennhak v Morgan* (1888) 20 QBD 635 to hold otherwise 'might lead to disastrous results to social life.'

Publication usually occurs intentionally. There may also be liability for any publication which is not intended but which can reasonably be anticipated. A letter containing defamatory material will be published if it is opened in the usual course by anyone other than the addressee, for example by a post clerk. If it is not marked 'confidential' this can reasonably be anticipated.

CASE EXAMPLE

Theaker v Richardson [1962] 1 All ER 229

A defamatory letter written by the defendant was put into an envelope similar to those used for election addresses. The envelope was addressed to the claimant but was in fact opened by her husband, believing it to be election material. It was held by the jury that this was a natural and probable consequence.

On appeal Lord Justice Pearson explained that it was a question of fact to be decided by the jury

JUDGMENT

'Was [the husband's] conduct something unusual, out of the ordinary and not reasonably to be anticipated, or was it something which could quite easily and naturally happen in the ordinary course of events?'

An interesting snapshot of domestic life in the early twentieth century is provided by the following case

CASE EXAMPLE

Huth v Huth [1915] 3 KB 32

Mr Huth sent his wife a letter in an unsealed envelope alleging that they were not in fact married and that their children were illegitimate. At the time, a wife could not sue her husband in tort but the children could sue their father. They alleged that publication had occurred when the letter had been opened by the butler before he handed it to Mrs Huth. As it is not part of a butler's duties to open letters addressed to his employers, Mr Huth could not reasonably have anticipated that the butler would in fact do so. Consequently there had been no publication and the children lost the case.

Once defamatory material has been put into circulation by the original publisher, there can be liability for repeated publications by others unless the repetition is unauthorised and/or is not a natural and probable consequence which can reasonably be foreseen.

CASE EXAMPLE

Slipper v BBC [1991] 1 QB 283

The BBC made a film about the claimant's unsuccessful attempts to bring a robber back from Brazil. Preview tapes were sent to journalists and the film was subsequently broadcast on BBC 1. The claimant claimed that the film was defamatory and alleged

(i) that the BBC knew and would foresee that the preview tapes were likely to be reviewed in the national press, alternatively

(ii) that it was the natural and probable consequence that such reviews would be published.

The Court of Appeal held that whether or not the reviews reproduced the sting of the libel and whether or not repetition was invited or could have been anticipated were questions for the jury to decide.

As will be seen, in section 14.4.5, the issue of responsibility for repeated publication has been addressed by Parliament in the Defamation Act 1996 which provides a defence in certain circumstances for 'innocent' publication.

ACTIVITY

Self-assessment questions

1. What are the main differences between libel and slander?
2. Explain the difficulties faced by the judge in deciding whether or not the words are capable of being defamatory.
3. What precisely is meant by 'innuendo'?

14.4 Defences

14.4.1 Justification

We have already seen that it cannot amount to defamation if what is published is the truth. It is for the defendant to prove the truth of the statement. What of the situation where most of what is published can be proved to be true but some parts of it cannot? The old defence of justification, namely that the substance of the statement is true even if there are some minor inaccuracies, is now explained in the Defamation Act 1952, s 5.

SECTION

's 5 . . . a defence of justification shall not fail by reason only that the truth of every charge is not proved if the words not proved to be true do not materially injure the plaintiff's reputation having regard to the truth of the remaining charges.'

It is therefore possible for the defendant to justify the 'sting' of the statement by proving its truth even though some details may be inaccurate. The inaccurate details must not add to the 'sting' of the statement.

CASE EXAMPLE

Alexander v Eastern Railway Co (1865) 6 B&S 340

The claimant alleged that he had been libelled by a notice which stated that he had been convicted of travelling without paying his fare. It went on to say that he had been fined £9 1s 10d with an alternative of three weeks in prison if he failed to pay. The notice was accurate save that the alternative period of imprisonment was in fact only 14 days. It was held that the defence of justification succeeded.

In an earlier case, *Edwards v Bell* (1824) 1 Bing 403, Mr Justice Burrough explained the defence saying

JUDGMENT

'. . . it is sufficient if the substance of the libellous statement can be justified … As much must be justified as meets the sting of the charge, and if anything be contained in a charge which does not add to the sting of it, that need not be justified.'

It has been tempting for people to try to protect themselves by stating that 'it is rumoured that . . .' but this is unlikely to work. The fact that there is such a rumour may be true but the defendant will have to prove that the facts alleged in the rumour are true (*Shah v Standard Chartered Bank* [1999] QB 241).

It is by contrast possible for a defendant to succeed where the statement makes it clear that the defamatory imputation is in fact false. Whether or not this in reality removes the 'sting' of the charge is debatable as the following case shows:

CASE EXAMPLE

Charleston and Another v News Group Newspapers Ltd [1995] 2 WLR 450

The claimants were actors who played husband and wife in '*Neighbours*', a popular television show. The defendants published, in a mass circulation Sunday paper, photographs of the claimants, which showed the stars apparently engaged in sexual activity. The banner headline read 'Strewth! What's Harold up to with our Madge' while another headline read 'Porn Shocker for Neighbours Stars'. The photographs had in fact been taken from a computer game which had superimposed the faces of the stars onto pornographic photographs. This had been done without their knowledge or consent. The article beneath the headlines and the photographs made the circumstances clear and described the claimants as victims.

The issue was what inference a reader would have drawn. It was conceded that provided a reader had actually read beyond the first paragraph of the article, the falsity of the impression given by the photographs would have been clear. It was argued that a significant proportion of the readership would only in fact have read the headlines and looked at the pictures. Such people would have understood the publication in the defamatory sense.

The House of Lords held that the readership must be treated as a whole and the article read as a whole. This meant that the allegation of defamation could not be sustained, the truth was made clear. Commenting on the suggestions that a proportion of readers would not in fact read the whole article, Lord Bridge said

JUDGMENT

'. . . if [such] readers, without taking the trouble to discover what the article was all about, carried away the impression that [the claimants] were . . . involved in making pornographic films, they could hardly be described as ordinary, reasonable, fair-minded readers . . .'

The judgments seem to show that the judges were aware that the publication was deeply offensive to the claimants but were 'not concerned to pronounce on any question of journalistic ethics' (per Lord Bridge). While this is undoubtedly true, the view can be of little comfort to the claimants.

It might also be thought that a claimant could ignore the true statements and bring an action based on only those parts of the statement which are untrue. Whether or not this can succeed depends on the nature of the charges. If they can be treated as distinct and separate (ie severable) this may work. If not, the defendant may be able to justify the actual charges complained of by showing that the charges, whether complained about or not, have a 'common sting' (*Polly Peck (Holdings) plc v Trelford* [1986] QB 1000).

It is for the defendant to show that the words complained of can be justified. This is usually done in the course of the pleadings in which the defendant will set out the facts on which reliance is placed. The defendant cannot seek to justify a meaning of which the claimant has not complained.

CASE EXAMPLE

Bookbinder v Tebbit [1989] 1 WLR 640

The claimant, the leader of a Labour council, complained only of a specific charge that the leadership of the council had squandered public money by having a caption 'Support Nuclear Free zones' printed on school stationery. The defendant's attempt to justify this by reference to alleged general squandering of public money was struck out by the Court of Appeal. The claimant had based his complaint on a specific allegation and it was for the defendant to justify that allegation.

During the 1960s some cases were brought by criminals who alleged that a statement that they were guilty of the crime was in fact libellous. In one notorious case, *Hinds v Sparks* [1964] Crim LR 717, the civil jury found that an allegation of murder by the claimant was in fact untrue even though a criminal jury had convicted him on the same facts. It was clear that the civil route of defamation was allowing convicted criminals effectively to have a retrial in a court where the standard of proof was lower. The loophole was closed by the Civil Evidence Act 1968 (as amended by the Defamation Act 1996) which provides that evidence of conviction of a crime is conclusive evidence that the crime was in fact committed by the claimant in a defamation case.

14.4.2 Fair comment

This defence, in recent times, is sometimes described as 'honest comment on a matter of public interest'. Many writers continue to use the original name for the defence and that approach is followed here.

Most people have opinions and express comments which may not always be reasonable. So-called 'experts' and commentators, journalists, critics and others are no exception, but their comments are likely to be widely circulated. An opinion can have as damaging an effect on reputation as an untrue statement of fact.

Comment distinguished from fact

It is sometimes difficult to distinguish between comment and fact. *Winfield and Jolowicz* (p 437) give a good example of the problem when he suggests 'calling a man a fornicator or a swindler looks like a statement of fact, but what is calling him immoral or dishonest? Are immorality and sin matters of fact or opinion?' The questions can only be answered by reference to the context in which the statements are made.

Comments are based on facts which may be explicitly stated or which are referred to by implication. Where the facts are explicit, it is generally easy to distinguish between fact and comment. Comment based in implicit facts is more difficult. The House of Lords, in

Kemsley v Foot [1952] AC 345, held that fair comment could be pleaded where there was sufficient indication of the subject-matter on which the comment was based.

The issue has been clarified by a more recent case

CASE EXAMPLE

Telnikoff v Matusevitch [1992] 2 AC 343

A national newspaper published an article by the claimant in which he criticised the BBC, his employers, for employing too many employees from the ethnic minorities of the USSR rather than those who 'associate themselves ethically, spiritually or religiously with the Russian people'. The defendant wrote to the newspaper in response, attacking the claimant's article as racist and anti-Semitic. The defendant also said that the claimant was asking the BBC 'to switch from professional testing to a blood test' and to dismiss 'ethnically alien' employees. The defendant raised the defence of fair comment.

The issue was whether the letter should be judged alongside the article. Could the two be read together? The majority of the House of Lords held that the letter must be read alone. Lord Keith explained

JUDGMENT

'the readers of the letter must have included a substantial number of persons who had not read the article or who, if they had read it, did not have its terms fully in mind . . . The matter cannot turn on the likelihood or otherwise of readers of the letter having read the article.'

For this reason, the letter should be considered by the jury to decide whether or not the statements in the letter amounted to fact or comment.

The underlying facts must be true

The facts on which the comment is based must be true. As it is for the defendant to prove the truth of the facts, this could present difficulties where something said by someone else has been repeated by the defendant who has no personal knowledge as to the truth or otherwise of the facts. Such a defendant is protected where the article reports statements which are subject to privilege, for example an account of the evidence given by a witness in court. Provided the comment is based upon those privileged statements, the defendant will be able to rely on fair comment even though the reported facts are in reality untrue.

A matter of public interest

The term 'public interest' when used in a legal context is notoriously difficult to define or explain. Does it mean in essence something which it may benefit society generally to be aware of or does it simply mean something in which the public generally are interested? If it is the latter, then it would appear that for those in the public eye, whether politicians, religious leaders, celebrities etc – the list could be endless – every aspect of their public and private life can be the subject of comment. In the absence of a law specifically protecting privacy (as to which see section 14.6.2), the courts have tried to draw some kind of line.

Lord Denning MR explained the concept of public policy in *London Artists Ltd v Littler* [1969] 2 QB 375 saying

JUDGMENT

'Whenever a matter is such as to affect people at large, so that they may be legitimately interested in, or concerned at, what is going on, or what may happen to them or others; then it is a matter of public interest on which everyone is entitled to make fair comment.'

This explanation appears to embrace both possible meanings. It is for the judge to decide whether or not the comment is on a matter of public interest. Recent years have seen a number of politicians subjected to comment about their privates lives. It is not difficult to appreciate that the fact that a politician who lacks personal integrity in personal life may also lack integrity in public life and thus the private life can become a matter of public interest.

Once a matter has been found to be one of public interest, it is for the jury to decide whether or not the comment is fair.

The comment must be fair

This does not mean that everyone has to agree with the comment but that it must be a comment which an honest person could make on the basis of the facts. Others may believe that the comment is wrong or misguided but this is irrelevant. The issue was discussed by the House of Lords in *Reynolds v Times Newspapers Ltd* [2001] 2 AC 127. Suggesting that the word 'fair' is meaningless, Lord Nicholls said

JUDGMENT

'Comment must be relevant to the facts to which it is addressed. It cannot be used as a cloak for mere invective. But . . . [t]he true test is whether the opinion, however exaggerated, obstinate or prejudiced, was honestly held by the person expressing it.'

The need is for honesty. In discussing matters of public interest concerning public figures, Mr Justice Eady commented that they must expect to have their motives 'subjected to scrutiny and discussed'. He went on to say

QUOTATION

'Nor is it realistic today to demand that such debate should be hobbled by the constraints of conventional good manners – still less of deference. The law of fair comment must allow for healthy scepticism.'

Branson v Bower [2002] 2 WLR 452

The test is objective thus the defendant does not need to prove honesty, it is for the claimant to disprove it. While the defendant may be a crank, prejudiced or obstinate this alone does not make the comment dishonest but may well influence a jury in deciding whether or not the opinion is genuine.

On the basis of the matters discussed above, the defence is important to protect freedom of speech. The jury is merely required to decide whether or not the comment is honest, not whether the jury agrees with it. In *Silkin v Beaverbrook Newspapers* [1958] 1 WLR 743, Mr Justice Diplock said

JUDGMENT

'. . . it would be a sad day for freedom of speech in this country if a jury were to apply the test of whether it agrees with the comment instead of applying the true test: was this an opinion, however exaggerated, obstinate or prejudiced, which was honestly held by the writer.'

It should be noted that even though the comment may be honest, the defendant's malicious motive may mean that the defence of fair comment in unavailable. A good example of this is found in

Thomas v Bradbury Agnew & Co Ltd [1906] 2 KB 627

A book was reviewed in Punch magazine published by the defendants. The review was extremely hostile but the defence of fair comment could perhaps have been used. However, the claimant was able to show, both from the words used in the review and from the demeanour of the reviewer in the witness box, that the reviewer was motivated by malice. The defence of fair comment failed.

For further discussion of the issue of malice see section 14.4.8 below.

14.4.3 Absolute privilege

It has long been believed that in certain circumstances people should be free to say whatever they wish without fear of being sued for defamation. The law recognises this and in limited circumstances will give the necessary protection by finding that the statement has absolute privilege; in other words the statement cannot be used as the basis of any legal action.

Parliamentary privilege

Statements made in either of the two Houses of Parliament have absolute privilege by virtue of the Bill of Rights 1688, art 9. This will not protect a Member of Parliament who makes a defamatory statement outside the House but it covers statements made

(i)   in the course of debate
(ii) during committee proceedings
(iii) by witnesses to committees.

By the Parliamentary Papers Act 1840, s 1 publication of the reports, papers, votes or proceedings of either House also has absolute privilege.

While the privilege does not extend to statements made outside the House, a claimant cannot rely on reports of privileged statements to prove malice (*Church of Scientology of California v Johnson-Smith* [1972] 1 QB 522). This apparently unjust situation has been mitigated in part by the Defamation Act 1996, s 13 which permits a member of either House to waive privilege to allow reference to be made to statements which could not otherwise be referred to. The Act only operates to permit a person to waive privilege in order to bring proceedings; it is of no help to a defendant (s 13(4)). The privilege which is waived in fact belongs to Parliament which has its own powers of enforcement, but the Act permits an individual to waive that privilege so far as it concerns that individual. This can be done even after the person has ceased to be a Member of the House (*Hamilton v Al Fayed* [2000] 2 All ER 224).

Judicial proceedings

Statements made in the course of proceedings before any court or tribunal whether by the judge, counsel, witnesses or the parties have absolute privilege (*Trapp v Mackie* [1979] 1 WLR 377). This can extend to statements made before the commencement of proceedings provided there is a link with possible proceedings (*Waple v Surrey County Council* [1998] 1 WLR 860) and to disclosure between opposing lawyers (*Taylor v Director of the Serious Fraud Office* [1999] 2 AC 177).

Absolute privilege also extends to 'fair and accurate report of proceedings in public before a court . . . if published contemporaneously with proceedings' (Defamation Act 1996, s 14(1)). By s 14(3) the courts covered by s 14(1) include

- any court in the United Kingdom
- the European Court of Justice
- the European Court of Human Rights

- any international criminal tribunal established by the United Nations or by international agreement to which the United Kingdom is a party.

Communications between officers of state

State business might grind to a halt were there to be a risk of action for defamation. This means that communications between senior officers of State have absolute privilege.

CASE EXAMPLE

Chatterton v Secretary of State for India [1895] 2 QB 189

An official had written a letter to the Under-Secretary for State which contained an allegedly libellous statement about the claimant.

Dismissing the claimant's action on the basis that the letter had absolute privilege, Lord Esher MR explained

JUDGMENT

'[The law] does not exist for the benefit of the official . . . the ground of its existence is the injury to the public good which would result if such an inquiry were allowed . . . An inquiry would take away from the public official his freedom of action in a matter concerning the public welfare . . .'

The extent of this rule is not clear. It covers communications between Ministers but it does not give blanket immunity for communications between civil servants. It seems that the rule is restricted to those few cases where it is essential that there should be total freedom of communication even though this results in a citizen losing any right to redress.

It should be remembered that the Crown can claim public interest immunity to prevent disclosure of certain classes of official documents (see a text on Constitutional and Administrative Law for details) although such a claim may well lead to political controversy.

The privilege also covers internal memoranda in a foreign embassy (*Fayed v Al-Tajir* [1988] QB 712) although it is likely that this is based on the idea that there should be no interference with the internal affairs of a foreign sovereign state rather than on the reasoning given in *Chatterton v SOS for India*.

14.4.4 Qualified privilege

The law recognises that there are other circumstances when a person needs to be free to tell the truth as they believe it to be, even though in reality they may be wrong. The protection which can apply in such circumstances is found in the doctrine of qualified privilege. Qualified privilege has the same effect as absolute privilege in that the statement cannot be used in a court of law. The rules are to be found in both common law and in statute. While reading this section, remember that the defence can be defeated if it is shown that the maker of the statement acted maliciously (see section 14.4.8).

The defence generally

Although in general an action will lie for publication of false and injurious statements, this will not be so where

QUOTATION

'[the statement] is made by a person in the discharge of some public or private duty whether legal or moral, or in matters where his interest is concerned . . . If fairly warranted by any reasonable occasion, and honestly made, such communications are protected for the common convenience and welfare of society.'

Parke B in Toogood v Spyring (1834) 1 Cr M&R 181

Whether or not such duty or interest exists will depend on the particular facts of the actual case in which the question arises.

The easiest example of how the defence works arises from giving an employment reference. Few contracts of employment require an employer to give a reference to an employee so that there is no legal duty to do so. In reality many employers do so when requested. If a reference is to be any use to a potential future employer, it is essential that an honest picture is given of the employee's competence and character. The employer has a duty to communicate what is believed to be a true picture while the potential employer has an interest in protecting his business to employ a suitable person. Provided the reference is given honestly, the employee will have no redress if it is unfavourable. It should be noted that the employee may have a remedy in negligence if the person giving the reference has failed to take reasonable steps to check the accuracy of what was said (see *Spring v Guardian Assurance plc* [1995] 3 WLR 354).

Duty situations

It is for the judge to decide whether or not a duty situation exists. As the duty can be based on moral or social grounds, it is difficult to formulate specific principles. Lord Justice Lindley in *Stuart v Bell* [1891] 2 QB 341 suggested

JUDGMENT

'I take moral or social duty to mean a duty recognised by English people of ordinary intelligence and moral principle.'

In *Watt v Longsdon* [1930] 1 KB 130 Lord Justice Scrutton stated the problem as follows

JUDGMENT

'Is the judge merely to give his own view of moral and social duty, though he thinks that a considerable portion of the community hold a different opinion? Or is he to endeavour to ascertain what view the great mass of right-minded men would take.'

It is clear that the judges try to be objective but inevitably their subjective view of what 'right-minded' people would think will influence the decision. Fortunately some principles are apparent from case law.

In *Adam v Ward* [1917] AC 309 it was said that the person to whom the statement is communicated must have 'a corresponding interest to receive it. This reciprocity is essential'. A good example of how this works is found in

CASE EXAMPLE

Watt v Longsdon [1930] 1 KB 130

The claimant was the overseas director of a company of which the defendant was also a director. A letter was sent to the defendant from a foreign employee suggesting that the claimant was dishonest and immoral. The defendant wrote back making defamatory comments about the claimant and asking for confirmation of the allegations. Without waiting for a reply, he then showed the letter to the chairman of the company and to the claimant's wife. The statements were in fact untrue.

The Court of Appeal held

(i) the letter to the foreign employee was privileged – they had a common interest in the company

(ii) publication to the chairman was privileged – the defendant as an employee had a duty to pass the information on

(iii) publication to the claimant's wife was not privileged – there was no legal, social or moral duty to inform her about unsubstantiated allegations.

In his judgment Scrutton LJ held

JUDGMENT

'. . . the principle is that there must be an interest in the recipient and a duty to communicate in the speaker, or an interest to be protected in the speaker and a duty to protect it in the recipient.'

In deciding whether or not a duty situation exists the court will take into account all relevant circumstances, in particular

(i) Was there a relationship of confidentiality between the speaker and the recipient?
(ii) Was the information given in response to a request or voluntarily?

From time to time defendants argue that certain types of statements should be treated generically as attracting qualified privilege. The courts have tended to reject this view.

In *Watts v Times Newspapers Ltd* [1996] 1 All ER 152 it was suggested that apologies by those making allegedly defamatory statements should form such a category. (The apology had in fact repeated details of the false accusations accompanied inadvertently by a picture of a third party totally unconnected with the matter.) Rejecting the idea that such apologies should generally attract qualified privilege, the Court of Appeal held that the usual principles must apply.

The courts have also considered whether there should be a generic category covering political information and debate.

CASE EXAMPLE

Reynolds v Times Newspapers Ltd [1999] 4 All ER 609

In 1994 a political crisis occurred in Ireland leading to the resignation of the claimant, the Prime Minister. The defendants published an article in the Sunday Times which the claimant said accused him of dishonestly and deliberately misleading the Irish Parliament about the reasons for the crisis and of lying to Parliament. The defendants claimed qualified privilege. At first instance the claimant succeeded. The defendants sought a new trial on the basis that the trial judge had erred when he refused to allow the defence of qualified privilege to be used. The Court of Appeal allowing the appeal suggested that qualified privilege can be argued by the press when

(i) the paper has a moral, social or legal duty to inform the public of the matter

(ii) the public has a corresponding interest in receiving the information and

(iii) the nature, status and source of the material and the circumstances of the publication are such as to warrant the protection of privilege.

The matter went to the House of Lords.

Holding that the question for the court is whether or not the duty-interest test is satisfied, the House of Lords found that the questions posed by the Court of Appeal were simply part of that test which takes account of all relevant circumstances. Emphasising the importance of freedom of expression and acknowledging the importance of the role played by the media to inform the public at large of political matters, Lord Nicholls said

JUDGMENT

'The common law should not develop "political information" as a new "subject matter" category of qualified privilege, whereby the publication of all such information would attract qualified privilege, whatever the circumstances.'

He went on to list 10 matters to be taken into account

(i) the seriousness of the allegation
(ii) the nature of the information and whether it is of public concern
(iii) the source of the information
(iv) steps taken to verify it
(v) the status of the information
(vi) the urgency of the matter
(vii) whether comment is sought from the claimant
(viii) whether the article contained at least the gist of the claimant's side of the story
(ix) the tone of the article
(x) the circumstances of the publication including the timing.

Lord Nichols emphasised that

JUDGMENT

'the list is not exhaustive. The weight to be given to these and any other relevant factors will vary from case to case.'

The House of Lords has subsequently considered the defence of public interest established in *Reynolds* in some detail. In *Jameel and others v Wall Street Journal* [2006] UKHL 44; [2006] All ER (D) 132 it was held that the defence should be treated as a question of law and not as a matter of fact to be decided in each case.

Interest situations

The defence may apply where the communication is made by a person who has a lawful interest to protect, to a person who has a corresponding interest or duty to protect. The interest may be personal to either party or an interest common to both. The latter is most usually found in the context of business and commerce; for example, an employee who reports dishonesty or other malpractice to management can use the defence. Despite the availability of the defence, employees who 'blow the whistle' are likely to be apprehensive about the reaction of management or colleagues. This has been partly dealt with by the Public Interest Disclosure Act 1998 which protects such an employee from disciplinary action or victimisation provided the disclosure was made to an appropriate person and provided the employee had an honest and reasonable belief in the truth of the allegation.

Some the cases already discussed demonstrate that duty/interest situations are often closely related. Examples include *Watt v Longsdon* and *Reynolds v Times Newspapers Ltd*.

Statutory provision

The defence of qualified privilege has been extended by statute. By the Parliamentary Papers Act 1840, s 3 extracts or abstracts of reports, papers, notes or proceedings published by order of Parliament have qualified privilege as, by the Broadcasting Act 1990 Sched 20, para 1 do publications of such extracts on television or radio.

The Defamation Act 1996 contains a Schedule that lists a wide range of documents which attract qualified privilege for any publication in any part of the media of any matter arising from such documents which are of public concern or of public benefit. Once this basic point of public interest is established, the extent of the protection is decided according to the part of the Schedule in which the document is listed.

Documents which appear in Schedule 1, Part 1 are privileged 'without explanation or contradiction'. These include fair and accurate reports of any parliament or court anywhere in the world and fair and accurate reports of proceedings at a public inquiry anywhere in the world.

Documents listed in Schedule 1, Part II are privileged 'subject to explanation or contradiction'. These include fair and accurate copies or extracts from documents produced by any parliament of a State which is a member of the European Union, by the European Parliament or by the European Court of Justice. It also includes fair and accurate reports of a general meeting of a United Kingdom public company and of the findings or decisions of various associations such as those formed for the promotion of sport, science, religion or learning.

Part II privilege is lost if the defendant is shown to have refused or failed to publish in a suitable manner a reasonable letter or other document by way of the claimant's explanation or contradiction of the report. The defendant may also be required to give the claimant a 'right to reply'.

14.4.5 Innocent publication

In theory some material is published many times over, for example in a book or newspaper – by the author to the editor, by the editor to the printer, by the printer to the wholesaler, by the wholesaler to the retailer and by the retailer to the reader! To deal with this situation, when in reality at least some of those involved may have no reason to know of the defamation, a defence is provided by the Defamation Act 1996, s 1. This states that it is a defence for the defendant to show that

- they were not the author or that they were not the editor or publisher, in a commercial sense, of the material
- all reasonable care was taken
- they did not know nor had they reason to believe that the material contained a defamatory statement.

The Act restates an older defence thus earlier cases can be helpful.

CASE EXAMPLE

Vizetelly v Mudie's Select Library Ltd [1900] 2 QB 170

The defendants subscribed to a publication in which publishers placed a notice asking for the return of copies of a book which contained defamatory material. The library ignored the notice and no member of staff had read the book.

The defendants had failed to make out the defence of innocent dissemination and were held to be liable for the publication. To succeed Romer LJ said that a defendant must show

JUDGMENT

'(1) that he was innocent of any knowledge of the libel in the work disseminated by him;

(2) that there was nothing in the work or the circumstances under which it came to him or was disseminated by him which ought to have led him to suppose that it contained a libel; and

(3) that, when the work was disseminated by him, it was not by any negligence on his part that he did not know that it contained the libel.'

The defence extends to those who provide access to information on the internet if the information is provided by a person over whom the service provider has no control. This is subject to certain limitations:

CASE EXAMPLE

Godfrey v Demon Internet Ltd [1999] EWHC 240 (QB)

The claimant was defamed when an anonymous person sent an obscene message to an internet user newsgroup which purported to come from him. He faxed the ISP, the defendant, telling them that the message was a forgery and asking for it to be removed. The defendant failed to do so. The claimant sought damages from the time he had given the necessary information to the defendant.

In his judgment Morland J commented

JUDGMENT

'. . . after receipt of the [claimant's] fax the defendant knew of the defamatory posting but chose not to remove it from its . . . service . . . In my judgment the defamatory posting was published by the defendant and, as . . . it knew of the defamatory content of the posting, it cannot avail itself of the protection provided by . . . the Act and its defence under section 1 is in law hopeless.'

It appears that an internet service provider will be liable once the defamatory content is drawn to its attention if it then does nothing to remove the offensive material.

14.4.6 Consent

A person who consents to publication cannot later complain that it is defamatory. This would cover someone who has given the defamatory material to the publisher or who has had editorial control over an article about themselves.

14.4.7 Offer of amends

This is not strictly a defence as it involves the defendant acknowledging that a defamation has occurred but it can have the effect of avoiding litigation and will therefore, in certain circumstances, have a similar effect.

By the Defamation Act 1996, s 2 a person who accepts that a complaint of defamation is well-founded may make a written offer of amends which includes offers to

- make a suitable correction and a sufficient apology
- publish the correction, etc in any way which is reasonable and practical
- pay compensation and costs.

By s 3 acceptance of the offer of amends brings the matter to an end save that the aggrieved party can apply to the court for an order that the terms of the accepted offer are fulfilled. If the necessary steps to fulfil the offer cannot be agreed, the defendant may make a statement in open court in terms approved by the court accompanied by an undertaking to the court for the manner of publication. In *Nail v News Group Newspapers* [2005] 1 All ER 1040 a newspaper had made false allegations about the sexual history of a well known actor. It made an offer of amends and the parties agreed the wording of an apology but could not agree on compensation. This was then determined by the court under s 3(5).

If the claimant does not accept the offer, by s 4 it can be pleaded as a defence provided that it can be proved that at the time the statement was made the defendant knew or had reason to believe that:

(a) the statement referred to the claimant or was likely to be understood as doing so and
(b) it was false and derogatory.

If this defence is pleaded, the defendant cannot rely on any other defence.

The offer can also be used in mitigation of damages, whether or not it has been relied on as a defence.

14.4.8 The role of 'malice'

It is only rarely that a person's motive for their actions is relevant in tort. One such situation arises in the context of private nuisance (see Chapter 9, section 9.4.2), another arises in relation to the defences of fair comment and qualified privilege in defamation.

In the context of fair comment, it is open to the claimant to prove that some improper motive lay behind the defendant's statement (see *Thomas v Bradbury Agnew & Co Ltd*, section 14.4.2 above, for an example of such a case).

Where the defence is qualified privilege it must be remembered that when the defence succeeds, what would otherwise be held to be defamatory is excused. To establish malice the claimant needs to prove that the defendant took advantage of the nature of the material to make statements which were not believed to be true or to vent spite or ill-will on the claimant or for some other improper motive. The protection of the defence is not lost because the defendant was negligent in checking the facts but in such a case the claimant may have an alternative action for negligence (*Spring v Guardian Assurance plc* [1993] 2 All ER 273).

The burden of proving malice rests on the claimant, who will seek to establish it from evidence of such matters as the relationship between the parties both before and after publication, from the words actually used which may be very excessive in the circumstances and from the defendant's demeanour when giving evidence.

Where more than one defendant is sued, malice on the part of one will not remove the availability of the defence to other, non-malicious defendants (*Telnikoff v Matusevitch*).

ACTIVITY

Self-assessment questions

1. Explain the defence of 'justification'.
2. What is the important principle established by *Charleston v News Group Newspapers*?
3. To what extent does the defence of 'fair comment' uphold the principle of freedom of speech?
4. Outline the circumstances in which a statement may be subject to 'absolute' privilege.
5. In the context of 'qualified' privilege explain how the courts approach the task of deciding whether a defendant has a 'duty' or 'interest' in making the statement complained of.
6. What are the limitations imposed in relation to the defence of 'innocent' publication?
7. Explain the effect of 'malice' in relation to defamation.

14.5 Remedies

14.5.1 Injunction

An injunction may be sought by the claimant in two circumstances:

1. in rare cases to prevent publication of a defamatory statement
2. to prevent the statement being repeated.

When a claimant becomes aware that a defamatory statement is about to be published, it would be natural to seek an interlocutory injunction to prevent that publication. The nature of an interlocutory injunction means that the substantive issue between the claimant and the defendant is not at that stage considered in detail – there is no trial of such issues. The result of this is that such injunctions are unlikely to be granted where a defendant can show that a defence, for example justification or fair comment, may be pleaded with some hope of success at the full trial.

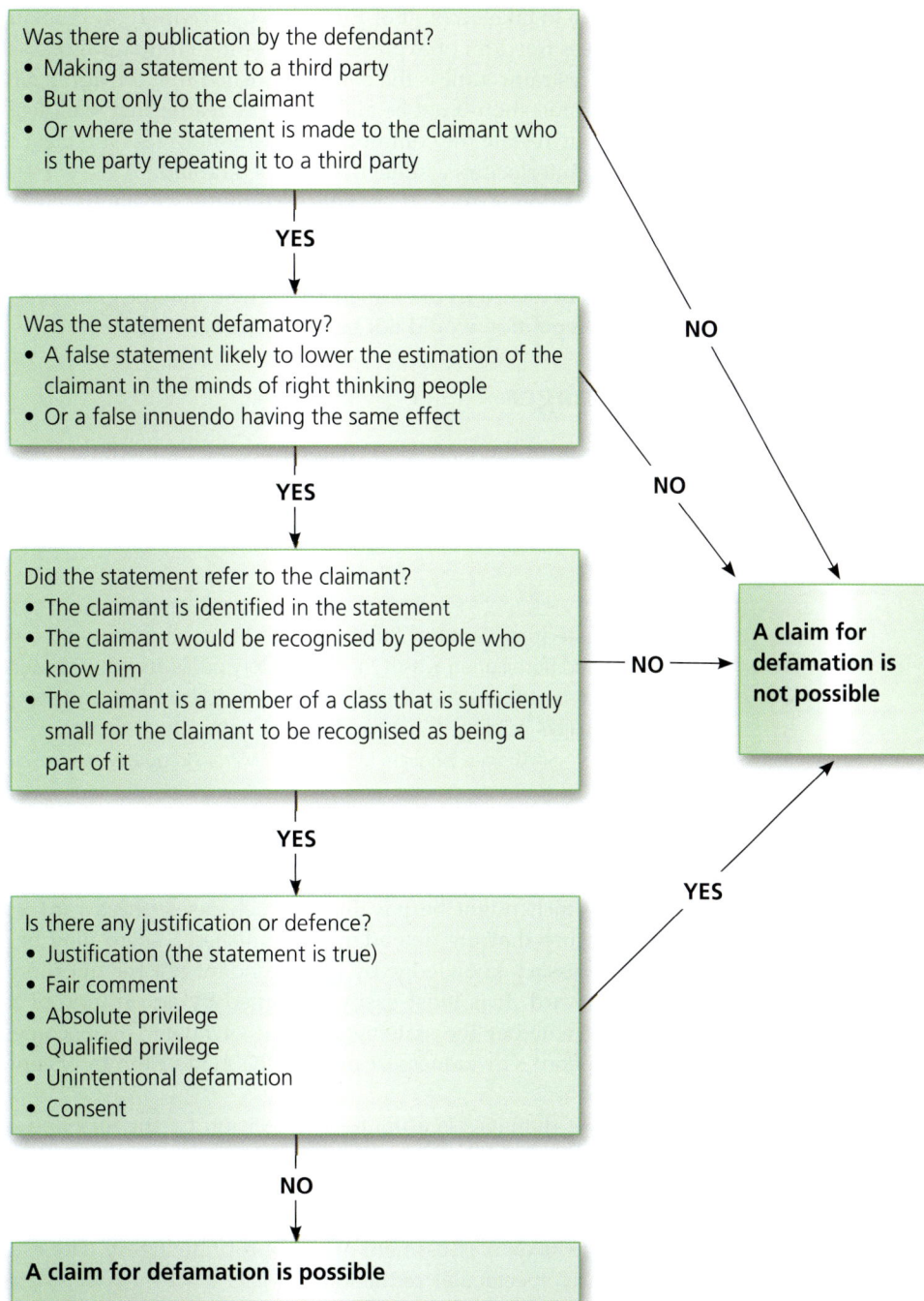

Figure 14.2 Diagram illustrating the essential elements for a claim in defamation

CASE EXAMPLE

Holley v Smyth [1998] QB 726

A squabble occurred between two people involved in a financial transaction. The defendant alleged that the claimant had acted dishonourably and sent him a copy of the press release which he proposed to issue. The claimant sought an interlocutory injunction but his application was refused. The defendant made it clear that were he to be sued after publication, he would be able to establish that what was said was true. The Court of Appeal said that an interlocutory injunction should only be granted when it was clear that the statement was untrue. The claimant's application was refused.

These rules have to take account of European Convention on Human Rights, Article 10 which guarantees freedom of expression and of the Human Rights Act 1998, s 12 which prevents prior restraint 'unless the court is satisfied that the applicant is likely to establish that publication should not be allowed'. The reader may well feel that the statutory provisions merely restate the common law position. Unless it is clear that any defence is likely to fail, no interlocutory injunction will be granted.

When an injunction is applied for after trial of the substantive issues, the claimant is more likely to be successful if it can be shown that damages alone will not provide a sufficient remedy in the particular circumstances. In *Tolstoy Miloslavsky v UK* (1995) 20 EHRR 442, ECtHR the Court of Human Rights held that the grant of a permanent injunction to prevent repetition would not be a breach of Article 10.

14.5.2 Damages

While the purpose of damages is to compensate the claimant for loss, defamation is one of the few torts in respect of which exemplary damages may be awarded. The usual award is compensatory damages to

QUOTATION

'. . . compensate [the claimant] for the loss of his good name; and take account of the distress, hurt and humiliation which the defamatory publication has caused . . . the extent of publication is also very relevant; a libel published to millions has a greater potential to cause damage than a libel published to a handful of people.'

Sir Thomas Bingham MR in *John v Mirror Group Newspapers Ltd* [1996] 2 All ER 35

Exemplary damages will only be awarded where the claimant can prove that the defendant knew that a tort was being committed (or was reckless on this point) and even so went ahead on the basis that the profits to be made from the publication would far exceed any damages which might be payable. In such cases, the award will include a sum designed to ensure that the defendant is 'punished'. There may be little difficulty in proving the necessary knowledge by the defendant but the question of recklessness is not straight-forward. It is most easily explained by an attitude of total disregard for the question of whether the statement is true or false. This becomes more believable when the defendant's awareness of profit to be made from publication is brought into consideration.

The amount of damages is a matter for decision by the jury and over the years the level of awards was so high that it was clear that damage to reputation was being valued more highly than damage due to personal injury. The Courts and Legal Services Act 1990 gave the Court of Appeal power to review the level of damages awarded by a jury and to substitute its own assessment of an appropriate figure. The use of this power has led to some fairly spectacular reductions. In *John v Mirror Group Newspapers* (1996) 146 NLJ Rep 13 the figure was reduced from £75,000 to £25,000 while in *Rantzen v Mirror Group Newspapers* (1986) Ltd [1994] QB 670 the figure was brought down from £250,000 to £110,000. The Court of Appeal does not always disagree with a jury assessment

CASE EXAMPLE

Kiam II v MGN Ltd [2002] EWCA Civ 43

The claimant had succeeded in a libel action in respect of a leading article published in the *Mirror* newspaper. The article was untrue in every material respect and the jury awarded damages of £105,000. The defendant appealed against the level of the award.

The jury award was upheld. Lord Justice Simon Brown re-stated a basic principle that

JUDGMENT

'this court should not interfere with the jury's award unless it regards it as substantially exceeding the most that any jury could reasonably have thought appropriate.'

In earlier cases a comparison with the level of damages awarded in personal injury cases had been ruled out. However, by the time this appeal was heard the maximum amount for general damages in such cases had been increased to £200,000. Lord Justice Simon Brown and Lord Justice Waller recognised that a comparison with the level of damages in personal injury cases was a relevant consideration but found that the award was not excessive and dismissed the appeal. Lord Sedley, giving a minority judgment, went so far as to say

JUDGMENT

'I would allow this appeal on the narrow ground that even by comparison with other libel awards, but especially by comparison with personal injury awards, the figure awarded by the jury as compensatory damages is wholly excessive.'

(For more detailed discussion of the principles governing awards of damages, see Chapter 20.)

14.6 Privacy, confidentiality and human rights

14.6.1 Introduction

It should be clear to the reader that almost the last thing that the existence of the tort of defamation does is to protect privacy or confidentiality. It is true that the tort allows for a remedy in the event that something which is not true is published. This may have a deterrent effect but in order to obtain a remedy, the claimant will be faced with bringing court action which more often than not is likely to have the effect of making even more people aware of the false allegation. We have seen that it is very rarely that an interim injunction will be issued to restrain publication.

Defamation provides no remedy for people who face publication of a fact which they would rather keep private but which is true. Even where the publication relates to a conviction which is 'spent' by virtue of the Rehabilitation of Offenders Act 1974, a defendant who has disclosed the existence of the spent conviction can use it to support a defence of fair comment or justification (s 8(3)), provided the publication was made without malice (s 8(5)).

A person who has something which they choose to hide may have some help available but as we shall see it is very limited.

14.6.2 Privacy

English law does not recognise a general right to privacy. The House of Lords in *Wainright v Home Office* [2004] AC 406; [2003] UKHL 53 considered this in detail and rejected the notion that there was such a right in English law. The European Court of Human Rights in *Wainright v UK* ECHR Application No 12350/04 has subsequently held that there was no breach of Article 3 but there were breaches of Article 8 and of Article 13. This is partly the result of the difficulty in framing an adequate definition. The difficulty is increased when it is remembered that too wide a definition could lead to

- the opening of the floodgates to large volumes of litigation
- an unreasonable restriction on the freedom of the media to report matters of public interest.

Too narrow a definition would fail to give adequate protection in all circumstances.

The issue was considered by the Calcutt Committee in 1990 which was investigating incidents of press intrusion. The Commission did not recommend the creation of a general tort of invasion of privacy considering that the right to privacy could be adequately protected by other means (Report of the Committee on Privacy and Related Matters (1990) Cm 1102).

The issue continues to be one which regularly troubles the courts. In the recent high-profile cases of *Campbell v MGN plc* [2004] 2 AC 457; [2004] 2 WLR 1232; [2004] UKHL 22 and *Douglas and Others v Hello! Ltd and Others* [2003] EWHC 786 (Ch) the judges were all concerned with the problem of giving effect to what they generally viewed as an underlying principle that privacy should be respected and protected. The conclusions were that this could be achieved by using existing English law rather than by developing a new general tort. In both cases the courts were prepared to accept that there were breaches of confidence.

Breach of privacy is in fact protected in various ways, most importantly by the development of the equitable remedy available for breach of confidence (see next paragraph). Other protections include

- Trespass to land for example where the media has come onto land to take photographs or seek other 'evidence' although *Bernstein v Skyviews and General Ltd* [1977] QB 479 suggests that this protection can be limited.
- Breach of copyright as for example in *Williams v Settle* [1960] 1 WLR 1072 where a claimant obtained damages for unauthorised use of a photograph in which he owned the copyright. (See also Copyright, Designs and Patents Act 1988 s 85 which gives the person who commissions a photograph or film for private and domestic purposes a right of privacy, in that publication of the work without consent is unlawful.)
- Breach of contract provides a simple remedy where the terms of the agreement are clear and impose a duty of confidentiality.
- Various statutes may also provide protection by regulating the way in which and the purposes for which information may be obtained (for example the Interception of Communications Act 1985 regulates the use of telephone tapping and the Data Protection Act 1998 sets out a detailed scheme for obtaining, storing and use of personal data).

14.6.3 Confidentiality

Breach of confidence is a concept established in equity and has not yet been recognised as a tort. Many cases are based on breach of confidentiality in commercial and business cases which often involve industrial espionage or inappropriate disclosure of information to a rival concern. These are not dealt with in this book. The concept is also available to those whose personal privacy has been invaded or is threatened by disclosure of information which they regard as private. The general circumstances were explained in *Argyll v Argyll* [1967] Ch 302. Mr Justice Ungoed-Thomas explained

JUDGMENT

'(1) . . . a contract or obligation of confidence need not be expressed but can be implied . . . ;

(2) . . . a breach of confidence . . . can arise independently of any right of property or contract . . . ;

(3) . . . the court in the exercise of its equitable jurisdiction will restrain a breach of confidence independently of any right at law.'

While the action remains rooted in equity, it will continue to allow the principle of privacy to be protected in various novel circumstances arising in a fast-changing world.

The right to confidentiality can be over-ridden where this is necessary on the ground of public interest. We have already seen the difficulties faced by the courts in such cases, especially when a balance has to be found between the public interest in maintaining a free press and the private rights of individuals. An interesting example is found in

CASE EXAMPLE

X v Y [1988] 2 All ER 648

A newspaper had found out that two doctors at a local hospital were being treated for AIDS. The paper argued that the names of the doctors should be disclosed in the public interest, that is so that patients could decide whether or not to be treated by the doctors.

Mr Justice Rose stated that he kept in the forefront of his mind 'the very important public interest in freedom of the press' but went on to say

JUDGMENT

'. . . in my judgment those public interests are substantially outweighed when measured against the public interests in relation to loyalty and confidentiality both generally and with particular reference to AIDS patients' hospital records.'

The judge was also concerned that to leave AIDS patients vulnerable to disclosure of their medical records would act as a deterrent to others who would be reluctant to come forward to seek diagnosis. Public interest would be better served by diagnosis of as many as possible of those infected by the disease.

14.6.4 Human rights

It is popularly thought that Article 8 of the Convention on Human Rights grants a right to privacy. In fact it guarantees a right to 'respect for private and family life'. We have seen in Chapter 1 that Article 8 can be used in a very wide range of cases. In the context of privacy, the European Court of Human Rights has considered the extent to which protection of privacy is granted.

CASE EXAMPLE

Peck v UK [2003] ECtHR, 36 EHRR 41

The claimant, while suffering from depression, was walking in a town centre with a knife in his hand and attempted to cut his wrists. The fact that he was carrying a knife was picked up on CCTV and the police were sent. The claimant received necessary help. The film was subsequently used to promote the use of CCTV and still photographs were published in a local paper. In neither case was the claimant masked and indeed people recognised him. The UK courts, while sympathetic to the claimant, found that he had no remedy. The claimant applied to the European Court alleging breach of Article 8.

Noting that the claimant did not allege that the use of CCTV as such infringed his rights under Article 8, the Court held that 'the disclosure of [the] record of his movements to the public in a manner in which he could never have foreseen' gave rise to such infringement.

JUDGMENT

'The disclosure . . . of the relevant footage constituted a serious interference with the . . . right to respect for his private life.'

14.6.5 Conclusion

The debate about privacy will continue but evidence to date suggests that the concept of privacy will continue to be regarded as a principle which underpins other aspects of the law. Equity is flexible so that confidentiality can be protected and the effect of Article 8 is gradually being understood in the context of English law. What is certain is that statute will play an important part. The Data Protection Act 1998 and the Freedom of Information Act 2000 have now been fully implemented. It may be that the statutory provisions and the codes of practice which are being developed at the present time will make a substantial contribution to the establishment of some clear rules.

ACTIVITY

Self-assessment questions

1. Why may a claimant be unable to obtain an interim injunction to restrain publication of defamatory material about the claimant?
2. When will the courts be likely to award exemplary damages for defamation?
3. Explain the equitable remedy for breach of confidentiality and the extent to which this can safeguard privacy of an individual.
4. In what circumstances is it likely that Article 8 of the European Convention of Human Rights will be used successfully to protect privacy?

SAMPLE ESSAY QUESTION

Discuss the extent to which the law on defamation achieves a balance between the right of a person to protect his reputation and the right of freedom of speech.

Outline the essential elements for a claim in defamation

- Publication
- Of a defamatory statement
- Referring to the claimant
- With no justification

Distinguish between the two forms

- Libel – permanent form and actionable *per se*
- Slander – transitory form – proof of damage required except imputation of criminal conviction, unfitness for office, contagious disease, unchastity of women
- Discuss any associated problems

Discuss the limitations of the tort

- Truth is always a defence so protects freedom of speech but could damage reputation
- Expensive to bring action so could limit ability to protect reputation
- Reputation is damaged as soon as the defamation occurs – unless prohibitory injunction is possible – but people rarely know about the defamation before publication

Discuss the effect of the defences

- Wide range favours freedom of speech possibly at expense of protecting reputation
- Absolute privilege and qualified privilege support freedom of speech at the expense of reputation
- Question whether fair comment gives too much license to the press and media
- Printed apologies rarely have the same space or impact as the defamatory comment

Discuss other relevant issues

- The difficulty in bringing a class action or being a member of a defamed class
- The rules relating to innuendo make it harder for a claimant to prove the defamation – so more difficult to protect reputation
- Lack of intention is no defence – so this restricts freedom of speech
- The effect of the Human Rights Act

Key facts on defamation

Libel generally	Case/statute
Untrue statement in permanent form Not necessarily in writing – includes broadcasts and TV performance of a play. Film. Actionable *per se*. Can be a crime but rare.	Defamation Act 1952 Theatres Act 1968 *Youssoupoff v MGM* (1934)
Slander generally	**Case/statute**
Untrue statement in transient form. Usually verbal but can be gesture. Actionable only on proof of special damage but note exceptions.	
Elements of defamation	**Case/statute**
Statement must be defamatory. It must refer to claimant. It must be published.	
Meaning of defamatory	**Case/statute**
Statement is untrue. It tends to lower a person in the eyes of others or to expose them to ridicule or contempt or to cause others to shun them. Note problem of deciding who is 'right thinking member of society': the ordinary good and worthy person the ordinary reader who is not unduly suspicious. Additional knowledge held by hearer or reader can make inoffensive statement defamatory.	*Cassell v Broome* (1972) *Parmiter v Coupland* (1840) *Youssoupoff v MGM* (1934) *Byrne v Deane* (1937) *Hartt v Newspaper Publishing* (1989) *Cassidy v Daily Mirror* (1929); *Tolley v Fry & Sons* (1931); *Norman v Future Publishing* (1999)
Reference to claimant	**Case/statute**
Usually explicit. Can be implied from other information.	*Cassidy v Daily Mirror* (1929); *Hulton v Jones* (1910); *Newstead v London Express Newspaper* (1940); *Morgan v Odhams Press* (1971)
Publication	**Case/statute**
Statement must be communicated to a person other than the claimant. Communication between spouses is not publication. Can be liability for unintentional publication where it can be reasonably anticipated that the material will be communicated.	*Huth v Huth* (1915); *Slipper v BBC* (1991)

Defences: Justification	Case/statute
The statement is true in substance.	*Alexander v Eastern Railway* (1865)
The untruthfulness of the statement is clearly stated.	*Charleston v News Group Newspapers* (1995)
Burden on defendant to prove justification.	*Bookbinder v Tebbit* (1989)
Note special provisions concerning criminal convictions.	*Hinds v Sparks* (1964)
	Civil Evidence Act 1968

Defences: Fair comment	Case/statute
Honest comment on a matter of public interest.	
Facts on which comment is based must be indicated expressly or by implication.	*Telnikoff v Matusevitch* (1992)
Facts must be true.	
Statement must be about a matter of public interest in sense that it is something in which the public is legitimately interested in what is going on or what may happen to them – a matter for the judge to decide.	*London Artists v Littler* (1969)
The comment must be honestly made even if no-one else agrees with it – claimant must disprove honesty note that malice will defeat this defence.	*Reynolds v Times Newspapers* (2001); *Thomas v Bradbury Agnew* (1906)

Defences: Absolute privilege	Case/statute
Statement cannot be used as the basis for any legal action.	
Applies to statements in either House of Parliament and to reports, etc published by order of either House.	Bill of Rights 1688; Parliamentary Papers Act 1840
Applies to statements made in proceedings before any court and to fair, accurate and contemporaneous reports of such proceedings.	
Certain communications between officers of state.	*Chatterton v Sec of State for India* (1895)

Defences: Qualified privilege	Case/statute
No action can be based on statement with qualified privilege.	
Statement must be made by someone who has a duty to make it to someone who has a duty to receive it.	*Toogood v Spyring* (1834)
Duty may be legal, moral or social.	*Stuart v Bell* (1891); *Watt v Longsdon* (1930)
Courts have refused to treat specific categories of statements as attracting qualified privilege.	*Watts v Times Newspapers* (1996); *Reynolds v Times Newspapers* (2001)

Defences: Innocent publication	Case/statute
Defendants will not be liable provided they are not the author, publisher or editor of the material, that they took all reasonable care and did not know of the defamatory material.	Defamation Act 1996, s 1
	Vizetelly v Mudie's Select Library (1900)
Defence extends to internet service providers but note	*Godfrey v Demon Internet* (1999)
Defences: Consent	**Case/statute**
Extends to those who are able to exercise editorial control.	
Defences: Offer of amends	**Case/statute**
Defendant acknowledges defamation has occurred but makes written offer to apologise, to publish the correction and to pay compensation and costs.	
Acceptance ends matter.	
Refusal allows offer to be pleaded as defence.	
Defences: Malice	**Case/statute**
Negates qualified privilege.	
Remedies	**Case/statute**
Injunction to prevent repeated publication but rarely available in advance of publication.	*Holley v Smyth* (1998)
Note effect of	European Convention on Human Rights, Art 10
and	Human Rights Act 1998, s 12
Damages – can be exemplary where defendant knew or was reckless that the material was defamatory – a matter for the jury but Court of Appeal has power to review and substitute a lower figure.	

KEY FACTS

Key facts on privacy, confidentiality and human rights

Privacy	Case/statute
No general legal right to privacy.	
Judicial view it is not needed as other parts of the law can be used.	*Campbell v MGN* (2003); *Douglas v Hello!* (2003)
Confidentiality	**Case/statute**
Equity may give remedy for breach of confidence.	*Argyll v Argyll* (1967)
Human rights	**Case/statute**
Protects right to respect for private and family life.	European Convention on Human Rights, Art 8
	Peck v UK (2003)

SUMMARY

- There are two types of defamation: libel (a permanent form) and slander (a transitory form) - libel is actionable *per se* (without proof of damage), but slander is not except where contagious disease, commission of a criminal offence, unchastity in women, or professional unfitness is alleged
- Defamation is defined as a publication to a third party of a defamatory statement which refers to the claimant and with no lawful justification
- A defamatory remark is one that lowers the estimation of the claimant in the minds of right thinking people or would cause them to shun or avoid him
- Implying decency or honesty cannot be defamatory
- Defamation can be by an innuendo
- The claimant must be able to show that the statement referred to him personally so class actions usually fail and only succeed where the claimant can show that he is identifiable as a member of the class
- There are many defences available including: justification (the truth can never be defamatory however hurtful); fair comment – where the press is entitled to express honest opinions on matters of public interest; absolute privilege (generally proceedings in Parliament or in court); qualified privilege (in certain confidential communications between privileged parties); unintentional defamation and innocent dissemination
- Remedies include both damages and injunctions

15

The economic torts

AIMS AND OBJECTIVES

After reading this chapter you should be able to:

- ■ Understand the essential elements for proving deceit
- ■ Understand the essential elements for proving malicious falsehood
- ■ Understand the essential elements for proving passing off
- ■ Understand the essential elements for proving conspiracy and inducing a breach of contract
- ■ Be able to critically analyse each tort
- ■ Be able to apply the law to factual situations and reach conclusions as to liability

We are used to the law of torts dealing with interference that has caused loss or damage to property or physical injury. We have already seen from the law on pure economic loss that the courts are less willing to become involved where economic loss is concerned (see Chapter 6, section 6.2). One of the traditional reasons given for this was that in character such loss was more appropriately compensated in the law of contract.

However, there are a number of torts that can be loosely grouped together and which are concerned with interference with a person's economic interests. They may represent an interference with a person's livelihood and include deceit and malicious falsehood and also can include passing off and a range of other specific ways of interfering with a person's trade.

15.1 Deceit

Deceit has a lot in common with and indeed is often associated with misrepresentation in contract law. It is a well-established tort that occurs when an entirely false representation is made that causes loss to a claimant who relies on the false statement. It was first recognised as early as the eighteenth century.

CASE EXAMPLE

Pasley v Freeman (1789) 3 Term Rep 51

In this case the defendant falsely represented to the claimant that a third party to whom the claimant wished to sell goods on credit was in fact creditworthy. In fact this was entirely false and the claimant suffered loss as a result of the transaction. He was nevertheless able to recover for his loss through the tort of deceit.

The significance of the tort is that a successful claimant is able to recover not just for financial loss but for physical loss or injury also.

CASE EXAMPLE

Burrows v Rhodes [1899] 1 QB 816

The claimant here was persuaded through a false representation to take part in the 'Jameson Raid'. He was able to recover under the tort for the physical injuries he sustained.

The tort is interrelated with the action for negligent misstatement and with misrepresentation in contract law. On this basis its significance may have reduced somewhat as a result of the *Hedley Byrne* principle and of the Misrepresentation Act 1967 since it is arguably harder to prove than either. However, the tort does enjoy a different measure of damages which may still make it a worthwhile cause of action.

The requirements of the tort of deceit are:

- that the defendant makes a false statement to the claimant or a class of people including the claimant
- that the defendant knows that the statement is false or is reckless in making it
- that the defendant intends that the claimant will rely for his conduct on the false statement
- that the claimant does indeed suffer damage as a result of having relied on the statement.

The making of a false statement

Generally a misrepresentation must concern a material fact in order to be actionable and must not be only a mere opinion.

CASE EXAMPLE

Bisset v Wilkinson [1927] AC 177

Here in response to a request by the purchaser of land the vendor made a false statement concerning the number of sheep that the land being sold would support. There was no liability. The statement could not be relied upon since the vendor had no knowledge or expertise in the area and it was merely an unsupported opinion.

Of course a misrepresentation concerning a material fact may be actionable where the person making it has specialist knowledge.

CASE EXAMPLE

Esso v Marden [1976] QB 801

In this case the petrol company represented the likely sales of petrol to the person who was contracting to take a franchise of a petrol station. The statement could be relied upon because of the superior specialist expertise of the party making it.

While opinions are not classed as statements of fact it may be a false statement of fact to misrepresent an opinion or knowledge which is not actually held.

CASE EXAMPLE

Edgington v Fitzmaurice (1885) 29 Ch D 459

The directors of a company falsely stated that a loan would be used to improve the company. In fact their intention all along was to use the money to repay very serious debts that were owed by the company. The misrepresentation of a future intent in these circumstances was sufficient to amount to an actionable falsehood.

It will also amount to a false statement to fail to correct a true statement that has later become false.

CASE EXAMPLE

With v O'Flanagan [1936] Ch 575

A doctor was selling his practice which was said during the negotiations for the sale to be worth an annual income of £2,000. The practice actually lost patients, and thus income, prior to the completion and the doctor's failure to inform the purchaser of this fact amounted to an actionable misrepresentation.

It is also possible that a person who makes a false statement can be personally liable for deceit even though the misrepresentation is made on behalf of another party if all of the other elements of the tort are satisfied.

CASE EXAMPLE

Standard Chartered Bank v Pakistan National Shipping Line (Nos 2 and 4) [2002] 3 WLR 1547

A company, Oakprime Ltd, agreed to supply bitumen to a Vietnamese buyer with payment to be by letter of credit issued by Vietnamese bankers and confirmed by the claimant bank. The letter of credit required delivery before a specific date but loading of the bitumen was delayed until after that date. Mr Mehra, the managing director of Oakprime, then agreed with the shippers to insert a false shipping date in the documents. The claimant bank then authorised payment but was unable to recover from the Vietnamese bank because it had failed to notice that the documents were not in order. The claimant successfully sued both the shippers and Mehra. Mehra was held liable even though he had engaged in the deceit for the company. The court rejected a defence of contributory negligence since the defence was held not to be available in the case of a fraudulent misrepresentation.

Knowledge that the statement is false

The appropriate test of knowledge is the classic definition explained by Lord Herschell in *Derry v Peek* (1889) 14 App Cas 337. The test identifies the need to show a fraud which is hard to show.

CASE EXAMPLE

Derry v Peek (1889) 14 App Cas 337

A tram company was licensed to operate horse drawn trams by Act of Parliament. Under the Act the company would also be able to use mechanical power by first gaining a certificate from the Board of Trade. The company made an application and also issued a prospectus to raise further share capital. In this, honestly believing that permission would be granted, the company falsely represented that it was able to use mechanical power. In the event the application was denied and the company fell into liquidation. Peek, who had invested on the strength of the representation in the prospectus and lost money, sued. His action failed since there was insufficient proof of fraud. Lord Herschell in the House of Lords defined the action as requiring actual proof that the false representation was made '. . . knowingly or without belief in its truth or recklessly careless whether it be true or false.'

The test required that fraud must be proved which would mean that the misrepresentation had been made:

- knowingly or
- without belief in its truth or
- reckless as to its truth.

It would appear that where an employee acts in the course of his employment in committing a deceit then the employer is likely to be vicariously liable for the false statement. The same principle is likely to apply in the case of agents and their principals also.

Intention that the statement should be acted upon

For the deceit to be actionable the defendant must also have intended that the statement would be acted upon. However, only those people falling within the class that intended to act upon the statement are able to sue.

CASE EXAMPLE

Peek v Gurnley (1873) LR 6 HL 377

Statements in a share prospectus were not intended to be acted upon other than by those to whom the prospectus was actually issued. As a result the court could not find that there was any liability for deceit.

In this way the representation need not be made personally to the person who relied on its truth.

CASE EXAMPLE

Langridge v Levy (1837) 2 M & W 519

The claimant bought a gun from the defendant who knew that the claimant intended his son to use it. The defendant falsely stated that the gun was sound and when the gun blew up in the son's face injuring him the defendant was held to be liable.

However, for the false statement to be actionable it is insufficient merely that it is foreseeable that the claimant might act on the statement.

CASE EXAMPLE

Caparo v Dickman [1990] 1 All ER 568

Here shareholders in a company bought more shares and then made a successful take-over bid for the company. When they wished to back out of the takeover they failed in their claim that they relied on the audited accounts prepared by the defendants that had shown a sizeable surplus rather than the deficit that was in fact the case. The House of Lords decided that the false statement could not found an action since the company accounts were a requirement of company law and are not prepared for those taking over the company. The fact that it was foreseeable that there was a possibility of the claimants relying on the audit was insufficient on its own for liability. It must have been in the defendant's mind at the time of the falsehood that the claimant was intended to rely on the falsehood.

Reliance on the statement

Actual reliance is also a necessary feature of the tort. The claimant must show that he did in fact act on the statement and suffer detriment as a result.

CASE EXAMPLE

Smith v Chadwick (1884) 9 App Cas 187

The claimant bought shares in a company whose prospectus falsely stated that a certain known influential person was a director of the company. In fact this false statement was of no significance at all since it was shown that the claimant had not in fact heard of that person and so could not have relied on the statement in entering the transaction. There was no liability.

The false statement need not be the only reason that the claimant acted as he did. It is sufficient in demonstrating reliance that it was one reason for acting.

Damage suffered by the plaintiff

For any action the claimant must inevitably have suffered loss or damage as a result of relying on the false statement for his course of conduct. The loss may be economic loss, or personal injury or property damage or indeed even distress and inconvenience.

CASE EXAMPLE

Archer v Brown [1984] 2 All ER 267

The claimant entered a partnership as a result of the defendant's deceit. In his successful action the court held that he should recover the cost of shares, interest on a loan needed to buy the shares, as well as loss of earnings and damages for injury to feelings all of which were losses caused by the deceit.

The claimant is able to recover for all losses that can be seen as a direct consequence of the deceit.

CASE EXAMPLE

Doyle v Olby (Ironmongers) Ltd [1969] 2 QB 158

In this case Lord Denning indicated that the measure of recoverable loss was based on direct consequences irrespective of whether or not the loss was foreseeable. The case involved a deceit made during the sale of a business that the business involved counter sales when it was in fact based on employment of a sales representative. The claimant was able to recover a sum equivalent to the difference in the value of the business acquired from that represented as being true during the sale and also expenditure in running the business, including the cost of employing a representative. The measure of damages was thus far superior to that which would have applied to the breach of contract.

ACTIVITY

Self-assessment questions

1. Is the action for deceit still relevant since *Hedley Byrne* and the Misrepresentation Act 1967?
2. What effect does specialist knowledge have in bringing an action for deceit?
3. What state of mind must a defendant have in order to be liable for deceit?
4. What degree of reliance does the claimant have to show in order to recover on the deceit?
5. For what loss can a claimant recover in a deceit action?

Deceit	Case
The tort has a lot in common with misrepresentation.	
The requirements of the tort of deceit are:	
The defendant makes a false statement to the claimant or a class of people including the claimant.	*Derry v Peek* (1889)
The defendant knows that the statement is false or is reckless in making it.	*Derry v Peek* (1889)
The defendant intends that the claimant will rely for his conduct on the false statement.	*Peek v Gurnley* (1873)
The claimant does rely on the false statement.	*Smith v Chadwick* (1884)
The claimant suffers damage as a result.	*Archer v Brown* (1984)
Damages can be recovered for all loss that is a natural consequence of the breach.	*Doyle v Olby (Ironmongers)* (1969)

In simple diagram form the tort can be shown as follows:

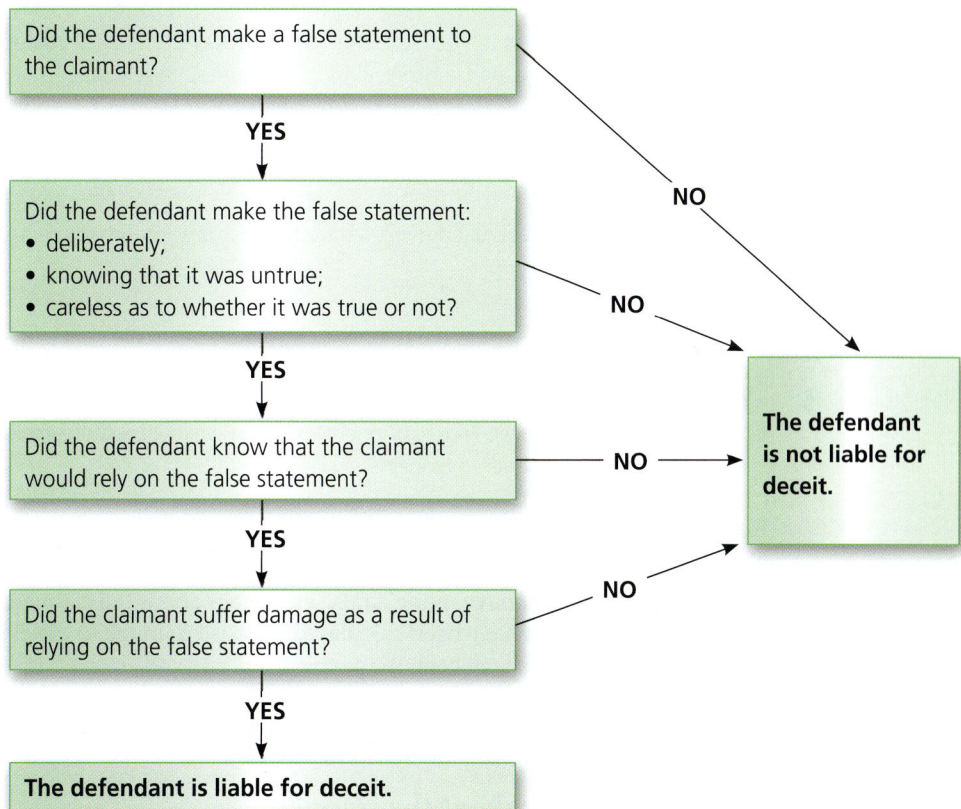

Figure 15.1 Liability for deceit

15.2 Malicious falsehood

Introduction

The tort is in fact probably less an individual tort in its own right and more a generalisation of specific cases and is also sometimes referred to as injurious falsehood. Inevitably it is to do with loss caused to a claimant's livelihood or reputation as a result of a false statement made by another. The significant addition is the 'malice'.

CASE EXAMPLE

Ratcliffe v Evans [1892] 2 QB 524

A newspaper printed an article falsely stating that the claimant had gone out of business. It did so with the intention of causing harm to the claimant and his business. He sued successfully for his resultant business losses. The Court of Appeal distinguished from the very specific requirements of defamation and decided that the tort could result in liability in respect of any malicious statement that resulted in damage even where defamation could not be shown.

The tort has its origins in an action formerly referred to as slander of title. This was a very specific action based on the false questioning of a person's title to land with the result that it became less saleable or even unsaleable. In the nineteenth century the tort extended to include slander of goods, based on similar principles.

More recently the tort has developed in a more general sense as a protection of people's economic and commercial interests.

CASE EXAMPLE

Kaye v Robertson [1991] FSR 62

This involved a famous television actor, Gordon Kaye. He was injured and journalists published photographs and a story about his injuries, falsely stating that the story was produced with the actor's permission. An action for malicious falsehood succeeded, the loss being that it prevented him from marketing the story himself and receiving payment for it.

In this way the tort can be used even where the loss is somewhat speculative in character.

CASE EXAMPLE

Joyce v Sengupta [1993] 1 All ER 897 CA

Here the claimant had been falsely accused in a newspaper article of stealing private letters from her former employer, Princess Anne. Her action was successful because of the potential damage to her employment prospects.

Even though it is potentially very broad in its scope, the tort has a number of distinct elements:

- The defendant must have made a false statement about the claimant.
- The statement must have been calculated to cause damage to the claimant.
- The statement must have been made to a third party.
- The statement must have been made maliciously.
- The statement must have caused damage to the claimant.

A false statement about the claimant

The statement must be false. A mere advertising puff is not accepted as being believable by the courts and so is not actionable, for example 'Carlsberg, probably the best lager in the world' need not be problematic.

However, false statements that actually run down a competitor's goods may well be.

CASE EXAMPLE

De Beers Abrasive Products Ltd v International General Electric Co of New York [1975] 2 All ER 599

Here the defendants published what was alleged to be a 'scientific study' falsely denigrating the claimant's products in order to boost sales of their own products. They were liable under the tort.

Where the statement does not refer to the claimant at all then it will not be actionable even if it causes damage to the claimant.

CASE EXAMPLE

Cambridge University Press v University Tutorial Press (1928) 45 RPC 335

The claimants argued that they had suffered damage when the defendants had falsely stated that it was their own book that was recommended by an examination board, when in fact it was the claimants' book that was recommended. There could be no liability within the tort since there had been no reference to the claimants, even though they had allegedly suffered a loss of sales.

Calculated to cause damage to the plaintiff

The word calculated in the context of the tort merely means that loss or damage to the claimant was foreseeable.

In this way only specific references to the claimant rather than general ones are likely to be actionable. Two cases can be compared on this point.

CASE EXAMPLE

Lyne v Nicholls (1906) 23 TLR 86

False and derogatory remarks made by a newspaper about the circulation of one of its rivals were specific and were, therefore, actionable.

CASE EXAMPLE

White v Mellin [1895] AC 154 HL

Here labels attached to containers of baby food stated that it was better than any other baby food. The statement was very general in character and as such did not attach any liability.

Statement made to a third party

Although different in other ways, the tort has some similarity with defamation. One of the obvious common characteristics is the requirement of publication of the statement to a third party.

The reasoning behind this requirement is that the claimant is only likely to suffer loss or damage if the false statement has had an impact on third parties.

The presence of malice

To succeed, the claimant must also show that the statement was made with malice and has the burden of proof on this.

Malice, as elsewhere in tort, is a difficult concept to define. It need not necessarily involve dishonesty on the part of the defendant. It does, however, involve the absence of just cause or of belief in the statement.

CASE EXAMPLE

Joyce v Motor Surveys Ltd [1948] Ch 252

The defendant wished to evict the claimant from a tenancy in order that he could sell the property with vacant possession. The defendant then falsely informed the Post Office that the claimant had changed address and also falsely stated to the Tyre Manufacturers Association that the claimant had ceased trading as a retailer of tyres. Both statements were clearly false and there could have been no belief in their truth. The defendant was held to have acted with malice and was liable for malicious falsehood.

Damage actually suffered by the claimant

The claimant also has to show that he suffered actual loss. The loss need not be a particular loss as in loss of a specific customer. A more general loss as in a reduction in overall takings is sufficient. The damage can include damage to property as well as a pecuniary loss.

The test of remoteness of damage is based on reasonable foreseeability. In certain circumstances there is no requirement for the claimant to prove special damage:

■ Where the statement is in a written or permanent form and was calculated to cause a pecuniary loss.
■ Where the statement was calculated to cause a pecuniary loss to the claimant in respect of any office or profession, calling, trade, or business he is in at the time of its publication – this is by s 3(1) Defamation Act 1952.

It is at times of course advantageous to sue in defamation instead of for damages for malicious falsehood.

CASE EXAMPLE

Fielding v Variety Incorporated [1967] 2 QB 841

The defendants in their magazine published a false statement about the play Charlie Girl and called it a 'disastrous flop' when it was in fact a success. The claimant was able to recover £1,500 in defamation but only £100 in malicious falsehood because the former included a sum for injury to feelings where the latter was based purely on the actual loss.

ACTIVITY

Self-assessment questions

1. What was the original purpose of an action for malicious falsehood?
2. Is this purpose still the same or has it changed?
3. What exactly does malice mean for the purposes of the action?
4. What advantages are there in bringing such an action rather than claiming under defamation?

```
┌──────────────────────────────────────┐
│ Does the defendant make a false        │
│ statement about the claimant?          │
└──────────────────────────────────────┘
              │ YES
              ▼
┌──────────────────────────────────────┐
│ Is the false statement calculated to   │
│ cause harm to the claimant?            │
└──────────────────────────────────────┘
              │ YES
              ▼
┌──────────────────────────────────────┐
│ Is the statement made to a third party?│
└──────────────────────────────────────┘
              │ YES
              ▼
┌──────────────────────────────────────┐
│ Is the defendant malicious in making    │
│ the statement?                         │
└──────────────────────────────────────┘
              │ YES
              ▼
┌──────────────────────────────────────┐
│ Does the claimant suffer damage as a    │
│ result?                                │
└──────────────────────────────────────┘
              │ YES
              ▼
┌──────────────────────────────────────┐
│ The defendant may be liable in the tort │
│ of malicious falsehood                 │
└──────────────────────────────────────┘
```

NO (from each question) → **The defendant will not be liable for malicious falsehood**

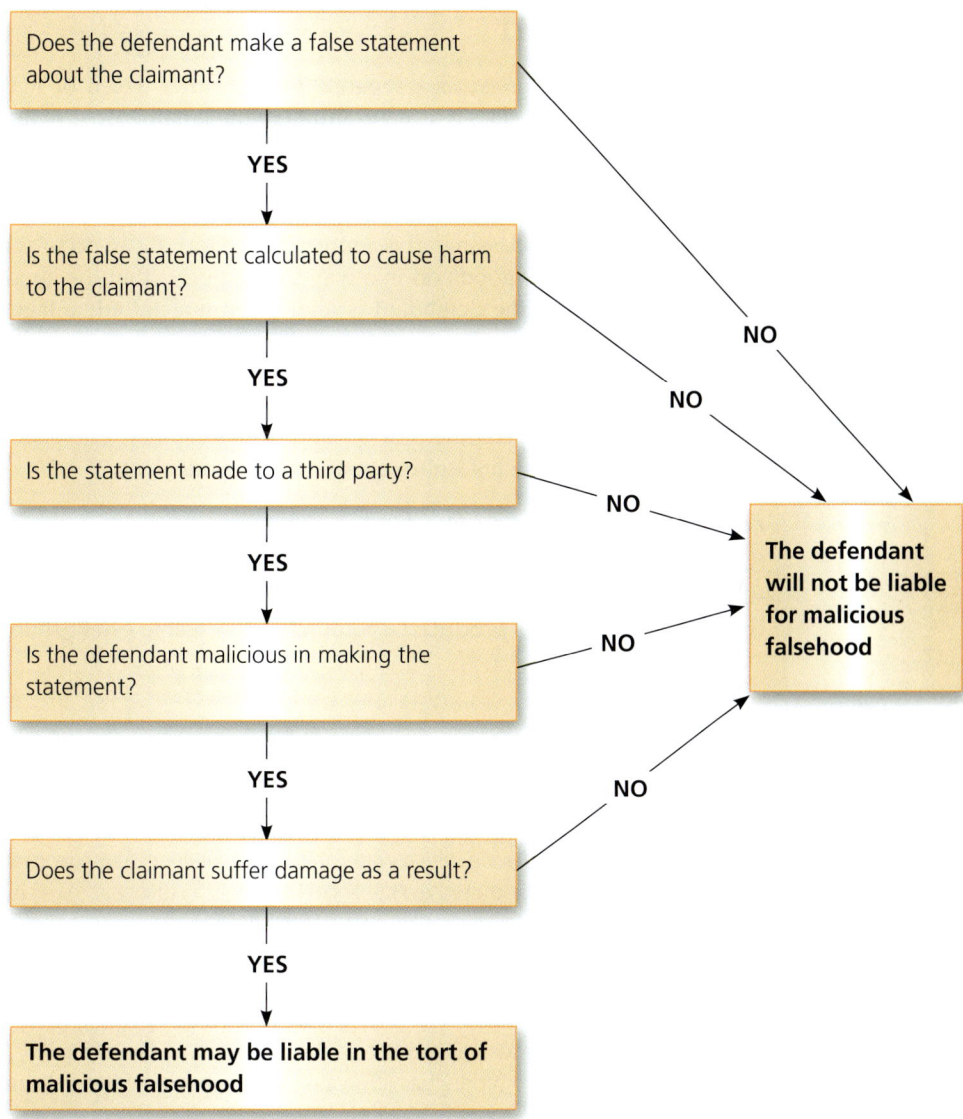

Figure 15.2 Diagram illustrating the essential elements for a claim in the tort of malicious falsehood

KEY FACTS

Malicious falsehood	Case/statute
A general class of torts covering loss to reputation through false statements – the elements are:	*Ratcliffe v Evans* (1892)
The defendant made a false statement about the claimant.	*De Beers Abrasive Products Ltd v International General Electric Co of New York* (1975)
The statement was calculated to cause damage to the claimant.	
The statement was made to a third party.	
The statement was made with malice.	*Joyce v Motor Surveys Ltd* (1948)
The statement caused damage to the claimant.	*Fielding v Variety Incorporated* (1967)

15.3 Passing off

Passing off is often classed as a separate tort to either deceit or malicious falsehood, although some writers class it as an example of the latter. It does in any case have much in common with these two torts.

Where deceit refers to those situations where a person is specifically a victim of a misrepresentation causing him loss and where malicious falsehood is concerned with any loss of reputation, passing off is a more precise tort. It can occur when the defendant has literally passed his goods off in a way that suggests that the goods are those of the claimant. In this way the defendant is taking commercial advantage of the claimant's goodwill or commercial reputation and in effect profiting from it.

Traditionally the tort would involve the defendant using the claimant's brand name or trademark in order to fool a customer into purchasing goods. As such in effect then it amounts to an unfair trading practice and is unacceptable and actionable because the claimant is likely to lose his legitimate trade as a result.

The characteristics of the tort

The tort has developed to include a variety of situations in which the defendant can be said to be trading unfairly at the expense of the claimant's legitimate business interests. The House of Lords has produced a comprehensive test to establish the tort.

CASE EXAMPLE

Erven Warnink BV v J Townend & Sons (Hull) Ltd [1979] AC 731

The claimants were the manufacturers of 'advocaat', an alcoholic drink made from egg yolks, spirit and wines. The defendants had for many years produced a drink called 'egg-flip', made from eggs and fortified wine which was significantly cheaper than advocaat. The defendants then introduced a drink known as 'Keeling's Old English Advocaat', which had the effect of capturing some of the advocaat market in the UK. The claimants sought an injunction to restrain the defendants from using the name 'advocaat', which they believed was specifically identified with their product. The House of Lords considered that nobody would be deceived into thinking that they were in fact buying Dutch advocaat. Nevertheless, the House also held that advocaat was still seen as a particular kind of drink and so the public had indeed been induced into buying the product as advocaat at the expense of the claimant's trade.

Lord Diplock in his judgment identified that the true test for passing off contained five essential elements:

- a basic misrepresentation
- made by a trader in the course of pursuing his trade
- directed towards prospective customers or ultimate consumers of his products
- that was calculated to, or would foreseeably damage the business of another trader
- and that damage was in fact caused to the trader bringing the action.

The ways of committing the tort (the basic misrepresentation)

The tort is about misrepresenting the truth in order to take advantage of the claimant's trade and goodwill. In this way the misrepresentation can actually arise in a number of different ways.

■ By using the claimant's trade name.

CASE EXAMPLE

Maxim's Ltd v Dye [1977] 1 WLR 1155

Here the defendant was prevented from opening a restaurant called 'Maxim's' because there was also a very famous French restaurant called 'Maxim's'. The court held that in the circumstances the public would inevitably be led to believe that the restaurant was associated in some way with the French business.

■ By using the claimant's trademark or brand name.

CASE EXAMPLE

J Bollinger v Costa Brava Wine Co Ltd [1960] Ch 262

Here the defendants were trading a product under the name of Spanish Champagne. Champagne, while it is often used in a general sense to refer to sparkling wines, in fact refers to the sparkling wines of a very specific region of France where the wine is produced by a very specific process, 'methode champenoise'. The defendants were held not to be able to apply the word champagne to their product which was merely taking advantage of the goodwill of the other product.

■ By claiming that the goods are those produced by the claimant when they in fact are not.

CASE EXAMPLE

Lord Byron v Johnston (1816) 2 Mer 29

Here the defendant sold books of poems and advertised them as being the works of Lord Byron, when someone else in fact wrote them. The court held that there was a clear misrepresentation designed to take advantage of a famous name.

■ By imitating the appearance of the claimant's product.

CASE EXAMPLE

Reckitt & Coleman Products v Borden Inc [1990] 1 All ER 873, HL

Here the claimants, among other things, were producers of lemon juice. They had marketed their product for more than 30 years in a yellow plastic container shaped like a lemon and thus the public very clearly identified with their product. When the defendants also sold lemon juice in a similar container the House of Lords held that this was passing off. The claimants were entitled to protect the very distinctive and original packaging of the product as well as the product itself. The court felt that it was clear that the public would be induced into believing that the lemon juice was produced by the same manufacturer and that the claimant's trade and goodwill was therefore threatened by the imitation.

■ By imitating the claimant's promotional or advertising material.

CASE EXAMPLE

Cadbury Schweppes Pty Ltd v Pub Squash Co Pty Ltd [1981] 1 All ER 213 PC

Here the claimants had introduced a new canned lemon drink, 'Solo', using an extensive and very effective television and radio advertising campaign to do so. The following year the defendants introduced a similar product, 'Pub Squash', and also advertised on both television and radio using very similar material and even slogans. The court was prepared to accept that such behaviour could amount to passing off. However, the case itself failed because the court was unable to find that there was in fact a specific misrepresentation that would have induced the public into believing that the goods were the claimants'. There was no possibility that the public would be confused into thinking that the two products were in fact the same.

■ By using a product name too similar to that used by the claimant.

CASE EXAMPLE

United Biscuits (UK) Ltd v Asda Stores Ltd [1997] RPC 513

Here the defendants produced and advertised a chocolate biscuit which they called 'Puffin'. The claimants had for a long time produced and sold a very popular chocolate biscuit snack called 'Penguin'. The court was prepared to accept that the two names were too close together and that the public could be deceived into believing that they were connected and that as a result the claimants' trade and goodwill was threatened. The product name was therefore held to amount to passing off.

The list is not exhaustive. Anything that imitates, or takes advantage of the claimant's product or even that suggests that the claimant's product is in any way inferior and that would have the effect of taking advantage of the claimant's trade or goodwill could amount to a passing off and be actionable as a result.

The other essential elements

It will not be a passing off unless the party accused is taking advantage of the claimant's goodwill for his own profit and is therefore passing off, unless the event occurs within a trade. Nevertheless, trade is quite liberally defined but not to the extent that it will cover every activity.

CASE EXAMPLE

Kean v McGivan [1982] FSR 119, CA

Here a political party was not able to protect itself against another person calling his own party the Social Democrat Party even though this could in effect lead to confusion. The court held that the concept of 'trade' did not extend this far.

The passing off must also be aimed at the customers or eventual consumers of the claimant's products for it to be actionable. Where the claimant and the defendant are involved in totally different businesses or activities then the court will not accept that damage could be caused to the claimant and there will be no actionable passing off.

CASE EXAMPLE

McCullough v May [1947] 2 All ER 845

A children's radio programme of the time was hosted by a person who was affectionately known as 'Uncle Mac'. The broadcaster failed in his attempt to show that a company producing a breakfast cereal which it called 'Uncle Mac's Puffed Wheat' could interfere with or take advantage of the goodwill that he had built up with the listening audience. The court held that there was no passing off because, even though the name was similar, it could not be shown to be aimed at the listeners in order to take advantage of the presenter's name.

The next requirement is at the very heart of passing off. The misrepresentation must be calculated to harm the trade or goodwill of the claimant. In this sense the tort is different to deceit where the intention to deceive is an essential element. With passing off the important thing is only that a misrepresentation has been made that will foreseeably deceive the customer of the claimant's product. If the consumer is unlikely to be confused by the misrepresentation then there can be no actionable passing off.

CASE EXAMPLE

Newsweek Inc v BBC [1979] RPC 441

An action was bought against the BBC on the basis that calling a news and current affairs programme 'Newsweek' injured the trade and goodwill of the claimants, who for some time had published a magazine of the same name. The court would not accept that there was a passing off because it would not be foreseeable that the readers of a magazine could confuse the product with a programme. The two were too distinctly different.

Finally it is sufficient that damage is a probable result of the passing off. There is no requirement that the claimant should show actual damage. To hold otherwise would prevent the most usual remedy, an injunction, from having any great effect. In *H P Bulmer Ltd and Showerings Ltd v Bollinger SA* [1978] RPC 79, CA the use of the term 'Champagne' could obviously have a misleading and damaging effect when applied to an inferior product. The key point of the action is that the defendant has taken unfair advantage of a market that has been created by another party.

Defences and remedies

While a number of defences may be possible, the obvious and potentially the most effective defence is consent. If the claimant is a willing participant to the deception then he cannot complain afterwards that it is unfair.

There are two potential remedies:

- damages
- injunction.

In the case of damages the claimant will obviously be seeking compensation for the loss of profits suffered as a result of any passing off and may also obtain damages for loss of reputation. It is also possible to use the equitable remedy of account on the profits made by the defendant out of the deception.

In the case of an injunction this will be used as a remedy to restrain the defendant from practising the deception. In this way the claimant is able to prevent the misrepresentation and protect his trade and goodwill.

ACTIVITY

Self-assessment questions

1. What is a defendant actually doing in order to be classed as 'passing off'?
2. What is the defendant hoping to achieve by the 'passing off'?
3. How does the effect of the deception differ between passing off and deceit?
4. In what ways is an injunction the best remedy for passing off?

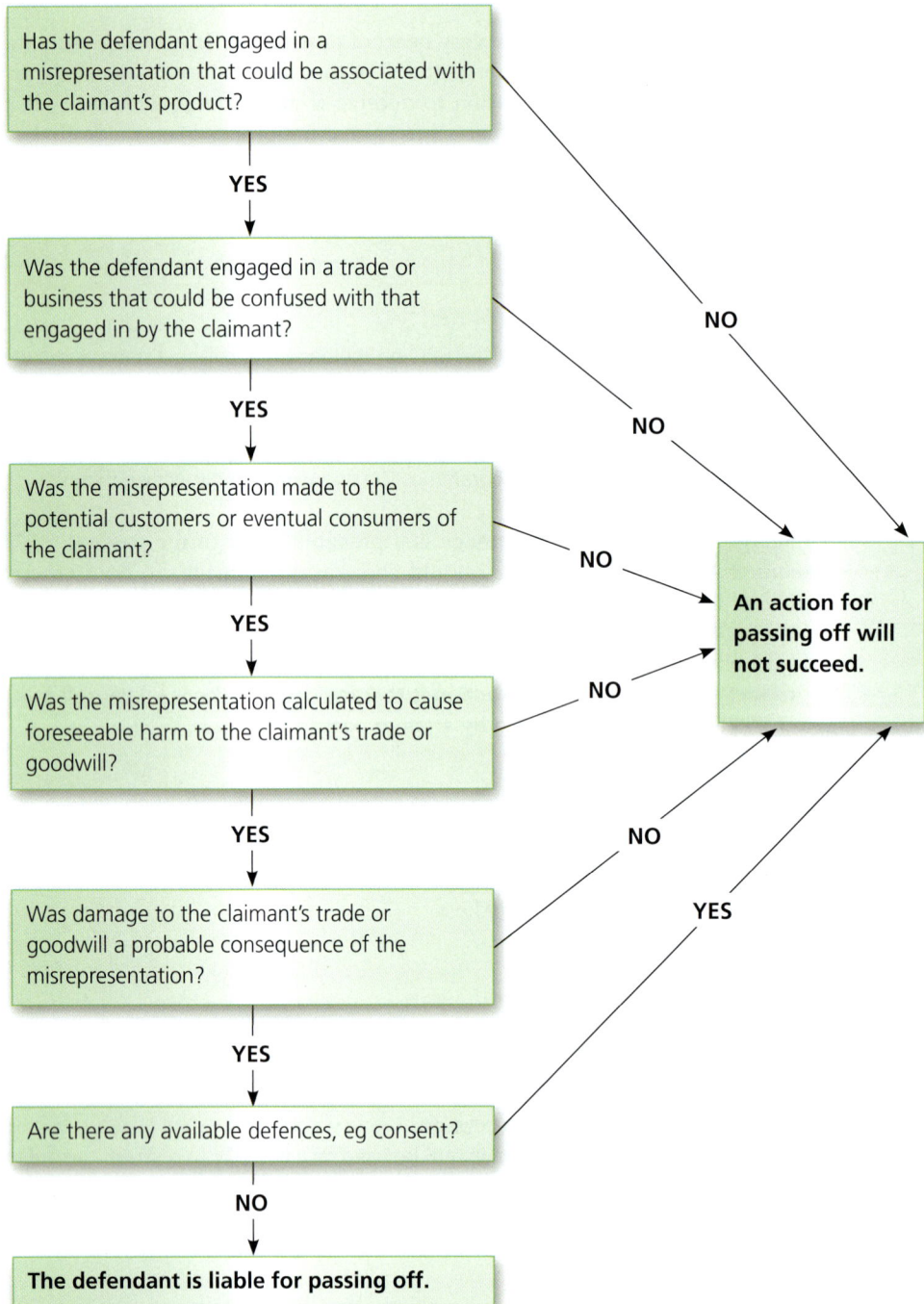

Figure 15.3 How an action for passing off is proved

Passing off	Case/statute
Occurs where the defendant through misrepresentation unfairly takes advantage of the claimant's trade or goodwill causing damage – the elements of the tort are defined in the misrepresentation, eg	*Erven Warnink BV v J Townend & Sons (Hull) Ltd* (1979)
using the claimant's trade name or	*Maxim's Ltd v Dye* (1977)
imitating the appearance of the claimant's product or	*Reckitt & Coleman Products v Borden Inc* (1990)
using a product name too similar to that used by the claimant.	*United Biscuits (UK) Ltd v Asda Stores Ltd* (1997)
The defendant must be acting in a trade or business.	*Kean v McGivan* (1982)
The misrepresentation is directed at the claimant's customers.	*McCullough v May* (1947)
The misrepresentation must be calculated to damage the claimant's trade or goodwill.	*Newsweek Inc v BBC* (1979)
It is sufficient that damage is a foreseeable consequence.	*H P Bulmer Ltd and Showerings Ltd v Bollinger SA* (1978)

15.4 Interference with trade

15.4.1 Introduction

This heading includes a strange and uncertain group of torts some of which were in former times used freely but have been overtaken by statutory rules, particularly those governing the actions of trade unions in trying to advance the conditions of their members. The common characteristic is that they concern interference with a person's trade or business by means other than a false representation that seems to characterise the three distinct torts in the three previous sections.

In the nineteenth century actions for numerous different torts were bought but there were two main ones:

- conspiracy
- inducement to a breach of contract.

Both were used successfully over a long period of time. More recently Lord Diplock suggested that there is a general class of torts of interfering with the trade or business of another person by doing unlawful acts (see *Merkar Island Shipping Corporation v Laughton* [1983] 2 AC 570).

What would actually fall within this general tort is unclear. Quite clearly a party will be held liable in tort for unlawful acts that damage a person's economic interests. However, there are problems in defining precisely what economic interests can be protected and what amounts to unlawful means.

With the former there may be a difficulty in showing that conspiracy and inducing a breach of contract are covered. The requirements of both conspiracy and inducing a breach of contract are quite specific and the torts possibly still exist independently.

With the latter there may for instance be the problem of demonstrating that statutory crimes also give rise to civil liability. At one point at least intimidation might have come within the necessary unlawful means in certain circumstances where there is a third party involved.

> ### *Rookes v Barnard* [1964] AC 1129
>
> At one time it was possible for trade unions to operate what was known as a 'closed shop'. By agreement with the employer all employees of a business were required to be members of a trade union. The union in question threatened a strike against an employer unless it dismissed an employee who had left the union. The employer did so and the employee then sued the employer. The House of Lords applied the law of intimidation and held that the union, by threatening an unlawful breach of contract by its members was liable. (The area of such trade union action is now covered by a variety of statutory rules.)

15.4.2 Conspiracy

A conspiracy in this context generally occurs when two or more people agree to injure another person in the course of his trade that will cause damage as a result.

There are three essential elements to the tort:

■ The conspiracy itself – this is a combination of parties with a common purpose (conspiracy law has been used to control a variety of combinations for unlawful purposes besides just a conspiracy that is aimed at harming someone's trade).
■ The purpose of the conspiracy – that the claimant's trade should be damaged.
■ That there is no justification for this – the law is not seeking to prevent competition, even fierce competition, but to prevent unlawful means being used.

The conspiracy

The conspiracy is rarely hard to show as it is merely a joining together with a common purpose to harm the other party. It might include husbands and wives (*Midland Bank Trust Co Ltd v Green (No 3)* [1982] Ch 529); and directors of a company (*Belmont Finance Corporation Ltd v Williams Furniture Ltd* [1979] Ch 250); and a variety of other combinations.

The important point is that the conspiracy has an unlawful purpose that is aimed at harming another party's trade.

The purpose of the conspiracy

Where a 'simple' conspiracy is involved (where the act is not unlawful in itself) the courts will only accept that the tort has been committed where the clear and major purpose of the combination is to damage the claimant's trade.

> ### *Crofter Hand Woven Harris Tweed Co Ltd v Veitch* [1942] AC 435
>
> The claimants produced tweed cloth in the Outer Hebrides for export using spun yarn from mainland Scotland. The defendants were trade union officials working for a rival firm that, as did most local firms, used yarn that was spun on the island. This firm was rejecting the men's demand for a wage rise, arguing that the competition provided by the claimants made it impossible. The union officials then pressured dockers at the port not to handle the yarn imported by the claimants, though the dockers were not in breach of contract when they agreed to do this. The claimants sought to prevent what they argued was an actionable conspiracy. The House of Lords considered that the major purpose of the combination was to promote the interests of the defendants, not to damage the claimants' interests, and the action failed.

In simple conspiracy therefore it will not matter that the conspirators are protecting their own interests if the major purpose of the conspiracy is damaging another party's trade. If that is the case then the conspiracy is actionable.

At one point it appeared that there was little difference when the conspiracy is to do an unlawful act by unlawful means. The courts would not accept that the conspiracy was actionable unless the conspiracy to do the unlawful act was not for the purposes of promoting or protecting the interests of the conspirators but was to damage the claimant's trade.

CASE EXAMPLE

Lonrho Ltd v Shell Petroleum Co Ltd (No 2) [1982] AC 173

At one point the government in Rhodesia (now Zimbabwe) had broken away from British rule and unlawfully declared independence. As a result the British Government imposed sanctions preventing UK companies from trading with the illegal regime. The defendants had traded with the regime in breach of the sanctions and made profits as a result that would not be available to those lawfully following the order, including the claimant. The House of Lords, however, held that even though the conspiracy was based on unlawful means, it could not be actionable unless the major purpose was to harm the claimant's trade rather than to advance its own.

The House of Lords has more recently identified that intention and motive are different. In this way where unlawful means are used, the defendant will not be able to excuse these means merely because the major purpose of the conspiracy was to advance the interests of the defendants.

CASE EXAMPLE

Lonrho plc v Fayed [1992] 1 AC 448

Here there was competition for the take-over of the House of Fraser, the chain owning the well-known department store Harrods. The defendant eventually won control and the claimant complained that this was only the result of false representations made to the Secretary of State for Trade and Industry by the defendant. The House of Lords accepted that an actionable conspiracy could be shown whenever there was sufficient proof of intent to harm the claimant's trade, and that, where the conspiracy was effected by unlawful means the fact that this intention to harm the defendant was not the major aim was irrelevant.

Justification

In a simple conspiracy it is sufficient to show that the major purpose of the conspiracy was to promote the interests of the conspirators. If this is shown then the action fails.

In the case of conspiracy by unlawful means it is much more difficult to show justification. In any case the use of the tort may be more limited in the light of the general tort of interference with trade.

15.4.3 Inducing a breach of contract

This tort originally developed so that there would be liability whenever one party knowingly induced a third party to breach his contract with the defendant causing the claimant a loss. Unlike conspiracy it would have been irrelevant whether or not the breach of contract was induced by unlawful means. The law seeks to protect freedom of contract. Once parties have entered a contract then interference with that contract can lead to liability in tort.

The origins of the tort in effect had more to do with the master and servant laws of the nineteenth century, as it had been recognised for some time that there could be liability for enticing a servant away from his master. However, there was no general liability for interference with a contract, but this was eventually developed to give an action to a party who had suffered loss because the other party had been persuaded to breach the contract.

CASE EXAMPLE

Lumley v Gye (1853) 2 E & B 216

A singer who was contracted to sing exclusively for the claimant was persuaded, in breach of that contract, to perform for the defendant. The court accepted that this gave rise to liability.

There are six essential elements to the tort:

- There is a breach of contractual obligations.
- The defendant induces the breach by either direct or indirect means.
- The defendant knows of the contract.
- The defendant intends that the contract should be broken.
- The claimant suffers loss as a result of the breach of contract.
- There is no justification.

Breach of contract

It was originally felt that the tort would only apply in the case of breaches going to the root of the contract and in effect destroying its purpose. However, it is now accepted that any breach of obligations is sufficient.

CASE EXAMPLE

Torquay Hotel Co Ltd v Cousins [1969] 1 All ER 522

During a dispute union action was used to prevent an oil supplier from fulfilling its contract with the claimant. The contract actually included an exclusion clause for damage caused by events beyond either party's control so there was in effect no actual breach of contract. An injunction was still granted to the claimant because there was still in effect interference with the contract. The exclusion clause only meant that the parties could be excused for breaches of their obligations. It did not mean that there were no obligations.

Inducement

The inducement will usually be either of two types:

- the defendant has persuaded a party to breach the contract or the defendant has prevented a party from completing his contract (direct means); or
- the defendant has prevented the party from carrying out his obligations often through industrial action (indirect means).

Lumley v Gye (1853) 2 E & B 216 is a classic example of the defendant persuading a party to breach his contract and the weight of the persuasion can be seen in the financial advantages on offer for breaching the contract. However, the persuasion can take a subtler form.

CASE EXAMPLE

Bent's Brewery Co Ltd v Hogan [1945] 2 All ER 570

Here a trade union official sent a questionnaire to pub managers for details of the trade and profits of the pubs they managed. This was held to have induced the managers into breaching their contracts by encouraging them to disclose confidential information.

Other forms of direct inducement include those making it impossible for a contracting party to perform his contract.

CASE EXAMPLE

GWK Ltd v Dunlop Rubber Co Ltd (1926) 42 TLR 593

Here car manufacturers had contracted with tyre manufacturers to use their tyres on cars exhibited at a motor show. The defendants actually removed those tyres and replaced them with their own. This unlawful action made it impossible for the car manufacturer to keep to their contract and was held to be an actionable inducement to a breach of contract.

Where the inducement is indirect then the inducement must also be achieved through unlawful means for the inducement to a breach of contract to be actionable. Historically many of the cases involve industrial action led by trade unions where members are in dispute with their employers.

CASE EXAMPLE

J T Stratford & Co v Lindley [1965] AC 269

Officials of the Waterman's Union were in dispute with the claimant. They instructed their members not to handle the claimant's barges as a result of which his business was damaged, as he was unable to complete contracts that he had formed with various customers. The House of Lords held that there was an inducement to a breach of contract, the breaches of contract by the union members with their employers, and this made it impossible for the employer to keep contracts with his customers, and that this had been achieved by unlawful means.

Knowledge of the existence of the contract by the defendant

This requirement is inevitably tied in also with the requirement that the defendant intends to cause the loss. It has generally developed that it is sufficient that the defendant has either actual or constructive knowledge of the existence of the contract. It is not for instance necessary that the defendant knew the terms of the contract. In this way it must have been obvious to the union in the *Stratford v Lindley* case that the barge company would have contractual arrangements with customers and that these would be breached and therefore cause loss to the claimants as a result of the industrial action by the members.

The intention that the contract should be breached

It is sufficient that the defendant intends that the contract should be breached. There is no requirement that the defendant should act with malice. Motive is in any case generally taken to be irrelevant in tort.

CASE EXAMPLE

Exchange Telegraph Co v Gregory & Co [1896] 1 QB 147, CA

Here the claimants were in exclusive possession of Stock Exchange prices which they sold under contract to subscribers who agreed not to reveal the information to others. The claimants also published the prices in a newspaper. The defendant, a stockbroker then induced a subscriber to breach the arrangement and used the information for the benefit of his own clients. The court held that there was an actionable inducement to breach of contract.

Damage resulting from the breach of contract

The claimant must show that he has suffered loss resulting from the breach of contract, so standard principles of causation apply.

CASE EXAMPLE

Jones Bros (Hunstanton) Ltd v Stevens [1955] 1 QB 275

The defendant, after hiring an employee, then realised that the employee was in breach of contract with the claimants by working for the defendant. Nevertheless, he continued to employ him. However, there was held to be no actionable inducement to breach of contract because the claimant could not be shown to have suffered damage when it was shown that the employee would not have returned to his employment with the claimant even without the new employment.

Justification

The tort is actionable because there is no justification for the defendant's actions. In rare circumstances, where justification can be shown this might provide a defence.

CASE EXAMPLE

Brimelow v Casson [1924] 1 Ch 302

Here a trade union representing theatrical workers persuaded a theatre manager to breach his contract with a theatrical company that was paying such poor wages that many of its chorus girls were forced into prostitution in order to make ends meet. The court held that the inducement to breach a contract was justified in the circumstances.

The common remedies in the tort are obviously damages or an injunction.

ACTIVITY

Self-assessment questions

1. What is the general characteristic common to all of the cases in this section?
2. What are the essential elements of a conspiracy?
3. What are the essential elements of an inducement to a breach of contract?
4. Why do so many of the cases involve trade unions?
5. What are the problems associated with Lord Diplock's suggestion of a general tort of interfering with trade through unlawful means in the *Merkar* case?

KEY FACTS

Nature of the tort	
There are a number of torts that involve interfering with a person's trade or business by means other than a false representation	
Two traditional ones are conspiracy and inducing a breach of contract	

The elements of conspiracy	Case
Two or more parties agreeing to damage another party's trade.	*Belmont Finance Corporation Ltd v Williams Furniture Ltd* (1979)
The purpose of the conspiracy is to damage the claimant's trade.	*Crofter Hand Woven Harris Tweed Co Ltd v Veitch* (1942)
If the conspiracy involves unlawful means then this is an absolute requirement.	*Lonrho Ltd v Shell Petroleum Co Ltd (No 2)* (1982)
There is no justification.	

The elements of inducement to breach a contract	Case
The defendant induces the breach by either: direct means; or	*GWK Ltd v Dunlop Rubber Co Ltd* (1926)
indirect means.	*J T Stratford & Co v Lindley* (1965)
Knowledge of the existence of the contract.	*J T Stratford & Co v Lindley* (1965)
Intention that the contract should be broken.	*Exchange Telegraph Co v Gregory & Co* (1896)
The breach of contract causes the claimant loss.	*Jones Bros (Hunstanton) Ltd v Stevens* (1955)
There is no justification.	*Brimelow v Casson* (1924)
A general tort	**Case**
Lord Diplock identified that there could be a general class of torts covering causing damage to a person's trade by unlawful means.	*Merkar Island Shipping Corporation v Laughton* (1983)
The scope of this tort is uncertain – it probably cannot cover conspiracy and inducing a breach of contract, and it is uncertain what sorts of loss could be covered and what the definition of unlawful means would include.	

ACTIVITY

Quick quiz

In the following examples consider which economic tort might be involved and the likelihood of a successful claim.

1. Dodi has begun to market a set of computer games covering football, cricket, rugby, athletics and other major sports. He is using the name 'Super Sports' as a brand name. There is already a national company manufacturing and retailing sportswear called 'Super Sports'.

2. Officers of the Allied and Amalgamated Union of Lecturing and Teaching Staff have called on members to strike because the Midshires University is paying its lecturing staff only 70 per cent of the usual rate for lecturing staff in universities.

3. Easyyears is a national company specialising in private warden patrolled residential housing for retired persons. In order to reduce overheads the company set up without gaining local authority licences for health and safety and minimum care standards as required by law. In its share prospectus Easyyears proclaimed to be local authority registered. The company have now had its homes shut because of breaches of safety and care standards after a local authority inspection. Adrian invested in what he thought was a very worthwhile project and has now lost his investment as a result of the local authority action.

4. Alan was a strong applicant for a position as Officer in Charge of a registered charity children's home. He failed to get the position after Belinda falsely stated that he had previous convictions for assaults on young children.

SUMMARY

Deceit
- Similar to misrepresentation but the defendant makes a false statement to the claimant or a class of people including the claimant, knowing that the statement is false or being reckless in making it, intending the claimant to rely on it, and the claimant does so and suffers damage as a result
- Damages are for all loss that is a natural consequence of the breach

Malicious falsehood
- Covers loss to reputation through false statements
- The defendant makes a false statement about the claimant to a third party, calculated to cause damage to the claimant, the statement is made with malice and causes damage to the claimant

Passing off
- Involves unfairly taking advantage of the claimant's trade or goodwill
- The defendant acting in a trade or business misrepresents the truth by using the claimant's trade name or imitating the claimant's product, and directs the misrepresentation at the claimant's customers, and this is calculated to damage the claimant's trade or goodwill

Interference with trade
- There are two main types of interference
- Conspiracy – where two or more parties agree to damage another party's trade
- Inducing a breach of contract – either by direct or indirect means intending that the contract should be broken

Further reading

Cooke, Professor J, *Law of Tort* (6th edn, Pearson, 2003), Chapter 21.
Murray, J, *Street on Torts* (11th edn, Butterworths, 2003), Chapters 7 and 8.

16

Breach of a statutory duty

AIMS AND OBJECTIVES

After reading this chapter you should be able to:

■ Understand the general character of statutory torts
■ Understand the circumstances in which these will give rise to civil liability
■ Be able to critically analyse the area
■ Be able to apply the law to factual situations and reach conclusions as to liability

16.1 Statutes creating civil liability

Commonly statutory duties are regulatory in character and in the case of breach a body such as the Health and Safety Commission will bring an action leading to a criminal sanction, usually a fine. However, often a statute imposing a duty may also give rise to civil liability. The ensuing civil action is then known in tort as an action for breach of a statutory duty.

Such actions can appear very similar to basic negligence actions but can differ in a number of key ways:

■ The standard of care appropriate to the duty is fixed by the statute and so is different from that in negligence where it is measured against the 'reasonable man'.
■ The duty may be strict (in which case there will be no requirement for the claimant to prove that the defendant was negligent); or alternatively the burden of proof may be reversed (in which case it is for the defendant to prove that he did not breach the duty); and either of these, or both, may be advantageous to the claimant by comparison to normal negligence actions.
■ Since the statutes in question are usually regulatory and often criminal in character the existence of civil liability is in any case often debatable.
■ In America a breach of a statutory duty may even be used as conclusive proof of negligence in a civil action – but in England this is not the case, if the statute gives rise to civil liability at all then in effect it gives rise to a separate tort action.

The result of all the above is that it is common to plead such a breach with negligence in the alternative in the same claim.

Certain statutory provisions more obviously concern civil liability than others as when they merely modify the existing common law. An obvious example of this is the Occupiers' Liability Acts 1957 and 1984 and also the Consumer Protection Act 1987, albeit that the latter was introduced to comply with EU legislation.

With others it is much harder to determine that civil liability is intended since the statute is predominantly regulatory and any civil liability that does exist may form only a very minor part of the statute as a whole. An example of this would be the Data Protection Act 1998.

Consequently the area is heavily dependent on statutory interpretation and therefore unpredictable since it is not always possible to assess which rule of interpretation a judge will rely on. Following the judgment in *Pepper v Hart* [1993] 1 All ER 42 there is also the question as to whether *Hansard* should be consulted.

The most common actions in which a claim for breach of statutory duties is made is industrial safety law. This itself runs alongside the basic common law principles of employers' liability (see Chapter 17). There is less evidence of success in other fields of law.

16.2 Proving liability

Actions are more complex than for normal negligence actions since the duty itself is invariably more complex. Claimants have a more complicated series of requirements that must be proved.

These propositions include:

- Does the statute create civil liability?
- Is there a duty of care owed to the claimant?
- Is there a duty of care imposed on the defendant?
- Has the defendant breached that duty by falling below the standard identified in the statute?
- Is the breach of duty the cause of the damage suffered by the claimant?
- Is the damage of a type which is contemplated in the statute?

Does the statute create civil liability?

First of all the claimant has to show that the Act in question actually confers an action for damages. This is not a problem where the Act gives specific guidance, an example of this being the Health and Safety at Work etc Act 1974. Here the general duties contained in ss 1–9 of the Act clearly do not give rise to any civil action because this possibility is expressly excluded by s 47. However, s 47 also states that certain regulations made under the statute do give rise to civil liability unless the regulation states otherwise.

However, problems can occur when the statute is silent on the issue. In this instance it is the role of the court in all cases to give effect to the intention of Parliament and again the claimant is subject to the application of the rules of statutory interpretation. This in itself can and has led to inconsistency in approach.

The modern test of whether a statute gives rise to civil liability is that of Lord Diplock in *Lonrho Ltd v Shell Petroleum Co (No 2)* [1982] AC 173:

- Firstly, the court should presume that if the Act creates an obligation which is enforceable in a specific manner then it is not enforceable in any other manner. In this way if the Act was intended for the general benefit of the community rather than for the granting of individual rights then it will not usually be possible to use the Act to bring an action in tort.

There are two exceptions to this basic principle:

- Where an obligation or prohibition is imposed under the Act to benefit a particular class of individuals.
- Where the provision in the Act created a public right but the claimant suffered particular, direct, and substantial damage different from that which was common to the rest of the public.

The test has been criticised because of two significant problems:

■ It gives the court significant discretion in determining how to define a particular class.
■ There does not appear to be a particular principle to determine the distinction between a statute creating a public right and one merely prohibiting what had formerly been lawful.

The courts in any case determine Parliament's intent by reference to various factors:

■ The more precise the wording of the statute the more likely it is that the breach of the duty will give rise to a civil action for damages. Two cases can be compared to illustrate this point.

CASE EXAMPLE

Monk v Warby [1935] All ER 373

This case involved breach of a duty under what is now s 143 of the Road Traffic Act 1988 not to allow an uninsured driver to drive a vehicle. The claimant, who had been injured through the negligence of the driver, was able to sue the owner of the car where there would have been no point in suing the uninsured driver. This was possible because the car had been used with the owner's knowledge.

CASE EXAMPLE

Atkinson v Newcastle Waterworks (1877) 2 ExD 441

Here no civil action was available where statute imposed a £10 fine for failing to keep water at a certain pressure. The claimant's premises had caught fire and burned down but, despite the breach of statutory duty no part of the fine was payable to an individual so the statute did not create individual rights to a civil action.

■ If the Act imposes a duty but there is a failure to mention a specific penalty then it is likely to give rise to a civil action.

CASE EXAMPLE

Cutler v Wandsworth Stadium Ltd [1949] AC 398

Here a breach of a statutory duty to allow a bookmaker entry to a dog-racing track gave rise to a civil action. There was no mention of a fine or a penalty.

■ Some groups commonly benefit from statutory duties and so in certain instances there are well established principles of civil liability.

CASE EXAMPLE

Groves v Lord Wimbourne [1898] 2 QB 402

Here the statutory duty was to fence machinery. The employee was injured as a result of a breach of that duty. A £100 fine was possible with part at least payable to the claimant, although there was no guarantee that he would receive it.

■ A civil action is also more likely where the duty of the welfare of an identifiable group is concerned.

CASE EXAMPLE

Thornton v Kirklees MBC [1979] QB 626

A statute creating an obligation to house homeless people was enforceable despite the fact that no specific remedy was identified.

■ However, there must be a direct link between the group and the purpose of statute.

CASE EXAMPLE

McCall v Abelsz [1976] QB 585

Here residential occupiers did not count as a class for the purposes of harassment actions.

■ For a civil action to be possible the purpose of the statutory provision must be for benefit of that class.

CASE EXAMPLE

R v Deputy Governor of Parkhurst Prison, ex parte Hague [1992] 1 AC 58

Here prisoners could not use alleged breaches of the Prison Rules to bring a civil action. The Prison Rules were for the regulation of prisons and did not provide any private law rights for the prisoners.

■ But a civil action will not be possible in any case where the court feels that the duty is intended to be enforced by other means.

CASE EXAMPLE

Cullen v Chief Constable of the Royal Ulster Constabulary [2003] 1 WLR 1763

Cullen was arrested and his right to see a solicitor was denied under s 15 Northern Ireland (Emergency Provisions) Act 1987. He was later given access to a solicitor and pleaded guilty to criminal charges. He then sought damages for the delay in giving him access to a solicitor. The trial judge and the Northern Ireland Court of Appeal held that the police had reasonable grounds to delay access and although they had breached the statutory requirement to give the claimant reasons for this delay at the time, this did not give rise to an action in tort. The House of Lords upheld the decision and held that there was no civil law duty because there would have been a possibility of judicial review. The House also commented that there was no issue under the Human Rights Act 1998 as there was no breach of Article 5 or Article 6 of the Convention on Human Rights.

One interesting recent development is the removal of the exclusion from civil liability in the Management of Health and Safety at Work Regulations 1999 under the Management of Health and Safety at Work and Fire Precautions (Workplace) (Amendment) Regulations 2003. Employees will now be able to bring a claim of breach of statutory duty where the regulations are not complied with. A particular requirement of the 1999 Regulations is risk assessment. In future a failure to assess risks or an inadequate risk assessment might give rise to liability. The changes in the regulations clearly gives employees much broader scope to claim.

Is there a duty of care owed to the claimant?

Unless the claimant can show that by the statute it was intended that a duty should be owed to him as an individual or as a member of a specific class of individuals then an action in tort will fail.

CASE EXAMPLE

Hartley v Mayoh & Co [1954] 1 QB 383

A fireman was injured in a fire at a factory. His claim for damages failed. No duty was owed under the industrial safety provisions on which he tried to rely since the fire was not at his place of employment which the precise wording of the statute required.

Even though a statute does appear on its wording to confer civil rights on an individual leading to a possible tort action this may not extend as far as the family of that individual. So an action by a relative might fail.

CASE EXAMPLE

Hewett v Alf Brown's Transport [1992] ICR 530

Here the wife of a lorry driver contracted lead poisoning through washing her husband's overalls. Safety regulations did create a duty of care in favour of employees such as the lorry driver here. Nevertheless the duty could not be extended to cover the wife in the case. Slightly different reasoning applied in *Maguire v Hartland & Wolff plc* [2005] EWCA Civ 01 in respect of a wife who had contracted mesothelioma after washing her husband's overalls which had been exposed to asbestos dust. At the time she was exposed to the dust it would not have been reasonably foreseeable that she was at risk.

Nevertheless the scope of the duty may be used in certain circumstances to recover damages.

CASE EXAMPLE

Atkinson v Croydon Corporation (1938) (unreported)

Here a father was able to recover damages when his daughter contracted typhoid as the result of a failure to provide a clean water supply. No duty was actually owed to the girl. However, the father, who was paying for the service, was owed a duty and could recover damages on that basis.

The scope for establishing the existence of a duty is in any case potentially very wide.

CASE EXAMPLE

Garden Cottage Foods v Milk Marketing Board [1984] 2 All ER 770

The duty in this action arose as a result of EU law.

However, in a series of joined appeals the House of Lords has clearly restated the need to show that Parliament intended to create private law rights before any action is possible: *X (minors) v Bedfordshire County Council; M (a minor) v Newham London Borough Council; Keating v Bromley LBC* [1995] 3 All ER 353.

Is there a duty of care imposed on the defendant?

The statute must impose civil liability on the defendant or there can be no possible action. This can only be established by reference to the precise wording of the statute.

CASE EXAMPLE

R v Deputy Governor of Parkhurst Prison, Ex Parte Hague [1992] 1 AC 58

Here a claim by prisoners that civil law rights were infringed was rejected. The Prison Rules were passed for the purposes of regulating the administration of prisons not in any way to impose duties on prisons that would operate in favour of prisoners.

However, it is of course possible the civil duty might extend to a broad range of defendants.

CASE EXAMPLE

Shell Tankers v Jeremson [2001] EWCA Civ 101

In this case the Court of Appeal recognised that regulations covering the asbestos industry would also extend to users of asbestos in other industries.

Quite simply if there is no civil duty on the defendant that is identifiable from the words of the statute then there can be no civil action.

Has the defendant breached that duty by falling below the standard identified in the statute?

In the case of breaches of statutory duties there is no single standard of care, since the standard is identifiable from the individual statutory provision, so the court must assess the exact standard by construing the statute itself.

This is inevitably subject to inconsistency in approach and inevitably policy has a key role to play. As Lord Denning remarked in *Ex parte Island Records* [1978] 3 WLR 23 '. . . you might as well toss a coin in order to decide the cases'.

Of course there are times when the words are so specific that the standard is self-evident.

CASE EXAMPLE

Chipchase v British Titan Products Co Ltd [1956] 1 QB 545

In this case the precise wording proved fatal to a claim. The defendant's injury was sustained when he fell six feet to the ground from a nine-inch wide platform. The regulations required that platforms over six feet six inches from the ground should be at least 34 inches wide. The specific wording of the provision was not breached and there was no possible action.

A precise and imperative wording in the provisions is likely to lead to liability being strict. Words such as 'must' or 'shall' are obvious examples of this general principle.

CASE EXAMPLE

John Summers & Sons v Frost [1955] AC 740

Section 14(1) of the Factories Act 1961 required fencing of machinery. The court refused to accept a plea that it was impracticable to fence machines. Liability was regarded as strict.

However, very often the standard may be only vaguely stated.

CASE EXAMPLE

Brown v NCB [1962] AC 574

Here the duty was to 'take such steps as may be necessary for keeping the road or working place secure'. There was held to be no liability when the court accepted that the manager had exercised reasonable skill and care.

Is the breach of duty the cause of the damage suffered by the claimant?

Causation is measured in similar ways to common law negligence. In this way the 'but for test' is significant in establishing a causal link.

CASE EXAMPLE

McWilliams v Sir William Arrol & Co Ltd [1962] 1 WLR 295

Here the claimant fell while not using a safety harness. Statute required that harnesses should be supplied. The defendant company was able to avoid liability because it was able to show that the claimant would not in any case have worn the harness.

So there must be a direct causal link between the defendant's breach of the statutory duty and the damage suffered by the claimant in order for a claim to succeed.

CASE EXAMPLE

Sussex Ambulance NHS Trust v King [2002] EWCA Civ 953

The claim was that injury was caused because of lack of specialist training required by regulations. The court accepted evidence showing that even without this specialist training the likelihood was that the claimant would still have suffered the injury. The court held that the employer was not liable.

However, the result might be different where the duty also extends to ensuring that the potential claimant complies with the safety provisions, for example by using or wearing safety equipment.

CASE EXAMPLE

Ginty v Belmont Building Supplies Ltd [1959] 1 All ER 414

While a failure to ensure that safety equipment is used may lead to liability, in this case the claim failed because the employer had done everything possible to ensure that the employee should use crawling boards provided for working on roofs. The claimant fell through the roof when not using the boards. The case is controversial however.

Is the damage of a type which is contemplated in the statute?

The final test for a claimant in respect of liability under a statutory duty in some senses mirrors the principle of remoteness of damage in normal negligence actions. The damage must be of a type that was contemplated by the statute or there can be no liability.

CASE EXAMPLE

Gorris v Scott (1874) LR 9 Ex 125

Here the claimant lost his sheep when they were swept overboard from the ship on which they were being carried. Even though there was a duty owed by statute, this was to prevent the loss of livestock through contagious diseases so there could be no liability.

The House of Lords in *Cullen v Chief Constable of the Royal Ulster Constabulary* also identified that the breach of duty in failing to warn of reasons for delaying access to a solicitor did not give rise to the type of damage that would normally be associated with a civil action. Tort damages are awarded for damage to property, personal injury and sometimes economic loss. The only possible action would have been for false imprisonment but the failure to warn would not amount to an unlawful detention.

On the issue of remoteness the case of *Young v Charles Church (Southern) Ltd*, *The Times*, 1st May, 1997, CA is also relevant. Here a claim was possible because nervous shock which was suffered by the claimant was a type of damage contemplated in the Construction (General Provisions) Regulations 1961.

16.3 Defences

There are generally two defences available in claims for breach of a statutory duty.

Volenti non fit injuria (voluntary assumption of a risk)

Consent is not normally available as a defence and this is on policy grounds. However, it may be in two situations:

■ where the claimant's wrongful act puts the defendant in breach – and *Ginty v Belmont Building Supplies* [1959] 1 All ER 414 is a good example of this

■ where the claimant tries to claim the defendant's vicarious liability as an issue.

CASE EXAMPLE

ICI Ltd v Shatwell [1965] AC 656

Two brothers who both worked in blasting ignored instructions and tested detonators without taking shelter as required by regulations. One brother who was injured as a result had ignored safety instructions and followed the guidance of the other brother. He then tried to fix the employer with vicarious liability for his brother's tort. The action failed because he had consented to the possible harm by accepting his brother's flawed advice and ignoring safety regulations himself.

Contributory negligence

The courts only very reluctantly accept this defence because regulations are often designed to protect workmen from their own carelessness. As Lord Denning remarked in *Caswell v Powell Duffryn Collieries* [1940] AC 152

JUDGMENT

'. . . the employee's sense of danger will have been dulled by familiarity, repetition, noise, confusion, fatigue, and preoccupation with work . . .'

The defence is still possible, however, where the claimant is genuinely at fault but liability is strict. Liability is not removed but the claimant's damages can be reduced to the extent to which he is at fault for his own loss or injury.

CASE EXAMPLE

Jayes v IMI (Kynoch) Ltd [1985] ICR 155

Reduction in damages of 100 per cent was awarded. The employer's obligation was not only to provide guards on machines but to ensure their continuous use when the machinery was turned on. The employee lost fingers when he failed to turn the machine off and tried to clear a blockage in the machine while it was still working.

ACTIVITY

Self-assessment questions

1. In what ways is the action similar to negligence?
2. In what ways is it different?
3. What advantages are there to a plaintiff in using the action?
4. What problems are there in proving the statute gave rise to an action in damages?
5. How imperfect is the test in *Lonrho*?
6. When will a claimant fail to show that a duty applies to him?
7. How is the standard of care measured?
8. How limiting are defences to the action?

Does the statute create civil liability?
- If the Act identifies a specific method of enforcement it is not enforceable in another way unless:
- The Act imposes an obligation to a specific class; or
- The claimant suffered damage different from that common to the rest of the public

YES ↓   NO →

Is a duty of care owed to the claimant?
- The Act identifies a duty owed to the individual; or
- The claimant is a member of a class identified by the Act as being owed a duty

YES ↓   NO

Is that duty of care owed by the defendant?
- The duty only exists if it is identified in the Act

YES ↓   NO →

There is no breach of a statutory duty

Has the defendant breached the duty?
- The defendant has fallen below the standard identified in the specific wording of the Act

YES ↓   NO →

Was the breach of duty the cause of the damage suffered by the claimant?
- There is a direct causal link between the defendant's breach of duty and the damage suffered; or
- The defendant has failed to ensure that the claimant follows required procedure and he is under a duty to do so

YES ↓   NO   NO

Is the damage of a type contemplated in the statute?
- The damage suffered is that identified in the Act as requiring the defendant to guard against

YES ↓

Liability for breach of a statutory duty is possible

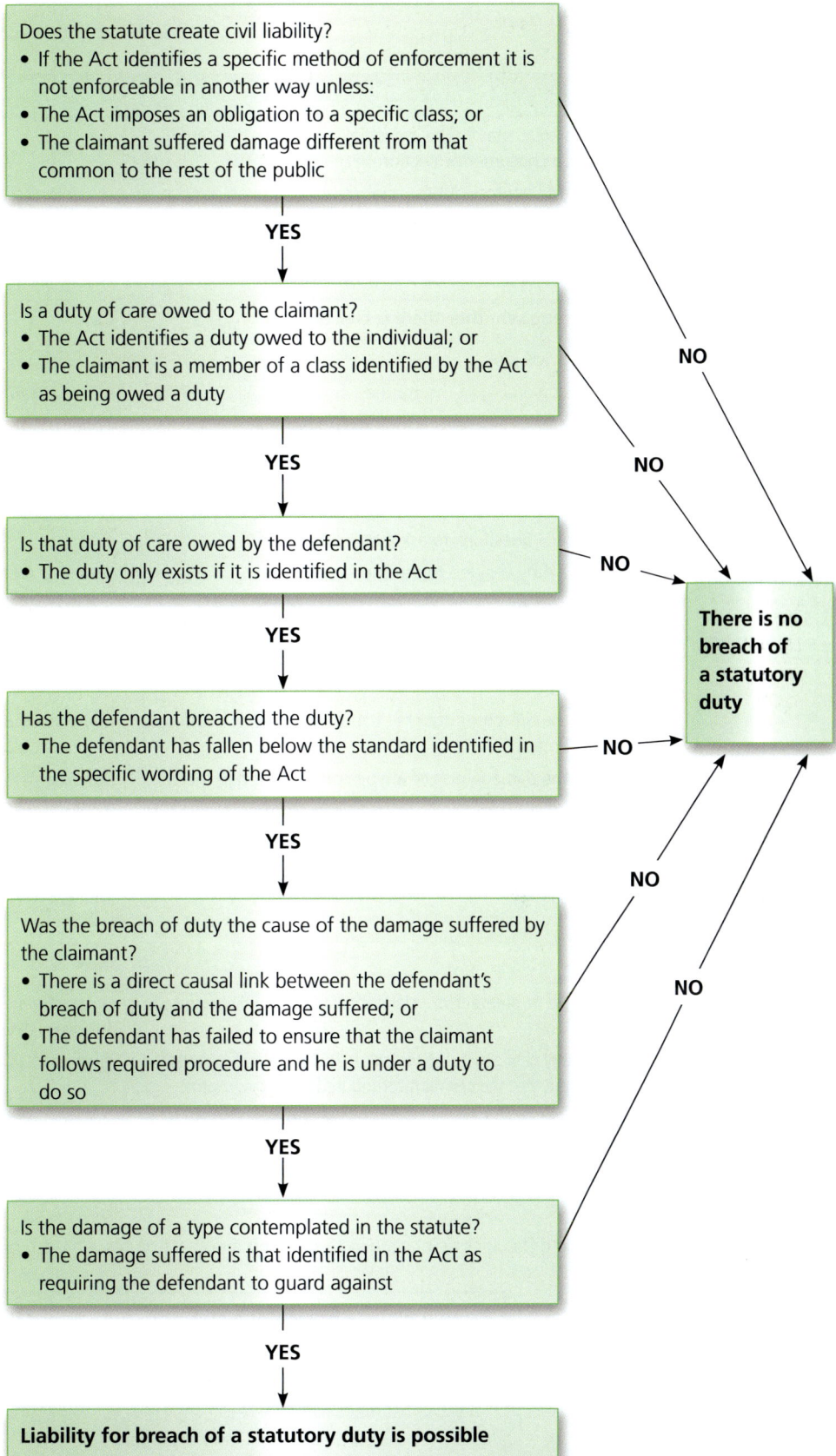

Figure 16.1 Diagram illustrating the essential elements of a claim for breach of a statutory

The nature of breach of a statutory duty	Case
Concerns areas mainly like industrial safety law, but can include, eg consumer protection. Breaches of statutory duties usually lead to criminal sanctions so the main problem is proving that there is also civil liability. A test has been developed by Lord Diplock in	*Lonrho Ltd v Shell Petroleum Co* (1982)
Determining whether there is civil liability	**Case**
The courts will look at: the precise wording of the statute whether a precise penalty is indicated whether the welfare of a definable class is a purpose of the statute. The essential questions to ask are: whether a duty is owed to the specific claimant whether a duty is imposed on the defendant whether the defendant has fallen below the appropriate standard of care whether the breach of duty has caused the damage suffered by the claimant whether the damage was of a type contemplated in the statute. The courts will in any case not impose a duty where they feel that an alternative remedy was intended in the statute.	*Monk v Warby* (1935) *Cutler v Wandsworth Stadium* (1949) *Thornton v Kirklees MBC* (1979) *Hewett v Alf Brown's Transport* (1992) *R v Deputy Governor of Parkhurst Prison, ex parte Hague* (1992) *Chipchase v British Titan Products Co Ltd* (1956) *McWilliams v Sir William Arrol & Co Ltd* (1962) *Gorris v Scott* (1874) *Cullen v Chief Constable of the Royal Ulster Constabulary* (2003)
Defences	**Case**
Volenti non fit injuria if the claimant has genuinely accepted the risk. Contributory negligence – in which case damages will be reduced to the extent that the claimant contributed to his own harm.	*Ginty v Belmont Building Supplies* (1959) *Jayes v IMI (Kynoch)* (1985)

SAMPLE ESSAY QUESTION

Discuss the difficulties associated with bringing a civil action for a breach of a statutory duty

Explain when a breach of a statutory duty might occur

- Often occurs in health and safety, industrial safety law, consumer protection etc
- Usually the statute is regulatory and makes criminal sanctions available to regulatory bodies

Discuss the basic problem

- Action for breach of statutory duty similar to negligence – but other considerations apply
- It is not always clear whether the statute does create civil liability since usually criminal in nature

Discuss how the courts decide if there is civil liability

- Examine precise wording of Act to see whether it intended to create civil liability
- Consider whether the claimant is owed a duty of care and that duty is imposed on the defendant
- Consider whether the defendant has breached his duty
- Decide whether the breach caused the damage and was a type of damage contemplated in the Act

Discuss the available defences

- *Volenti* which is only available only if the claimant's wrongful act caused the defendant breach

Discuss the difficulties associated with proving the existence of a civil action

- They usually impose criminal sanctions so the existence of civil liability is debatable
- It is often not stated whether is civil liability in Act
- Civil liability is more obvious where the Act modifies the common law
- But with other Acts it is harder to determine so the area is dependent on statutory interpretation
- As a result the area is unpredictable

Discuss the difficulties involved in succeeding in a claim

- The action is similar to negligence but it differs in significant ways
- The standard of care is usually fixed by the statute
- The duty can be strict, or the burden of proof may be reversed, either being advantageous to a claimant
- Treated as a separate tort
- So often it is pleaded together with negligence

ACTIVITY

Applying the law

Using the guide in Appendix 2 try the following problem question:

Gary works for Careless Contractors. On 14 November 2003 the foreman, John, ordered him to replace a glass panel in the seventh-floor window of Storer Tower where the contractors had completed re-glazing on 10 November 2003. Scaffolding on three sides of the building had already been disassembled. Gary took up position on scaffolding outside the window and waited for the new pane to be winched down to him from the roof. As it came to rest on the scaffolding boards they collapsed, and Gary fell onto the boards below injuring himself. The manager of the scaffolders suggested to John that the scaffolding was secure to work on but subjecting it to any great stresses should be avoided. Gary is hoping to claim under the Construction (Working Places) Regulations 1966 which state:

'. . . it shall be the duty of every contractor, and every employer or workmen, who is undertaking any of the operations or works to which these regulations apply –

a) To comply with such requirements as affect him, or any workman employed by him . . . provided that the requirements shall be deemed not to affect any workman if his presence in the place is not in the course of performing any work on behalf of his employer . . . and it shall be the duty of every contractor and every employer of workmen who erects or alters any scaffold to comply with such of the requirements as relate to the erection or alteration of scaffolds . . .'

Does Gary have an action for breach of statutory duty?

SUMMARY

- Mainly involves industrial safety law and some consumer protection
- Usually involves criminal sanctions so the problem is proving civil liability exists
- Courts consider the wording of the statute, whether a precise penalty is indicated, whether one purpose of the statute is the welfare of a definable class, whether the claimant is owed a duty of care, and the defendant owes the duty, whether the defendant has breached the duty, whether the breach caused the damage, whether the damage was of a type contemplated in the statute, whether an alternative remedy was intended in the statute
- *Volenti non fit injuria* and contributory negligence are possible defences

Further reading

Jones, M A, *Textbook on Torts* (8th edn, OUP, 2003), Chapter 9.
Murray, J, *Street on Torts* (11th edn, Butterworths, 2003), Chapter 21.

17

Employers' liability

AIMS AND OBJECTIVES

After reading this chapter you should be able to:

- Understand the essential elements of the common law duty
- Understand the ways in which the common law duty has been expanded
- Be able to critically analyse aspects of employer liability
- Be able to apply the law to factual situations and reach conclusions as to liability

17.1 Origins of liability

Employers' liability is a well developed principle that is to be found in both the common law and statute. It developed initially in the nineteenth century through very limited statutory controls following the Industrial Revolution. The very first industrial safety law was Sir Robert Peel's Health and Morals of Apprentices Act 1802.

Most often those controls applied only to children and sometimes to women and were aimed more at regulating employment practices than at providing legal rights for employees. The first Acts to provide protect adult male workers were the Factory Act 1833 (which created a Factory Inspectorate) and the Factory Act 1844 (which introduced the idea of fencing off dangerous machinery).

So it took a long time for civil liability to develop in the area, not until the Workmen's Compensation Act 1897, and workers rarely had the means of suing or gaining compensation for the injuries that they sustained through negligent practices.

The nature of the development has also meant that the area is quite complex and involves consideration of both common law and statutory provision.

Employment was traditionally seen, as it still is, as a contractual relationship, based on freedom of contract, so no remedies were available in tort. Employees were free to negotiate their own contractual terms, at least in theory, so if no reference to industrial safety was made in the contract then no civil action was available.

In the nineteenth century there were three further major barriers to workers' claims in respect of injuries sustained at work:

- The defence of *volenti* – the worker in accepting the work was said also to have consented to the risks and dangers inherent in the specific type of work.
- The defence of contributory negligence – this was a complete defence at that time so that if the employer could show that the employee was engaging in unsafe working

practices then there could be no claim and this would be the case even though the worker had been directed to pursue those practices by the employer.

■ The so called 'fellow servant rule' and the common law doctrine of common employment – where an employee was injured as the result of an unsafe practice of a fellow employee the employer could disclaim responsibility for that employee's actions and there could be no claim against the employer (and there would be little point in claiming against the 'fellow servant' who would inevitably be a 'man of straw').

The common law was generally hostile to workers and applied these three defences rigorously. Gradually, however, their severity was limited:

■ In *Smith v Baker* [1891] AC 325 the court accepted that *volenti* would only be available if the claimant freely accepted and understood the specific risk.

■ The Law Reform (Contributory Negligence) Act 1945 altered the character of the defence of contributory negligence making it a partial defence only affecting the amount of damages to be received rather than removing liability altogether as had formerly been the case.

■ Finally in *Groves v Lord Wimbourne* [1898] 2 QB 402 the 'fellow servant' rule was held not to be available as a defence to a breach of a statutory duty; and in the Law Reform (Personal Injuries) Act 1948 the defence was finally abolished altogether.

There were also further major positive developments in the law:

■ In *Wilsons & Clyde Coal v English* [1938] AC 57 the court identified that the employer owed a personal and non-delegable duty of care towards his employees.

■ Employers became liable for defective plant and equipment in the Employers' Liability (Defective Equipment) Act 1969.

■ The principle of the employer insuring workers against injury that was introduced in the Workmen's Compensation Act 1897 in respect of a limited range of named occupations was at a later stage extended to include all employees by the Employers' Liability (Compulsory Insurance) Act 1969.

Subsequent to all these developments there are in principle three means by which an employee might impose liability on an employer:

■ For a breach of a statutory duty, for example under the Health and Safety at Work etc Act 1974 or other regulatory provisions where they include civil liability (see Chapter 16).

■ For the tortious acts of another employee through the principle of vicarious liability (see Chapter 18).

■ For a breach of the employer's personal non-delegable duty of care.

All three have been subject to significant development. Proving the complexity of the area in a claim for an injury at work the pleadings will very often involve all three and there is the added further complication of regulations generated by the EU Framework Directive on Health and Safety 89/391 which may also provide civil liability actions.

17.2 The employer's non-delegable duty

17.2.1 Introduction

Firstly, it is important to remember that the whole area of employer's liability is complicated by virtue of there being not only basic common law duties but that these are interspersed with a huge number of statutory duties and regulatory provisions. Either might prove beneficial to a claimant since commonly with statutory duties, liability is strict or the burden of proof is reversed. Often also a common law duty is contained in any case within a statutory provision. For these reasons a claim is often a mixture of both, pleaded as alternatives.

With statutory duties there is the added complication of demonstrating that the statute does indeed provide a civil remedy (as seen in Chapter 16).

Besides this there is the added complication of EU law which, under Article 141 (formerly Art 119) and Article 138 (formerly Art 118A) EC Treaty, has the power to incorporate a wide range of employment duties, particularly in the field of industrial safety law.

The basic common law duty in essence derives from the judgment of Lord Wright in *Wilsons & Clyde Coal Co Ltd v English*. The basic duty is to take reasonable care for the safety of all employees while acting in the course of their employment.

Lord Wright identified the duty as personal and non-delegable and at the time saw the duty as having four key aspects:

- the duty to provide competent staff as working colleagues
- the duty to provide safe plant and equipment
- the duty to provide a safe place of work
- the duty to provide a safe system of work.

As the law has developed there has also now been established a general common law duty to protect the health and safety of the worker. This duty extends not only to physical health and well being but also to ensure the psychiatric health of the worker.

One significant fact that must be remembered is that these categories are quite simply stated and do not necessarily fully reflect the complexities of the modern workplace. In this sense the separate duties can quite easily overlap. In any case the likelihood is that a claim that an employer has breached his duties towards an employee will likely contain elements of more than one duty. Besides this, as has already been indicated, there is likely to be overlap also with many of the statutory duties and, if there are civil remedies attached, the claim will possibly include a range of evidence of the employer's breaches, both common law and statutory.

17.2.2 The different aspects of the duty

The duty to provide competent staff

It is clear that the employer must ensure that all employees are competent to carry out the duties they are required to undertake in their employment.

CASE EXAMPLE

General Cleaning Contractors Ltd v Christmas [1953] AC 180

Here a window cleaner was injured while cleaning sash windows, having been improperly instructed on the safest method of undertaking the work. The employer was held liable.

An employer must also ensure the good behaviour of all employees while at work. In this way an employer should not tolerate unsafe practices, including the playing of practical jokes that might cause harm to other employees. All unsafe practices should be dealt with and an employee who indulges in such practices should be disciplined and in extreme cases even dismissed.

CASE EXAMPLE

Hudson v Ridge Manufacturing Co [1957] 2 QB 348

An employee was injured when a fellow employee well known for such behaviour carried out a practical joke on him. The employer was in breach of his duty and liable for failing to discipline the employee at fault and prevent him from repeating such activity and was held liable.

However, the employer may not be liable if he is unaware that the employee causing damage or injury is likely to behave in that way.

CASE EXAMPLE

O'Reilly v National Rail & Tramway Appliances [1966] 1 All ER 499

Here labourers breaking up a disused railway line found what they believed to be an unexploded shell of some sort from the Second World War, some nine inches long and one inch in diameter. The claimant was injured when he followed the suggestion of work colleagues that he hit the object with a sledgehammer. One had said 'Hit it: what are you scared of?' The employer had no idea that his employees would be so silly and thus escaped liability for the severe injuries sustained by the claimant.

In modern times actions using this basic common law duty are rare because of the principle of vicarious liability. However, it may still be useful when the employee's act causing injury or damage falls outside the scope of employment.

The duty to provide safe working conditions is now supplemented by successful actions under s 3 Protection from Harassment Act 1997 – *Green v DB Group Services (UK) Ltd* [2006] EWHC 1989 (Ch) (see 13.6.2) and *Majrowski v Guy's & St Thomas's NHS Trust* [2006] UKHL 34 (see 18.3.1).

The duty to provide safe plant and equipment

The basic duty is that the employer must take care both to provide safe equipment and of course to properly maintain it.

CASE EXAMPLE

Smith v Baker [1891] AC 325

A quarry worker was hurt when stones fell on him from hoppers that crossed over the quarry bottom on a conveyor system. The employer was liable because the machinery was not properly maintained.

Lord Halsbury LC identified the position that the employee was faced with.

JUDGMENT

'The question of law that seems to be in debate is whether . . . on occasion when the very form of his employment prevented him from looking out for himself, he consented to undergo this particular risk . . . I do not think the plaintiff did consent at all. His attention was on a drill, and while he was unable to take precautions himself, a stone was negligently slung over his head without due precautions against its being permitted to fall.'

The employer may need to train employees how to use equipment properly.

CASE EXAMPLE

Mountenay (Hazzard) & Others v Bernard Matthews (1993) (unreported)

Here the employee developed a clinical wrist problem as the result of continuously handling dead poultry on a production line. There had been no attempt to rotate work to prevent workers constantly using the same wrist actions or to educate workers to the natural risks of the work, so the employer was liable.

However, the employer can still avoid liability if he actually provides adequate equipment but the employee misuses the equipment or fails to make proper use of it.

CASE EXAMPLE

Parkinson v Lyle Shipping Co Ltd [1964] 2 Lloyd's Rep 79

Here an employee was badly burned while trying to light a boiler. There was no defect in the boiler. It was quite safe and the employee had been properly instructed in how to light it. So there was no liability.

The provisions of the Employers' Liability (Defective Equipment) Act 1969 have now possibly superseded the common law duty in many respects. The Act has a seemingly precise definition of equipment. Section 1(3) defines 'equipment' as 'any plant and machinery, vehicle, aircraft and clothing'. Nevertheless, even the Act itself has been subject to conflicting interpretation.

CASE EXAMPLE

Coltman v Bibby Tankers [1988] AC 276

In this case the Court of Appeal held that an injury sustained because of a defect in the hull of a ship was not actionable, not falling within the definition. The House of Lords later reversed this and accepted that the definition within the Act could include the circumstances of the case.

As with all statutory provisions the definitions within sections of Acts may be challenged and the court will be called on to interpret. This may lead to some surprising results.

CASE EXAMPLE

Knowles v Liverpool City Council [1993] ICR 21

In this case the court found no problem in bringing a kerbstone within the definition for the purposes of imposing liability under the Act. The employee had been injured because of the negligence of the council in failing to ensure that kerbstones were not raised and it was liable as a result of the broad interpretation accepted by the court.

The duty to provide a safe place of work

The general duty here is to take all steps that are reasonably practicable to ensure that premises are safe.

CASE EXAMPLE

Latimer v AEC [1953] AC 643

An employee was injured when slipping on a greasy patch on the factory floor following flood damage. The employer was not liable, having done everything practicable to ensure that the floor was safe for use.

Since many forms of work depend on employees being mobile, the duty may also extend to premises other than the employer's own premises.

CASE EXAMPLE

Wilson v Tyneside Window Cleaning Co [1958] 2 QB 110

Window cleaners were injured while working on a client's premises. The employer had done everything within his capability to ensure that the men were safe so could not be liable.

It is also true, however, that most industrial premises, if not other places of work, are potentially hazardous. Where the employee exercises a particular skill or enjoys specific expertise liability may be avoided where the worker has failed to take account of his own safety. All people with a skill are expected to have an awareness of the risks that are associated with exercising that particular skill.

CASE EXAMPLE

Roles v Nathan [1963] 1 WLR 1117

Chimney sweeps were killed by fumes when they were cleaning flues in an industrial chimney stack while boilers under the chimney were still alight. Their own expert knowledge should have alerted them to the dangers, and claims for their deaths failed.

Lord Denning explained the position.

JUDGMENT

'These chimney sweeps ought to have known that there might be dangerous fumes . . . and ought to have taken steps to guard against them. They ought to have known that they should not attempt to seal up the sweep hole whilst the fire was still alight. They ought to have had the fire withdrawn . . . they ought not to have stayed in the alcove too long when there might be dangerous fumes about. All this was known to these two sweeps; they were repeatedly warned about it, and it was for them to guard against it.'

One final point is that since employers very often will be in control of the premises within which they operate there may also be liability under the Occupiers' Liability Act 1957 (see Chapter 7).

The duty to provide a safe system of work

There are two key aspects to the duty:

■ the creation of a safe system in the first place
■ a proper implementation of the system.

It is a question of fact in each case whether the work requires that a system is necessary and should be devised for safety purposes or whether safe practices should be obvious to the employee.

The employer is not able to rely on an unsafe practice merely because it is a common practice.

CASE EXAMPLE

Re Herald of Free Enterprise, The Independent, 18th December, 1987

It was irrelevant that it was not unusual for bow doors to be left open on roll-on roll-off ferries when entering or leaving port. Vessels could and did capsize as the result of such a practice.

The general duty is to provide an effective system of work which is sufficient to meet any foreseeable dangers.

CASE EXAMPLE

General Cleaning Contractors Ltd v Christmas [1953] AC 180

Holding on to the sill and without wedges while cleaning sash windows was clearly an unsafe system, although it was the one that had been explained to the employee by his immediate superior. In the event the sash cord failed and the window fell onto the window cleaner's hands, leading to the injuries and liability.

Inevitably in certain types of employment there are actual dangers presented by the nature of the work or by the people with whom the employee has to work. If the employer fails to operate systems to effectively avoid these dangers then the employer will be liable.

CASE EXAMPLE

Cook v Bradford Community NHS Trust [2002] EWCA Civ 1616

Here the employee worked in a psychiatric ward and was assaulted by a violent patient which in itself was a foreseeable risk. Because the systems in place failed to adequately address this risk the employer was liable.

The duty is also not just to devise the system but may also be to ensure that the system is carried out. A safe system is only safe if it is in fact followed. Thus, for instance, there is no point in an employer possessing safety equipment if employees are not provided with it.

CASE EXAMPLE

Bux v Slough Metals [1974] 1 All ER 262

An employee was provided with safety goggles but would not use them because he claimed that they misted up. The employer knew of this and when the employee was injured by a splash of molten metal the employer was liable for failing to ensure that the goggles were worn.

Again it is insufficient that an employer claims to have created a safe system if the employees are unaware of it. On this basis an employer might still be liable for a failure to warn of dangers inherent in the work.

CASE EXAMPLE

Pape v Cumbria CC [1992] 3 All ER 211

The employer was liable here for failing to warn that not wearing gloves might lead to dermatitis as a result of continuous contact with irritants.

The advances in modern technology and its effect on working practices may also have an impact on working conditions. In the case of use of VDUs for instance there are a range of provisions under regulations requiring safe working practices. The common law also demands that the systems for using such equipment should not damage the health and safety of the employee.

CASE EXAMPLE

Alexander and Others v Midland Bank plc [2000] ICR 464

Here employees worked under high pressure processing and continuously inputting information into computer databases. The employees successfully complained that the employer had consistently increased the work rate demanded and that as a result of unsafe practice they had suffered muscular injuries.

Where the employment involves contact with the public this in itself can very often present a potential hazard to the employee. The employer may well be expected to operate a system of work where the employee's safety was not unnecessarily threatened by public contact.

CASE EXAMPLE

Rahman v Arearose Ltd [2000] 3 WLR 1184

A restaurant worker was violently assaulted and seriously injured by customers. The employer was liable because it was identified that other members of staff had also been assaulted, the employer was aware of this, and had not introduced any effective system to prevent it.

Much of the duty here has probably now been superseded, for example by the duty to undertake risk assessment under the 'six pack' and other regulatory requirements on an employer.

One possible recent development of the duty is to ensure that the system of work does not cause undue stress to the employee.

CASE EXAMPLE

Walker v Northumberland CC [1995] 1 All ER 737

A second nervous breakdown of a senior social worker resulted in liability for the employers. This was because after the first they were aware of his susceptibility to stress and did nothing to reduce his workload or the pressure associated with it.

Colman J explained the development

JUDGMENT

'It is clear law that an employer has a duty to provide his employee with a safe system of work and to take reasonable steps to protect him from risks which are reasonably foreseeable . . . there is no logical reason why risk of psychiatric damage should be excluded from the scope of an employer's duty.'

ACTIVITY

Quick quiz:

Consider which aspect of the employers' duty may have been breached in the following circumstances:

1. Eric breaks his leg at the start of his shift at 6.00 am in December on his way into the factory when he stumbles into a pothole near to the main door. The entrance to the factory has not been resurfaced for many years and it is very dark because the bulb in the light outside the entrance has gone and has not been replaced.
2. Tariq suffers a severe back injury when a fellow employee, Angus, pulls Tariq's chair away as Tariq is about to sit down. Other employees have complained about Angus's practical jokes in the past but he has never been disciplined for them.
3. Bronwen has been forced to give up work because of a permanent bronchial complaint that has been caused in her work drilling panels of a toxic material. She has never been provided with a mask, there is no mechanism on the machine to prevent dust and she has never had any warnings about the dangers of inhaling the dust or received any health and safety training.
4. Olga works in a café. She has been badly burned and injured when the new Cappuccino machine spurted hot liquid all over her.

17.2.3 The character of the duty

As already identified the duty is entirely personal and non-delegable.

CASE EXAMPLE

Wilsons & Clyde Coal Co Ltd v English [1938] AC 57

Colliery owners had tried to delegate their responsibilities and liability under various industrial safety laws to their colliery manager by contractually making him entirely responsible for safety. However, when a miner was injured the colliery owners were held liable, the court refusing to accept that their personal liability could be delegated to a third party, who was in any case an employee.

However, the duty extends only as far as what is reasonable. There is inevitably no requirement to guarantee the safety of employees as seen in *Latimer v AEC* [1957] AC 643. The duty will extend to all reasonable and ancillary activities.

CASE EXAMPLE

Davidson v Handley Page Ltd [1945] 1 All ER 235

An employee slipped on a greasy duckboard on his way to his tea break and the employer was held liable. Breaks were a necessary part of the working day and even though the break might be out of the course of employment there must be a safe access to wherever the break is taken.

While the duty protects the employee it appears that the duty will not extend as far as protection of the employee's property.

CASE EXAMPLE

Deyong v Shenburn [1946] KB 227

The employee's clothing was stolen from a theatre in which he worked. There was held to be no liability on the employer.

Injuries that are sustained in the course of carrying out customary trade practices will not escape liability unless the practice itself is reasonable.

CASE EXAMPLE

Cavanagh v Ulster Weaving Co [1960] AC 145

Here the employee was expected to climb on a pitched roof while carrying a bag of cement and was injured when he fell. The employer argued that this was customary practice but it was clearly unsafe and he was held liable.

As in other areas of tort the 'thin skull' rule applies so the employer's duty extends to considering the possible extent of the injury to the particular employee.

CASE EXAMPLE

Paris v Stepney BC [1951] AC 367

Here the employee was already without sight in one eye. When failure to wear safety goggles resulted in the loss of his other eye the employer was liable to the extent of causing total blindness.

The employer of course is obliged only to guard against foreseeable risks and may take into account the practicability of any possible precautions.

CASE EXAMPLE

Charlton v Forrest Printing Ink Co Ltd [1978] IRLR 331

An employee was injured in an ambush while taking money to the bank on foot. The employer could have avoided the risk to the employee by arranging for a safer method of delivering the money and so was held liable.

The duty ultimately is to prevent accidents that are reasonably foreseeable. This is the basic *Wagon Mound* test. In this respect it is possible to compare two cases in determining how foreseeability is measured.

CASE EXAMPLE

Doughty v Turner Manufacturing Co Ltd [1964] 1 QB 518

In this case workmen were injured in an explosion when an asbestos lid negligently fitted on a chemical tank fell into the chemical. There was no liability because at the time it was not known that the specific chemical reaction causing the injuries would occur.

We have already seen in negligence that the precise damage or the precise circumstances in which it arises need not be foreseen as long as damage of the general kind caused can be foreseen.

CASE EXAMPLE

Bradford v Robinson Rentals [1967] 1 All ER 267

In this case, on the other hand, a driver was required to drive from Exeter to Bedford in a blizzard in a van with no heater and a broken window. The employer tried to claim that the resulting injury, frostbite, was unforeseeable. The court rejected the defence since some form of cold related illness was entirely foreseeable.

17.3 Developments in the common law duty

In recent times judges have begun to expand the boundaries of the employer's duties towards the employee's health and safety. These developments apply in both a general sense and in relation to more specific injuries.

Extreme pressures of work and excessive workloads have led to the introduction of a general duty to protect the health and safety of the employee.

CASE EXAMPLE

Johnstone v Bloomsbury Health Authority [1991] 2 All ER 293

A junior doctor brought an action against the health authority by whom he was employed, complaining that the fact that he was expected as a matter of course to work up to 48 hours overtime per week and had to be on call had damaged his general mental health. The court held that there had been a breach of a non-excludable implied term in his contract to take reasonable steps to care for his health and safety. The employer could not exclude this implied term by use of the specific express terms in the contract and was liable as a result.

This has opened up a whole field of law on stress-related illnesses and psychiatric damage caused at work. The action was not entirely novel. It is accepted now that there is a general duty to protect both the psychiatric health and well-being of the employee.

CASE EXAMPLE

Petch v Commissioners of Customs and Excise [1993] ICR 789

Here the employee was claiming for a breakdown that he argued was due to the stressful nature of the work undertaken. Dillon LJ in the Court of Appeal held that the employer was not negligent because the event was unforeseeable and also because the employer had done everything possible to try to persuade the employee not to return to work. Nevertheless the court did accept that an employer could be liable if he knows that the employee is susceptible to stress and allows the employee to continue working in stressful circumstances.

The result of these recent cases is that an employee is entitled to treat a psychiatric injury caused by negligent work practice in the same way that a physical injury would be dealt with.

CASE EXAMPLE

Walker v Northumberland CC [1995] 1 All ER 737

Here the case was actually given leave for an appeal to the Court of Appeal but was settled beforehand for £175,000. The significant feature of the case was that the employee had already suffered a nervous breakdown as a result of work related stress. On returning to work he had been promised that his workload would reduce but was actually faced with a huge backlog of work from his absence. The result was that he suffered a second breakdown causing him to leave work permanently after he was dismissed on sickness grounds. The employer was clearly liable because of placing a person who was already known to suffer from stress under even more stressful conditions and without having done anything about the understaffing and excess of work that had caused the first breakdown.

The *Walker* criteria can be straightforwardly applied. The employer is liable because (s)he is aware of the employee's susceptibility to stress and has worsened that condition by unsafe practices or unnecessary pressures of work.

CASE EXAMPLE

Young v Post Office [2002] EWCA Civ 661

After changes in work practices involving a change to computer systems without adequate training the employee became stressed, was put on anti-depressants, and suffered a nervous breakdown and was absent from work for months. The employer then agreed that the employee should return with a gradual reintroduction to work. In fact he had to attend a week's residential training course, and cover for a manager in his absence and suffered more stress, forcing him to leave permanently. The employer was liable because it did not follow its own agreed treatment of the employee.

The developments in this field have led to a variety of claims based on different aspects of stress at work that can be found reported in a variety of journals and newspapers.

Negligence claims in employment do not in any case have to result only from the workload. It is also possible for claims to be related to abuse or even physical danger in the workplace where the employer fails to protect the employee.

CASE EXAMPLE

Ingram v Worcestershire County Council, The Times, 11th January, 2000

Here a council worker who supervised a gypsy camp site as warden was attacked by residents of the site after the council changed its policies on the treatment of the residents. He had dogs set on him and was also shot at and was unable to work from 1997 onwards. The council was liable and the employee received considerable damages of £203,000.

Quite obviously bullying and harassment in the workplace can also be a breach of the employer's duty and can lead to liability in a similar way to the cases above.

CASE EXAMPLE

Ratcliffe v Dyfed County Council, The Times, 17th July, 1998

Here a claim for a stress related injury was accepted when a head teacher was found to have bullied a junior member of staff. The general duty to protect the health, safety and welfare of the employee applied.

Another category of stress claims has concerned the effects of redeployment and changing job roles. These are obviously stressful circumstances for an employee. If the employer fails to take care of the employee's general health and welfare in such circumstances then there may well be liability.

CASE EXAMPLE

Lancaster v Birmingham City Council (1999) 99(6) QR 4

The claimant was employed in a clerical capacity by a city council. She was redeployed but given no training or guidance in her new position as a housing officer. She then suffered three separate absences through stress and the employer failed to do anything about the problem so that she eventually had to retire on health grounds. The defendant council admitted liability 'in the door of the court' and compensated the claimant.

It is possible, however, that the courts are now pulling back and that there is no general duty to guard against psychiatric injuries. Instead courts are now accepting that a duty that arises when an ordinary bystander would foresee that the stress suffered is likely to be of such a degree as to cause a recognised psychiatric disorder.

CASE EXAMPLE

Rorrison v West Lothian College and Lothian Regional Council (Scottish Court of Session) IDS Brief 655 February 2000

The claimant was a nurse responsible for welfare duties and first aid in a college. A new personnel officer disciplined her, allegedly for no particular reason, took her first aid role off her, and changed the usual method of dealing with sick students without ever informing her. The claimant's GP then diagnosed anxiety depression and gave her sick notes for six weeks. When she returned to work the personnel officer gave her mainly clerical duties, allegedly harassed her, and frequently changed her duties afterwards. At one point she was given 30 minutes to accept a change of contractual terms or be fired. She then suffered distress, panic attacks and depression and was given beta blockers by her doctor. The court stated that her action against her employers could only succeed if she was able to show an identifiable psychiatric illness rather than mere stress, and was not prepared to accept anxiety depression as being the same as clinical depression. It was also suggested that the illness resulting from the work conditions should be foreseeable to a reasonable bystander, rather than to a doctor, to succeed. The case is only persuasive but it demonstrates a harsh application of the principles in Walker.

In any case *Walker* criteria must be satisfied before a successful claim can be made. This means that it is for the claimant to show that it is the actions of the employer, knowing of the employee's existing illness that has caused the later illness.

CASE EXAMPLE

Sparks v HSBC plc [2002] EWHC 2707 (QB)

The claimant had worked for the bank for many years when he began to suffer depression. The bank offered him retirement but instead he chose to work part time. Mistakes were found in his work but he was not disciplined and eventually he was also promoted. He suffered further depression and his work deteriorated and he was seen by the occupational therapist who recommended support although this was not given. He later retired on health grounds and claimed loss of earnings. The Court of Appeal would not accept his claim that the employer had caused or worsened the illness.

The area is a difficult one for judges to determine and the Court of Appeal has now produced guidelines for determining liability which appear to make it very difficult for claimants to bring successful claims for stress related psychiatric injuries.

CASE EXAMPLE

Sutherland v Hatton and Others [2002] EWCA Civ 76

This leading case involved a number of joined appeals on stress related illnesses at work. Two claims involved teachers. One concerned a local authority administrator and one a factory worker. All were claiming that they had been forced to stop working because of stress related psychiatric illnesses caused by their employers.

The Court of Appeal issued some important guidelines.

- The basic principles of negligence must apply including the usual principles of employers' liability.
- The critical question for the court to answer is whether the type of harm suffered was foreseeable.
- Foreseeability depends on what the reasonable employer knew or ought reasonably to have known.
- An employer is entitled to assume that an employee is able to cope with the pressures normally associated with the job unless the employer has specific knowledge that an employee has a particular problem and may not cope.
- The same test should apply whatever the employment.
- The employer will be obliged to take steps to prevent possible harm when the possibility of harm would be obvious to a reasonable employer.
- The employer will be liable if he then fails to take steps that are reasonable in the circumstances to avoid the harm.
- The nature of the employment, the employer's available resources, the counselling and treatment services provided are all relevant in determining whether the employer has taken effective steps to avoid the harm and in any case the employer is only expected to take steps that will do some good.
- The employee must show that it is the breach of duty by the employer that has caused the harm, not merely that the harm is stress related.
- Where there is more than one cause of the harm the employer will only be liable for that portion of damages that relates to the harm actually caused by his breach of duty.
- Damages will in any case take account of any pre-existing disorder.

'[W]hilst it is possible to identify some jobs that are intrinsically physically dangerous, it is rather more difficult to identify which jobs are intrinsically so stressful that physical or psychological harm is to be expected more often than in other jobs . . . With that guidance [*Sutherland v Hatton* [2002] EWCA Civ 76], courts are likely to be all the more willing to apportion and limit damages, to take account of the factors noted and if they do, the decision . . . will mark a significant development in the law . . .'

A Collender, 'Stress in the workplace' [2003] NLJ 248

The House of Lords has subsequently had the opportunity to review the principles laid down in *Hatton*.

CASE EXAMPLE

Barber v Somerset County Council [2004] UKHL 13; [2004] 1 WLR 1089

This appeal involved one of the original claimants in the joined appeals in *Hatton*, having lost his appeal in the Court of Appeal. The claimant was a maths teacher who was given additional co-ordinating and managerial responsibilities in order to maintain his current income following a restructuring of the school in which he worked. As a result his working hours increased to between 61 and 70 hours a week and after some months of trying to cope he complained of being overloaded to his deputy head teacher. Nothing was done and a few months later, after consulting his GP for stress and enquiring into the possibility of early retirement, he suffered a bout of stress and depression and was absent from work for three weeks. Again nothing was done by the school to address his problems and he continued to see his doctor for stress. He finally broke down, shook a pupil, and left the school permanently. Psychiatrists agreed that he was suffering moderate to severe depression. The claimant had won at first instance on the basis that the school ought to have appreciated that the risk to the claimant's health was significantly greater than to another teacher with a high workload and yet had done nothing. This was reversed by the Court of Appeal in the joined *Hatton* appeals. The House of Lords held that the Court of Appeal had failed to pay sufficient attention to the claimant's three week sickness absence and the medical reasons for it and held that the local authority was in breach of its duty of care by being aware of the difficulties that the increased workload were having on the claimant and the medical consequences but failing to do anything to remedy it.

Following *Barber* the Court of Appeal applied the *Hatton* criteria to individual cases in joined appeals, *Hartman v South Essex Mental Health & Community Care NHS Trust*; *Best v Staffordshire University*; *Wheeldon v HSBC Bank Ltd*; *Green v Grimsby & Scunthorpe Newspapers Ltd*; *Moore v Welwyn Components Ltd*; *Melville v The Home Office* [2004] EWCA Civ 06.

The Court of Appeal has more recently re-emphasised the point that a successful claimant must show that it was reasonably foreseeable that he would suffer a psychiatric illness as a result of the employer's breach of duty, not just that he would suffer from stress. However, in *Daw v Intel Corporation (UK) Ltd* [2007] EWCA Civ 76 the Court of Appeal held that 'indications of impending harm to health were plain enough for the [employer] to realise that immediate action was required'. The claimant had sent many notes to her employer drawing their attention to stress caused by overwork and confused lines of communication. The court also held that the mere fact of offering counselling was not sufficient to avoid liability.

Safety has always appeared to be a major preoccupation of the common law in the context of employment. Statutory obligations to the employee also demonstrate a clear concern with safety, but the health and general welfare of the employee are also key elements of the duty. It is significant that the common law is beginning to adopt a similarly broad attitude towards the employee's well being.

CASE EXAMPLE

Bonser v RJW Mining (UK) Ltd [2003] EWCA Civ 1296

The claimant was employed as a Technical Support and Training Manager. She often was forced to work beyond her contractual hours and the court accepted that her supervisor was overbearing and insensitive to her stress. This was despite the fact that her reference on taking up the post had said that she might not cope in a highly stressful environment. In 1996 she was reduced to a public display of tears when it looked as if the unreasonable demands by her supervisor were likely to lead to her having to cancel a holiday. Eventually in 1997 she suffered a stress related psychiatric illness and was forced to give up work. The trial judge held that, while in 1997 when the illness became obvious it was too late at that time for the employer to take steps to help the claimant, steps could have been taken after the crying episode in the previous year. They had not been and the employer was therefore liable. The Court of Appeal applied the *Hatton* criteria and held that there was insufficient in either the reference or the tears of 1996 to put the employer on notice of the foreseeability of a psychiatric illness resulting and found that the employer could not be liable in the circumstances.

The law has not only developed in this relatively narrow field. One area where employees may feel vulnerable is when they require references from employers in seeking new employment. Traditionally where an employee suffered from a poor and inaccurately written reference there was little chance of a remedy. The only action available was in defamation and the defence of qualified privilege might prevent the employee from seeing the reference unless he could show malice on the part of the employer (see Chapter 14, section 14.3.4). However, there has now also been developed a duty not to negligently prepare references for an employee. This removes many of the obstacles that an employee would have formerly faced.

CASE EXAMPLE

Spring v Guardian Assurance plc [1995] 3 WLR 354

Here the employee was dismissed and prevented from gaining a position with another company because of a negligently prepared reference provided by his employer. The House of Lords held that an employer has a duty when preparing a reference not to act negligently. The employer was held liable in the case. One other consideration was whether liability should be under *Hedley Byrne* or traditional negligence principles. The House was split on this point.

The rule on negligently prepared references has subsequently been developed in *Bartholomew v London Borough of Hackney* [1999] IRLR 246. The Court of Appeal identified that the duty was to ensure that only accurate information is provided and the impression created is not unfair. Even more recently in *Cox v Sun Alliance Life Ltd* [2001] IRLR 448 Lord Justice Mummery identified other key ingredients of the duty. The employer must believe in the truth of any information that he divulges and must also have reasonable grounds for that belief and make a reasonably thorough investigation of the facts before providing the reference (see also Chapter 6, section 6.3).

17.4 Defences

There are a number of defences that can apply from the general defences. However, there are two defences that are obviously very appropriate in the case of employer's liability.

Volenti non fit injuria (voluntary assumption of a risk)

Many if not most fields of work carry with them their own specific risks and dangers. Inevitably it is possible for the employer to argue that in accepting work the worker has accepted the risks that go with the work. However, the defence may be of more limited use since *Smith v Baker*.

However, the defence can still be claimed where the employee fully understands the risks involved and the agreement is free from pressure. There is contrasting case law to illustrate this.

CASE EXAMPLE

ICI Ltd v Shatwell [1965] AC 656

The claimant and his brother worked in the defendants' quarry. They ignored the defendants' orders and also statutory regulations by testing detonators without taking appropriate precautions. The claimant was then injured in an explosion and claimed that the defendants were vicariously liable on the basis of the claimant's brother, who instructed him not to follow the instructions, having been negligent and in breach of statutory duty. The court rejected his claim. By ignoring his employers and listening to his brother's unauthorised comments he had assumed the risk of injury by exercising his own free choice and the defence of volenti could apply.

Similarly where the employer by his negligence creates emergencies it is not then appropriate to try to apply the principles of *volenti* to the actions of those people responding to the emergency.

CASE EXAMPLE

Baker v T E Hopkins [1959] 3 All ER 225

An employer's workmen were subjected to danger by being exposed to petrol fumes in a confined space when the fumes overcame the men. A doctor attempting to rescue the men died as a result of his own exposure to the fumes. The employer tried to claim volenti on the part of the doctor. The court would not accept the application of the defence to the case. The doctor had not agreed to the specific risks involved. He was merely trying to do his best for the unconscious men. He had not consented to the risk of death.

The Court of Appeal explained the principle by referring to part of the judgment of Cardozo J in the American case *Wagner v International Railway Co* 332 NY 176 (1921) where he said

JUDGMENT

'Danger invites rescue. The law does not ignore these reactions . . . in tracing conduct to its consequences. It recognises them as normal. It places their effects within the range of the natural and the probable. The wrong that imperils life . . . is a wrong also to the rescuer.'

As a matter of policy the defence is generally unavailable for breach of a statutory duty. However, it may still be available where the claimant can be said to be the sole cause of his own misfortune.

CASE EXAMPLE

Ginty v Belmont Building Supplies Ltd [1959] 1 All ER 414

Here the appropriate safety equipment, duckboards, had been provided. It was the complete failure by the claimant to use safety equipment that actually led to injury.

Contributory negligence

As a partial defence only the defence may be available in the case of any of the duties where the claimant is partly responsible for his injury.

However, employees are generally treated more leniently by the courts (see *Caswell v*

Powell Duffryn Collieries [1940] AC 152). This is because it is accepted that the pressures of work mean that workers may take less than full care of themselves and should be protected from their own carelessness.

Even where the employee is careless in helping to create his own injury the employer may still be in breach of the duty to protect the employee from such carelessness (see *General Cleaning Contractors v Christmas* [1953] AC 180).

Nevertheless, where it is accepted that the employee has contributed to his own harm and that contributory negligence should apply then damages will be reduced according to the extent to which the employee did contribute to his own injury.

CASE EXAMPLE

Jones v Livox Quarries Ltd [1952] 2 QB 608

Here where the employee was injured in a collision caused by the defendant's negligence damages were reduced by 5 per cent. This was because the employee had contributed to his own injury by riding on the tow bar of a traxcavator despite the express prohibition of his employer.

Lord Denning identified the principles of the defence in the case.

JUDGMENT

'Although contributory negligence does not depend on a duty of care it does depend on foreseeability. Just as actionable negligence requires the foreseeability of harm to others, so contributory negligence requires the foreseeability of harm to oneself.'

The defence can be used even in situations where death has resulted from the negligent event but the employee also contributed to his own harm.

CASE EXAMPLE

Davies v Swan Motor (Swansea) Co Ltd [1949] 2 KB 291

Here a dustman was killed in a collision caused by the defendant's negligence. Damages were reduced because he had contributed to his injuries by riding on the step of the dustcart.

It is also possible for there to be liability on the defendant but 100 per cent contributory negligence awarded and consequent reduction in damages.

CASE EXAMPLE

Jayes v IMI (Kynoch) Ltd [1985] ICR 155

Here the employer was liable because a statutory duty in respect of guarding machinery was strict in terms of liability for ensuring that guards were maintained at all times when machines were working. 100 per cent contributory negligence was awarded when the employee lost fingers because the employee himself had taken the guard off the machine in order to clear a blockage while the machine was still running.

ACTIVITY

Self-assessment questions

1. Why did employers' liability develop so long after it was needed?
2. What were the major defects in the early law?
3. Was the common law always hostile to employees?

4. To what extent is an employer responsible for the actions of practical jokers within the workforce?
5. Which is more important the common law or statute in relation to safe plant and equipment?
6. To what extent can an employer follow an established trade practice which is dangerous?
7. What is the standard of care appropriate to maintaining safe premises?
8. What effect does causation have on the duty of an employer?
9. How easy is it for an employer to defend a case of breach of a common law duty?
10. How has the scope of an employer's duty of care expanded recently?
11. What difficulties confront an employee who is trying to bring a claim for a stress related injury?

ACTIVITY

Applying the law

Using the guide to answering problem questions in Appendix 2 try the following problems.

1. Bodgit & Fastfit Co are a light engineering firm. Some of their work involves cutting sheet metal on power guillotines. One day Stanley cuts a panel incorrectly, and, since the job is urgent, he agrees with his foreman, Oliver, to re-cut it without the safety guard in place. Because of the shape of the panel it slips and Stanley loses his hand as a result. Stanley had already lost his other hand when a fellow employee, Buster, a known practical joker, let off a banger behind Stanley. The shock caused Stanley to lurch forward and catch his hand in an unguarded press.

Advise Stanley of any possible course of action.

2. Spinnet & Weavit Co are textile manufacturers, who have recently installed central heating in their mill after complaints about the cold from their employees. In the weaving machine room, which is always warm, Fred becomes too warm, falls asleep, and injures his hand in the loom. The hot pipes cause some floorboards to warp. Jack, who is wheeling a trolley of hot dye, is badly burnt when a wheel catches an uneven board and the dye spills over his legs. This spillage also creates dangerous chemical fumes when the dye mixes with varnish on the floor. Tom, another worker, feels nauseous from the fumes and tries to open a window. This is impossible since the windows have been sealed following the complaints about the cold. Tom is overcome by the fumes and hits his head very badly when he passes out.

Advise Spinnet & Weavit Co of any liability it may have to Fred, Jack and Tom.

KEY FACTS

The scope of the duty	Case
The employer owes a non-delegable duty for the health and safety of the employee – so:	*Wilsons & Clyde Coal Co v English* (1938)
Must provide competent staff for duties undertaken.	*General Cleaning Contractors v Christmas* (1953
Must provide safe working colleagues.	*Hudson v Ridge Manufacturing* (1957)
Must provide safe plant and equipment and properly maintain it (but now Employers' Liability (Defective Equipment) Act 1969 applies).	*Smith v Baker* (1891)
Must take reasonable steps to provide safe premises (which may extend to other premises).	*Latimer v AEC* (1953)
	Wilson v Tyneside Cleaning Co (1958)

Must provide a safe system of work: must create and implement safe system and ensure system is carried out and system must meet dangers. Cannot rely on unsafe system just because it is common practice.	*Bux v Slough Metals* (1974) *General Cleaning Contractors v Christmas* (1953) *Re Herald of Free Enterprise* (1987)
Developments in the duty	**Case**
The duty now applies also to psychiatric health and wellbeing. The Court of Appeal has issued guidelines – must know of existing vulnerability, it must be foreseeable that the employment practices will lead to a stress-related psychiatric injury, and the employment practices must actually cause or worsen the psychiatric illness. There is also now a duty to provide references that are not negligently prepared.	*Walker v Northumberland CC* (1995) *Sutherland v Hatton* (2002) *Spring v Guardian Assurance Co* (1995)
The character of the duty	**Case**
The duty is non-delegable. The employer only need take reasonable precautions. The duty extends to reasonable and incidental activities. Duty does not extend to employees properly. Trade practices can only be relied upon if reasonable. The employer should consider the possible extent of injury. And may consider practicality of any precautions. And must prevent only reasonably foreseeable accidents.	*Wilsons & Clyde Coal Co v English* (1938) *Latimer v AEC* (1953) *Davidson v Handley Page Ltd* (1945) *Deyong v Shenburn* (1946) *Cavanagh v Ulster Weaving Co* (1960) *Paris v Stepney BC* (1951) *Charlton v Forrest Printing Ink Co* (1978) *Doughty v Turner Manufacturing* (1964)
Defences	**Case**
Volenti (consent) – has limited use – the employee must fully appreciate and consent to the actual risk. This is possible if the agreement is free from pressure and where the claimant is the sole cause of injury but it is not available for breach of a statutory duty. Contributory negligence – this is a possible defence to any duty. It is covered by the provisions of the Law Reform (Contributory Negligence) Act 1945. Damages may be reduced when the worker contributed to own injury and even 100% reduction is possible.	*Smith v Baker* (1891) *ICI v Shatwell* (1965) *Ginty v Belmont Building Supplies Ltd* (1959) *Jones v Livox Quarries Ltd* (1952) *Jayes v IMI (Kynoch) Ltd* (1985)

17.5 The importance of statutory protection and EU law

It should not be forgotten that many of the most effective aspects of industrial safety law come from statute. As industry developed in the nineteenth and twentieth centuries the sheer volume of accidents at work demonstrated the need for effective regulation. In the nineteenth century statutory regulation of employment conditions developed but was very limited. As an example of this the Factory Act 1844 created a Factory Inspectorate but only provided for four inspectors for the whole country.

By the late twentieth century the defects in the law as it had developed by statute were obvious:

■ It was found in too many Acts and so was very cumbersome.
■ The law was complex and often overlapped.
■ It was based on premises rather than people.
■ Many workers fell outside of cover.

The Robens Committee in 1970 reviewed the whole field, accepted all of the above and identified that too many bodies or ministries were also involved. As a result the Health and Safety at Work etc Act 1974 was passed. This imposed a basic duty to employees in s 2(1) '. . . to ensure so far as is practicable health, safety, and welfare of employees.'

The Act consolidated a number of other statutes and provided for safe plant, premises and systems; an obligation on employers to ensure absence of risks in handling, storing, transport, use of articles and substances; information, instruction, training and supervision; and also for the appointment of safety representatives. By s 7 all employees also have a duty to take care of themselves and other employees.

The Act also provides the means of enforcement with a Health and Safety Commission to supervise and administrate the law, and a Health and Safety Executive to enforce it. Much of the enforcement process is through the criminal law rather than through civil actions. Inspectors have wide powers to enter premises, investigate health and safety breaches, and indeed to use any other power necessary to carry out their duties. They can issue Improvement Notices and Prohibition Notices and even have the powers to close businesses until breaches of safety law are remedied.

The Act is supported by a variety of other Acts and regulations appropriate to specific industries, substances, processes etc. There are numerous instances of duties leading to civil liability but as we have seen in Chapter 16 there are also accompanying difficulties, not least very often the problem of proving that the provision in question does actually give rise to civil liability.

EC law has also become a major provider of health and safety protection in employment. Article 138 of the European Communities Treaty (formerly Art 118A inserted into the Treaty by the Single European Act 1986) creates the power to issue Directives in furtherance of health and safety at work. Many have already been implemented in the UK by statutory instrument and there are many more in draft form.

A major group of Regulations coming from Directives and often referred to as the 'six pack' was introduced in 1993; these have since been modified and updated. These include:

■ The Management of Health and Safety at Work Regulations 1999, which introduced the requirement of risk assessment.
■ The Workplace (Health and Safety and Welfare) Regulations 1992, which cover maintenance and repair and the general state of premises.
■ The Provision and Use of Work Equipment Regulations 1998, which cover all equipment and machinery.
■ The Personal Protective Equipment at Work Regulations 1992, which cover anything to be worn or held to protect employees from risks.
■ The Manual Handling Operations Regulations 1992, to reduce as far as possible any manual handling which carries risks.

■ The Health and Safety (Display Screen Equipment) Regulations 1992 which regulate the use of VDUs and workstations.

Another significant development resulting from EC law requirements, in the light of the long line of cases following *Johnstone v Bloomsbury* [1991] 2 All ER 293 and *Walker v Northumberland CC* (see section 17.3 above), is the Working Time Regulations 1998. These provide for:

■ a basic maximum working week of 48 hours
■ minimum daily rest periods of 11 hours
■ minimum weekly rest periods of 24 hours
■ minimum rest break periods of 20 minutes after six hours
■ minimum paid holiday entitlement of four weeks
■ higher minimums for young workers.

The Regulations are limited in scope because there are a number of exemptions in particular types of employment and it is also possible for employees to opt out of cover. Nevertheless, they introduce some significant basic standards of working conditions and health and safety protection. They are enforceable, as with most statutory health and safety law through criminal sanctions. However, they also provide for civil actions and civil remedies.

Common law duties
• Duty to provide competent working colleagues
• Duty to provide safe plant and equipment
• Duty to provide safe premises
• General duty to protect health and well being
• Duty to protect psychiatric health
• Duty not to give negligent references
Duties under The Health and Safety at Work etc Act 1974
The duty to ensure so far as is practicable the health, safety, and welfare of employees – including: • provide and maintain safe plant and systems • ensure absence of risks in handling, storing, transport, use of articles and substances • provide information, instruction, training and supervision where necessary • maintenance of premises, access, exits etc • safe working environment without risks
Duties deriving from EU Law
Management of Health & Safety at Work Regulations • Basic requirement of risk assessment • Appointment of safety officers • Must establish emergency procedures • Must provide necessary training

Workplace (Health & Safety & Welfare) Regulations
• Requires maintenance, repair, cleaning, to ensure all in efficient state
• Demands availability of pure air, reasonable temperature, adequate lighting
• Provision of seats when work can be done seated
• Controls construction of doors ladders etc
• Provision of adequate sanitary arrangements
• Provision for changing clothes where necessary
• Provision for changing clothing where necessary

Provision and Use of Work Regulations
• Work equipment must be suitable
• Employees to be given appropriate information
• Proper controls in respect of entry to machines, stopping controls etc and immediate isolation

Personal Protection Equipment at Work Regulations
• Covers anything to be worn or held to protect employees from risks
• Must conform to EC standards
• All such equipment must be compatible with any other used
• Should be kept in good repair
• Employer to ensure it is used properly

Manual Handling Operations Regulations
• Employer to reduce as far as possible manual handling which carries risks
• Employer must produce an assessment of operations
• Where such handling cannot be avoided employer to do everything possible to minimise risk

Health and Safety (Display Screen) Equipment Regulations
• Employer to analyse workstations to assess health and safety risks
• Duty to reduce such risks
• Provide planned periodic breaks or change of activity
• Provide eyesight testing
• Provide adequate information and training

The Working Time Regulations
• 48-hour week, though possible to average out over 17-week period
• Limits on night work – 8 hours in 24
• Minimum daily rest periods – 11 hours, 12 for young workers
• Minimum weekly rest periods – 24 hours, 48 for young workers
• Minimum rest break periods – 20 minutes after 6 hours (or 30 for young workers)
• Adequate rest breaks where the monotony of work puts the worker's health at risk
• Minimum paid holiday entitlement – 4 weeks
• Free health checks for night workers

Figure 17.1 Chart showing the extent of the various health and safety duties owed to employees

SUMMARY

- There is a non-delegable common law duty to provide competent fellow employees, safe plant and equipment, safe premises, a safe system of work, and more recently to prevent psychiatric harm
- The duty cannot be delegated, and is to do what is reasonable, even extending to ancillary activities, but not to property, only reasonable trade practices are accepted, and the employer must consider the possible extent of injury to an employee, and can take into account the practicality of any precautions since the duty is only to prevent foreseeable accidents
- *Volenti non fit injuria* and contributory negligence are possible defences
- The common law has also been supplemented with many statutory provisions regulating the workplace and some of these have originated in EU law

Further reading

Collier, A, 'Stress in the workplace' [2002] NLJ 248.

'Stress at work' IDS Brief 655, February 2000.

Zindani, J, 'Back to the future from the Court of Appeal' [2000] NLJ 1100.

18

Vicarious liability

AIMS AND OBJECTIVES

After reading this chapter you should be able to:

■ Understand the basic meaning of vicarious liability
■ Understand the purposes and justifications for imposing vicarious liability
■ Understand the tests for establishing employment status
■ Understand the circumstances in which an employer will and will not be liable for the acts and omissions of his employee
■ Be able to critically analyse the area
■ Be able to apply the law to factual situations and reach conclusions as to liability

18.1 Origins, purposes and criticisms

Vicarious liability is not an individual tort in the way that we have looked at other torts such as negligence or nuisance. It is a means of imposing liability for a tort onto a party other than the tortfeasor, the party causing the tort.

It was in fact originally based on the 'fiction' that an employer has control over his employees and therefore should be liable for torts committed by the employee. This was possibly less of a fiction in the nineteenth century when the 'master and servant' laws still accurately reflected the true imbalance in the employment relationship.

In a less sophisticated society with less diverse types of work control was indeed possible. In domestic service for instance the master could dictate exactly the method of the work done by the servant. This was in fact dramatically demonstrated by case law of the time.

CASE EXAMPLE

Latter v Braddell (1881) 50 LJQB 448

A young female domestic servant was asked to submit herself to an internal examination when her mistress suspected that the girl was pregnant. The girl very reluctantly and in great distress complied with the order as in the employment circumstances of the time she would have little chance to refuse. In her later action for assault her claim failed. She was held to have consented to the examination.

Modern forms of employment make control less evident. For instance the actual work done by a surgeon can hardly be said to be under the control of a hospital administrator with no medical expertise.

Nevertheless, the origins of the liability are important because it is rare that vicarious liability will exist outside of the employment relationship.

The rule has been criticised for being harsh and 'rough justice' since an apparently innocent party is being fixed with liability for something which he has not done. On this level imposing liability by this method is a direct contradiction of the principle requiring fault to be proved to establish liability.

There are a number of justifications for the practice, many of which have to do with ensuring that the victim of a wrong has the means of gaining compensation for the damage or injury suffered.

- Traditionally, as we have seen, an employer may have had a greater degree of control over the activities of employees. Indeed it may well be that an employee has carried out the tort on the employer's behalf, so it is only fair that the employer should bear the cost.
- The employer, in any case, is responsible for hiring and firing and disciplining staff. The employer may have been careless in selecting staff, and, if employees are either careless or prone to causing harm and the employer is aware of this, then he has the means of doing something about it. The internal disciplinary systems allow the employer to ensure that lapses are not repeated, ultimately to the extent of dismissing staff. The employer is also responsible for ensuring that all employees are effectively trained so that work is done safely.
- The major concern of an injured party is where compensation is likely to come from. In this respect the employer will usually be better able to stand the loss than the employee will. In any case the employer is obliged to take out public liability insurance and can also pass on loss in prices.
- This is itself a justification for vicarious liability since it is also a means of deterring tortious activities.
- In certain instances imposing vicarious liability makes the conduct of the case easier for the injured party in terms of identifying specific negligence. This is particularly so in the case of medical negligence.
- Proving vicarious liability first depends on satisfying a number of other basic tests:
  - Was the person alleged to have committed the tort an employee? There is only very limited liability for the torts of independent contractors.
  - Did that party commit the alleged tort 'during the course of his employment'? An employer is generally not liable for torts that occur away from work or while the employee is 'on a frolic on his own'.
  - Was the act or omission complained of a tort? Again an employer will not generally incur liability for other wrongs such as crimes carried out by the employee.

18.2 Tests of employment status

18.2.1 Introduction

It is not always possible to determine at first sight whether in fact a person is employed under a contract of service or not. It will often be in the interest of an 'employer' to deny that the relationship is one of employment. Definitions such as that contained in the Employment Rights Act 1996 that the employer is a person employed under a contract of employment are no real help in determining a person's employment status. It has been suggested in *WHPT Housing Association Ltd v Secretary of State for Social Services* [1981] ICR 737 that the distinction lies in the fact that the employee provides himself to serve while the self-employed person only offers his services. This is no great help in determining whether or not a person is employed.

There is in any case inconsistency in the methods of testing employee status according to who it is that is doing the testing. For instance the only concern of the tax authorities in testing employee status is in determining a liability for payment of tax, not for any other purpose. So the fact that a person is paying Schedule D tax is not necessarily definitive of their status as self-employed. Again industrial safety inspectors may have less concern with the status of an injured party and more with the regulations that have been breached.

Besides this a number of different types of working relationship are not so easy to define. 'Lump' labour was common in the past, particularly the 1960s and 1970s. Casual and temporary employment is possibly even more prevalent in recent times, and many major companies rely on the use of agency staff.

Over the years the courts have devised a number of methods of testing employee status. They all have shortcomings. Some are less useful in a modern society than others.

18.2.2 The control test

The oldest of these is the 'control test'. This test derived from the days of the 'master and servant' laws as we have already seen. In *Yewens v Noakes* (1880) 6 QBD 530 the test was whether the master had the right to control what was done and the way in which it was done. According to McArdie J in *Performing Right Society v Mitchell and Booker* [1924] 1 KB 762 the test concerns '. . . the nature and degree of detailed control.'

Lord Thankerton in *Short v J W Henderson Ltd* (1946) 62 TLR 427 identified many key features that would show that the master had control over the servant. These included the power to select the servant, the right to control the method of working, the right to suspend and dismiss and the payment of wages.

Such a test is virtually impossible to apply accurately in modern circumstances. Nevertheless, there are circumstances in which a test of control is still useful, in the case of borrowed workers.

CASE EXAMPLE

Mersey Docks & Harbour Board v Coggins and Griffiths (Liverpool) Ltd [1947] AC 1

Here the test was applied when a crane driver negligently damaged goods in the course of his work. In this case the Harbour Board hired a crane and the crane driver out to stevedores to act as their servant. Under the contract between the Board and the stevedores the crane driver was still to be paid by the Board and only they had the right to dismiss him, but for the duration of the contract he was to be regarded as the employee of the stevedores. The Harbour Board was still held to be liable for his negligence, however, since he would not accept control from the stevedores.

In the case above Lord Porter gave a very clear explanation of the control test.

JUDGMENT

'the most satisfactory [test] by which to ascertain who is the employer at any particular time, is to ask who is entitled to tell the employee the way in which he is to do the work upon which he is engaged . . . it is not enough that the task to be performed should be under his control, he must control the method of performing it.'

This can be seen in *Hawley v Luminar Leisure plc* [2005] EWHC 5 (QB) where a nightclub owner was held to be in control of and therefore vicariously liable for bouncers actually employed by a security firm. This was because the owner gave the men detailed instructions on how to do the job.

18.2.3 The integration or organisation test

Lord Denning in *Stevenson Jordan and Harrison Ltd v McDonald and Evans* (1969) 1 TLR 101 established this test. The basis of the test is that someone will be an employee whose work is fully integrated into the business, whereas if a person's work is only accessory to the business then that person is not an employee.

According to this test the master of a ship, a chauffeur and a reporter on the staff of a newspaper are all employees, where the pilot bringing a ship into port, a taxi driver and a freelance writer are not.

The test can work well in some circumstances but there are still defects. Part-time examiners may be classed as employed for the purposes of deducting tax, but it is unlikely that the exam board would be happy to pay redundancy when their services were no longer needed.

18.2.4 The economic reality or multiple test

The courts in recent times have at last recognised that a single test of employment is not satisfactory and may produce confusing results. The answer under this test is to consider whatever factors may be indicative of employment or self-employment. In particular, three conditions should be met before an employment relationship is identified:

■ The employee agrees to provide work or skill in return for a wage.
■ The employee expressly or impliedly accepts that the work will be subject to the control of the employer.
■ All other considerations in the contract are consistent with there being a contract of employment rather than any other relationship between the parties.

CASE EXAMPLE

Ready Mixed Concrete (South East) Ltd v Minister of Pensions and National Insurance [1968] 2 QB 497

The case involved who was liable for National Insurance contributions, the company or one of its drivers. Drivers were used under a new contract under which they drove vehicles in the company colours and logo that they bought on hire purchase agreements from the company. Under the contract they were also obliged to maintain the vehicles according to set standards in the contract. They were only allowed to use the lorries on company business. Their contracted hours, however, were flexible and their pay was subject to an annual minimum rate according to the concrete hauled. They were also allowed to hire drivers in their place. Although it might be seen to have operated unfairly on the claimant the drivers were held to be independent. The case is important because McKenna J developed the above test in determining their lack of employment status.

The test has subsequently been modified so that all factors in the relationship should be considered and weighed according to their significance. Such factors might include:

■ The ownership of tools, plant or equipment – clearly an employee is less likely to own the plant and equipment with which he works.
■ The method of payment – again a self-employed person is likely to take a price for a whole job where an employee will usually receive regular payments for a defined pay period.
■ Tax and National Insurance contributions – an employee usually has tax deducted out of wages under the PAYE scheme under Schedule E and Class 1 National Insurance contributions also deducted by the employer. A self-employed person will usually pay tax annually under Schedule D and will make National Insurance contributions by buying Class 2 stamps.

■ Self-description – a person may describe himself as one or the other and this will usually, but not always, be an accurate description.

■ Level of independence – probably one of the acid tests of status as self-employed is the extra degree of independence in being able to take work from whatever source and turn work down.

■ A recent addition is to determine who has the benefit of any insurance cover that might be available (see *British Telecommunications plc v James Thompson & Sons (Engineers) Ltd* [1999] 1 WLR 9).

All of these are useful in identifying the status of the worker but none of them are an absolute test or are definitive on their own.

18.2.5 Irregular situations

Certain types of work have proved more likely to cause problems in the past than have others. Not every working relationship is clear cut and judges and the members of tribunals have been called on to make decisions, sometimes based on the factors we have already considered. Often their answer will depend on the purpose of the case. In this way the court might seek to bring a person within industrial safety law although they appear to be self-employed.

Casual workers

Such workers have traditionally been viewed as independent contractors rather than as employed. This may be of particular significance since modern employment practices tend towards less secure and less permanent work.

CASE EXAMPLE

O'Kelly v Trust House Forte plc [1983] 3 WLR 605

Here it was important for 'wine butlers', employed casually at the Grosvenor House Hotel, to show that they were employees in order that they could claim for dismissal. They had no other source of income and there were a number of factors consistent with employment. However, the tribunal took the view that, since the employer had no obligation to provide work and since they could if they wished work elsewhere then there was no mutuality of obligations and they were not employed.

The House of Lords have also subsequently confirmed this lack of mutual obligation test of employment status in casual work.

CASE EXAMPLE

Carmichael v National Power plc [1998] ICR 1167

The case involved a tour guide at Sellafield, a nuclear power station. She was given work as required and paid for the work done and tax and National Insurance contributions were also deducted. However, the House of Lords eventually decided that the critical factors were that there was no obligation to provide work and no obligation on the woman's part to accept any that was offered. She was therefore held to be an independent contractor. It is interesting to note that the Court of Appeal had reached an entirely different result, which appeared to have recognised the difficult circumstances under which people are now often forced to accept what amounts to, but is not necessarily classed as employment.

Agency staff

Many large companies now hire staff through employment agencies. On past cases they have not always been seen as employees of the agency.

CASE EXAMPLE

Wickens v Champion Employment [1984] ICR 365

Here it was held that the agency workers were not employees since the agency was under no obligation to find them work and there was no continuity and care in the contractual relationship consistent with employment.

Workers' co-operatives

Again it is uncertain whether such workers would be employees or not. Usually we would expect them to be so. However, there are instances where such workers have been classed as self-employed.

CASE EXAMPLE

Addison v London Philharmonic Orchestra Ltd [1981] ICR 261

The orchestra operated as a co-operative. The musicians could do other work on their own account. It was held that they were subjecting themselves to discipline rather than control as employees and therefore were independent.

Outworkers

People who work from home, usually women with young children, are a very disadvantaged sector of the workforce. They tend to work for little pay and have few rights. There is obviously little control over the hours that they work. Nevertheless, working in areas such as the garment industry, they normally fall into a general framework of organisation. They were in the past always considered to be independent contractors, which is well illustrated in the case law. However, some cases have suggested otherwise.

CASE EXAMPLE

Nethermere (St Neots) Ltd v Taverna and Gardiner [1984] IRLR 240

Here workers in the garment industry were held to be employees because it was felt that they were doing the same work as employees in the factory, they were merely doing it at a different location, at home.

Trainees

Apprenticeships were traditionally subject to their own distinct rules but there are few of these traditional apprenticeships now. In the case of trainees the major purpose in their relationship with the 'employer' is to learn the trade rather than to actually provide work. Therefore they have usually not been classed as employees.

CASE EXAMPLE

Wiltshire Police Authority v Wynn [1980] QB 95

A female cadet tried to claim unfair dismissal, which required proving first that she was an employee. While she had been placed on various attachments, was paid a wage, could do no other work, and had set hours, she was only undergoing training with a view to becoming a police officer and it was held that she was not yet employed.

Labour-only sub-contractors (the lump)

At one time such workers were very common in the construction industry where they would do work for a lump sum. There are obvious advantages to both sides in not making tax and National Insurance contributions. These workers are classed as self-employed.

Crown servants

People working for the crown were traditionally viewed as not being under a contract of employment. This meant that they had very restricted rights. The trend in modern times has been to move away from this position.

Office holders

An office is basically a position that exists independently of the person currently holding it. So the general category might include ministers of the church and justices of the peace. The picture on these is confused but it has been held that there is no vicarious liability by the church.

Directors

A director may or may not also be an employee of the company. This will inevitably depend on the terms of the individual contract.

Hospital workers

Obviously vicarious liability for the work of people in health care can be critical. Nevertheless, the traditional view in *Hillyer v Governor of St Bartholomews Hospital* [1909] 2 KB 820 was that a hospital should not be vicariously liable for the work of doctors. This was justified on the grounds that hospitals generally lacked adequate finance before the creation of the National Health Service. The more recent view, expressed in *Cassidy v Ministry of Health* [1951] 2 KB 343 is that hospitals and health services should be responsible for the work done in them.

ACTIVITY

Quick quiz

Consider whether the following would be classed as employees using the tests above:
1. Sarah, a machinist, who works from home stitching shirts from pieces of cloth pre-cut and delivered by Tej, who also deducts National Insurance payments from her pay but leaves her to settle her own tax. Tej owns the sewing machine that Sarah uses.
2. Eric, a plasterer, who travels round building sites and works for cash payments. Neither he nor builders that he works for pay tax or NI for him. He uses his own tools.
3. Coco, a circus clown, who also sells tickets before performances and helps to pack up the big top when the circus goes on to the next town. He also drives one of the lorries that transports the circus. The circus owner says that Coco is self-employed.
4. Alistair is a consultant orthopaedic specialist. He is paid a full time salary by an NHS Trust but spends three days per week seeing private patients.

18.3 The test of liability

18.3.1 Torts committed in the course of employment

We have already discussed whether or not it is fair to impose liability on an employer for torts committed by his employee. Since it is a potentially unjust situation it is strictly limited and the employer will only be liable for those torts committed while the employee is 'in the course of the employment'.

What is and is not in the course of employment is a question of fact for the court to determine in each case. It is often difficult to see any consistency in the judgments. It seems inevitable that judges will decide cases on policy grounds and this may explain some of the apparent inconsistency.

Regardless of the reasoning applied in them, there are two lines of cases:

■ Those where there is vicarious liability because the employee is said to be acting in the course of the employment.

■ Those where there is no vicarious liability because the employee is said not to be acting in the course of employment.

It is very hard to find a general test for what is in the course of employment. However, courts have appeared to favour a test suggested by Salmond that the employer will be liable in two instances:

■ for a wrongful act that has been authorised by the employer;
■ for an act that, while authorised, was carried out in an unauthorised way.

Authorised acts

An employer then will inevitably be liable for acts that he has expressly authorised, and, since an employee is only obliged to obey all reasonable and lawful acts, he could refuse to carry out tortious acts that the employer instructed him to do.

The more difficult aspect of this rule is whether the employer can be said to have authorised a tortious act by implication and should therefore be liable. At least one case has suggested that this is possible.

CASE EXAMPLE

Poland v Parr [1927] 1 KB 236

The employee was a carter. He assaulted a boy in order to stop him from stealing from his employer's wagon. The boy fell under the wagon and was injured as a result. The employer was held to be vicariously liable for the assault since the employee was only protecting the employer's property, which by implication he had authority to do. He was acting reasonably and honestly in protection of the employer's property.

As Lord Atkin explained

JUDGMENT

'Any servant is, as a general rule, authorised to do acts which are for the protection of his master's property.'

Authorised acts carried out in an unauthorised manner

Most employment involves some form of discretion on the part of the employee. The employer may direct the specific work to be done and even to an extent the method by which it should be carried out. Almost inevitably employees will carry out work making decisions of their own as they go along. In some circumstances they may carry out acts that are completely unauthorised. The significant point to establish that the employer is still liable for their tortious acts is that they are actually still engaged in the work for which they are employed and that the tort arises out of this work. An employer can be liable then for unauthorised acts in a variety of ways.

■ Where the employee is still engaged in his own work but does something even though this has been expressly prohibited by the employer.

CASE EXAMPLE

Limpus v London General Omnibus Company (1862) 1 H & C 526

At the time of the case buses were horse drawn. Bus drivers had been specifically instructed not to race because of the dangers to themselves and to the public. When they did and the claimant was injured the employer was held vicariously liable. The drivers were authorised to drive the buses but not in the manner they did.

■ Where the employee carries out work that is authorised but is doing the work negligently.

CASE EXAMPLE

Century Insurance Co Ltd v Northern Ireland Transport Board [1942] AC 509

A driver of a petrol tanker was delivering to a petrol station. In lighting a cigarette he carelessly threw down a lighted match causing an explosion. The employer was still held liable since the driver was in the course of employment, and merely doing his work negligently.

■ Where the employee gives unauthorised lifts contrary to instructions.

CASE EXAMPLE

Rose v Plenty [1976] 1 WLR 141

Here a milkman continued to use a child helper despite express instructions from the employer not to allow people to ride on the milk floats. When the boy was injured partly through the milkman's negligence his employer was held liable. The milkman was carrying out his work in an unauthorised manner. Lord Denning suggested that the employer was liable because they were benefiting from the work undertaken by the boy.

In his judgment Lord Denning identified that

JUDGMENT

'An employer's express prohibition of the doing of an act is not necessarily such as to exempt the employer from liability, provided that the act is done not for the employee's own purpose, but in the course of his service and for his employer's benefit.'

Lord Scarman applied the principle to the case.

JUDGMENT

'Why was the plaintiff being carried on the float when the accident occurred? [He] was there because it was necessary that he should be there in order that he could assist, albeit in a way prohibited by the employers, in the job entrusted to the servant by his employers.'

■ Where the employee exceeds the proper boundaries of the job.

CASE EXAMPLE

Fennelly v Connex South Eastern Ltd [2001] IRLR 390

A ticket collector got into an argument with a customer whom he believed had not paid the appropriate fare and he then assaulted the customer. The Court of Appeal held that, since the act occurred within the course of employment the employer was liable for the assault.

■ Where the employee applies force in order to achieve the employer's objectives.

CASE EXAMPLE

Bayley v Manchester, Sheffield and Lincolnshire Railway Co (1873) LR 8 CP 148

Part of a porter's work was to ensure that passengers got on to the correct train. Here the porter pulled the claimant from the train in order to do so and the employers were vicariously liable for the assault.

■ Where the employee identifies himself as an employee even though the act is not to do with the employment.

CASE EXAMPLE

Weir v Chief Constable of Merseyside Police [2003] EWCA Civ 111

A police officer was helping his girlfriend to move flat and he used a police vehicle without permission for the purpose. He then caught a young man interfering with the girlfriend's property which was outside the flat. He assaulted the young man, identifying himself as a police officer at the same time. The court held that in the circumstances the young man was entitled to believe that he was being assaulted by a police officer and the employer was liable.

One recent important development is that it is now possible to impose vicarious liability where there is a breach of a statutory duty imposed on the individual employee rather than also on the employer. In this way a successful claim of vicarious liability can be made under s 3, Protection from Harassment Act 1997.

CASE EXAMPLE

Majrowski v Guy's and St Thomas' NHS Trust [2006] UKHL 34; [2006] All ER (D) 146

The claimant who was employed by the NHS trust claimed that he had been bullied and harassed by his departmental manager because of his homosexuality. He complained internally and following investigation his complaints were accepted and the Trust accepted that there had indeed been harassment. The claimant brought an action against the Trust under s 3, Protection from Harassment Act 1997. At first instance the claim was struck out but the claimant won his appeal in the House of Lords.

The case of *Green v DB Group Services* (UK) Ltd [2006] EWHC 1898 (Ch) (see 13.6.3) also represents a major development in respect of use of s 3.

Another important recent development is that dual vicarious liability is now also a possibility.

CASE EXAMPLE

Viasystems (Tyneside) Ltd v Thermal Transfer (Northern) Ltd, S & P Darwell Ltd and CAT Metalwork Services [2005] EWCA Civ 1151

The claimant hired Thermal Transfer to install air conditioning in its factory. Thermal Transfer sub-contracted ducting work to Darwell which in turn hired fitters from CAT on a labour only basis. One of these fitters, through his negligence, caused a flood damaging the claimant's property. Thermal Transfer was liable to the claimant under its contract. The trial judge held that CAT was also liable as the fitter's employer. CAT appealed that Darwell should be considered the fitter's employer in the circumstances and the Court of Appeal agreed and held both liable.

18.3.2 Torts committed outside of the course of employment

This area can be potentially confusing because many cases where the employer has been found not to be liable appear to cover similar areas as those that do fall within the course of employment. Usually there is some extra element but it is still confusing. In general though an employer will not be liable when the employee's tortious act fell outside of the actual scope of his own employment or where the employee was 'on a frolic on his own' (in other words he was acting on his own account and nothing to do with the employment at all). Again there are a variety of circumstances in which the employer can be found not to be liable.

■ Where the employee engages in expressly prohibited acts that have nothing to do with his own work.

CASE EXAMPLE

Beard v London General Omnibus Co [1900] 2 QB 530

Here a bus conductor drove the bus despite express orders to the contrary and injured the claimant. The employers were not vicariously liable. The conductor was not carrying out his own work but doing something outside of the scope of his own employment.

■ Where the employee is 'on a frolic of his own'. An employer will not be responsible for acts that occur outside of the normal working day such as travelling into work. The same will apply where the employee does something outside of the scope of the work. An employee who leaves work unofficially and goes off on an unauthorised escapade may be said to be 'on a frolic'.

CASE EXAMPLE

Hilton v Thomas Burton (Rhodes) Ltd [1961] 1 WLR 705

Workmen took an unauthorised break and left their place of work. On returning to work one employee, who was driving the work's van, crashed the van and killed somebody. The employer was held not to be liable since the workmen were 'on a frolic'.

■ Activities that are nothing to do with the employer's business.

CASE EXAMPLE

Storey v Ashton (1869) LR 4 QB 476

A delivery driver was persuaded to divert from his journey to pick up coal for another man. Through his negligence the driver then caused an accident. The court would not accept that there could be vicarious liability. The employee was 'on a frolic on his own'.

■ Giving unauthorised lifts.

CASE EXAMPLE

Twine v Beans Express (1946) 62 TLR 458

A hitchhiker was injured through the negligence of a driver who had been forbidden to give lifts. The employers were held not to be liable. This contrasts with what appears to be a fairly similar situation in *Rose v Plenty* [1976] 1 WLR 141. The significant difference is that here the employer was gaining no benefit from the prohibited lift.

■ Acts that exceed the proper boundaries of the work and cannot be said to form part of the employment.

CASE EXAMPLE

Makanjuola v Metropolitan Police Commissioner, *The Times*, 8th August, 1992

The claimant was persuaded into allowing a police officer to have sex with her in return for not reporting her to immigration authorities. The court accepted that there could be no possible liability on the employer. The actions of the employee were anything but part of his job and the officer was not doing anything that could be described as falling within his work responsibilities.

Some situations still defy easy analysis. As we have seen an employer will generally not be responsible for the employee while the employee is travelling to and from work. In some situations, however, this may not be the case. This for instance might include where the employee works from home and travelling is an essential part of the work.

CASE EXAMPLE

Smith v Stages [1989] 2 WLR 529

The employees in question were laggers and were sent from where they were working in the Midlands to deliver some urgent supplies to a power station in Wales. They were paid wages and also travelling expenses equivalent to rail fare, although there was no stipulation as to how they should travel. They went by car and as a result of one employee's negligent driving they were both seriously injured in a car crash. The employer was held to be liable here because the employees were paid both travelling expenses and travelling time and therefore the journey was accepted by the court as falling within their employment.

Goff LJ of Chieveley identified the operation of the principle.

JUDGMENT

'[this involves] an employee, who has for a short time to work for his employers at a different place of work some distance away from his usual place of work . . . in all the circumstances of the case, S was required by the employers to make this journey . . . and it would be proper to describe him as having been employed to do so.'

ACTIVITY

Applying the law

Consider whether the employer would be liable in the following circumstances:

1. Roger is employed by 'Eazi-build', a DIY warehouse. While driving to work one morning his negligence causes a car crash in which Parminder is injured and her car is damaged beyond repair.
2. Simon is a travelling salesman for 'Eazi-build' who works from home. While driving to his first call he negligently collides with a car driven by Oona, injuring her and damaging her car.
3. Taru is a delivery driver for 'Eazi-build'. One day after completing his last morning delivery instead of returning to work as he should he goes to the Red Lion for a few beers. On driving back to work he negligently runs over a pedestrian, Nellie, killing her.

Is the wrongdoer an employee?

- There is an agreement to provide skill in return for a wage
- The hirer exercises a degree of control over the worker
- The terms of the agreement between them are not inconsistent with an employment relationship

NO →

YES ↓

Is the wrong committed in the course of employment?

- Employee is carrying out an authorised wrongful act
- Employee is carrying out an authorised act in an unauthorised manner
- Employee is not 'on a frolic on his own'
- Employee is not travelling to or from work in own time

NO →

There is no vicarious liability on the part of the employer

YES ↓

The employer may be vicariously liable for the torts of the employee

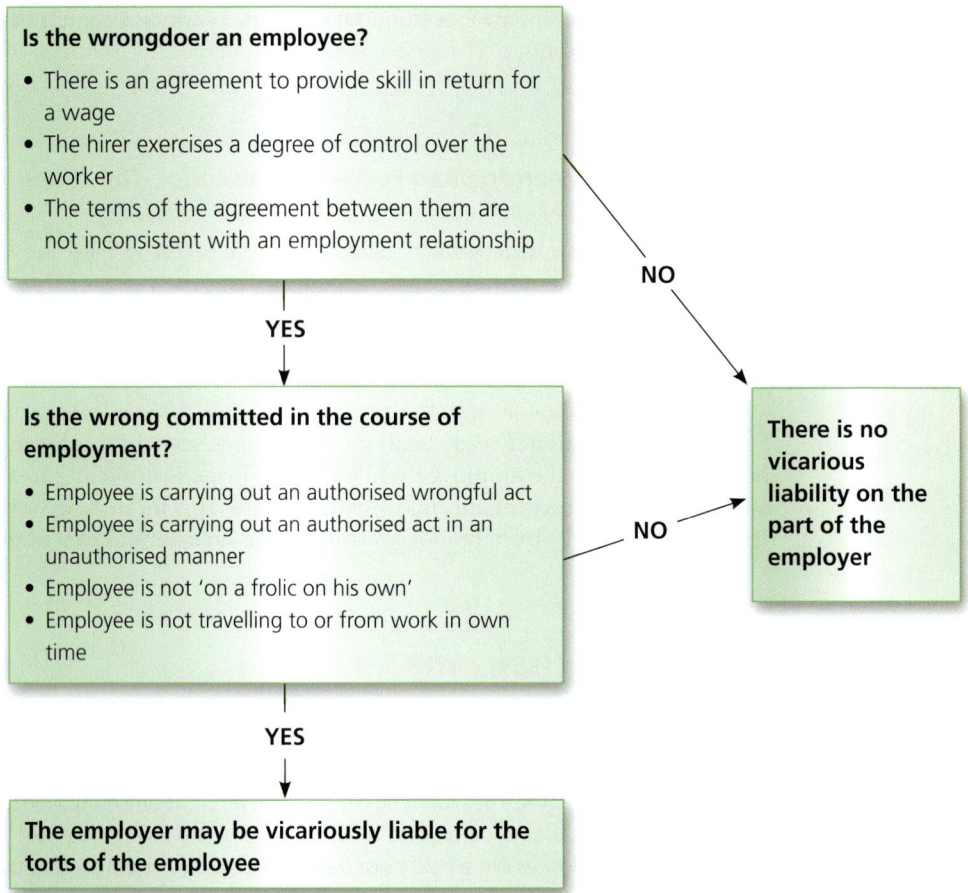

Figure 18.1 The straightforward process of testing vicarious liability

18.3.3 Liability for the crimes of employees

In general an employer will not usually be liable for the crimes of an employee that also amount to torts so that there can be civil liability.

CASE EXAMPLE

Warren v Henleys [1948] 2 All ER 935

Here a petrol pump attendant assaulted a customer who he believed was intending not to pay. The court was not prepared to hold that the assault took place in the course of employment. It was not an essential part of his employment that he engaged in criminal activity.

The courts are more prepared to consider that the dishonesty of an employee falls within the course of employment and therefore to impose liability on the employer. This might apply in the case of fraud.

CASE EXAMPLE

Lloyd v Grace Smith & Co [1912] AC 716

The employee was an unsupervised conveyancing clerk. The solicitors who employed him were held liable for the fraud when the clerk fraudulently induced a client to convey her property to him. The court identified that the clerk was engaged in the job that he was hired for and the fraud occurred because he was given insufficient supervision by his employers.

However, the courts will generally not make an employer liable for an employee's fraudulent activities where they occurred partly in and partly outside the course of the employment.

CASE EXAMPLE

Credit Lyonnais Bank Nederland NV v Export Credits Guarantee Department [1999] 1 All ER 929

Here two parties were involved in a fraud on the bank but some of the activities fell outside of their employment. Therefore the court would not hold that the employer could be vicariously liable for these specific frauds.

Vicarious liability can also apply and an employer can therefore be held liable in the case of thefts by the employee.

CASE EXAMPLE

Morris v Martin & Sons [1966] 1 QB 792

The employee, who was a cleaner in the employer's dry-cleaning business, stole a customer's fur coat. The employer was held liable to compensate for the theft since the employee was doing the work that he was engaged to do but in an unauthorised manner.

One area that has caused difficulty for the courts in recent years is where public bodies are accused of being responsible for abuses carried out by their employees.

On the basis of implied duties owed by employers to their employees, employers have been held liable in cases of sexual harassment by other of their employees (*Bracebridge Engineering v Darby* [1990] IRLR 3 EAT), and also in the case of racial harassment (*Jones v Tower Boot Co Ltd* [1997] 2 All ER 406).

However, the difficulty of identifying abuse as an 'unauthorised mode of carrying out an authorised act' had already led the Court of Appeal to rejecting claims of vicarious liability for sexual abuse.

CASE EXAMPLE

Trotman v North Yorkshire County Council [1999] IRLR 98

Here the claimant was a pupil at a special school. He alleged vicarious liability against the local authority after being sexually abused by his deputy headmaster while on a holiday with the school. The teacher was sharing the boy's bedroom for nocturnal supervision because of the boy's fits. Butler Sloss LJ found it difficult to reconcile the case with either the harassment cases based on an employer's implied duties to the employee, or with the cases based on fraud. The general feeling of the court was that the more extreme the act of the employee, the less likely that the employer would be held vicariously liable for it.

The approach of the Court of Appeal in such cases was not without criticism. Brenda Barrett argued for a broader approach:

QUOTATION

'This commentator always argues forcefully for the importance of the employer's personal responsibility for maintaining a safe system of operation . . . investigation would have been likely to have disclosed that in both Bracebridge and Jones there was some fault on the part of the employer in permitting such conduct to occur on its premises. If that were so then liability might have been attached to those employers without resort to debate about the boundaries of vicarious liability . . .

Jones v Tower Boot seems likely to have determined beyond dispute that vicarious liability is to be interpreted broadly in cases which are bought under discrimination legislation. On the other hand it is equally likely that *Trotman* will not be viewed as the final statement of the limits of vicarious liability at common law even in the narrow context of child abuse.'

B Barrett, 'The limits of vicarious liability' (1999) 3 The Law Teacher 1;
Trotman v North Yorkshire County Council [1999] IRLR 98

More recently, then, the House of Lords have developed a newer test based on inherent risk to cover such situations and enable liability to be imposed more easily.

CASE EXAMPLE

Lister v Hesley Hall Ltd [2001] 2 All ER 769

This case is a major development in vicarious liability. Three claimants were sexually abused over a period of time by the warden of the school for children with emotional difficulties where they were all resident. The warden was then convicted of criminal charges. The claim against the school was on the basis that it had actual or constructive knowledge of the abuse and had failed to prevent it. The trial judge, despite being bound by *Trotman*, allowed the claim on the basis of breach of a duty to the claimants. The Court of Appeal reversed this finding of vicarious liability on the ground that the wrongful behaviour could not be considered to be 'in the course of employment' according to the established definitions. In the House of Lords the judges rejected the test in Trotman and held that the key test was whether there was sufficient connection between the employment and the torts carried out by the employee. Here the employee's torts were carried out on the school's premises and at times when the employee should have been caring for the claimants. The House was satisfied that there was an inherent risk of abuse that the employer should have guarded against and that vicarious liability was appropriate in all the circumstances, despite appreciating the applicability of the 'floodgates' argument that was presented in the case.

The judgment in *Lister v Hesley Hall* is clearly a major development of the law on vicarious liability in respect of the victim of the tort.

QUOTATION

'Whatever the reluctance of their Lordships to set forth the social and policy considerations behind the principle of vicarious liability, it is to be concluded from the decision that the question "who should be the loser" between the "two innocent parties", namely the employer and the victim, is answered by a finding that the risk should fall upon the enterprise . . . provided that there is a sufficient connection between the acts of the employee and the employment. The suggestion that the greater the fault of the servant, the less the liability of the master reflects the wrong approach.'

R Coe, 'A new test for vicarious liability' [2001] NLJ 1154

Nevertheless it has also been argued that the case leaves both legal difficulties unanswered and has far reaching practical implications.

QUOTATION

'Lister . . . fails to resolve the underlying rationale of vicarious liability and, if anything, adds further difficulties. By failing to distinguish between primary and vicarious liability in an area of law in which an institution may be sued on both bases the House missed a valuable opportunity to clarify the law. . . . Lister has inevitably raised concerns as to the application of the "close connection" test, provoking comment that following Lister, "authorities" liability insurers will be anxiously manning the floodgates. Litigants, their advisers and insurers will all be concerned as to the boundaries of the decision and will turn to the judgments of the House for guidance. Unfortunately they will find limited assistance.'

R Coe, 'Lister v Hesley Hall Ltd' (2002) 65 MLR 270

The principle from *Lister* was given further explanation in *Dubai Aluminium v Salaam* [2003] 2 AC 366.

Lord Millet stated that it would be no answer to a claim of vicarious liability that

JUDGMENT

'the employee was guilty of intentional wrongdoing, or that his act was not merely cautious but criminal, or that he was acting exclusively for his own benefit, or that he was acting contrary to express instructions, or that his conduct was the very negation of his employer's duty.'

The reasoning in both cases has subsequently been approved and applied.

CASE EXAMPLE

Mattis v Pollock [2003] EWCA Civ 887; [2003] 1 WLR 2158; [2003] ICR 1335

A bouncer employed by a nightclub got involved in a fight with customers and the claimant intervened. The bouncer then left the club went home, returned with a knife and intent on revenge stabbed the claimant outside the club. In the Court of Appeal Lord Justice Judge identified that the simple question that the court had to decide was whether what the bouncer did was so closely connected to what his employer expected of him that the employer should be held vicariously liable. The court held that this was indeed the case. The whole point of the bouncer's employment was that he should physically manhandle customers and he was encouraged and was supposed to intimidate them and be able to win any fight.

The close connection test has subsequently been used with quite different results. In *Gravill v Carroll and Redruth Rugby Club* [2008] EWCA Civ 689 the club were held vicariously liable for a punch by one of its players causing a serious eye injury to the claimant. The court held that the punch was very closely connected with the type of employment, and that the club had various measures at its disposal, including disciplinary sanctions, to deter misconduct.

In *N v Chief Constable of Merseyside Police* [2006] EWHC 3041 (QB), however, there was no vicarious liability when an off-duty police officer, dressed in his uniform, agreed with a first-aider from a night club to take a young woman who was ill for medical attention but instead took her to his home, drugged her and raped her over a period of hours. The police officer's actions were held not to be closely connected with his employment. He had merely been using his uniform as a way of being able to commit assaults against women.

18.3.4 The employer's indemnity

Where the employer is vicariously liable then both he and the employee are in effect joint tortfeasors. The consequence of this is that the claimant could actually sue either. One further consequence is that the employer who is sued may then sue the employee for an indemnity.

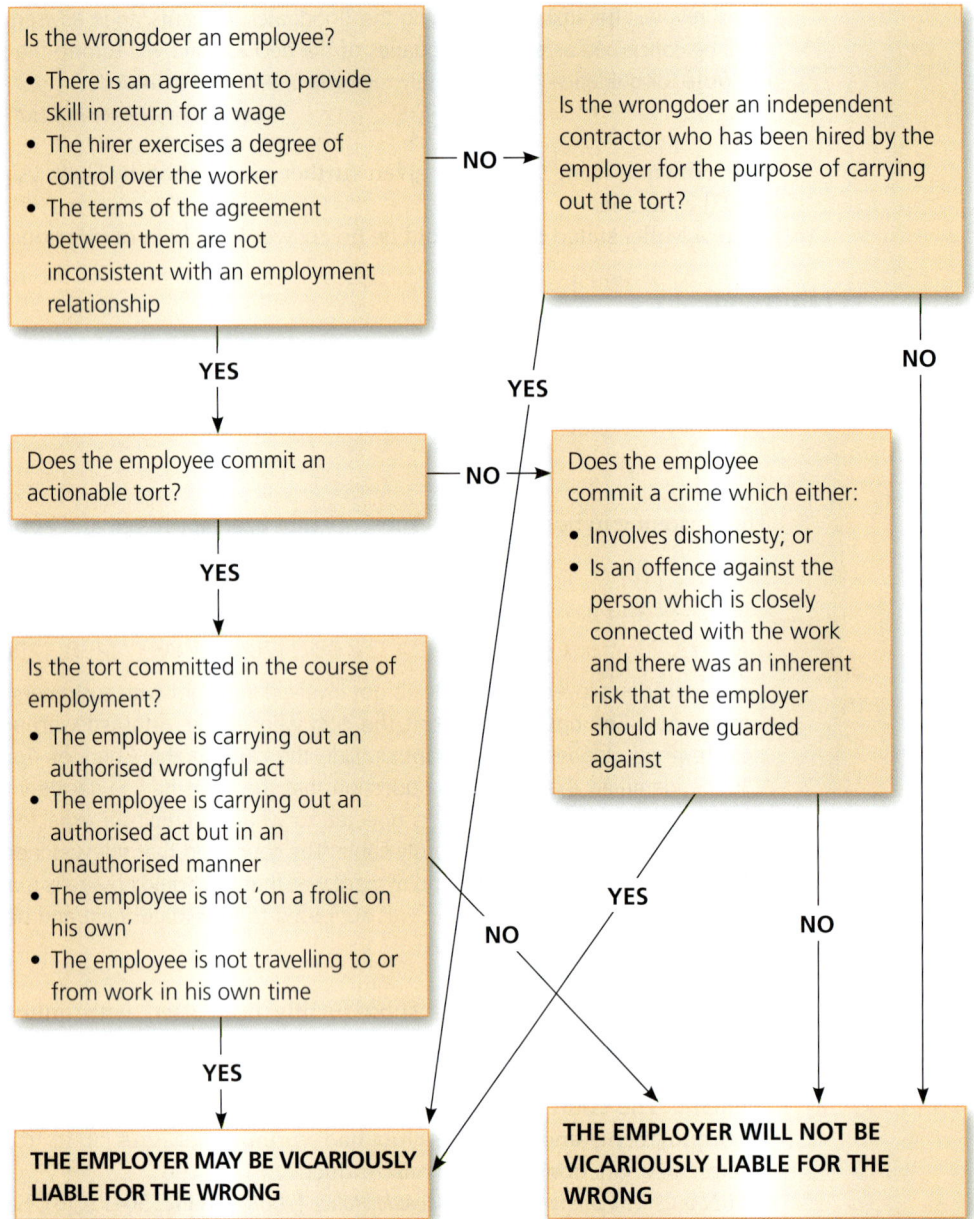

Figure 18.2 Diagram illustrating the process of establishing vicarious liability including more complex situations

CASE EXAMPLE

Lister v Romford Ice & Cold Storage Ltd [1957] AC 555

A lorry driver knocked over his father who at the time was his driver's mate. The father then claimed compensation from the employers. The employers' insurers on settling the claim then exercised their rights of subrogation under the insurance contract and sued the driver. The House of Lords accepted that this was possible.

The case has been strongly criticised, not least because it destroys the purpose of imposing vicarious liability. As a result insurers do not generally exercise their rights under the principle.

18.3.5 Liability for the torts of independent contractors

An employer will not usually be liable for the tortious acts of independent contractors whom he has hired. The reason is the lack of control that the employer is able to exercise.

Nevertheless there are some very limited circumstances in which an employer has been shown to be liable for the acts of independent contractors.

These include:

■ If the contractor has been hired for the purpose of carrying out the tort then the employer may be liable, as he would be for his employees.

CASE EXAMPLE

Ellis v Sheffield Gas Consumers Co (1853) 2 E & B 767

The defendants without having sought any actual authority to do so hired contractors to dig a hole in the road. The contractors failed to properly replace the hole and the claimant was injured as a result. The defendants were held vicariously liable because the contractor had only been carrying out the task set by the defendants who had in effect sanctioned the tort.

■ Where the employers are under a non-delegable duty of care imposed by statute. This might for instance apply where there is an obligation not only to provide but also to ensure that industrial safety equipment is used.

■ Where a similar non-delegable duty of care is owed in common law.

CASE EXAMPLE

Honeywill & Stein v Larkin Bros Ltd [1934] 1 KB 191

Employers were held to be vicariously liable for a breach of the implied duty to provide competent staff and a safe system of work when a freelance photographer set fire to a cinema when using magnesium flares for lighting.

18.4 Vicarious liability of lenders of cars

Another area that creates problems apart from travelling to and from work is the practice of lending vehicles. The area includes a strange group of cases, not easily classified and in many ways quite confusing. In establishing whether the owner of the vehicle is vicariously liable for the acts of the driver, the defining difference appears to be whether or not the vehicle is being used for a purpose in which the owner has an interest.

CASE EXAMPLE

Britt v Galmoye (1928) 44 TLR 294

Here there was no liability on an employer when the car was lent to the employee for the employee's own personal use.

The result will be different where the owner has requested that the other party should borrow the car to carry out the purposes of the owner.

CASE EXAMPLE

Ormrod v Crosville Motor Services Ltd [1953] 1 WLR 1120

In this case the owner of a car asked another party to take the car to Monte Carlo where the owner would later join him and other friends for a holiday. The friend drove the car negligently and collided with a bus, causing damage to both vehicles and injuries to the occupants of the car. The Court of Appeal held that the owner of the car was liable. Even though the driver was benefiting from the use of the car and using it for his own purposes he was also driving the car with the express authority and for reasons of the owner, who was thus vicariously liable for the accident.

As Lord Denning explained

JUDGMENT

'The trip to Monte Carlo must be considered as a whole . . . it was undertaken with the owner's consent for the purposes of both of them, and the owner is liable for any negligence of the driver in the course of it.'

Though in some instances it appears that the logic of the decision is merely that the judges wished there to be liability, which does not necessarily produce a fully justifiable result.

CASE EXAMPLE

Morgans v Launchbury [1973] AC 127

A wife allowed her husband to use her car knowing that he was going out drinking on the express promise that he would not drive while drunk. The husband did have too much to drink and so he allowed another drunk and uninsured driver to drive him home. When there was an accident the Court of Appeal imposed vicarious liability on the wife in order that a claim could be made against her insurance. Lord Denning felt that the fact that the wife had given permission to use the car was sufficient to make her responsible. In the House of Lords Lord Wilberforce rejected this argument because it was impossible to pinpoint the exact basis on which a court could fix liability in such circumstances. He also felt that it was not for judges to interfere with the interrelationship between liability and insurance.

Lord Wilberforce identified the unfairness of the Court of Appeal's reasoning in making the owner of the car liable when put in the context of the general rules on vicarious liability.

JUDGMENT

'The owner ought to pay, it says, because he has authorised the act, or requested it, or because the actor is carrying out a task duly delegated, or because he is in control of the actor's conduct. He ought not to pay (on accepted rules) if he has no control over the actor, has not authorised or requested the act, or if the actor is acting wholly on his own purposes.'

ACTIVITY

Self-assessment questions

1. What justifications are there for making an employer liable for the torts of his employee?
2. In what ways can vicarious liability be said to be unfair?
3. What will a claimant need to show in order to establish liability on the part of the employer?
4. To what extent is it easy to demonstrate that a person is an employee?
5. Why is the 'control test' an ineffective test on its own?
6. How does the 'economic reality' test operate?
7. What factors are useful indicators of whether a person is employed or self-employed?
8. Is an employer liable for acts done in protection of his property?
9. Explain what is meant by an authorised act done in an unauthorised manner.

10. Why exactly was the dairy liable in Rose v Plenty?
11. What exactly is a 'frolic on his own'?
12. Why were Limpus and Beard decided differently?
13. In what circumstances is an employer liable for the crimes of his employee?
14. Why is Lister v Hesley Hall such an important case?
15. Why is the principle in Lister v Romford criticised and why is it not followed?
16. What consistency, if any, is there between Morgans v Launchbury and other cases on vicarious liability?

KEY FACTS

The nature of vicarious liability	Case
Vicarious liability is where one person is held liable for the torts of another.	
This is usually where an employer is liable for the tortious acts of an employee.	
For the employer to be liable: (i) the tortfeasor must be an employee; (ii) the tort must take place during the course of employment.	
The tests of employment status	
Various tests have been developed to determine whether or not someone is an employee rather than an independent contractor (self-employed) – these include the 'control' test, the 'indicia' test, and the 'organisation' (or integration) test.	
The most modern test is the 'economic reality' test – all factors should be considered and their importance weighed.	*Ready Mixed Concrete v Minister of Pensions and National Insurance* (1968)
A number of types of work defy easy description, eg casual workers.	*Carmichael v National Power* (1998)
Torts in the course of employment	**Case**
Course of employment can include:	
authorised acts	*Poland v Parr* (1927)
acts done in an unauthorised manner	*Limpus v General London Omnibus Co* (1862)
negligently carried out work	*Century Insurance v Northern Ireland Transport Board* (1942)
exceeding the proper bounds of the work.	*Bayley v Manchester, Sheffield & Lincolnshire Railway* (1873)
Torts outside of the course of employment	**Case**
There is no liability for:	
being on a 'frolic on his own'	*Hilton v Thomas Burton* (1961
things outside of the scope of employment.	*Twine v Beans Express* (1946)

Liability for the crimes of an employee	Case
An employer is not usually liable for an employee's crimes. This will apply to fraud and also to crimes generally. But now a distinction is made where the criminal act of the employee is an inherent risk that the employer should guard against.	*Lloyd v Grace Smith* (1912) *Warren v Henleys* (1948) *Lister v Hesley Hall* (2001)

Liability for torts of independent contractors	Case
There is usually no liability for torts of independent contractors. It is rare but possible to recover the loss from the employee. In some cases it is possible for owners to be liable for torts committed in cars that they have lent to the tortfeasor.	*Ellis v Sheffield Gas Consumers* (1853) *Lister v Romford Ice* (1957) *Morgans v Launchbury* (1973)

ACTIVITY

Applying the law

Using the guide in Appendix 2, try the following problem question:

Barry recently secured work as a delivery driver for 'Dodgy Transport' driving a 15 hundredweight Luton bodied Transit van, the only qualification being production of a valid driving licence. Barry has a clean licence but expressed concern at the time of his interview as he was only used to driving motor bikes. He signed a document called 'Document of Service' in which it was written that he must work such hours as the firm require, wear their uniform at all times while at work, and that he accepts work from no other delivery business, except as authorised by 'Dodgy' officials. 'Dodgy' owns the van that Barry drives and they pay him a gross amount, leaving him to settle his own tax and National Insurance contributions. In his first week Barry was delivering to 'Rocky Co', a very good customer of 'Dodgy'. Alex, the manager of Rocky, asked Barry if he would take a parcel in need of urgent delivery to 'Steady Co', a customer of 'Rocky' that is 5 miles away and in the opposite direction to Dodgy's premises. Despite being unable to contact Dodgy on his mobile phone, Barry took the parcel. When he arrived at Steady's offices Barry had to reverse into their loading bay and negligently ran over the warehouseman, Stan.

Advise Dodgy whether they will be liable for the injuries caused by Barry's negligence.

student mentor tip

"Applying tort to real life situations is the best way to remember the facts and principles of the topic areas."

Gayatri, University of Leicester

SAMPLE ESSAY QUESTION

Discuss the argument that vicarious liability is unjust as it places liability on someone other than the person at fault.

Explain the basis of vicarious liability
- One party (usually an employer) is fixed with liability for the torts (and sometimes the crimes) of another party (usually an employee)

Explain the requirements for liability
- There is an established tort
- The tortfeasor is an employee
- The tort occurred in the course of employment

Describe the tests of employment status

- Control test
- Integration test
- Economic reality (multiple) test

Discuss the meaning of 'in the course of employment'

- Authorised acts
- Authorised acts carried out in an unauthorised manner
- Authorised acts carried out carelessly
- Where the employer benefits from the tort *Rose v Plenty*
- Paid travelling time
- But not frolics, activities not within the scope of employment, and giving unauthorised lifts

Discuss whether the principle is unjust

- It contradicts the basic fault principle
- An employer can incur liability even though he has expressly prohibited the unsafe practice
- The rule may operate inconsistently or arbitrarily
- The tort often occurs before the employer realises that the employee has behaved badly and should be disciplined

Discuss whether the rule can be justified

- The employer benefits from work so should be responsible
- The employer should ensure that work is carried out safely
- The employer can more easily stand the loss
- It ensures that the claimant can be compensated
- The fact of compulsory insurance so only pays the premiums
- Increased premiums may act as a deterrent
- The employer can discipline employees for unsafe practices

Discuss the close connection test and its application – and whether it is any more or any less just

SUMMARY

- Vicarious liability is not a tort but refers to liability being with a person other than the tortfeasor usually an employer
- And it is possible now for there to be joint vicarious liability
- For the employer to be liable there must be a tort carried out by an employee during the course of employment
- Tests of employee status include the 'control' test, the 'indicia' test, and the 'organisation' (or integration) test, but the most commonly used now is the 'economic reality' test
- Acts in the course of employment can include: authorised acts, acts done in an unauthorised manner, negligently carried out work, exceeding the proper bounds of the work
- But there is no liability for: being on a 'frolic on his own', or anything outside of the scope of employment
- An employer is not usually liable for an employee's crimes, but may be in the case of fraud and dishonesty – and now also where there is a close connection with the work and the criminal act of the employee carries with it an inherent risk that the employer should guard against
- In rare situations a person can be vicariously liable for the torts of independent contractors
- There is a theoretical possibility of the employee indemnifying an employer

Further reading

Coe, R, 'A new test for vicarious liability' [2001] NLJ 1154.
Coe, R, '*Lister v Hesley Hall Ltd*' (2002) 65 MLR 270.
'Vicarious liability' IDS Brief 655, February 2000.

19

General defences

After reading this chapter you should be able to:

- Understand the essential elements of the general defences
- Be able to critically analyse the area
- Be able to apply the law to factual situations and reach conclusions as to liability

19.1 Introduction

As you have gone through the book, general defences which are of particular importance to a tort have been highlighted and those which are applicable only to a particular tort have been discussed. In this Chapter, we look at the general defences available to most torts.

19.2 Voluntary assumption of risk (*volenti non fit injuria*)

This defence has been discussed in detail in Chapter 13 relating to trespass to the person and in Chapter 5 in the context of negligence. The defence is, however, relevant to other torts, for example in relation to claims under the Animals Act 1971. It is also specifically referred to in the Occupiers' Liability Acts 1957 and 1984.

A person who consents to damage or injury or to the risk that either may occur cannot later complain and make the defendant liable for what has happened. Consent may be express, for example where a person signs a consent form for a surgical procedure, or implied, for example taking part in a contact sport.

The principal issue is whether or not the claimant has in fact consented. To decide this it must be shown that the claimant

(a) was aware of the risk and
(b) accepted it freely.

19.2.1 Knowledge of the risk

Claimants must be aware of the broad nature of the risk which they are taking, in other words they must know what they are doing and what the possible outcomes may be. As has been seen, in the context of consent to medical treatment, this does not mean that they need to understand all the detail of the treatment but they must understand why the treatment is advisable, what it involves, what any side-effects may be and the intended outcome. Failure to ensure such understanding may amount to negligence on the part of the health practitioner involved. In medical cases consent is usually express.

In the context of sport, the claimant consents to the risk of injury which is inherent in the game played according to the rules. This is an example of implied consent. An action may lie for trespass to the person if injury occurs as a result of something which is against the rules of the game.

What both examples have in common is the knowledge by the claimant of the nature of the risk which is being taken.

19.2.2 Free acceptance of the risk

It is not enough to show that the claimant had knowledge, whether specific or general, of the risk that was being taken. It must also be shown that it was freely accepted by the claimant when undertaking the activity. Case law illustrates this in relation to various categories of claimants:

- employees
- rescuers
- spectators at sporting events
- passengers in vehicles.

Employees

The defence is often important in cases where an employee has been injured during the course of employment. The courts take a realistic view that an employee may be under pressure for all sorts of reasons to keep the job. Saying that there is always a right to leave the employment is certainly true but would be impractical for most people.

The position of many employees was explained in *Smith v Baker* [1891] AC 325 when Lord Herschell, while acknowledging that an employee 'no doubt voluntarily subjects himself to the risks inevitably accompanying the job' said that 'mere continuance in service, with knowledge of the risk' cannot amount to consent to the risk.

Employees may also feel that they put their jobs at risk if they make a complaint. The latter problem has in theory been dealt with by the Employment Rights Act 1996 which gives protection to employees who complain about unsafe practices. Although the Employment Tribunal could order reinstatement should the employee have been dismissed, there is no guarantee that the employer will comply. In times of high unemployment, the protection may appear to be flimsy to say the least.

While it is not denied that the defence can apply in employment situations, it only exceptionally does so. An example of this type of case is found in *Imperial Chemical Industries Ltd v Shatwell* [1964] 3 WLR 329 (see Chapter 17, section 17.4).

Rescuers

The courts have been reluctant to find that a rescuer has consented to the risks inherent in the rescue.

CASE EXAMPLE

Baker v T E Hopkins & Sons Ltd [1959] 1 WLR 966

Two workmen had been overcome by fumes from a pump while trying to repair a well. Dr Baker had himself lowered by rope to try to rescue the men but was himself overcome when the rope jammed and he also became trapped. He died.

The Court of Appeal found that the defendants owed the Doctor a duty of care, thus the issue of whether Dr Baker had voluntarily consented to the risk was irrelevant. Holding that the act of a rescuer in the circumstances was a foreseeable consequence of the breach of duty owed to the workmen, Lord Justice Willmer said

JUDGMENT

'. . . it would certainly be a strange result if the law were held to penalise the courage of the rescuer by depriving him of any remedy.'

This case appears to say that a duty of care will be owed to a rescuer. This has been refined in *White v Chief Constable of South Yorkshire Police* [1999] 2 AC 455 which says that where the injury amounts to nervous shock, a rescuer must satisfy the same tests as any other primary victim (discussed earlier in Chapter 6, section 6.1.4).

Spectators at sporting events

While participants in sport consent freely to the risks involved in the sport, what about spectators? Some sports, for example motor racing, are inherently dangerous and spectators are from time to time injured by accidents. The issue was discussed by the Court of Appeal in *Wooldridge v Sumner* [1962] 2 All ER 978. Lord Justice Diplock explained the position

JUDGMENT

'A person attending a game or competition takes the risk of any damage caused to him by any act of a participant . . . notwithstanding that such act may involve an error of judgment or a lapse of skill, unless the participant's conduct is such as to evince a reckless disregard of the spectator's safety.'

The rules seems therefore to be that provided the cause of the incident was not due to negligence, the spectator will have consented to the risks which are inherent to watching the sport.

Passengers

Anyone who is a passenger in a motor vehicle driven by someone they know to be drunk or otherwise incapable is factually likely to have assumed the risk that they might be injured by the driver's negligence. In *Dann v Hamilton* [1939] 1 All ER 59 Mr Justice Asquith, while finding in the particular case that the defence did not apply, nonetheless acknowledged the possibility that in extreme cases it might be successfully pleaded.

JUDGMENT

'There may be cases where the drunkenness of the driver . . . is so extreme and so glaring that to accept a lift is like . . . inter-meddling with an unexploded bomb or walking on the edge of an unfenced cliff.'

The position of passengers in a motor vehicle has been settled by the Road Traffic Act 1988, s 149(3). Where a person is carried in a vehicle in circumstances such that compulsory third party insurance is required:

JUDGMENT

'The fact that a person so carried has willingly accepted as his the risk of negligence on the part of the [insured] shall not be treated as negativing any . . . liability on the part of the [insured].'

Although the defence of voluntary assumption of risk cannot be used, the defence of contributory negligence remains open when a passenger can be seen to be aware of the risk and to have consented to it.

While passengers in motor vehicles are not vulnerable to the defence, passengers in other forms of transport may find that the defence can be successfully used against them.

CASE EXAMPLE

Morris v Murray and Another [1990] 3 All ER 801

The claim was brought against the estate of a deceased person. The claimant and the deceased met at a pub and later, after several drinks, the claimant accepted the deceased's invitation to go for a ride in the deceased's plane. Flying from the aerodrome had been suspended because of bad weather but nonetheless they took off. The plane crashed, seriously injuring the claimant.

The Court of Appeal found that the claimant had been fully aware of the risk that he was taking. Fox LJ held that

JUDGMENT

'He knowingly and willingly embarked on a flight with a drunken pilot.'

It was held that the claimant voluntarily assumed the risks inherent in the flight due to the condition of the pilot.

19.2.3 Where are we now?

As will be seen, the defence of contributory negligence enables the court to apportion blame between the claimant and the defendant to the extent that the facts suggest that each has some part to play in the events leading to the injury.

Common sense however suggests that a person would be unlikely to consent to the risk that another person would be negligent. Although in *Dann v Hamilton* the door was left open to the use of the defence in cases involving negligence, it seems clear that where negligence is involved the defence will rarely be successful. A hint of this was given by Lord Denning MR when he said

QUOTATION

'Now that contributory negligence is not a complete defence . . . the defence of [voluntary assumption of risk] has been closely considered and, in consequence, it has been severely limited . . . Nothing will suffice short of an agreement to waive any claim for negligence.'

Nettleship v Weston [1971] 2 QB 691

Although the defence was successfully used in *Morris v Murray* [1990] 3 All ER 801, both that case and the later case of *Pitts v Hunt* [1991] 1 QB 24, make it clear that the defence will only apply in the most extreme case of lack of care by the claimant.

CASE EXAMPLE

Pitts v Hunt [1991] 1 QB 24

The claimant was seriously injured when he was a passenger on a motor bike, driven by Hunt. Both the claimant and Hunt were very much the worse for drink. The evidence showed that the claimant had actively encouraged Hunt to drive in a dangerous manner, to frighten other road users, and that he knew that Hunt was underage, drunk and uninsured. The effect of the Road Traffic Act 1988 meant that the defence was unsuccessful but Lord Justice Beldam in the Court of Appeal said that the defence would have applied were it not for the statute.

19.3 Contributory negligence

19.3.1 Introduction

Unlike voluntary assumption of risk which is a total defence, contributory negligence is a partial defence which allows the court to apportion blame between the claimant and the other parties.

This has proved particularly effective in cases involving negligence and is discussed in detail in Chapter 5. It is however a general defence and can be used in the context of most torts.

The principle is found in the Law Reform (Contributory Negligence) Act 1945 s 1(1) which states

SECTION

's 1(1) Where any person suffers damage as the result partly of his own fault and partly of the fault of any other person . . . a claim in respect of that damage shall not be defeated by reason of the fault of the person suffering the damage, but the damages . . . shall be reduced to such extent as the court thinks just and equitable having regard to the claimant's share in the responsibility for the damage . . .'

The Act makes it clear in s 4 that the defence does not apply only to a case where the claimant alleges negligence by the defendant.

The effect of the provisions is to give the court true flexibility. Once the defendant's liability for the tort is established, the judge is then free to decide whether, and if so to what extent, the claimant must bear some part of the blame. In deciding the extent of the claimant's responsibility, the court will compare the claimant's behaviour with the way in which a reasonable person having regard for their own well-being would behave.

CASE EXAMPLE

Davies v Swan Motor Co (Swansea) Ltd [1949] 2 KB 291

The claimant's husband was killed while riding on the back of a dustcart.

In considering the defence of contributory negligence Lord Denning explained

JUDGMENT

'The real question is not whether the [claimant] was neglecting some legal duty, but whether he was acting as a responsible man and with reasonable care.'

19.4 Illegality (*ex turpi causa non oritur actio*)

ex turpi causa non oritur actio

A defence that may be raised against a claimant whose claim arises from their own criminal actions

The Latin phrase translates as 'an action cannot be founded on a base cause'. This is clearly demonstrated in the rules governing illegal contracts, which are unenforceable as a matter of public policy (see C Turner *Unlocking Contract Law* for details of the rule in contract). It would be reasonable to suppose that a person who suffers a tort while engaged in illegal or unlawful activity would, for the same reason, be unable to bring a successful claim. Such a blanket rule would however cause injustice and the courts have tended to decide whether or not the illegality should have the effect of barring a claim on a case by case basis according to the particular circumstances.

It might seem obvious that a crime should be regarded as disallowing any claim but this is not always the case.

In *Revill v Newbery* [1996] 1 All ER 291 the claimant succeeded although he had been injured while attempting to commit burglary. The defence of illegality was rejected, Lord Justice Evans saying

JUDGMENT

'It is one thing to deny a [claimant] any fruits from his illegal conduct, but different and far more far-reaching to deprive him even of compensation for injury which he suffers and which otherwise he is entitled to recover at law.'

In *Clunis v Camden and Islington Area Health Authority* [1998] QB 978 the court reached a different conclusion:

CASE EXAMPLE

Clunis v Camden and Islington Area Health Authority [1998] QB 978

The claimant had been convicted of manslaughter on the ground of diminished responsibility. He sued the defendants for negligence in failing to make a proper assessment of his mental condition. Had this been done, he argued, he would not have been released from detention in a psychiatric hospital and the killing would not have taken place.

The claim was rejected on the basis that it was based essentially on his own illegal act, that he must be taken to have known what he was doing and that it was wrong.

The essential difference between the two cases seems to be that in *Revill* the injury was in a sense separate from the claimant's criminal activity. Had he been a lawful visitor a claim would certainly have succeeded. In *Clunis*, however, the injury suffered by the claimant was the fact that he had committed a crime. Admitting the claim could perhaps have been seen as profiting from the crime.

The courts have sometimes argued that 'it would be an affront to the public conscience' to allow a criminal to recover damages. This approach was explained in the judgment in the case of *Euro-Diam Ltd v Bathurst* [1988] 2 All ER 23, where Lord Justice Kerr said, the defence will not apply

JUDGMENT

'if, in all the circumstances, it would be an affront to the public conscience to grant the [claimant] the relief which he seeks because the courts would thereby appear to assist or encourage the [claimant] in his illegal conduct or to encourage others in similar acts.'

Lord Justice Kerr's approach in *Euro-Diam v Bathurst* [1988] 2 All ER 23 when read alongside Lord Justice Evans' approach in *Revill* encapsulates the confusion in this part of tort law. The Law Commission has published a consultation paper ('The Illegality Defence in Tort', Law Com No 160, 2001) in which it suggests that the defence should remain, but subject to reform. The Commission proposes

1. The court would have discretion to reject a tort claim when it arises from or is connected to an illegal act by the claimant.
2. The discretion would be exercised taking into account specified matters, for example whether denying the claim is proportionate to the wrong-doing, the extent of the illegality and the knowledge of the claimant.

The Commission also expresses doubt as to whether the defence should ever apply in personal injury actions.

For an interesting discussion of the proposals see M A Jones, *Textbook on Torts* (8th edn, OUP, 2002), para 25.20, p 866.

19.5 Inevitable accident

This defence is available where the defendant can show that despite exercising all reasonable care and taking all reasonable precautions, the accident could not have been avoided. In *Fardon v Harcourt Rivington* (1932) 146 LT 391 (for facts see Chapter 11) Lord Dunedin said

JUDGMENT

'People must guard against reasonable possibilities, but they are not bound to guard against fantastic possibilities.'

The defence exists but its usefulness is very limited.

19.6 Act of God

This defence is available only to the tort of *Rylands v Fletcher* (1868) LR 1 Exch 265. For full discussion see Chapter 10.

19.7 Necessity

Necessity may justify what would otherwise amount to a tort. The defendant's actions must be for the purpose of protecting

- the public
- a third party or
- himself
- from what is perceived to be a greater danger.

The essence of the defence is that the action was prompted by a reasonable perception that it was required to avoid an immediate and imminent danger judged by the circumstances at the time. There is no room for hindsight so that if the perception of the risk is reasonable, it does not matter that the danger never in fact materialises. The defence has been discussed in some detail in relation to trespass to the person where it may be used to justify medical treatment and trespass to land where it may justify commission of the tort (see Chapters 8 and 13).

19.8 Statutory authority

We have seen that statutory authority may be a defence in several contexts, in particular in relation to

- nuisance
- *Rylands v Fletcher*
- breach of statutory duty
- and reference should be made to Chapters 9, 10 and 16 for discussion of the defence.

19.9 Self-help

This generally takes one of three forms
1. self-defence, which has been discussed fully in Chapter 13 in relation to trespass to the person
2. ejectment in relation to trespass to land, discussed in Chapter 8
3. abatement, which is relevant to nuisance and discussed in Chapter 9.

Key facts on general defences

Voluntary assumption of risk (*volenti non fit injuria*)	Case/statute
Complete defence.	
Claimant must know the nature of the risk.	
It must be freely accepted.	
Court reluctant to find employee *volenti*	*Smith v Baker* (1891)
but will do so in appropriate case.	*ICI v Shatwell* (1965)
Rescuers traditionally not held to be *volenti*	*Baker v T E Hopkins* (1959)
but note	*White v Chief Constable of S Yorks* (1999)
Spectators at sporting events *volenti* to risks inherent in watching the event.	*Wooldridge v Sumner* (1963)
Note passengers in a motor vehicle cannot be *volenti*	Road Traffic Act 1988 s 149(3)
but can be *volenti* in respect of other forms of transport.	*Morris v Murray* (1990)
Volenti used less frequently since contributory negligence became available.	
Contributory negligence	**Case/statute**
Governed by	Law Reform (Contributory Negligence) Act 1945
Partial defence allowing blame to be apportioned.	
Illegality *(ex turpi causa non oritur actio)*	**Case/statute**
General principle that a person should bear the consequences of acting illegally.	
Courts aware of potential for injustice.	*Revill v Newbery* (1996)
Cases decided on circumstances relevant to the particular case.	*Clunis v Camden & Islington AHA* (1998)
	Euro-Diam v Bathurst (1988)
Inevitable accident	**Case**
Rarely used.	
Defendant must show that despite taking all precautions the accident could not have been avoided.	*Fardon v Harcourt-Rivington* (1932)
Act of God	**Case**
Only relevant to	*Rylands v Fletcher* (1868)
Necessity	**Case**
Tortious act will be excused provided defendant acted for the protection of himself or others – can extend to protection of property.	
Action must be prompted by reasonable perception of immediate an imminent danger.	

Statutory authority	Case
See discussion in relation to nuisance, breach of statutory duty and *Rylands v Fletcher*.	

Self help	Case
Self-defence (see Chapter 13 – Trespass to the person). Ejectment (see Chapter 8 – Trespass to land). Abatement (see Chapter 9 – Nuisance).	

SUMMARY

There are many defences that are specific to individual torts – but there are also many general defences that could be applied to any torts:

- *Volenti non fit injuria* – means that there will be no liability to a person who voluntarily accepts a risk of harm – so must understand nature of risk and freely accept it
- Contributory negligence under the Law Reform (Contributory Negligence) Act 1945 – reduces damages to the extent that the claimant is responsible for his own harm – so claimant must fail to take proper care of himself and this is partly the cause of the damage suffered
- Illegality (*ex turpi causa no oritur actio*) – no claim possible where the damage occurs in a criminal venture to which the claimant is a party
- Inevitable accident – no liability where the incident could not have been avoided and is pure accident
- Act of God – basically involves the damage being caused by extreme weather conditions beyond the control of the claimant
- Necessity – where the defendant's actions are prompted by imminent danger to himself or others
- Statutory authority – if the activity is authorised by Parliament then it cannot lead to tortious liability

20

Remedies and Limitations

AIMS AND OBJECTIVES

After reading this chapter you should be able to:

■ Understand the way in which different remedies are awarded
■ Understand the significance of limitation periods
■ Be able to critically analyse the area
■ Be able to apply the law to factual situations and reach conclusions

20.1 Damages

20.1.1 Nature and purpose of damages

In many cases where physical damage to property has occurred, the purpose of damages is clear – to compensate the claimant for the loss suffered, which usually means the cost of repairs and other quantifiable financial loss caused by the tort. It is less clear where personal injury is involved, as the court may also seek to compensate for future financial loss which can only be estimated as well as the pain and suffering which has been caused.

In the case of torts actionable *per se* no actual damage needs to be proved. So what then is the purpose of an award in such cases? Here the court seeks to mark its disapproval of the interference with the claimant's legal interest whether in relation to bodily integrity (trespass to the person), goods (trespass to goods), land (trespass to land) or reputation (libel and those situations where slander is actionable *per se*). The award is compensation for violation of such interest.

One particular feature of the system raises a very real difficulty. As a general rule, all awards of damages are final. The case cannot be re-opened and the award reassessed at a later date. How can one predict the future? This is of real concern in personal injury cases. As we shall see, this rule has been somewhat relaxed in such cases but a crystal ball is still needed.

20.1.2 Types of damages – general and special

Damages are either general or **special damages**. Special damages must be specifically pleaded and consist of quantifiable financial losses including loss of wages, value of clothing or other property which has been lost or destroyed, cost of repairing damaged property and other out of pocket expenses. General damages are by their nature unable to

---

special damages
Not to be confused with special damage – generally refers to damages for financial losses and expenses incurred up to the date of trial which have to be pleaded separately from the claim itself

loss of amenity

Damages are awarded where the claimant is unable to do things that he could before the wrong occurred

be quantified precisely and cover such things as pain and suffering and **loss of amenity**. In certain circumstances general damages may be awarded in different forms to achieve slightly different purposes:

- contemptuous
- nominal
- aggravated
- exemplary.

Contemptuous damages

The award of contemptuous damages, often the value of the smallest coin in the realm, marks the fact that

- the claimant has established that a right has been infringed
- in the court's view the action should never have been brought.

The latter may be because of the actual circumstances of the case, for example where a 'one off' trespass to land has occurred but was no more than a limited incursion causing no actual damage. The court may also use contemptuous damages to mark its belief that morally at least, although not legally, the claimant 'got what they deserved'. Such awards are not uncommon in libel actions.

One consequence of contemptuous damages is that the claimant may find that the award of costs is affected. Although an order is usually made in favour of the successful party, the judge has a discretion to order that both sides bear their own costs or even to order the claimant to pay the costs of both sides.

Nominal damages

nominal damages

A small sum of damages awarded where there has technically been a wrong but no actual damage has been caused

Where **nominal damages** are awarded the claimant's right has been infringed but little damage has occurred. The judge will be satisfied that the claimant has acted reasonably in bringing the case. Such awards are not unusual in cases where the tort is actionable *per se* such as trespass or where the remedy of choice is an injunction or a declaration. In the recent case of *Ms B v An NHS Trust* [2002] EWHC 429 (Fam) the declaration sought by the claimant was granted and a nominal sum awarded for damages for the trespass to her person. In that case the claimant also received full costs but it should be remembered that the judge may exercise discretion whether or not to award costs and may decline to do so.

Aggravated damages

Aggravated damages are awarded to compensate the claimant for injury to feelings and distress which have been increased by the defendant's bad motive or wilful behaviour.

The Court of Appeal gave an explanation of the circumstances in which aggravated damages should be awarded in the case of *Thompson v Metropolitan Police Commissioner* [1997] 2 All ER 762. Explaining that aggravated damages are awarded in addition to the basic figure which would usually be the sum for general damages, Lord Woolf MR said

JUDGMENT

'Such damages can be awarded where there are aggravating features about the case which would result in the [claimant] not receiving sufficient compensation for the injury suffered . . . Aggravating features can include humiliating circumstances . . . or any conduct of those responsible . . . which shows that they had behaved in a high-handed, insulting, malicious or oppressive manner . . .'

Aggravated damages have been awarded for claims relating to torts such as battery, trespass to land, deceit and racial or sexual discrimination but there is authority to say that this should not happen in cases involving claims of negligence (*Kralj v McGrath* [1986] 1 All ER 54 – a case involving medical negligence).

As the award is basically for hurt feelings, it would be inappropriate for a company to receive such an award – a company has no feelings to be hurt!

Exemplary damages

The purpose of exemplary damages is two-fold:

(i) to punish the defendant and
(ii) to deter others from similar behaviour.

At first sight, the difference between exemplary and aggravated damages is not clear. In both cases, the disapproval of the defendant's action is seen to merit an additional award based largely on the view taken of the defendant's behaviour. The distinction is drawn between behaviour which adds to the claimant's hurt feelings (aggravated damages) and behaviour which deserves punishment even if the additional hurt to the claimant is minimal.

The availability of exemplary damages

The modern approach dates from a case in 1964:

CASE EXAMPLE

Rookes v Barnard [1964] AC 1129

The case involved an industrial dispute at Heathrow Airport. The claimant was an employee who had left the union which operated an informal closed shop agreement with the employers, British Overseas Airways Corporation. The defendant was an unpaid union official and as a result of union action, the employers were told that unless the claimant was dismissed there would be a strike. The claimant was dismissed and brought a civil action against the defendant and others for conspiracy. The claimant succeeded in his action. The important point for discussion here was whether he could be awarded exemplary damages.

Lord Devlin explained the distinction between compensatory damages and exemplary damages. The former, including aggravated damages, are intended to compensate the claimant for loss suffered. The latter are awarded to mark disapproval of the defendant's conduct and to deter others from similar behaviour. Lord Devlin concluded that there are two categories of cases where an award of exemplary damages could be appropriate:

JUDGMENT

(i) 'oppressive, arbitrary or unconstitutional action by the servants of the government'
(ii) 'those [cases] where the defendant's conduct has been calculated by him to make a profit for himself which may well exceed the compensation payable to the [claimant].'

The judge noted that a third category of case existed where 'exemplary damages are expressly authorised by statute'.

The availability of exemplary damages has continued to be controversial. Lord Devlin in *Rookes v Barnard* took the view that there were

JUDGMENT

'certain categories of cases in which an award of exemplary damages can serve a useful purpose in vindicating the strength of the law . . . and thus admitting into the civil law a principle which ought logically to belong to the criminal.'

When it is remembered that the general purpose of damages in civil law is to provide compensation rather than to punish a defendant, the basis for this view is clear. However, what about those cases where the criminal law provides no remedy but the conduct of the defendant is in the eyes of many people deserving of punishment? It is in this area that the issue of exemplary damages becomes of particular importance and, at the same time, particularly controversial. The courts have struggled with the problem and have shown reluctance to allow any extension of the categories for which exemplary damages can be awarded.

In *Broome v Cassell & Co Ltd* [1972] AC 1027 it was held that the categories of torts for which exemplary damages could be awarded was limited to those cases where such an award had been possible prior to 1964 (the 'cause of action approach'). This view, although the subject of academic argument and criticism, has been re-considered by the House of Lords in *Kuddus v Chief Constable of Leicestershire* [2002] UKHL 29

CASE EXAMPLE

Kuddus v Chief Constable of Leicestershire [2002] UKHL 29

The claimant had come back to his flat to find that many items were missing. The police officer attending the scene said that the matter would be investigated but two months later forged the claimant's signature on a statement withdrawing the complaint of theft. The claimant brought an action for misfeasance in a public office against the defendant as the employer of the police officer. The issue for the courts was whether the actions of the police officer could be the basis of an award of exemplary damages.

In considering its judgment, the members of the House of Lords bore in mind the report of the Law Commission, which in 1997 recommended that the availability of exemplary damages should extend to all torts regardless of whether such categories had been recognised prior to 1964 (Report on Aggravated, Exemplary and Restitutional Damages (1997) (Law Com No 247). Discussing this issue, and supporting the view of the Law Commission, Lord Mackay said

JUDGMENT

'The issue is determined by whether the factual situation is covered by either of Lord Devlin's formulations.'

Rejecting the 'cause of action' approach taken in *Broome v Cassell*, Lord Nicholls said that it represented

JUDGMENT

'an arbitrary and irrational restriction on the availability of exemplary damages.'

Lord Nicholls went on to say

JUDGMENT

'On occasion conscious wrongdoing by a defendant is so outrageous, his disregard of the [claimant's] rights so contumelious, that something more is needed to show that the law will not tolerate such behaviour. Without an award of exemplary damages, justice will not have been done.'

The present position

Accepting as one must, that the position is now that explained by the House of Lords in *Kuddus v Chief Constable of Leicestershire*, it is informative to consider examples of those cases where the courts have considered the issue of exemplary damages in those circumstances suggested by Lord Devlin in *Rookes v Barnard*.

In the case of oppressive, arbitrary or unconscionable action by servants of the government it is clear that there can be a punitive remedy for blatant abuse of power by civil servants or other agents of the government. An example of this is found in the following case.

CASE EXAMPLE

Huckle v Money (1763) 2 Wils 205

The defendant was detained pursuant to a search warrant for no more than six hours, during which time he was given 'beefsteaks and beer'. Notwithstanding this good treatment, the court held that the fact that the warrant was issued to obtain evidence,

QUOTATION

'is worse than the Spanish inquisition . . . it is a more daring public attack upon the liberty of the subject.'

The purpose of the category seems to be to ensure that executive powers are not exercised in an abusive way. Police officers are not strictly servants of the government but their actions are covered by these rules. Actions by publicly owned corporate bodies are only covered if the body is exercising an executive function. In *AB v South West Water Services Ltd* [1993] 1 All ER 609 it was held that a publicly owned monopoly supplier of water did not exercise executive functions and was not covered.

Lord Devlin's second category is intended to catch behaviour by the defendant which shows

(i) cynical self-interest in calculating that profit will exceed any compensation to which the claimant may be entitled; and

(ii) knowledge that the action is against the law or a blatant disregard of whether the action is or is not lawful.

Mere carelessness by the defendant will not suffice. No precise definition of what will suffice can be given but it seems that the courts are looking for some evidence of deliberate, calculated action. It is clear that there is no need to show that the defendant made any precise calculation.

In *John v MGN Ltd* [1997] QB 586, a case in which the singer Elton John was the subject of a libel, it was suggested that

(i) a general calculation that publication would aid sales of the newspaper and

(ii) any negotiated settlement or even any award of damages would be less than the profit from the increased sales was enough.

20.1.3 Damages for personal injury

Assessing unliquidated damages for personal injury is fraught with difficulty. How can such injury be compensated for by money? The award is divided into three parts:

1. pre-trial pecuniary loss
2. loss of future earnings and
3. **non-pecuniary loss**.

non-pecuniary loss

Compensation for pain, suffering and loss of amenities where judges have developed rates of compensation

We will look at the first two categories together and then turn to the third.

Pecuniary loss

It is possible for losses falling into this category to be assessed in money terms. The claimant will be able to provide evidence of actual expenditure relating to the injury and future earnings can be quantified.

Expenses

Many items of expenditure can simply be proved by the production of receipts or similar evidence. This can include the cost of private medical treatment actually incurred as there is no requirement to use the National Health Service (Law Reform (Personal Injuries) Act 1948, s 2(4)). Where it is used, the NHS has the right to recover costs relating to treatment resulting from a road traffic accident from the third party's insurers (Road Traffic (NHS Charges) Act 1999) but this does not apply to the cost of future treatment.

The claimant may claim the cost of future private medical care but once the award has been made, the court has no supervisory powers and it is for the claimant to decide whether or not to use NHS facilities after all. At the time of the award, the court may take into account the cost of care which the claimant will be unable to receive privately and indeed, if the court is satisfied that private treatment will not in fact be used for whatever reason, no award can be made to cover private costs.

Apart from the choice to use private medical care, there is a requirement that the expenditure is reasonably incurred. By way of example, a claimant is free to choose between permanent care in an institution or at home. The difference in cost is not decisive but the basis of the choice must be reasonable. It will be more difficult for the claimant to show that the choice of home-care is reasonable where the alternative cost of institutional care is much less.

Where a relative or other person provides necessary care rather than a person employed for that purpose, the carer has no direct claim. Since *Donnelly v Joyce* [1974] QB 454 the cost of such services, whether actually paid for or not, has been recoverable by the claimant. This would certainly cover net loss of earnings by a family member who has given up work to care for the claimant but will not otherwise amount to the commercial rate for the services.

Loss of future earnings

The court has to calculate the sum which will, when invested, produce a sum representing the claimant's lost earnings. This is done in two stages:

1. assessment of net annual loss and
2. multiplying this figure by the number of years such loss is likely to continue.

The net annual loss is usually gross wages less tax, social security contributions, pension contributions and any other deductions which would have been made from gross income. At first sight this looks simple but how many people can be certain of what the future holds? Opportunity may knock, enabling the claimant to increase earnings, or unemployment may strike, causing a drastic reduction. A claimant may argue that the injury has resulted in the loss of a chance of fame and/or fortune. In such cases, the court will make as realistic assessment as possible of the chances of the claimant actually achieving the goal. This happened in

CASE EXAMPLE

Doyle v Wallace [1998] PIQR Q146

The claimant was unable to work following a car accident. She had been planning to qualify as a drama teacher but, if she was not successful, to work as a clerk. As it was too early to say on the basis of her studies to that date whether or not she would have qualified, the court assessed her chances of qualifying at 50 per cent and her net future income at halfway between what she would have earned as a clerk and the higher pay she could have expected as a teacher.

Once the net annual loss has been calculated it would seem a simple calculation to multiply this figure by the relevant number of years throughout which it might have been earned. The courts will however take account of what have been described as 'the normal vicissitudes of life', for example, that the claimant might not have worked until retirement age.

Even after these figures have been assessed, it is not simple to calculate the lump sum payable. The court needs to decide what capital sum must be invested to produce an annual income of the right amount. This takes into account the fact that interest will accrue on the investment and the fact that the claimant will be expected to use part of the capital to supplement the income. A major problem is caused by inflation, which can fluctuate widely over a long period of time with the result that the return on the invested income can be seriously affected. The courts use actuarial tables (the *Ogden Tables*) prepared by insurance experts as well as guidance issued by the Lord Chancellor (presumably now by the Department of Constitutional Affairs) as to the likely rate of return on investments. By the Damages (Personal Injury) Order 2001 (SI 2001 No 2301) the rate is presently set at 2.5 per cent. The courts do not have to follow the guidance, the Damages Act 1996 s 1 granting discretion to depart from it where appropriate.

Deductions

It is a basic principle that a person should not be compensated from more than one source for the same injury. There are exceptions for certain social security benefits and for some other sources of compensation.

Social security benefits: For many years the sum awarded to the claimant was reduced by the amount of social security benefits payable. In 1989 this was changed to enable relevant benefits to be recouped from the defendants or their insurers but the result was that on occasions the claimant would be left without any compensation and it continued to allow the insurers to avoid payment of compensation in full. The position is now governed by the Social Security (Recovery of Benefits) Act 1997 which provides that damages may only be reduced if certain benefits equivalent to particular heads of damage have been paid. Schedule 2 specifies the relevant benefits which will be set against loss of earnings, the cost of care and the loss of mobility. By way of an example, attendance allowance is taken into account against the heading 'loss of care' and income support is set against 'loss of income.'

The result of this complex legislation is that the claimant will receive full compensation although some of it may come from social security benefits which are then paid back to the State by the defendants or their insurers.

Other sources of compensation: Sums paid by way of sickness benefit by an employer are taken into account but not a disability pension paid by an employer, insurance payouts from personal accident cover taken out by the claimant or payments made on a charitable basis. This obviously means that the claimant does in fact 'profit' in the sense that income is increased.

The approach has been criticised by the Law Commission ('Damages for Personal Injury: Collateral Benefits' Consultation Paper 147, 1997) but continues to be used by the courts. The reasoning seems to be that to do otherwise would

(i)   discourage employers from making proper arrangements for their employees
(ii) discourage people from obtaining sensible insurance cover
(iii) be an unreasonable rebuff to those seeking to act benevolently in response to another's misfortune
(iv) allow tortfeasors to escape full liability.

CASE EXAMPLE

Parry v Cleaver [1970] AC 1

Considering the issue of collateral benefits, the House of Lords held that by ignoring insurance payments under an employer's scheme the court acknowledged the fact that the claimant had in fact 'paid for' the benefit either directly through contributions or indirectly through past service to the employers. In relation to policies taken out by the claimant, the public interest was served by encouraging people to protect themselves in this way, and to deduct such sums might discourage them from doing so.

Discussing charitable payments Lord Reid said

JUDGMENT

'It would be revolting to the ordinary man's sense of justice, and therefore contrary to public policy, that the sufferer should have his damages reduced so that he would gain nothing from the benevolence of his friends or relations or the public at large, and that the only gainer would be the wrongdoer.'

Non-pecuniary loss

The difficulty of assessing such awards is immense. In an Australian case, *Todorovic v Waller* (1987) 37 ALR 481, Gibbs CJ and Mr Justice Wilson, in a joint judgment commented

JUDGMENT

'Although the aim of the court . . . is to make good to the [claimant], as far as money can do, the loss which he has suffered, it is obvious that it is impossible to assess damages for pain and suffering and loss of amenities . . . by any process of arithmetical calculation.'

Despite the difficulties some principles have evolved to enable the courts to assess such damages. This is dealt under two heads namely damages for

(i) pain and suffering; and
(ii) loss of amenity.

The meaning of pain and suffering is clear and will include worry about the future as well as mental suffering caused by knowledge that life expectancy may have been reduced. It can also include awareness of impending death unless the circumstances of the accident are such that the claimant would have been unaware (*Hicks v Chief Constable of South Yorkshire* [1992] 2 All ER 65 – one of the Hillsborough cases where no award was made for the victims of suffocation for the pain preceding death). A victim who remains unconscious may receive a reduced sum taking account of the fact that there is no awareness.

The term 'loss of amenity' refers to the changes in life style which the claimant will suffer as a result of the injury. A keen amateur sportsperson may recover under this head for inability to continue the sport. It is an objective judgment so that an award under this head will be made to someone who is permanently unconscious. While it may seem odd that a person is compensated even when unable to comprehend their loss, the award for loss of amenity continues.

The principles governing awards under these heads were explained by the House of Lords in 1980.

CASE EXAMPLE

Lim Poh Choo v Camden and Islington Area Health Authority [1980] AC 174

The claimant was the victim of medical negligence which caused her to suffer extensive and permanent brain damage. As a result for most of the time she was barely aware and at all times she needed total care.

Lord Devlin explained that damages for pain and suffering

JUDGMENT

'depend on the [claimant's] personal awareness of pain, her capacity for suffering.'

Damages for loss of amenity

JUDGMENT

'are awarded for the fact of deprivation, a substantial loss, whether the [claimant] is aware of it or not.'

He went on to acknowledge that

JUDGMENT

'. . . comparability matters. Justice requires that such awards . . . be consistent with the general level accepted by the judges.'

The consequence of the requirement that awards should be comparable is that the courts have created a 'tariff' of the amounts appropriate to different categories of claim involving loss of amenity. This normally takes the form of lower and upper brackets within which the particular award will fall. Over the years, the awards decreased in value and the Law Commission concluded that they were far too low ('Damages for Personal Injury: Non-pecuniary Loss', Law Com No 257, 1999). This finding was accepted by the Court of Appeal in *Heil v Rankin* [2001] QB 272. Although the Court refused to raise the tariffs by the amount suggested by the Law Commission, it recommended that certain categories of awards should be increased where the injuries were more serious. The scale amount will now be increased by about one-third for very serious cases, for example quadriplegia and severe brain damage, tapering down to no increase in awards of £10,000 and below.

Once for all settlement

We have seen the difficulties inherent in calculating an appropriate amount of compensation. The claimant, the defendant and the court are forced to rely on assessments of what the future holds. The need for a crystal ball to predict the future may be particularly acute in the context of certain types of injury where later deterioration may occur, but whether or not it does in fact do so is unpredictable.

Only one award can be made

Public policy dictates that only one action can be brought based on the same wrong. A later action cannot be brought if the consequences turn out to be worse than was taken into account at the time of the trial.

In the case of compensation for personal injuries, the problem has been partly addressed by the Senior Courts Act 1981 s 32A. This applies where there is a known chance that the claimant's health may seriously deteriorate at some time in the future but where there is no certainty when or if it will happen. In such cases an award of provisional damages can be made based on the assumption that such deterioration will not occur, but allowing the claimant to obtain further compensation should it do so.

Another way to address the problem is found by splitting the hearing into two parts, the first concerned with liability, the second with assessment of damages. This allows the medical situation to be come clearer and a more accurate assessment of the claimant's loss to be made.

Structured settlements

An obvious solution to the problem would be to introduce a mechanism for re-assessment of the claimant's position at fixed intervals. This has been rejected by the Law Commission (Law Com No 56 HC 373, 1973) although it was supported by the Pearson Commission.

In the meantime one potentially helpful development has occurred with the creation of structured settlements. These are governed by the Damages Act 1996, s 5 which provides:

> 's 5(1) . . . a "structured settlement" means an agreement settling a claim . . . for personal injury on terms whereby
> (a) the damages are to consist wholly or partly of periodical payments; and
> (b) the person to whom the payments are to be made is to receive them as the annuitant under [annuities] purchased for him by the person against whom the claim is brought . . . or his insurer.'

The section goes on to provide that the amounts may be for life or specified periods and may be for a fixed sum subject to increases or re-assessment to ensure that its value in real terms is maintained.

The court has no power to order structured settlements nor is there any mechanism to take account of later deterioration in the claimant's health. Not surprisingly, the Law Commission did not recommend that the court should have power to impose such settlements ('Structured Settlements and Interim and Provisional Damages', Law Com No 224, 1994).

20.1.4 Damages for damage to property

The basic rule is that the claimant must be restored to the position prior to the damage to, or destruction of, the property.

In the case of damage to property, the claimant is entitled to a sum which represents the amount by which the value of the property has been diminished. This will usually be the cost of repair unless this outweighs the market value of the property. In the latter case only the diminution in value will normally be payable. Where property has been destroyed, the market-value of property at the time of destruction will be awarded.

In both cases an additional sum for loss of use until repair or replacement will be awarded where this is reasonable. In the case of a business this can include a sum for loss of profit.

20.1.5 Damage to land and buildings

Although the basic principle is the same as for other damage to property, the issue of reasonableness is more important when the cost of restoration exceeds the value of the land. It may make commercial sense to re-build on the same site rather than move elsewhere in which case the cost of rebuilding might well be reasonable and thus the basis of the award (for a more detailed discussion of this issue see Chapter 8, section 8.7.1).

20.1.6 Some general principles

We have already seen the first important principle that the claimant should only be compensated for actual loss. This was re-affirmed by Lord Justice Otton in *Indata Equipment Supplies Ltd (t/a Autofleet) v ACL Ltd* [1998] 1 BCLC 412 when he said that the correct measure of tortious damages is

JUDGMENT

> 'such sum as would . . . put the [claimant] into the position it would have been in had it not been for the tort . . .'

The second principle is that the claimant has a duty to mitigate their loss by taking any steps which it is reasonable for them to take. A claimant seeking compensation for personal injury is expected to undergo medical treatment which may improve the situation. Where such treatment has unreasonably been refused, damages will be assessed as if the treatment had been given and effected the anticipated improvement.

A claimant who is unable to pursue former employment because of the injury is expected to take reasonable steps to obtain alternative employment. The fact that the new work may be lower paid will be reflected in the calculation of lost earnings.

Where property has been damaged, we have already seen that consequential losses will only be recoverable if they have been reasonably incurred. A business which is deprived of the use of essential equipment may recover the cost of hiring similar equipment if by that means the loss of profit is minimised.

20.1.7 The problem of death

As a general rule, the fact that the claimant or the defendant has died will not affect liability as the cause of action will survive for the benefit of or against the estate (Law Reform (Miscellaneous Provisions) Act 1934, s 1). A deceased claimant's estate cannot benefit from an award of exemplary damages nor can loss of income include any period after the date of death. Funeral expenses can be claimed where the defendant's tort is responsible for the death.

By virtue of the Fatal Accidents Act 1976 (as amended) certain relatives of a deceased person may bring a separate action against a person who has caused the death. The action, which is brought by the personal representatives of the deceased, lies for the benefit of

- **(i)** a surviving spouse, former spouse or common law spouse
- **(ii)** a parent or person treated by the deceased as a parent
- **(iii)** children
- **(iv)** a brother, sister, uncle or aunt of the deceased.

Damages are assessed on the basis of the extent to which the claimant was dependent on the deceased. The purpose of the award is to compensate for the loss of financial support, although an additional sum can be awarded for loss of services and emotional support.

A surviving spouse or a parent of a deceased child is entitled to damages for bereavement. The amount of such damages is set by statute and currently stands at £11,800.

20.2 Injunction

20.2.1 Generally

An injunction is an order of the court which must be obeyed. Breach of injunction amounts to contempt of court and as such is punishable by imprisonment in more serious cases. The remedy is theoretically available in respect of all torts but is perhaps most commonly used to prevent recurrence in cases of private nuisance, trespass to land and defamation.

It must be remembered that the remedy is equitable which means that it is discretionary. The court must be satisfied that the grant of an injunction is appropriate in the particular circumstances. Unlike damages, which are granted as of right where a legal right has been infringed, there is no right to an injunction. It will be refused, for example, where the claimant has acquiesced in the sense that the defendant has been led to believe that the claimant does not object to the infringement of the claimant's right. Where the claimant has acted to mislead the court or the defendant in some way, the order may well be refused. It must be remembered that the maxims of equity will always apply. (For further discussion of equitable maxims, you may care to consult a text on Equity and Trusts.)

20.2.2 Damages in lieu?

While there is discretion to award damages in lieu of an injunction, the courts are concerned to ensure that the right to break the law should not be available for purchase by those who are in a position to pay. This could amount to endorsing the conception that there is one law for the rich and one for the poor. As Lord Justice Lindley commented in *Shelfer v City of London Electric Lighting* [1895] 1 Ch 287:

JUDGMENT

'. . . the court has always protested against the notion that it ought to allow a wrong to continue simply because the wrongdoer is able and willing to pay for the injury he may inflict.'

(For a more detailed discussion of this principle in the context of nuisance see Chapter 9, section 9.6.2.)

It is clear that where the wrong is trivial or very temporary, damages may be awarded in lieu of an injunction. Winfield cites another, perhaps more practical, approach when referring to a New Zealand case, *Bank of New Zealand v Greenwood* [1984] 1 NZLR 525. A nuisance arose from the glare of a building. The case was adjourned sine die when the judge intimated that the installation of blinds at the defendants' expense would solve the problem! (*Winfield and Jolowicz*, p 797.)

We have already seen that in cases of nuisance the courts may 'tailor' an injunction to reach a sensible compromise between the interests of the claimant and the defendant (*Kennaway v Thompson* [1980] 3 WLR 361).

The courts also try to balance the public interest against private rights. In *Miller v Jackson* [1977] QB 966 Lord Denning MR took the view that where public and private interests conflict, the public interest should prevail

JUDGMENT

'The public interest lies in protecting the environment by preserving our playing fields in the face of mounting development, and by enabling our youth to enjoy all the benefits of outdoor games such as cricket and football.'

Lord Denning's view has been criticised and the principles set out in *Shelfer* have been re-affirmed. An injunction should only be refused and damages awarded in lieu where

- **(i)** to grant an injunction would be oppressive to the defendant; and
- **(ii)** the injury to the claimant's rights is small and is capable of being estimated in money and
- **(iii)** monetary compensation is adequate.

See *Kennaway v Thompson* and for discussion see Chapter 9.

20.2.3 Types of injunctions available

Mandatory injunctions

A mandatory injunction requires the defendant to take some active step to put matters right. It is rarely granted. The principles which will guide the court were set out in

CASE EXAMPLE

Redland Bricks Ltd v Morris [1970] AC 652

Excavations by the defendants on their land had meant that part of the claimant's land had subsided and the rest was likely to slip. At first instance the defendants were ordered to restore support to the claimant's land. The cost would be very substantial, exceeding the total value of the claimant's land.

On appeal to the House of Lords Lord Upjohn set out some general principles:
(i) There must be a very strong probability that substantial damage will be caused.
(ii) Damages would be inadequate as a remedy.
(iii) The defendants' behaviour is relevant – have they tried to 'steal a march' on the claimant or the court or have they behaved reasonably albeit wrongly?
(iv) It must be possible to frame a mandatory injunction in such a way that the defendants are very clear as to precisely what needs to be done.

For further discussion of these issues, particularly the reasonableness of the defendants' action, see Chapter 8, section 8.7.

Prohibitory injunctions

This is an order of the court to prevent a recurrence of the tort. It is most commonly found in actions for nuisance, trespass to land and defamation where there is a risk that the tortious behaviour may be repeated.

Quia timet injunctions

In rare cases it may be clear that a tort is about to be committed. In such cases, it is possible for the claimant to anticipate matters and to ask the court to prevent the defendant from proceeding. The injunction is rarely granted as the claimant must show that:

(i) there is a high probability of substantial damage; and
(ii) the probability is imminent.

It is tempting to believe that this would be an effective remedy to prevent publication of allegedly defamatory material in those rare cases where the claimant has prior warning. This has become less likely since the Human Rights Act 1998 came into effect. The provisions of s 12 are very relevant and are discussed in the next paragraph.

Interim (interlocutory) injunctions

Where it can be shown that an order is urgently necessary to prevent substantial damage, the court can sometimes be persuaded to grant an interim injunction. This has the effect of stopping the allegedly tortious behaviour for a short time pending a full hearing of an application for a prohibitory injunction. If an interim injunction is granted, the claimant will normally be required to give an undertaking to the court to pay damages and costs if the later action fails. In cases involving alleged defamation, the Human Rights Act 1998 s 12 is very relevant. The Act provides that where the court is considering a matter which raises the right to freedom of expression

SECTION

's 12(3) no [interim] relief is to be granted so as to restrain publication before trial unless the court is satisfied that the applicant is likely to establish that publication should not be allowed.'

The Act goes on in s 12(4)(a), to require the court to consider the extent to which the material is likely to be available to the public and whether it is in the public interest that the material should be published.

The court will not grant such an injunction where the defendant alleges an intention to rely on the defence of justification or fair comment.

20.3 Other remedies

We have already discussed self-help remedies which are applicable to specific torts:

(i) self-defence in the context of trespass to the person
(ii) necessity in the context of trespass to the person, negligence and trespass to land
(iii) abatement in the context of nuisance

and reference should be made to the appropriate sections for further detail.

20.4 Limitation periods

20.4.1 Generally

It is a fundamental principle that people should not be at risk of having an action brought against them for an indefinite period of time. In addition to the unfairness caused to that person, a very practical difficulty can arise in finding the evidence. Documents may have been lost or destroyed, witnesses may have disappeared and memories fade with time. For this reason a claimant is required to seek a remedy within a specified period. In Chapter 1 we saw the effect that this requirement can have in *Letang v Cooper* [1965] 1 QB 232 where the claimant sought to use the old forms of action in order to avoid a limitation period. As we shall see, in some cases it may be possible for the claimant to obtain the court's leave to bring an action after the limitation period has expired. The court will in such cases be very concerned to ensure that justice is done to both parties.

The present law is found in the Limitation Act 1980 as amended by the Latent Damage Act 1986 and the Defamation Act 1996.

20.4.2 The basic periods

These are as follows:

- claims which do not involve personal injury – six years
- claims involving personal injury, even if only part of the claim – three years.

In each case the time is calculated from the date on which the cause of action accrued. In most cases this is clear – the event happens, damage is immediately known to have happened and it is immediately possible for an action to be brought. The cause of action accrues on the date the event happened.

This is easy to see in relation to those torts which are actionable *per se* and in many others, but what of the cases where the damage lies hidden for some time? Special rules dealing with these cases are considered in the next sections.

20.4.3 Latent damage to property

In those cases where damage has to be proved, the damage can lie hidden for some time and not become apparent within the limitation period.

The problems became apparent in cases about defective buildings heard during the 1970s and 1980s. In *Sparham-Souter v Town & Country Developments (Essex) Ltd* [1976] QB 858 it had been held, by the Court of Appeal, that the limitation period would run from the date on which the claimant knew or ought reasonably to know that damage had occurred. This was known as the 'reasonable discovery' test. Some years later, in *Pirelli General Cable Works Ltd v Oscar Faber & Partners* [1983] 2 AC 1, the House of Lords over-ruled the reasonable discovery test.

CASE EXAMPLE

Pirelli General Cable Works Ltd v Oscar Faber & Partners [1983] 2 AC 1

The defendants were consulting engineers who had designed tall chimneys. As a result of negligent design, cracks appeared in the chimneys. The damage was not discovered for some considerable time by which date the limitation period for a claim in negligence had expired. The claimants argued that time did not begin to run until the damage could have been discovered using reasonable diligence.

Time would start to run when physical damage occurred regardless of whether or not it was at that time discoverable. The claim was accordingly out of time and barred.

As a result of the confusion and apparent injustice, the Latent Damage Act 1986 was passed which inserted new provisions into the Limitation Act 1980.

By s 14A(4)(b) a new period was available of three years from the date on which the claimant knew or reasonably could have known about the defect and that it was due to the defendant's negligence. This meant that a claim could be brought many years after the expiration of the usual limitation period of six years.

It was still considered that it would be unjust for defendants to be at risk for an indefinite time. To deal with this, s 14B provides that there is a 'long stop' of 15 years running from the date of the last act of negligence which could be the basis of the claim. By way of example, in *Pirelli* the defendants would have remained at risk for a total period of 15 years from the date of the negligence which caused the defect.

Property may well have changed hands during the limitation period. This could mean that the right to bring an action was lost as the person who originally had a cause of action would no longer be able to bring a claim. This has been dealt with by the Latent Damage Act 1986, s 3(1) which provides that the right of action vests in a successor in title to the property. The limitation period is still calculated from the date on which the original owner would have been able to claim.

20.4.4 Personal injuries

As we have seen, the basic limitation period for any claim which is concerned wholly or partly with personal injury is three years from the date the cause of action accrues. This has always caused problems, particularly in the case of certain industrial diseases, where the injury may not become apparent for many years.

When an injury has occurred the Limitation Act 1980, s 11(4) provides that the limitation periods runs for the period of three years from the date of the injury or, where this is not immediately apparent, for a period of three years from the date on which the claimant has knowledge of the injury. A claimant is deemed to have the necessary knowledge in circumstances set out in s 14(1) namely:

- the claimant is aware that the injury is significant and
- the injury is due in whole or in part to the defendant's negligence, nuisance or breach of duty and
- the claimant knows the identity of the defendant and
- if the alleged wrongdoer was someone other than the defendant, for example an employee in cases where the defendant has vicarious liability, the claimant knows the identity of that person and the necessary additional facts to support the claim, for example the fact that the person was employed at the relevant time by the defendant.

Injury is regarded as 'significant' if a claimant would reasonably have regarded it as sufficiently serious to bring an action against a defendant who did not dispute liability. This complicated meaning was interpreted by the Court of Appeal in *Spargo v North Essex District Health Authority* [1997] PIQR P235:

1. The claimant needs broad knowledge of the act or omission which caused the injury.
2. There must be a real possibility that the act or omission in question is the cause of the injury.
3. The claimant will be regarded as having the necessary knowledge when matters have reached the stage where it would be reasonable for the claimant to investigate whether or not there is a cause of action, for example by seeking legal advice.
4. A claimant who

   - believes that the cause is known but who is mistaken or
   - one whose knowledge is so vague that they cannot reasonably be expected to investigate a possible claim or
   - one whose knowledge is such that they would need to check with an expert for more information, will not have the necessary knowledge to start the limitation period running.

A claimant must seek the advice and information which it is reasonable to seek but will not be deemed to have knowledge of matters only available as the result of failure by an expert to identify the problem.

CASE EXAMPLE

Marston v British Railways Board [1976] ICR 124

The claimant suffered injury when a piece of metal flew off a hammer. An expert who conducted a hardness test on the hammer failed to notice the defect which caused the accident. It was held that the claimant was not deemed to be aware of the cause of action and a later claim was allowed.

Where death has resulted and a claim is to be made under the Fatal Accidents Act 1976, the limitation period is three years from the date of death or the date on which the deceased had the necessary knowledge whichever is the later (Limitation Act 1980, s 12(2)).

20.4.5 Other statutory provisions

Various statutes impose specific limitation periods.

By the Defamation Act 1996, which inserted s 4A into the Limitation Act 1980, an action for defamation or malicious falsehood must be brought within a period of 12 months from the date of the publication. A cause of action in defamation does not survive the death of the person defamed.

As we have seen, an action under the Consumer Protection Act 1987 is subject to a 'long stop' of 10 years from the date the product is put into circulation (Limitation Act 1980, s 11A(3)).

The Merchant Shipping Act 1995 ensures that actions brought for damage to a vessel, cargo or persons on board the vessel caused by another vessel must be brought within two years.

20.4.6 The court's power to extend the limitation period

By the Limitation Act 1980, s 33 the court has power to over-ride the statutory time limits where it is equitable to do so. This power cannot be exercised in cases:

- brought under the Consumer Protection Act 1987
- involving trespass to the person where the limit is six years.

The court must have regard to all relevant circumstances and in particular, but not exclusively, to

- the length of and reasons for the delay
- the effect, if any, on the evidence in the case, for example have documents been lost or destroyed or have witnesses become untraceable or unavailable
- the behaviour of the defendant after the cause of action arose, for example what replies were given to requests for information
- if the claimant has been disabled for any cause arising after the cause of action, how long that disability lasted
- did the claimant act promptly and reasonably once the possibility of an action was known
- steps taken by the claimant to obtain appropriate information from, for example, doctors, lawyers or other experts.

The discretion can only apply where no proceedings have been issued within the relevant period. A claimant who issues a claim and then does not proceed with it, will usually be unable to take advantage of s 33. This is of particular importance now that the courts are taking a pro-active role to ensure that claims are dealt with expeditiously. In such cases the claimant may have an action in negligence against professional advisers who have failed to take steps required. This is likely to mean that s 33 cannot be used, but there is no general rule that this will follow. The judge's discretion is unfettered and the decision will reflect a balancing act between the prejudice caused to both parties by the delay.

The issue of discretionary extension of the limitation period has recently been considered by the House of Lords in a series of joined appeals, *A v Hoare and conjoined appeals* [2008] UKHL 6, which involved claims for sexual abuse brought out of time. While discretionary extension of the three-year period for personal injury claims applies to 'negligence, nuisance or breach of duty' the House of Lords in *Stubbings v Webb* [1993] AC 498 had held that there was no such discretion in the case of deliberate assault. In *Hoare* the House of Lords overruled *Stubbings v Webb* arguing that there was no rational explanation why Parliament would make the law harder for a person bringing a personal injury claim caused by a deliberate assault than one caused by negligence.

20.4.7 Legal disability

A claimant who suffers legal disability is not thereby disadvantaged. The limitation period will run for the relevant period from the time the disability ceases or the claimant dies. This means that a minor can bring an action for personal injury within three years of attaining majority (18 years of age) unless an action has previously been brought on their behalf. Someone who is of unsound mind when time begins to run is similarly protected. Where a person becomes of unsound mind after the date of accrual, the disability has no effect.

20.4.8 Fraud and concealment

The law is concerned to ensure that a person cannot benefit from fraud or other dishonest behaviour. The limitation periods are therefore subject to extension in some cases.

Where the claimant's action is based on fraudulent action, for example the tort of deceit, time only begins to run once the claimant has discovered, or ought by reasonable diligence to have discovered, the fraud.

In cases where the claimant's right of action has been deliberately concealed by the defendant, time will only start to run once the claimant has discovered, or ought to have discovered, the concealment.

20.4.9 The future?

The reader will have realised that the law in this area is extremely complex and confused. The Law Commission has recommended that

1. the limitation period in all cases should be three years running from the date the cause of action is discoverable
2. there should be an absolute 'long stop' of 10 years
3. in personal injury cases, the court should continue to have a discretion to extend the limitation period and no long stop would apply.

Law Commission, Limitation of Actions, Report No 270, July 2001.

The reforms would continue to make special provision for actions under the Consumer Protection Act 1987 allowing for an absolute long stop of a different period.

In the case of those suffering legal disability, the Law Commission proposes that

1. In the case of infancy (minority) although the initial period would not run, the long stop would apply provided it did not come to an end before the minor reached 18.

2. In the case of adults, the initial period would not run but the overall long stop would apply.
3. Where a claimant is under a disability and has suffered personal injury but is in the care of a responsible adult 10 years after the date of accrual or the date when they became disabled whichever is the later, the periods will run from the date the responsible adult knew or ought to have known the relevant facts. This would be subject to the court's discretion to grant leave to bring proceedings even after the end of the limitation period.

The reader is likely to agree that reform is needed. Whether the proposals would in reality simplify the situation is a matter to be seen if and when reform is implemented. To date, there is little sign that the Law Commission's proposals will be adopted.

KEY FACTS

Key facts on damages

General and special damages	Case/statute
General damages not capable of being precisely quantified – awarded, eg for pain and suffering and loss of amenity. Special damages – costs which can be precisely quantified.	
Categories of general damages	**Case/statute**
contemptuous nominal aggravated exemplary	
Contemptuous damages	**Case/statute**
Marks court's view that the action should not have been brought to court. Can be influenced by fact that actual damage is minimal or by fact that claimant in some way 'asked for what they got'. Note potential costs penalty.	
Nominal damages	**Case/statute**
Awarded where little actual damage is caused. Court satisfied that action properly brought. Often linked to application for injunction or declaration.	*Ms B v An NHS Hospital Trust* (2002)
Aggravated damages	**Case/statute**
Awarded to compensate injury to feelings and distress. Increased by defendant's bad behaviour.	*Thompson v Metropolitan Police Commissioner* (1997)
Exemplary damages	**Case/statute**
Purpose to punish defendant **and** to deter others from similar behaviour. Available for blatant abuse of executive power or where defendant has calculated that profits will outweigh any damages that may be payable. Note controversy as to when exemplary damages should be available now apparently settled.	*Rookes v Barnard* (1964) *Kuddus v Chief Constable of Leicester* (2002) *Kuddus* (2002)

Damages for personal injury	Case/statute
Pecuniary loss – covers actual expenditure including cost of medical treatment or private care if actually incurred or to be incurred in the future if reasonable. Loss of future earnings involves assessment of actual net annual loss multiplied by number of years of productive life – figure needs to represent that which will produce the necessary income over the period taking into account the gradual use of capital and the rate of inflation. Certain sums can be deducted from net loss of earnings including social security benefits and sickness benefits but not employers' disability pension, claimant's own health insurance or charitable payments. A good example of the court's approach.	*Parry v Cleaver* (1970)

Non-pecuniary loss	Case/statute
Includes a sum for pain and suffering which claimant must actually experience.	*Hicks v Chief Constable of S Yorks* (1992)
Additional sum is awarded for loss of amenity, ie necessary changes in life-style – awarded even when claimant unaware of the changes.	
For court's approach in particular see judgment of Lord Devlin.	*Lim Poh Choo v Camden & Islington AHA* (1980)

Problems with damages for personal injury	Case/statute
Only one award can be made – claimant cannot go back to court if situation changes.	
Problem partly alleviated by voluntary use of structured settlements which can be subject to re-assessment.	Damages Act 1996, s 5

Damages for damage to property	Case/statute
Sum represents diminution of value of the property.	
Usually cost of repair plus sum for loss of use until repair or replacement.	
Loss in value of property usual award where cost of repair outweighs value.	
Market value where property destroyed.	

General principles	Case/statute
Claimant is only compensated for actual loss – there should be no element of profit.	
Claimant under a duty to take reasonable steps to mitigate the loss.	

Death	Case/statute
Generally action will survive death of claimant or defendant, personal representatives acting on behalf of the estate.	
Deceased claimant cannot receive exemplary damages nor loss of income after the date of death.	
Relatives who were financially dependent on deceased claimant have action in their own right.	
Surviving spouse or child entitled to damages for bereavement, presently £7,500.	

Key facts on injunction

Generally	Case/statute
Equitable order breach of which amounts to contempt of court and is punishable.	
Cannot be granted as of right – court must be satisfied that it is appropriate in the particular circumstances.	
Damages can be awarded in lieu but court must be wary not to allow a wrongdoer to buy the right to continue the wrong.	*Shelfer v City of London Electric Lighting* (1895)
Modern tendency for court to tailor the injunction to try to achieve balance between parties	*Kennaway v Thompson* (1980)
Mandatory injunction	**Case/statute**
An order to do something.	
For principles see	*Redland Bricks v Morris* (1970)
Risk of substantial damage, damages would be inadequate, defendant's behaviour is relevant, defendant must know exactly what needs to be done.	
Prohibitory injunction	**Case/statute**
Prohibits wrongful act.	
Quia timet – granted in anticipation to prevent to future wrong doing – very rarely available.	
Interim (interlocutory) injunction	**Case/statute**
Will stop allegedly unlawful action pending full hearing for prohibitory injunction.	
Claimant usually required to give undertakings as to costs and payment of damages if action unsuccessful.	
Rarely available in defamation cases.	Human Rights Act 1998, s 12(3)
Generally	**Case/statute**
Law found in	Limitation Act 1980 as amended
Action must be started within prescribed period.	
Failure to do so means action barred.	
Basic period 6 years for claims not involving personal injury, 3 years for claims any part of which relates to personal injury.	
Latent damage to property	**Case/statute**
Time runs from when claimant knows or ought reasonably to have known the damage has occurred due to defendant's negligence.	s 14A(4)(b)
Longstop of 15 years running from the date of the last act of negligence which could be the basis for the claim.	s 14B

Personal injuries	Case/statute
Normally 3 years from the date of injury. In cases where injury is not immediately apparent, eg industrial disease, 3 years from date claimant has knowledge of the injury and the potential for a claim against the defendant.	s 14(1) *Spargo v North Essex DHA* (1997)
Other limitation periods	**Case/statute**
Defamation – 12 months from date of publication. Consumer protection – long stop of 10 years from date product put into circulation. Damage to shipping cargo or person on board – 2 years. Trespass to the person – 6 years.	Defamation Act 1996 Consumer Protection Act 1987 Merchant Shipping Act 1995
Power to allow action out of time	**Case/statute**
Found in Cannot be used in relation to action under or in cases of trespass to the person. Court must be satisfied that it is reasonable in all the circumstances to grant leave taking into account relevant history and the conduct of both parties as well as the likely availability of evidence.	Limitation Act 1980, s 33 Consumer Protection Act 1987
Legal disability	**Case/statute**
A child has 3 years from attaining 18 if no previous action brought on the child's behalf. Someone of unsound mind has 3 years from recovery unless previous action brought on their behalf.	
Fraud and concealment	**Case/statute**
Time will only begin to run from the date when the claimant discovers or ought to have discovered the fraud or the concealment.	

Conclusion

The rules are complex. The Law Commission proposes change to simplify matters but there is as yet so sign that reform will occur.

SUMMARY

Remedies include:
- Damages – which can be: general, special, contemptuous, nominal, exemplary, non-pecuniary
- Injunctions – which can be: mandatory, prohibitory, interim (interlocutory)

There are statutory limitation periods beyond which no action can be brought:
- Six years generally from the tort
- Three years from the tort or the date of knowledge in personal injury claims
- There are other fixed periods for other specific torts
- There is also the means for a court to allow an action that is out of time in very strict circumstances

Appendix 1

Essay writing

Below is a sample essay title and a guide on how to prepare to answer it.

It has been suggested that 'it is generally recognised that the rules governing recovery for damages for nervous shock lack coherence, logic, justice and even plain common sense' (FA Trindade, 'Reformulation of the Nervous Shock Rules' (2003) 119 LQR 204).

In the light of the above statement, compare and evaluate the different rules applied by the courts to primary and secondary victims in cases of nervous shock.

Answering the question:

There are usually two key elements to essays in law:

■ Firstly you are required to reproduce a series of factual information on a particular area of law as identified in the question.

■ Secondly you are required to answer the question set, which usually is in the form of some sort of critical element, ie you may very probably see the words discuss, analyse, critically consider, explain, etc.

Students for the most part seem quite capable of doing the first, and also generally seem less skilled at the second. The important points in any case are to ensure that you only deal with relevant legal material in your answer and that you do answer the question set, rather than one you have made up yourself, or the one that was on last year's paper.

For instance, in the case of the first, in this essay you might say the following: Nervous shock is an area of negligence. Negligence requires proof of the existence of a duty of care and breach of that duty and damage caused by the defendant that is not too remote a consequence of the breach. But you do not need to treat the examiner to everything that you know about the standard of care, or the 'but for' test, etc, because none of that is relevant. In the case of the second the essay asks you to 'compare and evaluate' the rules applicable to different types of claimant in nervous shock cases. This clearly indicates that you must compare the different rules for dealing with primary and secondary victims, and since you are asked to evaluate you will need to pass some sort of comment on whether the law treats both fairly, adequately, etc.

Relevant law:

The appropriate law appears to be:

■ That nervous shock is one of those novel duty situations in negligence and thus all the other rules of negligence apply.

■ Nervous shock involves recognised psychiatric illnesses such as PTSD but not mere grief or other distress – compare *Reilly* and *Tredget*.

■ The rules on who can recover in what situation are now contained in *Alcock*.

■ The law distinguishes between primary victims – those present at the scene of an incident and directly affected or injured by the defendant's negligent act or omission – and secondary victims – those indirectly affected by the trauma caused by the defendant's negligent act or omission.

■ Primary victims can recover if they suffer physical as well as psychiatric injury, or if physical harm is foreseeable and they suffer nervous shock as a result – *Dulieu v White* or *Page v Smith*.

■ Secondary victims must have a close tie of love and affection with a primary victim and close proximity in time and space to the traumatic event or its immediate aftermath –

McLoughlin v O'Brian – or be a professional rescuer – *Chadwick v British Railways Board* and *Hale v London Underground* – note also that such people must be of reasonable fortitude – *Bourhill v Young* and that the psychiatric injury must result from the trauma being witnessed by their own unaided senses, either seeing or hearing.

Evaluation:

The commentary in the essay requires you to compare the treatment of primary and secondary victims and to evaluate their treatment. Relevant comments might include:

- That the range of injuries that will allow liability is limited, although floodgates argument and state of medical knowledge may justify this and it has had some expansion – *Vernon v Bosely*.
- That primary victims generally have no problem recovering.
- Consideration that since *White v Chief Constable of South Yorkshire*, professional rescuers must be identifiable as genuine primary victims in order to claim.
- Consideration that, according to *Greatorex v Greatorex*, a rescuer could also claim if he could be classed as a genuine secondary victim, ie conform to all of the requirements in *Alcock*.
- That close tie of love and affection is quite limited in scope – *Alcock*.
- And perhaps unfairly does not include close friendships or working relationships – *Robertson and Rough v Forth Road Bridge* and *Duncan v British Coal*.
- That immediate aftermath is quite narrowly defined – *Alcock* – and the widest point predates the test now – *McLoughlin v O'Brian*.
- That bystanders are treated unfairly in comparison to professional rescuers although they might suffer the same psychiatric injuries – *McFarlane v EE Caledonia*.
- That professional rescuers were originally treated more fairly in determining liability than were the relatives of primary victims – *Alcock* – but that the courts recognising the possible injustice have changed their stance on professional rescuers in relation to the 'Hillsborough' litigation – compare the Court of Appeal in *Hicks v Chief Constable of South Yorkshire* [1992] 2 All ER 65 and the different approach taken by the House of Lords in *White v Chief Constable of South Yorkshire*.
- That public policy plays an important role in deciding on liability in nervous shock, particularly the 'floodgates' argument.
- That numerous cases seem to be out of line with the 'strict' rules – eg *Attia v British Gas* and nervous shock following witnessing damage to property, *Owens v Liverpool Corporation* and primary victim being a corpse, *Dooley v Cammell Laird* and primary victim being a work colleague of the claimant, *Tredget v Bexley Health Authority* where the nervous shock seemed to be based on profound grief at the death of a child, *Hevican v Ruane* [1991] 3 All ER 65 where the nervous shock followed the claimant being informed of the death of his son and witnessing the body was long after the immediate aftermath.

Of course it will usually be required of you in producing a discussion that you make references also to the arguments of academic commentators either in leading texts or journal articles.

You should also take care to follow whatever system for citation and use of tables and bibliography you have been given.

Appendix 2

Applying the law

Below is a reasonably straightforward problem question and a guide on how to answer it.

There are always four essential ingredients to answering problem questions:

- Firstly, you must be able to identify which are the key facts in the problem, the ones on which any resolution of the problem will depend.
- Secondly, you will need to identify which is the appropriate law which applies to the particular situation in the problem.
- Thirdly, you must apply the law to the facts.
- Finally, you will need to reach conclusions of some sort. If the question asks you to advise, then that is what you need to do. On the other hand if the problem says 'Discuss the legal consequences of . . .' then you know that you can be less positive in your conclusions.

Problem:

Homer, his wife Marge and children Bart and Lisa go to the Springfield Holiday Camp for two weeks in August. In their holiday contract is the following clause: 'Neither the Springfield Holiday Camp nor their servants or agents will be liable for death or injury to visitors, howsoever caused.' A large notice to the same effect is placed at the entrance to the camp. The camp is owned and managed by Springfield Leisure Co.

Late one night while returning to the holiday chalet, which is high up on a slope, Homer falls down the steep steps that lead to the chalet from the road below. There is no guardrail to the steps and the steps are also unlit. Homer suffers severe head injuries in the fall.

Marge is electrocuted and badly burnt when she plugs in the kettle in the chalet's kitchenette. The socket has actually been left live due to the negligence of Shoddy Electric Co who recently rewired the chalet.

Bart cuts himself badly and wrecks his jacket with a sharp knife when he sneaks into the kitchen in the camp restaurant to make himself a sandwich. The door is not locked but a notice on the door of the kitchen reads: 'Danger. Staff only.'

Lisa suffers a very bad stomach upset when she eats berries on a bush growing by the chalet front door. The berries are poisonous.

Advise Homer, Marge, Bart and Lisa of any remedies that they might have for their injuries and against whom.

The facts:

It is important to have a clear idea of what the principal facts are, particularly as here where there is a number of different people and different problems involved. The main facts seem to be:

1. Springfield Leisure Co own and manage the Springfield Holiday Camp.
2. Homer, Marge and their children Bart and Lisa contract for a holiday at the camp for two weeks in August.
3. The contract contains an exclusion of liability for death or injury, however caused.
4. A notice to the same effect is posted at the entrance to the camp.
5. Homer is injured when he falls at night down steep unlit steps to his chalet with no hand rail.
6. Marge is electrocuted and badly burnt when plugging in the kettle.
7. The socket is live due to the negligence of Shoddy Electric Co who rewired it.

8. Bart cuts himself on a knife in the restaurant kitchen.
9. A notice on the kitchen door reads: 'Danger. Staff only.'
10. Lisa is poisoned when she eats berries growing on a bush by the front door.
11. Bart and Lisa are both children.

The appropriate law

It is very important when answering problem questions that you use only the law that is relevant to the precise facts, if for no other reason than that you are not getting any marks for using law that is irrelevant and so you are wasting valuable writing time. By looking at the various facts we can say that the following law may be relevant in our problem here:

1. The area involved is the Occupiers' Liability Acts.
2. (a) The 1957 Act covers liability towards 'visitors' – those lawfully on the premises.
   (b) The 1984 Act concerns trespassers – and is appropriate only to personal injury, not property damage.
3. There are three key issues:
   (i) what counts as premises
   (ii) who is an 'occupier' and so who can be sued
   (iii) who can claim under the Acts and under which one.
4. There is no real definition of premises in either Act – the common law applies and is widely defined (ie wide enough to include a ladder in *Wheeler v Copas*).
5. Occupier is again not defined in either Act – again the common law applies, an occupier is 'anybody who is in control of the premises' – *Wheat v Lacon*.
6. Under the 1957 Act a 'visitor' is anybody with a lawful right to be on the premises.
7. Under s 2(1) a 'common duty of care' is owed to all visitors.
8. Under s 2(2) the duty is to take all reasonable care to keep the visitor safe for the purposes for which he has legitimately entered the premises.
9. The standard of care is as for negligence so the same sorts of principles apply.
10. Under s 2(3) an occupier must be prepared for children to be less careful than adults would be.
    (a) The occupier must not do anything to 'allure' the child into danger – *Taylor v Glasgow Corporation*.
    (b) An occupier may be able to rely on the duty of parents to supervise very young children – *Phipps v Rochester Corporation*.
11. An occupier will not be liable for the harm caused by the work of independent contractors provided that:
    (i) It is reasonable for the occupier to entrust the work to someone else – *Haseldine v Daw*.
    (ii) A competent contractor is hired – *Ferguson v Welsh*.
    (iii) The occupier carries out checks on the work if appropriate – *AMF v Magnet Bowling*.
12. An occupier may avoid liability under s 2(1) in a number of ways:
    (a) Warning notices, provided they are effective – *Rae v Mars* (and nothing short of a barrier may possibly be sufficient for children).
    (b) Exclusion clauses in contracts – but these would be subject to the Unfair Contract Terms Act 1977, and a clause excluding liability for death or injury caused by negligence is invalid under s 2(1).
    (c) The defences of contributory negligence and consent (not relevant here).
13. The 1984 Act applies by s 1(1)(a) to persons other than visitors.
14. Under the 1984 Act an occupier is liable under s 1(1) in respect of dangers 'due to the state of the premises or things done or omitted to be done on them'.
15. Under s 1(3) the occupier will be liable if
    (a) he is aware of the danger,
    (b) he knows that the trespasser may come into the vicinity of the danger, and
    (c) the risk is one against which the occupier might be expected to provide some protection.

Applying the law to the facts

1. We know that Springfield Leisure Co own and manage the holiday camp so we can feel that they 'control' the premises and are occupiers and therefore defendants under the Act.
2. We know also that Homer and his family have paid for their holiday and so will be 'visitors' and therefore may claim under the 1957 Act. The common duty of care applies to them all and they are entitled to expect the same standard of care.
3. 'Premises' presents no problems here – the holiday camp clearly is.
4. It is easier past this point to take each individual in turn:

   Homer:
   - The question is whether not providing a hand rail on the steep steps and not having them lit is a breach of Springfield's duty – it would certainly seem to fall below an appropriate standard of care and the facts in any case seem to resemble those in *Wheat v Lacon*.
   - The exclusion clause cannot apply because of s 2(1) of UCTA.
   - Similarly, the warning notice outside the camp would fail to relieve liability unless it covered specific risks – *Rae v Mars*.

   Marge:
   - Leaving sockets 'live' clearly falls below an appropriate standard of care.
   - The question here is whether it is Springfield or Shoddy who is responsible.
   - It will obviously depend on whether Shoddy is a reliable contractor or not.
   - Clearly it is appropriate for Springfield to delegate that type of work and they do not have the expertise to check it, they are relying on the contractors – *Haseldine v Daw*.
   - The exclusion clause and warning notice would fail for the same reasons.

   Lisa:
   - Lisa is a child so under s 2(3) is entitled to expect greater care than an adult.
   - The bush appears to be a possible 'allurement', certainly if we compare it with the facts in *Taylor v Glasgow Corporation*.
   - It would be hard to expect the parents to take full responsibility here where the bush is outside the front door and so it is unlikely that *Phipps v Rochester Corporation* could apply in the circumstances.
   - Again the exclusion clause cannot apply and the notice is even less appropriate here because Lisa is a child.

   Bart:
   - Bart has entered a part of the premises from which he is barred – this may make him a trespasser.
   - Bart is a child and a kitchen may well be an allurement to a hungry child – Springfield may expect some risk of trespassers to such parts of the premises if they do not keep them locked up – *BR Board v Herrington*.
   - Furthermore, kitchen implements, sharp knives, etc are clearly dangerous if unattended.
   - The notice on the door is unlikely to be sufficient warning since it is imprecise in respect of the risk and in any case Bart is a child.
   - The 1984 Act applies only in respect of injuries so Bart may be unable to claim in respect of his damaged jacket.

Conclusions

We have shown how the law applies to each of our four central characters and would be able to advise them to sue with confidence.

- Homer and Lisa could both sue Springfield for their injuries under the 1957 Act.
- Marge can sue for her injuries, but unless Shoddy are disreputable contractors whom Springfield should not have hired, then her action will be against Shoddy rather than Springfield.
- Bart is a trespasser and will sue Springfield under the 1984 Act, but for his injuries only, not for his other damage.

You should also remember to use references and citations and tables and bibliography in the accepted way.

Glossary of Legal Terminology

actionable *per se*
an action for a tort where the claimant does not have to prove that damage occurred only that the tort occurred

but for test
the main test for establishing factual causation in an action for negligence – but for the defendant's breach of duty the damage would not have occurred

claimant
the person who brings an action in tort

damages
refers to the compensation awarded by the court in a successful claim

damnum sine injuria
where harm is caused without a legal wrong

defendant
the person against whom a claim in tort is made

distress damage feasant
the right to keep an object that has been left unlawfully on a claimant's land that has caused damage until the damage is paid for

economic loss
refers to a loss that is purely financial, eg loss of profit – in contrast to personal injury or damage to property

exemplary damages
a form of damages which is not related to compensation for damage suffered but which the court makes to show its disapproval of the defendant's action

ex turpi causa non oritur actio
a defence that may be raised against a claimant whose claim arises from their own criminal actions

interlocutory injunction
an injunction given before the actual dispute is heard – to avoid harm that may be caused to the claimant before the action comes to court

joint tortfeasors
where the wrongful act is carried out by more than one person they are joint tortfeasors and any or all of them can be sued

loss of amenity
damages are awarded where the claimant is unable to do things that he could before the wrong occurred

malice
motive is generally unimportant in most torts but in some circumstances acting maliciously is an element of the tort, eg malicious falsehood and nuisance

mesne profits
used in trespass to land – allowing the claimant to claim for damage done by the trespasser and for any costs incurred in recovering possession of the land

misfeasance
this is where the defendant has acted wrongly

neighbour principle
a test used in negligence to establish whether a duty of care is owed

nervous shock
a recognised psychiatric injury such as clinical depression and Post Traumatic Stress Disorder caused by a single shocking event

nominal damages
a small sum of damages awarded where there has technically been a wrong but no actual damage has been caused

non-feasance
this is where the defendant has a duty to act and is liable for a failure to act

non-pecuniary damages
compensation for pain, suffering and loss of amenities where judges have developed rates of compensation

novus actus interveniens
means 'a new act intervenes' – refers to situations where the defendant is excused liability because another intervening act has broken the chain of causation

occupier
in liability for damage caused by the state of premises the occupier is the person in actual control of the premises when the damage occurs – so there can be dual occupation

pecuniary damages
damages that can be calculated in financial terms, eg loss of earnings

prescription
a defence in private nuisance where the thing complained of had been active for 20 years or more and the claimant had known about it and not complained before

proximity

refers to the fact that the defendant should contemplate that his actions may have an effect on potential claimants – rather than physical closeness

remoteness of damage

also known as causation in law – refers to damage which is foreseeable and therefore which the courts are prepared to compensate – they would not compensate for damage that was too remote a consequence of the defendant's breach

res ipsa loquitur

literally means 'the thing speaks for itself' – where the claimant is unable to show details of the negligence but the damage was obviously caused negligently the defendant will be required to show that he was not negligent

several liability

where there are joint tortfeasors each one can be separately liable for the whole damage – so if one lacks funds to pay compensation the claimant can bring the action against the one that can pay

special damage

occurs in slander where the claimant usually has to prove that he has suffered damage as a result – also occurs in public nuisance where the claimant has to show that he has suffered damage over that suffered by the public generally

special damages

not to be confused with special damage – generally refers to damages for financial losses and expenses incurred up to the date of trial which have to be pleaded separately from the claim itself

strict liability

refers to torts where the claimant does not have to show fault on the part of the defendant – the most obvious ones are under the Animals Act 1971 and the Consumer Protection Act 1987

thin skull rule

also known as the 'eggshell skull rule' – means that the defendant has to take extra care of a claimant who is susceptible to a certain type of harm

tort

a French word meaning 'wrong' – so is a general word used to describe civil wrongs

tortfeasor

will be the defendant in a tort action – the person who commits the wrong

trespass

torts based on trespass tend to involve interference, eg with rights over land, or property or indeed with their 'bodily integrity'

trespass *ab initio*

in the case of people who have a legal right to enter land such as a meter reader if they commit wrong while on the land they are said to be trespassers from when they entered

trespasser

a person who enters premises without permission or who exceeds the permission they are given

vicarious liability

not a tort in itself but a means of imposing liability on somebody who is responsible for the tortfeasor usually an employer

visitor

usually refers to somebody who enters premises lawfully

volenti non fit injuria

literally means 'no injury can be done to a willing person' – so is a defence where the claimant understands the risk of harm and willingly accepts it

Index

UNLOCKING TORTS